P9-CDD-948

By the same author

MR ATTLEE: AN INTERIM BIOGRAPHY

PURSUIT OF PROGRESS

MR BALFOUR'S POODLE

SIR CHARLES DILKE: A VICTORIAN TRAGEDY

THE LABOUR CASE

ASQUITH

ESSAYS AND SPEECHES

AFTERNOON ON THE POTOMAC?

WHAT MATTERS NOW

NINE MEN OF POWER

PARTNERSHIP OF PRINCIPLE

TRUMAN

BALDWIN

TWENTIETH-CENTURY PORTRAITS

EUROPEAN DIARY

A LIFE AT THE CENTER

PORTRAITS AND MINIATURES

GLADSTONE

GLADSTONE

A Biography

Roy Jenkins

RANDOM HOUSE
NEW YORK

Published in the United States by Random House, Inc., New York.

This work was originally published, in slightly different form, by Macmillan, an imprint of Macmillan General Books, London, in 1995.

Library of Congress Cataloging-in-Publication Data
Jenkins, Roy.
Gladstone: a biography/Roy Jenkins.
p. cm.
Originally published: London: Macmillan, 1995. With forenote to the American ed.
Includes bibliographical references and index.
ISBN 0-679-45144-7
1. Gladstone, W. E. (William Ewart), 1809–1898. 2. Great Britain—Politics and government—1837–1901. 3. Prime ministers—Great Britain—Biography. 4. Liberal Party (Great Britain)—Biography.
I. Title.
DA563.4.J45 1997
941.081'092—dc21 96-49632
[B]

Random House website address: http://www.randomhouse.com/
Printed in the United States of America on acid-free paper
2 4 6 8 9 7 5 3

Contents

PART THREE

The First Premiership and the First Retirement 1868–1876

PART FOUR

The Rebound into the Second Premiership 1876–1885

PART FIVE

Ireland Dominates and Age Withers
1885–1898

List of Illustrations

Section One

Section Two

Section Three

Section Four

Preface

This attempt to write a full-scale but not multi-volume biography of Gladstone is by far my rashest literary enterprise. It is like suddenly deciding, at a late stage in life and after a sedate middle age, to climb the rougher face of the Matterhorn. I hesitated for some time after the idea was suggested to me. But eventually the fascination of the subject, aided maybe by an inherent liking for taking a risk, overcame my caution at the presumption of the task.

The fascination arises from Gladstone's own peculiar qualities and pre-eminence. He was the quintessential Victorian statesman, fitting the reign, although not latterly the prejudices of the Queen, like a hand into a glove. He first briefly held office two years before Victoria's accession and he predeceased her by only two and a half years. Of the other great politicians of the age, Peel survived little more than a fifth of the Queen's reign, Palmerston was always more of a throwback to the Regency than a true Victorian, Disraeli was an exotic exile from lusher civilizations cast up on the shore of England, and Salisbury, although undoubtedly English and looking like a caricature of a Victorian, practised a detached statecraft which would equally well have been pursued at the time of the early Cecils or from such another capital as Vienna.

Gladstone, however, was uniquely matched to nineteenth-century Britain. The evolving size of the electorate suited him perfectly. During his active lifetime and keeping very good step with his increasing democratic enthusiasm it moved from half to a million to a little over five million, large enough to accommodate his taste for mass audiences but restrictive enough to prevent his instinctive sense of hierarchy becoming obviously anomalous. It also suited him well that Britain was the most powerful country in the world. He hated 'jingoism' (a phrase coined only in his sixty-ninth year) and deeply disapproved of the showy imperialism which he saw as Disraeli's hallmark. The Concert of Europe was his frequently reiterated lodestar. *'Securus judicat orbis terrarum'* (the united verdict of the whole world must be accepted as conclusive), which was Newman's ultimate reason for joining the Church of Rome, did not lead Gladstone in that particular direction. The concept nonetheless had a most powerful impact upon his later policy positions, in relation particularly to justice for Ireland. As, however, he liked pronouncing with great moral force upon international issues, it suited him well that he was able to do so from such a pulpit of power. Britain's reduced late-twentieth-century status would have been less suited to his style.

He was also lucky that his sixty-three years of active politics embraced no war which threatened Britain's vital security. The Napoleonic Wars were over when he was five. The First World War was nearly a generation after his retirement. Of the two medium-grade conflicts, the South African War began in the year after his death, and the Crimean War was the only one for which he bore any responsibility. He had no natural martial spirit and his uneasy experience with the Crimean conflict underlined his good fortune in not having, like Asquith, to try to turn himself from a peacetime to a wartime leader. Unlike the two Pitts, Lloyd George and Churchill, therefore, he was not tested in a fight for survival.

Perhaps for this reason I hesitate to claim that he was Britain's greatest Prime Minister. He made many mistakes, failed to carry his last endeavour of Home Rule for Ireland, and left a squabbling Liberal party which was excluded from office for a short generation after his withdrawal. But I have no doubt that he was the most remarkable specimen of humanity of all the fifty who, from Walpole to Major, have so far held the office of British Prime Minister. This was partly a question of his prodigious energy. He lived for nearly eighty-nine years, a more unusual feat a hundred years ago than it is today, and although he spent a surprising amount of time on a sickbed he always bounced back with devastating vigour. He read over 20,000 books. He chopped down innumerable trees. He could walk vast distances in Snowdonia or the Scottish Highlands, but sometimes just in the ordinary course of his life, from Chester station to Hawarden, or around the less respectable parts of the West End of London, trying to redeem prostitutes, but filling himself as a result of these irresistible excursions with far more guilt than self-righteousness. He was a great classicist, although perhaps a powerful rather than a subtle scholar. Homer and Dante were his literary heroes, but he also read contemporary fiction (and in the prolific mid-Victorian period there was a lot of it) in a way that no subsequent Prime Minister has done.

At the same time he claimed, and to some extent justified the claim, that religion was more important to him than politics. He was deeply involved in all the theological and liturgical battles of the nineteenth century. He was a compelling orator who, despite his addiction to endless sentences, convoluted constructions, and classical allusion and quotation, could hold both the House of Commons and popular audiences transfixed for hours at a time. This was largely a function of his physical magnetism, his flashing eye and the eagle's swoop of his cadences. He had all the earnestness of Victorian England, yet he was rarely dull. He was always the biggest beast in the forest, and he had inherent star quality, difficult to define but on the rare occasions when it exists easy to recognize. Everything he did he infused with a touch of magic. In this respect he was comparable among his near contemporaries with Newman, with Tennyson, with Darwin, maybe Carlyle, and some (but not I) would say with Dickens. In any event it was a select company.

To attempt to write afresh about such a creature, by and about whom the number of books is already incomparable and whose papers, in the British Library Catalogue, amount to 750 volumes, is obviously a formidable undertaking. This mammoth bibliography, at least ten if not twenty times that relating to Asquith for instance, does not however comprise much in the way of recent general biography. In this category Disraeli has proved far more of a modern honeypot. One or two long essays apart, there has been nothing written as complete biography since Sir Philip Magnus's *Gladstone*, which appeared forty one years ago. Magnus still reads freshly and is in the idiom of modern biography, although to my mind wrong on a number of points, including in particular Gladstone's motivation in his prostitute-reclaiming activities. And the interval back to Magnus is now almost as long as the fifty-one years separating his work from John Morley's massive and splendid three volumes which appeared simultaneously only five years after Gladstone's death. Morley's was a commissioned 'tombstone' life, although one at the very top of this category, and inevitably therefore now appears somewhat dated in format and over-respectful in content.

Complete biographies apart, there is the dense, informative and controversial half-life by Professor R. T. Shannon of Swansea. The first volume (up to 1865) appeared in 1982, and was obviously intended to be followed by another, but as that has not yet been forthcoming there arises some doubt whether the half will become a whole. Then there are the collected introductions of Professor H.C.G. Matthew, the doyen (in spite of his relative youth) of Gladstone experts, who has just brought to triumphant completion the fourteen-volume edition of Gladstone's diaries, which work of dedicated and brilliant scholarship he took over from Professor M.R.D. Foot twenty-three years and twelve volumes back. The two volumes of Professor Matthew's introductions between them cover the complete life, with an 1874 break point, but they were not written as a whole or with an explicit biographical intention, even though the result, almost as a by-product, has been a considerable biographical achievement.

Nonetheless Gladstone biographical territory is not over-populated, and, although I encountered many difficulties in comprehending some facets of Gladstone's multifarious interests and activities, I never found myself short of new things to say about him. My book is written from published sources. I have no new cache of material, as I did in the case of Asquith with the then unused letters to Venetia Stanley. But the published sources are in Gladstone's case so vast and variegated that I in no way felt that this constrained me to move only along over-trodden paths.

Throughout I have been anxious to set Gladstone in the context of other British Prime Ministers and proximate political figures, those who have come after him as well as those who came before. I have also tried to relate nineteenth-century patterns of political life to those of today, although often more by contrast than by affinity. For this purpose I have drawn extensively on the details of Victorian habits, travel arrangements, meal-times, property values, for which Gladstone's diaries are an unusually rich and detailed source, as well as on my own experience of modern political life. I have also tried to retain Gladstone's vivid interest in landscape and buildings. Relating Victorian *mentalité*, particularly in matters of religion, to that of today has presented a more difficult problem. Yet it is impossible to write adequately about Gladstone, even more during his first forty than during his last twenty years in politics, without engaging closely with both the framework and the content of his religion.

This has been the more necessary because I have to some extent adopted a policy of 'front-end loading'. The image of Gladstone which readily springs to most people's minds is that of a somewhat wild-eyed and wild-haired old man in a hurry, a prophet from the Midlothian hills to his admirers, a destructive obsessive concerned only with Ireland to his detractors. Yet Gladstone's career cannot possibly be seen in perspective if his old age is allowed to obscure either his talented if somewhat priggish youth or his occasionally unhinged but immensely productive middle age. He was a Cabinet minister at thirty-three. He was Chancellor of the Exchequer for fourteen budgets between his forty-third and his fifty-seventh birthdays and was so successful that he enhanced not only his own career but also the long-term status of the office. And until almost his sixtieth year his interest in Ireland was less than that of the average British politician.

His life will not be seen in focus if it is looked at primarily through the telescope of his last two or even his last three premierships. I have therefore given full weight to the earlier period, devoting nearly half the book to the years before even the first of his four premierships. This was made easier by my belief that he led the most interesting pre–Prime Ministerial life of any of his predecessors except for the Duke of Wellington.

I have accumulated many debts in the process of bringing the large ship of Gladstone into some sort of harbour. My agent Michael Sissons and my then publisher Roland Philipps were responsible for the original idea. Michael Sissons has remained an invaluable adviser and Roland Philipps's successors at Macmillan, William Armstrong and Tanya Stobbs, have provided much publishing skill and attention. Peter James has once again, as with my autobiography *A Life at the Center*, been an exceptional freelance editor, and Douglas Matthews, former librarian of the London Library, has once more compiled a complicated index. None of them would, however, have been able to function had not Mary Rundell transformed my increasingly elusive handwriting into a series of typescripts of diminishing inaccuracy.

Outside the process of book-making my largest debt is to Professor H.C.G. Matthew. The Gladstone diaries, in spite of their author's taste for obscurity, are made almost pellucid by the quality of his editing. And, once understood, they constitute a unique background of detailed fact, like a fine tapestry dominating one wall of a library, against which to construct a Gladstone narrative and try out Gladstone theories. In addition Colin Matthew was good enough to apply his eagle eye to any inaccuracies in my manuscript, while standing well back from its opinions and interpretations.

My second debt is to Sir William Gladstone, the present holder of the baronetcy which Peel conferred upon old John Gladstone in 1846, and also the proprietor of both the Hawarden and the Fasque estates. By several times welcoming me to Hawarden and straightening out some of my topography (and occasionally my history as well) he has greatly facilitated my task.

East Hendred
February 1995

ROY JENKINS

Forenote to the American Edition

This forenote, which did not appear in the London edition, endeavours to set the context of the England into which William Ewart Gladstone was born (of Scottish parents) and in which he lived his long life. At the date of his birth Britain was in the eighteenth year, the brief peace of Amiens apart, of the Napoleonic wars, and there was no light of victory on the horizon. Bonaparte was supreme in continental Europe. Britain's European toeholds were confined to Sicily and an insecure presence in Portugal, from which latter country tentative expeditions into Spain could be mounted. At the beginning of 1809, Sir John Moore had been forced to end such a foray with a skillful (but for him fatal) retreat to embarkation at Corunna. It was a success in the sense that the 1940 evacuation from Dunkirk was a success, and in much the same way indicated what a long haul it was to be to victory.

Yet comparisons between that war and World War II, particularly as circumstances into which an Englishman was born, are invalid for one central reason. Both wars, it is true, had a decisive effect upon the future. The history of the nineteenth century would have been very different had Napoleon won, as certainly would that of the second half of the twentieth century had Hitler done so. In this way they were qualitatively distinct from the Crimean War, which was the only European war of Gladstone's long career as a minister, or the South African War, which began in the year after his death. Nevertheless, the degree of British concentration upon beating Napoleon was not comparable with that on the defeat of Hitler after 1940. Between Gladstone's second and fifth birthday Britain allowed its eye to be diverted sufficiently far from the ball to fight the War of 1812 with the United States. Winston Churchill would hardly have allowed a similar diversion to have occurred in 1942 and 1943. Of course there had been a vast change both in United States power and in Anglo-American relations in the meantime. The 'continental divide' of the latter process was Gladstone's 1872 acceptance as Prime Minister of the *Alabama* Award with its vast damages by the standards of the time. This was despite an unfortunate speech by him during the Civil War itself having been unhelpful to the Union. Yet his acceptance at the plenitude of Britain's power of the supremacy of the international rule of law in a way that neither Palmerston nor Disraeli would have been likely to do, far outweighed this. Behind 1872 lay a hundred years of fluctuating hostility. Ahead of it lay two world wars fought in partnership as well as NATO, the American-led but partly British-created alliance which won a (Cold) war without ever firing a shot.

Internally to Britain a still more striking difference between the Napoleonic Wars and 1939–45 was that the impact of the former on life at home was negligible. Those years of the earlier war were the years of Jane Austen's novels. In 1809, having moved to Chawton in the north-east corner of Hampshire, she was busy preparing for the press both *Sense and Sensibility* and *Pride and Prejudice*. Yet there is not the slightest suggestion that it ever occurred to Willoughby or Darcy, the heroes of those books, or to their demure but sharp heroines, that vigorous young men of good family and patriotic views ought to be doing anything for the war effort. Nor were there even many ripples of economic inconvenience. The squirearchy and the more prosperous clergy were subject to Pitt's income tax and to some general inflation, but they were more than compensated for the effects by the high rents and tithes which followed from the strong market for corn and other agricultural products. G. M. Trevelyan wrote of precisely this time that "at no period had the upper class been wealthier, or happier, or more engrossed in the life of its pleasant country houses."*

Gladstone was not born into a family of landed proprietorship and established membership of the ruling class. He was nonetheless even more free of the privations of war than were Miss Austen's squires. His father was not merely floated up on a general tide but was one of the new class of mercantile or industrial princes whose prosperity was exploding, and who were becoming eager to use their wealth to buy political power as well as to secure material ease.

The benign effect of the war upon both the traditional ruling class and the 'new men' of the North was in no way matched by any benign impact upon the mass of the population. This again was a sharp differ-

* *British History in the Nineteenth Century and After*, p. 129

ence between the Napoleonic wars and 1939–45. So far from promoting social cohesion the former struggle made divides deeper and resentments greater. This broadly applied to both the agricultural labourer and the new industrial proletariat. Late eighteenth century enclosures and agricultural improvements greatly increased land productivity but destroyed many of the supplementary benefits of rural life, such as cottage industries and grazing rights on common land, without raising agricultural wages. Furthermore the so-called 'Speenhamland system', which began in 1795, took the pressure for providing a living wage off the landowner or prosperous farmer and put it on the parish, thereby leading to a deadening rural pauperization.

A sullen alienation which expressed itself in hayrick-burning and a vicious poaching war, with the most horrendous penalties for the most venial crimes, rather than 'Merrie England' and maypoles, was the spirit of much of the countryside at the time of Gladstone's birth. And in the new industrial areas the same spirit showed itself in the loom-breaking of the Luddite riots which began in Nottingham in 1811 and spread to Lancashire, Yorkshire and the Lowlands of Scotland in 1812. The reaction of government to these discontents was almost totally negative. Having repealed the old fair wage legislation, Parliament forbade any combination of workmen and thereby ensured that there could not be fair free bargaining. And when at the end of the war a faltering price for wheat showed some prospect of producing cheaper food, this possibility was repulsed by the Corn Law of 1815, which provided for a high degree of protection (and incidentally provided the basis for Gladstone—at Peel's side—to fight his first reforming battle thirty years later). At least up to the 1819 massacre in St Peter's Fields, Manchester, after which a hesitant liberal reaction began to set in, the only answer of executive, legislature and judiciary alike to these injustices was repressive legislation backed by cruel punishments.

The England into which Gladstone was born was thus far from being the stable and relatively humane society, with improving condition for most of the population, which set in around 1850 and persisted, even if less certainly in the fourth than in the third quarter of the century, for the rest of his life. It was a harsh and divided society, in which no one assumed much more stability for British institutions than was achieved across the Channel in France. The King was declining into permanent madness, the Prince of Wales (soon to be Regent) redeemed his shop-soiled self-indulgence only by flashes of aesthetic taste, and had long retreated from any liberal sympathy. Temporarily presiding over a far from inspiring government was the man who, of all nineteenth century Prime Ministers was the least like Gladstone. Spencer Percival was a *Mann ohne Schätten.* He came from nowhere and he left little behind him, except for the distinction of being the only British Prime Minister to be shot dead. But it was not even a grand assassination with him falling victim to an insurrectionary upsurge. His killer merely had an individual grievance so obsessive that his counsel pleaded insanity, which plea did not however prevent his being hanged within a week of the attack. Justice (and/or punishment) was at least quick in that rough epoch. Its violence was illustrated from another angle by that year of Gladstone's birth also being marked by the two principal Tory statesmen, Castlereagh and Canning, fighting a serious duel on Putney Heath, a sign of party disunity greater even than anything recently displayed. Brutality was thus not confined to the lower orders, as was illustrated by the vicious man-trap against poachers which many gentlemanly squires introduced upon their land, or the notorious Eton fight several years later when a nephew of the Marquess of Londonderry killed a brother of the future Earl of Shaftesbury in a fight which lasted two hours with half the school looking on.

The other educational institution, the University of Oxford—which was to be even more intertwined with Gladstone's life than Eton—was hardly beginning to rub its eyes after its long eighteenth century torpor. The four Scottish universities (England still had only two) were more professorially interesting, even though the students were taught as though they were at an austere high school away from home, as indeed their age made appropriate. Edinburgh, although the youngest of the Scottish four, was in the van. There Thomas Carlyle arrived (on foot) from Ecclefechan at the age of not quite fourteen, six weeks or so before Gladstone's birth. He was five years older than John Henry Newman, another of Gladstone's co-evals amongst the brightest stars of the nineteenth century, who had just gone to a quiet school in Ealing, while Edward Bouverie Pusey was at a preparatory school in Mitcham. John Keble however was already an Oxford undergraduate at Oriel. Henry Manning and Alfred Tennyson were both still in swaddling clothes, the future Cardinal Archbishop in a Hertfordshire country house, the future Poet Laureate in a Lincolnshire rectory. Disraeli was a precocious five in his father's book-lined Bloomsbury house—it was another seven or eight years before Isaac D'Israeli became both a Christian and a country gentleman. Palmerston, although only twenty-five, was already a minister of the Crown.

Britain, divided and discontented, was also advancing. The population was growing rapidly, although this led more to the dismal doctrines of Malthus and Ricardo than to any upsurge of national optimism. In 1801 there were ten and a half million inhabitants of Great Britain, and in 1811 there were twelve million. (The last figure compared with six million for Ireland, seven million for the United States and a massive thirty million for France.) National wealth, difficult to measure at the time, was probably increasing still more rapidly, although, needless to say, not nearly as fast as that of the Gladstone family. The twelve million people and the towns in which they increasingly lived were connected by substantially improved roads. A coherent railway network was still three or four decades into the future, but McAdam with his hard surfacing and Telford with his bridges and turnpikes were greatly increasing the ability of the mobile classes to get about the country. Better roads brought lighter and much faster post chaises. It was the short-lived golden age of the fast (perhaps fifteen miles per hour) public coaches which made the yards of the principal inns of the country towns of England the more intimate precursors of railway termini and airport concourses. London to Bath could be done in eight hours, and, more relevant to the much-travelling Gladstone family, London to Liverpool in twenty hours.

It was still however the case that journeys between some of the principal cities—London to Edinburgh or Liverpool to Glasgow—could more conveniently be done by boat. London to Dublin, a still more vital link since Pitt had forced through the union of the Irish with the British Parliament eight years before Gladstone's birth, remained a tenuous link. The only remotely speedy route involved a land journey of 280 miles, followed by a sea voyage of sixty. Most nineteenth century English and Scottish politicians solved the problem by not going to Ireland (Disraeli never, Gladstone only effectively once) even though it then contained a third of the total population of the British Isles. Many large landowners in Ireland followed the example of the politicians and remained firmly based on the London side of the Irish Sea. Their rents however were expected to make the eastward journey with regularity. There, already fermenting a quarter century before the great famine, lay the roots of the intractable Irish problem which was to dominate the last two decades of Gladstone's life.

By then it was a vastly different England from that into which he had been born. The Regency had given way to the 1820s with George IV fully on the throne, and then to the adjectiveless seven-year reign of his brother William IV. And by 1880 the early-Victorian period had ceded to the mid-Victorian period, which in turn was evolving into late Victorianism. Gladstone shadowed the Queen's life. That was perhaps part of her trouble with him. He was always there, or at least always turning up. He had come to appear to her almost like a 'stalker'. She was ten years his junior, but she enjoyed only two and a half years after his death. As she succeeded so young she was his sovereign when he was still a young MP of twenty-seven. Already, however, he had been a junior minister in a brief administration under her predecessor. This gave him a unique seniority after Derby had died in 1869 and Russell, much withdrawn for some time previously, had followed him in 1878.

For the first part of Queen Victoria's reign, difficult although subsequent events made it to believe this, Gladstone was something of a court favourite. So long as the Prince Consort was alive (until December 1861), the improving earnestness of Gladstone, Peel and Aberdeen, chimed well with the spirit of Windsor. It was only in his first spell as Prime Minister (1868–74) that Gladstone's relations with the Queen seriously deteriorated. A combination of his own clumsy royalism and Disraeli's cynical but skillful flattery made her a Conservative partisan for the rest of her life. This caused Gladstone dismay and displeasure but could not undermine the fact that he stamped the Victorian age even more than did Victoria herself, and represented it almost as much.

Although Gladstone lived nearly to the end of the Queen's reign, through the two jubilees of 1887 and 1897, and dominated the politics of these years (although without commanding the success of his Irish policy) the late-Victorian age was not really his period. It was too imperialist, too flamboyant, too drum-beating for his taste. As Britain's superiority became more challenged, by Germany from the east and America from the west, so paradoxically but perhaps typically, it began to be more noisily asserted. The imperial jingoism of the 1897 golden jubilee celebrations would have been unimaginable under Peel, Aberdeen, Derby, Russell or even Palmerston. Gladstone, although respecting aristocracy and the acquiring of money but not its lavish expenditure, was much more at home in the good solid bourgeois Britain of the third quarter, the mid-Victorian years, the nineteenth century equivalent of West Germany's unostentatious and unassertive Federal Republic. In mid-Victorian Britain, as in the Germany of Adenauer and Erhard, wealth multiplied but, a few Palmerstonian pyrotechnics apart, power was not brutally asserted. They were also years of much greater religious intensity and controversy than were the last decades of the century, when, Welsh revivalism apart, there was an ebbing of the mid-century liturgical disputes.

Gladstone was not a Regency man despite his date of birth. He was not exactly an early Victorian; he was as unlike Melbourne as it is possible to imagine, and he was also very much at sea from his own political and intellectual moorings during the beginning of the Queen's reign. Essentially he was a mid-Victorian. Those were his golden years when he made his reputation as Chancellor of the Exchequer, and was most in tune with the spirit of the age. Paradoxically, these years were nearly all over even before the first of his four premierships.

During these last thirty years he could not be regarded as a beached whale, for he remained by far the dominant politician of the age, and beached whales do not dominate, except for a small area of sand around them. But although his one central idea on Ireland was farsightedly right, he became rather out of touch with other aspects of the 1890s, whether they were the decadence of Beardsley's *Yellow Book*, or the heavy opulence of the furniture, or the 'constructive radicalism' of new semi-socialist Liberalism from which he remained very detached. In the twentieth century he would have found it still more difficult to operate. His death marked not merely the fall of a great and more venerable oak than any of those he himself felled, but also the effective end of the century.

September 1996 ROY JENKINS

Part One

A TALENTED AND TORTURED YOUNG MAN

1809–1852

I

A Liverpool Gentleman?

William Ewart Gladstone was born in Liverpool at the end of 1809. When, just over half a century later, he had introduced the pattern-setting budget of 1860, Walter Bagehot recorded this description of him: 'Ah, Oxford on the surface, but Liverpool below.'[1] Bagehot, founder of the *Economist*, was in many ways the nineteenth century's best substitute for Dr Johnson. He could aphorize at the drop of a hat, and often with wisdom. But was he right on this occasion? Gladstone undoubtedly became a great Oxonian, an accomplished scholar in his youth, a member of Parliament for the University for seventeen years in middle age, and towards the end of his life its most famous ornament. The town of his birth, on the other hand, faded into the background while he was still a very young man. Did he nonetheless remain 'Liverpool below'?

He was indisputably born in the heart of that metropolis of ships and commerce which from about 1790 to 1925 had a high claim to be the second city of England. Its population in 1810 was 94,000, below that of Manchester (and of Dublin, Glasgow and Edinburgh, but they were not English), but it was growing more rapidly and had more metropolitan quality than its inland rival. The day of Gladstone's birth was 29 December and the place was 62 Rodney Street. The late-December date meant that he was always a year younger than was signified by a superficial calculation, although his morbidity made him stress the reverse. Furthermore, despite his longevity and the fact that he was Prime Minister later in life than any other holder of the office, he was the youngest among his best-known near contemporaries, Newman or Disraeli, Manning or Tennyson. The Rodney Street address meant that it was a good modern 1793 town house, less than a mile from the waterfront. Over the two centuries that have since gone by Rodney Street property has experienced two transitions: first from merchants' semi-mansions to consultants' rooms and residences in what became outside St Marylebone the most eminent medical street in Britain (at the end of which from 1912 onwards there arose the massive solidity of

Giles Gilbert Scott's Anglican cathedral); and then, much more recently, the further change to the sad decay of the Liverpool 8 of the late twentieth century.

Gladstone did not have many years of the town life of Rodney Street. He was there long enough to be brought downstairs at the age of barely three and shown off at a large dinner party which his father, John Gladstone, was giving for George Canning, whom Gladstone *père* was instrumental in persuading to stand and be elected for Liverpool against Henry Brougham the future Lord Chancellor. Thereafter Canning remained for William Gladstone a hero until and indeed well beyond his early death six months after he had become Prime Minister in 1827. But John Gladstone was at this period of his life both socially and geographically mobile, and Rodney Street could not long contain him. His wealth, which he had estimated at £15,900 in 1795, had risen to £145,600 by 1812 (and continued to climb to £502,000 by 1828).

There is no difficulty about knowing the exact current cash value of John Gladstone's assets. He kept very careful stock of them, and when in 1815 he built two churches, St Andrew's in the city and St Thomas's at Seaforth, he entered them in his balance sheet at £10,000 and £4000 respectively, and endeavoured to get a 5 per cent return, mainly through pew rents, on these amounts. What is more difficult is to make a rough estimate of what his wealth was worth in modern terms. If this is to be done simply it must also be done crudely, and the best working rule I have been able to devise is to multiply all nineteenth-century values by a factor of fifty in order to turn them into late-twentieth-century terms. This obviously leaves jagged edges. The last century compared with the present enjoyed relative currency stability. But there were fluctuations from decade to decade for which no allowance is made. There have also, between the centuries, been variations within this general price level, the cost of services rising much more rapidly than that of manufactures. But the 'fifty factor' produces results which rarely defy common sense and give a vivid and reasonably accurate impression of the command over resources that went with the relatively modest cash sums which were involved in the various Gladstone family transactions. On this basis John Gladstone's 1828 fortune would be worth a modern £25 million.

From where did it come? In his early Liverpool days he had been primarily a corn trader, bringing with him to the Mersey the skill which he had developed in Leith, and making mostly Baltic purchases. Then he was a partner in an East Indian house, dealing mainly with the sub-continent, and coming up against the restrictive privileges of the East

India Company. This and Liverpool's natural direction made him look more westward. In 1789–90 he spent a year buying cargoes in what had just become the United States. He did some cotton trade with Brazil. But it was on the West Indies and particularly on the two territories of Demerara and Jamaica that he became increasingly concentrated. By 1833, which was the peak of his trading activities, he showed total assets of £636,000, of which £296,000 were in Demerara and £40,000 in Jamaica. By 1843, however, he had turned himself from a merchant adventurer into a rentier. The West Indies stake was down to £53,000 and his shareholdings (mainly in railways) were up to £213,000.[2] Sugar was the core of his West Indies activity, but tobacco and cotton were also important. He did not trade in slaves, even before the slave trade was outlawed in Britain in 1807, but the plantations he owned operated on slave labour throughout his time as a West Indian magnate.

In 1811 he began the building of Seaforth House, a full-scale country residence (except that it was not really in the country, having the mouth of the Mersey on one side and the beginning of Liverpool on the other) set in an estate of a hundred acres. By 1815 the family had effectively removed themselves five or six miles downstream to this new location. In 1817 he sent his eldest son, Thomas Gladstone, to Eton. Liverpool wealth did not intend to be shut out from privileged education, and already by 1811, according to William Ewart, a business partner of John Gladstone's whose name was immortalized in W. E. Gladstone, there were 'enough Liverpool Etonians to fill a coach'.[3]

Then in 1818 John Gladstone became a member of Parliament. His parliamentary career never prospered. He was too old (fifty-four) when he started. But there was more to it than that. He was like an elderly philanderer who always had to buy his favours, and failed to make neat transactions. Liverpool rejected him, and he went to Lancaster. Most of his two years as member for that borough was occupied with fighting off a petition alleging that he had been corruptly elected. In 1820 he transferred to Woodstock, where the Duke of Marlborough had a seat going cheap – for £877 to be exact. But by 1826 the market seemed to have improved and John Gladstone failed to come to terms with the Duke for the renewal of his mandate. With a fine indifference to locality he once more removed himself, this time to Berwick-on-Tweed. There he was elected in second place (in a two-member borough) by a margin of three votes, but was once again subjected to a petition for corrupt practices. This time it succeeded, and his far from splendid parliamentary career (much of it devoted to defending the rights of West Indian slave-owners, of which he was a leading example) came to an end in 1827. But these nine years at Westminster, inglorious though they may have been, required five or six months a year of London residence, for which 5 Grafton Street, between Bond Street and Berkeley Square, was rented, and which constituted a further extension of the horizons of Rodney Street.

After the débâcle of Berwick John Gladstone never again sat in Parliament. It was not for want of trying. He was humiliatingly defeated at Dundee in 1837 and flickered towards the prospect of a nomination for either Aberdeen or Leith in 1841, when he was seventy-seven. He did, however, largely turn his back on England. He regarded his £500,000 as adequate (although it grew to £750,000 by 1850), and he abandoned Liverpool, the base of his West Indian trading fortune. At the end of 1829 he bought Fasque, a Scottish estate on the northern slope of the Mearns, between Dundee and Aberdeen, for the very considerable sum of £80,000 and supplemented it with an Edinburgh New Town winter house in Atholl Crescent. Fasque was (and is) a fine mansion, as elegant as it is substantial, built in the year of William Gladstone's birth. It has a delicate staircase and a particularly good first-floor library with a commanding view to the south-west.

John Gladstone took time to move in to these two houses, and for the years around 1830 led a somewhat nomadic existence taking his invalid second wife (William Gladstone's mother) and his invalid elder daughter (William Gladstone's senior by seven years) on an ineffective search for health at some of the watering places of England. Thus when William Gladstone was at Oxford he several times did the forty-five-mile walk to join his family at Leamington, and when he was summoned to Newark for the beginning of his first election campaign in September 1832 he was at Torquay and had to do some hard posting to get there via London in forty hours.

After about 1834, however, John Gladstone settled down in his two Scottish houses. He was seventy that year, he had already lost his elder daughter and in 1835 he was to lose his second wife. His old age was long and prosperous but lonely and sometimes irascible. He was eighty-seven when he died in 1851. He had been made a baronet in Peel's resignation honours list of 1846, but this was more of a tip to William Gladstone than a mark of personal regard to his father, who was a very reluctant Peelite. John Gladstone made the money on which his sons lived in near affluence. He was shrewd, mostly generous to his children and sometimes more broad-minded in family matters than they were. But he was dominant and demanding. He imposed upon his only surviving daughter a lonely isolation at Fasque which helped to turn her into a drug addict and a religious fanatic. And he treated his distinguished fourth son even when he had been a Cabinet minister – and no doubt so treated the other three too – as though he was still at the end of his adolescence. William Gladstone was pietistic and used habitually to spend a couple of autumn months at Fasque. During these visits he had to superimpose on his own voluminous letter-writing the copying out of dictated replies to his father's correspondence.

John Gladstone had not been born a gentleman. Nor indeed was he born Gladstone. His own father was called Gladstones, and John Gladstone abandoned this usage, simply on the ground of euphony, it appears, only after he went from Leith (the port of Edinburgh) to Liverpool in 1787. Thereafter the 's' never appeared south of the border, not in his own name, his trading designations or the names of his children, although he waited until 1835 to formalize the change by letters patent. There is no suggestion of social climbing in the change, although it is difficult to imagine the more tentative name of 'Gladstones' ringing down the nineteenth century with quite the clear-cut authority of 'Gladstone'. What was more to the social point was that John Gladstone, although his father (who had come from the Lanarkshire town of Biggar in 1746) had evolved into a modestly successful Leith corn merchant, left school at thirteen. He was fully literate and for seventy years and more could write business letters of singular pith and force. But the Scottish Enlightenment, which was pulsating through the Edinburgh of his youth, was as alien to his experience as it was to a crofter on the most remote Hebridean island.

John Gladstone had two wives, who were both nearly as 'delicate' in health and as retiring in tastes as he was vigorous and domineering. The wives had little else in common. The first, Jane Hall, was the daughter of another Liverpool merchant but one of less note and fortune than himself. He married her soon after his 1790 return from America, which was the only oceanic journey that he ever made, despite his controlling so many argosies and speaking with such dogmatic authority of the beneficial conditions in which slaves lived on the West Indian sugar plantations. Jane Gladstone was the first mistress of Rodney Street, but filled it with neither children nor local society. She quietly subsided and survived only six years of marriage.

Two years later in 1800 John Gladstone married Anne Mackenzie

Robertson, whose father (dead in 1796) had been a gentleman lawyer and Provost of the little Ross-shire county town of Dingwall. Her mother was also of Highland gentry stock. Anne Robertson was twenty-eight years old and a distinct beauty. It was surprising that she had not been married before, although what was even more surprising (and unexplained) was how John Gladstone found her. The Gladstones, father and sons, both before and after the onset of the railway age, were remarkably mobile within Britain, but it was a long way from Dingwall to Liverpool, or even to Leith, and there was no obvious reason for John Gladstone to go to the far north or for Miss Robertson to come south.

Once they had met, however, there was no obstacle to the match. There was a suggestion that John Gladstone wished he had been better educated for the polite society of Dingwall (which must have been very select, for the total population of the town was only 750) but his wealth more than made up for this. He carried his bride-to-be off to Liverpool for marriage. They arrived almost simultaneously with two Raeburn portraits of his parents which he had commissioned for the Rodney Street dining room. The wedding took place in the parish church of St Peter's, for Anne Robertson was a Scots Episcopalian and John Gladstone, although brought up in the strictest tradition of the Presbyterian Church of Scotland, had slipped over to the Church of England in Liverpool. But he did not do so in a latitudinarian way. Both he and his wife embraced the most determinedly Low Church Evangelicalism, which was very different from the High Anglicanism to which their fourth son shifted as a young man. There is a paradoxical suggestion that they rejected the Scottish kirk in Liverpool because it was too easy-going and did not produce a sufficient fervour of hell-fire preaching for their taste.

As her health declined, which it did fairly steadily at least from 1815, Evangelical religion became the central feature of Anne Gladstone's life. This did not separate her from her husband, for he, although engaged in the most vigorous pursuit of mammon, professed an equal attachment. Furthermore, Anne Gladstone, unlike her predecessor, produced six children, all born between 1802 and 1814, rather liked entertaining provided she could spend most of her days reclining upon an invalid's couch, and survived until the age of sixty-three.

William Gladstone's brothers and sisters had no qualities of personality, energy, intellect or success comparable with his own. As he was by any standards among a handful of outstanding figures of the Victorian age this was hardly surprising. What was perhaps more so was that, although his three brothers were almost as drawn to politics (local Liverpool politics in the case of the second) as he was himself, and although in theory at least he was naturally family minded, they constituted no continuing close-knit phalanx of support or even of companionship. After his marriage in 1839* he saw far more of his wife's family than he did of his own. This was not only true of her brother, Sir Stephen Glynne, where there was the special factor of Gladstone's gradual taking over of his Hawarden estate, although Glynne continued to live there, almost as a guest in his own house, until his death in 1874. It was also so with his wife's sister's husband, Lord Lyttelton, whose Hagley Hall outside Birmingham became almost a second country house for the Gladstones. An account of the political and religious differences, and largely ineffective ambitions, of the other brothers belongs to later in the story, as does the tragedy of the surviving sister Helen Gladstone. William Gladstone was mostly detached from them during their lives, although occasionally interfering and intolerant, particularly with his sister, and immensely solicitous at the times of their deaths.

When William Gladstone left Liverpool to go to Eton for the first time in 1821, his eldest brother Tom had been there for four and a half years, most of the time as unhappy as he was unsuccessful, and his second brother Robertson had just been removed from the school after two years. So far the Gladstones were a determined rather than a successful Etonian family. Tom had several times asked to be taken away. He was no good at composing Latin verse, which was the basis of the very limited curriculum. He quarrelled constantly with his 'dame' (house matron) and with Keate, the famous flogging headmaster. He found the atmosphere harsh and irreligious, and he made few friends. But his father was determined that he should not leave. To do so would mean that the Gladstone attempt to infiltrate the citadel of upper-class education had failed at the first encounter. So Tom accepted not merely that he could not leave voluntarily but that he must submit to several Keate floggings in lieu of expulsion.

Robertson was different. He was not the eldest son, and when it was decided, entirely with his own concurrence, that his future lay in continuing in Liverpool the mercantile tradition of the family, he was

* This seems to have been the watershed, for at the first (1832) election he was supported by his two brothers who were not themselves fighting seats. They were indeed in the constituency before he arrived.

smartly removed from Eton. John Gladstone's approach to education was strictly vocational. He was willing to pay to turn his sons into members of the ruling class. But if they were going to become merchants rather than rulers there was no point in paying. And the cost was surprisingly high, particularly as Eton was not well run at the time, with too few masters, and those that there were of uncertain quality. Its main advantage was the opportunity to make influential friends. For this the total cost in Tom's case, according to the meticulous Gladstone accounts, was £261 for a year, a figure which was somewhat above the average for the all-in expenditure of an Oxford undergraduate 120 years later.

Robertson, who had been doing rather better at Eton than Tom but had acquired no affection for it, was then despatched to Glasgow College, as the 270-year-old university was known at the time. It was still on its old High Street site around the cloisters of which Adam Smith had recently paced, and its curriculum, while far from narrowly commercial, was thought more suitable for Liverpool trade than an almost exclusive diet of hexameters. Glasgow seemed to do well for Robertson, an effective and intelligent man of business, who became Mayor of Liverpool before he was forty. Like his youngest brother but not many others, he moved across the political spectrum to the left as he got older, but his habits of thought and pattern of life were never remotely like those of William Gladstone. He was an immense mountain of a man, over twenty stone in weight, and he aged early, leading a disorganized and even dishevelled life after the death of his wife in 1865 until he too died in 1875.

The third son, John Neilson Gladstone, just short of three years older than William, was also entered for Eton. But he was resolved to go into the navy, although it was a bad time to do so – in the aftermath of the Napoleonic Wars when the south coastal counties were spattered with small Regency gentleman's residences from which redundant naval officers looked out in vain for ships to command. His determination however was great and he went to the Royal Naval College at Portsmouth in 1820. His career at sea was over at the age of twenty-eight, but although he could not thereafter get a ship he got some promotion and ended as a captain RN. He lived the second half of his life as a Wiltshire country gentleman, settling at Bowden Park, near Chippenham, preceding Lord Weinstock by a century and a quarter in the acquisition of that estate. He was also intermittently an MP, never tempted by his brother's transition to fluctuate from his Tory faith.

Although he appeared to have the most robust health and least neurotic temperament of all the Gladstone children, he died the first of the brothers, in 1863.

On the day in September 1821 when William Gladstone for the first time accompanied his brother Tom to Eton, there was no reason for him to feel exhilarated. He had hitherto had only slight schooling experience. He had been taught, but not very much or very skilfully, by the Evangelical vicar of St Thomas's, Seaforth, the church which his father had built and entered in his balance sheet. The Revd Mr Rawson was imported from Cambridge by John Gladstone and ran a school for about twelve boys in the parsonage.

This instruction singularly failed to excite him: 'To return to Mr Rawson,' he wrote at the 1892 beginning of his unfinished autobiography. 'Everything was unobjectionable there. I suppose I learnt something there. But I have no recollection of being under any moral or personal influence whatever. . . .'[4] But if he thought little of Rawson he thought still less of himself as a child. He had a strong conviction, in retrospect at any rate, that he was neither a good nor an engaging child. 'The best I can say for it is that I do not think it was actually a vicious childhood,' he continued in 1892. '. . . But truth obliges me to record this against myself. I have no recollection of being a loving or a winning child.'[5] The confluence of his lack of response to Rawson and lack of esteem for himself no doubt accounted for the remarkable absence of any nostalgia for childhood when he paid a return visit to Seaforth Rectory and indeed to the Rawsons thirty-two years later.*

In these circumstances it was lucky that such a wide new window opened to him when he went to Eton in 1821. The journey to South Buckinghamshire was a formidable one for an eleven-year-old boy, although he already had a remarkably wide geographical experience for a child of that age in the pre-railway years; he had travelled to London, Cambridge, Bristol, Edinburgh and Dingwall. His 1821 journey (to deduce backwards from his diaries, which he began just under four years later) involved departure from Seaforth in the early afternoon, leaving Liverpool by the Birmingham coach at 3.30 p.m. and getting to that Midland town at about 5.30 the next morning, making an interchange and proceeding onwards by a coach sometimes called the 'Hibernian', which presumably came from Holyhead, and allowed its passengers to breakfast at Leamington and dine at Benson (between Oxford and

* See pp. 179–80 below.

Henley) before depositing them at Slough in time to get to Eton at 7.00 p.m.[6] Tom's presence may have given some reassurance, particularly as William was to be in the same house and also to do his fagging under him. But it must also have been something of a wet blanket, for Tom can hardly have fired him with Eton enthusiasm.

However, William took to Eton like the proverbial duck to water. Despite his later tendency self-consciously to defer to rank, there is no suggestion that he ever felt or suffered from any sense of inferiority because of his northern trading origin. Magnus thought that he was 'never a popular boy' because of his lack of interest in games, but this is implausible. Gladstone was at school well before the mania for the football field and the cricket pitch spread from Thomas Arnold's Rugby into the new 'imperial' public schools and reached its apogee in Henry Newbolt's end-of-the-century Clifton-inspired 'bumping pitch and a blinding light'. Regency England, which was only a year over when Gladstone got to Eton, thought more of gaming than of games. He was also there before that new wave of schools imposed on their pupils the standard accent of the southern upper middle classes.

The old schools never did this. Addington, Winchester's one Prime Minister, nicknamed 'the Doctor', spoke like the mixture of Reading apothecary and Hampshire yeoman which was his provenance. Peel, who went to Harrow from a rich but parvenu northern background very similar to that from which Gladstone came twenty years later, always spoke with a distinct Lancashire accent. And Curzon, who was a notable Etonian half a century after Gladstone, was famous for his short Derbyshire *a*s, as in bräss and gläss (when complaining that the Foreign Secretary's inkstand was that rather than silver and crystal).

In Gladstone's case, as opposed to Addington's or Peel's, there are faint and scratchy wax cylinder recordings which give some indication of the authority, but not of the depth or melodiousness, of his voice late in life. The accent is faintly northern. Seventy years earlier Gladstone must, if anything, have spoken with more and not less of a Liverpool accent, but this was neither unusual nor inhibiting to him at Eton. He was an early and central member of the Eton Society (Pop as it later came to be called, or the Literati, giving it a rather different connotation, as it was known at the time) and at its meetings first showed his unusual command over an oratory which was classical in structure and illustration, yet infused with a fervour and expounded with a profligacy of words which made it hardly Roman. The stylized nature of the framework, even if not always of the contents, of the debates was accentuated by the strange convention, an exaggerated inversion of the 'fourteen-day rule' in the early years of political television, that no issue which had arisen in the past fifty years could be debated. It at least gave the participants a need for historical knowledge and a taste for argument by analogy.

Gladstone's mind meshed well with Eton teaching. He later claimed that 'we knew very little indeed, but we knew it accurately'.[7] This was perhaps true so far as the limited and severely classical curriculum was concerned. Gladstone liked conventional learning, and was good if not brilliant at Latin and Greek composition. He had great application and muscular intellectual strength. But he had no special verbal facility in English, and probably not in the dead languages either. For an outstanding orator, which he was already on the way to becoming, he was singularly lacking in neatness of phrase. He was too periphrastic and too addicted to qualifying subordinate clauses. His force depended essentially on his flashing eyes and the physical authority of his presence. Thus the printed records of his speeches do not compare with those of Chatham or Burke or Canning or Abraham Lincoln, or even with the contrived epigrams of Disraeli, whose flippancy was so antipathetic to Gladstone. There was also a degree of sentimentality about Gladstone's later speeches, 'intellectual sentimentality' Morley called it with a well-chosen oxymoron, which was absent from the oratory of the other five just cited. Even in the sentimental category, however, John Bright made finer arches out of hackneyed but emotive images. Gladstone's oratory was a most powerful vehicle for moving men's minds on a particular issue rather than an art form which stood on its own because of the limpidity of the construction.

Nonetheless Gladstone did a good deal better at Eton than Lincoln or Bright would have been likely to do. Unlike Tom he attracted the interest of and got on well with the best masters. Although occasionally beaten by Keate, he appears to have both liked and respected him. Certainly he persuaded himself that this was so and wrote in his last years of Keate's enthusiastic reception at an 1841 banquet to celebrate the 400th anniversary of the school as 'one of the most moving spectacles that in my whole life I have witnessed'.[8] But it was E. C. Hawtrey, Keate's successor as headmaster from 1834, later Provost and the maker of Victorian Eton, from whom Gladstone claimed that, about Easter 1822, he first received a spark – *divinae particularam aurae* – which opened his mind and set him on a determined course of acquiring knowledge.[9]

Hawtrey was a great schoolmaster, but he was unlikely to have been as necessary an agent as Gladstone retrospectively suggested. Gladstone had phenomenal energy, both mental and physical, a blotting-paper mind, and an imbued sense that the highest challenge of life was to satisfy God of the most effective possible use of time. William Gladstone respected the minutes as much as John Gladstone respected money. Just as the father meticulously kept count of how he spent his pounds so the son equally meticulously kept count of how he spent his quarter hours. His diary, which he began in July 1825 at the age of fifteen and continued until he was eighty-five, with an entry for each day of nearly seventy years, was as unique and impressive a document in the round as it was often bleakly factual in its individual entries. It mostly eschewed comment, for its essential quality, as Gladstone expressed it when trying to persuade his youngest son to follow his example, was as 'an account-book of the all-precious gift of Time'.

Gladstone's combination of energy, eclectic interest and feeling of intellectual accountability to God made him develop at Eton into a voracious reader. Throughout the whole seven decades of the diary he kept a comprehensive (although sometimes cryptic)* record of what he read, whether books or pamphlets, everything indeed except for newspapers, which he also devoured although without individual record. As a result it is possible in a way that cumulatively is almost without parallel to see the whole vast sweep of his literary input: theology, politics, history, science, poetry, fiction, all the main controversial publications of the year, but also many chance works of information which just happened to catch his interest made up the almost unbelievable total of nearly 20,000 works which he recorded as having consumed in the course of his life. He started early. Thus on 28 February 1826, when he was just sixteen, he 'Read Memoirs of Sir Rt Walpole in Biograph. Dict; finished *L'Avare*: read a speech of Huskisson's on Silk Trade. Capital. Began Lyrics (Greek iambics, instead of usual) and read about 160 lines of the second Georgic. . . .'[10]

Gladstone's command over Greek as well as Latin was already considerable, and remained with him throughout his life. He read the Bible every day and often in a Greek text. Homer was a constant companion, and indeed his Homeric studies were a long-term intellectual hobby, into which he would retreat, sometimes at inappropriate

* 'Ar. Pol', for instance, requires the help of the expert editors of the diaries to become a clear indication that he had been reading Aristotle's *Politics*.

moments, and led to his producing some fantastical and unscholarly theories about the roots of Christianity. French he was working at hard with Monsieur Berthomier, a sort of supernumerary Eton master. German was still beyond him, but he later acquired enough to be able in middle life to hold theological discussions with Ignaz von Döllinger in Munich. Italian he taught himself more thoroughly, and Dante (although not until 1834) ranked with Homer as his most sustaining literary refuge. His attitude to modern languages was reminiscent of a tank cutting its way through undergrowth. It was not subtle. His letters, even in French, whether to station masters or statesmen, lacked much sense of elegance, or idiom, or the subjunctive (which had he been French would have been made for him), but he could say what he wanted to.

His concepts of a common civilization and of a united Christendom, which were strong, convinced him that an educated Englishman (which his Anglicanism and his Thames Valley school and university inevitably made him even though his blood made him the most Scottish of all Prime Ministers, with the possible exception of Ramsay MacDonald) ought to be able to communicate in all the principal languages of civilized Europe. So he did so. He conversed with Döllinger in German. He corresponded with Guizot in French notwithstanding that the latter's command of English was such that he had translated all thirteen volumes of Gibbon. And when he was briefly (and eccentrically) Commissioner for the Ionian Isles he made a major policy speech to the Corfu National Assembly in Italian. (It is possible on this occasion that speaker and audience were united in an equal imperfection in their grasp of the language which he had decided should be the bridge between them.) His ability, from his first Italian visit in 1832 to his last in 1889, to listen to vernacular sermons from Milan to Naples and appraise their theological worth was more impressive. In any event he despised allowing languages to be a barrier in the Concert of Europe, a concept which for him had a lively and consistent meaning.

Gladstone's six and a quarter years at Eton were also rewarding on the plane of personal friendship. With the exception of the Earl of Lincoln, later Duke of Newcastle, who was to perform a crucial role in the advancement of Gladstone's early career, he made no grandee friends. But there were plenty of figures of Eton and subsequent note. There was Francis Doyle, who became a fellow of All Souls in 1839, succeeded to a baronetcy, was best man at Gladstone's wedding, and after thirty years as a Customs official became Professor of Poetry at

Oxford in 1877. There was James Milnes Gaskell, whose Unitarian mother first opened Gladstone's mind to the possibility that all true Christians, whatever their liturgical faults, might look forward to salvation rather than to eternal damnation. There was George Selwyn, Bishop of New Zealand at thirty-two and then of Lichfield at a more normal episcopal age, in whose memory Selwyn College, Cambridge, was founded. There was Gerald Wellesley, only nepotically ducal, who was to be Dean of Windsor for nearly thirty years, the strongest Anglican influence upon Queen Victoria (although that was not saying a great deal) in the plenitude of her widowhood, and the man with whom Gladstone most liked to discuss the ever fascinating subject of ecclesiastical patronage during his first premiership.

Above all there was Arthur Hallam, the *jeune homme fatal* (in several senses of the last word) of his age, the Rupert Brooke of the early nineteenth century. He lived only twenty-two years, but achieved an entry in the *Dictionary of National Biography*, which was richly deserved by anyone who could captivate Gladstone and then inspire Tennyson to write *In Memoriam*. Arthur Hallam, the son of a constitutional historian, was two years younger than Gladstone – a big gap in their late teens – and thought dazzlingly beautiful. Gladstone was also very handsome as a young man. There is no evidence of any homosexual behaviour, but it is impossible to believe that there was not the electricity of infatuation and jealousy between them. Hallam was a Foxite Whig, and he appears to have been the one person at Eton, not Lincoln, or Wellesley, who gave Gladstone some sense of inferiority of background. 'He had evidently, from the first,' Gladstone wrote, 'a large share of cultivated domestic education: with a father absorbed in diversified business, I had little or none'.[11] Hallam leaves the impression of being not only a Whig but also a minx. In 1826 he wrote to his sister that he was 'walking out a good deal, and running the changes on Rogers, Gladstone, Farr and Hanmer'. This was after Gladstone had managed to arrange that, although they were in different and widely separated houses, they could breakfast for alternating weeks in each other's rooms. Gladstone went to Oxford in 1828 and Hallam, after more than a year in Italy, to Trinity College, Cambridge, where he met Tennyson, in 1829. But already before they separately left Eton their relationship was over its crest. Gladstone, late in 1829, wrote an account of it which combines the flavour of a shop-girl's romance with that of the prickly and etiolated jealousies of Maynard Keynes and Lytton Strachey in the Cambridge of seventy years later:

> The history of my connection with [Hallam] is as follows.
> It began late in 1824, more at his seeking than mine.
> It slackened soon: more on my account than his.
> It recommenced in 1825, late, more at my seeking than his.
> It ripened much from the early part of 1826 to the middle.
> In the middle [Farr?] *rather* took my place.
> In the latter end [of 1826] it became closer & stronger than ever.
> Through 1827 it flourished most happily, to my very great enjoyment. . . .
> Middle of 1828 [Hallam] returned and thought me cold. (I did not increase my *rate* of letters as under the circumstances I ought to have done.). . . .
> At present, almost an uncertainty, very painful, whether I may call [Hallam] my friend or not.[12]

Prickly and defensive this may have been, but it was a good deal better than the pompous and dismissive letter which Hallam wrote to Gladstone nine months later:

> My dear Gladstone,
> I read the latter part of your letter with much sorrow. . . . I am utterly unworthy of the admiring sentiments you express. . . . Circumstance, my dear Gladstone, has separated our paths, but it can never do away with what has been. The stamp of each of our minds is upon the other. . . . I am aware that your letter points to something more. . . . If you mean that such intercourse as we had at Eton is not likely again to fall to our lot, that is undoubtedly, a stern truth. But if you intimate that I have ceased, or may cease, to interest myself in your happiness, indeed, Gladstone, you are mistaken.[13]

Three years after writing this tiresome missive Hallam died of apoplexy in a Vienna hotel. Gladstone heard the news (a month late) during the first of his autumn visits to his father at Fasque and 'walked upon the hills to muse upon this very mournful event, which cuts me to the heart'. Nonetheless he intermingled reality with nostalgia and wrote on that same day of Hallam as 'my earliest near friend', and of his 'attaining almost to that ideal standard, of which it is presumption to expect an example in natural life'.[14] Tennyson felt less need for qualification and wrote of:

> My Arthur, whom I shall not see
> Till all my widowed race be run
> Dear as the mother to the son
> More than my brothers are to me.[15]

What was most remarkable, however, was that, as Professor Robert Martin's life of Tennyson points out, 'sixty years after his [Hallam's] death the Prime Minister and the Poet Laureate were still jealous of each other's place in his affections'.[16] Gladstone and Tennyson, whom Martin jointly and uncompromisingly described as 'the foremost of all Victorians', spoke well of each other in public but met only occasionally and with some restraint over their relationship until they went together on a Scandinavian cruise in 1883, during which the Prime Minister persuaded the Laureate to accept the rare offer of a literary peerage.

On 10 October 1828 Gladstone and about half of his Eton friends went to Oxford, and almost without exception to Christ Church. However, Hallam and Wellesley went to Trinity, Cambridge, and Selwyn to St John's College in that university. Christ Church then had an Oxford dominance much greater, leading and unusual a college though it has remained, than it has enjoyed in the twentieth century. When Gladstone was matriculated there had been twenty-one Prime Ministers and six of them had been at Christ Church. In addition another two – Peel and Derby – who were subsequently to attain that office had already passed through the House, the somewhat solipsistic sobriquet, derived from *Aedes Christi*, which it liked to give itself. Another four came after Gladstone.

As a seedbed for Prime Ministers, from Grenville in 1763 to Home in 1964, Christ Church has been unmatched in either university. However, its 1828 prestige cannot be measured solely by its position in the Prime Ministerial stakes. Despite having to accommodate a cathedral and the canonries which went with the diocesan church it was a genuine college for the education of the young, and not merely a closed society for the delectation of the fellows, as was then the case with a number of other Oxford houses. It had well over a hundred undergraduates, and, although predisposed to the rich, the titled and the potentially famous, was not much bound by obligation to founder's kin (Henry VIII's three regnant children were not in any event fecund) or to special localities producing dim but entitled aspirants. There were perhaps too many from Westminster School (with which there was a more formal link than with Eton), and Christ Church began to suffer from this as the quality of Westminster declined towards the middle of the nineteenth century from its high seventeenth- and eighteenth-century level. But this was after Gladstone's day. In 1831, Gladstone's final year, five of the ten first classes awarded in the University examinations went to Christ Church men. In addition the college had managed to get a proprietary grip on one of the two Oxford University seats in Parliament. The second might be competed for among the other eighteen or nineteen colleges* which then made up the University, but the first was a *chasse gardée*. Paradoxically this was a disadvantage for Gladstone when he contested the University in 1847. The other seat was already in the Christ Church hands of Sir Robert Inglis, who until he died in 1855 always polled better than Gladstone. For Christ Church to take the second one as well was presumptuous even for the House.

Nor were the other main colleges then in a position to mount much of a challenge. Oxford was only hesitantly rubbing its eyes after its long eighteenth-century sleep, when it had mostly been little more than a seminary for the Anglican Church. Christ Church unusually had kept its grip upon secretaryships of state as well as rectories. In the 1820s Oriel, where was congregated the remarkable constellation of Pusey, Newman, Keble and Samuel Wilberforce, led the awakening. But it was essentially a religious awakening. None of these four was exactly a blushing violet. Pusey had a movement named after him and Keble a college. Newman became the most famous British cardinal since the Reformation, and Bishop Wilberforce of Oxford and Winchester, although sometimes known as 'soapy Sam', was more widely given the admiring label of 'the great diocesan'. But they all became religious leaders rather than rulers of the state, and although the Oriel Common Room was at the time the most brilliant and vital in Oxford, it was unworldly, if not notably saintly, in the vehemence (and even vindictiveness) with which its doctrinal disputes were pursued. Nonetheless, as Newman reflected in his 1852 Dublin *Idea of a University* lectures, there was at that time a unique spirit working within the 'hemmed-in small plot of ground' which was Oriel. It might well have attracted Gladstone, but the possibility does not seem even to have been considered, so well trodden was the path from Eton to Christ Church.

Christ Church was the most privileged college, but Gladstone (or his father) did not claim the most privileged status there. Unlike several of his friends (the Acland brothers and Lincoln) he did not pay the extra fees to be treated as a gentleman-commoner (sometimes called nobleman-commoner). Whether such a status was open to him is not clear. No Gladstone had attained rank as opposed to wealth by that stage, but money has always been a great lubricant of the transition to nobility.

* There was some ambiguity about the status of Magdalen Hall, later Hertford College, at this stage.

Whether or not because of this abstinence William Gladstone at first did not get good rooms. He was turned out of one set. Then he was in a dark ground-floor corner of Chaplain's Quadrangle (since demolished), which required distempering to make the rooms even tolerable. Then he moved (probably when after four terms he had been made a student – a special and elevated rank at the House, more or less equivalent to a fellow elsewhere) to what he described to his mother as 'the most fashionable part of the college'. This was on the first floor to the right (on entering) of the back gate in Canterbury Quadrangle which had been designed by James Wyatt thirty-five years earlier. And writing of the Oxford of a hundred years later John Betjeman in *Summoned by Bells* still envied 'the leisured set in Canterbury quad'. These rooms were for a time preserved as a sort of Gladstone shrine (a rare Oxford distinction shared by Newman but by very few others) and were for some years devoted to the editing of the Gladstone diaries by Professor H. C. G. Matthew.

From this base on what might be called the University side of Christ Church (with Oriel, Corpus and Merton within a few yards, whereas the other side of the college, looking on to the Meadow or St Aldate's, has more the feel of a great liner moored off the shore of the rest of Oxford), Gladstone was a highly successful undergraduate. His continuing Eton friends were Gaskell (who had rooms alongside his), Doyle, Charles Canning, a younger son of the Gladstone-family hero who himself later became Governor-General of India and an earl, Bruce, who succeeded as eighth Earl of Elgin and punitively burnt the Summer Palace in Peking, Walter Kerr Hamilton, who later became Bishop of Salisbury, and Henry Clinton, Earl of Lincoln, who succeeded as Duke of Newcastle in 1851 and was a Peelite Cabinet colleague of Gladstone both in the Aberdeen and in the second Palmerston governments. From outside Eton there were Thomas and Arthur Acland, Rugbeian scions of an old Devon family, Joseph Anstice, who came from Westminster School and became the first Professor of Classical Literature at King's College, London, before dying at the age of twenty-six, and Robert Phillimore, also from Westminster, who became a considerable jurist and short-term MP, which roles he combined with being something of a Boswell to Gladstone, who eventually rewarded him with a baronetcy in 1883.

From outside Christ Church there were two Harrovians who were later to play a considerable and at times intimate part in Gladstone's life: Sidney Herbert, a younger son of the Earl of Pembroke, who was at Oriel and who later became another Peelite colleague of Gladstone, and also, in Morley's words, 'perhaps the best beloved of all his friends'; and Henry Manning, who at Balliol was then a rather Low Church Anglican, with his ambitions directed more towards marriage and archdeaconries than towards cardinals' hats and ultramontanism. But these last two at that stage were more acquaintances than close friends. James Hope (Hope-Scott after, by marrying Sir Walter Scott's granddaughter, he acquired Abbotsford, Scott's house on the Tweed), with whom Gladstone was to have one of his intense friendships in the 1840s, was then in the same category. F. D. Maurice, who had come from Cambridge to Exeter College in 1830, and Edward Pusey, who became a canon of Christ Church on becoming Professor of Hebrew in the same year, were also influential acquaintances of Gladstone at Oxford. With Keble and Newman, on the other hand, he had little direct contact, although much aware of them as eminences of the University.

Gladstone was thus far from being a lonely undergraduate. But nor was he a generally popular one. He surrounded himself with a defensive coterie who were all of some distinction but to whom he was the central figure. When towards the end of his first year he organized them into an essay club, which he hoped might be a counterpart to the Cambridge Apostles, it was known as the Weg, after his own initials; whether or not because of this label it achieved neither the fame nor the permanence of the Society, as the Apostles were alternatively known. He was much less vulnerable than the reclusive brass-rubber, Paul Pennyfeather, whose dismayed reaction to 'the sound of the English county families baying for broken glass' was immortalized by Waugh's *Decline and Fall* portrait of Christ Church a century later. But Pennyfeather and Gladstone were beaten up in somewhat similar circumstances, although in Gladstone's case the incident started no sequence of tragi-comic events. Late on a March night in the middle of his second year, Gladstone's rooms were invaded by a boisterous party of Christ Church 'bloods' who had clearly decided that Gladstone was priggish, pious and self-righteous. Unfortunately his diary reaction was an orgy of holier-than-thou self-abnegation which had it been available to his assailants would have confirmed them in their worst suspicions:

> Here I have great reason to be thankful to that God whose mercies fail not ... 1) Because this incident must tend to the mortification of my pride, by God's grace.... It is no disgrace to be beaten for Christ was buffeted and smitten....
>
> 2) Because here I have to some small extent an opportunity of exercising the duty of forgiveness.... And if this hostile and unkind

conduct be a sample of their ways, I pray that the grace of God may reveal to them that the end thereof is death. Even this prayer is selfish. I prayed little for them before, when I knew that they were living in sin and had rejected Christ their Saviour. . . . I ought to have prayed before as much as now. . . .'[17]

This was Gladstone at his worst, particularly as he was only twenty at the time. But in general the immense seriousness of his purpose was tempered by the width of his interests, which prevented his work being too obsessive, just as the delicacy of his conscience was tempered by a sense of fun and a liking for companionship. He did not work excessively hard at Oxford, except perhaps in the late summer and autumn of 1831, which culminated in his taking two 'Schools', *Literae Humaniores* and Mathematics, between 7 November and 14 December, and getting secure firsts in both. The feat was the greater because he was not really interested in mathematics. He merely absorbed the subject in order to get the coveted scalp of a double first.

Even during this period of pressurized preparation he took five days off in early October to go to London and listen to fifty hours or more of the House of Lords debate which culminated in the rejection of the Reform Bill. His listening stamina was formidable, even though he was 'compelled to leave the House by exhaustion' before the reply of the Prime Minister (Grey). But he was already both a gourmand and a gourmet of rhetoric. During the debate he thought that Brougham's speech was 'most wonderful', Grey's (opening) speech 'most beautiful' and Lansdowne's 'very good',[18] even though they were all on the wrong (Whig) side from his point of view.

In the same way his appetite for sermons stemmed as much from his growing connoisseurship of oratory as from his devoutness. On a normal Sunday, whether in Oxford or at home in Liverpool or with his family in one of their spa towns, he would almost invariably listen to two and occasionally to three sermons. His diary for 6 March 1831 provided a fairly typical example of such a day, except that the Newman comment added a special piquancy:

Chapel & sermon twice. Newman preached in the afternoon – much singular not to say objectionable matter if one may so speak of so good a man. Bible [reading] – D. Wilson – Leighton's *Praelect[iones Theologicae]* – writing a little – heard Buckley preach most admirably – walked to Marsden [should be Marston, about two and a half miles from Christ Church] to see a poor man – heard a prayer at a Dissenting Chapel (standing at the door) on my way back.[19]

In and around Oxford Gladstone walked a lot and also rode. But he engaged in no country sports nor in any organized games, although he occasionally watched both cricket and rowing, including an expedition to Henley (which he described as 'an exceedingly pleasant day') to see the first Oxford and Cambridge boat race in June 1829. His principal recreations were conversation and debating. He gave and went to frequent wine parties, and paid some attention to the quality that was served. He was never censorious about alcohol indulgence in himself or others, and noted with satisfaction the delivery of wine stocks to his rooms.

Gladstone's debating was centred upon the nascent Union Society, which had been founded less than five years before, and was then very different from the imitation Palace of Westminster, gothic-designed and pre-Raphaelite-decorated, in which Asquith, Curzon and F. E. Smith later disported themselves. Gladstone was the first of the household gods of the Union but he had to make do with a primitive version which was more frequently and prosaically called the Debating Society, had only just acquired permanent but rented and modest premises in the High Street (the St Michael's Street site was not acquired until 1853), and attracted audiences of very limited size. On the evening of 14 November 1830, when Gladstone was elected president (for a term), his motion to censure the Wellington government for its pusillanimity in accepting Catholic emancipation was carried by only 57 to 56 votes, as compared with the nearly 600 who voted at the end of the Munich debate in 1938. After his most notable speech in the Union, on 17 May 1831 and in vehement opposition to the Reform Bill, he carried the motion by 94 votes to 38. He spoke for forty-five minutes. The debate was an ingrowing affair for he came immediately after Gaskell, who had followed Lincoln. It was his first speech of compelling power. 'When [he] sat down,' Francis Doyle wrote, 'we all of us felt that an epoch in our lives had occurred.'[20] Charles Wordsworth, nephew of the poet and son of the Master of Trinity (Cambridge), described it as 'the most splendid speech, out and out, that was ever heard in our Society'.

It was hardly a moderate speech. Its thesis was that the Reform Bill, if carried, would break up the social order not merely in Britain but throughout the civilized world. Chesterton's satire on F. E. Smith's claim ninety years later that the Welsh Church Disestablishment Bill had 'shocked the conscience of every Christian community in Europe' could have been applied with an equally deflating mockery to Gladstone's onslaught on the immorality of reducing the number of rotten boroughs.

Gladstone himself in later life was to be only mildly embarrassed by the direction and extremity of his views at this time. When Disraeli in 1866 not unreasonably mocked him for these opinions, he replied, semi-complacently: 'My youthful mind and imagination were impressed with some idle and futile fears which still bewilder and distract the mature mind of the right honourable gentleman.'[21] And he also claimed, latterly and blandly, that 'while I do not think that the general tendencies of my mind were, in the time of my youth, illiberal, there was to my eyes an element of the anti-Christ in the Reform Act'.[22] His more serious and self-critical mature view was that while Oxford taught him to respect truth it did not teach him to love liberty.

Nor did it teach him to avoid excess. But excess was always one of his salient qualities. He could lie back from a subject because he thought that the time for it was not ripe. But, once he had engaged with it, he did so with a commitment which excited his allies on the issue (who were often surprising because of the oscillating nature of his interests and views), affronted his opponents and filled his long-term friends with apprehension. As a result many of his most memorable speeches did him more direct harm than good, although at the same time they built up, as a stalagmite grows, the respect for and fear of the most formidable orator in Parliament.

His Oxford Union anti-Reform effusion, by contrast and measurably, brought the most direct benefit. It led Lord Lincoln, in no way offended by being out-orated, successfully to recommend him as a parliamentary candidate to his father. This fourth Duke of Newcastle, whose distinctions were mainly the accidental ones of holding the dukedom for fifty-six years and of having so many boroughs more or less at his disposal that the great Reform Act, which he opposed as vehemently as Gladstone but less articulately, merely ruffled his feathers in this respect. One of his boroughs, Newark in Nottinghamshire, he bestowed upon Gladstone. It was a fine parliamentary property to acquire at the age of twenty-two, but it came very much as a leasehold and not as a freehold.

2

A Grand Tour Ending at Newark

THERE WAS A YEAR between Gladstone leaving Oxford and his election to Parliament, and he spent half of it making his grand tour. He was always a natural traveller, geographically somewhat restless in spite of his great powers of concentration and love of book learning, curious to see new sights, and powerfully resilient against the fatigue of long days and nights in bumping coaches. He liked planning journeys and he enjoyed moments of departure, particularly if they came after periods of high strain. Thus, on 14 December 1831, the day on which he did his last examination papers in the morning, and received the news of his mathematical (and hence double) first in the afternoon he managed after an evening of letter-writing, packing and farewells to leave by the night coach to London, where he stopped only for breakfast before proceeding to Cambridge for a five-day visit (during which he was 'excellently lodged' with the Master of Trinity). In much the same mood, when he was a leading politician and the railways had come, he would mark the beginning of a holiday from London business by a dawn departure from Euston to Chester (for Hawarden) or Birmingham (for Hagley), sometimes walking the final six or twelve miles from the railway stations to the country mansions which were his destinations.

Thus, when in early 1832 the time for a major European excursion became as available as the money had always been, Gladstone was eager to undertake the journey. The only surprising element was that he chose to do so with his naval-officer brother, temporarily but not unusually without a ship, and not with one or more of his Christ Church friends. John Neilson Gladstone was then twenty-five and William Ewart Gladstone only twenty-two, but there emerges (admittedly from William Gladstone's own diary) the strong impression that William was nonetheless the senior partner in the enterprise. What was more important, however, was that they got on well together, much better than William would then have been likely to do with either of his other brothers. This was, to say the least, fortunate for the expedition lasted 179 days and they were rarely apart for more than a few hours.

Their experiences abroad were similar to those of most English travellers of the eighteenth and early nineteenth centuries: uncomfortable post-chaises, with a lot of ill-tempered haggling over prices; small-town inns of very variable quality, but the discomfort of these relieved by long stays in spacious lodgings or well-kept hotels in the principal cities, where they enjoyed thorough but leisurely sight-seeing and social contact with other English visitors as well as, although to a lesser extent, with local notables. They were sufficiently cosmopolitan to assume that language was not an obstacle, at any rate with the educated classes, and sufficiently English to have a good deal of concern about the cleanliness of the beds and the strangeness of the food. (They were of course purely Scottish by birth, but it would not have occurred to them so to describe themselves or to enquire for anything other than the *English* Legation, the *English* church or the *English* tea rooms.) On balance, however, they were a good deal more integrated with local life and customs than are most British visitors to France or Italy today.

They left London on 1 February, were in Belgium for five days and then in Paris for another twelve from 11 February. They crossed the Mont Cenis pass on 1 March and descended into Turin for a week, then to Genoa for a weekend, and then by Lucca, Pisa and Livorno to Florence for ten days. They eventually reached Rome a month after crossing the Piedmontese frontier. Rome was then given a full four weeks until the southward journey was resumed and twenty-five days were spent in Naples and around its bay. Every Italian city was given carefully graded allocations of time, with Rome being put in its place above Naples with an additional ten-day sojourn on the way back.

They finally left the Eternal City as summer was beginning and struck north on 5 June. (Most English travellers in those days scampered back across the Alps before even the vernal sun might attack them with heat and fevers.) They got to Venice after two nights in Ravenna and three in Bologna and stayed there for ten days. Then they went *via* Verona and Bolzano to Innspruck (as Gladstone rather quaintly called it) and back by the lakes of Garda and Como to a final Italian pause of four days in Milan, which impressed Gladstone as having 'an appearance of wealth, abundance, and activity' lacking in the rest of Italy. Another three days brought them to Geneva, from where Gladstone accepted the Duke of Newcastle's offer to sponsor him as candidate for his borough of Newark, on the understanding, distinctly generous for a duke, that he would pay half the election expenses (estimated at £1000 but turning out to be £2000) provided that John Gladstone paid the other half.

This prospect filled William Gladstone with awesome excitement. He wrote of it as a 'bold and terrible experiment'. He hoped, in the words of the second collect for evensong, that his decision had been taken 'in a spirit not of utter forgetfulness of Him, who is the author of all good counsels, all holy desires, and all just works'. But he also laid a great deal of weight on the counsel of his father in the flesh as well as of his Father in God. And he seasoned it all with some electoral caution: 'there cannot be, I should think, anything approaching certainty in a case where the constituency consists of 1600 voters'.[1] But he did not hurry home. He and his brother proceeded across Switzerland to Basle, by steamboat down the Rhine valley (the scenery of which failed to impress him) to Cologne, overland to Brussels and Ostend and to London by the morning of 28 July. The Kent country looked 'well cultivated and the towns along the route beautifully clean'. In addition he had found the Dover 'Customhouse officers civil, reasonable, and expeditious – and of a genus infinitely superior to the foreign doganieri. No winking nor cheating, little bowing and scraping.'[2] He was a good traveller ('always look after your luggage yourself', he recorded as a sensible precept), and an instinctive European, but not free of the traditional prejudices which, at least since the Reformation, have separated England from the Continent.

One of the several paradoxes which racked his life was that while he believed passionately in the unity of Christendom (and in its political manifestation, the Concert of Europe), he also felt that idolatry began at Calais. He had been brought up in what Magnus described as 'the narrowest form of Evangelical religion',[3] although Matthew is perhaps more accurate when he calls the atmosphere of the household 'moderately Evangelical'.[4] The Gladstones never contemplated leaving the Church of England, which many Evangelicals did, and were therefore necessarily in some contact with the other strands of Anglicanism. Even when John Gladstone had added two to the number of Evangelical churches in Liverpool there were no more than a total of three. Secondly, the home atmosphere was argumentative and questioning rather than flatteningly authoritarian. The children were encouraged to engage in courteous dispute.

This moderation did not make the family cool Evangelicals. Coolness indeed was one of the last qualities it would be appropriate to attribute to anything to do with William Gladstone. He could sometimes be patient, as shown by the immense quantities of time which he was prepared to devote to listening in the House of Commons or by the meticulousness with which he would refute the most minor points of argument. He was never good at understanding positions opposed to his own, but he was good at taking trouble to expose error. Yet his patience never stemmed from coolness. He had a consistently tumultuous nature. It was often (but not always) held in check by rigid discipline. The result, however, was not a calm lake but a mill-race controlled by a dam of steel.

The other two *dévotes* in his family were his mother and his sister Anne. They were not tumultuous personalities in William Gladstone's sense. Their invalidism would have made it difficult for them to emulate his turbulence. But they were dominated by religion, and his sister in particular was a powerful spiritual influence upon him. Her death in February 1829 was the greatest trauma that he experienced during the mounting success of his school and Oxford years. The effect was to increase both his morbidity and his religiosity. It strengthened his view that the central purpose of his life, not only spiritually but also organizationally, should be the upholding of religion. He felt (and announced in a turgid and sometimes incomprehensible 4000-word letter to his father) that this should take the form of his becoming a clergyman, but when John Gladstone firmly opposed this course William Gladstone was quite easily turned away from it, even though the moment of decision was little more than a year after his sister's death.

He persuaded himself that this was because of a combination of the duty that he owed his father and of his own feeling that he could perhaps better serve the cause of religion as a political warrior on its ramparts than as a priest protected within the citadel. Yet he accepted the turning away sufficiently easily that it is difficult to believe that there was not an element of relief. As a forum for his powers a cathedral close, even in the days of thundering bishops and liturgically authoritative deans, could not have compared with Parliament when Britain was powerful and politicians were treated as heroes. He attempted to square the circle by always insisting that his primary task in politics was to uphold religion. However, his view of how best this could be done changed drastically over the years.

Although there can be no doubt of the depth, dominance and consistency of Gladstone's religious passion, it is nonetheless surprising, this being so, that an Evangelical from Liverpool took so easily to the virtually pagan Eton (as both Morley and Magnus put it) and to the worldly Erastianism, tempered only by the first stirrings of Tractarianism, of Christ Church. At Eton, Gladstone wrote much later, 'the actual teaching of Christianity was all but dead', and Magnus made much of Gladstone's disappointment at the 'empty show' of his 1827 Confirmation service. But the only criticism that Gladstone committed to his diary was that 'the Bishop [of Lincoln was] not dignified in appearance'.[5] As Bishop Pelham died six days later it would perhaps be unfair to stress his demeanour on that particular occasion. What was undoubtedly the case, however, was that Eton religious teaching and observances during the reign of George IV were much more a hangover from eighteenth-century scepticism than a harbinger of Victorian fervour. Gladstone would have wished it otherwise, but it did not put him out of joint with the school.

At Christ Church the cathedral services were conducted almost as perfunctorily as those in Eton Chapel. Gladstone at the end of his first term wrote: 'Sacrament: as cold and unprepared as usual'.[6] He attended frequently but he got more spiritual sustenance from St Mary's, the University church in the High Street, of which Newman had just become vicar, from a variety of Oxford shrines most of which have since become ecclesiastically redundant, St Ebbe's, St Martin's at Carfax, St Peter's-in-the-East, and even from the extra-mural activities of the Revd Mr Bulteel. Bulteel was a curate at St Ebbe's when Gladstone arrived in Oxford, but soon got himself expelled from that church for preaching in Dissenting chapels (that is, outside the communion of the Church of England) or in the open air – it is not clear which was the worse. He was an early exponent of 'born-again' Christianity who invited his hearers to experience an apocalyptic conversion.

Gladstone never underwent such a single experience, although he liked listening to Bulteel, even if he did so with enough circumspection that when he observed his outdoor revivalism it was from an open window and not among the crowd. There was perhaps a certain symbolism in this position. Gladstone as a young man retained a good deal of the spirit and language of Evangelicalism (which indeed persisted throughout his life), but his position was firmly within the tabernacle of the Apostolic Church, with institutional religion, not in the formal and material sense of the pomp and emoluments of a rich state Church, but in the historical and theological sense of the Church as a carefully ordained unity which uniquely represented Christ on earth, becoming increasingly important to him.

There were at that time three main parties within the Church of England. They could perhaps be better described as tendencies, for not everybody belonged to one or other of them and many who did held their tenets fairly loosely, often, if they were of a non-ideological turn of mind, combining some aspects of one outlook with some of another. As a result, while the parties provided plenty of ground for dispute and even bitterness, they were not so fissiparous as to make impossible coexistence within the frontiers of the established Church. They were like three hillocks in a landscape, on each of which the more disputatious leaders could stand, while their varyingly committed followers could occupy, closer or further away from the hillocks at will, the intervening folds of ground.

The most intellectually exciting, although in other ways the weakest of the three parties, was the Apostolic, or Catholic, or as they later came to be called when the Oxford Movement had gathered momentum the Tractarian party. For them the Bible was all very well in its way, but it needed the sacred authority of an apostolic, sacramental, priestly Church to interpret it properly, and the Prayer Book was at least an equally important textbook of faith. And the lives of the saints and of the early fathers were just as worthy of attention as were the doings of the titans of the Old Testament. The label most abhorred by the adherents of the tendency was that of Protestant. They were Catholics, although those who were not tempted over the dreadful border disapproved of many of the pretensions and abuses of the Church of Rome. Since the Reformation, which provided an awkward kink but not a full break in tradition, they had been Anglicans. But they were no more Protestants than they were Dissenters. The Apostolic Church was the only means to salvation. To dissent from it was to exclude oneself from the hope of grace. The Church was *the* Church in the realm, but this was so because it was Christ's Church rather than because it was the King's Church, although it was desirable that it should be that also. But the state should serve the Church, rather than the Church serve the state. Indeed the Erastian view of the Church in which archbishops were as subordinate to Prime Ministers as were parsons to Whig magnates was so intolerable that disestablishment might be better. 'Church and King' was a tolerable motto but not 'State and Church'.

The Evangelical party did not much involve itself with this competing institutionalism for it was primarily concerned with the direct relationship of the individual with his God, and did not allow high place to either Church or state. Its tradition stemmed from the Puritans and had been much fortified by the Wesleys and by Whitefield in the middle of the eighteenth century. For its adherents the Bible rather than the Church was man's essential route to God. Personal salvation could be achieved by personal conversion. Ministers of God's word might assist in this process, but they were not essential agents. They were the organizers and, maybe, the inspirers of congregations but they were not 'the stewards of the mysteries of God'.

Evangelicals provided much of the energy and of the enthusiasm of the Church of England. They sustained the Biblical Societies and the Protestant Missions throughout the world. Most of the great practical reformers and philanthropists – William Wilberforce or Shaftesbury – were Evangelicals. It was a form of religion which released energy rather than satisfied intellectual sophistication. As Gladstone wrote when he looked back on his youth: 'The Evangelical movement . . . did not ally itself with literature, art and general cultivation; but it harmonized well with the money-getting pursuits.'[7]

The third party in the Church were the liberals or Latitudinarians. They dated back at least to the reign of Charles I, but their wonderful century had begun in 1688. They did not much believe in religious glory, regarding as almost equally far-fetched Anglo-Catholic views about grace transmitted through the priesthood and Evangelical views about grace spontaneously generated by an inner experience of conversion. They were the religious beneficiaries of the Glorious Revolution. Their cool rationalism, which had made them hostile to Stuart claims of divine right, made them at home with a Whig oligarchy and well attuned to the mannered cultivation of the so-called Augustan age. They were somewhat insular (although, if they were rich enough, venturing into the occasional grand tour and the importation of Italian works of art), which made them anti-Catholic, and they were against excessive enthusiasm, which made them anti-Evangelical. They thought that religion should be an affair of sense, morals (within reason) and good behaviour. John Locke and Bishop Butler were their philosophers and Jane Austen was the best chronicler of the background against which they flourished.

This liberal (in ecclesiastical terms) or Broad Church approach has over the three centuries since the Whig Revolution shown a persistent if fluctuating strength and has been the dominant trend within the Church under different manifestations alike in Butler's Durham, Trollope's Barchester and Runcie's Canterbury. But it was at a relatively low ebb *circa* 1830, when the clerical spirit of eighteenth-century Oxford had encouraged Latitudinarianism to degenerate into lethargy. In any event it never held much appeal for Gladstone. It was too cool and detached for him, and it was not religious liberalism but the rival enthusiasms of the Apostolic and the Evangelical Churches which, as in Housman's *Welsh Marches*, 'ceased not fighting, east and west, on the marches of [his] breast'.

An important engagement of that continuing conflict occurred during his Italian sojourn in the spring of 1832, when he was just over twenty-two years of age and poised between his Oxford academic triumphs of December 1831 and his election to Parliament in December 1832. He had travelled for two months, mostly finding English services for Sunday mornings (although having to make do with Prussian Protestantism in Turin), but also taking in, generally with disapproval, a wide range of Roman Catholic observances. The low mass at the Cathedral of St Gudule in Brussels was 'an unmeaning and sorrowful ceremony'.[8] In Florence he saw two baptisms administered in the Baptistery and wrote of himself as 'dissatisfied with the matter, disgusted (I cannot use a weaker term) with the *manner* of the service'.[9] The next day he went to a minor church and was at once sad and severe: 'It is painful to speak disrespectfully of any religious services but these certainly seemed no better than mummery.'[10] The underlying causes of his trans-European censoriousness were idolatry, the elevation of the Virgin to a position almost above Christ, and the disengaged mumbling of the services by unprepossessing priests (although he ought to have become used to the last fault by 'the mumblings of toothless fellows', as he had expressed it, in Eton Chapel).

On 31 March, his first day in Rome, he went to St Peter's. He was not at first impressed by the architecture ('my humble homage is reserved for that Gothic style, which prevails in our own English cathedrals')[11] and could not easily equate the baroque with a religious atmosphere. Yet the great basilica achieved what must be adjudged its central purpose and set him meditating on the unity of Christendom in a way that he had never done before. In so doing he made few concessions to the authority of the Holy See:

> In entering such a Church as this, most deeply does one feel the pain and shame of the schism which separates us from Rome – whose guilt (for guilt I at least am well persuaded there always is where there is schism) surely rests not upon the Venerable Fathers of the English Reformed Church, but upon Rome itself [there then follow nine balancing subordinate clauses of a convolution which make the net effect almost impossible to follow]. . . . May God bind up the wounds of his bleeding Church.[12]

Yet for all his instinctive disputatiousness (six weeks before, in Paris, he had self-revealingly written: 'Unhappily my manner tends to turn every conversation into a debate')[13], this visit to the areopagus of Christianity did shift his mind. Already the next day, after Vespers at Trinità del Monte, Gladstone, while regretting that the litany was to the Blessed Virgin and, combining his usual opaqueness with an unusual casualness of introduction, wrote: 'Speaking of the Virgin, surely we are as much too remiss, yet not the Church of England, but her members, in commemorations of saints as the Romish Church is *officious and audacious*.'[14] And six weeks later, in Naples, he recorded:

> Of late and today in particular, I have been employed in examining some of the details of the system of the English Church, as set forth in the Prayer-book, with which I was before less acquainted. To coming into Catholic countries, and to some few books, I owe glimpses which now seem to be afforded to me of the nature of a Church, and of our duties as members of it, which involve an idea very much higher & more important than I had previously had any conception of.[15]

This was Gladstone's contemporary version. Nearly sixty years later he provided a grander but not incompatible account of the same occasion. After testifying that 'the impression [of that Naples day] has never been effaced', he wrote:

> I had previously taken a great deal of teaching direct from the Bible, as best I could, but now the figure of the Church rose before me as a teacher too, and I gradually found in how incomplete and fragmentary a manner I had drawn divine truth from the sacred volume, as indeed I had also missed in the Thirty-Nine Articles some things which ought to have taught me better. Such, for I believe that I have given the fact as it occurred, in its silence and its solitude, was my first introduction to the august conception of the Church of Christ. It presented to me Christianity under an aspect in which I had not yet known it: its ministry of symbols, its channels of grace, its unending line of teachers joining from the Head: a sublime construction, based throughout upon historic fact, uplifting the idea of the community in which we live, and of the access which it enjoys through the new and living way to the presence of the Most High. From this time I began to feel my way by degree into or towards a true notion of the Church.[16]

Thus, in one of the several major paradoxes of his life, was Gladstone moved by his experience in Roman Catholic Europe towards a position which was (and remained) as firmly anti-Roman as, within the terms of the Anglican debate, it was both emotionally and terminologically Catholic.

Back in England in the late summer of 1832, Gladstone turned his attention from religion to politics. This has to be qualified to the extent that he would never have admitted that politics was allowed to exclude religion. For the absence of dichotomy he would have argued first on the inner and therefore incontestable if not wholly convincing ground that politics were for him merely a means to religious ends; and second, and more empirically, by always being able to show that political preoccupation never interfered with the intensity of either his religious observances or his theological reading and thought.

Nevertheless Newark, about which his electoral caution was justified, did require and receive considerable attention. His visit in late September 1832, for which he had posted so hurriedly from Torquay because he was informed that 'the canvass' had already begun, lasted well into October. Apart from general canvassing, which took a surprisingly modern form, with Gladstone recording the few occasions when he was refused a handshake ('principally by *women*'), he had to underpin his position with the Duke of Newcastle, whom he had not previously met. He was 'most kindly' received at Clumber and indeed subsequently wrote to his father about the Duke almost in terms which might have been employed by the Revd Mr Collins of Lady Catherine de Burgh. Patron and protégé both dismayed and comforted each other with agreement on the awful impending threats to the social and moral order. Gladstone appears to have thrown in the possibility of the downfall of the Papacy, to which the Duke looked forward with more complacency than did Gladstone. What they mutually accepted as more decisively good were 'the virtues of an ancient aristocracy, than which the world never saw one more powerful or more pure' than that epitomized at Clumber.[17]

The Duke, however, was by no means all-powerful in Newark, and Gladstone had to deal not only with independent-minded burghers of that borough but also with magnates who had segments of influence smaller than but separate from those of the Duke. The Earl of Winchilsea and Nottingham was wholly supportive but regretted that his tenants had not been as 'warm and unanimous' towards Gladstone as he would have wished. He would endeavour to apply corrective measures. Lord Middleton, on the other hand, replied from Wollaton House, the fine Tudor mansion on the edge of Nottingham, with a heavy rebuke for Gladstone's approach to him: 'as an entire stranger to me, I must be allow'd to express my surprise that you should thus early have applied to me'.[18]

However, despite this, a bumpy passage on the slavery issue and other rebuffs within the town, where it does not appear that his candidature aroused much enthusiasm, Gladstone did win. Indeed, in an election for two seats, he came top of the poll, an experience which, even though he had then become famous, was subsequently to elude him in Oxford, South Lancashire and Greenwich. At Newark there were three candidates for the two seats. The second Tory, Handley, was quasi-anonymous. The sole and defeated Whig was far from this. He was already a well-known lawyer, bearing the rumbustious advocates' title of 'Serjeant'. Later, transformed from Serjeant Wilde into Baron Truro, he was to be Lord Chancellor in Lord John Russell's first government. Gladstone, who on the day of nomination spent six and a half hours on the hustings, was even at twenty-two a near match for him in debating skill and stronger in influence, polled 887, the dim Mr Handley 798 and the future Lord Truro 726.

On the declaration of the poll, which was at nine in the morning of 14 December 1832, Gladstone spoke for 'an hour or more – Serjeant [Wilde] procured me a hearing – but a cold one'.[19] This might seem early evidence of Gladstone's life-long taste for inflated oratory in even the most inappropriate circumstances. But the point of the example is somewhat weakened by the fact that Serjeant Wilde followed him for one and a half hours.

There had been a number of the features of Eatanswill (Dickens's caricature of a corrupt borough in *The Pickwick Papers*) to the Newark contest, not least the distribution of far more money on Gladstone's behalf than he was aware of or subsequently approved. However, it was not quite scandalous enough to lead to a petition against corrupt practices, the usual Gladstone family experience. There was also a good deal of boisterousness, with stones missing Gladstone's head by only 'twelve inches' (his usual precision), but he had sufficient cohorts to be 'most powerfully escorted [back] to the Clinton Arms'. In that hostelry, appropriately named to mark the Newcastle influence, Gladstone dined on the evening of his election in the company of the members of the 'Red Clubs' which were vigorous in the constituency. Red was the local Tory colour, evoking a loyalty almost as fierce as that which was to be inspired by the 'bloody shirt' in the American Civil War, and even seventy years later (although this was after the words of the 'Red Flag' had been added to the tune of 'Tannenbaum' to make a socialist hymn)

Morley recorded without irony that the most intense Tory partisan and cheerleader had proclaimed: 'I was born Red, I live Red, and I shall die Red.'[20] The most notable feature of Gladstone's own speech was an attempt, based no doubt on the new confidence of having the seat under his belt but also somewhat bumptiously maladroit for twenty-two, to solve the problem of his dependence on the Duke of Newcastle with a syllogism. 'You need not ask', he said, 'whether I am your man or the Duke's man, for the answer is that we are both of us, the Duke and I, equally your men.'

The new Parliament met two months later, and Gladstone first entered the House of Commons as a member on 7 February 1833. He and his brother Tom walked down together from Jermyn Street, where they were both temporarily lodging, although removing to Albany a month later, and took their seats side by side among the ranks of 160 which was all that the Tories were able to muster in the first reformed Parliament. In George Hayter's painting of the old chamber, done in 1834 a few months before the fire which destroyed most of the Palace of Westminster, they are visible, still together, sitting on the back row but one. Tom, misleadingly, looks the more distinguished. They were nonetheless shown as being remarkably alike, and Tom's first speech in that Parliament (he had been in the previous one for about a year), which he delivered on 21 February, was attributed by Hansard to William. This misattribution created lasting confusion and led to William's alleged maiden speech being described as late as 1971 as 'a dim début'.

Dim that February speech certainly was, with much of it inaudible and the subject the hardly inspiring one of the defence of the alleged corrupt parties in Liverpool local elections. But it was not by William Gladstone, who did not make what he and others regarded as his maiden speech until 3 June, although he had uttered a few sentences on both 30 April and 21 May when presenting petitions. Then (on 3 June) the subject-matter was little more elevating for he chose to speak in opposition to a Slavery Abolition Bill and did so very much as a 'West Indian' representative. Both the Gladstone boys made pietistic starts in the House, defending not only their father's interests but his name as well. However, it was a fully effective speech, which Gladstone recorded in his diary as having lasted for fifty minutes and being 'very kindly' received by the House so that 'my *friends* were satisfied'.[21]

Thereafter the House of Commons careers of the two Gladstones could hardly have diverged more sharply. William went on to be the dominant parliamentarian of the century, outpacing Canning, Peel and Disraeli by the sheer length of his span in the House of Commons, and elbowing aside Palmerston and Lord John Russell by the greater fervour of his oratory. Tom Gladstone's parliamentary experience, by contrast, was if anything still less glorious than that of his father. He suffered in an extreme form from the family disability of rarely being able to keep a seat over two elections without either defeat or unseating on petition. For the 1830 election the almost unknown Kent town of Queensborough, lurking in the shadows of the Isle of Sheppey, had been procured for him. He lost his seat on the poll, but a few months later retrieved it on petition. For the 1832 election he transferred to the Irish Midlands borough of Portarlington and secured a majority of its 150 electors. But by the next general election in 1835 he had got on to such bad terms with almost every local interest that there was no question of his even contesting Portarlington. He contemplated both Nottingham and, bizarrely, Orkney, but settled upon Leicester. He sat for this town until 1837, when for the last time a change of sovereign involved the dissolution of Parliament, which resulted in Tom Gladstone's temporary disappearance from it. At the 1841 general election he contested Peterborough, and although again defeated reversed the result at an 1842 by-election. But he had overdone his enticements to the electors and was unseated on petition. For the remaining forty-seven years of his long life he was never again in the House of Commons.

John Neilson Gladstone had an almost equally chequered electoral experience. When he could no longer get a ship he sought a seat, and in 1841 he won a by-election at Walsall. He was petitioned against for corrupt practices, but that year's general election intervened and the petition was overridden by his defeat. In 1842 he won another by-election at Ipswich and sat there until the next general election of 1847, when he was again beaten. In 1852 he secured at Devizes a seat in a county which was his own (by adoption at least) and survived there until his death eleven years later, which was a long constituency association by the standards of all members of John Gladstone's family other than William, and a moderate one even by his.

William Gladstone's parliamentary service covered sixty-two and a half years, with a break of twenty months in 1846–7. But this great span was divided between five constituencies as disparate as Newark, Oxford University, South Lancashire, Greenwich and Midlothian.

The inescapable conclusion is that John Gladstone and his three parliamentary sons were both peripatetic and opportunistically cold-hearted in their approach to constituencies. The father and the two elder sons were unsuccessfully so; William by contrast, despite the problems which might have been caused by his move across the political spectrum, had an almost complete command over what he wanted. He changed constituencies like an exigent hunting man demanding a new horse whenever he felt the old one was tiring. Admittedly much greater mobility in this respect was usual in the nineteenth century. Canning, Peel, Russell, Palmerston, Disraeli were all wanderers, although the last two, after early strayings, settled down to thirty years in, respectively, Tiverton and Buckinghamshire.

The single constituency throughout a political lifetime and the geographical identity which goes with it came in only with Joseph Chamberlain, whose pattern in this respect if not in most others was followed in the twentieth century by such diverse figures as Lloyd George, R. A. Butler, Harold Wilson, James Callaghan and Margaret Thatcher. In the nineteenth century before Chamberlain there was by contrast no figure of the first rank who stuck to a single constituency. Nevertheless the Gladstones, taken collectively, were unusually fickle. Between them, and including constituencies considered as well as fought, they spattered the map of England, Scotland and even Ireland with as many red spots as did the British Empire on an old globe. Only Wales was free from their attentions, which was strange both because it provided much of the hinterland to Liverpool and because William Gladstone lived there, even if barely over the border from Cheshire, for half a century. However, his brother-in-law, with whom Gladstone cohabited at Hawarden, was a Flintshire member for fifteeen years and thus repaired the Gladstone omission.

The residence, the brother-in-law and the tenuous Welsh parliamentary connection followed from his marriage into the Glynne family. This, however, did not occur until 1839, shortly before his thirtieth birthday, and in his seventh year as a member of Parliament. This was despite determined attempts from 1835, involving two failures, to find himself a bride. Those refusals, and his ultimate success with Miss Glynne, belong to the next chapter.

3
A Clumsy Suitor

The ten years from his 1833 entry into the House of Commons to 15 May 1843, when he was promoted to Peel's Cabinet as President of the Board of Trade, were on the surface a period of vaulting success for Gladstone. In politics it was mostly a Whig decade, but nonetheless one in which the cohesion and reforming zeal of the 1832 majority gradually dissipated themselves, and the Tories, although requiring three general elections over which to do so, came back from the rump of 160 among whom Gladstone first sat to a party of approximately 360 with a majority of 80. Each of the general elections had gone smoothly for Gladstone. In 1835 and 1837 he was unopposed at Newark, and in 1841 he was top of the poll, with Lord John Manners, his new running mate, three votes behind him, and the sole Whig challenger nowhere near either of them.

Gladstone had also got as early (and substantial) a bite at office as the minority position of his party made possible. At the end of 1834, when William IV rashly dismissed his Whig ministers, Peel hurried back from a Roman holiday to form a government. He took several weeks on the journey, for the railway age was still just over the horizon. After his arrival, however, he quickly sent for Gladstone, who was also inconveniently placed in Edinburgh, but who managed to get back to London in time to accept a junior lordship of the Treasury on Christmas Eve. The January election brought a gain of nearly a hundred seats but no majority for the new government and a fortuitous outcome for Gladstone. The Under-Secretary for War and the Colonies (J. S. Wortley) was defeated in Forfar and Peel gave Gladstone the vacancy.

This was a desirable slot because the Secretary of State was Lord Aberdeen, and the under-secretaryship therefore carried the sole spokesmanship for a major department in the Commons. It also fitted Gladstone well. It matched what he thought of as his continuing 'Liverpool' interests (there was also room for embarrassment there, but the government did not last long enough for them to develop), and he formed a lasting affection and respect for Aberdeen, whom he had not previously met. Aberdeen, in turn, was equally impressed, although he stated his first approbation in terms which failed to do justice to Gladstone's force and turbulence. 'He appears to be so amiable that personally I am sure I shall like him,' he wrote.[1] Aberdeen quickly corrected the blandness of this view and became an affectionate and occasionally amused connoisseur of the eccentricities and extravagances of Gladstone's genius. Their lives were closely intertwined for a quarter of a century, and Aberdeen's political influence upon Gladstone was second in intensity only to that of Sir Robert Peel. Furthermore he was able to exercise it for ten years after Peel had fallen off his horse.

George Gordon, fourth Earl of Aberdeen (1784–1860) is the most elusive of all the post-1832 Prime Ministers. He was cultivated, pacific and public-spirited, with a withdrawn charm. His reclusiveness was perhaps to be explained by a combination of his lonely childhood and grief-ridden second twenty-five years. His father died when he was seven, his mother when he was eleven. His grandfather, the third Earl, neglected both his heir and his estate and was not on speaking terms with his daughter-in-law, who when widowed had migrated with George (who had then become Lord Haddo) and her other sons to England. After her death Haddo was taken into the London household of Dundas (later Lord Melville), the legendary manipulator of Scottish patronage under Pitt, and saw much of both Prime Minister and proconsul. They, rather than the reprobate and remote third Earl, procured his education, first at Harrow and then at St John's College, Cambridge.

He saw little of Scotland, however, which he never visited between the ages of eight and twenty-one, even though he had succeeded to the earldom, Haddo Castle and large surrounding tracts of land when he was seventeen. When he did see them, in 1805, he was appalled, disliking equally the house, the neglected bog-ridden countryside and the neighbours. A decade or so later, with considerable improvements already effected, he was converted to the attractions of Haddo, began to retreat there as frequently as possible, and became a great Scotsman, much involved for instance in the Scottish Church controversies leading to the schism of 1843, although showing a much cooler religious spirit than Gladstone would have done.

His bereavements began with and were always dominated by the death of his first wife, the daughter of the then Marquess of Abercorn, when he was twenty-eight. He was exceptionally devoted and continued to wear mourning for her throughout the remaining forty-nine years of his life. She left him with three daughters under five (the couple had also had a stillborn son), all of whom died before they were twenty-one.

In 1815 Aberdeen had made a second marriage to his first wife's sister-in-law, the widow of Abercorn's recently dead heir. She died in 1833, when Aberdeen was still under fifty. Their fifteen-year-old daughter followed the next year. Three sons, however, survived, one of whom (Arthur Gordon) makes several subsequent appearances in Gladstone's life and in this narrative.

In view of all these tragedies Aberdeen's reclusiveness was hardly surprising. A note of disinterested would-be withdrawal was one which he frequently and genuinely struck. 'You look for interest and amusement in the agitation of the world and the spectacle it affords; now I cannot express to you my distaste for everything of the kind. . . . I have had enough of the world . . . and would willingly have as little to do with it as is decent.'[2] So he wrote to the Princesse de Lieven in 1838.* And in 1845 he informed Sir Robert Peel, 'I have no wish ever to enter the House of Lords again.'[3]

Nonetheless he was always a sought-after figure and had in many ways a dazzling career, in both early and middle life. And although his premiership, like the end of Asquith's, was vitiated by his being a man made for the arts of peace caught up in the toils of war, he was venerated in old age, at least by those who knew him well, which category notably included Gladstone. Because of his early succession, he was, together with Rosebery, the only Prime Minister since 1832 who never served in the House of Commons and one of only a few even before that date. His range of public service over half a century was nonetheless wide. He was offered but refused the embassy to Sicily at the age of twenty-three. He was a Knight of the Thistle at twenty-four (and a Garter at seventy-one, again with Rosebery one of the few men ever to hold the two orders). He accepted at the age of twenty-nine the embassy to Austria, which involved not the comforts of Vienna but a rough mission to the field headquarters of the Emperor Franz II during the campaign which extruded Napoleon from the Germanic lands. The rigours of this involved bivouacking for a night in a Thuringian hayloft with Chancellor Prince Metternich – himself then only thirty-nine. Fortified by these

* It was an odd quirk that he should chose the exhibitionist wife of the Russian Ambassador, first in London then in Paris, Antoinette de Lieven, as a frequent recipient of letters of personal confidence, and an even odder one that she should also have been the acknowledged mistress of the austerely intellectual François Guizot, Louis-Philippe's chief minister in the 1840s when he and Aberdeen (as Foreign Secretary in the Peel Government) produced better Anglo-French relations than at almost any other time in the nineteenth century.

experiences Aberdeen became Foreign Secretary for the first of several tours in 1828 at the age of forty-four.

At the beginning of his association with Gladstone Aberdeen was thus already a great European figure, his fame temporarily equal to that of Palmerston, his repute higher. He was also later to be described by Gladstone as 'the man in public life of all others whom I have *loved*'.[4] And although Gladstone sometimes said almost exactly the same about Sidney Herbert this rendered the high compliment neither insincere nor unduly diluted. Aberdeen was a mentor, Herbert a contemporary. Altogether it was a fine thing for Gladstone to be his under-secretary at the age of twenty-five. The disadvantage was that it lasted for only three months, at the end of which came the collapse of the last attempt by a sovereign to override the House of Commons in his choice of ministers.

Gladstone then spent six and a quarter years without office. During much of this period he was concerned more with seeking a wife than with obtaining a department (and was considerably less adept at the former pursuit). He had started so young that he could sustain this patch of slack water and still be a Privy Councillor at thirty-one and a Cabinet minister at thirty-three. He was older at the time of Cabinet entry than Pitt or Harold Wilson, but younger than Canning or Peel or (by three weeks) Winston Churchill, and than all the other participants in the 250-year history of British Cabinet government. His period of slack water between the ages of twenty-five and thirty-one cannot therefore be accounted as even an approach to a serious setback.

Yet, if this conveys a sense of a favoured and carefree youth striding to triumphs which were as joyous as they were glorious, it is almost wholly misplaced. Palmerston and Churchill, to take two statesmen who, like Gladstone, both succeeded early and lived long, got far more obvious pleasure out of life and politics than did Gladstone, perhaps ever, certainly as a young man. He was tortured and he was somewhat awkward, both in movement and in words. He was frequently dissatisfied, alike with his performance and with the direction of his effort. Although by the late 1830s he had moved far from the Evangelicalism of his youth, he always retained a legacy from his early Low Church instruction. Sin, condemnation and fear played a great part in his religion. God's mercy was always more problematical.

Despite ease of material circumstance and reality of political achievement, the first half of Gladstone's adult life had in it more of the nature of a painful pilgrimage through a vale of sorrows (and temptations) than of a triumphal walk back to the cricket pavilion after scoring a debonair double century. Several of his aspects and attributes which made this so showed themselves in his determined but flat-footed search for a wife which dominated the years from 1835 to 1839.

Fragmentary but converging evidence strongly suggests that Gladstone had a sexual drive to match the flash of his eye, the force of his oratory and the vigour of his intellectual and physical energy. It is also the view of Professor Matthew, the unmatched cicerone of Gladstone's life and *œuvre*, that he was a virgin when he married. The conjuncture of these two considerations must necessarily have introduced some urgency into his desire for matrimony. But they did not secure its rapid fulfilment.

Gladstone as a young man appears to have been at once moderately susceptible to the attractions of women and singularly ill at ease in their company. The word 'moderately', usually inappropriate to Gladstone, is appropriate here because of the paucity of references to girls in his diaries. There was no question of his falling happily in and out of love with the sisters of his friends. In 1830 there were some references to the two daughters of a Leamington colonel, rather unpromisingly named Pocklington, whom he encountered on one of his Oxford-vacation visits to his spa-waters-imbibing family. One sister, Jane Pocklington, aroused more interest than the other and as he curiously put it, he 'got upon delicate ground [with her] about the Vicar's preaching'. How he escaped from this delicate ground is not recorded but his appallingly priggish (and syntactically awkward) summing up of this holiday foray does not suggest that it produced many transports of joy for either side: 'But it seems to me that female society, whatever the disadvantages may be, has just & manifold uses attendant upon it in turning the mind away from some of its most dangerous & degrading temptations.'[5] Then during his 1832 grand tour he was temporarily moved by the beauty of Henrietta Milnes (the sister of Richard Monkton Milnes, later Lord Houghton), whom he encountered in Rome. But again it appears to have been no more than an ineffective flutter towards a flame. And that is all the romantic contact with 'respectable' females that is recorded before his approach to (very) serious wooing in 1835.

Perhaps aided by his idealization of the pure and ethereal qualities of his sister Anne, and to a lesser extent (because she was not so close to him) of his mother, he found it difficult to establish a bridge between his generalized sexual urge and individual women, particularly if they were of his own social class. Thus the temptations to which he referred so frequently and so darkly were essentially those of fascination with sex as an abstract and generalized concept rather than the pursuit of specific girls: masturbation, about which he got into a tremendous state, pouring post-indulgence abuse on to his own head in many diary passages; and pornography, the enticements of which were still making his visits to Munich bookshops, during the intervals of his 1845 theological conversations with Dr Döllinger, into a wearing mixture of excitement and shame.

There were also early traces of his later obsession, at once semi-innocent and self-indulgent, with 'rescue' work among prostitutes. Thus, on his first night of a preliminary visit to Oxford in August 1828, at the age of eighteen and before he was even a member of the University (which might have been as well if the Proctors had been on a patrolling expedition), he went out, encountered a lady of the night and had a long conversation with her. The following night he again met the 'poor creature'.[6] Eleemosynary though part of his motive may have been, and restrained although the outcome undoubtedly was, it is impossible to believe that frissons of excitement did not guide his steps on at least the second evening and that he found it easier to talk to this girl redolent of sin and sexual mystery than to chatter to Miss Pocklington.

None of these temptations, however, was conducive to finding Gladstone a wife. This he set about without guilt but also without guile. His first target was Caroline Farquhar, the sister of an Eton friend and the daughter of a Surrey baronet of considerable and somewhat older wealth than that of the Gladstones. The family did not therefore regard Gladstone as a particularly good match, but nor would they have been likely to be resistant had Miss Farquhar, who was considered by Gladstone and others to be a 'beauty', been responsive.

She was exactly the reverse. Gladstone persuaded himself that her religious position was satisfactory, but may well have over-estimated the aphrodisiacal effect of telling her this. He also mistakenly believed that appeals to her father and brother would advance his suit. He had no idea how to interest her. She had no insight to the qualities behind his awkwardness. Her main contemporary comment (a little unreliably recorded in Farquhar family lore) was the exclamation, when she saw Gladstone walking across her family's park at Polesden Lacey with a case in his hand: 'Mama, I cannot marry a man who carries his bag like that.' What sort and size of a bag it was is not recorded – it was well before the days when he gave his name to that somewhat commercial-traveller-like receptacle, the Gladstone bag. Nor is the fault of style (unless it was the mere fact of doing it at all) in his porterage. It was presumably akin to his alleged bourgeois stiffness, which provoked Emily Eden over twenty years later to complain to Lord Clarendon that there was 'something in the tone of his voice and his way of coming into a room that is not aristocratic'.[7]

Miss Farquhar was probably a fairly silly woman. She subsequently married (General) Charles Grey, a younger son of the Reform Bill Prime Minister, who became first the Prince Consort's and then Queen Victoria's private secretary. General Grey always treated Gladstone with respect and friendliness, but Mrs Grey followed up 1830s unresponsiveness with 1880s sourness. There is a story of her finding herself next to Gladstone at the communion rail in the Savoy Chapel in 1886, and immediately getting up and leaving. Prejudice took precedence over the sacrament. Gladstone was lucky to have escaped her, but his trouble was that it was not only the luck which (understandably at the time) he could not accept, but also the fact of the escape. For nearly a year he continued with his embarrassing siege and his foolish attempts to use her male relations as his Trojan horses.

Gladstone's discontent at the Farquhar outcome was increased by two of his brothers successfully contracting marriages during 1835. The unesteemed Tom, his brief parliamentary career already almost over, married the daughter of a substantial Norfolk squire. There could be no objection to the background of Miss Fellowes, but William Gladstone nonetheless managed to be distinctly unenthusiastic about her personality. In the case of the intended wife of the second brother, Robertson, William was subject to no such limitation. Mary Ellen Jones, indigenous to Liverpool, was a Unitarian. William Gladstone treated this affiliation as bringing about the disgrace and damnation of the entire Gladstone clan. The tolerance of Unitarians which Mrs Milnes Gaskell was alleged to have taught him on a Yorkshire visit with her son seemed to have been dissipated during his first Parliament. He made a portentous and Pharisaical fuss, aided by his younger and then twenty-year-old sister Helen, who was always a hysteric in anything to do with religion, and in a good many other things too. (On this occasion she was the ally of her brother's Anglican intolerance, although when she later became a Roman Catholic she was to be very much the victim of it.)

William Gladstone's behaviour towards his brother was appallingly presumptuous and made the more unedifying by a strong whiff of snobbery. The implication was that it was time Robertson grew out of Liverpool trade as well as away from dangerous religious unorthodoxies. Eventually John Gladstone, rather impressively, called his youngest son to order, reminded him of his family duties (perhaps also of the source of his family wealth), and made him desist from his sanctimonious preaching. William Gladstone was a reluctant, if not a convivial, guest at the wedding, in Liverpool, in January 1836.

From there he skulked off to a large landed estate on the borders of Cheshire and North Wales. It was called Hawarden and his host was Sir Stephen Glynne, a well-connected baronet who, like Farquhar, had been somewhere between an acquaintance and a friend at Eton and Christ Church, and who was currently sitting silently in Parliament as member for Flintshire. Glynne's immediate family was composed of a widowed and valetudinarian mother, a younger brother, the Revd Henry Glynne, who had briefly been an MP himself before taking orders and who held the local living, which had the remarkable characteristic of being worth £3000 a year (more than many bishoprics), and two sisters, Catherine, aged twenty-four and Mary, two years younger. He also had about 8000 acres of land which was of reasonably good quality by English standards and spectacularly so by Welsh ones, a substantial park with fine trees and wide views, a moderate-sized eighteenth-century house which had been gothicized by his father, an adjacent ruined fort on a small hill which justified the rather grand postal direction of Hawarden Castle for the whole establishment, and a substantial estate village.

This domain was to be the centre of gravity of the last two-thirds of Gladstone's life, but during this visit of recuperation from the strains of witnessing a Liverpool marriage no impact was made upon him by Catherine Glynne. It was she, however, who eventually solved his matrimonial problems, became his partner for fifty-nine years of stable and sustaining but often physically separated marriage, and enabled him gradually to imbue Hawarden with a Gladstone rather than a Glynne spirit and give it a late-nineteenth-century fame unparalleled among properties of a similar size. Perhaps she was away during his visit. Perhaps his mind was still on the dying embers (not that they ever had much warmth in them) of his Farquhar hopes. In either event he was to mount another matrimonial foray before his beam settled in a Glynne direction.

This second attempt was conducted from the base of his father's Atholl Crescent house in Edinburgh, and was as unsuccessful, for much the same reasons, as his Surrey assault on Caroline Farquhar. The object was Lady Frances Douglas, daughter of the eighteenth Earl of Morton, who came of a long line of Scottish notables and whose wealth, while less impressive than his lineage, was sufficient for there to be no attraction in a Gladstone match unless it was infused by a romantic passion on the daughter's part. Yet once again Gladstone tried heavy-footedly to use the reluctant parents as stepping-stones to the citadel. Lady Frances (only eighteen years old) remained unmoved, Lord Morton had formally to request Gladstone to desist, and the only positive outcome was to increase the enthusiasm of everyone except Gladstone for Frances Douglas's early marriage to Lord Milton, the heir to the third Earl Fitzwilliam. She lived until 1895 and, unlike Miss Farquhar, showed subsequent friendliness to Gladstone. In 1837, however, she cast him down even more than the previous failure had done, and he wrote of the 'icy coldness' in his heart and of living 'almost perpetually restless and depressed'.

Restless he may well have been, and no doubt depressed in bursts, but certainly not perpetually so, or to the extent of being driven to lethargy. Lethargy was the last thing from which Gladstone ever suffered, and there is no evidence that it attacked him in the interval between the Douglas rejection and the Glynne acceptance. He had not been particularly active in the House of Commons in 1836 or 1837, but in March 1838 he delivered the first of his marathon speeches. He filled thirty-three columns of Hansard with a defence of negro apprenticeship schemes on West Indian plantations. This long speech, delivered by a young man of twenty-eight holding no official position who nonetheless did not hesitate to detain the House for well over two hours, may leave room for doubt about his wisdom, his modesty, even his motives, but not about his energy. Moreover it was regarded as a successful *tour de force* which considerably enhanced his oratorical reputation.

Later that spring he attended in the Hanover Square Rooms a fashionable series of lectures (at one the packed audience included seven bishops and the Duke of Cumberland) by Thomas Chalmers, a famous Edinburgh divine, on the role of the state in relation to established Churches. Gladstone knew Chalmers well. During the two previous Edinburgh winters he had been considerably more successful in achieving relations with him than with Lady Frances Douglas. But he did not approve of Chalmers's relatively liberal doctrine, which left the state unconcerned with theology, and able, comfortably and calmly, to support one form of establishment in England and another in Scotland. Gladstone was shocked by this easy-going attitude, incompatible as it was with his belief in a theocratic state, which he assumed, both curiously and complacently, would uphold exactly his own doctrinal position. Whether he would have seriously advocated imposing Episcopalianism upon Scotland is not clear, but he was certainly then terrified by the dangers for the (Anglican) Church of Ireland which might follow from the easy acceptance of the national position of the Scottish Presbyterian Church.

Negatively inspired by Dr Chalmers, although not in direct refutation of him, he set about producing the first of his books, and did so, as became his frequent habit, with white-hot enthusiasm. He wrote most of the manuscript of *The State in its Relations with the Church* during late June and July 1838. This was a substantial work of 500 or so pages. Gladstone was never economical with words. To do it in little more than a month was to do it in a foolish hurry, particularly as he had been warned that continuous writing or reading was bad for his eyes. But this hurtling-torrent approach was always Gladstone's way. Packages of manuscript were rushed off to his currently trusted friends and advisers, John Murray the publisher was persuaded to bring the book out by the end of the year, and then the parcels began to fly to Murray as quickly as they came back from the advisers. The rush was as unnecessary as it was potentially dangerous for a young and at least half-ambitious politician, of not notably steady judgement, writing without experience on a delicate subject on which he held extreme views. His first plunge into authorship begins to give point to Archbishop Tait's superficially most surprising remark about him. 'What I fear in Gladstone', he said much later, 'is his levity.'[8]

Gladstone's principal friends and advisers for the purposes of the book were James Hope, Henry Manning, Philip Pusey and Thomas Dyke Acland. Only Acland had been continuously close to Gladstone since Oxford. He and Pusey, the elder but less interesting brother of Edward Pusey, whose name symbolized High Anglicanism after the mid-century defections to Rome, were members of Parliament. Manning was a rural dean and Hope was a lay *dévot*; if anyone took Hallam's place in Gladstone's affections it was Hope. Although Manning in particular seemed miles away from this precipice in 1838, they were together to shatter Gladstone by being received into the Roman Catholic Church on the same day in April 1851. Gladstone petulantly struck out Hope-Scott (as Hope had become) as an executor of his will, but he was later more forgiving of him than he was of Manning. They had both come strongly into Gladstone's life in 1836–7. Manning had the devout air and cool but black-and-white mind which made the Barchester-like (and married) clergyman of the 1840s become such a convincingly ultramontane prince of the Church under Pius IX by 1870. Hope was a much less cool zealot who until 1851 was a strong but unsteadying influence on Gladstone.

As he completed his book Gladstone made one of his then rare descents on the House of Commons to speak and vote against the renewal of the government grant to the Catholic seminary at Maynooth in County Kildare. He argued that the £9000 subvention to the cause of indigenous education and religion in Ireland 'contravened and stultified the main principle on which the Established Church of England and Ireland was founded'.[9] Both the future Roman Catholic converts were in favour of this act of unyielding intolerance, which was to build up vast trouble for Gladstone in the mid-1840s. It must be said, however, that there was no greater irony in Manning, the future leader of the authoritarian populist tendency, largely Irish supported, in British Catholicism, being against Maynooth than there was in Newman, the future patron of a gentler, older, more educated, more English approach to an apostolic and universal Church, having played a key role in driving Peel out of his Oxford University parliamentary seat because of his support for Catholic Emancipation in 1829.

With his book at the press, and somewhat disenchanted with the British scene, both political and matrimonial, Gladstone set off in August 1838 on another six-month European tour. First he spent nearly a month at Bad Ems, a spa near Koblenz which was to achieve fame during his first premiership by producing the famous diplomatic telegram which sparked off the Franco-Prussian War.* His purpose there was to help settle in his sister Helen, who was causing trouble already but not nearly as much as she was to do in the 1840s, and who, it was felt, needed a season away from Fasque, where domesticity and being her father's sole companion were sitting oppressively on her unstable and exhibitionist temperament. He also dealt at Ems with his proofs and sent them back to Hope, who was an eager intermediary.

The crucial although intermittent companions of this tour were the Glynne family. All of them, two brothers, two sisters and fragile mother, were committed to an autumn and early winter in Italy, and the prospect

* In July 1870 King (later Emperor) Wilhelm I, taking the waters at Ems, gave an audience to Benedetti, the French Ambassador, about that perennial question of the Spanish Succession. He sent an account of the audience by telegram to Bismarck in Berlin. Bismarck, with von Moltke, proceeded to alter the telegram so as to make it appear that the Ambassador had been peremptorily dismissed (which was not so) and then published it. Napoleon III, frivolously and disastrously, chose to treat the altered version as a *casus belli*.

of joining them in Rome was sufficient to keep Gladstone heading south when he was seized by doubts in both Milan and Florence about whether concern for Helen, or his father, or his eyesight, or even his constituents, ought not to send him back to Ems or England. However, there was also a Gladstone pull on the Glynnes for they turned up briefly in the Rheingau spa at the end of August, and Ems was by no means a necessary staging point on the road to Italy. When Gladstone began to concentrate his attention on Catherine Glynne is not clear. He had noted her presence, with that of her sister, at a London 'breakfast' (really an early luncheon) party in July, but it seems that it was the whole family, although no doubt with her as the salient point, which was assuming a special attraction for him. This was at once strange and symptomatic. It was strange because the Glynnes, with the exception of Catherine, had become a somewhat effete family, singularly lacking in his own quality of pulsating energy. It was symptomatic because Gladstone did in a sense marry the whole family. So far as way of life went he transferred his allegiance from Fasque to Hawarden and took over many Glynne values (although never quite mastering their self-conscious private language) before gradually taking over their estate as well. It was Gladstone rather than Catherine who left home on marriage.

He also left the Glynnes in Naples quite soon after he had found them in Rome and set off on a most testing twenty-five-day tour of Sicily and Calabria, accompanied by Arthur Kinnaird, Whig MP for Perth, who had been his travelling companion southward over the Alps but who, except on the road, was never one of those closest to him. Storms raged, fleas bit, crowds surged, bandits threatened, Etna erupted, but Gladstone survived it all, including 400 miles on a mule for which he could form no affection, and of which he was reminded, with himself in the role of the mule, by the coolness of Queen Victoria's final farewell to him as Prime Minister in 1894.* There was, one suspects, an element of bravado about it, of showing to Miss Glynne that he had a vitality and toughness to which she was unused.

He was nonetheless very glad to be back in Naples with her and 'the luxury of a reasonably good bed',[10] although certainly not both at the same time. Indeed so far was he from contemplating such an arrangement that when he went to see the San Carlo ballet he was shocked enough to leave abruptly. (But why, in view of his Munich bookshop

* See below, p. 621.

temptations of seven years later? Was it only to impress the Glynnes? But it is not certain that they were even present.) Thus, by a fine irony, the 'Murderer of Gordon', as he was hyperbolically to be described during his second premiership, reacted in exactly the same way to 'les femmes à demi-nues' (Gordon could bring himself to write about them only in French) as that somewhat brandy-sodden general was to do when he passed through Naples forty-two years later. The Bourbon monarchy might have fallen in the interval but the undress of the San Carlo *corps de ballet* was more stable.

Gladstone then returned to Rome and received almost simultaneously copies of his book and the news that Helen had used the Ems autumn to engage herself to marry a Russo-Polish count, and that her conversion to the Orthodox Church and removal to Russia seemed to be imminent. Perhaps the allure for an author of copies of his own book, particularly the first, and the knowledge that the Glynnes were following him from Naples helped to steady his mind, for he did not rush off to Ems. This was wise, for the Count's parents satisfactorily (to the families at least) killed the marriage, and Gladstone settled down to a rewarding Advent, Christmas and New Year in Rome.

Apart from the Glynnes, with whom there were constant dinners, teas and expeditions, the city was sprinkled with Gladstone's friends and acquaintances. Lord Lincoln, Gladstone's Christ Church friend, was there with his Scottish ducal wife of six years' standing, which made the circumstances very different from those in which Gladstone was next to engage with Lady Lincoln in Italy in 1849. Thomas Babington Macaulay, standard-bearer of Whig intellectual commentators, was there and amicably encountered Gladstone as they emerged after observing from different angles of scepticism the Pope at Christmas Eve Vespers in St Peter's. Macaulay had not then seen *The State in its Relations with the Church* and was as unaware as was Gladstone that he was to subject it in the April 1839 number of the *Edinburgh Review* to one of the most famous of mid-nineteenth-century critical polemics. (Macaulay was more vicious against Peel than against Gladstone, whom he treated with a polemicists' well-known trick as an honest and clear exponent of the views which his leader held but wished to obfuscate.) Manning was also in Rome, and Gladstone persuaded that slightly suspicious Rural Dean, who then disapproved of the Roman tendencies of the Oxford Tractarians, to accept introduction to Monsignor Wiseman. (In 1838 Wiseman was head of the English College in Rome. In 1851, with the setting up of the hierarchy in Britain, he became the first Cardinal Archbishop of

Westminster. In 1868 Manning succeeded him in that metropolitan see.)

Miss Glynne, as was indeed to be her experience throughout life, had thus to face considerable competition for Gladstone's attention. In this Roman winter she triumphantly overcame this competition. But whether this was then her intention is by no means clear. She was certainly not repelled by Gladstone as had been Miss Farquhar and Lady Frances Douglas. But neither did she find him an easy suitor. She and her family called him Gia, a name suggesting a mixture of affection and faintly mocking respect. Gia chose well his *mise en scène* for a declaration. It was in the Colosseum under a full moon on 3 January 1839. But his words may have lacked the clarity and even the glow of the moon's beam. When, a fortnight later, he put his proposal to her in writing (at least not on this occasion to her father or brother) she claimed to be taken by surprise. His letter was unmistakable in intent if not succinct in expression. Lord Attlee, Gladstone's successor but eleven as head of a government and not normally regarded as one of the most romantic of Prime Ministers, when he read it reproduced in Magnus's 1954 biography, was almost as shocked by it as Gladstone had been by the San Carlo ballet. 'He really was a frightful old prig,' Attlee wrote. 'Fancy writing a letter proposing marriage including a sentence of 140 words all about the Almighty. He was a dreadful person.'[11]

Gladstone was not a dreadful person. He was in many ways the greatest figure of the nineteenth century, and taken in the round the greatest British politician of that or any other parliamentary century. But he could be portentous and a little ridiculous, particularly when dealing with young women, and his twenties, which were nearly but not quite over when he wrote this letter, were not his best decade. It was understandable that Attlee should take against the letter, but it was both a little narrow and carrying his laconic dismissiveness too far to build a general censure upon it. Fortunately Miss Glynne took a more perceptive view. She did not say yes, but she did not say no, and Gladstone travelled back to London at the end of January, in the company of her elder brother and in a state of reasonable hope.

4
Peel's Apprentice

The first half of 1839 was not politically prosperous for Gladstone. After his return to England on 31 January he came gradually to understand that his *State and Church* book had not been a success. Macaulay's *Edinburgh Review* polemic, which appeared at Easter, he could have dismissed as the howling of the Whig dogs. It at least suggested that the book was attracting attention, and it put into the English language the first of several phrases which are inseparable from Gladstone's name: 'the rising hope of those stern and unbending Tories' has retained its resonance after a century and a half. Like most of the best phrases, however, it was doubtfully accurate. Not only was it to be belied by Gladstone's future political development. In addition the book was at the time ill regarded by the most influential Tories, and their distaste for it was such as temporarily to hinder Gladstone's prospects of rising.

They mostly considered it a foolish book, making up in portentousness (it was, for instance, dedicated to the University of Oxford) for what it lacked in sense and judgement. Gladstone noticed their silence more than he divined the cause. 'Not a word from him [Peel], S[tanley] or G[raham] yet,'* he wrote on 9 February, 'even to acknowledge my poor book.'[1] Peel was reported as having thrown it on the floor in annoyance at Gladstone's crassness in gratuitously giving to fortune the hostage of such an extreme and impractical piece of writing. It was probably lucky for the author that, when Melbourne offered his resignation as Prime Minister in May of that year, the Queen's stubbornness in refusing to install some Tory ladies of the bedchamber led to Peel's declining to form a government. Had he done so, Gladstone might well have been excluded.

The only self-protective aspect of *The State in its Relations with the*

* Lord Stanley, later fourteenth Earl of Derby and three times (briefly) Tory Prime Minister, and Sir James Graham, Home Secretary 1841–6, were two of Peel's principal colleagues.

Church was that it was extremely difficult to read. Few can have penetrated its opaqueness to the full monstrous intolerance of the doctrine, which broadly amounted to a policy of no public service jobs throughout the British Isles (although maybe the pass had been most undesirably sold in Scotland) for anyone who was not a communicating member of the Church of England. The plenitude of Gladstone's extremity was underlined by his one 'moderate' concession: the doctrine might be difficult to apply in India.

Among the scarce benefits to flow from the book, and almost the only bonus of Gladstone's 1839 spring, was that one of the few who did get through it from beginning to end was Miss Catherine Glynne. She even copied out some chosen passages and endeavoured to learn them by heart. It was perhaps the only way in which she could avoid the immediate erasure from her mind of what she had read. Many years later her daughter Mary (Drew) thought that this indicated that her mother who, despite her many gifts of character, personality, and a spontaneous even if disorganized intelligence, rarely then read a book or even a newspaper, must have been something of an intellectual in her youth. It seems more likely that it was a sign of her growing absorption in Gladstone. Had Gladstone been more worldly or less literarily vain he would surely have regarded a detailed acquaintance with *State and Church* as a certain sign that he had at last succeeded as a suitor. As it was he remained on tenterhooks until 8 June, when she formally accepted him during a riverside walk away from the concourse at a Fulham garden party.

Although Gladstone had come to her via the Farquhar and Douglas setbacks, and although one reason why she may have been so slow to accept was that she had been heavily jilted in 1837 by Colonel Francis Harcourt,* neither approached the marriage as in any way a *pis aller*. They were totally engaged with each other, and each recognized from the beginning, as indeed turned out to be abundantly so, that they had been lucky to be available because rejected.

Catherine Glynne was almost perfectly suited to be Gladstone's wife. In the first place she was healthy, unlike the female members of his own family, out-survived him by two years (in full vigour until nearly the

* Although his own career was obscure he was the uncle of the William Vernon Harcourt, who was to be one of Gladstone's Home Secretaries and Chancellors of the Exchequer as well as his successor as Liberal leader in the Commons; the girl who supplanted Miss Glynne was Lady Charlotte Jenkinson, a daughter of the third Earl of Liverpool and a niece of the long-serving Prime Minister.

end) and died only in 1900, at the same age of eighty-eight which he had attained. She was also buoyant, self-confident and high-spirited, as well as physically graceful and on the edge of beauty, less fashionably and glossily but more vitally so than Miss Farquhar. She was moderately careless of convention and well at ease within her own skin, very much a part of which were her high family connections – Grenvilles, Pitts, Wyndhams – and her chatelaineship of Hawarden, exercised almost since girlhood owing to her mother's valetudinarianism and her brother's bachelordom. Her commitment to Hawarden, which was her home for the whole of her eighty-eight years, fortified much less crucially by a large London establishment, meant that she never showed signs of sulky neglect in the face of the frequent preoccupations and occasional infatuations of Gladstone.

It could be argued that their marriage was not particularly close. They were often and sometimes unnecessarily in different houses, conjoined only by regular but not notably intimate letters. Gladstone nearly always signed himself to her 'Ever yours affty., W. E. Gladstone'. Later in life he occasionally alternated this with 'From your old WEG'. For decades, however, he never varied in writing 'Mrs W. E. Gladstone', as though it were a business communication, across the bottom of the letter. But when the last of the wives of his three elder brothers had died, he suddenly shifted, with an extraordinary sense of precedential precision, to writing 'Mrs Gladstone'.

Catherine Gladstone was passionately engaged with the success and wellbeing of her husband, but not very interested in either politics or the intricacies of religious doctrine and observance, the two subjects which most interested him. On religion her (1956) biographer describes her as *Anima naturaliter Christiana*[2] – a soul turned instinctively towards God – which was a description Gladstone had applied to Arthur Hallam. This might be interpreted either as a tribute to her spontaneous piety or as a determination to put the best possible explanation on her lack of interest in religious instruction. She never reacted against Gladstone's religiosity, being affronted neither by the letter which so upset Clement Attlee nor by his engrossment within minutes of her Thameside acceptance of his proposal, in explaining his attitude to the Church. She was appropriately regular as a parson's sister and a famous layman's wife in her own public devotions. Yet she cannot be regarded as a wifely sycophant. Her middle-life 'Oh, William dear, if you weren't such a great man you would be a terrible bore'[3] must be accounted a rarely illuminating expression of exasperated affection.

On politics she never betrayed any views of her own beyond a fierce loyalty to her husband and a more moderate one to others whose personality and behaviour earned her approval. This ideological detachment, which put her firmly in the category of a Mrs Baldwin or a Mrs Attlee rather than a Mrs Asquith or a Mrs Roosevelt, was perhaps as well in view of the meteoric progress across the political sky which Gladstone pursued in the course of his marriage. It also meant that Gladstone's early decision to tell her all his political secrets (in a typically Manichaean way he thought the alternative was to tell her none), to which he stuck throughout his life, was made safer. In the early days she occasionally betrayed one through carelessness, but never at any stage by malevolent or even benevolent intent. The ideological detachment was, however, accompanied by a willingness, when in London and after the birth of her eighth and last child more or less coincided with the completion of Barry's new Palace of Westminster, to spend long hours in the old grille-covered ladies' gallery of the House of Commons. It was indeed a legend of the pre-1941 House that, just as the despatch boxes bore indentations caused by the vehemence with which over the years Gladstone had pounded them with his heavy rings, so in the ladies' gallery there was a patch of brass railing in front of her habitual corner seat which Mrs Gladstone had polished bright with her gloved hand. (The length of her husband's speeches ensured that both the despatch boxes and the railing had plenty of time in which to receive punishment or massage.)

The question which arises is whether Catherine Gladstone's disorganized self-confidence amounted to a gushing self-satisfaction. There are one or two signs which point in that direction. 'Glynnese', the private family language, which Gladstone had the independent good sense never fully to master, was surely a most tiresome affectation. The use of 'young mawkin' for stranger, of 'hydra' for disorder or of 'with a magpie' for underdone was surely more a search for exclusivity and a sign of self-regard than an aid to clear communication. Glynnese makes Winchester 'notions' appear almost rational. And Catherine Gladstone was near to being the keeper of the shrine of this piece of nonsense. Her familiar names were also a little arch. As girls she and her younger sister Mary were known as the 'two pussies'. Gladstone, happily, never took to this name and preferred 'Catherine' or 'Cathie' or 'C'. However, on her side of the family Mary surrendered the joint claim and taught her own children (an even greater quiverful of twelve) to refer to 'Aunt Puss' or 'Auntie Pussy'.

Catherine's influence upon Mary was so strong that the latter announced her own engagement three days after her sister's betrothal with Gladstone. When her sister had hesitated, so did she. When her sister decided, she followed suit. Mary's husband-to-be was George Lyttelton, of Hagley Hall, Worcestershire, who had succeeded as the fourth Lord Lyttelton of the second creation in 1837 when he was still an undergraduate at Trinity College, Cambridge. He was only twenty-one at the time of the engagement (four years younger than Mary Glynne) and had a somewhat immature appearance. Nonetheless his later achievements were considerable. He became a fellow of the Royal Society, received honorary degrees from both Oxford and Cambridge, was the first Principal of Queen's College, Birmingham, and the first President of the Midland Institute there. He was the leader of West Midlands intellectual life.

Among his children (he added three by a second wife to make a total of fifteen) were Lucy, who married Lord Frederick Cavendish, the assassinated Chief Secretary for Ireland in Gladstone's second government; Lavinia, who married Edward Talbot, the effective founder of Keble College, Oxford, and later Bishop of Rochester, Southwark and finally Winchester; and Alfred, the great cricketer who was Colonial Secretary under Balfour. George Lyttelton himself was as enthusiastic a cricketer as he was an intellectual, and one of the reasons for his excessive number of children, which led to the searing death of his wife, aged forty-three, in 1857, was said to be his desire to produce a family eleven. He was a tragic as well as a gifted figure. In a fit of melancholia he committed suicide at the age of fifty-eight.

In 1839, however, he like Gladstone was an eager husband-to-be and they agreed to a double marriage at Hawarden in July. Both the bridegrooms, against more recent custom, took themselves there nearly two weeks before the wedding and naturally attracted considerable attention in the estate village, where Gladstone, taller, more handsome and eight years older, contradicted the impression that he had made on Caroline Farquhar at Polesden Lacey by causing a group of villagers mistakenly to murmur: 'It is easy to see which one is the lord.' The wedding passed off well on 25 July as a great estate and families celebration (John Gladstone was delighted with the match), and the two bridegrooms were sufficiently pleased with each other and their brides that, after a brief separation when the Lytteltons went to Hagley and the Gladstones stayed at Hawarden, they all four set off on what proved to be a rain-sodden tour of the Scottish Highlands.

Then the Gladstones settled down for a quiet October and most of November at Fasque. After that they did a month's tour of Edinburgh, the Borders, Yorkshire, Lincolnshire, and Nottinghamshire, including a brief visit to Newark (and Clumber), before returning to Hawarden for Christmas.

They spent two days at Dalmahoy, Lord Morton's house in Midlothian. Lady Milton, as Lady Frances Douglas had become, was there, and Gladstone wrote of her in his diary with somewhat elephantine delicacy:

> Cath. walked a little with Lady Milton & liked her very much. In appearance she is just as two years ago. She dresses in excellent taste *plainly*, evincing thereby a higher tact. She seems to me in all respects now the same person as she seemed then. No one of the family alluded ever so indirectly to my having been here before. They were most kind to us.
>
> Dearest C. not very well here.
>
> There was some awkwardness in meeting Lady (F.) M. She felt it too and lingered on the handle of the door when she entered. But why should she? She has nothing to regret. I have a precipitancy blamable [*sic*] in itself though I do not believe that it at all affected the issue. In other respects, I received here a sharp instruction which I believe will chasten me for my life long with respect to all objects of my desire: combined, that is to say, with what preceded it in 1835. And I say deliberately, & I think not self-deceived, that I now see how much more wisely God judged and ordered for me: C. & I talked over these matters for two hours and read Scr[ipture].[4]

Gladstone was always incapable of glossing over things where others might have thought it wiser to do so. Thus, well before this marriage excursion, he had already taken Catherine through the Farquhar and Douglas campaigns. She had retaliated by giving him the names of her previous suitors, rejected and rejecting, which he wrote in his diary in a continuous stream of Greek characters, presumably as a modification of his habit of always there expressing difficult or prurient thoughts in French or Italian. This had the effect, when translated, of sounding like either a cricket team (which should have pleased his brother-in-law) or a courtesan's engagement sheet: 'Seymer Newark Hill Vaughan Egerton Anson Harcourt Lewis Mordaunt'.[5]

However, they both appeared to survive these mutual bombardments without undue casualties, and on 14 January 1840 they left Hawarden together and proceeded by railway to Wolverhampton, where they separated, Catherine going to Hagley and he on to London. A week later he went for a few days to Hagley and then brought her to London on the 27th. Gladstone was a great early user of railways. He had so travelled from Euston to Crewe (and then on by road) before his wedding, and had then written: '9–9. 200 miles to Hawarden. Dust from engine annoying to the eyes and filthy in the carriage. I had dreaded the motion backward.'[6] Of the shorter journey from Hagley he merely wrote: '11¼ to 7½ . . . by B[irmingha]m Railway. C. weary.'[7] On 8 February he concluded an arrangement with the Marquess of Cholmondeley to take over his deceased mother's house at 13 Carlton House Terrace. Three days later, having taken over most of the furniture as well, they were able to move in.

It was a very grand house for a young MP of bourgeois origin, even one who had married into the upper squirearchy. However, the Gladstones survived in proximate grandeur for thirty-five years. He transferred to 6 Carlton Gardens, which his father made over to him, in 1847. And then in 1856 he moved back the few hundred yards to Carlton House Terrace, this time not to No. 13 but to No. 11, which was a bigger house. Only in 1876 did he finally abandon the 'Carltons' and retreat to Harley Street. After he lost his Prime Minister's salary of £5000 a year, he complained that he was left with a residual and encumbered £6050 of his own, while everyone else in the Terrace had £25,000 or more. In 1840 he calculated his income at £4260 and his expenditure at £2168. By 1846 the figures had risen to £6987 and £4007. The near doubling of expenditure was more surprising than the surge in income, which was, however, very much the boom before the slump.

In the summer of 1840 Catherine Gladstone gave birth to their first child and William Gladstone to his second book. The book was entitled *Church Principles Considered by their Results*, was written in the same spirit of intolerant Anglicanism as was the first, but fell much flatter. Manning and Hope-Scott had again been his principal consultants. Those others who noticed it at all (for instance Dr Thomas Arnold) thought it as theologically unsound as it was politically opinionated.

The only parliamentary significant event for Gladstone in his first session after marriage was his speech on 8 April 1840 denouncing the so-called Opium War which Palmerston as Foreign Secretary had launched against China. It was his first major speech since his defence of the West Indian sugar planters three years before, and was very different from it both in motivation and in impact. Unusually the diary gives some indication of preparation: 'Wrote to Mr Campbell – Mrs Hickey, read on China. House 4–6 + 7–10½. Spoke 1¼, heavily: strongly agt the Trade & the war....'[8] Of the motivation he wrote (several weeks later), 'I am in dread of the judgements of God upon England for our national iniquity towards China.'[9] Undoubtedly, however, another part of it was his growing dislike and distrust of Palmerston, whom he saw as bumptious, chauvinist, libertine without guilt, and compounding his sins by claiming to be the heir of Canning. Gladstone in general, while moralizing easily on issues, was personally tolerant about political opponents and allies – his progress across the political sky meant that at one time or another most were both – but there were two major figures who, throughout his middle political years, he could not abide. The one was Palmerston and the other was Disraeli. His desire to keep away from both of them had an almost astronomic quality to it. It was, however, impossible in the cosmology of mid-nineteenth-century politics to do both at the same time, and for the last six years of Palmerston's life Gladstone was his independent, powerful and warily detached Chancellor of the Exchequer. Palmerston was the earlier of the two in engaging his antipathy, for by 1840 Gladstone had had little more contact with Disraeli than meeting him at a dinner party of Lord Lyndhurst's in 1835 and finding him 'rather dull', although noticeable for the foppery of his clothes. Disraeli compensated by irritating Gladstone for sixteen years after Palmerston had gone.

This Opium War speech was both Gladstone's main political incursion in that flat session of 1840, during which the Melbourne government subsided and the Whig decade came to an end, and his first foreign policy foray. Eighteen-forty-one, by contrast, saw a general election with a major turnover of seats, and a new government which marked as dramatic a change of political weather as 1906 or 1945 or 1979. The new model Conservative party (as the Tories were coming to be called) of the Tamworth Manifesto, accepting the Reform Bill and attempting to embrace a good proportion of the new manufacturing class as well as the Church and state squirearchy, was in office with a majority of eighty. And Peel, who was the epitome of the new Conservative balance, was beginning his first period of secure power.

Peel was not only Gladstone's leader but his political mentor. He and Gladstone had a similar social provenance, and even more strikingly, with a gap of a short generation (twenty-one years) between them, did their careers follow similar courses. They were both the sons of rich first-generation baronets who had made their money in Lancashire. Peel's father was more a manufacturer than a merchant, and somewhat richer even than John Gladstone. The sons both retained distinct accent traces of their county of origin. Peel was one of Harrow's seven Prime Ministers rather than one of Eton's eighteen, but he was as naturally a Christ Church man as was Gladstone, and there produced as notable an academic result as Gladstone was to do.

Within a year of Oxford, again as with Gladstone, Peel was in the House of Commons, in his case as member for Cashel, a Co. Tipperary borough which made Gladstone's election for Newark look positively democratic. They were later both members for Oxford University over sizeable spells, and were both eventually turned out by the electorate of graduates (a high proportion of whom were then country clergy) for liberal sins, Peel for promoting Catholic emancipation, which he had hitherto strongly opposed, and Gladstone for a cumulative list of similar offences. As a young MP Peel's career prospered even more than Gladstone's was to do. He became Chief Secretary for Ireland (the post which Gladstone coveted in 1841) for a six-year period at the age of twenty-four, and Home Secretary for five years at the age of thirty-four.

They both began their effective premierships in their fifties, having each fashioned a new-style political grouping to sustain him in that role. Peel at fifty-three became in 1841 the first *Conservative* Prime Minister with a majority (there had previously been Tories), and Gladstone at fifty-eight became in 1868 the first *Liberal* Prime Minister who had nothing of Whiggery about him, except for some of the followers by whom he was sustained. And towards the end of their lives they both caused considerable mayhem in the parties they themselves had created. They both had phenomenal energy, and were by any standards towering statesmen, Peel the most effective between Pitt and Gladstone himself, and Gladstone still more pre-eminent, dominating both the third and fourth quarters of the nineteenth century at least as completely as Peel had dominated the second quarter.

Beyond this, however, there were very substantial differences. In the first place Peel had no old age and no possibility of return to Downing Street after 1846, whereas Gladstone had the longest twilight and the greatest number of encores in the history of politics. Peel was cut down at the age of sixty-two, falling off his horse on Constitution Hill, and dying dramatically in his Whitehall Gardens house three days later. It needed the nature of his death to infuse his end with drama, for he was in many ways a cool man, even in external manner a cold one. There is some doubt whether it was his smile which Daniel O'Connell compared to the silver plate on a coffin, but there was in any event some applicability about the simile. This could never have been said of Gladstone.

Peel was a commanding figure, prickly and vain, although attracting loyalty and even affection, but never tempestuous. Bagehot's critical view of him was that he had 'the powers of a first-rate man and the creed of a second-rate man'. By that he meant that Peel, who in the case of 'almost all the great measures with which his name is associated ... attained great eminence as [their] opponent before he achieved even greater eminence as their advocate',[10] always changed his mind at the time when the average man and not the pioneer did so. This made him a wise and truly Conservative man of government, but it did not give him Gladstone's swoop of an eagle's flight.

The other gulf between them was in their attitude to religion. Peel is said to have gone beyond the demands of observance normal in the first half of the nineteenth century and to have been on the threshold of private devoutness. But he was not tortured or obsessed by religion, and he did not allow it to obtrude on to his political decisions. Professor Gash, his 1972 biographer, wrote: 'Peel's own religion was a simple, rational, pious Protestantism. The enthusiasm of the "Saints", the high sacerdotal principles of Gladstone, were as foreign to him as the intellectual pessimism of Melbourne or the tortured self-examination of Lord Ashley [Shaftesbury].'[11] He may have been less cynical than Melbourne but, adjusting for the fact that he was the leader of a more clerical party, he was nearly as Erastian as any Whig. Although he had a fine rational mind, he was essentially unable (perhaps because unwilling) to understand what Gladstone was going on about. Whether or not he threw *State and Church* on the floor, the depth of the chasm which separated them on the issue with which it dealt is even more strongly (because more calmly and dismissively) expressed by his reported comment: 'that young man will ruin a fine career if he writes books such as these'.[12]

Gladstone was Peel's political heir. As Morley puts it: 'we cannot forget that Peel and Mr Gladstone were in the strict line of political succession',[13] and Morley, relying on his own experience as a minister under Gladstone (which experience only began thirty-six years after Peel's death), then proceeds to pay eloquent tribute to the way Gladstone's whole habit of conducting public business still owed a great deal to Peel's assumptions, his methods and even his phrases (as revealed in his published correspondence). Gladstone also proudly called himself a Peelite for a full decade after the death of the eponym. Of the distinguished band who originally bore this label the others – Aberdeen, Goulburn, Graham, Sidney Herbert – were all dead by 1861. But Gladstone's pre-eminence stemmed from much more than a capacity for survival. He was indeed the one political figure of the nineteenth century whose quality and fame came to exceed that of Peel himself. And it may be that a presentiment of this – on both sides – was part of the reason why, despite all the centripetal factors, relations between Gladstone and Peel were never as close as might have been expected. There was always some delicate curtain between them. Gladstone was loyal to Peel, but not with quite the spontaneous and affectionate loyalty which he had felt towards Canning as a very young man, and which the memory of Canning continued to excite in him. Peel used, recognized and three-quarters admired Gladstone's qualities, yet stood a little back from him and queried his sense of proportion. 'That young man [might] ruin a fine career' was a phrase which almost perfectly expressed his conditional benevolence.

Nothing is more difficult in the chemistry of politics than to bridge the time gap and to think how two men who served together in a senior–junior relationship would have adjusted had the age of the junior moved upwards while that of the senior remained constant so that they had to coexist as near equals. Asquith and Churchill (between whom the age gap was exactly the same as that between Peel and Gladstone) got along thoroughly well so long as Churchill could regard Asquith as a great if somewhat detached judge and Asquith could regard Churchill as a talented but amusingly impetuous young minister. What balance would have been struck had they been in a competitive position is another matter.

When Peel died in 1850 Gladstone's reaction was surprisingly cool. This was the more striking because of the dramatic nature of the tragedy, with the former Prime Minister lying poised between life and death for eighty hours in the heart of the capital, with the street outside his house thronged not only with the carriages of a stream of enquiring callers but also with a sympathetic concourse of the general public. Official and popular London hung upon his fate, and when he eventually succumbed he was mourned as the greatest statesman of his time and the nation operated at half-mast for several days. The House of Commons suspended effective business, except for tributes, for two days. Gladstone seconded the motion for the adjournment on the first, the moving of which apparently took him by surprise, and he spoke no more than a few sentences, recalling however Walter Scott's lines in memory of Pitt,* and adding to them the comment, at once measured and convoluted, that these words had been addressed 'to a man great indeed, but not greater than Sir Robert Peel'.[14]

Yet Gladstone did not attend the funeral, which took place at Drayton (Peel's house outside Tamworth in Staffordshire) six days later, although Aberdeen, Graham, Goulburn and three other prominent political supporters acted as pall-bearers, and Sidney Herbert was also present. 'I mourn to be absent,' he wrote in the diary,[15] but without explanation. He spoke in the House of Commons late that night, although on what was hardly a compelling occasion. There is also the impression that he had come to regard Peel as something of an incubus. On the day of Peel's death he wrote to Sir John Gladstone: 'I thought Sir R. Peel looked extremely feeble during the debate last week [that is, immediately before the accident]. . . . I observed that he slept during much of Lord Palmerston's speech, that he spoke with little physical energy. . . .'[16] Then, a week later, he wrote again to his father: 'People feel, I suppose, that Sir Robert Peel's life and continuance in parliament were of themselves powerful obstacles to the general reorganisation of the conservative party,'[17] of which, still counting himself a Conservative, he pronounced himself in favour. And in 1876, just over a quarter of a century later, reflecting on this period Gladstone wrote: 'I do not, therefore, think, and I did not think, that the death of Sir Robert Peel at the time when it occurred was a great calamity so far as the chief question of our internal politics was concerned.'[18]

All these criticisms were immediately qualified by protestations of how great a man Gladstone nonetheless thought Peel to be. Indeed, even in the case of his 1876 retrospect he was at pains to make it clear that he was referring only to the key contemporary issue of whether or not the 'protectionists' could in 1850 be trusted with office (Gladstone thought yes, Peel thought no). 'In other respects it [the calamity of his death] was indeed great; in some of them it may almost be called immeasurable. The moral atmosphere of the House of Commons has never since his death been quite the same. . . .'[19] Yet the impression of

* Now is the stately column broke,
The beacon-light is quenched in smoke,
The trumpet's silver sound is still,
The warder silent on the hill.

emotional detachment given by the about-to-be-qualified comments cannot be erased, particularly when taken in conjunction with the remark of the somewhat forgotten George Cornewall Lewis (Chancellor of the Exchequer for three years and Home Secretary for two years, 1855–61) that 'upon Gladstone the death of Peel will have the effect of removing a weight from a spring'.[20] Lewis's aphorism caught an echo nearly ten years later when Aberdeen, contemplating the apparent collapse of Gladstone's political prospects after the débâcle of his unsuccessful six months as Commissioner in the Ionian Isles, said: 'Ah, but he is terrible in the rebound.'[21]

Weight released or rebounding, Gladstone's reaction to Peel's departure was not straightforwardly that of a loyal lieutenant. It may be that he was crushed throughout that summer of 1850 by the harrowing death of his five-year-old daughter Jessy from meningitis on 9 April, and had no emotion to spare for even the most revered political chief. Yet this is not wholly convincing, for Gladstone's morbidity made him at home with death. There is some truth in Professor Shannon's flippancy that 'he was a connoisseur of nineteenth-century death-beds'.[22] He dwelt on them, his mother's, his sister's, in particular his father's (which occurred in December 1851) and constantly contemplated his own mortality. When he became thirty-five (at the end of 1844), a young and highly successful Cabinet minister, it was reasonable for him as a Dante enthusiast to temper a sense of the great opportunities which lay before him with an awareness that he was 'nel mezzo del cammin di nostra vita', but to add to that, as he did, 'Now commences as it were the downhill of my life . . . I am older than was the Redeemer in the flesh,'[23] might be regarded as a striking combination of his morbidity and religiosity.

On the surface he had taken with Christian resignation his daughter's death after nearly two weeks of fluctuating struggle and anguish. 'It is all over and all well,' he wrote. 'The blessed child was released at two o'clock in the morning compassionately taken by her Saviour into the fold of his peace.'[24] Three days later he subjected himself to taking her small coffin with him in a compartment from Euston to Fasque. He had her nine-year-old brother with him to Blisworth Junction, from where he was consigned to a Northamptonshire school. Then he 'closed my blind to have no other company than the thought of her' until he reached Fasque and its family vault just over twenty-four hours later. But the journey was not satisfactorily uninterrupted. Intermingling a railway legislator's acumen with a parent's grief, he noted that 'notwithstanding precautions and assurances I had to pay in five parts and to make three changes of carriage'.[25]

This experience was certainly a major contributory cause of Gladstone's being around the middle of the century in a state of what Morley described as 'extreme perturbation' and what others might regard as nearly unhinged. But this hardly explains the relative coolness of his reaction to the death of Peel. On the contrary it might have been expected to make his reaction the more extreme. He was in general inclined to overreact to bad news. In the 1880s Lord Granville (his Foreign Secretary at the time) wrote a splendidly comic description of Gladstone, at a dinner, receiving the news that the Duke of Argyll could not come because he had a cold and throwing up his arms in horror as though he had just received news of a new Bulgarian atrocity.

The paradox (one of the many in Gladstone's life) therefore is that the foremost Peelite had some reserve about Peel. It is reminiscent of the remark about Captain Alfred Dreyfus that, had he not been Dreyfus, he would have been a natural anti-Dreyfusard. Gladstone would never have been a natural anti-Peelite. But he had his reserves, which may well have dated from his continuing resentment of Peel's treatment of him in 1841.

That year's general election was spread over the end of June and the first ten days of July. Gladstone was returned at Newark on 29 June, but it was 9 July before Stephen Glynne, despite strong Gladstone assistance, was defeated by forty votes and faggotry (the artificial splitting of estates to give owners extra votes), against which Gladstone was to fulminate for decades. On 18 August Gladstone went to London by railway from Chester. 'Arrived well, thank God,' he wrote.[26] A safely completed rail journey still deserved the applause of relief, rather like a safe trans-Andean aircraft landing. On the 21st he was summoned to a conclave of ten at Peel's house, to determine the form of the amendment to the Address which ended the Melbourne government. He assumed from this that he was to be in the Cabinet. He had some but not complete justification. Two of the others, Lord Granville Somerset and Sir Thomas Fremantle, had to wait like himself a few years for this. But the rest were all included. When, on the 21st, Peel offered him the vice-presidency of the Board of Trade – or 'a post in the Admiralty' – he was bitterly disappointed. He was dismayed by both the rank and the department in which he was required to perform. He had set his eye in particular upon the chief secretaryship for Ireland. The Board of Trade he regarded as pedestrian. It provoked his *cri du cœur* that, while he had hoped to concern himself with the affairs of men, he found himself set 'to governing packages'. Nor was he assuaged by Peel's assurance that Lord Ripon, who was to be his chief and as Goderich had been an unsuccessful and short-lived Prime Minister between Canning and Wellington in 1827–8, was pre-eminent in the management of packages.

This assurance, perhaps fortunately, proved false. Ripon, if he knew anything about packages, had largely lost interest in them and was happy to let Gladstone do all the work and even take some of the credit. But his under-promotion in 1841 (in contrast with his over-promotion in 1835) rankled with Gladstone as did his subordination to Ripon. On his famous eight-day visit to All Souls College, Oxford, in 1890, Gladstone was recorded as saying: 'The man who knew least about finance who was ever head of the Treasury was the first Lord Ripon.'[27] As Ripon, Robinson when he was Chancellor, before becoming first Lord Goderich and then Earl of Ripon in 1833, was by 1890 thirty-one years dead and sixty-three years away from the Exechequer, this was a striking indication both of the sweep of Gladstone's memory and of his resentment at being given a subordinate post in 1841.

Where Peel was powerfully right, however, was in seeing that Gladstone would take to the details of customs reduction, commercial treaties and the intricacies of railway legislation with almost as much enthusiasm as he had hitherto reserved for liturgical disputes. It was of this period that James Graham, who was then Home Secretary, noted that 'Gladstone could do in four hours what it took any other man sixteen to do and that he [nonetheless] worked sixteen hours a day'. Contrary to his own expectations, the Board of Trade fascinated Gladstone. Until he himself in the next decade infused the Treasury with a new authority and made the budget into a great annual national event, the presidency of the Board carried with it at least an equal responsibility for the fiscal regime. Of a total tax revenue in 1840 of no more than £47 million, £35 million came from custom and excise duties. Sugar, tea, tobacco, wine, spirits, timber and coffee made the principal contributions, but there were about 750 separate and mostly wholly illogical duties. Gladstone quickly became the master of this haphazard pattern and of the conflicting special-interest lobbies which it spawned. In the course of acquiring this mastery the relentless logic (and extremism) of his mind, which applied in different fields had led him to the romantic intolerance of *The State in its Relations with the Church*, brought him near to a rational utilitarianism, which disposed him towards free trade and made him more than ready for each step in this direction which Peel took between 1841 and 1845.

The other major subject with which Gladstone concerned himself at the Board of Trade was providing a legislative framework for the avalanche of railway construction which was the major socio-economic development of the decade. His 1844 Railway Act put the equivalent of a finely arched train-shed roof over the hitherto uncoordinated mass of private railway bills. It stipulated that on each line there had to be what became known as a 'parliamentary train' at least once a day, with a fare of no more than one penny a mile. It also reserved to the state powers of nationalization should private enterprise fail to provide an adequate system.

This absorption in departmental business did not prevent Gladstone being frequently on the brink of resignation. In May 1843 Ripon was shunted to the Board of Control (the forerunner of the India Office in pre-Mutiny days) and Gladstone became President of the Board of Trade in his place. In one sense this did little more than regularize the authority which he had already been exercising. But in another it enabled him, awkwardly but logically, to make fresh difficulties about whether he was sufficiently in accord with all aspects of government policy to be able to accept. As a junior minister, he held, he could just keep his head down on issues beyond the purview of the Board of Trade. Even within this limitation, however, he had incurred what he described as Peel's 'sulky displeasure' by threatening at the beginning of 1842 to resign (or 'retire' as he at the age of thirty-two a little prematurely put it) when he got out of step with and in advance of Peel in the move away from the protective duty on corn. But once he had achieved what he regarded as the overdue offer of a Cabinet seat, all sorts of wider concerns became open to him.

At a meeting with Peel on 13 May, so far from expressing a simple enthusiasm and gratitude for the offer, he raised difficulties about the opium trade (which Peel said was the responsibility of the East India Company rather than of the government), about certain education clauses, which Peel said he did not think could pass the House of Commons, and about the proposed amalgamation of the North Wales bishoprics of Bangor and St Asaph in order to make room for a new see of Manchester. This had been provided for by Parliament in 1836, but its implementation depended on the death of the Bishop of St Asaph, which in 1843 appeared to be imminent, but which was providentially postponed until 1846 and a Whig ministry.

But it was this issue which Peel appeared to take most seriously, ostensibly on the ground that it might be the most imminent for decision, but perhaps because his patience was running out by that stage, particularly as Gladstone kept saying that it might be better if he left the government altogether. Peel then delivered a well-deserved if gentle rebuking lecture on the accommodations and sense of proportion necessary to enable any group of men to work together in a Cabinet of fourteen, and the issues were circumnavigated (as Gladstone probably always intended they should be) so that he could enter the Cabinet and stay there for twenty-one months. But at least twelve of these months were occupied with his teetering towards resignation, with the issue one on which his position made his previous hesitancies look like those of a simple man of bluff common sense.

Since the Act of Union of 1800 the British government had made an annual subvention of £9000 to the Roman Catholic seminary at Maynooth near Dublin. In relation to the major endowments of Trinity College Dublin and indeed of the whole Anglican establishment in overwhelmingly Catholic Ireland it was a drop in the ocean. Gladstone, however, in the spate of his *State in its Relations with the Church* intolerance had denounced it as a cowardly selling of the pass which would endanger the tradition of Bishop Berkeley, Dean Swift and every other Anglo-Irish divine of the previous 150 years. By 1842 he had recovered enough balance to vote for a renewal of the paltry grant. But in 1844 when Peel, seeking a conciliatory gesture towards indigenous Ireland, proposed to raise the subvention to £30,000, make it permanent, and incorporate the college, Gladstone was thrown into a great state.

He saw that the demands of good government pointed in precisely these directions. But he also feared that it might be a backdoor undermining of the position of the Church of Ireland; and that it might be dishonourable if he, who had written as he had done in 1838, even though he had two-thirds changed his mind in the meantime, were to remain a member of a government which implemented a policy contradictory to his previous beliefs. He therefore spent the whole of 1844 plaguing his colleagues with his conscience. As at that time the Conservative Party was racked by the issue of whether it would allow Peel to usher in the much more stable and prosperous Britain of the third quarter of the nineteenth century or whether it would respond to what became the atavism of Disraeli, Stanley and Bentinck, and as on the big issue Gladstone was wholly on the side of Peel, his obsession was totally lacking in proportion. Peel's comment that 'I really have great difficulty sometimes in comprehending what Gladstone means' seems in the circumstances remarkably restrained.

Into the midst of this troubled year Gladstone threw a bizarre spanner. In July he wrote to Peel suggesting that he should resign his Cabinet post, his parliamentary seat and almost anything else within striking distance in order to become special British envoy to the Vatican. (Peel and Aberdeen, the Foreign Secretary, were thought to be contemplating the opening of diplomatic relations.) He told Peel that if he did not like the suggestion he need not reply. Peel took him at his word and did precisely that. And fifty years later Gladstone provided his own commentary on his 1844 behaviour. 'I have difficulty at this date [1894] in conceiving by what obliquity of view I could have come to imagine that this was a rational or in any way excusable proposal: and this, although I vaguely think my friend James Hope had some hand in it, seems to show me now that there existed in my mind a strong element of fanaticism.'[28]

Although diverted from this particular piece of foolishness, Gladstone continued for another six months (two and a half of them at Fasque, fortunately for ministers' patience) to keep his colleagues on tenterhooks about whether or not he would resign on the Maynooth issue. They combined an irritated amusement at the delicate twists of his conscience with a surprisingly strong desire that he should not go – a fine tribute to his other qualities of energy, intellect and eloquence. Eventually, on 3 February 1845, he did resign, and explained his reasons to the House of Commons in an hour-long speech on the following day. No one was much the wiser at the end, but his opacity at least had the advantage that the danger of bitterness was drowned in incomprehension.

Disraeli, without ill will, complacently thought that Gladstone's career was finished, and Sir Robert Inglis, with whom Gladstone was soon to share the representation of the University of Oxford, assumed that he was freeing himself to join him in the fight for diehard causes, beginning with opposition to the Maynooth Bill itself. Inglis could not have been more mistaken. The resignation was not the first but the last departing swallow of Gladstone's theocratic intolerance. Since 1838 he had lost his faith, not in God, but in the ability of any government or state to act as the agent of God. His ideal of rule by a clerisy was not possible. It was better therefore for government (if not necessarily for the Church) to respect different routes to God. In fact Gladstone's 1844 support for the Dissenting Chapels Bill (which underpinned the rights of Unitarians and others to their buildings and endowments) was more significant for the future than his Maynooth resignation.

He confounded Inglis and confused a great many other people by not only voting for the Maynooth Bill but speaking (for two and a half hours) in its favour. His resignation was the discharge of a debt to the past, and maybe an expiation of what he was coming to see as the foolishness of *The State in its Relations with the Church*. His support for the bill, even though he confessed it 'opposed to my own deeply cherished predilections', was an obeisance to the cause of sense in government. That was something which he was learning, even if slowly and unevenly, from Peel.

5
Orator, Zealot and Debtor

Gladstone's behaviour during the 1840s was nevertheless distinctly erratic. Although it was to be another twenty years before he achieved his unique quality as a platform orator, which both set him apart from all his contemporaries and scandalized many of them, he was already a formidable and fearsome parliamentary performer. He did not have a great advocate's gift of rendering complexity wholly lucid. He had the still rarer gift of keeping his meaning convoluted and often obscure, yet making his presentation of it compelling and persuasive. It stemmed from the intensely physical nature of his eloquence: 'his falcon's eye with strange imperious flash' in Morley's unforgettable phrase, and his 'great actor's command of gesture, bold, sweeping, natural, unforced', which also had something of 'an eager and powerful athlete' in it.[1] And it explained the paradox that he was often as unreadable in prose as he was riveting in speech.

His oratory aroused apprehension as well as admiration. This was particularly so when, as in the 1840s, his always tempestuous nature became like a huge wheel spinning loose. After his Maynooth speech his next significant House of Commons eruption (and his last for two and a half years) was in July 1845, when from his new independent position he replied for another two and a half hours to a Palmerston attack on the government for its handling of colonial sugar duties in relation to its treaties with Spain. When he sat down Peel turned round to him and said, 'That was a wonderful speech, Gladstone.' This gave him particular pleasure, for as he also noted, 'Peel was the most conscientious man I ever knew in spareness of eulogium.'[2] But there was probably relief as well as praise in Peel's reaction. For once the big gun had pointed in the right direction. It had done a fine job, but an ensuing period of silence from it could be borne with equanimity.

Apart from his generally unquiet nature there were a number of special reasons for Gladstone's perturbation in these years. The first was the reception of his sister Helen into the Roman Catholic Church in May 1842. Dr Wiseman, Gladstone's acquaintance in Rome at the end of 1838, was the agent of her conversion, which took place at Oscott College near Birmingham, where three and a half years later Newman was to go to be confirmed, also by Wiseman, immediately after he had made his first Roman confession at Littlemore.

Gladstone took Helen's move as a major family scandal and a direct personal affront. His relations with her were close – much more so than with any of his brothers by this time – but not easy and often unfriendly. As his attitude to his brother Robertson's marriage had shown, he regarded himself as in charge of family discipline on religious matters. In the six years that had gone by since then he may have begun to move to greater tolerance in public policy, but this did not extend to what he thought was permissible within the family. And Helen was more serious to him than was Robertson. He in no way identified with the latter, but he might well have seen in Helen something of his own susceptibility to temptations. Furthermore he always felt a special responsibility for defending the narrow and crucial line between his own High Anglicanism and what he regarded as the insinuating indulgences of the Church of Rome. He saw himself, in a phrase he (not then dreaming of the apostasy which was to come from that quarter) was to use about Hope-Scott, 'as one of the sentinels of the Church of England on the side looking towards Rome'.[3]

He was therefore in favour of the most unforgiving sanctions. He advised his father to turn Helen out of Fasque and himself forbade her to see his children. Once again John Gladstone was more tolerant and sensible. He quite rightly regarded Fasque as Helen's home (much more than it was William Gladstone's), continued to make her welcome and permitted her (much to William Gladstone's disgust) to be visited there by her confessor. This gentler treatment did not prevent her becoming increasingly addicted to opium and anxious to get away from any family interference or supervision. In the autumn of 1845 she was in a terrible state in Baden-Baden, and William Gladstone, always the most officious member of the family, set off to bring her back, although it was a task which could probably have been more neatly exercised by any of the other brothers. But he was the one who, in spite of being much busier, always had the energy to be available.

He appeared to have given up denunciation and even went to Birmingham to get a letter from Dr Wiseman telling her that she should obey her father (from whom Gladstone also had a letter) and return. In Birmingham Gladstone was in a relatively ecumenical mood, recording himself as being 'most kindly received' and visiting the new Catholic cathedral of St Chad.[4] Having got the letter, however, he did not rush to Helen but spent two weeks on the way, calling on Guizot in Paris, and devoting six days to theological discussion with Dr Döllinger in Munich.

When he eventually reached Baden-Baden he found Helen worse than he had expected. There was an horrific scene when, having taken the vast dose of 300 drops of laudanum and become partly paralysed, she had to be held down by force while leeches were applied. Gladstone stayed in and around Baden for five gloomy weeks, doing his clumsy best. Eventually, assisted more by his father's threats to cut off money than by his own persuasiveness, he got Helen to travel with him (and a priest and a doctor) to Cologne. There, however, she stuck, and Gladstone 'after much deliberation' had to go home alone. After three weeks she followed, but to her father's house in Carlton Gardens and certainly not to her brother's a couple of hundred yards away.

While Gladstone was away, indeed almost exactly when he was witnessing Helen's convulsions, John Henry Newman was being received into the Roman Catholic Church. Rather as with Hallam's death, Gladstone did not learn of this until some time later, and then it was more of a depressant than a shock to him. Magnus, indeed, says that he accepted the news 'with equanimity', but that is an exaggeration. Gladstone reacted to very few things with equanimity, and insofar as he was not bowled over by the Newman news it was because he had been expecting it for nearly two years. He knew the contents of the letters which Newman had written to Pusey and Manning in the autumn of 1843. When he received this 1843 intelligence he was thrown into a state of extreme shock and himself wrote to Manning: 'I stagger to and fro like a drunken man. I am at my wit's end.' He was censorious as well as shocked. Some of Newman's language struck him as, 'forgive me if I say it, more like expressions of some Faust gambling for his soul than the records of the inner life of a great Christian teacher'.[5] But censorious although he might be – his next letter to Manning referred to Newman as 'a *disgraced man*' – he could not doubt the disintegrating blow that the departing enchanter had delivered to the High Anglican movement, a cause which had been gathering momentum only a short time before and about which Gladstone cared deeply.

Gladstone and Newman were never close to each other. They both had too much star quality for either to be comfortable too close to the other. But there were several similarities as well as some sharp contrasts between them. Almost without trying, they both infused nearly everything they said and did with an excitement which was in no way diminished by uncertainty about what would come next. Beyond this their religion had much more in common than the obvious apostolic historicism. They both retained considerable traces of the Evangelicalism of their youth. 'Fear', Geoffrey Faber wrote in *The Oxford Apostles*, 'is the driving force of [Newman's] arguments. . . . Again and again in his sermons it seems as if he had to force himself to speak of God's love and mercy.'[6] Condemnation and sin were more real to him. This was equally true of Gladstone, who had a pervading sense of human sin, and of his own special contribution to it. They were both essentially religious pessimists, trying to erect ramparts, whether in the form of a new church building, a new argument or a new hymn, against man's terrifying prospects.

Their eloquence was at once a similarity and a difference. They were both remarkable although utterly contrasting orators. Newman was the more delicate. Matthew Arnold's description of his preaching in the University Church of St Mary's at Oxford (of which he was vicar from 1828 to 1843) is not easily forgotten. Arnold wrote of 'that spiritual apparition gliding in the dim afternoon light through the aisles of St Mary's, rising into the pulpit and then, in the most entrancing of voices, breaking the silence with words and thoughts which were a religious music – subtle, sweet, mournful'.[7] Newman's sentences were always carefully prepared, which was in contrast with Gladstone's flashing eye, thundering tone and cascades of spontaneous words. But this did not mean that Newman was more austere in his use of rhetoric, or that, although he never addressed great multitudes, his command over the spoken word was a less necessary part of his armoury of argument. To quote Faber again: 'Other men have known better how to stir up a sudden tempest of emotions; others have argued as skilfully, but few, if any, have equalled him in the art of using reason as a lever for the prising of hearts.'[8]

Another quality which Newman had in common with Gladstone was the ability to recover from a failure, which sometimes led in his case to a collapse. Faber says he did so in a way which 'went just as far above normality as the collapse had fallen below it'. Aberdeen's remark about Gladstone 'in the rebound' immediately springs to mind. Even though detached from and even censorious of Newman, Gladstone therefore had quite enough understanding of his power and importance to know that it shattered the movement which had begun with Keble's Oxford 'Assize Sermon' in 1833 and in the slipstream of which Gladstone had hitherto lived his whole adult life. Since leaving Christ Church Gladstone's religious life had never been physically centred on Oxford, although he had closely followed the liturgical controversies which had convulsed the University in those schismatic years.

Gladstone's London spiritual home had gradually become the Margaret Chapel north of Oxford Circus, which the polychromatic architect William Butterfield later rebuilt as All Saints, Margaret Street. Here he became part of a Tractarian lay brotherhood with a membership of fifteen, which included the Acland brothers (who were the initiators), Frederic Rogers, J. T. Coleridge, Roundell Palmer (who as Lord Selborne became one of Gladstone's Lord Chancellors), Butterfield himself and James Hope. The rules of the brotherhood mainly related to liturgical observance, but they also contained provisions for devoting proportions of both time and energy to 'some regular work of charity'. This 'engagement' as it came to be called was at first directed towards male or female destitution and was centred on the House of St Barnabas in Rose Street, Soho. But as the 1840s wore on it came in Gladstone's case to concentrate on the attempted reformation of prostitutes, many of whom were far from destitute.

This concentration led Gladstone somewhat to disengage from the brotherhood, which in any event showed signs of faltering. However, the framework of his work among the ladies of the streets was eminently respectable, even if there is more room for doubt about some of his motives.* When in 1848 he set up the Church Penitentiary Asociation for the Reclamation of Fallen Women his principal collaborators were Bishop Blomfield of London and Bishop Wilberforce, who had just been translated to the see of Oxford from the deanery of Westminster; and when a few years later he helped to found (for the same purpose) the Clewer House of Mercy at Windsor his wife too was closely involved in the project.

He was also centrally involved in major ecclesiastical building. His plans for a new church in Leicester Square proved abortive, although he did establish a small chapel of ease off St Martin's Lane, but in Scotland he was more successful. He got Trinity College, Glenalmond, an Episcopalian public school for 160 boys on a greenfield site in Perthshire, built and opened by 1846. And in the grounds of Fasque there arose a public St Andrew's Chapel.

His collaborator in most of these enterprises was James Hope.

* See Chapter Seven below.

Throughout the 1840s Hope and Manning were Gladstone's closest politico-religious advisers. But Gladstone loved Hope, whereas he did not love Manning. He said many years later that he could only look 'at him [Manning] as a man looks at the stars';[9] and the stars are clearest on a cold night. Hope, he said, possessed 'the most rare gift, the power of fascination, and he fascinated me'.[10] Hope was one of the three men whom Gladstone loved. The first was Hallam, and the second and the third (it is difficult to place these two in chronological or other order) were Hope and Sidney Herbert.* The only one of the three who did Gladstone no harm (although he was sometimes obstructive to him in Cabinet) was Herbert. Hope did him the considerable harm, given Gladstone's already surging temperament, of always stirring him up and not calming him down. He was like a wife who encouraged rather than corrected her husband's misjudgements. Mrs Gladstone was if anything the reverse, but she did not much engage with matters for decision. And Hope, who was very close – the godfather (with Manning) of Gladstone's first child, an executor of his will – egged him on, over the hurried publication of his book, over his Maynooth resignation, over Helen, over disapproval of Newman. And then, to crown it all, Hope himself deserted his post on the ramparts and betrayed Gladstone, as the latter saw it, by being received as a Roman Catholic on the same day in April 1851 that Manning went over.

To add to these various destabilizing factors there came in 1847 the major financial embarrassment of Oak Farm, a curiously rural and gentle name for an establishment which was to cause such upheaval in Gladstone's life and wreak such havoc in the fortunes of his wife's family. At the time of the Gladstone–Glynne marriage in 1839 Sir Stephen Glynne had been a rich bachelor, not extravagant (except perhaps on election expenses), who pottered comfortably along on an annual income of over £10,000 (about £500,000 at present-day values) coming mainly from agricultural rents. Of this, £2500 went under a generous settlement to his mother, who took to living mostly with her Lyttelton daughter at Hagley. But he had few other family obligations, for the Gladstones were self-supporting and his younger brother, as already noted, had the £3000 a year benefice at Hawarden. However, great possessions, even among the gentle and unthrusting, by no means always provide an immunity against the desire to accumulate more. When therefore Stephen Glynne saw other landlords becoming mag-

* But see Gladstone on Aberdeen, p. 42, above.

nates as a result of turning their fields into coal mines or ironworks, and when Oak Farm, a property of his detached from the main Hawarden estate and on the edge of Worcestershire and Staffordshire, near Stourbridge, showed itself rich in mineral deposits, he was tempted.

Glynne began to exploit Oak Farm in 1835. When the double marriage took place in 1839 he got both Lord Lyttelton and Gladstone to take one-tenth shares in it. In 1840 he sold land for £55,000 in order to put the money into the ironworks. In that same year Oak Farm provided a revenue of £9454 as against £12,300 from the traditional estate rents. But by 1841 the first clouds were gathering. John Gladstone had to provide credit, and disliked doing so, partly because of his distrust of Boydell, the manager, and partly because his old merchant's nostrils (although he was never an industrialist) disliked the smell of the business. It was, however, six years between then and the crash, and it seems almost incredible that, during that period and so forewarned by the only close observer who knew anything about business, the three partners could not at least staunch the potential liability. On the contrary it became a pre-enactment of Charles Kingsley's poem of 1869 immortalizing the legend of the sands of Dee, visible appropriately enough from the mock battlements of Hawarden, and from which, once the mist came down and the suction set in, there was no escape.

In late 1844, when John Gladstone had become more urgent (disengage 'at almost whatever sacrifice may be required'; 'events the most disastrous are possible'),[11] the three partners tried to end their unlimited liability by retiring to the position of mortgagees. But they could not avoid the fact that the future of the whole Hawarden estate was committed to the declining fortunes of approximately ninety-four acres of ill-fated and ill-managed land on the edge of the Black Country.

In the autumn of 1847 there was a Stock Exchange crash and a general financial shake-out. Oak Farm fell under its impact as predictably as does a windfall apple to the puffs of autumn wind. It left a liability on Hawarden of approximately £250,000 (£12½ million today). There were bankruptcy proceedings at Birmingham provoked by Lord Ward (the future Earl of Dudley), who was the principal creditor. For the handling of these (including what he called an 'indecent cross-examination') Gladstone accepted responsibility, Glynne having been packed off to Constantinople, for it was thought he was better out of the way. Gladstone then devoted himself with portentous care and some ingenuity to clearing up the mess. He had been little use so long as there was life in the company. But, true to his longstanding proclivity for deathbed scenes, the closing of the eyelids released a storm of activity from him. Freshfields were the solicitors and they received from him no fewer than 140 letters on the subject. They must have groaned when yet another franked envelope in the well-known handwriting arrived.

At the decisive family conclave Sir John Gladstone advocated the financially sensible course of selling off the whole Hawarden property, which would enable Stephen Glynne to discharge the Oak Farm debt and be left with a comfortable income of approximately £4500 a year. But it would also have left him rootless, a Lord Lieutenant (who would probably have had to resign) without a county base. And it would have left Gladstone without a dimension which had already become important to his life over the previous nine years (Tom Gladstone and not he was the heir to Fasque), Catherine Gladstone without the house in which she had been born and was to live in for nearly nine decades, and Henry Glynne as a squire–parson sitting on a very isolated branch.

So they decided on a more heroic course. They kept the estate and paid off the Oak Farm debts by a period of stringent economies. Sir Stephen Glynne tried to live on £700 a year. Hawarden Castle was closed with the thought of letting it (a tenant was never found) and did not reopen until early 1852. Even old Lady Glynne suffered a reduction in her jointure from £2500 to £1500. Gladstone, who was largely the instigator of this plan of economies, suffered no reduction in his own circumstances comparable with those of Stephen Glynne (but nor should he have done; he was only a one-tenth partner). His own income was, however, reduced for a time by about 30 per cent, and from first to last he sank £267,500 of his own or his father's money into the Hawarden estate. But he was also the ultimate beneficiary. After the 1852 return to the big house he increasingly became the head of Hawarden. In 1851, with the death of Parson Henry Glynne's wife, the likelihood of a Glynne male heir had disappeared (although Henry Glynne caused agitation with one or two lurches towards remarriage), and Stephen Glynne, securely unmarried, was apparently content, not only to become a subsidiary figure in his own house, although he always sat at the head of the table, but also to see the property settled on the Gladstone children. In 1867 Gladstone paid £57,000 to secure its full reversion to himself and his heirs after the deaths of the two Glynne brothers (which both occurred within seven years).

The only (ambiguous) indication of resentment which Stephen Glynne ever showed was to develop a habit of referring to the Gladstones as 'the great people'. But so of course they were. Gladstone gave

Hawarden a fame comparable with that which Franklin Roosevelt gave to his Hyde Park mansion on the Hudson seventy or so years later. And Gladstone should not fairly be regarded as a cuckoo in Stephen Glynne's nest. He did not tip him out but treated him with affectionate regard. And, apart from anything else, there would, without Gladstone's prodigal expenditure of energy in the late 1840s, have been no remaining nest. Far busier than anyone else, he was the only one on the scene who had the vigour to engage with and clear up a disastrous situation. He always subsequently claimed that this immersion into private business was an immensely valuable training for his several chancellorships of the Exchequer. Without it he could not have understood the commercial problems of mid-Victorian England. This was Gladstone in his self-flagellating mood, thanking God for His goodness in allowing him to be beaten up by the bloods of Christ Church in 1829 or brutally examined by the Birmingham inspector in bankruptcy in 1847. The connection between private and public financial skill is minimal. Pitt was a great public financier who left his own affairs in confusion. Most of those who have best served their country have done so at the expense of their own personal wealth. Oak Farm was in no way necessary to make Gladstone a great Chancellor. What it did, before giving him the important and safe harbourage of Hawarden, was substantially to increase both his burden of work and the sense of personal strain and perturbation which was such a feature of his late thirties and early forties.

6

Mid-Century Frenzy

On top of these several sources of dismay, Oak Farm, Helen, Newman's conversion, Gladstone lost his parliamentary seat. When he returned to England on 18 November 1845 from his two-month Helen-retrieving German trip he found that a combination of factors – the Irish famine, a poor harvest in England, a public announcement (on 22 November) by the Whig leader Lord John Russell of his conversion to Repeal – was leading Peel to take the issue of the Corn Laws* more quickly than he had hitherto intended. Previously he had been content to rest on the doctrine of 'unripe time', one to which Gladstone, despite his generally impetuous nature, was always inclined to defer.

The anti-Corn Law position was not an easy one for Gladstone. It divided him from his father, which he disliked not only because of his naturally filial loyalty but because the Oak Farm troubles increased his paternal dependence. It also separated him from his borough patron, the Duke of Newcastle. Once the issue had become actual, however, he did not doubt that he had to be on Peel's side. Nevertheless he rushed into no frenzy of political activity. He spent only one night at Carlton House Terrace before joining Catherine at Hagley for the last two weeks of November and then only another four days in London before going to Hawarden for ten mid-December days. His correspondence was more religious and Helen-related (with a strong dash of Oak Farm) than it was politically centred. And his reading was much directed to Newman, probably with a view to a refutation, which he did not, however, complete or publish. He recorded only three serious political conversations, all of them with Lincoln, who had been in the Cabinet

* The basic Corn Law had been introduced by the Liverpool government at the end of the Napoleonic Wars and provided for a prohibitively high duty on foreign corn if the domestic price fell below 80 shillings a quarter (eight bushels). It was a measure of high protection for the landed interest at the expense of the consumer. In 1828 a sliding scale of duty had replaced this sudden activation of full protection. In 1842 Peel had reduced this sliding scale. The argument which dominated the remainder of his government was about whether the duty should be completely eliminated.

since 1844 as Commissioner of Woods and Forests: the first on 6 December and the latter two in the week before Christmas.

The day before the first conversation Peel had resigned, feeling that without the support of a wholly united Cabinet he should leave it to Russell to carry Repeal. The Cabinet was disunited only to the extent that the Duke of Buccleuch and Stanley (Derby after 1851 and the only man before Gladstone to be Prime Minister more than twice, although his triple occupancy of the office amounted to a cumulative total of only three years and ten months) could not accept Peel's lead. It was not a major split but the two peers (Stanley had been called up to the House of Lords in 1844) paradoxically represented a lot of House of Commons feeling.*

After two weeks of hesitation Russell declined to pick up the poisoned chalice which Peel, via the Queen, had handed him. He said that he could act effectively only with both Palmerston and Sir George Grey in his Cabinet, but Grey would not serve if Palmerston were Foreign Secretary and Palmerston would not serve in any other position. In addition Russell claimed that Peel offered him inadequate guarantees of support on what they both knew had to be done. So, without great reluctance, Peel took up office again. It was at once a tribute to his public spirit and a criticism of his party leadership that, having seen that Repeal was essential, he had a positive zest, more than the querulous Russell, for carrying it through himself. This was central to the subsequent count against him as a party splitter. Had he just leant back and franchised Russell to do the necessary job, he might have been forgiven. The 'protectionists' half knew that it was necessary to abandon protection, which, within six years, they themselves proceeded to do. But they did not want a leader who put country before party. Sixty-four years later the precedent led even so fastidious a politician as Arthur Balfour to say that he could not become another Robert Peel to his party: 'Peel twice committed what seems to me the unforgivable sin. . . . He simply betrayed his party.'[1] Peel chose the path of activity rather than of lying back, and as a result became both excoriated and the architect of the calm and prosperous third quarter of the nineteenth century,

* The dukes were pretty strong on the issue, and put on almost a dress rehearsal (although there were a few changes of cast in the meantime) of their 1893 and 1909 performances against Home Rule and the Lloyd George budget. Both Newcastle and Marlborough refused to let Peel supporters be re-elected for their family boroughs, while Richmond and Buckingham went even further and demanded resignations from sitting MPs.

relatively the most unchallenged period of material and moral superiority in British history.

In order to do this, however, he had to plug the gaps in his Cabinet. Buccleuch, mysteriously, plugged his own gap. Having helped to precipitate a Cabinet crisis on 5 December he calmly returned to office on the 21st, and indeed in January 1846 advanced from being Lord Privy Seal to being Lord President of the Council. Stanley was a more resolute resigner and Peel turned to Gladstone to replace him as Secretary for War and Colonies (as it was still quaintly called until 1854, although Sidney Herbert as Secretary *at* War was already in charge of the War Office). Gladstone was still only thirty-five, but he was looked to as almost a veteran, temporarily in the reserve, whom it was useful to bring back into the front line. It was a relatively young era. Peel was fifty-seven and Russell fifty-three, but Buccleuch only thirty-nine and the resigning Stanley forty-six.

Gladstone had little hesitation about accepting Peel's offer. He did so, he wrote to his wife, 'with a clear conscience but with a heavy heart',[2] which for Gladstone was almost the equivalent of saying that he leapt at it. This was curious, for it involved a serious risk of the loss of his seat in Parliament. Until after the First World War the acceptance of Cabinet office necessarily involved vacating a seat and seeking re-election. And a few fell at the hurdle, most notably Winston Churchill in North-west Manchester in 1908. Gladstone did not take the hurdle. He played with the idea of contesting the seat against the Duke of Newcastle, who was a virulent protectionist, but discovered that he did not have enough support in the town and that his former 'principal and best supporters' produced an alternative candidate with humiliating speed and ease. This was ironical, for it was discussion with Newcastle's son Lincoln which had been most mind-clearing for Gladstone in his approach to office.

On 22 December he almost kissed hands with Peel ('we *held* hands instinctively & I could not but reciprocate with emphasis his "God bless you"').[3] And over the Christmas holidays (only five days at Hawarden, most exceptionally, followed by a New Year forty-eight hours at Windsor)* and the first weeks of January he gradually reconciled himself to his exclusion from Newark. He then sought another seat with more urgency than discrimination. There was talk of North Nottinghamshire, Wigan, Liverpool, Dorchester, Chester and South Lanca-

* While the Prince Consort was alive Gladstone was on good and close terms with the Queen.

shire. Later Oxford City, Scarborough, Aberdeen and Montrose Burghs were all subject to feelers. For a variety of reasons none of them came to anything.

Wigan, in the early spring of 1846, approached the nearest to reality. The Tory (and Peelite) member who had been elected at a bye-election in the previous October was in danger of being unseated on a petition. As he was a son of the Earl of Crawford and Balcarres, who was also Lord Wigan, he had some territorial strength (which Gladstone after Newark, and indeed because of his own views, was bound to treat with respect) and he was willing to let the Colonial Secretary in only for the bye-election and not for the subsequent general election when his own disqualification would have ceased. Gladstone was prepared to accept this somewhat stringent condition, for the short lease would at least have solved his immediate governmental problem. He got as far as writing his election address and preparing to take the night mail to Lancashire. But it was in vain. On 8 April he wrote, 'My Wigan vision is dissolved.'[4] The reason could be regarded as a parliamentary compliment. The Whigs had withdrawn the petition, thinking it well worth while to forgo a bye-election in order to keep Gladstone out of the House of Commons.

No other seat presented itself, and the main reason for which Peel wanted Gladstone to replace Stanley was thus frustrated. He could make administrative decisions in his Secretary of State's office, but he could bring no debating thunder to the government's aid in the House of Commons. For his six months' tenure of the Colonial Office, the first and only time that he was a Secretary of State, he could get no nearer to the despatch box than the distinguished strangers' gallery. There he often sat, for it was a momentous six months for parliamentary clashes and for the fashioning of the shape of mid-Victorian politics. On 23 January 1846, Disraeli delivered the first of his insolently devastating attacks on Peel, rallied the protectionist forces in the Conservative Party and went on to form with Lord George Bentinck (MP for King's Lynn, a younger son of the Duke of Portland and hitherto more interested in racing than in politics) his improbable but effective partnership: 'the Jew and the jockey', as it was irreverently known.

So effective was it that on the first important division on Repeal, at the end of February and after twelve nights of debate, including another philippic from Disraeli, Peel carried only 112 Tories into the lobby with him; 242 of his 'supporters' voted against, and he carried his motion to go into committee (by 97) only with the help of 227 Whigs and Radicals.

From that moment the Tory party in which Gladstone had grown up was irrevocably split and it was to be another twenty-eight years before another Conservative Prime Minister commanded an independent majority in the House of Commons. Repeal got through (the House of Lords was strangely quiescent), but the moment the bill was safe the Whigs joined with the Radicals, the Irish and a hard core of only seventy (but enough) Disraeli–Bentinck rebels ('a blackguard combination' in the Duke of Wellington's view) to defeat the government on an Irish coercion bill.

Peel resigned four days later, ending up with an encomium of Richard Cobden, the Radical leader of the victorious anti-Corn Law campaign, which shocked Gladstone, and of his own performance as Prime Minister which displeased both sides of the House of Commons. Russell became Prime Minister of a Whig government. The anomaly of Gladstone's position as a non-parliamentary Secretary of State was ended, but not his seatlessness which continued for more than a year. Gladstone had suffered two major blows. Having seen Newman in 1843–5 shatter the high hopes of the apostolic revival within the Church of England he watched Peel producing equally devastating effects upon the Conservative party in 1845–6. There were differences. On the merits of the issue Gladstone agreed with Peel and disagreed with Newman. Furthermore he was never central to Tractarianism (much though it occupied his mind) in the way that he was to the movement away from protectionism in the Peel-led Conservative party. On both issues, however, he found himself in the final stages a spectator rather than a participant.

Would it have made any difference had Gladstone been in the House of Commons in the first half of 1846? Certainly his presence would have ensured that the government's case was presented with more brio. The more or less simultaneous loss in different directions from the Treasury bench of Stanley and Gladstone was gravely weakening to the government in the House of Commons. It left Peel effectively alone to face the *banderillas* of Disraeli and the lesser weapons of Bentinck (for Aberdeen was in the Lords, Goulburn, Graham and Sidney Herbert not great debaters, and Lincoln, not a great one either, was in Ireland). This had the effect of making the Prime Minister unusually sullen and wooden. Gladstone himself, forty-five years later, told John Morley that the performances against Peel of Disraeli (in whose favour he was hardly biased) were 'quite as wonderful as report makes them. Peel altogether helpless in reply. Dealt with them with a kind of "righteous dullness".'[5]

With Gladstone at his side he might have been more buoyant and less alienating, but the lines of the split were unlikely to have been significantly different. What would have been significantly reduced was Gladstone's sense of frustration.

Nor did his Colonial Office achievements provide any relief. To leave Gladstone as an administrator without providing him with a parliamentary sounding-board was like putting Napoleon in charge of army supply while forbidding him to fight any campaigns, except that Napoleon would have been better at *intendance* than Gladstone was at exercising calm judgement on delicate colonial issues. Gladstone was at best an indifferent Colonial Secretary, as Morley, normally admiring although not sycophantic, delicately makes clear. 'To colonial policy at this stage,' he circumspectly wrote, 'I discern no particular contribution, and the matters that I have named are now well covered by the moss of kindly time.'[6] These 'matters' were first Gladstone's unfortunate advocacy of the resumption of convict despatch to Australia, which provoked a sharp reaction there and was promptly vetoed by his Whig successor (the third Earl Grey); and second his clumsy sacking of the Governor of Tasmania, one Eardley-Wilmot. Wilmot probably deserved recall for general inefficiency, but Gladstone, like a sermonizing judge, added to the dismissal letter a homily on the retiring Governor's private character, details of which he had got, typically, from the local bishop, but by which that dignitary refused to stand when the point became a matter of public and (to Gladstone) damaging controversy.

The politics of the mid-1840s therefore provided Gladstone with no stabilizing counterbalance to his various personal and religious troubles. And when he eventually regained a seat in Parliament at the general election in the late summer of 1847, neither his new constituency nor the party configuration of the new House of Commons was helpful to his equanimity. The constituency was the University of Oxford. From 1604 to 1950 the University returned two 'burgesses' to Parliament. The thought of this unusual constituency excited Gladstone, but as his need was more for calming down than for stirring up there was by no means a clear gain. That subjective factor apart, the seat had some advantages and some disadvantages. The first of the advantages, by no means irrelevant in the year of the Oak Farm bankruptcy, was that it was cheap. There were several grounds of objection to the university constituencies, but an electorate inviting corruption was not one of them. Indeed the voters were so physically elusive that it was difficult to incur even the normal expenses of an austere campaign. This, however, carried its disadvantages from Gladstone's point of view. In a seat that was never safe for him the man who was becoming the foremost orator of his age was almost uniquely prevented from exercising this form of persuasion upon his constituents.

Furthermore Oxford exaggerated his natural tendency to mingle politics and religion. The worst convulsions of the Tractarian earthquake were over by the time Gladstone became member, but Oxford nevertheless remained the central battleground of liturgical and theological dispute, and the representation of the University was determined at least as much on religious as on political grounds. It is difficult to believe that Peel, for example, with his own unsatisfactory 1817–29 experience there, not to mention his desire to see Gladstone treat Church matters more calmly, could ever have counselled him to sit for Oxford. Beyond that the pulls of the University electorate were still strongly conservative and even intolerant. It was Gladstone's early reputation as 'the rising hope of those stern and unbending Tories' which gave him his initial attraction as a candidate. But already by 1847 he was moving away from that position, and was to do so with gathering momentum over the eighteen years for which he remained a member for the University. This meant that relations with his constituency introduced an additional dimension of turbulence into an already tempestuous period of his life. Yet once the possibility of election for Oxford opened before him there was no question of his refusing. He had great need of a seat, and he loved and respected the institution which on his deathbed he was to salute as 'the God-fearing and God-sustaining University of Oxford'.

The two members for the University in the Parliament of 1841 had been Sir Robert Inglis of Christ Church, who had beaten Peel in the immediate aftermath of Catholic emancipation, and Thomas Bucknall-Estcourt of Corpus Christi College, who had sat obscurely since 1826. Inglis was a genial man of reactionary views. His geniality endeared him to the House of Commons (Peel in 1847, and in spite of 1829, came to Oxford to vote for him – and for Gladstone), as his views did to a large part of the Oxford electorate. He was impregnable in his seat.

Estcourt wished to retire, and Gladstone's name as a possible replacement began to be actively canvassed in May. Edward Cardwell, recently Financial Secretary to the Treasury, later to be Gladstone's Secretary of State for War, was already in the lists with Peel's support, but he was bundled out of the way. Gladstone was formally nominated in the Sheldonian Theatre on 29 July by the Rector of Exeter (Richards) in a

Latin speech of notable succinctness. Inglis was nominated on the same occasion by a canon of Christ Church, and a third candidate, Professor Charles Round, by the Master of Balliol (Jenkyns). Round was an Evangelical, procured with some difficulty to run against Gladstone. It was not thought worth running against Inglis.

Gladstone, however, had considerable High Anglican and liberal Church support. Helpfully from the point of view of rallying the Anglo-Catholics, Keble surprisingly described him as 'Pusey in a blue coat'. By 'blue coat' he probably meant no more than that Gladstone was not 'of the cloth', but it was surprising because there were few people who were less inclined to carry the flashier fashions of the Regency into the Victorian age than was Gladstone; and in any event there was by 1847 hardly anyone other than the first Marquess of Anglesey who habitually wore a blue coat in London.

So the Anglo-Catholics, rallied by Keble, liked Gladstone because they thought (rightly) that he was a Tractarian sympathizer and because they knew that he had come specially to Oxford in 1845 to vote (unavailingly) against the Heads of Houses and in favour of W. G. Ward, fellow of Balliol and father of Newman's first biographer, being deprived of his degree for heresy. The liberals meanwhile hoped that Gladstone would be in favour of reform of the University, if need be by Parliament. This looked to the curbing of the oligarchic power which the Heads of Houses had appropriated to themselves and which they had used against Ward and attempted to use against Newman's 'Tract 90'.

As a result Gladstone was supported by very few of these Heads – only four, as against the sixteen who voted for Round. But this was balanced by a strong Gladstone preponderance among the fellows of colleges, particularly those who had achieved firsts, double firsts or University prizes. His named supporters included John Ruskin, Arthur Hugh Clough, Frederick Temple (future archbishop and father of another future archbishop) and Benjamin Jowett, who as a future and still more notable Master of Balliol balanced Richard Jenkyns.

His opponents were equally varied and some distinctly intemperate. He called on Dr Routh, the ninety-two-year-old President of Magdalen, who had held that office since 1791 and had another seven years still to go, but found him adamantly opposed to having a second Christ Church member for the University. This indeed was one of the counts used against Gladstone throughout the election, but it was inoffensively factual compared with some of the other charges against him. One was that he was tainted by his sister Helen's apostasy, and a secret Roman himself. Ashley (then a Whig MP, later Shaftesbury) showed that an Evangelical philanthropist was well capable of partisan invective by describing Gladstone as a 'mystified, slippery, uncertain, politico-Churchman, a non-Romanist Jesuit'.[7]

Another and largely contradictory count against Gladstone was that he had already shown his liberalism by voting for the Dissenters' Chapels Bill in 1845. This charge, however, was a dangerous one for Round, who was the candidate not only of the Evangelicals but also of the old high-and-dry faction in the University, which was horrified when it came to light that Round had not only favoured tolerance to Dissenters but was on the verge of being one himself. He had actually attended a Dissenting chapel, once in 1845 and three times in 1846, so he reluctantly confessed. The fact that the Oxford election was fought among an elevated electorate and on religious rather than political issues appeared to increase rather than diminish the petty backbiting.

A supporter whom Gladstone had difficulty in attracting was his eldest brother Tom. Either out of jealousy or because of the genuine strength of his Low Church principles he wrote to William to tell him that, while blood might be thicker than politics, it was not thicker than religion, which in his view was what the election was about. William Gladstone was merely offended, but Sir John Gladstone was outraged. With an even-handed authority matching that which he had exercised against William at the time of Robertson's marriage a decade earlier, he dealt with Tom, who duly voted for his brother.

The margin was not such that this was crucial in terms of anything except family relations, but it was not handsomely wide either. Inglis soared away with 1700 votes, Gladstone polled 997 and Round 824. Gladstone was at Fasque when he heard the result on 5 August and did not come south until 20 October, or visit Oxford until five days later. There was probably nobody much there to visit until October, and the victory, while it satisfactorily put him back in the House of Commons, was not so glorious as to call for celebration. In any event he had other things heavily on his mind – Oak Farm and family illness. In the second half of September his five-year-old daughter Agnes nearly died of erysipelas ('Just twelve years ago my Mother died in this same house of the same terrible complaint,' he wrote in his diary before going into a comparison of that deathbed and the current sick room).[8] Agnes recovered and lived to marry Edward Wickham, the headmaster of Wellington College, but the Gladstones were sufficiently oppressed by the threat that when it was removed they installed a window of thanksgiving, replete with a fine Latin inscription done by William but which he cautiously and modestly noted as needing to 'pass under the eyes of a fresher and better scholar than myself'.[9]

Relief from this anxiety uncovered the problem of his sister. On 3 October he wrote: 'In the evg I saw poor Helen & was greatly shocked. I thought her voice quite altered, her frame more emaciated but more utterly shattered; and although she conversed rationally about others her mind quite gone in relation to herself.'[10] Altogether it was not an easy early autumn and was made no more so by the fact that Catherine Gladstone was in her fifth and perhaps most difficult pregnancy.* When the Gladstones came to London by railway on 20 October (filling a second-class compartment) they had a hostile Helen with them until Rugby, where she was handed over to Tom, who installed her in a Roman Catholic convent at Leamington. The various family tensions during that long day of primitive rail travel must have been formidable.

In London they were confronted with the prospect not only of a new baby, a new Parliament and a new constituency but also of a (to them) new house. John Gladstone no longer came to London, and particularly with the drain of Oak Farm it had become a ridiculous extravagance to keep up both 13 Carlton House Terrace and 6 Carlton Gardens within a couple of hundred yards of each other. The William Gladstones accordingly prepared to give up the former and take over the paternal house.

Despite these preoccupations Gladstone paid significant attention both to Oxford and to Parliament during the remainder of the autumn. But what he did in Parliament, while courageous, was not strengthening of his position in Oxford. He paid two five-day visits to the University (with calls on all the Heads of Houses) within a single fortnight, which was far more than he had ever done at Newark after his 1832 introduction to the town and more too than he was to do anywhere else until he got to Midlothian in 1879. Oxford might free him from the rigours of an actual campaign but it certainly did not free him from the need for courtesy visiting and patient discussion.

Gladstone balanced these social obeisances with no concessions to the politico-religious prejudices of the University. His first House of Commons speech for two and a half years was in favour of a minor Roman Catholic Relief Bill, and he made an appropriately minor speech. But it was not calculated to propitiate his Oxford critics. Then, eight

* This fifth child, Mary, sometimes called Mazie, was born on 23 November 1847.

days later on 16 December, he made a more substantial speech on a more important issue, that of 'the Jew Bill', as it was habitually called. It arose out of the election of Baron Lionel de Rothschild, the current head of the Rothschild banking house and the father of the first Lord Rothschild, as member for the City of London (jointly, as it happened, with the new Prime Minister, Lord John Russell). Rothschild could not sit because he could not take the 'Church and state' oath. (Disraeli, thanks to his father's sudden lurch towards baptizing his children, was subject to no such inhibition.) Russell moved a bill to allow his City and Whig colleague to take a Jewish oath. Gladstone, to the surprise of almost all his supporters from his father to Edward Pusey, and to the collective indignation of the University, on whose behalf Sir Robert Inglis presented a petition of opposition from Convocation, spoke and voted for the bill, which got through the Commons but failed in the Lords. Rothschild, several times re-elected, had to wait until 1858 to be allowed in. It was a less convulsive pre-run of the drama of Bradlaugh (who was an Anglo-Saxon atheist and not a theocratic Jew), which from 1880 onwards was to dominate the life of the second Gladstone government, and substantially limit its effectiveness.

Why did Gladstone do it? His speech, which it is difficult to believe can have been one of his more successful, provides neither directly nor indirectly much explanation of motive. His old friend Thomas Acland had begged him beforehand, if he had to speak, to be direct. Despite this advice, which Gladstone engagingly believed he had followed, the subordinate clauses hung like candelabra throughout his oration with few of his sentences containing less than seventy words, and some twice as many.

His conclusion has long seemed overwhelmingly right, but most of his arguments must have appeared specious. First he erected a very pompous theory about his duty as member for Oxford University. This, he claimed, put him in a different category from other members. They were superior to their constituents 'in mental cultivation and opportunities of knowledge', and were therefore clearly entitled to exercise their own judgement. His constituents, on the other hand, were 'either superior or, on the least favourable showing, equal to myself'. Nevertheless he must also be free to speak for himself and not for them, a worthy Burkeian sentiment, but one which made the distinction pointless.

Much of his argument was a *de minimis* one. There were not going to be many Jews in Parliament even with the removal of the disability. This was a perfectly sensible argument of expediency, but it sat ill with any high statement of principle. The central theme of the speech was, however, an uncharacteristically defeatist piece of historical analysis which probably stemmed from his difficulty in evacuating the untenable ground of *The State in its Relations with the Church* without allowing the withdrawal to become a rout. He said: 'we have now arrived at a stage in which, after two or three generations had contended for a Church Parliament, and two or three generations more contended for a Protestant Parliament, each being in succession beaten, we are called upon to decide the question whether we shall contend for a Christian Parliament.'[11] And his answer to that was only the very modified affirmative implied by his argument that there would not be many Jews elected in any event.

His attitude to the 'Jew Bill' did not (just) prevent Gladstone being given an honorary degree by Oxford in the following July. It had long been the custom for the University to confer a DCL (doctorate of civil law) upon its burgesses. There was some attempt to break the convention with Gladstone, but the Hebdomadal Board held firm to precedent, and on 5 July 1848, not without trepidation, he duly presented himself. The Encaenia, as described by Gladstone, was not very different from today, although it appears that Chancellor Wellington (then aged seventy-nine) was not present:

> joined the V.C. and doctors in the Hall at Wadham: and went in procession to the Divinity Schools provided with a white neckcloth by Sir R. Inglis who seized me at the Station in horror and alarm when he saw me in a black one. In due time we were summoned to the Theatre where my degree had been granted with some non-placets [negative votes] but with no scrutiny. That scene so remarkable to the eye and mind, so pictorial and so national, was I think trying to Cath. but she has no want of strength for such things. There was great tumult about me mite that I am:* the hissers were obstinate and the fautores [supporters] also very generous and manful. 'Gladstone and the Jew Bill' came sometimes from the gallery, sometimes more favouring sounds. The proceedings lasted till two. Then we went to luncheon and speeches at University [College]†

* A very odd phrase; there seems to be no other example implying that Gladstone (in fact of medium height or a little more for the period) thought of himself as small, except when he was a boy and grew late. Precision about his height is, however, elusive. Professor Shannon resolutely attempts it by saying that in 1859 he was 5 feet 10 inches 'in slippers' (but how thick were the slippers?), and weighed 11 stone 10½ pounds in 1861. Gladstone himself recorded that he was 5 feet 9 inches when he was eighty-four, but had been 5 feet 11 inches.

† All Souls had not then assumed its generous catering role.

> then to a long but interesting concert at 4: after this and a rest for C. in New College Gardens to the Provost of Oriel's for tea; finally to town at half past nine. . . .[12]

A year later, in July 1849, Gladstone indulged in a fresh burst of eccentricity verging on the unbalanced. The Countess of Lincoln, born Lady Susan Douglas, daughter of the tenth Duke of Hamilton, after seventeen years of marriage to Gladstone's long-standing Eton, Christ Church and political friend, had bolted to Italy with Lord Walpole, heir to the Earl of Orford, and descendant of the first Prime Minister. She left not only her husband, who was dismayed although less agitated than Gladstone became on his behalf, but also her five children, for whom Catherine Gladstone unsuccessfully provided vice-parental care,* and her prospect of becoming a duchess (her father-in-law was to die in 1851). Most people other than the impetuous and beneficently interfering Gladstones would have assumed that she knew what she was about. Gladstone, however, strongly supported by his wife, decided that it was his duty to go in search of 'dearest Suzie' (as Catherine addressed her in an accompanying letter), persuade her of her sin and bring her back. Manning was an alternative candidate for the task, but the then Archdeacon and future Cardinal shrewdly decided that his Sussex parochial duties made him much busier than an ex-Colonial Secretary and opposition front-bencher. Catherine was within two months of her sixth confinement, which produced the second Helen Gladstone (the choice of name marked some improvement in his relations with his sister), who became vice-principal of Newnham College, Cambridge. Otherwise Catherine Gladstone might have come too.

As it was William Gladstone set out alone on 13 July 1849, with Europe still in a considerable state of chaos following the 1848 revolutionary upheavals and with some ambiguity both of destination and of what his function was going to be when he reached it. Obviously his optimum objective was to redeem the fallen and bring Lady Lincoln back to a renewal of conjugal duty. But did he also envisage the fall-back role, which he ended up playing, of acting as a witness of her adultery before the House of Lords, when her husband in the following year sought a divorce by private Act of Parliament, then the only possible way of proceeding? And did he apprehend that such a position might leave him looking ridiculous and even a little squalid?

But he rarely feared ridicule, he was a keen traveller, he loved Italy,

* With one exception, they all turned out disastrously.

he thought Naples the most promising site for his quarry, and he set off with enthusiasm on a journey according to his own most careful calculations of 3010 miles and twenty-seven days, during which he spent only eleven nights of an average length of five hours 'in bed ashore'.[13] He was preoccupied by his sad mission, but not to the extent of wasting his time or missing any sightseeing. He arrived in Marseille (which he had not previously visited) in great heat and after a testing fifty-hour journey from Paris, and had to wait there for a couple of days before getting a boat to Genoa, Livorno and Civitavecchia. During this delay he dealt with a lot of travel arrangements, read three books, climbed up to Notre Dame de la Garde, 'purchased a cask of the wine of the country to send home' (not too locally of the country, one hopes), dined twice at the table d'hôte of the (extant) Hôtel Beauvau, on the first occasion talking animatedly to an Italian neighbour on one side and a Peruvian on the other, and after one dinner going to a play and after the other to hear Donizetti's then relatively new *Lucia di Lammermoor*.

He reached Naples eleven days after leaving London, but discovered that the birds had flown, probably to Milan, and so set off north again, mainly by sea. Five days later he got to Milan, and there had a splendid day except for the thought that 'the business I was about was really horrible'. Having reached the city at 10.30 a.m. he:

> Breakfasted (luxuriously) at the Albergo della Città & then set out on my search for Lady L. . . . This kept me till past 3. I was too late for the Brera [gallery] – went to the Duomo and S. Alessandro, bought some books arranged to go to Como tomorrow morning: dined at the Table d'Hôte and then went to work with pen & ink & my books. . . . At 8 went to the Teatro Ré and heard the Masnadieri [an unfamous Verdi opera which had been first performed in Rome the year before] sung with two good basses & good Choruses – home at midnight but my sleep was bitten away.[14]

At Como the pursuit turned into an encounter of a sort, with an obtruding mixture of farce and tragedy (from the point of view of the Lincoln marriage, which Gladstone regarded as sacrosanct).

> It was a day of great excitement, constant movement, overpowering sadness. I saw the Govr. of the Province – the head of Police – the landlord [of the rented villa where Lady Lincoln who had assumed the alias of Mrs Lawrence had been staying] – the (false) Mrs L's courier – the *levatrice* [midwife] (at night) – & had the lacquais de place [odd-job man] incessantly at work – he did it well & we went at the proper time to

watch the departure. I wrote fully to Lincoln in the evening except the horror reported to me.[15]

The 'horror' was that Lady Lincoln was heavily pregnant, not, it need hardly be said, by Lincoln, and that 'the departure', really a flight from Gladstone's heavy intrusion, brought on her confinement. Magnus thought that the flight was to Verona, but as Gladstone followed by steamer this would have been an improbable journey. In fact she went to Lecco, at the foot of the other arm of the lake, and Gladstone had an agreeable lake cruise to Varenna, higher up that same arm, and then down to Lecco to discover that she had decamped to Bergamo. Although the city of Montagues and Capulets was not on the itinerary, the *Kiss Me Kate* couplet ('we opened in Verona, we went on to Cremona') was beginning to sound appropriate to the musical-comedy aspects of the tour. These had included his being disguised as a mandolinist in order to get near the villa and observe the departure from Como.

After that Gladstone never again glimpsed Lady Lincoln. At Lecco he called off the chase. Perhaps he was beginning to accept her determination not to see him or to respond to his numerous letters. He returned to Como, collected evidence from Dr Balzari, who sounds like a good Donizetti character, and from the Villa Mancini, which had been her *nid d'amour*, and departed for Varese, Lake Maggiore and Switzerland. In Lausanne he was desolated by there being no Anglican Sunday afternoon service (he had rushed 'unwashed and unshaven' to the late-morning holy communion), contemplated going to the Free Church, but thought better of it, and reflected on the failure of his mission and the tragedy of the errant wife:

> Oh that poor miserable Lady L. – once the dream of dreams, the image that to my young age combined everything that earth could offer of beauty and of joy. What is she now! But may that Spotless Sacrifice whereof I partook, unworthy as I am, today avail for her, to the washing away of sin and to the renewal of the image of God.
>
> At midnight, started for Besançon.[16]

This was classic Gladstone: sanctimonious and judgemental, perhaps over-concerned, made prurient by the recollection of the beauty of the fallen one, oppressed by her sins, yet in no way reduced to inactivity by this or by the rejection of his overtures. It was not even as leisurely as 'off to Besançon in the morning'. It was off that night and in London four days later. Failure could leave Gladstone dismayed and censorious, but almost never without energy for the next move.

Yet a combination of filial duty and conventional acceptance of the view that the autumn was not a season for London led him into four subsequent months of bucolic Scottish quietism. Soon after his return from Italy, Catherine's sixth confinement took place in the Rectory at Hawarden (the Castle being closed as a result of Oak Farm) and five weeks later the whole family sailed from Liverpool to Greenock and hence across to Fasque by train. They stayed there until the end of January 1850, interrupted for Gladstone only by three days with Lord Aberdeen at Haddo, one night in another Scottish house and a twenty-four-hour dentist excursion to Edinburgh. It was the penultimate autumn at Fasque. For the following one they were in Italy, and in December 1851 Sir John Gladstone died within a few days of his eighty-seventh birthday (sixteen months younger than the age his fourth son was to attain), and Fasque passed to Tom, the new baronet. Thereafter William Gladstone virtually severed his connection with Fasque. His 5000 books were moved to Hawarden. At intervals of about five years, sometimes nearer ten, he would call in for a very few days during a round of visits to other Scottish houses, at which the sojourns were mostly appreciably longer.

During that lengthy autumn and early-winter visit of 1849–50 Gladstone's days were not passed in idleness or even (much) in country pursuits, but were gripped in his usual rigid framework of unrelenting activity, conducting his voluminous correspondence (as well as his father's), writing a long essay on Giacomo Leopardi for the *Quarterly Review*, teaching Latin to his nine-year-old son, pursuing his variegated reading, and making the fullest possible use of the new and adjacent St Andrew's Chapel. It was nonetheless odd that at a period of such agitation in his life he should for so long have accepted such geographical and domestic confinement. There was hardly any non-family company, apart from his three specified overnight visits away there was virtually nowhere outside the estate that he could go, and, substantial though the house was, the presence of his father, his wife, his six children, his sister Helen and numerous servants inevitably made it a restricted terrain.

This might have been satisfactory had his mood been more contented and calm. It was far from that. During the long visit he reached his fortieth birthday. It is at once a tribute and a surprise that all his previous achievements, vicissitudes and eccentricities should have occurred in his twenties and thirties and before he even reached that early climacteric. Yet he marked it with no sense of satisfaction:

> And this day I am forty years old. Forty years long hath God been grieved with me – hath with much long suffering endured me! Alas I cannot say better of myself. The retrospect of my inward life is dark.... In some things I may seem to improve a little: but the flesh and the devil if not the world still have fearful hold upon me.[17]

Some reasons for this late-1840s dismay have already been indicated: the undermining of his 'Church and state' certainties and the defection of Newman; the break-up of Peel's Conservative party; the trouble with Helen; and the Oak Farm disaster. This last he singled out in his birthday budget as the 'only one personal [item] that I venture to indicate in conditional prayer: it is for a lightening of the load of pecuniary cares and anxieties upon me'.

Helen had achieved what was literally a miraculous cure in Edinburgh during the autumn of 1848. She produced a near repeat of her Baden-Baden condition, with locked jaw, clenched hands and an insistent demand for oblivion-promoting drugs. Dr Wiseman arrived with a holy relic, apparently the knuckle bone of a female saint, conducted some sort of makeshift service, touched her jaw with the bone and effected an instantaneous cure. The proceedings were watched and reported with some cynicism by the (presumably Scots Presbyterian) Edinburgh doctor under whose care she had been placed. Gladstone regarded his sister as having been subject to a 'deplorable illusion', typical of the showy trickery of the Church of Rome at its worst. But, if trickery it was, Helen was delighted to take part in a trick which enabled her to recover with drama. She became well enough to resume looking after her father for the last couple of years of his life, and then to withdraw first to the Isle of Wight and subsequently to Germany, where she caused no more trouble until her death.

The Helen amelioration apart, however, the upheavals of Gladstone's early forties were if anything worse than those of his late thirties. In April 1850 there came the harrowing and already described death of his daughter Jessy. Over that spring there also hung the shadow of the Gorham judgement, which dismayed Gladstone, as it did all Anglo-Catholics, and which was the major cause of the next great secession to Rome. G. C. Gorham was a Low Church clergyman, a fellow of Queens' College, Cambridge, who at the somewhat advanced age of sixty was in 1847 nominated to the living of Brampford Speke in Devon by the Lord Chancellor, the patron of the parish. It was part of a pattern of Whig Erastianism. In the same year Dr Hampden, whom Oxford had pronounced heretical seven years before, was made Bishop of Hereford. But the Bishop of Exeter (Phillpotts) was not a man for running before the storm. He simply refused to install Gorham on the ground that his views on baptismal regeneration were not those of the Church of England. Bishop and vicar were equally intransigent, and fought each other through a series of legal actions. The Court of Arches – an ecclesiastical court – upheld the Bishop, but when Gorham appealed from it to the Judicial Committee of the Privy Council – a lay court, although one which took the precaution of enrolling the Archbishop of Canterbury (Howley), the Archbishop of York (Musgrave) and the Bishop of London (Blomfield) as assessors – they overturned the Court of Arches, found against the Bishop of Exeter, and by so doing proclaimed the rights of the courts of Queen and Parliament to overturn those of God and Church on a matter of religious doctrine. It was this which outraged those who believed that, even in the Church of England, doctrinal authority descended from St Peter and not from the Glorious Revolution.

The Judicial Committee pronounced on 8 March 1850, and it was another thirteen months before Manning and Hope-Scott were received into the Roman Catholic Church. The Gorham judgement was nonetheless a crucial cause of their action. Gladstone was never tempted to move with them, greatly though he felt the severance, particularly from Hope-Scott. Nevertheless the traumatic effect of the judgement was probably greater upon him than upon them. It marked the final stage of his disillusionment with the view that the Church could and should live in the bosom of the state. At the time of his 1838 book he had believed that such a partnership should impose the doctrines of the Church upon everyone who wished to be a full citizen. During the 1840s he had come to see that as impractical, and maybe indefensible. But Gorham made him apprehend that a Church which looked for privileges from the state was likely to have to pay for them by depending for its doctrine more upon Acts of Parliament and judgements of lay legal luminaries than upon apostolic truth. In reality this was a liberation for him, because it opened the way to his accepting first Irish and then Welsh Church disestablishment for the very good reason that he was henceforward only half happy with establishment even in England. But at the time it left him floundering, yet unwilling to strike out for the shore of Roman certainties which welcomed Manning and Hope-Scott.

The second reason why Gorham became a peculiarly unhappy issue for him was that he failed to go through with the wave of opposition which he originally helped to mount. There were plans for a declaration of protest to be signed by the most prominent Anglo-Catholic laymen and to be addressed jointly to the bishops. Although the plans were partly hatched at meetings in his own house on 12 and 14 March, Gladstone began to hedge. Manning thought it was because he became doubtful whether, as a Privy Councillor, he ought to sign a denunciation of the Council's Judicial Committee. But that did not appear to be his motive. It was a more general and uncharacteristic sense of caution and tactics. Manning and Hope-Scott thought that he had blown unsatisfactorily hot and cold, and forty-five years later Purcell, Manning's combative and unreliable biographer, delicately compared Gladstone's role in the whole affair to that of Judas Iscariot. This produced a vehement denial from Gladstone (then aged eighty-six) of Manning's whole version of events. But what cannot be denied is that it was the beginning of his separation from his two closest religious associates (one of whom was also his closest friend at the time). As a result he suffered full dismay at the Gorham judgement without having the compensating stimulus of treating it as a call to arms. 'It was a terrible time,' he wrote in 1894, 'aggravated for me by heavy cares and responsibilities of a nature quite extraneous: and far beyond all others by the illness and death of a much-loved child, with great anxieties about another. My recollection of the conversations before the declaration [which he declined to sign] are little but a mass of confusion and bewilderment.'[18] And at the time he wrote (in Italian) on 19 August 1851 of 'these two terrible years . . . [which] may yet succeed in bringing about my ruin, body and soul'.[19]

7

Ladies of the Night

The mid-century years of 1850 and 1851, and the period of preliminary vicissitudes which led up to them, were not only terrible, they were also frenzied. Between October 1845 and July 1851 (that is from his thirty-sixth to his forty-second years) Gladstone experienced four religio-sexual emotional crises, which were perhaps exceptional more for the abjectness of the guilt which they produced than for the strength of the temptation. But temptation and guilt in combination indisputably produced high states of neurotic tension.

The first was at Baden-Baden, during the long, dismal and solitary sojourn which he sustained in the autumn of 1845 in the hope of being able to bring his sister back to England, and when the circumstances therefore provided considerable excuse for any aberrations of either behaviour or thought. He had been for a couple of days of sightseeing to Strasbourg, where he had looked at everything in a jaundiced light ('I was disappointed with the Cathedral except the West front and the stained glass. There is no proportion between the Western mass and the building in general; even the spire has not the harmony of our best: the transepts add nothing . . . the arches of the nave want elevation'),[1] and returned to Baden on the Saturday evening with the prospect of a depressing Sunday ahead of him. The English service occupied him for no less than four hours from 11.15 to 3.15. One feels he must have been like a cinema-goer who saw the film several times round, for it is difficult to believe that even in that age of relative fervour there were many subjects of Her Majesty who in a fashionable and pleasure-seeking foreign spa town required that length of devotion. Then he got down to the construction of a remarkable table of introspection. It was separate from and folded into the diary for that day. Additions to it must have been made up to four and a half years later, but it started life on that German October Sunday.

It was Gladstone's habit to set everything down. But it was also his habit to do so in forms so obscure that the meaning was often incomprehensible. And sometimes it was not only the mode of expression but the thought itself which was so cloudy as to defy rational interpretation. When he went into Italian, which he frequently did when dealing with 'delicate' subjects, he was generally clear enough. It was in English that obfuscation became an art form. This was peculiarly so in parts of this budget of guilt which he set out at Baden. It was divided into four sections, which were entitled 'Channels', 'Incentives', 'Chief actual dangers' and 'Remedies'. The 'Channels' section is impenetrable. In both the heading and the contents perfectly simple words seem to be used in a way and an order which render them meaningless. The next section 'Incentives' is comparatively lucid and sets out the factors which particularly exposed him to temptation. They are listed as '1. Idleness; 2. Exhaustion; 3. Absence from usual place; 4. Interruption of usual habits of time; 5. Curiosity of knowledge a) as such. b) πρός τι [in respect of things of a certain kind, an Aristotelian term which Gladstone habitually used for erotically stimulating subjects]; 6. Curiosity of sympathy.' It may be thought that the meaning of the first three is perfectly clear, that of the fourth a little elusive, the fifth somewhat curiously expressed, and the sixth back to the higher meaninglessness of 'Channels'. However, the fourth section on 'Remedies' has for most of its length something of the naive clarity of a primitive painting, although even here cryptic elements enter towards the end:

1. Prayer for blessing on any act about to be done.
2. Realising the presence of the Lord crucified or Enthroned.
3. Immediate pain
4. Abstinence
5. Examination
6. Withdrawal from *presumption and first appearances* of any exciting cause.
7. Interpreting every case of doubt on that side.
8. Not to deviate
9. Not to linger
10. Until D[ecember] 29. 46* not in E[ngland] to look over books in bookshops except known ones.
11. Do. as to looking into printshop windows.
12. Till E[ngland] to apply 6 to 13 to 8, 10, 11
13. Withdrawal upon first affect.[2]

It is something of an anti-climax to know that the sins which were obsessing Gladstone when he wrote out this elaborate schedule of

* The date of his thirty-seventh birthday; but why he thought this anniversary should free him from the proscription does not begin to be clear.

temptation and guilt and possible cures were almost exclusively those of reading pornography. And the sense of anti-climax is increased, although perhaps this is balanced by a diminution of dismay at the contrast between his secret vice and his public persona, when it is realized how very restrictive was the frontier over which he felt he ought not to step. Restoration poetry, some classical authors and what he refers to as the *Fabliaux* were all treated by him as most dreadful black holes of temptation and sin.

Thus on 13 May 1848, he described (in Italian) how he had encountered the several volumes of *Fabliaux et contes des poètes français du XI–XV siècles*:

> I bought this book because it had within it the name of Mr Grenville,* to whom it had belonged: and I began to read it, and found in some parts of it impure passages, concealed beneath the veil of a quite foreign idiom: so I drank the poison, sinfully, because understanding was thus hidden by a cloud – I have stained my memory and my soul – which may it please God to cleanse for me, as I have need. Have set down a black mark against this day.[3]

Then five days later, after another go at the *Fabliaux*, he wrote:

> But it seems to me necessary to shut up these last two volumes for good, having fallen yet again among impurities: how strong and subtle are the evils of that age, and of this. I read sinfully, although with disgust, under the pretext of hunting soberly for what was innocent; but – criminal that I am – with a prurient curiosity against all the rules of pious prudence, and inflaming the war between the better qualities of man and the worse.[4]

Nine months later, in February 1849, however, he was back at the *Fabliaux*, just as in July 1848 he had stumbled upon 'two vile poems' of Rochester's. Although he had avoided ('I believe', he rather doubtfully added) reading some earlier objectionable material, he nonetheless read these 'with disgust I hope but certainly with a corrupt sympathy' and under the pretext 'of acquiring a knowledge of the facts of nature and the manners of men'.[5]

It all appears venial and rather pathetic, the picture of this ex-Cabinet minister, already of commanding presence and authority, two-thirds accusing himself and one-third excusing himself over the guilty reading

* Thomas Grenville (1755–1846), statesman and book-collector, as he is described in the *Dictionary of National Biography*. Parts of his huge library were sold after his death two years earlier.

of the most marginally salacious material. Yet the weakness and for him the sin depended not on the objective strength of the pornographic content of what he read, but on his having decided he ought not to do it, and nonetheless succumbing time after time to the recurring temptation; and also on mild depravities being obviously sufficient to arouse in his mind the most lustful thoughts. Thus, in April 1849, he accused himself of committing 'adultery in the heart', and also of 'that which is well called *delectatio morosa* [enjoying thinking of evil without the intention of action]'.[6]

His recurring but not very frequent surrenders to temptation are shown by one of the two lists which he subsequently and gradually added to his 1845 schema. Twenty days, one in 1845, one in 1846, three in 1847, ten in 1848, and five in the first four months of 1849, were marked with an ×, the symbol which made the 'black mark against the day', already exemplified by 13 May 1848. That there were no dates recorded subsequent to April 1849 does not mean that a 'cure' was then effected, although it could be that this was nominally so. It could equally be that he merely gave up keeping records on that particular piece of paper, which also contained another list, and was becoming full.

The second list was made up of six dates between 13 January and 29 April 1849 against each of which there was placed the symbol ᛣ, presumably, as is suggested by the editor of the diaries, because of its resemblance to a whip. As a mixture of retribution and possible cure Gladstone had from the beginning of 1849 adopted a policy of scourging or self-flagellation. Exactly how he applied it, and to which part of his anatomy, bearing in mind that the most obvious part must surely have been excluded by the fact that the discipline was self-administered, or exactly what form the instrument took, is not clear. What seems certain, however, is that the chastisement was solitary and that there was never any other person, male or female, involved in administering it. Nor did any spiritual counselling seem to have been sought, either before or after the punishment. Gladstone, perhaps surprisingly, for its absence separated him from many of his Anglo-Catholic friends, never sought relief from his tensions in the confessional box. Judged by the ethos and outlook of today it must seem highly unlikely that, even had he done so, he could easily have discussed, still less found any encouragement for, his self-scourging practices. By mid-nineteenth-century standards, however, this is far less implausible.

Newman used a scourge and, with considerable attention to detail, described one 'studded with nails' in his 1848 novel *Loss and Gain*.

Edward Pusey asked James Hope-Scott to bring him such an instrument from France (in view of French views about *le vice anglais* this might be regarded as an example of coals to Newcastle), and hoped that Keble, his confessor, would advise him to use it. Another curious feature about Gladstone's self-punishment was that, while it was undoubtedly solitary, it did not require excessive privacy. When he first used the scourge at the beginning of 1849, he was at Fasque, in the family surroundings already described, which while not exactly overcrowded were certainly not hermit-like.

If there was a lifting after three months' use of the scourge of the temptations of erotic reading it seems likely that this was not so much a cure as a transference to a different, more famous and interesting, maybe more dangerous 'vice'. This was Gladstone's well-known involvement with prostitutes. In some form this dated from as far back as 1827 when he paid his pre-matriculation visit to Oxford (in 1848 he also dated his pornographic 'plague' as having lasted 'more than twenty years'), and in the mid-1840s he had directed the charitable efforts of the Margaret Street brotherhood towards the redemption of 'fallen women'. But it was only in May 1849 that he began systematic late-night encounters with identifiable women, several of whom he saw many times over, occasionally accompanying them back to their rooms for long conversations. Moreover he came to regard some of them not as poor, deprived and bedraggled creatures but as ethereal dreams. 'Half a most lovely statue', he wrote (in Italian) about one Elizabeth Collins on 1 July 1852, 'beautiful beyond measure'.*

The traditional view of Gladstone's activities in the field, which was long accepted apart from a few sniggers of cynicism, was that it was no more than a particularly bold form of charitable work in which he had chosen to engage (and continued with until well into old age). It clearly exposed him to certain risks, but his mixture of innocence and moral authority enabled him to stride through the murk while hardly accumulating a single stain. He might equally well have applied himself to rescuing deserted children or caring for elderly alcoholics. Instead he applied himself to what was in a sense a nobler task because it was work which very few men of substance, even had they not been Privy Councillors and potential Prime Ministers, would have dared to undertake.

This was probably the view of most of his contemporaries, including

* 'La metà di una statua bellissima, bella oltre misura' (*Diaries*, iv, p. 440).

those who knew him best, although his friends were frequently frightened for his reputation, and maybe a little puzzled themselves. There is an 1882 story of Granville and Rosebery tossing a coin to determine which of them should undertake the intimidating task of delivering a warning to the Grand Old Man. Granville was then his Foreign Secretary and the urbane and easy-going Whig (a group from which Gladstone's close friends did not often come) with whom he found it easiest to get on. Rosebery, who lost the toss and therefore had to perform, was over thirty years younger, more prickly, less nice and altogether less suitable for the task, but was at the time close to Gladstone because he had been his host and sponsor during the Midlothian campaign of 1879–80. What were the assumptions (perhaps hidden from each other) on which these two worldly figures proceeded? What is certain is that Rosebery got nowhere with his *démarche*, Gladstone blandly assuring him that he was not going to break the habits of half a century and that the night walks were beneficial to his health. In 1886, when Gladstone's vulnerability to calumny had been made greater by the bitterness of the Home Rule split, Edward Hamilton, his principal Downing Street secretary, got a somewhat more forthcoming response from the seventy-six-year-old Prime Minister to a similar warning. Even then, however, Gladstone did not entirely desist.

Morley in his massive 1903 biography virtually ignored the whole subject. Later, in 1927, Herbert (Viscount) Gladstone, former Home Secretary and Governor-General of South Africa, assisted by his elder brother Henry (Lord Gladstone of Hawarden), managed to circumnavigate the general rule that courts of law cannot be used to protect the reputation of the dead. One Captain Peter Wright published a book which contained some scurrilous material about William Gladstone's relations with his prostitutes, whereupon Herbert Gladstone countered with an attack of such vehemence that it took Henry Gladstone's breath away.[7] He sent it first direct to Wright, who did not immediately rise, and then to the secretary of the Bath Club, of which Wright was a member and Herbert Gladstone one of the founders. The Committee decided to expel Wright, nominally on the ground that he had used the club's address in controversial public correspondence on the issue, but omitted to give him a hearing. Wright then mounted two legal actions: one against the club, which he won on the procedural point and was awarded £125 damages; and the other against Herbert Gladstone, which became a very much bigger affair. The case turned on the truth or otherwise of Wright's original allegations. He failed to sustain them under a destructive cross-examination from Norman Birkett, and the outcome was a triumph for Herbert Gladstone and his father's reputation. Mr Justice Avory delivered a withering summing up against Wright, and the jury requested permission to add a rider recording their unanimous view that the evidence had 'completely vindicated the high moral character of the late Mr W. E. Gladstone'. When the Gladstone brothers came out of the Law Courts into the Strand they were greeted by a cheering crowd. Rarely has a statesman been able to arouse a favourable public demonstration twenty-nine years after his death.

Magnus in 1954, while devoting far more attention to the street-walking issue than Morley had done, took as wholly exonerative a view as did the 1927 judgement. He wrote:

> [Gladstone] had schooled himself early in life to sublimate absolutely the tensions which seethed inside him. The rescue work was an important aspect of that process of sublimation. He had experienced a call to enter the Church, and he had not responded to it. He had nursed the ideal of a sacred union between Church and State, and he had watched it dissolve into air. In his rescue work he found a priestly office which he could fulfil as a layman, and in which his duty to God and man could be discharged together.[8]

Following the publication of the diaries, it is no longer possible to take so sacerdotal a view. Nor, still more to the point, did Gladstone himself. What is indisputable from the diaries is that, while there was a strong beneficent aspect to his rescue work, and while his self-discipline held him back from a full use of his protégées' services, there was also (at least during his middle-life crisis) a powerful element of sexual temptation, which he found impossible to resist, about his nocturnal forays. So far from having 'schooled himself early in life to sublimate absolutely the tensions which seethed inside him', he was irresistibly led by them to actions which filled him with remorse. On one occasion Gladstone referred to his 'rescue' activities as 'Carnal, or the withdrawal of them would not leave such a void'.[9] On another he described them as 'the chief burden of my soul'.[10] And, after the first months of its use as an anti-pornography corrective, he began to use the scourge as a possible but on the whole ineffective remedy against excessive involvement with prostitutes.

This self-punishment appears to have continued until the summer of 1859, when the λ sign appears in the diaries for the last time. Yet it is not always easy to tell whether Gladstone's records, meticulous and self-accusing though they were, embraced all his peccadilloes (or worse, as he regarded them) or what was the exact sin for which, on a particular occasion, he was endeavouring to punish himself. On Sunday, 22 April 1849, he both brought to an end his lists opened in October 1845 (except for a solitary subsequent entry for the following Sunday, 29 April, but with no indication of the reason), and summed up his three months' experience of the use of the scourge. He thought he might have been depending upon it too much (as opposed to the observance of his other rules) and he doubted whether it was proving as useful as he had at first found. He thought 'the sin of impurity', while not showing quite the force of the previous year, had 'lingered more'. As a result he abstained from taking holy communion for two successive Sundays.

There is a sense of a change of gear at this stage, but to what exactly? There is no mention of any concourse with prostitutes until 25 May, as indeed there had not been since the generalized and clearly charitable rehabilitation efforts of the mid-1840s. And it then comes in such a casual entry as to raise a doubt whether it could have been the beginning of a new pattern. At this time he was leading a very active parliamentary and social life. On Thursday the 24th he spoke in the House of Commons in the early evening, gave a small dinner party (ten) at Carlton Gardens for the intriguing combination of Manning and the Duchess of Buccleuch (they both subsequently became Roman Catholics) before returning to the House for the wind-up. On Tuesday the 25th he (briefly) spoke again, dined at Lord Wenlock's, went to an evening party given by Lady Essex and then 'Conv with one of those poor creatures, a very sad case'.[11]

Five weeks later there occurs the only ʎ sign for that summer but without any explanation. As there is no reference to any night walk it was presumably for the old pornographic sin, although his reading list for the day does not provide much sustenance for this: 'Read Irish Eviction papers – Lords Railway Audit Report. Quintilian – Simpson – Newman on the Soul.'[12] Perhaps Quintilian was the trouble, although it was not the first diary entry showing that he was engaged with that exponent of classical oratory and literature, who is not in any event widely regarded as notably corrupting or depraving. His Lady Lincoln expedition occupied him in the late summer of that year, and then, after a Hawarden interlude, there was his long October–January visit to Fasque. During this period there were his self-abasing fortieth-birthday reflections but no return either to the sign of the whip or to accounts of late-night encounters until May 1850, three weeks after the tragedy of Jessy. Then on 2 May he laconically recorded, 'Conv at night with an unhappy woman', and on 4 May after the Royal Academy Banquet he encountered her again and was more informative, although in a way which indicated much more charitable concern than erotic excitement. 'Found again the same poor creature at night. She has a son to support: & working *very* hard with her needle *may* reach 6/- per week as a maximum: pays 5/- for lodging – sends her boy to school at 6d a week. Lives No 6 Duke's Court.'[13]

These two diary entries were indeed wholly compatible with the most innocent view of Gladstone's nocturnal activities. There was no indication of his being in a high state of tension during the days concerned. On 4 May he spent nearly three hours looking at the Academy summer exhibition – 'there was much to see' – and in the evening he had been sufficiently relaxed to write of the banquet, 'there I sat by Disraeli who was very easy and agreeable'.[14] But a week later he again abstained from holy communion, 'for I have had much wicked negligence to reproach myself with of late as respects particular temptations';[15] and when he approached the beginning from 1 June of a new manuscript volume (each one normally covered just under two years) he instituted a new system of noting days of 'impurity'. However, it appeared to lean even more on the side of catching the venial as well as the vicious. 'I now think of marking days in two classes,' he wrote: 'one those of distinct offence against my rules: the other that of ill impressions without such distinctness of offence. Thus I hope to cover the debatable ground. . . .'[16] And he marked 1, 4, 6, 7, 10, 11, 13, 19, 20, 21 and 22 June as being within his new broad category; 13 and 22 June were also days which received the symbol indicating the use of the scourge. The diary entries for none of these days contain any indication of the nature of the transgressions. At the end of that manuscript volume (which went up to February 1852) he added another table which, in addition to 1–21 June (which he repeated without differentiating between the days), he added 7, 21 and 28 July and 2 September, all in 1850. These dates were accompanied by a gnomic series of figures, letters and signs, of which even Professor Matthew has failed to provide an interpretation, and which might have been qualifying, or exacerbating or merely otiose.

This second series of dates does, however, bear more relationship to relevant events recorded in the diary than did the first June list. On 7 July he was still much concerned with the death of Peel, which had taken place on the 2nd, and with his funeral on the 9th. But on the 8th he recorded an attempted rescue of a prostitute named South. Then around, although not exactly coinciding with, the two late-July dates, he became much preoccupied with a lady called Emma Clifton. At this time he took up a 'beat' opposite the Argyll Rooms in Great Windmill Street (off Piccadilly Circus). This was a choice of locale which compounded his habitual rashness, for the Rooms were the best-known centre of upper-class dissipation in London. It was therefore the place where, a hundred years before the television age made leading politicians recognizable by the masses, he was most likely, next perhaps to the entrances of the Carlton Club (of which he was still a member), Westminster Abbey and the House of Commons, to be identified. But in Great Windmill Street, if his innocence allowed him to contemplate the risk, he could perhaps have assumed a mutual desire for anonymity. There, on 22 July, he first took up his stand and encountered one E. Herring. But it was on the following (Tuesday) night that Emma Clifton, who became a much more immanent figure, first appeared in the diary.

He saw Miss Clifton again on the Wednesday evening from 6.00 to 7.30, and again on the Friday, and on the Saturday, when he wrote: 'Saw E Clifton at night and made I hope some way – But alas my unworthiness.' It sounded altogether a day of frenzied and disagreeable activity: 'Worked on letters, papers and accounts and on draft of will,' he recorded after the meeting with Miss Clifton (but his diary was not always chronological within a day). 'My cough very bad and headach [*sic*] almost unmanageable.'[17] On the Sunday he composed an 'MS [manuscript] meant for E.C.'.

On the Tuesday he saw her at night. On the next evening (1 August) he went into a spate of activity: 'Before nine I went to find E.C.: but failed: after 1¼ hours came home . . . went again at 11½ to O[range?] Street, and again failed. Resolved to go to E.C.'s lodgings: I found her there, and left her with the resolution declared of going in the morning by my advice and with her child at once to Mrs Tennant [at the Windsor Clewer House].'[18] He returned late to Carlton Gardens, and after only two and a half hours in bed took the early train to Birmingham for Hagley.

Then came ten days of relative peace there, followed by another three in the Rectory at Hawarden. But on 15 August he wrote: 'Mrs Tennant's letter this morning showed that matters had not moved with respect to E. Clifton: and after consulting with C[atherine] I thought it my duty to go to town. I reached my house at 8pm – failed in finding E.C. for the evening, although I did all I could.'[19] The next day he devoted himself to seeing the officers of various charities which might (if she wished) have provided Emma Clifton with support, but concluded, 'I failed in getting at night a separate commun[icatio]n.' On the following morning he returned to North Wales – '5¾–2½ from my door to Hawarden',[20] as for those who like precision and railways he satisfactorily put it. Euston to Chester (179 miles) must have consumed about six of the eight and three-quarter hours of journey time.

Hawarden, after four hard years, was looking faintly up in that summer. 'I am now at the bottom I think of his [Stephen Glynne's] difficulties, which although lessened are still frightful,'[21] Gladstone wrote on 28 August. All the family were still in the capacious Rectory, but there was a prospecting visit of William and Catherine Gladstone to the Castle and discussion of the possibility of setting up a joint residence there with Stephen Glynne. This was in a way made easier by another family tragedy in early October. On 15 September, when the Gladstones were at Fasque for three weeks, Lavinia Glynne gave birth to a fourth daughter, who lived until 1940 and as Lady Penrhyn became chatelaine of the vast stone castle of that name which at the time of her birth was arising out of both the profits and the products of the North Wales quarries. But two weeks after the birth the mother died and with her went the likelihood of a Glynne male heir. The way to the passing of the Hawarden property to the Gladstone side of the family was thus opened up.

At the time of this event, at once tragic and seminal, Gladstone was in London, and indeed engaged in two further fruitless sorties for Emma Clifton, but that seemed to be the end of his preoccupation with her. He went back to Hawarden for the Glynne funeral, then grouped his party of wife, daughters and servants in London, and on 18 October set off for another long Italian expedition, of which the centrepiece was a sojourn of over three months in Naples. He did not return to London until 26 February 1851, and Catherine Gladstone and the children were away until 10 April.

This Naples winter was immensely agitating to his mind on the iniquities which he discovered within the Bourbon kingdom and led to his putting into circulation the first of the great liberal phrases which came to be associated with his name. 'This is the negation of God erected into a system of Government,' he wrote in a public letter to Lord Aberdeen in April 1851.* It did, however, appear to calm his

* In fact he disclaimed authorship of the phrase, said that it was one that he had heard used in Naples, and for good measure gave it also in the original Italian: '*E la negazione di Dio eretta a sistema di governo*'.

sexual tension and to diminish both the forms of temptation to which it gave rise. He recorded no 'days of impurity' or encounters with 'fallen women' while he was away, and in consequence there were no applications of the scourge or deep outbursts of remorse. (He inverted the habits of many rich Victorian Englishmen who did things 'abroad' which they would not have dreamt of doing at home. He, on the contrary, was far more rash in Covent Garden than outside the San Carlo theatre, or even at the top of the Duke of York's steps, where a famous incident was to take place in 1882, than in the Place de la Madeleine.)

Even on his birthday, normally a day for great diary self-prostration, he was relatively restrained in Naples. After noting that the year had been 'one of anxiety and of labour', he complained that he 'would to God I could add that it has been one of progress in obtaining the mastery over my most besetting sins which I think are impurity and lukewarmness'. ('Lukewarmness' was surely a most extraordinary fault for the raging tornado that was Gladstone, who was currently engaged in gratuitously – although admirably – stirring up a Europe-wide agitation against the Neapolitan government, to attribute to himself.) The year 'has sorely taught me . . . how little even sorrow has in *itself* a virtue to overcome sin . . .'.[22] But this was very mild stuff by the standards of some other years.

Turmoil began again when he got back to London. Although he had always intended to return in advance of his family, a short-term political upheaval brought him across the Channel from Paris more quickly than would otherwise have been the case. The excitement was occasioned by the defeat in the House of Commons and resignation of Lord John Russell, which led to the Queen offering Stanley the commission to form a Conservative government. For this, Stanley felt he needed the support of the Peelites and offered Gladstone almost any position within it. But he proposed to restore a small duty on corn and that for Gladstone and the others was a sticking point. Although Gladstone psychologically needed office (he had been out for four and a half years) it took him only about six hours after his morning arrival at London Bridge Station on 26 February to dispose of Stanley's offer. In general he admired Lord Stanley (he had described him on 17 June 1850, as making on the Greek question, that is against Palmerston's Don Pacifico policy, 'the finest speech I ever heard from him', and almost exactly a year later at the Merchant Tailors' banquet, he was to bring his acclamation up to the absolute by writing that 'Lord Stanley made the best after dinner speech I ever heard'). But he was not willing to countenance any return to protection.

This refusal had the effect of leaving him on his own and relatively unoccupied in London for a month and a half, gloomily awaiting the defection of Manning and Hope-Scott from the Church of England, which event duly occurred on 6 April. The combination of circumstances amounted to an almost perfect recipe for sending him back to his night prowls. On both his third and his fourth and again on his seventh, eighth and tenth evenings in London he was scouring the purlieus of Shaftesbury Avenue for Emma Clifton. On these nights he never found her. But he had a number of other encounters, some specified and some anonymous and, perhaps because this more generalized intercourse strengthened the missionary and weakened the sexual aspects to his activities, he recorded no evidence of subsequent remorse.

Then at the end of March he became more particularly involved with P. Lightfoot (her Christian name never emerged). On the first evening (28 March) that he met her he recorded, 'Saw . . . P.L. a singular case indeed,' which was his way of confessing to a special interest. The next evening he searched for her, it appears in vain. On the third day, a Sunday, he gave Manning an argumentative paper he had written for him, and thereby provoked a depressing, indeed shattering, discussion, followed by another encounter with Miss Lightfoot which led him to the already quoted confession of carnality in his habitual obscurity:

> [Manning] smote me to the ground by answering with suppressed emotion that he is now upon the *brink*: and Hope too. Such terrible blows not only upset & oppress but I fear demoralize me: which tends to show that my trysts* are Carnal or the withdrawal of them would not leave such a void. *Was* it possibly from this that thinking P.L. would look for me as turned out to be the fact, I had a second interview and conversation indoors here [Carlton Gardens?] and heard more history: yet I trusted without harm done.[23]

The next evening he was less sanguine about the absence of harm:

> Saw P.L. again indoors and said I thought it must be the last time: as I fear lest more harm was done than good. There seems to be little guilt, & good affections, but an ill-informed conscience, & a want of depth & strength in impressions. I was certainly wrong in some things and trod the path of danger.[24]

* The editor of the *Diaries* transcribes this word as 'trusts', but 'trysts' makes more sense and is an equally possible interpretation of Gladstone's handwriting.

Then followed a period of relative calm on this front, even though it included the actual (although already somewhat discounted) reception of Manning and Hope-Scott into the Church of Rome. On 9 April Gladstone was in Paris to meet his wife and daughters and bring them back to London. He indicated pleasure at having them back, but in less than another week was off, without them, on nearly a month's Easter visit to his father at Fasque. There he reverted on 'Easter eve' to writing one of his budgets of guilt. 'But I must write a bitter thing against myself. Whether owing (as I think) to the sad and recent events (of the 6th) or not, I have been unmanned & unnerved & out of sheer cowardice have not used the measure which I have found so beneficial to temptations against impurity. Therefore they have been stronger than usual in Lent: and I had no courage!'[25]

In July, that aspect of his courage revived and there were three Λ symbols, the first for more than a year. They coincided with the peaks of his erotic obsession with young women whom he was genuinely (but almost always unsuccessfully) endeavouring to rescue from their life of sin. In May he had been only mildly involved, although he saw P. Lightfoot again on the 28th, but on 11 June, after listening to Stanley's oratorical gem in the Merchant Tailors' hall, he had his first meeting with Elizabeth Collins, who was to be an obsession for the rest of that summer: 'Saw Collins – Seymour – and a person from Stourbridge – in the first I was much interested.'[26] He did not, however, record seeing her again until the 27th, although there was the 'sad case of some flowergirls' on the 16th. Then he was with her for an hour and a half, maybe saw her again on the 30th (the text is corrupt) and then on 4 July, after writing to her in the morning, went unavailingly to meet her in the evening. He wrote to her again on the 7th and saw her at night, mysteriously writing 'and closed with advising a day visit and appeal to C[atherine] for advice'. Then next day he again saw her 'but did not advance in the matter'.[27]

He again looked for her unsuccessfully on 12 July, and on the 13th: 'Went with a note to E.C.'s – received (unexpectedly) and remained 2 hours: a strange and humbling scene – returned to Λ.' The next day was something of an anti-climax, except for its diary entry encapsulating the contradictions of his life: 'Saw Bp of Oxford – Ld Aberdeen. H of C [where he spoke] 5–7¼ and at home in evg. except a short time looking for E.C.' So was the next day's, although ending less quietly: 'Attended the Dentist and saw the D[owage]r. Dss of Beaufort. Mr and Mrs Gaskell dined with me. Corrected proofs. Fell in with E.C.

and another mixed scene somewhat like of 48 hours before – ƛ afterwards.'[28]

The day after that P. Lightfoot created a diversion from Elizabeth Collins; on this occasion his conversation with her seems to have been confined to her conditions of life. On 19 July he looked unsuccessfully for Elizabeth Collins, and on the 21st he found her: 'Saw E.C. again in the same [?] manner: and did not ƛ afterwards: thinking there was a change.'[29] On the 23rd there was a dinner at the Clarendon Hotel in New Bond Street for the American Minister (Lawrence) and Palmerston, then Foreign Secretary and already by no means a favourite of Gladstone's. Gladstone spoke, as did several others, but 'At half past twelve I came away: the first to do so. I then in a singular way hit upon E.C.: two more hours, strange, questionable, or more: followed by ƛ. Whether or not I have been deluded in the notion of doing good by such means, or whether I have sought it through what was unlawful I am not clear. God grant however not for my sake that the good may be done.'[30]

That was the trough of his mid-century crisis of nerves and sex. He was away at Hagley and Hawarden for the first half of August. He wrote to Elizabeth Collins on the 17th and again on the 19th. He looked for her unsuccessfully that evening having returned to London in the afternoon, saw her alone on the following evening for two and a quarter hours and wrote extensively in Italian after this meeting. But the tension sounded in some way relaxed. He moved on easily from describing the meeting – 'Things went partly as before' – to her relations with a prospective husband, to his relations with God and to the devastation caused in him by the defections of Manning and Hope-Scott. On the 20th he left London for five months, spent mostly at Fasque.

Throughout the 1850s (and for decades beyond) he continued with sporadic rescue work. In 1859 he got considerably involved with a courtesan called Marion Summerhayes. He found it necessary to write of their relations, 'My thoughts of S. require to be limited and purged,'[31] but everything was then, and had been for seven or eight years past, on a somewhat quieter plane. The frenzy of 1845, 1848, 1849, 1850 and above all 1851 was never repeated.

Did Gladstone believe that he was doing much good with his rescue efforts? Probably not, for although sometimes priggish he was not basically hypocritical. In 1854 he recorded that, in differing circumstances, he had over five years or so engaged with between eighty and ninety prostitutes of whom 'there is but one of whom I know that the miserable life has been abandoned *and* that I can fairly join that fact with influence of mine'.[32] He was perfectly aware that his motives were mixed and that his obsession must be explained by temptation and could not be justified by results.

What did his involvements amount to on the occasions when he was filled with remorse and even felt it necessary to apply physical correction to himself? The *locus classicus* for this is the 1896 statement which he made to his clergyman son Stephen, who together with the Bishop of St Andrews was his main pastoral confidant at the end of his life. This was that he had never 'been guilty of the act which is known as that of infidelity to the marriage bed'.[33] The denial was obviously both precise and limited, and while this may have carried conviction it also led to a decision, on counsel's advice, at the time of the Wright–Herbert Gladstone trial in 1927, that more harm than good would be done if the statement were put in as evidence.

One reason why the tide of mid-century madness, which at its height threatened to engulf Gladstone, began to recede after the summer of 1851 was that he became more engaged politically, although the future for him as a Peelite, a disciple without a messiah, a Conservative (just) who had lost his faith in most Conservative causes, remained hazardous.

8

The Tremendous Projectile

Gladstone's preoccupations and derangements of 1850 and 1851 did not prevent his making occasional major political forays. Indeed it could be argued that it was during these two years that he made the breakthrough, both at home and abroad, from being merely a figure of promise and interest, of whom there were perhaps thirty in the House of Commons, to being one of a handful of four or five whose names had world resonance. Yet it was a confusing time for him politically as well as emotionally. He was losing a lot of old moorings while only tentatively edging towards new ones, and making the crossing among the swirling waters of both political and religious uncertainties. As a result some of his forays pointed to his future Liberalism while one or two pointed back to the Toryism of his early years in Parliament. It was a period when he came to justify Morley's famous description of his 'formidable powers of contention and attack which were before long [Morley was writing of 1843] to resemble some tremendous projectile, describing a path the law of whose curves and deviations, as they watched its journey through the air in wonder and anxiety for its shattering impact, men found it impossible to calculate'.[1]

The first of these forays owed more to old Toryism than to new Liberalism. In April 1850 a motion for the setting up of a Royal Commission to enquire into the affairs of Oxford and Cambridge was brought before the House of Commons by a Radical backbencher. Gladstone was at this stage strongly opposed to the proposal, despite the hopes that he had aroused among the University reformers in 1847. Rather surprisingly, he did not speak in this debate, but left it to Inglis to fulminate for Oxford obscurantism. He had been brought 'very reluctantly to town' (from Brighton, where Catherine Gladstone with the younger children was convalescing after the death of Jessy) and applied himself to caballing against the proposal, including a call on the Duke of Wellington as Chancellor of the University.

However, the Prime Minister of the day was more important to the issue than one of twenty-one years before, even if a field-marshal as well as a duke. Lord John Russell was persuaded by the debate and, a few months later, announced the setting up of such an enquiry. Gladstone then intervened heavily but ineffectively. On 18 July he delivered himself of one and a half hours of the most intransigent opposition, but was as unavailing as Inglis had been. The Commission was appointed in August, began work in October and produced by May 1852 a report which was as expeditious as it was effective. Its competent chairman was Samuel Hinds, the dry and donnish Bishop of Norwich, and its secretary was the future Dean Stanley (then a fellow of Balliol). Among its members were Tait, then Dean of Carlisle and later Archbishop of Canterbury; Liddell, then headmaster of Westminster and later one of the most famous of Christ Church deans; Jeune, then Master of Pembroke College, Oxford, and later Bishop of Peterborough; and Baden Powell, Savilian Professor of Geometry at Oxford and grandfather of the future Chief Scout.

Its report converted Gladstone. The 'tremendous projectile' swooped into an awesome curve. Gladstone then devoted the equivalent of what for most men would have been a major part of their energies (but could not be for him as he was a particularly active Chancellor of the Exchequer over most of the relevant period) to devising and carrying through Parliament a bill implementing its main recommendations. In the two years over which this secondary activity was spread his correspondence on the issue amounted to 520 letters of substance. This might be thought to be natural. He had a peculiarly literate constituency and the subject was of most vital and direct interest to his electors. But what was not natural was that Gladstone wrote 350 of them (in his own hand) and that only 170 came from the Heads of Houses, professors, fellows and outside ecclesiastical dignitaries who made up the collectivity of his constituency. This inversion of the normal proportion illustrated one facet of the qualities which made Gladstone unique.

His second foray in that summer of 1850 was in the Don Pacifico debate. As long previously as Easter 1847, a Greek mob which included several well-connected youths had pillaged the Athens house of a merchant by the name of David Pacifico, who liked to call himself Chevalier Pacifico, but who became known to history as Don Pacifico. Pacifico was a Spanish Jew who had been born in Gibraltar (which entitled him to British citizenship) but had lived much of his life in Portugal, had acquired Portuguese nationality and had indeed been the consul of Portugal in Athens until dismissed for forgery. He had wisely acquired a British passport before the pillaging took place and as a result Palmerston was willing to add Pacifico's vast claim for damage to the house (totalling £31,000, the equivalent to a good £1½ million today) to other claims and grievances against the Greek government. When Pacifico's claims (*inter alia*) were not met, Palmerston proclaimed the doctrine of *Civis Romanus sum* (that a British connection, however tenuous, entitled the holder to the full panoply of imperial protection) and ordered a naval blockade of the Greek coast.

The imperious action of the Foreign Secretary, which set him at odds with both Russia and Austria as well as leading to a sufficiently serious diplomatic quarrel with France for the French ambassador to be withdrawn from London, was challenged first by a motion of Stanley's in the Lords, which was carried against the government, and then in the Commons. As a parliamentary occasion, that Commons debate was the great setpiece of the nineteenth century, just as the Norway debate of 7–8 May 1940 was that of the twentieth century. They were both characterized by the participation of almost every member of the first rank, and by the continuing resonance of the phrases used by at least some of them. Eighteen-fifty has the edge over 1940 in that the debate lasted four nights (with no cut-off point) rather than two (with an 11.00 p.m. close-down) and that the speeches, led by Palmerston with an oration of over four and a half hours and buttressed in this respect by Gladstone with one of nearly three hours, were immensely longer. The 1940 debate has the edge in that much more flowed from it.

Palmerston had spoken from dusk to dawn on the second night of the debate, and Gladstone on the third night was almost as late if not as long. It was nearly two o'clock before he sat down. His speech was not a *sur place* triumph comparable with that of Palmerston, who not only secured the division but in Gladstone's description, 'through the livelong summer's night [made] the British House of Commons, crowded as it was, hang upon his words'.[2] There was some straying of attention during Gladstone's second hour, to which he responded with pained rebuke. Despite this mixed reception the speech extended Gladstone's range into foreign affairs, made a considerable outside impact and contained some remarkable passages which presaged the distaste for chauvinism which was to inform the four Gladstone administrations. He took *Civis Romanus sum* head on:

> [The noble Viscount] vaunted amidst the cheers of his supporters, that under his administration an Englishman should be, throughout the world, what the citizen of Rome had been. What then, Sir, was a Roman citizen? He was the member of a privileged caste; he belonged to a conquering race, to a nation that held all others bound down by the strong arm of

power. For him there was to be an exceptional system of law; for him principles were to be asserted, and by him rights were to be enjoyed, that were denied to the rest of the world. Is that the view of the noble Lord as to the relation that is to subsist between England and other countries?

More surprisingly, Gladstone then contested and mocked the doctrine of Britain as a universal moral arbitrator:

Does he make the claim for us that we are uplifted upon a platform high above the standing-ground of all other nations? It is, indeed, too clear, not only from the expressions, but from the whole spirit of the speech of the noble Viscount, that too much of this notion is lurking in his mind; that he adopts in part that vain conception that we, forsooth, have a mission to be the censors of vice and folly, of abuse and imperfection, among the other countries of the world; that we are to be the universal schoolmasters; and that all those who hesitate to recognise our office, can be governed only by prejudice or personal animosity, and should have the blind war of diplomacy forthwith declared against them. And certainly if the business of a Foreign Secretary properly were to carry on such diplomatic wars, all must admit that the noble Lord is a master of the discharge of his functions. What, Sir, ought a Foreign Secretary to be? Is he to be like some gallant knight at a tournament of old, pricking forth into the lists, armed at all points, confiding in his sinews and his skill, challenging all comers for the sake of honour, and having no other duty than to lay as many as possible of his adversaries sprawling in the dust? If such is the idea of a good Foreign Secretary, I, for one, would vote to the noble Lord his present appointment for his life. But, Sir, I do not understand the duty of a Secretary for Foreign Affairs to be of such a character. I understand it to be his duty to conciliate peace with dignity. I think it to be the very first of all his duties studiously to observe, and to exalt in honour among mankind, that great code of principles which is termed the law of nations. . . .

Very near the end Gladstone sustained this argument with a subtle and sensitive piece of national self-criticism:

Sir, I say the policy of the noble Lord tends to encourage and confirm in us that which is our besetting fault and weakness, both as a nation and as individuals. Let an Englishman travel where he will as a private person, he is found in general to be upright, high-minded, brave, liberal, and true; though with all this, foreigners are too often sensible of something that galls them in his presence, and I apprehend it is because he has too great a tendency to self-esteem – too little disposition to regard the feelings, the habits, and the ideas of others. Sir, I find this characteristic too plainly legible in the policy of the noble Lord.

Gladstone's speech, as well as these fine excursions on to the high moral ground, also and less characteristically contained some brilliant pieces of raillery against the extravagance of Pacifico's claims. It is an interesting comment on mid-nineteenth-century values that Pacifico was thought to be broaching the top end of the market when he specified £170 for a couch, £53 for a chest of drawers, £60 for a carpet, £150 for a bed, £24 for a card-table, £120 for a pair of mirrors, £170 for a dinner service and £64 for tea and coffee services. Yes, said Gladstone, you could find such articles at such prices in shops in London, but the only people who bought them were those who, apart from their possessions, had incomes of £20,000, £50,000 or £100,000 a year. Yet Monsieur Pacifico, 'who thus surpassed nearly all subjects and equalled almost any prince, according to his own account, in many articles of luxury, who had £5,000 worth of clothes, jewels and furniture in his house, had not outside of it, except plate pledged to the Bank of Athens for £30, which he had not been able to redeem, one single farthing! So, Sir, having his house crammed full of fine furniture, fine clothes and fine jewels, Monsieur Pacifico was in all other respects a pauper.'[3]

Gladstone in this speech may not have rivalled Palmerston. But he probably made the next best speech of the great debate, better than Disraeli's, whom he recorded as 'being below his mark though he seemed in earnest', better than Russell's, whom he allowed as being 'about par', and stronger than what proved to be Peel's swan-song. It was, however, the result not the speeches which aroused his anger. 'The division was disgusting, not on account of the numbers simply but considering where they came from.'[4] The ground for this bitter complaint was that with the exception of Cobden, Bright and Joseph Hume, the Radicals as well as the entire Whig party voted for Palmerston, for jingoism (a word not then invented) and for the big stick, thus giving the Foreign Secretary a Commons majority of forty-six to compensate for the Lords defeat which Stanley had inflicted upon him. And an equal irony was that the restrained internationalism outlined in Gladstone's speech was one of the few issues of the day in favour of which the scattered parts of the Conservative party, protectionists and Peelites alike, united in a single lobby. The debate also fortified Gladstone's hostility to Palmerston. Hitherto he had mildly disapproved of his character. Henceforward he deeply distrusted his policy.

Gladstone's next burst of political (although not parliamentary) activity could be regarded as somewhat incompatible with the high non-assertiveness which he preached in the Don Pacifico debate. Before he left for Italy he had little intention of political involvement during his Naples winter of 1850–1. The object was an improvement in the health of his daughter Mary, a rest for his wife after the strains of pregnancy, illness and death in the family, and perhaps some repose too for his own uncalm nervous system. The chief vacation task which he set himself, that of translating the three Italian volumes of L. C. Farini's history of *Lo Stato Romano 1815–1850*, was half a help and half a hindrance to this end. In the first place it involved him in sustained work, sometimes on his own and sometimes with L. J. Barber, the British vice-consul in Naples, as an assistant. When they were working together he recorded that they had done 303 pages in seventy-one and three-quarter hours, a considerable pace at which to copy let alone probe Italian meanings and search for appropriate English words and phrases. Given his energy, however, this task probably provided a more steadying influence than sightseeing alone could have given. On the other hand the work he had chosen tempted him towards Italian politics. It was perhaps for him the equivalent, in another context, of lingering in front of a bookshop window. Farini was a very moderate liberal, but his history of the post-Napoleonic exercise of papal temporal power was highly critical and could not fail to set the mind of his translator on to the question of whether post-1848 conditions in Naples were not even worse.

Gladstone's interest in what went on under the regime of King Ferdinand of the Two Sicilies,* 'King Bomba' as he was devisively known in England, had been aroused in London by (Sir) Anthony Panizzi, then deputy keeper of the British Museum and the creator of the Round Reading Room, who although of Lombard origin kept Neapolitan affairs very much under his eye. As soon as Gladstone arrived in Naples Panizzi's influence was fortified by that of another and almost equally remarkable Anglo-Italian knight-to-be (Sir) Joseph Lacaita, later Professor at King's College London, and secretary to Gladstone on his Ionian Isles mission in 1859. Lacaita was at that time a Neapolitan subject and legal adviser to the British Legation, which was headed by William Temple, Palmerston's younger brother.

Through Lacaita, Gladstone became much involved with the case of

* One of the 'Sicilies' in the odd title was the so-called Regno or mainland part of the kingdom, with Naples as its capital.

Baron Carlo Poerio, who had been briefly a Neapolitan minister in the frightened days of 1848 but who by 1850 was put on trial for subversion and sentenced to twenty-four years in irons. Gladstone attended with deep disapproval some of the court proceedings, and then visited Poerio at the Bagno di Nisida prison. The conditions in the dungeons where Poerio was habitually confined were of the classic quality of operatic incarceration. Chained prisoners lay in foetid darkness and were occasionally handed out a portion of filthy food. On the day of Gladstone's visit a veritable *Fidelio* scene was enacted.

> For half an hour before noon on Thursdays perhaps rather more the prisoners may come out to see their friends, or rather relations. About ten of the political prisoners came out two and two. . . . My conductor signified to Poerio in part who I was, and he then came aside to me. We conversed most of the time: for the rest of it I spoke with Pironti to whom he was chained and Braico the nephew of Madame Dekker as whose friend or escort I went in.*

Gladstone recorded in great detail the conditions in which the prisoners were held, and in Poerio's case had been held for sixteen months before trial. He recorded the length and heaviness of the chains which were never taken off night and day, observed the 'stinking soup' which was taken in as food, ascertained that the dungeons were damp and hardly lit, and noted that the political prisoners were forced to wear the rough dress of 'common malefactors' including 'the felon's red cap'. These facts whipped up Gladstone's indignation, but the main purpose of his visit was to get assurance from Poerio that public intervention would not do more harm than good. Gladstone had been warned against this a few days before by the Prince San Giacomo, who had been ambassador to London in the false Neapolitan dawn of 1848 and of whom he thought highly. And Poerio himself was at first somewhat hesitant. He told Gladstone that he feared 'his case had been made worse by Mr Temple's intervention: not in the least blaming Mr T or considering it officious. But he said to speak without reserve the Kings [of Naples] had a great hatred of the English generally.'[5]

Gladstone then asked Poerio a question which, as a protesting man of

* Pironti, also sentenced to twenty-four years, was a Neapolitan lawyer and judge. Braico was a young man of twenty-six who had the advantage of an aunt who combined temerity and ingenuity. She accompanied Gladstone and told the gaolers that he was a halfwit named Michele di Santo, who 'understood nothing up there' (pointing to his head). Not even Leonora's kindly gaoler father Rocco would have been taken in.

courage, it would have been very difficult for him to answer other than as he did. 'Matters standing thus,' Gladstone said,

> I saw no way open but that of exposure; and might that possibly exasperate the Neap. Govt. & increase their severity? His reply was 'as to us, never mind – we can hardly be worse than we are – but think of our country for which we are most willing to be sacrificed. Exposure will do it good. The present Govt. of Naples rely on the English Conservative Party. . . . Let there be a voice from that party showing that whatever Govt. be in power in England, no support will be given to proceedings such as these – it will do much to break them down.'[6]

Having got the assurance,* and boiling with indignation against the Neapolitan government, Gladstone was anxious to be back in England and to have the opportunity to rally the Conservative party against the iniquities. This at first was his limited objective. Palmerston, he assumed, could be got to fire off a protest at the drop of a hat, but the Foreign Secretary had devalued such *démarches* by their too frequent use, and it was conservative opinion, both with a large and a small 'c', that Gladstone thought was likely to be most effective in Naples. It was also the case that he still instinctively thought of himself as a Conservative and that what most aroused his ire against the tyranny of the Neapolitan government was that it was specifically directed against the bourgeoisie: 'The class persecuted as a whole is the class that lives and moves, the middle class, in its widest acceptation, but particularly in the upper part of the middle class which [it] may be said embraces the professions, the most cultivated and progressive part of the nation.'[7]

These considerations may have persuaded him to couch his anti-Bourbon manifesto in the form of a letter to Lord Aberdeen, who was the last previous Conservative Foreign Secretary and was looked to as

* Whether the giving of it was a damaging act for Poerio remains an open question. His imprisonment continued for another eight years, after which 'King Bomba', almost at the end of his own life and apparently fearful of the effect on European opinion if the Baron should either die in chains or become insane as a result of ten years in them, commuted his sentence and that of sixty-five others to life exile in the New World. At Lisbon they were transferred to an American ship, the captain of which put in at Queenstown (now Cobh) in Ireland, no doubt to pick up Irish immigrants. But he there lost at least some of his Italian prisoners, including Poerio, who made his way to Bristol, where he was given a public banquet, and then to London, where Gladstone gave him a Carlton House Terrace dinner party of sixteen on 6 April 1859. (Morley, *Life of Gladstone*, I, p. 401, and *Diaries*, V, p. 384.) In 1867, in return, Poerio presided over a dinner given to Gladstone in Florence (the temporary capital) by the Chamber of Deputies of the newly united Italy.

the leader of the Peelites after the death of the former Prime Minister. Aberdeen had also long been looked upon as having a special position in Austria, which was rightly regarded as the paramount power in Naples. Gladstone wrote the letter (more a pamphlet) in one of his 'white-heat' moods, and had it ready for despatch on 7 April (1851), despite the distractions of a major, difficult and unpopular speech in the House of Commons on 25 March,* the final arguments with Manning on the 30th and with Hope-Scott on 3 April, and the news that they had both made the fateful break on the 6th. Gladstone pronounced himself 'smitten' by this last event. He was also irrepressible. 'One blessing I have is total freedom from doubts.' And later on that same evening of the despatch of the letter to Aberdeen he wrote: 'Dined at the Palace: when I had most interesting conversations especially with the Queen about Naples.'[8] The still young Sovereign obviously had an early experience of enjoying Gladstone's lecturing style.

Aberdeen liked Gladstone but he also liked a quiet life and a quiet pattern of politics in Europe. This for him meant the upholding of as much as possible of the 1815 settlement of Vienna, which had been rudely enough shaken by the events of 1848, and he saw Gladstone's activities as a likely source of future trouble. Nevertheless his sense of justice and humanity made him accept the horror of the evidence put before him, and his sense of caution made him tremble at the signs of movement in the 'tremendous projectile' and desire to exercise some influence over its 'curves and deviations'. Accordingly he had a friendly meeting with Gladstone on 13 April, offered one or two suggestions for small changes to the letter, and promised to make a private approach to Prince Schwarzenberg, the Chancellor of the Austrian Empire.

He was not however in a hurry and it was nearly three weeks before he wrote a gentle letter to Schwarzenberg pointing out the disadvantages to conservative Europe of a conservative statesman of Gladstone's repute feeling he was forced to make public remonstrance. Aberdeen's dilatoriness was minor compared with that of Schwarzenberg, who took another seven weeks to reply. Maybe the Ballhausplatz officials needed these weeks to polish the insolent ripostes with which the Chancellor embellished his cold reply. The British government's treatment of political prisoners in Ireland, Ceylon, the Ionian Islands and even in England (the case of Ernest Jones the Chartist was specified) was recriminatingly deployed. Finally, throwing a bone to a dog, Schwarzenberg told

* On the Ecclesiastical Titles Bill. See pp. 131–2 below.

Aberdeen that, as it had not been formally requested (if it had he would have refused), he would pass Gladstone's statement to His Sicilian Majesty.

The sheer efflux of time (it was four months since his return from Naples) quite apart from the dismissive nature of the reply had severely tried Gladstone's patience by this date, and he decided to publish and to do so under the title of *Letter to the Earl of Aberdeen*. Immediately before the event, but after he had written to his publisher, John Murray, giving instructions to go ahead, which instructions presumably embraced the title of the pamphlet, he had at least four meetings with Aberdeen, and at his request agreed to postpone publication by a few days to 15 July. Aberdeen subsequently complained that he had never given his consent to publication. Gladstone's response was that it had been implied in conversation, and it is difficult to believe that this was not so in view of Gladstone's agreement to postpone. But it may be that Aberdeen felt he was confronted with an unnegotiable position so far as a decision to publish was concerned, with room for discussion only on the exact date.

What is certainly the case is that Gladstone inappropriately associated Aberdeen's name with a polemical publication of vast impact. And what is probably the case is that Aberdeen only became seriously embarrassed and somewhat (but not lastingly) resentful when he discovered how much Gladstone made his (Aberdeen's) name resound throughout Europe and how strongly conservative opinion across the Continent disapproved of Gladstone's content wrapped in Aberdeen's flag. Even the friendly and anglophile Guizot wrote a letter of courteous rebuke. Others were less courteous. An unconnected and (so far as is known) inoffensive Gladstone was blackballed for a Paris Club on account of his name alone.

On the other hand Gladstone aroused enormous enthusiasm in liberal circles, particularly but not only in Italy. At home Palmerston expressed his support, allied to pleasure at being able to stir a party political pot, by distributing copies of the Gladstone pamphlet to all British heads of mission in Europe with instructions that it be communicated to the governments to which they were accredited. And when the Neapolitan minister in London countered by asking for the distribution of an exculpation which his government had produced Palmerston dismissed it as 'a flimsy tissue of bare assertions and reckless denials mixed up with coarse ribaldry and commonplace abuse'.[9]

In view of the quietist approach of Aberdeen to Don Pacifico and one or two other issues this cavalier attitude was (and was intended to be) a source of embarrassment for him, and should perhaps have been so for Gladstone too. The latter, however, so far from showing any sign of dismay, compounded his sin by publishing a *Second Letter to the Earl of Aberdeen*, dated the day before the publication of the first and incorporated with it in subsequent or translated editions of the pamphlet. The second letter, only half the length of the first's 13,000 words, was a less impressive document than its predecessor. In the first Gladstone achieved a compelling tautness of style which was unusual for him, and dealt authoritatively with the travesty of justice involved in the trial of Poerio and others, as well as with the cruel squalor in which they were held. In the second letter he reverted to his more convoluted style, got over-involved with the articles of the Neapolitan constitution, and attempted to make far too much of a 'Philosophical Catechism' for use in elementary schools published in 1850, which he claimed must be the work of the government because nothing was printed or taught in Naples without its consent. He also dealt unhappily with the Naples government's refutation of his claim that there were 20,000 political prisoners in the Regno. The true number, they said, was 2000. Two thousand was bad enough, was in effect his reply, and over twice that number had been semi-officially suggested to him in Naples.

The longer-term effects of the whole chapter were that it gave Gladstone great fame and much increased his standing with the liberals of Europe while sowing a new distrust of him among the conservatives. It also slightly loosened his relations with Aberdeen and his other Peelite colleagues, who doubted his steadiness. It did not reconcile him to Palmerston, but it did incline his mind towards Italian unity, the importance of which he had not hitherto apprehended. It made little direct difference to the conditions in the dungeons of Naples. If anything, it made conditions even worse in the short run, but it assisted the undermining of the Bourbon regime in the Two Sicilies, and thus helped to prepare the way for Garibaldi and his patriotic invasion of 1860.

In the midst of composing the first letter to Aberdeen, on Tuesday, 25 March 1851, Gladstone delivered another of his marathon parliamentary speeches, and the one which was probably his most distinguished to date. Morley indeed thought it 'in all its elements and aspects one of the great orator's three or four most conspicuous masterpieces'.[10] It was on the second reading of the Ecclesiastical Titles Bill, and was made on the seventh night of the debate, which had begun, almost unbelievably, on the previous Friday week and had occupied every intervening parliamentary day except for the then short Wednesday sitting. Gladstone at the beginning of his speech admitted the truth of the earlier statement of Russell (the Prime Minister) that the debate was already exhausted, that the best arguments for and against the bill had already been deployed. His excuse for speaking in spite of this was that he was the only member for an English university, and thus the only representative of a large body of Anglican clergy (with whose predominant view he strongly disagreed) who had not hitherto done so.

Having admitted Russell's point he then proceeded to contradict it by making the best speech of the whole debate, and deploying a unique authority on the subject with more unforced ease and equable temper than he habitually showed, despite the fact that he was addressing a largely hostile and occasionally noisy House. But he took thirty-two columns of Hansard and nearly two and a half hours of the time of the House to do so. And although, as usual, there was no diary evidence that he had devoted time to direct preparation, the prospect of the speech seemed to agitate him more than usual. He had tried to speak on the previous night, but had not been called, and had written: 'H of C 7–12½: *waiting* – wh[en] so much prolonged produces great nervousness.' And on the night when he did speak and was in the House from '5–6½ and 8¼–3', he recorded that 'My head being hot I poured water over it with a large sponge before dinner, and this seemed at once to clear the brain.'[11]

The Ecclesiastical Titles Bill has been described by Professor Owen Chadwick as 'the most foolish act of Russell's political career'[12] (which lasted sixty-five years). The bill arose out of the decision of Pope Pius IX, announced in mid-October 1850, to re-establish, for the first time since 1584, the Roman Catholic hierarchy in England. The flamboyant, high-living and Romano-centric Dr Wiseman was to be Cardinal Archbishop of the metropolitan see of Westminster, and the rest of the country was to be divided into twelve dioceses. His new Eminence (whom, partly as a result of his high living, his Irish servant was said to be in the habit of addressing as 'Your Immense') proclaimed the new regime in a pastoral letter of more resonance than tact addressed from 'out of the Flaminian Gate'. 'Catholic England', it said, 'has been restored to its orbit in the ecclesiastical firmament, from which its light had long vanished.'

The concession to English susceptibilities was that the new sees did not duplicate the names of Anglican dioceses. To some Protestant minds, however, this did not nearly make up for the presumption of any territorial titles, and in particular for the taking of a name so central to the tradition of the English state as Westminster for the archbishopric. Papal aggression became the widely used term. However, neither the head of Bagehot's 'dignified' part of the state nor the head of his 'efficient' part at first reacted strongly. The Prime Minister wrote to the Queen on 25 October (from the Archbishop of York's palace at Bishopsthorpe):

> [Lord John Russell] has also read the Pope's Bull. It strikes him that the division into twelve territorial dioceses of the eight ecclesiastical vicariats is not a matter to be alarmed at. The persons to be affected by this change must be already Roman Catholics before it can touch them.
>
> The matter to create rational alarm is, as your Majesty says, the growth of Roman Catholic doctrines and practices within the bosom of the [Anglican] Church. Dr Arnold said very truly, 'I look upon a Roman Catholic as an enemy in his uniform; I look upon a Tractarian as an enemy disguised as a spy'. . . . Sir George Grey [the Home Secretary] will ask the Law Officers whether there is anything illegal in Dr Wiseman's assuming the title of Archbishop of Westminster. An English Cardinal is not a novelty.[13]*

The Queen did not demur. Under the influence of the Prince Consort she liked a Protestant Church, and under the influence of her position as its Supreme Governor she liked an Erastian one. So did Russell. His rigid Whiggery made him believe in religious liberty, but not in religious presumption. It was only when the two ran counter to each that he got into difficulties, and he did not for the moment see the papal action as creating such a conflict.

Ironically the immediate reaction of some old English Catholics to the actions of the Pope and of Wiseman was more hostile than was that of the Queen and her Minister. The old Catholics liked a quiet and gentlemanly religion and were already somewhat disturbed with the attention which the new elements in their Church were devoting to populist authoritarianism for Irish labourers on the one hand and to the drama and opulence of new churches for middle-class converts on the other. The proclamation of the hierarchy acted as a catalyst which brought these discontents to the surface. Lord Beaumont declared that English Catholics could not accept the hierarchy without violating their

* The calm final sentiment was based on a long view. The last previous English Cardinal had been in the reign of the Sovereign to whom those in the tradition to which the Russell family firmly belonged were inclined to refer as 'Bloody Mary'.

duties as loyal subjects of the Queen, and the thirteenth Duke of Norfolk took his disapproval to the extent of proclaiming himself an Anglican convert (on the issue) and receiving holy communion in the Arundel parish church. Newman, who was sympathetic to much of the spirit of the old Catholics, even though he was a very new one himself, was also unenthusiastic. He thought seminaries and education were more important than sees. But, somewhat typically, he allowed himself to be persuaded that it was his duty to preach a supportive sermon, and did so on 26 October in the new St Chad's Cathedral at Birmingham. His voice was barely audible, but his arguments only too resonant and provocative. Lord Shrewsbury, who was instinctively sympathetic to what was sometimes known as pageant Catholicism and the romanizing of the English recusant tradition, was almost the only grand Catholic layman to be enthusiastic for the Pope.

With these internal stresses in English Catholicism, particularly when accompanied by his own calm initial reaction, a wise Prime Minister would surely have allowed the popular storm (there were a few minor anti-papist riots) against the proclamation of the hierarchy to blow itself out, and the Roman Church to draw up its own balance sheet of the value or otherwise of the change. Russell, however, although brave and dedicated, was frequently unwise. He got himself committed, in a way which although half accidental served him right, to attempt legislation against the Pope. But as the Pope was manifestly outside the jurisdiction, this in practice meant against those who obeyed papal instructions on a matter relating to the organization of their religion.

This, to say the least, was an unhappy position for a quintessential Whig who had based his whole career on being for liberty and against the pretensions of authority, whether in state or Church. Russell was led into this course by too much converse with Whig prelates. There were not many of them, but they nearly all seemed to cause him trouble. In this instance it was the most senior, Maltby, who had been sent to Chichester by Grey in 1831 and to Durham by Melbourne in 1836, who lit the fuse. Too old at nearly eighty to be considered for York or Canterbury, Maltby lived remotely but grandly in his northern fastness and disapproved of Tractarians as much as they distrusted him. He wrote to Russell – an old friend – towards the end of October denouncing the Pope's aggression as insolent and insidious. Russell replied on 4 November, agreeing with Durham and promising that the existing law would be examined and if found deficient to deal with the aggression new legislation would be considered. This was the essential and fatal import of the letter, although he surrounded it with *obiter dicta* which combined some of the dismissive good sense which he had expressed to the Queen with a few insults to the Pope ('a foreign prince of no great power') and an attempt to use popular indignation against Rome to damage Anglican Ritualists who led 'their flocks . . . step by step to the very verge of the precipice'. His final sally was that 'the great mass of the nation looked with contempt upon the mummeries of superstition'.[14]

The letter having been written on the eve of Guy Fawkes day, Russell was subsequently blamed for instigating the more than usually boisterous celebration of that anti-papist feast. In fact more violence was threatened than took place. A few Catholic churches were besieged, a few windows broken and a few priests menaced. But insults were more rife than physical damage. A typical 'celebration' was that at Salisbury where guys in the shape of Wiseman, the Pope and the twelve diocesans were all destroyed on a giant bonfire which was ignited after a torchlight procession and the singing of the national anthem. The not very serious words of the twentieth-century revolutionary song,

> Build the burning pyre,
> Higher up and higher
> Pile the bleeding bishops on,
> One by bleeding one,

achieved a rare and not very serious approach to reality, in effigy at least.

Whatever was responsible for these manifestations, however, it was not the Prime Minister's letter, for that was published only on 7 November, at the request of Durham and with the consent of Russell. And it was Russell himself and not the Pope or the new Cardinal, or the twelve adjutants, that it then harpooned. From then onwards, for no very clear reason, the whole government became mesmerized with the idea that legislation was inevitable. This was in spite of few ministers being in favour of it. Russell's letter was deeply disapproved of, inside and outside the government, as being ill-considered and beneath the dignity of a Prime Minister. The Queen disapproved, so did Lansdowne, Lord President and Russell's closest colleague, so did Clarendon, the President of the Board of Trade, so from outside did John Bright, the moral voice of Nonconformity, who rebuked Russell most mightily for unnecessarily offending eight million of his Catholic countrymen.* Yet

* To get to his eight million, Bright included the Irish.

the Cabinet decided on 13 December to go ahead with legislation. The third Earl Grey, Secretary for War and Colonies, who had bought Gladstone's Carlton House Terrace house but had been very slow to pay, probably caught the general mood as well as providing a classic example of an argument for bad legislation. 'I disapprove of such legislation very much', he wrote in his diary, 'and most reluctantly assent to its being attempted, but the country has got into such a state that I believe still greater mischief would result from doing nothing.'[15]

The bill which was presented to Parliament in February 1851 provided for a penalty of £100 to be imposed on any archbishop, bishop or dean who assumed a territorial title. More severely it also provided that the endowments of any such sees or persons should be forfeited to the Crown. It was against this bill and against this background that Gladstone spoke late at night on 25 March. The main thrust of his argument was that the bill could be defended only by those who were prepared to turn their backs on the whole Whig tradition of extending religious liberty. Early in his somewhat extended but nonetheless extremely effective peroration ('one unbroken torrent of energetic declamation', Stanley called it) he used a (then) well-known and evocative Virgil quotation* to illustrate the benefits of the burying of religious strife and the consequent ebbing of religious bitterness. 'Are you', he turned upon the Whigs,

> going to spend the second half of the nineteenth century in undoing the great work which with so much pain and difficulty your greatest men have been achieving during the first half...? Your fathers and yourselves have earned a brilliant character for England. Do not forget it. Do not allow it to be tarnished. Show, if you will, the Pope of Rome that England as well as Rome has her *semper eadem*: and that when she has once adopted the great principle of legislation which is destined to influence her national character and make her policy for ages to come, and affect the whole nature of her influence among the nations of the world – show that once she has done this slowly, and with hesitation and difficulty, but still deliberately, but once for all – she can no more retrace her steps than the river which bathes this giant city can flow backwards to its source.... We cannot turn back the profound tendencies of the age towards religious liberty. It is our business to guide and to control their applications. Do this you may, but to endeavour to turn them backwards is the sport of children, done by the hands of men; and every effort you

* Which begins 'Scilicet et tempus veniet, cum finibus illis / Agricola, incurvo terram molitus aratro'.

> may make in that direction will recoil upon you with disaster and disgrace.[16]

So the monumental peroration rolled to its conclusion, and so Gladstone, still aged only forty-one, began to assume his best-remembered parliamentary style of a prophet who came down from the hills and denounced the sins and errors of his opponents.

There were a number of subsidiary points: that if the territorial titles of Roman Catholic prelates were to be forbidden, so must also be suppressed, unless there were to be the most blatant anti-papist discrimination, those of bishops in the Episcopal Church of Scotland, which, given that it was not the Queen's Church north of the border, were equally presumptuous; that a diocesan structure was in fact the enemy of the centralization of power in Rome, for it gave to the diocesan bishops certain rights against the Pope and it gave to the diocesan clergy certain rights against their bishop, which existed not at all so long as the Roman Church in England was treated as a missionary Church and administered by vicars-apostolic who were under the direct control of the Office of Propaganda at the Vatican; and that the appointment of bishops within a non-established Church was a spiritual not a temporal act, and therefore one with which Parliament had no right to meddle. All this was argued with an impressive wealth of historical and canonical knowledge and allusion. But it was essentially subordinate to the central argument of the peroration, which was the almost determinist one that in the second half of the nineteenth century the movement towards religious equality could not be set back. And Gladstone was right to the extent that the bill was the last promoted by a British government which endeavoured to discriminate between religious denominations.

When Gladstone sat down at 1.00 a.m. he was followed by Disraeli and a brittle sharpness replaced the uplifting orotundities with which the member for Oxford University had endeavoured to persuade the House. This does not, however, count as the first in the series of great Gladstone–Disraeli duels of the third quarter of the century. That memorable event came only at the end of 1852. On Ecclesiastical Titles they did not sufficiently engage with each other. They each spoke as from a different planet. Disraeli continued until half-past two in the morning. Then the vote was taken. Although few speakers had supported the bill with any enthusiasm, Russell and Disraeli between them had the big battalions, and the opposition of Gladstone, most of the other Peelites, thirty or so Irish Catholics, John Bright and Joseph Hume was

The two new Liverpool houses of Gladstone's childhood:

62 Rodney Street, sixteen years old when it became his birthplace

Seaforth House, five miles down river, which John Gladstone began building in 1811 and to which he removed his family in the summer of Waterloo.

Facing page: George Canning (by Lawrence), Member for Liverpool 1812–22, and an early and continuing Gladstone family hero. A striking declamatory picture, but why is he addressing an empty House of Commons from the middle of the floor?

Left: Arthur Hallam, the *jeune homme fatal*, who excited Gladstone, Tennyson and several others before his early death in 1833.

The Oxford, and in particular the Christ Church (on the left, Merton College on the right) at which Gladstone arrived in 1828.

Fasque, the fine Kincardineshire mansion which John Gladstone acquired in 1829, when it was twenty years old, and in which William Gladstone spent many autumns in his twenties and thirties.

Hawarden, Flintshire, older but much remodelled at about the time of the creation of Fasque. Gladstone married into the Hawarden estate in 1839 and increasingly made it his home for the remaining sixty years of his life.

Catherine Gladstone (formerly Glynne) painted by F. R. Say around the time of her marriage in 1839.

Gladstone (second from left) as the new MP for Newark seated alongside his elder brother, Thomas (third from left), in one of the last (1834) pictures of the old House of Commons, which was destroyed by fire within a few months.

Gladstone as a young man, a possibly flattering portrait done in 1838 by William Bradley.

The founder of the fortune and the dynasty, and by then the hard laird of Fasque: Sir John Gladstone, painted by Bradley about the time of his 1846 baronetcy.

The Tory deities of Gladstone's early political years. Sir Robert Peel towers over the Duke of Wellington in this 1844 drawing by Winterhalter.

crushed by 438 votes to 95. It was a discreditable vote in the sense that the huge majority was mostly provided by those without conviction of the merits of the measure but who believed they might assuage popular sentiment by voting aye.

The bill was then considerably amended in committee. The forfeiture of endowment clause was removed with only the £100 penalty on individual clerics remaining, and special adjustments were inserted to except the Scottish bishoprics, thereby making the measure still more discriminatory against Roman Catholics. But it mattered little. The bill received royal assent on 31 July 1851, but was never implemented. It was largely ignored by the Roman Catholic community, but there were no prosecutions. After twenty years as a dead letter it was repealed, appropriately by the first Gladstone government, in 1871.

His famous speech and other interventions on the bill did not do Gladstone much good with the electors of the University of Oxford. But they did not do him much harm either. He took his stand absolutely, but he took it on narrow ground. He was not in favour of the 'division of England into Romist dioceses'. 'Amicable prevention' he desired. 'Spiritual and ecclesiastical resistance', he approved. But he would not countenance discrimination by law: 'I would far rather quit parliament for ever than vote for so pernicious a measure.'[17] As is usually the case when resolute Burkeism is proclaimed, Gladstone gained in respect at least as much as he lost through disagreement, and at the general election in the summer of 1852 he markedly improved his result over that of 1847. He got 1108 votes against Inglis's 1368 (which was a halving of the 1847 gap) and was comfortably ahead of the challenging and 'protestant' candidate, Warden Marsham of Merton, who received only 758.

The Ecclesiastical Titles Bill further enhanced Gladstone's reputation as a dominant parliamentary figure, and marked an important stage in his move towards liberalism, although not towards the leaders of the Whig party. It also underlined the slightly self-righteous separateness of the Peelites – 'a limited but accomplished school' as Disraeli mockingly called them. But it did not begin to provide Gladstone with any firm moorings for his political future. He looked powerful but idiosyncratic and isolated rather than on the verge of the glorious blossoming of his career which was to come in 1852–3.

Part Two

A MIDDLE-AGED MID-VICTORIAN STATESMAN

1852–1868

— 9 —

The Chancellor Who Made the Job

The Russell government staggered on for another seven months, with Parliament in recess for most of them, after the sad farce of the passage into law of the Ecclesiastical Titles Bill in July 1851. It had tried to divest itself of office, for which it had lost all appetite, in the late winter of 1851. But Stanley, the alternative Prime Minister as the leader of the majority of the Conservative party which had opposed Peel in 1846, took one look at his followers and decided that, when he had failed to add Gladstone or Graham to them, they were simply not up to constituting a government. 'These are not names I can put before the Queen,' Disraeli recorded him as dismissively concluding the attempt to create an administration.[1]

For Disraeli the lesson was clear. He noted: 'every public man of experience and influence, however slight, had declined to act unless the principle of Protection were unequivocally renounced'.[2] He therefore redoubled his efforts to get rid of the old policy for the sake of which he had broken Peel and on which he had elevated himself to the Conservative leadership in the Commons. Stanley was a little less ruthless, but equally aware of the weakness of a protectionist party.

The unsettling effect which, after 1846, Peel had upon British politics ('former Prime Ministers', Gladstone said, with Peel very much in mind, 'are like great rafts floating untethered in a harbour') was spectacularly illustrated by the fact that nearly a year after his death the leaders of neither party had faith in their own ability to govern with confidence, although Russell was in general fond of office. Stanley's awareness of his own party's unfitness could not, however, prop up the Whigs for long. In December 1851, Russell decided under considerable pressure from the Queen and Prince Albert that he must make a desperate effort to recover his authority against the overt insubordination of his Foreign Secretary, who had unilaterally congratulated Louis Napoleon on his *coup d'état*. As is often the case in such circumstances, he overreached himself.

Palmerston was dismissed and became determined to have his 'tit-for-tat with Johnnie Russell'. He effectively if blatantly achieved that within a few weeks of the reassembly of Parliament on 4 February 1852. He united with Disraeli to defeat Russell on the Militia Bill and the five-and-a-half-year Whig government came to an end. Stanley this time had no other choice than to form an administration or contract out of serious politics.*

The government which Derby formed was not much better than that which he had declined to present a year before. It contained only three members (Derby himself, Lonsdale and J. C. Herries) who had ever held office before, and consequently only three Privy Councillors. The rest had to be sworn in as part of a mass baptism which Robert Blake compared with the installation of the first Labour government in 1924; and, Blake suggested, there was an almost equal feeling of the arrival of the barbarians within the gates, which was unmitigated by the Cabinet (of thirteen) containing one duke, one marquess and four earls. The sense of the backwoodsmen taking over was captured for posterity by the deaf and declining Duke of Wellington having the glory of the list explained to him by Derby in the Lords chamber and responding to most names with an increasingly penetrating and incredulous 'Who? Who?'

So the 'Who Who' ministry was born, and Disraeli began his official career, which was to be so intertwined, symbiotically if without much mutual sympathy, with that of Gladstone. The symbiosis was immediately to the fore. Disraeli, who was the only possible choice to lead the House of Commons, became Chancellor of the Exchequer. Although Pitt had progressed from the Exchequer to his great premiership and Althorp had led the House of Commons from the Treasury in both the Grey and the first Melbourne governments, it was then by no means the second post or the most natural one from which to lead in the Commons if the Prime Minister were a peer – as he was for just over half the nineteenth century. Both the Home and the Foreign Offices were more likely bases. But each of these ministers saw much more of the Queen than did the Under-Treasurer, the clerkly title which the Chancellor is significantly given in Court documents, and this was thought to preclude

* To add to the general confusion he had by this time changed his name. He became the fourteenth Earl of Derby when his father died on 30 June 1851. This resulted in the Prime Minister Derby's son, later the fifteenth Earl, who was himself to be Foreign Secretary under Disraeli and Colonial Secretary under Gladstone, ceasing to be Mr Edward Stanley and becoming Lord Stanley, although not a peer. Differentiation was not made simpler by their all being christened Edward.

Disraeli's appointment as a Secretary of State. The Queen had indeed specifically registered such an objection during the previous year's abortive attempt to form a Conservative government, pegging it to Disraeli's treatment of Peel in 1846. So he became Chancellor (Derby brushing aside his demurral that he had no knowledge of the Treasury with 'You know as much as Mr Canning did. They give you the figures'). By so doing Disraeli not only made himself a target which brought out the full force of Gladstone's parliamentary wrath but also increased the status of the post which that rival was soon to occupy.

This time round it was Palmerston rather than the Peelites whom Derby tried to capture for his government. But here too he was inhibited by royal disfavour, for the Queen, although for different reasons, was as unwilling to see Palmerston as Disraeli at the Foreign Office (at this stage her prejudices were remarkably similar to those of Gladstone). And, as Palmerston was tempted by no other post, that settled the matter. Without such independent Whig adherence, Derby had no alternative but to accept the Peelite terms for support from outside, which were that there should be a general election in the summer (of 1852) followed by a late-autumn session of Parliament during which the government must bring forward its fiscal proposals and thus show its hand on how thoroughly it was abandoning protection.

These arrangements led to an indecisive result in a July election, and to the unusual and inconvenient event of a December budget, which proved fatal for the government and triumphant for Gladstone. The election, as already indicated, led to a secure return for Gladstone from Oxford, and to the 'Derbyites' gaining some seats but not enough to give them a dependable majority. In a House of 654 their strength was varyingly interpreted as between 290 and 310. The rest were about 270 'Liberals' as they were coming loosely to be called, 35 to 40 Peelites, and about the same number of variegated Irish. (The numbers are imprecise because MPs were often imprecise about the labels they wished to attach to themselves.)

The December budget fell unhappily for Disraeli as a neophyte Chancellor. He was due to present it on the 3rd, and he had had a wretched November. When the new Parliament met at the beginning of the month it was necessary for the government quickly to declare where it stood on the Corn Laws. Charles Villiers had put down a provocative motion which stated that repeal had been 'a wise, just and beneficial measure'. The protectionists of 1846 were anxious to be rid of their albatross but to ask them to vote for this motion was to ask them to canonize Peel, to the revolt against whom they owed their origin and their leadership. Gladstone and Sidney Herbert then drafted a compromise motion which, through the agency of Palmerston, Disraeli was glad to accept. But he had to go through three uncomfortable nights of debate to get it carried and to avoid the government being washed away before he could even present his budget in the following week. He was suffering from severe influenza, which meant that he spoke only with difficulty, and he had to sit and listen to a scornful indictment of himself from Herbert, who, as a loyal Peelite, pilloried Disraeli for his shameless opportunism in first destroying Peel and then adopting his policy.

Perhaps aided by his illness, Disraeli listened with the pallid impassivity which was to become his stock-in-trade. But his maintenance of such dignity was not aided by other circumstances. The Duke of Wellington had died between the election and the meeting of Parliament, and one of Disraeli's early duties as leader of the House of Commons was to pronounce an encomium upon him. His words were noble, but by what Blake charitably calls 'a curious trick of memory' they turned out to be a word-for-word translation of those which Thiers had used for an obituary of Maréchal St Cyr in 1829. The exposure of this coincidence caused much mockery at the Chancellor's expense. In addition, far from finding that, in Derby's reassuring phrase, 'they give you the figures', he found himself bereft of a private secretary, who had caught his own influenza, and grubbing around in desperation and solitude to make his budget add up.

What he had determined to do, perhaps more for reasons of politics than of justice, was to accept free trade, but to ease by taxation concessions the position of the principal groups which were alleged to have suffered from it. These were thought to be the landed, the sugar and the shipping interests. To be able to do something in these directions in what looked a tight budgetary situation (in fact the out-turn for the financial year was more favourable than he expected and he would have done better to wait for a spring budget) required some imaginative juggling, and Derby congratulated him on having successfully 'doctored' his figures.

Disraeli presented these results in a five-hour speech, which Macaulay said he himself could have done more clearly in two. The debate did not begin until a week later and lasted over four nights. Disraeli and his proposals were heavily battered. On the first night (a Friday) Gladstone spoke on the house and income tax aspects of the budget (it was taken in parts), and was in the Commons until '12¾'. Then, having got home, 'I sat up for the night: and fell to work on my arrears of letters and papers' until, as he recorded for the next morning, 'off by six o'clock train to Birm. & Hagley which I reached before one: falling in with a nice boy on the road [that is, on his twelve-mile walk from Birmingham station], Nanny's grandson. Saw Griffiths [an agent, probably on Oak Farm business] in evg. but was sleepy enough.'[3] It is a comfort to know that his energy was subject to at least that degree of human limitation.

Gladstone was back in London on the Monday evening and at the House later that night and on the Tuesday for the continuation of the budget debate. On the Thursday (16 December) he spoke in 'the very exciting debate early in the evening' about a procedural question, and then, after going home to Carlton Gardens for dinner, returned to the House for Disraeli's reply to the whole debate, which lasted from 10.20 until 1.00. Gladstone thought Disraeli's speech brilliant, even if insolent and at times vulgar. The drama of the occasion was increased by the noises off of a violent thunderstorm, an almost unique December event. Towards the end Disraeli employed what became one of his most quoted aphorisms. He was faced, he said, by a coalition of opposition: 'The combination may be successful. A coalition has before this been successful. But coalitions although successful have always found this, that their triumph has been brief. This too I know, that England does not love coalitions.'[4]

When Disraeli sat down, exhausted by two and a quarter hours of mordancy, the House, collectively tired by that time, assumed an immediate division. It was an hour after midnight and the Chancellor of the Exchequer had just wound up four days of budget debate. But they reckoned without Gladstone who, amazingly as it now seems and uninhibited by having already spoken twice in the four days, decided that a full-scale reply could and should be imposed upon the House. He accordingly stood in his place on the opposition side below the gangway, which was where the Peelites then sat, and the chairman (the House being in Committee, which meant there was no rule against multiple speeches) had reluctantly to call him.*

* For budget debates and other tax-raising proceedings the House traditionally sat as a Committee of Ways and Means, with the chairman of committees presiding from a seat at the clerks' table and no one in the Speaker's chair. This symbolized, as did the mace being below and not on the table, somewhat more informal rules of business, the most significant difference being the ability (in committee) of members to speak more than once in the same debate. The same considerations apply when the Committee Stage of a bill is being taken on the floor of the House. Recently, however, the tradition has been modified so that the Speaker now presides over the opening of a Chancellor's budget.

The House was at least as reluctant to hear him, and to begin with he spoke through considerable noise. 'It was a most difficult operation . . .', he informed his wife. Although he defined his 'great object [as being] to show the Conservative party how their leader was hoodwinking and bewildering them', he himself began with a fair piece of sophistry. 'I am reluctant . . . to trespass upon the attention of the Committee, but it appears to me that the speech we have just heard is a speech which ought to meet with a reply, and that, too, on the moment.' This impression of spontaneity provoked by affront might have been more convincing had he not written to his wife (she was at Hagley) thirty-six hours before: 'I am sorry to say that I have a long speech fomenting in me, and I feel as a loaf might in the oven.'[5] In addition he had for much of the morning 'worked up the Exchequer loan business* and made notes for speaking'.

In other words the speech counted for him as a more than usually prepared one, and there can be little doubt that his deliberate intention had been to trump Disraeli's ace and to seize from the government its normal right to the last word. From the moment of Disraeli's rising Gladstone confessed himself 'on tenterhooks, except when his [Disraeli's] superlative acting and brilliant oratory from time to time absorbed me and made me quite *forget* that I had to follow him'.[6] Earlier in the evening, when he had been in his own house between seven and nine, he had dined alone, read *Travels in Tartary, Thibet and China* by E. V. Huc and 'actually contrived . . . to sleep in the fur cloak for . . . quarter of an hour'. Despite these attempts at relaxation he described his brain as being 'strung very high'[7] for his own speech.

This speech lasted another two hours until after three o'clock in the morning. During the first quarter of an hour or so, while he was rebuking Disraeli for his cheap personal attacks, there was a lot of interruption. Then, as he gradually got control of the House, there was a change of pace. He was, as usual, somewhat periphrastic with occasional dark pools of obscurity as he piled negative upon negative and one subordinate clause upon another. Yet the whole is curiously easy to read. He proceeds throughout on the assumption that he knew more about government than did Disraeli. This was supplemented by frequent appeals to the authority of Sir Robert Peel, compared with whom Disraeli was treated as a lightweight charlatan. The result,

* Which was important to the dispute about the spuriousness or otherwise of Disraeli's surplus.

Gladstone suggested, was a decline in the conscience and repute of the Conservative party, which filled him more with sorrow than with anger.

This did not prevent his delivering some good dismissive jokes. He gradually built up a picture of Disraeli as a frivolous fellow who lacked clarity of execution, consistency of purpose, or the honesty to admit that his surplus was fictitious. Gladstone's peroration was powerful and not too florid. He did not however go in for understatement. He would vote against the budget because it was 'the most subversive in its tendency and ultimate effects which I have ever known submitted to this House'.[8] He would vote in support of Conservative principles, and particularly those which were enshrined in the great name and the great days of Sir R. Peel.

In voting for Conservative principles, however, he took good care to do so on a motion and in circumstances which would give him plenty of Whig and Radical allies. That was the point of Disraeli's jibe about coalitions. When Gladstone left the House at four o'clock in the morning he may have proclaimed Conservative principles but he had destroyed the only flicker of a Conservative government between 1846 and 1858. It was therefore surprising and perhaps insensitive that on his way home he went into the Carlton Club (as now exclusively Conservative and then in Pall Mall) to write a letter.*

That visit provoked no reported reaction – the club was presumably fairly empty at 4.30 in the morning, even after a critical division – but when Gladstone next went into the club, after dinner on 20 December, and was sitting reading, he was mildly harassed by a baying group of young members who threatened to throw him across the road into the Reform Club, where, they insisted, he properly belonged. However, he clung on to his Carlton membership for another seven years, despite or perhaps because of the fact that in 1855, when he had turned against a continuation of the Crimean War, the Duke of Beaufort tried to have him expelled. Eventually, in 1860 when he had passed over most watersheds away from Conservatism, he allowed his membership to lapse. It was probably the only club in which he ever felt at home. He had been a member for a long time, and it was very convenient for his various residences in Carlton Gardens and Carlton House Terrace. At the end of his life he was a member of the Athenaeum and of the United Universities Club, as well as being the literal founder – he laid the

* Requesting the renewal of the private-secretary services of Stafford Northcote, at that time a civil servant. (See p. 165, below.)

foundation stone – of the National Liberal Club. But he never belonged to the Reform Club or to the Whig citadel of Brooks's where, however, he was frequently entertained by his private secretaries in his later governments.

When he got home from his Carlton Club letter-writing he managed only two hours' sleep: 'My nervous system was too powerfully acted upon by the scene of last night. A recollection of having mismanaged a material point (by omission) came into my head when I was half awake between 7 and 8 and utterly prevented my getting more rest.'[9] Then he was agitated by the fact that *The Times* that morning contained only 'a mangled abbreviation' of his speech. (It might be thought a feat far beyond modern technology that it contained even the semblance of a report of a speech delivered in the middle of the night.) He was somewhat mollified by the following day's edition containing a laudatory comparison between his style and that of Disraeli.

In the subsequent days Gladstone could contemplate with increasing satisfaction the repercussions of his oration. Indeed, one reason the atmosphere had been so charged in the Carlton Club on the evening of Monday 20 December was that the government had that afternoon announced its resignation, Derby with petulance in the Lords and Disraeli with good humour in the Commons.

Aberdeen became Prime Minister of a Whig–Peelite coalition. Russell was a used-up man and the Queen and the Prince were set against Palmerston. So a Whig premier was effectively excluded. These two eagles of Whiggery occupied the two senior secretaryships of state, but Palmerston was kept out of the Foreign Office because of his rashness over Prince Louis Napoleon (who had in the meantime become the Emperor Napoleon III) and Russell was kept out of the Home Office because of the mess he had made of the Ecclesiastical Titles Bill. So they each went to the department for which they were less suited. For the rest the Peelites, who provided barely a tenth of the new government's parliamentary backing, got the pickings. Apart from the Prime Minister and the Chancellor of the Exchequer, they filled the War Office, the Admiralty and the Colonial Office, as well as holding the Privy Seal.

For the chancellorship Russell as the leader of the Whigs would have preferred Graham (who, however, preferred the Admiralty), and Delane of *The Times* tried to promote Charles Wood, who had been at the Treasury from 1846 to 1851. The most resolute for Gladstone were the Queen and Prince Albert. Aberdeen was content to fall in with their wish, and Gladstone for once accepted without demur or agonizing or conditions. In reality it would have been nonsense to have had anyone else. He had destroyed the previous budget and he obviously had to make the next one. After two and a half days at Hawarden, where he arrived in a hurricane at five o'clock on Christmas morning, he went to Windsor to be sworn in on 28 December, one day short of his forty-third birthday. His introspective musings on the year which was past, while mildly self-critical, were only a tithe in length (and self-abasement) of what had been his recent annual habit. It was a sign of his absorption, for the moment at least, in public business. He prepared to engage with the nation's finances, the control of which he was to dominate for most of the next twenty years. But first he engaged between January and March 1853 with Disraeli about the furniture of 11 Downing Street (then numbered 12) and the Chancellor of the Exchequer's robe.

Disraeli had paid his Whig predecessor, Wood, £787 12s 6d for the furniture of the house, and had subsequently got a refund from the Office of Works of £479 16s for that part of it which related to the public reception rooms. He therefore wanted £307 16s 6d from Gladstone for the rest. (The figures help to put Don Pacifico's claims into perspective.) Gladstone thought that Disraeli should get the money from the Office of Works, which under a new disposition had assumed responsibility (subject to charging ministers for wear and tear in the private rooms) for the whole. Disraeli thought that this should apply only to future transfers, knew that the Office of Works was dilatory and was probably not averse to a private *casus belli* with Gladstone, to whom he had hardly been endeared by the events of the previous December. He may also have wished to create a diversion under the smoke of which he could hope to escape from the obligation to transfer the Chancellor's robes, which he believed had been made for Pitt, and which he wished to keep.

As a result there occurred the most childish epistolatory quarrel. Gladstone wrote courteously if stiffly on 21 January ('My dear Sir. . . . I remain, my dear Sir, faithfully yours, W. E. Gladstone') proposing Office of Works payment for the furniture (on which point he was probably in the wrong) and requesting the transfer of the robes on the normal terms. Disraeli replied only on 26 February in nominally courteous but even stiffer terms ('I have the honour to remain, dear Sir, your obedient servant, B. Disraeli') rejecting the role of the Office of Works and ignoring the robes. Gladstone wrote again two days later, sticking a little woodenly to his two points. Disraeli on 6 March mounted into the high and disdainful saddle of the third person. 'Mr Disraeli regrets very much that he is obliged to say that Mr Gladstone's letter repudiating his obligation to pay for the furniture of the official residence is not satisfactory. . . . Mr Disraeli is unwilling to prolong this correspondence. As Mr Gladstone seems to be in some perplexity on the subject, Mr Disraeli recommends him to consult Sir Charles Wood,* who is a man of the world.'

Gladstone the next day wrote a pained reply, also in the third person. He agreed to pay 'without in any degree admitting the justice of Mr Disraeli's assumptions', and by omission gave up on the robes. He concluded: 'It is highly unpleasant to Mr. W. E. Gladstone to address Mr. Disraeli without the usual terms of courtesy, but he abstains from them only because he perceives that they are unwelcome.'[10] Gladstone sent his cheque, but Disraeli kept his robes, wore them during his two subsequent chancellorships, and left them as treasures of Hughenden Manor, his Buckinghamshire house.

Gladstone had to have a new set made, which descended without difficulty until Sir William Harcourt in 1886. Harcourt, however, took these 'Gladstone' robes with him when the government went out. Lord Randolph Churchill therefore had another new set made, but Goschen, who quickly succeeded him, declined to buy and preferred to have yet another set made. The 'Churchill' robes were subsequently worn only by Winston Churchill in 1924–9. These 'Goschen' robes appear to be the ones still in use today. There have therefore been at least three breaks in the apostolic succession since Pitt, even assuming the uncertain fact that Disraeli's robes were Pitt's.

On 3 February, robeless and with the furniture still unpaid for, Gladstone had moved into 12 (11) Downing Street, which house or its next-door neighbour he was to have at his disposal for twenty-two of his remaining forty-five years of life. He had already overcome the first obstacle to the success of his chancellorship, which was the need to get re-elected by Oxford. This was more than a formality, for clerical opinion was distinctly unenthusiastic both about the defeat of the short-lived Conservative government, in which event Gladstone had played so notable a part, and about the Peelite decision to coalesce with the Whigs. Archdeacon Denison of Taunton, Gladstone's senior by a year

* Wood, later the first Viscount Halifax, was not only the outgoing Chancellor from whom Disraeli had bought the furniture and the robes, but also Gladstone's current Cabinet colleague as President of the Board of Control.

at both Eton and Christ Church and one of his leading High Church mentors, had written him a terrible letter on the day after Christmas. 'I wish to use few words', Denison wrote, 'where every word I write is so bitterly distressing to me, and must be little less so, I cannot doubt, to yourself and to many others whom I respect and love. I have to state to you, as one of your constituents, that from this time I can place no confidence in you as representative of the university of Oxford, or as a public man.'[11]*

Denison was naturally disputatious, and was soon to get involved in a quarrel with his diocesan of Bath and Wells which led to his being prosecuted before an ecclesiastical court, but on the occasion of his letter to Gladstone, unattractively though he licked his lips over the pain it caused, he had some legitimate grievance against the author of *The State in its Relations with the Church*, the extremism of which work had contributed to Gladstone being elected for Oxford in the first place. Now Gladstone had just joined a government which was overwhelmingly dependent on Whig parliamentary votes, of which the Prime Minister was a Scots Presbyterian, the Foreign Secretary, who was also leader of the House of Commons, was the nominator to Hereford of the allegedly heretical Bishop Hampden as well as the heir to all the Erastian and despoiling traditions of the Russells, and the Chancellor of the Duchy of Lancaster (important for ecclesiastical patronage) was the Radical Sir William Molesworth, who was accused of being a Socinian, which was more or less the equivalent of a Unitarian.

At the by-election which followed from Gladstone's appointment as Chancellor, a standard-bearer for these grievances was found in the shape of Dudley Montagu Perceval, son of the assassinated Prime Minister of 1812. Spencer Perceval is not (except for his end) one of the most remembered heads of government, but he was a model both of statesmanship and of amiability compared with his son, who mounted a scurrilous but damaging campaign against Gladstone. He polled 892 to the Chancellor of the Exchequer's 1022, the narrow result a temporary relief but an early harbinger of the mutual disenchantment of the University constituency and its member which was to end in divorce twelve years later.

Once this hurdle was surmounted, even if narrowly, Gladstone got

* Denison was true to his word. As late as 1885 he wrote and published what the *Dictionary of National Biography* describes as 'a violent political diatribe against Gladstone'.

down to the long straight run of preparation for his first budget, which he presented on Monday, 18 April. Even by his own Herculean standards he worked unusually hard in those spring weeks, although Morley's claim that he put in 'thirteen, fourteen, fifteen hours a day' at his Treasury desk seems an exaggeration. Most nights Gladstone needed seven or eight hours of sleep, and he continued to dine out frequently, to give almost daily Latin lessons to one or other of his two elder sons, to go to two if not three church services on Sundays, to attend Cabinets, to discharge his normal House of Commons voting duties, and even to do a little 'rescue' work. So Morley's arithmetic does not quite add up, even though Gladstone compensated for his excursions into both social and sinful London by many hours of subsequent late-night work on income tax or customs duties.

The budgetary prospect in the spring of 1853 was more strategically challenging than tactically menacing. Nineteenth-century Chancellors, at least in peacetime, were subject to none of the short-term pressures by which, in the decline of the British economy, their post-1930 successors have been frequently buffeted. In the 1850s there was no danger of a weak budget leading to a run on sterling. Furthermore, and with greater particularity, the short-term financial prospect had become relatively easy. The official estimates on which Disraeli had framed his December 1852 proposals were pessimistically false, a somewhat persistent Treasury habit. On the basis of them he had to perform some considerable sleights of hand to pretend that he had a surplus, and on those premisses Gladstone had been right in criticizing its hollowness. But by the spring the out-turn had produced a genuine surplus of £2½ million and Gladstone had no immediate problem.

The challenge which he had to meet, if he was to be a major Chancellor, was at once a more subtle and a longer-term one. Whig financial policy between 1846 and 1851 had been unimpressive, and Charles Wood, the Chancellor throughout these years, had not compared in influence within the government with Russell himself, with Palmerston as Foreign Secretary, with George Grey as Home Secretary or with Lansdowne as Lord President of the Council. (The low regard in which his chancellorship was held did not, however, prevent Wood as President of the Board of Control from being a querulous Cabinet critic of Gladstone's 1853 proposals.) Then Disraeli, in his two 1852 budgets, had been looking more for a smokescreen under which his party could escape from the incubus of protection than for a rational framework of finance for the country. The result was a series of unconnected improvisations. The second Disraeli budget particularly had been a conjuror's rather than a philosopher's or even a political economist's budget. That at least was the ground on which Gladstone had destroyed it.

This left him, as the incoming Chancellor, with a heavy obligation to coherence, as well as an heir's desire to revive the Peel tradition of probity and courage. His need was not so much a budget for a year as a system of finance for the third quarter of the century. This he was held to have produced, and his achievement in this respect, made the greater by his having to get his proposals through a disparate Cabinet made up of men unused to working together and a House of Commons in which the government had no secure majority, laid the foundation of much of his subsequent reputation. And rightly so, it may be said, for the 1853 budget (and its two 1854 successors) enabled the country to go through the Crimean War, which subverted the public finances of France and Russia, in such a way that when he returned to the Exchequer in 1859 he found a platform of sound fiscal strength and a national wealth which had increased by nearly a fifth since his first impact on the Treasury.

Alternatively it could be argued that the 1853 budget was a triumph more of personality than of prescience, that Gladstone got at least as many things wrong as Disraeli had done, and that the centre-piece of his presentation was just as much of a rabbit out of a hat as anything which Disraeli had produced. What Gladstone indisputably did, however, was to set his proposals in a schematic framework, and to argue for them from first principles, as well as with a wealth of historical and comparative fiscal analogy. The result was that he gave the impression of having brought a large ship into a constricted harbour with unusual deftness controlling latent power.

The speech in which these qualities were displayed fully matched the importance of the ship which it steered. It took four and three-quarter hours, from approximately five o'clock to just before ten on the evening of Monday, 18 April. The speech occupied seventy-two columns of Hansard and was the longest (although not by a very wide margin) that he ever made in the House of Commons or anywhere else. Yet the sums of money with which it dealt were by modern standards derisory. The total size of the budget was £52 million. Even making a full allowance for the change in the value of money and applying a factor of fifty, this would be the equivalent of a modern budget of just over £2½ billion, about 2 per cent of today's actual total. The income tax, the treatment of which was the central issue of suspense and controversy in Gladstone's budget, brought in £5½ million, the equivalent, after the application of the fifty factor, of £275 million today, an amount shifted by the most minor modern adjustment of allowances.

None of this prevented the budget of 1853 sending out large political ripples, and maybe a few economic ones too. Gladstone had difficulty in getting it through the Cabinet. In this respect, as well as in its length and in the near nullity of one of his principal measures, it was a worthy forerunner of the famous budget of 1909. Among those who were most querulous were Wood, the unsuccessful Chancellor of the Russell administration, and Graham, close Peelite colleague though he was, who might himself have become Chancellor, but did not, when Aberdeen formed his government. Palmerston also was strongly opposed to the succession duty on landed property which Gladstone introduced, and so indeed, in their hearts at least, were nearly the whole of the Cabinet.

On Saturday, 9 April, there began the nine-day climax of Gladstone's several months of budgetary preparation. Fortified by a visit on the previous day to see the plans and site for Panizzi's Round Reading Room at the British Museum, he expounded his proposals to Prince Albert from 1.00 to 2.00 p.m. (unlike the more recent practice a pre-budget visit to the Sovereign herself did not then seem to be necessary) and almost immediately afterwards gave the Cabinet a three-hour exposé. This left his colleagues sufficiently stunned (the Duke of Argyll, who was to sit in Cabinets with Gladstone for another twenty-eight years, wrote that he 'never heard a speech which so riveted my attention') that there was practically no discussion at that stage. But in the following week there were four argumentative Cabinets between the Monday and the Saturday. Morley summed up the position after the first of these with almost the blandness of a Cabinet Secretary (which official was not to exist for another sixty-three years): 'At the end of a long and interesting discussion, there stood for the whole budget Lord John [Russell], Newcastle, Clarendon, Molesworth, Gladstone, with Argyll and Aberdeen more or less favourable: for dropping the two extensions of income tax and keeping half the soap duty, Lansdowne, Graham, Wood; more or less leaning towards them, Palmerston and Granville.'[12]

Gladstone seems to have dealt with this unpromising situation with exemplary patience. He did not fulminate and he did not for once threaten resignation, except on one point which he described as 'the breaking up of the basis of the Income Tax'. He relied on his mastery of the detail and on the solidity and consistency of his scheme, which he rightly opined would lead to the waves of opposition breaking in contrary directions and leaving his steadily steered ship to sail down the middle. It took fifteen and a half hours of Cabinet discussion to get the budget approved, but it eventually emerged unscathed: 'Thus the whole Cabinet after finding that the suggested amendments cut against one another ended by adopting the entire Budget – the only dissentients being Ld. Lansdowne, Graham, Wood, S. Herbert. Graham was full of ill auguries but said he would assent and assist. Wood looked grave and said he must take time.'[13]

It was permission to move to the next and public stage, but it was hardly a confidence-giving endorsement for a young and first-time Chancellor. Clearly the other putative Chancellors, Wood and Graham, sat glowering like the two ugly sisters. Lansdowne was a very senior Whig, seventy-three at the time, who had himself been Chancellor nearly fifty years before. And Gladstone's beloved Sidney Herbert, it might be thought, behaved with less than the loyalty of a close friend, particularly as he had just taken the Gladstones to the Herbert family house at Wilton for a four-day Easter week break, the Chancellor's only interlude in the long run-up to the budget.* Nor was the solidarity of the Peelite front wholly restored at this stage by the Prime Minister. Aberdeen's salient comment, 'You must take care your proposals are not unpopular ones,' was no more notably constructive than it was supportive.

Gladstone was undismayed. On the Sunday after the last of the five Cabinets he went to church twice, wrote a small ration of letters, saw Herbert and Newcastle and read Dante's *Paradiso*, but 'was obliged to give several hours to my figures'. On the Monday he 'devoted [himself] to working on [his] papers and figures for this evening', but drove and walked with his wife before going to the House at 4.30 and starting his marathon oration a quarter of an hour later: 'my strength stood out well thank God'. At eleven o'clock, about an hour and a quarter after sitting down, 'the Herberts and Wortley's came home with us and had soup and Negus [hot sweetened wine and water]'.† By that time he knew that the presentation of the budget had been a triumph, but recorded it

* Gladstone on this visit was in a very benign sightseeing mood, in sharp contrast with, say, his attitude at Strasbourg seven and a half years before. He was enchanted with Salisbury Cathedral, then unrestored, and thought it 'a wonder of harmony and beauty', and impressed by Stonehenge, 'a noble and an awful relic, telling much, and telling too that it conceals more'. The Bishop (of Salisbury) coming to dinner was 'another treat'. Compared with these excitements he was unmoved by the classical splendours of Wilton House.

† J. A. Stuart-Wortley was a fellow of Merton College and later Solicitor-General.

modestly, merely writing 'Many kind congratulations afterwards.' By the next day, however, he had graduated to: 'I received today immeasurable marks of kindness, enough to make me ashamed. . . . But my life is wholly unworthy of these consolations.'[14]

How was the triumph secured, and what made a budget which had received such a battering in the Cabinet so acclaimed in the House of Commons, and hence, when the crunch was over, the subject of so much enthusiastic congratulation by his hitherto querulous colleagues? Primarily, it was the sense of command over both circumstances and his material which he conveyed, and in particular the *tour de force*, at once masterly and impudently bold, with which he dealt with the vexing and central subject of the income tax. Gladstone's essential dilemma was that nearly everybody, including himself, had pronounced themselves against this unpopular tax, but that there was no way in which he could attain his main objectives of prudent finance and a further simplification and reduction of indirect taxes (in the conviction that such reduction would in the medium term increase both national prosperity and the tax yields) without relying on the income tax for at any rate some years to come.

The history of this tax was that it had been first introduced by Pitt in 1799 after six years of improvident financing of the French War, was allowed to lapse in 1802 with the Peace of Amiens, but was reintroduced in 1806 in a stronger form and was retained until after the victory of 1815. When in operation it transformed the basis of war finance and enabled most of the cost to be covered by current revenue. Nevertheless the overhang of debt from previous borrowing in the years of poor trade and unrigorous finance between Waterloo and Peel's coming to power in 1841 was formidable in relation to the small resources available to successive Chancellors. In the quinquennium from 1836 to 1840 debt charges accounted for 58 per cent of central public expenditure, leaving 25 per cent for defence and only 10 per cent for the whole business of civil government.*

Peel in 1842, when he wished both to replace Whig deficits with Conservative rigour and to lead an attack on the labyrinth of indirect taxes, reintroduced Pitt's income tax, and did so at the same rate of sevenpence in the pound (or 3 per cent) which had applied from 1806 to 1816. He did it upon a three-year basis, which meant that, with two reluctant renewals, it survived until 1851. Then Stanley brought the

* By the end of Gladstone's life these proportions had changed to 21 per cent for debt servicing, 37 per cent for defence and 20 per cent for civil government.

Tories strongly out against the tax, and Russell's dying Whig government succeeded in getting it extended, for one year not three, only by accepting a select committee to improve the methods by which it was assessed and collected. Gladstone wisely refused to serve on that committee, which searched for a method of differentiating between realized and precarious incomes, or unearned and earned ones as they would be called today, but ended by finding this as impracticable as it was desirable. Disraeli, however, first jettisoned the declaration of Stanley (by then both Derby and Prime Minister) by renewing the tax for another year in his 1852 spring budget, and then attempted differentiation (which implied permanence) in his ill-fated December one. An attack on the illogicality which flowed from this ill-thought-out attempt was one of the principal arguments on which Gladstone had led the Peelites and the Whigs into the lobby to defeat that budget.

This was the unpromising background against which Gladstone had to square the circle of justifying his dependence on an excoriated tax and, if he was to transcend the short-term improvisations of both Whig and Disraelian finance, escape from the constriction of a year-to-year renewal. He did so with a strategic daring worthy of Alexander the Great and a thundering eloquence worthy of Demosthenes. By admitting its disadvantages he touched the base that most of those who had to provide his majority were committed against the tax:

> there are circumstances attending its operation which make it difficult, perhaps impossible, at any rate in our opinion not desirable, to maintain it as a portion of the permanent and ordinary finances of this country: The public feeling of its inequality is a fact most important in itself. The inquisition it entails is a most serious disadvantage; and the frauds to which it leads are an evil which it is not possible to characterize in terms too strong.

At the same time he built the tax up as a most formidable instrument of public policy, giving it the same brooding strength which Stonehenge had imprinted on his mind eighteen days before – 'an engine of gigantic power for great national purposes' were his exact words. He reviewed the history of the tax in terms which, while inevitably tendentious, were at once sonorous and relevant. We can almost feel him holding the House in the hollow of his hand as he describes how this tax changed the financing of the Napoleonic Wars from a debauch to a model of probity. The words and the terms he employs capture a sense of what may be called historic actuality which is alien to the House of Commons today: 'Now the scene shifts. In 1798 Mr Pitt first initiates the income tax, and immediately a change begins.' Then he moves on to its revival by Peel, but hardly in the flat prose of normal bureaucratic fiscalese:

> Sir Robert Peel, in 1842, called forth from repose this giant, who had once shielded us in war, to come and assist our industrious toils in peace; and if the first income tax produced enduring and memorable results, so, I am free to say, at less expenditure by far in money, and without those painful accompaniments of havoc, war and bloodshed, has the second income tax. The second income tax has been the instrument by which you have introduced, and by which I hope ere long you may perfect, the reform, the effective reform, of your commercial and fiscal system; and I for one am bold enough to hope – nay, to expect and believe – that, in reforming your own fiscal and commercial system, you have laid the foundations of similar reforms – slow perhaps, but certain in their progress – through every country of the civilized world.'[15]*

This was a classical passage, illustrating nearly all the facets of Gladstone's middle-phase oratory. There was the initial grandiloquence, almost but not quite over the hill. There were the archaisms, as they appear today and were even then on the edge, of 'ere long' and 'nay', there were the platitudes of 'I, for one, am bold enough to hope', there was the profusion of subordinate clauses, there was the argumentative use of the second person plural, 'you have introduced', 'you may perfect', and there was the utopian international optimism of mid-century England, the hope of freedom seeping down from the centre to the lesser limbs. There was, above all, the compulsive persuasiveness, the almost anaesthetizing quality of the eloquence.

Such a touch of chloroform was indeed necessary, for the next stage of the argument was breathtaking enough to inflict a considerable trauma upon any non-prepared mind. He announced a seven-year prolongation of the tax, more than twice what Pitt or Peel had ever ventured, seven times the hesitant fumbling of 1851 and 1852. He also extended the tax to Ireland and reduced the exemption limit from £150 of annual income to £100. But he did it in a way which, while fiscally responsible, made it extraordinarily difficult for the opponents of the income tax to engage with him. The tax was to be at sevenpence in the pound from 1853 to 1855, at sixpence from 1855 to 1857, and at

* Some of the phrases in this passage have a slight sense of bathos when it is recalled that the total yield of the tax at that stage was no more than £5½ million a year.

fivepence for three years from then. 'Under this proposal,' he concluded the passage, 'on the 5th of April, 1860 the income tax will by law expire.'

He had pre-empted the decade, harnessed the income tax to his immediate need for room to reduce indirect imposts while enticing its opponents by what appeared to be a realistic programme for its abolition, and also put them on good behaviour to support the Chancellor in his rigorous control of public expenditure in order that his and their objective might be achieved. He appeared to have reconciled imagination with rigour. (He did not of course foresee the Crimean War, but in this he was no more and no less prescient than his listeners.) And in the slipstream he was able to carry much further the central Peelite policy of getting rid of protective, discriminating and labyrinthine customs duties: 123 articles were entirely removed from the tariff in the 1853 budget, and the duties on another 135 were significantly reduced. The excise duty on soap also went completely. Lansdowne, Graham and Wood had tried to retain half of it, but Gladstone resisted this, and brought cleanliness twice as near to godliness as their compromise would have done.

From the moment that he sat down (after a final sentence of 344 words) Gladstone's triumph began to reverberate throughout the political world. Russell, as leader of the House, wrote to the Queen that the budget statement was 'one of the most powerful financial speeches ever made. Mr Pitt, in the days of his glory, might have been more imposing, but he could not have been more persuasive.'[16] Aberdeen both passed on the Queen's expression of delight 'at the great success of Mr Gladstone's speech last night' and added his own congratulations, which were made much more than formal by his concluding 'if the existence of my government shall be prolonged, it will be your work'.[17] Clarendon, the Foreign Secretary (who had changed jobs with Russell a few weeks earlier), wrote that it was 'the most perfect financial statement ever heard within the walls of Parlt. for such it is allowed to be by friend and foe'.[18] Charles Greville, clerk to the Privy Council and most sensitive appraiser of the market value of political reputations, recorded that the budget 'had raised Gladstone to a great political elevation, and what is of far greater consequence than the measure itself, has given the country assurance of a *man* equal to great political necessities and fit to lead parties and direct governments'.[19] Prince Albert said that he would 'certainly have cheered had [he] a seat in the House'; and at the French imperial court they appeared to discuss little else except 'the boldness and comprehensiveness' of the British budget.

This acclaim was more than sufficient to carry Gladstone over a misjudgement which might in other circumstances have been damaging. He attempted a major conversion operation designed to reduce the rate of interest on a portion of the national debt to 2½ per cent, but got a take-up at the reduced rate of only a couple of million pounds, whereas he had hoped for twenty or thirty million. He attributed the failure partly to Disraeli's 'malignant opposition', which crucially (and improperly, he alleged) delayed the date of the offer past a major turning-point in the sentiment of the market. But in a long-distance (1897) retrospect he also blamed himself for 'an incessant course of sailing near the wind', which habit of 'daring navigation' he attributed to his Oak Farm and Hawarden estate experience, where he had learnt to choose this course because 'there was really no other hope'.[20]

Despite the setback, the wave of success on which he emerged from the budget and its aftermath was such as to make hubris a more likely danger than dismay. There was however remarkably little indication of even the most extravagant praise going to his head. Gladstone, like de Gaulle, was conceited rather than vain. He had great certainty about his intellectual positions, frequently although they could change (but not under pressure from others), and this meant that he was both undismayed in adversity and unflattered in success. He did not greatly need the approval of his peers, although in later life, again like de Gaulle, he became addicted to *bains de foule* (immersions in enthusiastic crowds). He could castigate himself for moral weakness, but that was a matter between himself and his God. On matters of intellectual and oratorical performance he knew his strength and did not much need others to tell him of it. Like all human beings he did not reject praise, but he did not wallow in it. In his diaries he took it all in his stride, and in his summing up of the year, eight months later, he did not mention his spring triumph. 'The singular blessing of this year', he wrote, 'has been *health*. Without this among them I do not know how I could have gone through its labours. It has not I grieve to say been a year of advance towards purity, taken as a whole.'[21]

The 1853 budget marked not only an enhancement of the office of Chancellor and of the importance of his spring festival, but also a major strengthening of Gladstone's personal position among his colleagues. After 18 April he would have had much less difficulty in getting his proposals through the Cabinet than he experienced in the ten days before it. The truth of the adage about success having a thousand (or, in the case of this Cabinet, fifteen) parents, while failure was an orphan, has rarely been better illustrated.

A short time later Gladstone drew attention to the composition of the fifteen and to his position among them. 'No Cabinet could have been more aristocratically composed than that over which Lord Aberdeen presided,' he said. 'I myself was the only one of fifteen noblemen and gentlemen who composed it, who could not fairly be said to belong to that class.'[22] While it may be doubted whether Gladstone's social origin was markedly different from that of Molesworth, there was nonetheless general validity in the point, which he no doubt made with as much pride as humbleness, even though he always had a certain deference for rank. There could be no question, after April 1853, of his being employed as a professional to roll the pitch as well as to score the runs. Aberdeen was right. Gladstone had given the government such hold on life as it possessed, and he was more pivotal to it than the Foreign Secretary (Clarendon), the leader of the House of Commons (Russell), perhaps even than the Prime Minister (Aberdeen).

His only political equal was Palmerston, temporarily languishing in the Home Office, and contention between them (and indeed almost total difference of political outlook) ran through the next twelve years of Gladstone's career. It was more an incompatibility than a rivalry – the twenty-five-year difference in age was too wide for the latter, and Disraeli was already ensconced as the rival *en titre*. But Palmerston and Gladstone were to spend eight years of the next twelve within the same Cabinets, whereas Disraeli and Gladstone were never colleagues, although the margin by which they missed being so was at times narrow. And, as is well known, personal tensions within parties are mostly greater than those across parties. However that may be, there was no doubt after the spring of 1853 that Gladstone, with Palmerston and Disraeli, was one of the trio of stars of British politics, although one who could shoot down as well as up. It took him a couple of decades more to outshine both the others, but that he eventually and assuredly did.

10

The Decline and Fall of the Aberdeen Coalition

Despite the personal triumph Gladstone had achieved with the budget of 1853, he at that stage was essentially an isolated figure, even though one of great individual power. He wished to work neither with Palmerston nor with Disraeli. In addition, although he did not exactly disapprove of him as he did of the other two, he and Russell were instinctively quarrelsome with each other. This three-directional repugnance on Gladstone's part meant that he was out of office (even though no one else was very stably in) for three-quarters of the 1850s.

The Peelites gradually subsided around him. The five most prominent other than himself, Aberdeen, Sidney Herbert, Goulburn, Graham and Newcastle (Lincoln), all died between 1857 and 1864, and only Herbert and Newcastle held office after 1855. Gladstone's passage into the full embrace of Liberalism was solitary and hazardous. At times his political prospects looked at least as bleak as after his perverse resignation from the Board of Trade in 1845. In 1856 Aberdeen wrote to him with avuncular concern: 'With an admitted superiority of character and intellectual power above any other member, I fear that you do not really possess the sympathy of the House at large. . . .'[1] And two years later, when his acceptance of a bizarre mission to the Ionian Isles took him out of British politics for a whole winter, he looked like a man who was marginalizing himself before he was fifty. Yet within three months of the not very successful conclusion of that mission, Gladstone boxed all compasses by first voting to keep Disraeli (and Derby) in office and then, when that vote had proved ineffective, accepting a return to the Treasury under Palmerston and remaining Chancellor, in contentious but continuing partnership with him, for longer than anyone had done since the unmemorable Vansittart in the first decade of the Liverpool government. This 1859 return was the beginning of the second and much more governmental phase of his political life. The first phase, from his election for Newark, had covered twenty-seven years, of which he had been in office for only six and a half. The second was to extend over thirty-five years, with nineteen of them in office. This nevertheless meant that, during the sixty-two and a half years between his first entry into the House of Commons and his leaving it for the last time in 1895, he was for thirty-seven of them a private member. His ration of office was substantial, but by no means such as to make him essentially a Treasury-bench politician, one who was out of his natural element when he could not put his feet upon the Commons table from the government side, as had been the case with Pitt and Palmerston and was to be so with Asquith and Baldwin.

In the spring of 1853, however, and on his 'great political elevation', Gladstone had nearly another two years of his first term as Chancellor to go until the collapse of the Aberdeen government, and his unwillingness to continue in the Palmerston one which followed it, sent him on his second excursion into the political wilderness. Broadly speaking the first of these two years was highly productive and the second vexatious. Essentially the Crimean War was the cause of the degression. It was a war with which Gladstone was always ill at ease. He did not oppose it at the outset. Indeed in one notable and maybe decisive conversation with his Prime Minister he took a markedly more pro-war line than did Aberdeen.* But he never had his heart in it, brought no urgency to its winning, financed it only reluctantly and became an early advocate of peace without victory. As a result, rather like R. A. Butler at the time of Suez, he got the worst of both worlds and offended all parties, including himself, becoming guilt-ridden for his initial attitude. He liked issues on which he could fulminate with moral certainty. The Crimean War was the reverse of that, and he accordingly tried to circumnavigate it. The war was not fatal to him, as it was to 18,000 British soldiers and to the premiership of Aberdeen, but it was damaging, and was a substantial cause of his quinquennium of political setback which began in the mid-1850s. Contemplating these years, it is difficult not to be struck by Gladstone's luck in being able to fit his whole career into the long years of mostly unbroken peace which followed Waterloo and without having to engage with the Boer War, let alone 1914–18 and the slaughter on the Somme. He was not made for war, not from want of courage or of

* 'He [Aberdeen] said how could he bring himself to fight for the Turks? I replied we were not fighting for the Turks, but we were warning Russia off the forbidden ground.' (Entry for 22 February 1854, *Diaries*, IV, p. 595n.)

patriotism, but because the martial arts stirred in him a sense more of waste than of excitement or admiration.

Nonetheless the long-running dispute about the respective rights of protection over the Christian holy places in Palestine enjoyed by the Greek and the Latin faiths, which was as much the trigger of the Crimean War as the Sarajevo assassination was of the First World War (although with a slower-acting mechanism) was a subject which might have been expected, by virtue both of its religious content and of its geographical location, to excite Gladstone's interest and imagination.

This dispute entered a dangerous phase early in 1853. There is, however, little evidence that the issue engaged Gladstone's mind until after a long Scottish holiday visit from 17 August to 1 October, and not seriously until after the outbreak of war between Russia and Turkey later in that October and the destruction of much of the Turkish fleet off Sinope on 30 November. This was partly because, although it was a good period for Gladstone with more sense of political momentum, less financial or family worries and less sexual frenzy than in at least the four preceding years, he was heavily occupied with two half-connected subjects. The first was the reform of the University of Oxford and the second was the reform of the British civil service.

The report of the Oxford Commission had been published in the spring of 1852, but it was only a year later, with Gladstone's first budget behind him and with his authority enhanced by the reputation which it gave him, that he began to take the lead in University reform. Bitterly though he had opposed the setting up of the Commission in 1850, denouncing it as illegal as well as undesirable, he had been impressed by its deliberations and report, and decided that the Oxford's best chance of preserving as much as possible of its traditional and clerical pattern was to seize the opportunity of guiding its own reform. In the Queen's Speech of November 1852 the Derby government had envisaged legislation after the University had been allowed a year for reflection on the recommendations. The Aberdeen government could have repudiated the undertaking, but under guidance from Gladstone it decided not to do so, and the Chancellor of the Exchequer, acting more in a constituency than a Treasury capacity, took responsibility for devising a government measure and for piloting it through Parliament.

This bill was not ready for introduction to the House of Commons until 17 March 1854, but it had been central to Gladstone's thoughts for much of the preceding twelve months and dominating, more so indeed than the 6 March budget of that year, since the beginning of

January. Not only did he engage in the vast correspondence already cited; he also immersed himself in detail, carefully studying, for example, the statutes of the individual colleges. On 8 March, only two days after the budget, Gladstone's presentation of which, with unusual restraint, was confined to two hours, he was up until 4.30 in the morning working on the Oxford bill. It was formally introduced by Russell as the leader of the House of Commons, but Gladstone made the substantive speech replying to the debate, which moved A. P. Stanley, who had been the secretary of the Commission and was to become Dean of Westminster in 1864, to describe it as 'a superb speech . . . in which, for the first time, all the arguments for our report were worked up in the most effective manner'. Stanley produced two penetrating comments on Gladstone's parliamentary style. First he criticized him for a vain endeavour to reconcile his new with his old position: 'with this exception I listened to the speech with the greatest delight'. And then he praised him with an unusual slant. 'One great charm of his speaking is its exceeding good humour. There is great vehemence but no bitterness.'[2]

The Oxford bill then ground its way through committee, report stage and third reading until it went to the Lords in early July, where it was not greatly mutilated, in spite of the opposition of Derby (who had become Chancellor of the University in 1853 following the death of Wellington). What did it do? Essentially it broke the Anglican monopoly and opened the way for Dissenters to matriculate and proceed to bachelors' degrees. There were supporting changes. The Hebdomadal Board, hitherto confined to Heads of colleges, was replaced by an elected council. This may sound a somewhat technical change, but when seen against the background of the vast oligarchic powers which the Heads of Houses (who never retired even if, as in the case of Dr Routh of Magdalen, they reached the age of ninety-nine and had occupied the post for sixty-five years) had presumed to exercise in the 1830s and 1840s, it was a change of significance for the tone of Oxford. The elected and more heterogeneous body never attempted to exercise the absolute powers which were epitomized by its predecessor's 1843 action of forbidding Pusey, then Regius Professor of Hebrew and a canon of Christ Church, to preach in the University for two years, or their 1845 action of reducing W. G. Ward, Fellow of Balliol, to the status of an undergraduate, and being frustrated in their attempt to condemn Newman's Tract 90 only by the veto of dedicated High Church proctors. It is now a long time since the formula of proctorial veto – *Nobis*

Procturatoribus non placet – has rung around the Sheldonian Theatre in opposition to the Vice-Chancellor.

The Vice-Chancellor was empowered to open private halls. This was a provision to which Gladstone attached considerable importance and carried in committee by 205 votes to 113. It could be described as a Christ Church man's attempt half to democratize the University without endangering the privileges of the House. It was a two-tier solution. Let the core colleges continue to be mostly the preserve of the rich, but let there be a periphery around them through which those of more modest means could get Oxford degrees and participate (to some extent) in the life of the University. It has proved an effective even if somewhat condescending provision. Permanent private halls (which has become the term of art) continue to exist today, although many of the earlier ones have graduated into full colleges of the University, as have the five women's foundations, to which it also opened the way.

In the wake of legislation there were other significant changes. College statutes were reformed, non-resident clerical sinecures were weeded out and tutorial supervision much improved. The honours examinations, hitherto restricted to Literae Humaniores and Mathematics, were widened to include Schools of Law and Modern History and later Natural Science, English and other faculty subjects.[3]

There are several points, some of them contradictory, to be made about Gladstone's role in promoting this bill. First, his performance was heroically self-reliant. He did it nearly all himself. Russell, without whom the Commission and therefore the bill would never have existed, faded after the early stages. This was as well, for there was great mutual prickliness, exacerbated by a long-running row which escalated into a major cause of Cabinet dissension over Gladstone's determination to dismiss for general maladministration the Commissioner of Woods and Forests, T. F. Kennedy, who was senior enough to be a Privy Councillor, and whom Russell was equally determined to protect. Gladstone was assisted on the Oxford bill in the House of Commons by the Solicitor-General, Richard Bethell, later the first Lord Westbury and Lord Chancellor under Palmerston, and outside it by his old friend Robert Phillimore, who was a good draftsman. He also received a lot of often self-cancelling advice from Oxford. But the responsibility which he himself undertook, not only for sustaining the bill in the House of Commons but for the detail of its provisions, was something which no minister would contemplate today.

It also showed remarkable courage on his part. He was always a controversial member for the University. He had been opposed when he first stood in 1847 and again in 1853 at the 'technical' bye-election made necessary by his appointment as Chancellor of the Exchequer and was to be so yet again on reappointment to the Exchequer in 1859. This was very unusual in the history of the Oxford seat. After Gladstone was defeated there in 1865 there was no contested election in the constituency until 1918. And that 1865 defeat (the surprising thing was that it did not occur earlier) was made almost inevitable by Gladstone embracing the dangerous issue of University reform in the 1850s. Yet he did so, when convinced that it was necessary, against his earlier views, and against the wishes of many of his former supporters, with a determination which was as complete as was his clear-sightedness about the risks that he was running.

On the other hand one of the most important provisions of the bill was carried against his opposition. He spoke and voted against the matriculation (admission) of Dissenters. He did not do so with great passion, for he had got himself into one of his convoluted positions. He was at least half in favour of such liberalization, but thought it should be a reserved question, and dealt with, if by Parliament at all, in a separate measure. Fortunately the House of Commons was less convoluted and defeated Gladstone and the government by a decisive 251 to 162. He did not seem to take it tragically and wrote to various Oxford dignitaries saying that 'Parliament having unhappily [so] determined', they had better make the best of the matter. In the course of the further stages of the bill the freedom at matriculation was extended to the bachelors' degree, and then, seventeen years later and under Gladstone's first premiership, religious tests were removed for all except the strictly ecclesiastical appointments.

On the other issues which produced a government defeat in the House of Commons Gladstone was on the advanced side and the majority of the House of Commons on the reactionary side, and he responded to this with more dismay than he had to the defeat on Dissenters. On 16 June a new clause moved by Roundell Palmer (as Lord Selborne one of Gladstone's future Lord Chancellors) to protect closed scholarships and traditional school–college links (Winchester –New College and Westminster–Christ Church, to take the two most powerful Oxford examples) was carried against the government: 'a great blow' for the Oxford bill, Gladstone noted. None of this, however, much detracted from the unusual phenomenon of a considerable non-financial legislative triumph for the Chancellor of the Exchequer.

Gladstone's parallel efforts to produce a civil service recruited on the basis of talent rather than of patronage were less immediately fruitful, but it may be that this acorn eventually led to a more important tree than did the Oxford changes. To some extent, however, Gladstone saw the two issues as linked, and both placed him in somewhat surprising alliance with the liberal Erastian Benjamin Jowett, who was anxious to turn Oxford (and Balliol in particular) from a mixture of Anglican seminary and gentlemen's finishing school into a serious forcing house for those who governed Britain and the Empire. And certainly Jowett himself, when he became Master of Balliol in 1870, was a superb practitioner of the art of turning out young men who were well qualified for the best jobs, and then making sure, through a network of college influence, that they got them. Thus in a sense a new patronage came to replace the old one of aristocratic connection and political jobbery, but it interposed a hurdle of intellectual merit over which the applicant had to be able to jump.

Despite Jowett's very different religious approach this was much in accordance with Gladstone's evolving views about how he wanted to see the public service recruited. He by no means wanted it democratized in the sense of being open to those who had not been burnished with a classical education in the most privileged academies. He was eager that the public service should be staffed by 'gentlemen', and that their fine minds should not be wasted on the mechanical aspects of the work, which should be separated as rigidly as possible from the intellectual aspects, thereby foreshadowing the administrative grade and its mandarin denizens which was to be such a feature of British public administration for a hundred years. But he was equally keen that they should be educated gentlemen able to surmount any test of merit. It was a modified version of the 'clerisy' approach, although now with much less religious restriction, which fifteen years before he had hoped could run the whole polity of Britain.

The running was made in the Indian public service, which was thrown open to competition for any British-born applicant in an 1853 bill, sponsored by Charles Wood, President of the Board of Control, and assisted by Robert Lowe, then at the beginning of his career, later to be Chancellor of the Exchequer under Gladstone, a difficult, uncompromising, brave man. Partly inspired by this Indian example, Gladstone in April of that year commissioned Sir Stafford Northcote and Sir Charles Trevelyan to produce a report dealing with the home civil service, including the Colonial Office but not the Foreign Office, in which latter department

Palmerston had introduced a very limited measure of meritocracy, based mainly on the possession of a clear bold handwriting, a few years before.

Northcote, who had succeeded to a baronetcy in 1851 and was to go on to become both Chancellor and Foreign Secretary, as well as Conservative leader in the House of Commons, where he was a somewhat over-awed *vis-à-vis* to Gladstone in his second premiership, before ending up as Earl of Iddesleigh, was then thirty-five years old and Gladstone's private secretary at the Treasury. He had been with him in that capacity at the Board of Trade in 1842 and had been urgently summoned back in Gladstone's Carlton Club letter on the night of the latter's great defeat of Disraeli in 1852.

Trevelyan was ten years older than Northcote and had served for the first fifteen years of his adult life in India (during which time he had married Macaulay's sister) before spending the two middle decades of the century as an assistant secretary (the equivalent today of a second permanent secretary) in the Treasury. He had administered Irish famine relief, perhaps with more logic than humanity, in 1845–7, and he was to go back to India in 1859, first as Governor of Madras and then as finance member of the Viceroy's Council. He was the epitome of a mid-Victorian public servant.

Between them they produced for Gladstone by late November 1853 what became known as one of the great state papers of the nineteenth century. Gladstone read it, interlaced with a report on decimal coinage, some of Horace Walpole's letters and a few chapters of Jane Austen's *Pride and Prejudice*, at Hawarden on 30 November. The two central recommendations were competitive examinations and a central board for recruitment to all the home departments. He reacted with enthusiasm to both, although later he became somewhat impatient with signs of tactical backsliding on the part of the authors. They thought it wiser to exclude (for the moment at any rate) the Treasury satraps of Customs and Excise and the Inland Revenue, although as Gladstone correctly pointed out it was in precisely these two departments that the largest number of posts lay. And they also suggested that, between those who had passed the examination, the First Lord of the Treasury should be allowed to choose after giving 'due weight to the recommendations of his colleagues and also of his Parliamentary supporters'. As Gladstone again pointed out, this would be to pretend that patronage had been slain while allowing it to wriggle back. 'Pray let this disappear,' he magisterially wrote to Trevelyan on 3 December.

Yet Trevelyan and Northcote had a more lively sense of political realities than did the famous politician at the head of their department. The Queen grumbled and, unusually in this phase, was not brought into line on Gladstone's side by Prince Albert. 'Where is the application of the principle of public competitions to stop?'[4] she asked apprehensively, perhaps influenced by Lord John Russell's view that the 'harshly republican scheme was as hostile to the monarchy as it was to the aristocracy'. Russell's extreme Whiggery made him fairly indifferent, except for purposes of argument, to the former aspect, but he certainly cared about the latter, and proved a jagged rock of opposition which Gladstone could not bulldoze out of the way. On 20 January 1854 he wrote Russell a powerfully argued, but not wholly tactful, letter which concluded with a 115-word sentence. In it he claimed that the Glorious Revolution had marked the change from prerogative to patronage, that since then there had been a movement from bribery to influence, and that this was a process which must continue. This was peculiarly rash ground, for Russell regarded himself as the keeper of the bones of the Glorious Revolution and also believed that, occasional limited extensions of the franchise apart, it had settled constitutional issues for all time. It did not require upsetting by the moralizing son of a Liverpool merchant, with dangerous religious enthusiasms and no adequate respect for the Whig cousinage. His reply to Gladstone's ten pages was dismissively brief: 'I hope no change will be made, and I certainly must protest against it.'[5]

Gladstone's error was that he did not make an obvious deal with Russell, who was currently engaged in promoting one of his Reform Bills. It found little favour within the government, let alone on the other side of the House of Commons. Palmerston was opposed to the extent of threatening to resign, Aberdeen was lukewarm, and Gladstone wholly unhelpful. He deployed a 'too clever by half' argument, 'This is *my* contribution to parliamentary reform,' he wrote on 3 January to Graham (First Lord of the Admiralty) about his civil service plans. It would have been much more sensible for Gladstone to have moved more quickly to the position on the franchise which he was to occupy within less than a decade and to have at least tempted Russell with a pact of mutual support for each other's pet reforms.

As it was, Gladstone ran into a wall of Whig hostility at the crucial Cabinet on 26 January. The Peelites were mostly content to go along with what he wanted, although Graham was cool, but with the exception of Granville the Whig half of the coalition, which provided most of the votes in the House of Commons, was unanimously hostile. As a result

1854 was much less productive for civil service than for Oxford reform. It was not until after the fall of the Aberdeen government that Gladstone was able to make his trio of notable parliamentary speeches on open entry to the public services, two in the summer of 1855 and one in the spring of 1856. Nevertheless the seed which he had sown in 1853 was an unsuppressible one which, like so many other burgeoning mid-Victorian reforms, came to full fruition during his first and most fructuous 1868–74 premiership. This 1854 dispute illustrated the capacity for mutual irritation between Gladstone and Russell, and the incompatibility of both provenance and instinctive political attitudes which lay behind it. It was within a year to prove fatal to the Aberdeen government.

On 27 March 1854 Russell had written pointedly but with apparent good humour to Gladstone, 'I fear my mind is exclusively occupied with the war [which Britain and France had that day declared, an event unnoticed in Gladstone's diaries] and the Reform Bill, and yours with University reform.'[6] On 25 May, however, when Gladstone had unavailingly wound up a debate on a maladroit second attempt by Russell to resolve the Rothschild difficulty about the parliamentary oath, he petulantly wrote: 'H of C 4½–7½. Spoke 1h. & voted 247:251 on Lord J R's Oaths Bill: wh Bill was from the first a great mistake of his and his only.'[7] (For a great orator reluctantly to be persuaded to give succour to a disapproved-of colleague and to fail to bring it off is no doubt an almost perfect recipe for exasperation.) Then the row about the Commissioner of Woods and Forests gathered a momentum of bitterness over the summer, and at church on Christmas morning Gladstone put first among his thoughts and self-reproaches his worry about his 'cabinet feud' with Russell.

The two leading Whigs, Russell and Palmerston, badly though they often got on with each other, were united in finding the Peelite elements in the government inadequately bellicose. And with Aberdeen Prime Minister, Gladstone Chancellor, Graham First Lord of the Admiralty, Sidney Herbert Secretary at War, and Newcastle Secretary for War and the Colonies (under the curious split system which prevailed until 1857) the Peelites were very powerfully placed to obstruct a war. Palmerston resigned in December 1853 against the dilatory approach to support for Turkey, and was persuaded by Aberdeen to remain as Home Secretary only on terms which pushed the Prime Minister in a more warlike direction than he would have wished.

After the war began, however, it was Russell who made the more trouble. The Whigs in 1852, like the Tories in the Asquith coalition of 1915, had accepted an unsatisfactory set of portfolios and retaliated for their own bad bargaining by complaining about the lack of adequate war direction. Russell, with a presumption much exceeding that of Bonar Law just over sixty years later, thought that he ought to be Prime Minister, and indeed believed that he had some sort of assurance from Aberdeen that he would soon make way for him. ('Soon', however, as Eden found with Churchill and Erhard with Adenauer, is not a precise contractual term.) Russell also thought that Palmerston should replace Newcastle.

These beliefs led to growing acrimony. Already by 15 February 1854, a Cabinet dinner lasted from 7.45 p.m. to 2.15 in the morning, and it was not conviviality which accounted for the lateness of the break-up. By December of that year relations were in a permanent state of bitterness, with Russell threatening to resign on the 4th, another dreadful Cabinet dinner on the 6th, and 'a childish scene' at a Saturday Cabinet on the 10th. Russell's resignation remained in a state of suspended animation over the brief Christmas holidays. When Parliament met on 23 January 1855 Newcastle had decided to resign out of honourable guilt.

Roebuck, Radical MP for Sheffield, had put down a motion for a parliamentary committee of enquiry into the war, and Russell announced that he could not conscientiously oppose the motion and must therefore reactivate his suspended resignation. Palmerston incongruously took Russell's place as leader of the House of Commons, but made a very weak reply to Roebuck. He was no better as an 'air-raid shelter' for Aberdeen than Churchill was accused of being for Chamberlain in May 1940. Gladstone tried harder three days later, and denounced the presumptions of the legislature in trying by means of the committee of enquiry to invade the functions of the executive. But denouncing the jury is rarely a wise way of winning a verdict, and the House voted by the massive majority of 304 to 148 for Roebuck. That was the end of the Aberdeen government. The Cabinet met only for 'friendly adieus' on the following day, 30 January.

This collapse did not necessarily mean even the temporary end of office for Gladstone. The uncertainty which resulted from the fall of the Aberdeen coalition was extreme even by the standards of instability which marked the whole period between the end of the Peel government in 1846 and the accession of Gladstone himself to the premiership in 1868. There were at least three possible Prime Ministers, all of whom were prepared, perhaps even eager, to keep Gladstone as Chancellor. Gladstone, however, with an uncanny stubbornness, attached himself to the one manifestly impossible solution, which was the return of Aberdeen to 10 Downing Street, and did so with a sophistical ingenuity which must have infuriated nearly every other player in the game, and ended up by generally damaging his own reputation and ensuring an ignominious end for the Peelites as a collective and influential group.

During the four weeks between the farewell meeting of the Aberdeen Cabinet and Gladstone's surrendering the seals of the Exchequer to George Cornewall Lewis on 28 February, almost every combination was mooted or tried, and Gladstone (and some others as well) displayed a skill in thinking up difficulties which was a fine tribute to his resourcefulness. It was perhaps less of a tribute to his constructive statesmanship in the middle of a war which, while not threatening Britain's survival, was nonetheless taking a severe toll of men and reputations.

First Palmerston came to Gladstone with a proposition that they should both serve under Derby, for whom the Queen had sent. Palmerston was to lead in the Commons and Gladstone was to remain at the Exchequer. This meant Disraeli giving up both the posts which he had occupied in the 1852 government. He was however willing to make the sacrifice. Sidney Herbert for the Peelites was also to be included, but not Graham. Gladstone made Graham's exclusion a sticking point, and as Palmerston was not very keen, really wanting the foreign secretaryship or indeed the premiership for himself, and Derby, who never had much thrust to office, was not enthusiastic either, the combination collapsed. Disraeli thought at the time that this was a major missed opportunity, and Gladstone came to think so later. Certainly it was the last real chance of Conservative reunion (although that might have been more coherently achieved without Palmerston), and as Gladstone subsequently told the Queen that 'she would have little peace or comfort in these matters [stable ministries] until parliament should have returned to its old organisation in two political parties',[8] he might have done more to bring it about.

Next, Gladstone went to see Lord Lansdowne at the latter's request. Lansdowne, then aged seventy-four, was a trusted and moderate Whig who had served in Cabinets since that of Grenville in 1806. He might have made an acceptable although hardly dynamic Prime Minister, and had been sounded out at Windsor that morning. Gladstone and he then made a leisurely *tour d'horizon* in which Gladstone poured cold water on the possibilities first of Russell, then of Palmerston and finally of

Clarendon as Prime Minister, and said that of the Whigs Lansdowne himself would be the best. Lansdowne then asked him if he would continue as Chancellor under him. If so, he would persevere. If not, not. Gladstone in effect said no. He was disillusioned with the previous coalition, and was not prepared to try it again under anyone other than Aberdeen. He thought it would be better if Lansdowne tried to form an homogeneous Whig government. As Lansdowne had already excluded this course it was not a constructive suggestion. Forty-two years later Gladstone more than endorsed this view. It was his second error in two days. 'This I think was one of the greatest, perhaps the greatest, errors I ever committed.'[9]

On the following day Russell came to see Gladstone. He too had been asked if he could form a government. Would Gladstone continue in his office under him? Gladstone recorded Russell's tone as 'low and doubtful'. It cannot have been made any less so by Gladstone's refusal, rejecting the suggestion that he might take time to think. So, in three days' short work, Gladstone had in effect achieved by default the solution he least wanted, which was to make Palmerston Prime Minister, an outcome for which public opinion appeared to be clamouring. Palmerston received the commission on 4 February and came to see Gladstone that afternoon, once again offering the Exchequer. Once again Gladstone declined, but not perhaps as definitely as he had done with Russell. The following day was spent in a scurry of consultation among the Peelites, the process made more complicated by Graham being ill in bed. But they were in a greater difficulty than that. They tried to hold the line that they would not serve in a Cabinet which did not include Aberdeen, preferably as Prime Minister, but if not at least as a member and as a guarantor of a sensible attitude (that is, not too bellicose) to 'war and peace'.

Aberdeen himself did not agree with them. He knew that his return to the premiership was out of the question, and he had no intention of serving in a subordinate capacity under Palmerston. But he believed that the others ought to accept office. The matter then came to turn on the extent to which Aberdeen would endorse the government, although not a member of it, in the House of Lords. On the Monday (5 February) he would commit himself only to expressing the hope that 'it might do right'. Gladstone gasped with relief. He had a new excuse for standing out, and that day closed with the Peelites still refusing. On the Tuesday, however, Aberdeen said that he would endorse, and the little band publicly changed their mind and agreed to join. Gladstone wrote of their submission in almost biblical terms: 'I had a message from P[almerston] that he would answer me but at night I went up to him.'[10] He spoke in equally emotional terms to Aberdeen – '... I hoped our conduct and reliance on him would tend to his eminence and honour' – and said, 'you are not to be of the Cabinet, but you are to be its tutelary deity'.[11] Gladstone remained as Chancellor, Graham as First Lord, and Herbert as Colonial Secretary.

The public shilly-shallying of 5–6 February was bad enough, but what followed was worse. These Peelite ministers were sworn in at Windsor on the 8th. On the 21st they all three resigned. Two other Peelites, Argyll and Canning, remained in the Cabinet. The ostensible and at least half the real reason for going was the decision of Palmerston and of the majority of the Cabinet to accept the committee of enquiry arising out of the Roebuck motion. Gladstone felt passionately that this was an unacceptable dilution of the power of the executive as well as a slur upon the Aberdeen government. He also felt that Palmerston's believing this was inevitable showed that the new government did not effectively command the confidence of the House of Commons. But nearly all resignations have an underlying as well as a triggering cause, and Gladstone's was that he had been unhappy at each of the three meetings of the Palmerston Cabinet which he had attended, and that his discontent was not made less by the knowledge, which cannot have been absent from his mind, that it had been his own conduct, as much as anything else, which had created the premiership of which he so disapproved.

So ended Gladstone's second substantial experience of office. He claimed that his resignation speech (of one and a half hours) on 23 February had led to his being 'much satisfied with the feeling of this House'. On this occasion even Gladstone must have been overshadowed by John Bright's unforgettable if somewhat florid eloquence on the same day when he had called up an image of 'the angel of death [who] has been abroad throughout the land' so that 'you may almost hear the beating of his wings'. But more important than oratorical upstaging was that Gladstone's departure and his behaviour over the previous month had left an impression of self-regard, bad judgement and wavering mind. Only his extraordinary force and talent enabled him to recover so spectacularly from such a setback.

— 11 —
Health and Wealth

After the 1853 budget Gladstone, while psychologically in much better shape than during his mid-century crisis, became exhausted and fell into indifferent physical health. The reaction from his budget strain and triumph followed a familiar time pattern. At first he was buoyed up. Then after about ten days he began to sleep badly and felt washed out. On 29 April he recorded in characteristically opaque terms: 'I felt at length a good deal overset: and had recourse to blue pill at night.' The next day he wrote: 'I only had 6 or 6½ hours of business but was all the worse for it and repeated the Blue Pill [presumably a sedative; it had moved to the upper case over the preceding twenty-four hours] – absenting myself from the H. of Commons.'[1]

Two days after that there occurred the unfortunate Wilson affair. A pathetic young Scot of that name, an unemployed commercial traveller, having seen Gladstone talking to two prostitutes near the Haymarket, tried to blackmail him with the threat of exposure unless he procured him a public service post, preferably in the Inland Revenue department. Gladstone was both too innocent and too wise to fall for that, and handed Wilson over to the police. As a result he had to visit Vine Street police station that night, make depositions at Marlborough Street magistrates' court three days later, and attend (silently) the trial at the Old Bailey five weeks after that. Wilson was sentenced to twelve months' hard labour, but was released after two of them as a result of Gladstone's pleas to Palmerston as Home Secretary.

The case did not do Gladstone much harm, although it occasioned a few raised eyebrows and no doubt further agitated him at a time of strain and pressure. 'This day my work touched 17 hours very nearly,' he recorded between the committal and the trial, and two days after that he developed erysipelas in his leg (a febrile disease which although local had killed his mother in 1835 and nearly killed his daughter Agnes in 1847). He was half confined to bed for three or four days. His immediate verdict (some time before that at the Old Bailey) on the Wilson incident was: 'These talkings of mine are certainly not within the rules of worldly prudence: I am not sure that Christian prudence sanctions them for such a one as me, but my aim and intention did not warrant the charge which doubtless has been sent to teach me wisdom and which I therefore welcome.'[2] It produced no increase in prudence, however. That summer his 'rescue work' was intense, seven such encounters being recorded in the last week of June. Yet there is a strong impression that the motivation was less frenzied than had been the case two or three years before.

Mainly as a result of concern about his health, he began that summer a frequent and dutiful habit of riding in London. For 11 May he recorded: 'Rode: an adventure, after so long a cessation.' He kept up the habit for nearly two years, except during the periods when the after-effects of his recurrent attacks of erysipelas precluded it, and often four or five times a week. Mostly it was a session of three-quarters of an hour in Hyde Park, but on one day in April 1854 he recorded himself as having ridden for an hour and twenty minutes 'into the country'. (What did that mean at the time? Chiswick?) Early that year he rode regularly with Sidney Herbert, but for the most part it was a solitary and somewhat contrived pursuit. On 4 April 1855, as abruptly as he had taken to the saddle in May 1853, he decided that he had had enough and assumed a policy of complete renunciation. 'Rode: my last; I am glad to get rid of a personal luxury and indulgence.'[3] However, he continued over that and subsequent summers and autumns in the country occasionally to get on a horse with one or other of his older children, who were beginning to grow up. Willy was fifteen, Agnes thirteen and Stephen eleven that year. And then, from the following spring, he began to ride again in London, but always, in contrast with his habit before the renunciation, with a child. This, accompanied by his other habits of giving them regular Latin lessons and seeking religious conversations whenever possible, meant that they saw much more of him than was common in upper-class families of the time, even when the father was far less occupied than was Gladstone.

Whether riding did his health any good, which was its ostensible purpose, seems more doubtful. He was in bed for most of two or three days (again with erysipelas in a leg) in early June 1853, he described himself as 'pretty well knocked up' at the end of the session in mid-August, and two weeks into his Scottish holiday trip he became severely ill. On 3 September he (and Catherine and Willy Gladstone) arrived at Dunrobin Castle on the Moray Firth to stay with the Duke and Duchess of Sutherland. On the 4th he took to his bed with his old friend 'erysipelas inflammations' (as he then put it) and remained there for eight days. Then he got gently better, but was unable to leave Dunrobin until his projected visit of a week or so had turned into a twenty-six-day one. Fortunately, as he recorded, 'the welcome was the kindest possible'. Then the Gladstones proceeded on a westerly arc which took them via Oban and Greenock to Drumlanrig in Dumfriesshire, where they stayed with the Buccleuchs for two days only, and without mishap.

They regained Hawarden on 1 October, but did not settle down there for an extended autumn, as had been Gladstone's habit at Fasque in the 1840s and was to become so, although a little more intermittently, at Hawarden itself in the later 1850s and 1860s. This was not simply a function of his being in office. No habit of presence in London, let alone a regular attendance at the Treasury, was expected of a Chancellor, or forthcoming even from one as diligent as Gladstone, during the months when Parliament was not sitting. It was more a function of the main house at Hawarden, which the Gladstones shared with Stephen Glynne until his death in 1874, only gradually being got back into shape after its Oak Farm-induced closure from 1847 to 1852. There were also frequent commands, issued more on a personal than a political basis, to stay with the Queen and Prince Albert at Windsor, which led him to graft on to these Windsor excursions London visits, which he used for encounters with both his Cabinet colleagues and his ladies. Thus he was at Windsor for two nights on 25 and 26 October (followed by one in London) and for three nights (this time with Catherine) from 9 to 12 November (followed by twelve in London and a veritable flurry of nine late-night excursions), and then at Windsor yet again from 4 to 6 January 1854. It was a strong indication of how good were Gladstone's relations with the royal couple during that noontide of their marriage. The relations of court and government were also generally closer than today.

Gladstone's first absence from Hawarden that autumn of 1853 was however occasioned more by his first tentative approach to demagogy than by any courtly devotion. On 10 October he went on a five-day visit to Manchester. He had never done anything like it before, and he was not to do so again until nine years later when he went to Newcastle and its surrounding shipyard towns, was received with even more enthusiasm and spoke with still less discretion than at Manchester. Thereafter these excursions among the populace were regarded as a Gladstone speciality, and one which became considerably disapproved of by, among others, the Queen and the majority of metropolitan politicians who, partly because they could not themselves evoke much enthusiasm in the provinces, decided that such activity was a vulgar pandering to the appetites of the masses.

This side of Gladstone's activities was to reach its peak in the Midlothian campaigns of 1879 and 1880, but it all began in Manchester in 1853 where the enthusiasm of his welcome and the continuing demands for oratory pleasantly surprised him as much as it dismayed his opponents when reports seeped back. The visit took place under the most respectable of auspices. The central purpose was to unveil a memorial statue to Sir Robert Peel on a site which was then in front of the old Royal Infirmary but which has since become Piccadilly Gardens. The Mayor and all the principal civic leaders and men of business were involved in welcoming and entertaining the visitor. He was accompanied throughout by his old friend 'Soapy Sam', the redoubtable Bishop Wilberforce of Oxford, who, whenever there was a pause in Gladstone's oratory, obligingly intervened with a powerful sermon. The double act was much in evidence at the luncheon in the Town Hall (which was not Waterhouse's 1868 masterpiece but its less exciting predecessor). Gladstone, who had gone on 'to the cracking of my voice' at the morning unveiling ceremony, gave them a further one and a quarter hours at the luncheon before the Bishop 'laid a strong hand upon the company'.[4]

Manchester, then known as 'Cottonopolis' and perceived throughout the world as the epitome of the whirling fierceness of the industrial revolution, was approached by the visitors with the slightly bewildered awe with which European travellers looked at New York and Chicago in the first half of the twentieth century. They were appropriately impressed with the size and advanced nature of everything from 'Mr Whitworth's tool manufactury to Mr Walton's innovating card-setting and other most curious machines'. But it was the size and composition of his audiences which most impressed Gladstone. His Peel speech was 'before a great assemblage – of men almost exclusively, and working men'. His Town Hall one and a quarter hours 'was greatly helped by a singularly attentive and favourable audience'. And on the next day, at the laying of the foundation stone for a new school, 'I had again to speak to an assembly of the *people*.'[5]

All these speeches, most of them impromptu, were made by Gladstone in the immediate aftermath of the outbreak of the Russo-Turkish war, and attention was naturally much focused on what tilt he could give to British government policy, hitherto unannounced on this issue. Morley wrote in rare criticism that he was 'cloudy', whereas Shannon thought that he 'ranged himself ostentatiously beside Aberdeen' (as opposed to the bellicosity of Palmerston, the leader of the pro-Turkish faction within the government). The two judgements are not incompatible. For Gladstone both to be cloudy and to put himself firmly alongside the Prime Minister required only an adequate degree of cloudiness in the attitude of Aberdeen, and that he was fully willing to supply. Gladstone committed himself to the maintenance of the integrity and independence of the Ottoman Empire, although with so many reservations about the 'political solecism' of a Muslim (or, as he called it, Mahometan) sovereign exercising despotic power over twelve million Christians as to drain away any possible enthusiasm for fighting to uphold this integrity. Furthermore he extolled all the non-martial virtues, denounced the 'glare of glory' and regretted that the policy of peace and negotiation, which was the only basis of the 'real moral and social advancement of man', sometimes failed to sustain itself against the false glamour and romantic excitement of war.

It was a good speech for the city which John Bright represented in Parliament and where Richard Cobden lived, although viewed critically it could be accused of encapsulating exactly the approach which caused the Aberdeen government to walk backwards into the Crimean War, and then to conduct it without either vigour or efficiency. However, the reports satisfied the Prime Minister ('Your Manchester speech', he wrote, 'has produced a great and, I hope, a very beneficial effect upon the public mind . . .'),[6] and the reaction of the audiences more than satisfied Gladstone, who departed for Hawarden on the Friday afternoon (having arrived in Manchester on the Monday), with the Bishop of Oxford still in tow, and full of new-found enthusiasm for northern industrial audiences and self-improving working men.

His main enterprise at Hawarden that autumn was the creation of what became known, perhaps a little pretentiously, as the Temple of Peace. This involved his building a medium-sized library, running back from the main drawing room, which itself filled the south-west corner of the house on the park side. This new or 'north room' became an intensely crammed work-room and a repository for books, for papers and mementoes. Much later he built on to it a small circular tower with gallery as well as a ground floor which was entirely a book and paper storehouse. The Temple of Peace itself had two good windows. To the west it looked out to the original ruined castle on a hillock, to the path (about three-quarters of a mile long) which Gladstone made to the church and which at that stage ran alongside the ruin. It was also open to the evening clearness and bright but unstable sunsets which, often at the end of wet and cloudy days, are a compensation for the 'Western approaches' weather pattern.

It is one of the most vividly evocative political shrines in the world, comparable perhaps only with Churchill's Chartwell and Franklin Roosevelt's Hyde Park. All three make it possible without great effort to imagine the physical presence of the commemorated heroes. But both Hyde Park and Chartwell produce the atmosphere of a theatre piece with other characters surrounding the hero on the stage. In the Temple of Peace at Hawarden, on the other hand, the image created is essentially a solitary one. The house might be full of other people, whom Gladstone might join for church or meals or walking or evening music, but in the room which for forty-four years was central to his life away from London he was nearly always alone on the stage. He needed no supporting players. There, for many hours of each Hawarden day, he sat solitary, driving his pen through his letters and pamphlets, pursuing his vast and eclectic range of reading, sealing his envelopes and packages, sorting his books and papers, fighting his endless battle for the victory of activity over time.

The first reference to the Temple of Peace in Gladstone's diary was in the entry for Saturday, 15 October 1853. 'Arranging books papers & c in the north room to wh. I migrate.' It was not, however, until the following year that the full frenzy of his book arrangement developed. The 5000 or so which he began to move from Fasque soon after his father's death seem to have taken some time to find their permanent home. His London book rooms were also in a state of flux. When he moved into Downing Street in 1853 he kept 6 Carlton Gardens, the house which his father had transferred to him in 1849, but when his two last children, Henry (or Harry) and Herbert, had been born in April 1852 and March 1854 he began to feel that this hardly bijou town house was not big enough for the whole family, and in 1856 he exchanged it for 11 Carlton House Terrace (next door to the smaller No. 13, which had been his first married house in London).

With Oak Farm behind him and with the bonus of £5000 a year (£250,000 today) as the large although insecure salary of a senior minister and in addition to the total assets of *circa* £150,000 (about £7½ million at today's prices) which came to him from his father, some towards the end of John Gladstone's life and some on his death, William Gladstone's affairs gave a considerable impression of affluence during the mid-1850s. In the summer of 1853 he had bought Murillo's *Virgin and Child*, which became the *chef d'œuvre* of his modest picture gallery.

He was also frequently engaged on china-shopping expeditions, accumulating a considerable collection of Wedgwood and other porcelain, which he eventually sold in 1875 when, after the end of his first premiership, he suddenly decided that he was a relatively poor man, sold 11 Carlton House Terrace, abandoned the grand and convenient neighbourhood in which he had lived for thirty-five years, and retreated to Harley Street.

There is some dispute about the quality of his china collection, as indeed there is about his general aesthetic taste. Francis Birrell, in a penetrating 1933 Gladstone essay, was mildly mocking about his over-enthusiasm in 'explaining the beauties of his rather chipped collection of old china'. But over-enthusiasm was always an essential part of Gladstone's power, as well as, for some people at least, of his charm. And there can be no doubt that the china, chipped or not, absorbed him. As Matthew points out, a diary entry of 'Worked on China' (Gladstone mostly gave it the upper case) from the 1850s and 1860s almost invariably referred to porcelain and not to the Middle Kingdom.

The books were more numerous if individually less valuable and still more time-consuming. In the autumn of 1854, still Chancellor, when he was at Hawarden for October and the first ten days of November and then in London until the day before Christmas Eve, he was equally occupied with them at either end, packing up in Carlton Gardens and unpacking and arranging at Hawarden. 'Worked 3½ hours on my books,' he wrote of 10 November, his first full day back in London. And this was fairly typical at both ends. Throughout his life he had both a physical and an intellectual obsession with books. One of the most vivid and symbolic pictures from his extreme old age was 'the wheeling of the books'. When he had built and endowed the St Deiniol's Library in Hawarden village as a place of study for visiting students and a final repository for his collection, he himself spent several days at the age of eighty-six pushing barrows full of the contents of his own library along the connecting route.

It was not just that the handling of books appeared to give him the same sort of satisfaction that a dedicated old-style grocer might get from cutting and wrapping pounds of butter or cheese. He also believed that, in his unending battle against the efflux of time, he might gain a few yards of territory by unrelenting and often indiscriminate reading. Birrell again, who was far from an unfriendly critic, thought that he would always prefer to fill in a spare few minutes by reading a second-rate book than by giving himself the opportunity to think a first-rate thought. (Such a rigid dichotomy surprisingly assumes that a first-rate thought can be ordered up at will.) This wild and almost pointless eclecticism was splendidly illustrated by Gladstone's recording that on 28 October 1853 he read 'Colt on his revolvers'.[7] This meant that, in the first year of his first chancellorship of the Exchequer, he had at least perused a recently published work by the American inventor of a type of pistol (a side-arm in which Gladstone was neither in theory nor in practice particularly interested) and which bore the unpromising title of *On the Application of Machining to the Manufacture of Rotating Chambered-Breach Fire-arms and their Peculiarities.*

There were two other private events during that autumn of 1853 which provoke comment on Gladstone's idiosyncrasies. In early November he went for two and a half days to Liverpool, mainly to keep an eye on the Seaforth property. Curiously in view of his other preoccupations and of the powerful and prosperous presence of Robertson Gladstone in the city, this had been included in William's share of his father's assets.* On this and other occasions he stayed with Robertson in the latter's large house (as he was well over twenty stone he needed space) called Court Hey, at the other end of the city from Seaforth. Robertson was at that time (and thereafter) the brother with whom William got on best, even though his religious position remained as unsatisfactory as William feared at the time of his Unitarian marriage. They were both moving to the left in politics, although Robertson was at this stage several paces in advance of his brother.

There was a Liverpool dinner party on the first evening, with which William seemed entirely content, but his main interest was to get across to Seaforth on the next morning and to inspect in particular the churches which his father had built. (That he was more concerned with the litany than with the state of the roofs may have had something to do with the ill-management of the property.) After dismissing the sermon as 'well-meant', he went off into a very natural retrospective reverie, but one which seemed to give him peculiarly little nostalgic pleasure:

> the occasion was one of interest to me. The memory of my ungodly childhood came thickly upon me. Others may look back upon that time

* William Gladstone (assisted by Robertson) could not be said to have managed the property well, favourably placed though it was to benefit from the northward growth of the docks. He allowed the house to become derelict instead of selling it while it was in good condition, and eventually lost £12,000 (or nearly half a million at today's values) on the whole enterprise.

> as one of little strain; for me it offers nothing in retrospect but selfishness and sin. May the Eternal Priest absolve it and the Manhood wh. has followed. I sat an hour and had luncheon with the Rawsons.[8]*

Immediately before Gladstone's Liverpool visit he had been confined to bed for a day with a return of the erysipelas which had laid him so low for so long in Scotland. It again attacked him in the leg and prevented his riding, which he was most anxious to resume, until the middle of January. He therefore experienced a total of three bed-confining bouts of this tiresome complaint, one of them severe and sustained, in the course of a single year, as well as a general period of malaise causing him to miss some House of Commons occasions soon after his budget. This makes mystifying his birthday summing up of 1853, which baldly stated: 'The singular blessing of this year has been *health*.'[9]

Something of an explanation, but hardly a complete one, may lie in the fact that 1853 was by no means an exceptional Gladstone year for illness. In the following one he had chicken pox for a week in early July, five days of digestive incapacity during a family seaside holiday at Broadstairs in early September, and a month later at Hawarden started another five mostly bedridden days on account of diarrhoea followed by a heavy cold. The truth was that Gladstone, despite his exceptional vigour and longevity, did not exactly have robust health. He was not often seriously ill, but he was always liable to be struck down by some bug or self-generated complaint, and habitually made a good deal of fuss about the attacks, summoning doctors and demanding doses of physic. It was a rare year in which he did not several times retreat to his bed.

This was despite his taking considerable care of his health. The riding was very much directed to that end. He always walked several miles a day, both in the country and in London, where the late-night rescue expeditions helped, and was capable of occasional prodigious feats of

* The Rawsons were the Revd William Rawson, the Cambridge Evangelical who had been Gladstone's first schoolmaster more than thirty-five years before, and his wife. The diary passage has a secondary interest in that it is the first mention in that vast journal of 'luncheon' as a meal or a social occasion. Socially and nutritionally his London life had all been geared to late breakfasts and relatively early dinners. The fashionable meal pattern did change substantially in the third quarter of the nineteenth century, with breakfast diminishing, dinner becoming later, and lunch emerging. But it was an odd reversal of the normal dissemination of fashion that Liverpool led while London followed, and Gladstone's first experience of a luncheon party was in a parsonage beyond Bootle.

self-propulsion. In September 1855 on a North Wales tour he walked forty miles one day and on another added at least fifteen road miles to the ascent and descent of Snowdon. He was also a determined sea-bather. 'I find it a very *powerful* agent,'[10] he wrote in 1859, without specifying of what it was an agent, but clearly of something beneficial. It was this which took him to Broadstairs in 1854, although that was an unusual and not repeated destination for a full-scale holiday. It also led him in 1855 to pay the first of many visits to Penmaenmawr, between Conwy and Bangor, where under some of the highest cliffs in Europe he rented a variety of substantial seaside houses for about a month in the late summers of that and several subsequent years. Between 1859 and 1868 the Gladstones were there in eight Septembers.

The main purpose in Gladstone's case was sea-bathing, which he sometimes continued to do, with a fine indifference to the North Wales weather, into the early days of October, and on one occasion at least immediately after rising from one of his sudden sickbeds.* In 1861 he recorded twenty-seven bathes between 15 August and 10 September. But there were some other attractions too. He liked the dramatic Caernarvonshire scenery and found Penmaenmawr a good base for excursions into the misty mountains. He had Dean Liddell of Christ Church, the great Greek lexicographer and the father of Alice (in Wonderland), as a near holiday neighbour. And he felt at home with the spirit of the Anglican Church in Welsh Wales, which Flintshire hardly was, even occasionally listening (without understanding the words but appreciating the rhythm of the oratory) to a sermon in Welsh, which language however he found inadequately latinate to be a good vehicle for the traditions of Christendom.

It was in that first 1855 Penmaenmawr summer that he seriously embarked on one of the most bizarre of all his intellectual exercises. Homer had long been the Greek writer from whom he derived most satisfaction. 'Old Homer', at once respectful and familiar, was often Gladstone's form of diary reference to him. His niche in Gladstone's literary pantheon predated that of Dante, his only possible rival in the temple, by at least ten years, and Homer never ceased to keep a sporadic place in his voracious reading. But it was only in 1855, out of office and with some energy to spare, that Gladstone took to serious work as opposed to literary browsing on the slopes of the blind epic poet. On 7

* Catherine Gladstone, however, upstaged him in 1861 by bathing at Rhyl as late in the year as 7 November.

July at Hawarden (that he was at something of a loose end, insofar as that phrase can ever be applied to Gladstone, is indicated by his presence there for three weeks at that time of year) he recorded that he had 'looked into my papers on Homer [accumulated in 1847 and 1848] and I am strongly tempted to undertake something, avoiding Scholarship however on account of inability'.[11]

A few days later he went to London for three weeks, but returned to Homer as soon as he got back to Hawarden. 'Began the Iliad,' he wrote on 6 August, 'with serious intentions of working out something on old Homer if I can.'[12] Thereafter he worked at the *Iliad* or the *Odyssey* or the writings of others on Homer for a substantial part of every day (except Sundays) of the next two months, half of them at Hawarden and half of them at Penmaenmawr, to where he seemed to have transported enough books and other material to be equally well equipped as in the Temple of Peace.

The exclusion of Sundays was an odd habit. Gladstone did not practise a strict sabbatarianism. He normally went to church twice, but in London he frequently dined out, and he used part of the day for his general correspondence as well as for reading, which while not strictly devotional had more of a religious bias than was his pattern on weekdays. When, for instance, in the spring of 1858, a few months after its publication, he read *Barchester Towers* (as he did most of the great mid-Victorian novels, although rather eschewing Dickens) he consumed it in six days, which pointed to a high degree of interest and engagement. He nonetheless missed the intervening Sunday, substituting A. F. Rio's study of four martyrs, which he obviously regarded as more suitable for the day than a portrayal of diocesan life if seen through eyes as worldly as Trollope's.

Homer might have been expected to rank more with Rio than with Trollope, for a main part of Gladstone's object in writing about him was to propound the improbable thesis that his work was part of the headwaters of Christianity. This gave it more of a religious than of a scholarly or aesthetic purpose. Gladstone was no doubt not alone in feeling some unease at the contradiction between a ruling ethos which elevated godliness above everything else and an educational system (for the upper classes and educated bourgeoisie) which was based almost exclusively on a study of the literature and history of pagan civilizations. In the easy-going eighteenth century it had not seemed to matter much. The fervour of Victorian religion made the contradiction more awkward. Where Gladstone was almost alone, however, was in believing that he might resolve the issue by proving that part of the same divine revelation was made to the Greeks before it was made to the Jews. The attempt – in Magnus's good formulation 'to catholicize Hellenism and to canonize Homer' – was a tribute at once to his innocence and to his daring. It was not a success.

The Oxford University Press (perhaps influenced by his position as senior burgess for the University, Inglis having died in 1855) published *Homer and the Homeric Age* in three volumes in 1858. The critical response was unfavourable. No one thought that Gladstone had advanced classical scholarship or shown a high critical facility. What he had done was to try to promote a religious cause and in so doing to provide himself with an intellectual hobby which lasted intermittently over the next twenty years. It was Gladstone in his Lord Longford mood, showing indifference to mockery, vast reserves of both energy and self-confidence and more enthusiasm than scholarly fastidiousness. Fortunately he did not himself suffer from great illusions about either the academic or the popular quality of the work, and he advised a friend to start with the third volume because it was probably the 'least unreadable'.

At the beginning of March 1857, Gladstone delivered another of his thundering, government-shaking parliamentary orations. Palmerston was engaged in punitive action against the Chinese for arresting a British registered boat on a charge of piracy.* Cobden moved a vote of censure. Gladstone spoke, relatively briefly for him – he was a little less than two hours – at 9.30 on the night of the vote. The faithful Phillimore wrote of the speech as 'the finest delivered in the memory of man in the House of Commons'.[13] Even allowing for elements both of exaggeration and of sycophancy in this judgement, it was undoubtedly a polemic of the highest class, and helped to secure an 'aye' lobby of 263 (containing not only Cobden and Gladstone, but such variegated auxiliaries as Disraeli, Bright and Russell) against the 247 which was all that Palmerston, who was surprised as well as discomfited by the result, could rally. The next laugh, however, lay very much with the Prime Minister. He dissolved, and was strongly vindicated by the result of the general election. Cobden and Bright both lost their seats, as did most of the other Manchester School 'pacifists'. In Flintshire, where Gladstone did most of his campaigning, Sir Stephen Glynne also went down.

* The incident and surrounding circumstances were well chronicled in *The Arrow War*, written in 1967 by Douglas Hurd, who subsequently achieved an alternative claim to fame.

Gladstone himself was lucky to be unopposed at Oxford. However, he treated the national outcome as a personal rebuff and as an invitation to observe a period of silence. He hardly opened his mouth in the House of Commons for the next four months, and attended only fitfully. Carlton House Terrace was let for six weeks from late May (for the remarkably large sum of a hundred guineas a week – about £5000 today), and he spent most of June at Hawarden. He was not proud of his disengagement, and on 29 May, for the first time for several years, scourged himself as a retribution for 'half-heartedness'.

He was brought back into committed politics, and for no more than a short month, only in order to fight what turned out to be his last pitched illiberal battle. The Palmerston government followed its election victory by introducing a bill for what could be roughly described as the opening to the middle classes of the possibility of divorce. Hitherto the upper classes had been able to proceed by the prohibitively expensive method of private Act of Parliament. This bill made it possible to proceed, even if over very considerable obstacles, by ordinary civil suit. This aroused Gladstone to a frenzy of opposition, although the Aberdeen government had published but not proceeded with a very similar measure. He regarded it as a major depredation of the authority of the Church, despite the fact that in the House of Lords, where the bill had started, it had been supported by the Archbishop of Canterbury and nine other prelates, including even the normally intransigent Dr Phillpotts of Exeter. (The equally formidable Bishop Wilberforce was, however, on Gladstone's side.) And he fought it *à outrance*, despite his being peculiarly vulnerable to the charge of hypocrisy in view of the part that he had played in collecting evidence in support of the Lincoln divorce – carried through by private Act, of course. Furthermore his period of strenuous opposition coincided with the slow decline to death, following her twelfth pregnancy, of Catherine Gladstone's forty-three-year-old sister Mary Lyttelton. It might be thought that he could have done more practical good for the institution of marriage by sustaining his own distraught wife at Hagley than by vainly fulminating for its inviolable principle in London.

Up to his middle age Gladstone was always a little unhinged on anything to do with the institution of marriage. Its disciplines had to be preserved at all costs. It was reminiscent of an intoxicated guardsman who could prevent himself falling over only by standing too rigidly to attention. This lack of balance was shown by his uncharitable censoriousness towards the unions, projected and actual, of three of his brothers and sisters, by his foolish gallivanting for the sake of Lady Lincoln's virtue, and above all by his frenzied opposition to the 1857 legislation. He made seventy-three interventions against that bill, twenty-nine of them in the course of one protracted sitting. He was in a small minority which often failed to muster more than a few dozen votes.

Fortunately and surprisingly, however, he did not carry his intolerant censoriousness into the next generation and his role as a father-in-law. Five of the seven surviving Gladstone children married during their father's lifetime (Helen, the vice-principal of Newnham, never did, and Herbert, the future Home Secretary, did so only in 1901) and their spouses were a fairly mixed bag (and a less fashionable one than that acquired by the Asquith offspring a generation later): one curate, one headmaster, one daughter of a Tory Scottish landowning peer, one of another peer who was a late Gladstonian creation, and one of a Liverpool doctor. William Gladstone appeared content with them all as sons- and daughters-in-law, although one of the latter (Mrs Henry Gladstone) was to evolve into a silly and pretentious middle-aged lady.

12

A Short Odyssey for a British Ulysses

The Divorce Bill apart, Gladstone followed a pattern of political detachment in 1857 and 1858. He let the Palmerston government get on with it, and he got on with Homer. Between 18 August 1857 and 16 February 1858 he was in London only for ten days in early December and four days in late January. He slept 153 out of 172 nights at Hawarden during that long parliamentary recess, the highest proportion of static rusticity in any year of his life until 1886–7. His Carlton House Terrace residence was closed, and even when he at last removed himself semi-permanently back to London in February it was to lodge at the convenient address of 18 Great George Street, Westminster, with a Mrs Talbot, who was a distant family connection through the Lytteltons.

Within three days of his return he had the satisfaction of both speaking and voting for the defeat of the government on the Conspiracy to Murder Bill. It was an ironical issue, for Palmerston was arraigned for being too subservient to a foreign government. An Italian terrorist, Felice Orsini, operating from a British base, had attempted to assassinate the Emperor Napoleon III. Responding to a strong despatch from Foreign Minister Walewski, whose birth and office were in combination a symbol of the continuity of the First and Second Empires, Palmerston introduced one of those criminal justice measures which fall within the category more of gesture than of efficacy. Gladstone was torn between his dislike of Palmerston and his belief in the Concert of Europe, but he was able to resolve the issue by bringing in a third libertarian factor, and voted '234:215', a remarkably small vote (on both sides) for a division which toppled a government. Palmerston, although within nine months of his 1857 electoral triumph, nonetheless resigned.

Derby came in, for the third of those Conservative attempts at government which punctuated the 1850s like short showers in a fine (or at least a non-Tory) summer. He asked Gladstone and other Peelites to join him. The offices were not specified. For once the Exchequer does not seem to have been on offer. But the Colonial Office, then a major secretaryship of state, almost certainly would have been, particularly as it was eventually filled by Derby's son, who must have been expendable. The offer clearly embarrassed other Peelites, at least Herbert and Graham. These two and Gladstone met together with their erstwhile chief in an almost instinctive feast of abnegation at Aberdeen's house after (for Gladstone) evensong at Westminster Abbey. There was no particular reason why they should refuse: Gladstone liked and even admired Derby, and was going through one of the less vehemently anti-Disraeli phases. Refuse they nonetheless did. The Peelites were becoming a group of vestal virgins. Their enthusiasm for saying no had become a form of self-indulgence. 'The case though grave was not doubtful,' Gladstone wrote. '. . . we separated for the evg. with the fervent wish that in public life we might never part.'[1]*

Despite this wish the Peelites were in disarray, with Graham and Herbert pulling increasingly towards the Whigs, while Gladstone was experiencing the last Conservative tug upon his heartstrings. On 19 April he delivered a friendly speech on the budget, in sharp contrast with the denunciation which Disraeli's previous budgetary essay had called forth five and a quarter years before, and in contrast too with his hostility to Cornewall Lewis's efforts in 1855–7. On 4 May Gladstone followed this with one of his major moralizing foreign policy philippics, this time in favour of the rights of the inhabitants of Wallachia and Moldavia (later Roumania) against both the Turks and the Austrians. This was much more critical of the government, but it was not conducive to a Whig alliance either.

In mid-May Lord Ellenborough, who had been intermittently President of the Board of Control since 1828, resigned from that office as a result of a dispute with Gladstone's old Eton and Christ Church contemporary Charles Canning, who was Governor-General in Calcutta. Indian affairs were at a crucial juncture, with the Mutiny only a few months over and the governor-generalship and the presidency of the Board of Control about to be turned into respectively a viceroyalty and a secretaryship of state. Derby sent an envoy to offer Gladstone the vacancy, accompanying it with the alternative offer of his old office of Colonial Secretary. This was presumably designed to cover the possibility

* The meaning of the 'we' is a little obscure in the context, but probably refers only to himself and Sidney Herbert rather than to the wider group.

that he might be disposed to enter the government while remaining unstirred with the challenge of India, a department of public affairs from which he remained almost wholly detached throughout his career. The offer was maladroitly made. It was confined to Gladstone alone at that stage, for it was to fill a specific vacancy (but the Colonial Office alternative made rather a nonsense of that), although there were hints that other Peelites might be brought in later, and more than a hint that Disraeli might be prepared to give up the leadership of the House of Commons to Graham. The existence of these nuances made it the more mysterious that Derby (who always had a good relationship with Gladstone) did not see him himself rather than using Spencer Walpole, the Home Secretary, as an intermediary.

Three days later, having returned a negative but not perhaps totally door-slamming reply to Derby via Walpole, Gladstone received a more surprising but equally maladroit letter from Disraeli. This was in sharp contrast with the coldly affected style of his 'Exchequer robes and Downing Street furniture' 1853 letters. Disraeli began without prefix and on a note of almost gushing urgency:

> I think it of such paramount importance to the public interests that you should assume at this time a commanding position in the administration of affairs, that I feel it a solemn duty to lay before you some facts, that you may not decide under a misapprehension.
>
> Listen, without prejudice, to this brief narrative.

Disraeli then deployed three or four points designed to show that he had always been prepared to behave unselfishly to promote the reunion of the Conservative party.

> Thus you see, for more than eight years, instead of thrusting myself into the foremost place, I have been, at all times, actively prepared to make every sacrifice of self for the public good, which I have ever thought identical with your accepting office in a conservative government.
>
> Don't you think the time has come when you might deign to be magnanimous?
>
> Mr Canning was superior to Lord Castlereagh in capacity, in acquirements, in eloquence, but he joined Lord C. when Lord C. was Lord Liverpool's lieutenant [that is, leader of the House of Commons], when the state of the Tory party rendered it necessary. That was an enduring, and, on the whole, not an unsatisfactory connection, and it certainly terminated very gloriously for Mr Canning.
>
> I may be removed from the scene, or I may wish to be removed from the scene.

> Every man performs his office, and there is a Power, greater than ourselves, which disposes of all this.

He then continued for another page before concluding, still in a gush: 'Think of all this in a kindly spirit. These are hurried lines, but they are heartfelt.'[2]

G. W. E. Russell, devoted Gladstone acolyte and chronicler of his later life (Russell, nephew of Lord John and himself an MP and junior minister, was born only in 1853) interpreted this letter (in a short, hagiographic but often perceptive biography of Gladstone which was published in 1891) as a coldly machiavellian ploy by Disraeli to turn Gladstone into his creature, with 'the satisfaction of knowing that the one contemporary statesman whose powers and ambition were equal to his own was subordinated, in all probability for ever, to his imperious will'.[3] This was ludicrous. Disraeli's motives may well have been mixed, but there was more (possibly self-deceiving) spontaneity than plotting about them, and he would never have been so foolish as to believe that he could permanently turn Gladstone into a subordinate.

What is certain, however, is that Disraeli's letter was not well directed to achieving its immediate objective of getting Gladstone into the government. The flattery was too transparent, the attempt to persuade him that he could be Canning to Disraeli's Castlereagh (was Disraeli suggesting that he might follow Castlereagh in committing suicide?) was too blatant an appeal to Gladstone's ambition rather than his duty. Above all, however, Gladstone was not going to have Disraeli lecturing him about 'a Power, greater than ourselves'. His reply was much more superficially courteous but fundamentally just as chilling as Disraeli's 1853 brush-off:

> My dear Sir,
>
> The letter which you have been so kind as to address to me will enable me, I trust, to remove from your mind some impressions with which you will not be sorry to part. . . .
>
> At the present moment I am awaiting counsel which at Lord Derby's wish, I have sought. But the difficulties which he wishes me to find means of overcoming are broader than you may have supposed. . . .
>
> I state these points fearlessly and without reserve, for you have yourself well reminded me that there is a Power beyond us that disposes of what we are and do, and I find the limits of choice in public life to be very narrow.
>
> I remain, etc[4]

The 'counsel' which Gladstone took was with Aberdeen and the other members of the little band of Peelites, and the result, arrived at more or less unanimously but on what all agreed was a narrow balance of considerations, was to confirm the negative. Thus passed Gladstone's last sight of the shore of serving in a Conservative government. The refusal was in a sense instinctive, but it gave Gladstone no sense of the exhilaration of freedom. He was beginning to feel the futility of his political position. Having played a material part in bringing down Palmerston in February, he was inhibited from doing the same with the only practical alternative government. Yet he did not feel enough affinity to join it. It was the old 'devil and the deep blue sea' paradigm between Palmerston and Disraeli which afflicted him throughout the 1850s. He attempted to resolve (or at least to escape) it by retreating to Hawarden for much of June and July and then by accepting an unlikely overseas mission for the autumn and winter which kept him abroad for four months.

That flaccid summer led him partly to fill the vacuum with what became the most famous recreational activity of the second half of his life. For 31 July 1858 one of his diary lines read: 'Spent the afternoon in woodcutting & the like about the old Castle: my first lesson.'[5] Thereafter the felling of trees became a central occupation. In Lord Randolph Churchill's unforgettable phrase of a quarter of a century later, 'The forest laments, in order that Mr Gladstone may perspire'.[6] There were another seven arboreal assaults during that August. One even took priority over accompanying Bishop Wilberforce (who was staying at Hawarden) to a Society for the Propagation of the Gospel meeting at Mold.

In that third summer out of office, without even the compensation of having a clear thrust to oppose the government, there was something which Gladstone needed more than either an opportunity for sweating or even a new subject for holiday studies, and that was some public occupation into which he could get his teeth. The morsel which he succeeded in masticating was the very modest one of the string of a dozen islands which run down the west coast of Greece from Corfu to Zante, and the status in which he performed was that of a quasi-constitutional governor-general. The islands had been made a British protectorate in an almost absent-minded disposition of the spoils of victory in 1815.

It was in several senses a preposterous undertaking. Edward Bulwer Lytton, the Colonial Secretary who got Gladstone to accept the commission, was one of the most amateur of all nineteenth-century politicians, which made it the more remarkable that he got Gladstone, who was the most accomplished and in that sense the most professional politician of the same period, to agree to be temporarily one of his satraps.

Lytton, although primarily a novelist, was an MP for twenty-four years, first as an advanced reformer and then as a Conservative. His year as Colonial Secretary, which he became as a direct result of Gladstone's refusal, was his only experience of office. It was not, however, felt that he was showing gratitude towards Gladstone. Indeed the general view was that Gladstone by going to Corfu was conferring a wholly bizarre favour upon the government rather than that they were discharging any obligation by offering him the appointment. All the Peelites except Newcastle, who had much the worst judgement, were strongly against his accepting the mission. Graham thought it would ruin his career. Herbert, his 'best friend', was the most exasperated, probably because he was the one who most minded Gladstone being away. Herbert thought Gladstone had got himself into 'an infernal position' and that he 'really is not safe to go about out of Lord Aberdeen's room'. Aberdeen was calmer but thought him too 'headstrong' for the task.

It was of course precisely this headstrong quality which made him accept against all the advice, and indeed against all rational evaluation of the prospects. The chances of achievement, or indeed its significance even if attained, would never have been adequate in the eyes of a calmly calculating politician of stature to compensate for the probability of failure and the possibility of ridicule. Nonetheless sheer rashness would not have been enough on its own to send Gladstone off for nearly half a year to the eastern Adriatic. He needed some supporting motives, and there were several available.

First, he loved the Mediterranean, both in romantic anticipation and in reality, and he had not been there for nearly eight years. He also thought a winter sojourn would be good for Catherine Gladstone after the oppression of her sister's death, and he planned that their sixteen-year-old daughter Agnes should also be of the party. Third, his head was still full of Homer, and an odyssey of his own around the famous islands had much attraction. Fourth, he was always attracted by the Greek Orthodox Church, and the thought of seeing a whole new group of archbishops and bishops with whom he could engage in theological and Christian reunion conversation was an intoxicating one. But, above all, he was disenchanted and even a little bored (a most unusual condition for Gladstone) with the home political scene, and wanted a new stimulus, even if it was concerned only with the unpromising affairs of 250,000 people. Therefore, the idea having first surfaced at the beginning of October, he was ready by the end of the month to give a definite acceptance. He was sworn in at Windsor on 5 November 1858 and he left London on the 8th.

Although his acceptance was definite, the offer to which he was giving this clear answer was itself a good deal less so. He was asked to go out as Commissioner Extraordinary and to report and make recommendations to the government on the situation in the islands and the possible remedies. But there was already a High Commissioner there. Sir John Young was both a friend of Gladstone's from Eton and Christ Church days, and a senior man, being a Privy Counsellor and a former Chief Secretary for Ireland in the Aberdeen government. Gladstone said that he could have had him recalled, and he was no doubt right. But he did not wish to do so. This rendered his own position ambiguous from the beginning.

Nor was his staff entirely satisfactory, although it was in a sense both high-powered and notable. As secretary of the mission he enlisted Joseph (soon to be Sir Joseph) Lacaita, his former amanuensis at the time of his Neapolitan gaol investigations, who had since become a professor at King's College, London. Arthur Gordon, the fourth and then twenty-nine-year-old son of Aberdeen, who subsequently governed several colonies and ended as Lord Stanmore, also described himself as the secretary of the mission, but was intended to act more as an aide-de-camp to Gladstone. In the role he was lackadaisical and by the time they got to Brussels on the way out had already irritated Gladstone by casually making both of them late for dinner with the King of the Belgians. His slackness eventually led to Gladstone steeling himself for a great scene of rebuke (he was of course torn between his regard for Aberdeen and his impatience with his son) and the arrival of another ADC at the end of January.*

* Gordon, however, was more easily replaced than got rid of. This may have been because he had become infatuated with Agnes. In any event he was still around until Gladstone returned to England, and indeed frequently reappeared in the Gladstones' lives, sometimes at Hawarden, over several decades. In Corfu he had the compensating advantage (more obvious perhaps to a biographer of his chief than to the chief himself) that he wrote vivid letters of detailed description of Gladstone's adventures and encounters. Also, by writing much later in his life the good standard biography of his father Aberdeen and also a memoir of Sidney Herbert, he had the last word on many issues.

Lacaita was an altogether more serious adviser. Inevitably however he gave a somewhat italianate tilt to the delegation, and may have been responsible for Gladstone's decision to deliver all his major addresses in Italian. This was doubtfully good for comprehension and certainly not good for giving an impression of evenhandedness. For several centuries Venetian influence had been dominant in the islands, and the upper classes, such as they were, were italianophone. But the demotic language was Greek, and the predominant sentiment was for *enosis* or union with Athens. Gladstone had a lot of underlying sympathy with this philhellenism, but he was persuaded that it was not politically practical or opportune, and set himself the intractable task of persuading (in Italian) the Greek-speaking population through their representatives in the Assembly (which had been set up in 1849) that this was so. The result was that he was regarded with suspicion by the leaders of both the main currents of opinion. The proponents of *enosis* rejected his constitutional schemes, while the agents of British colonialism (above all the garrison, and those who clustered under its shade), thought him a dangerous and ignorant native-lover. He was shocked by their lack of interest in Homer. They were even more shocked by his kissing the ring of a Greek Orthodox bishop.

In addition to these inherent difficulties there was a considerable overhang of ill luck. It struck first and most conspicuously when Gladstone was in Vienna on the way to embarkation in a British warship at Trieste. In eight typically vigorous days of train travel and sightseeing he had traversed Germanic Europe, taking in Cologne, Brunswick, Magdeburg, Berlin, Dresden and Prague before reaching Vienna. It was his first all-rail journey across the continent, but he was complaining rather than dazzled: 'We reached Erzherzog Karl* past eight,' he wrote for 18 November, 'train late, as seems common'.[7] As it was eight in the morning, however, the lateness did not prevent his visiting the Stefansdom, the Augustinus Kirche and the picture gallery in the Belvedere before dining in a restaurant, where in good Viennese style he read the newspapers, and then going to a theatre.

The next day he was told by the British ambassador that an 1857 despatch sent from Corfu by Sir John Young had leaked (or, more precisely, been stolen from a pigeonhole in the Colonial Office) and

* The most fashionable hotel, in the Kärntnerstrasse, although the construction of the Ring which was then in progress meant that the age of the Imperial and the Sacher was only just over the horizon.

sold or given to a London newspaper, its publication in which had caused considerable repercussions throughout the capitals of Europe. Young had advocated the partition of the Ionian Isles, with the seven southern ones being incorporated in Greece, and Corfu and Paxos moving from protected status to becoming straightforward British Crown Colonies. Apart from suggesting a unilateral abrogation of the 1815 settlement this document pre-empted a large part of the purpose of Gladstone's mission. Its status was somewhat reduced by Young writing a few days later to say that he had changed his mind, but that letter of withdrawal unfortunately escaped stealing, and might well not have achieved publicity even had it been available.

Gladstone then had to spend most of the day endeavouring to repair the damage in Vienna, although it was alleged to be at least equally great in Paris and St Petersburg, which were clearly outside his reach. He called on Buol, Metternich's successor as Chancellor, as well as on Metternich himself, then aged eighty and in the last year of his life, and on Brück, the powerful Minister of the Interior. He also saw *The Times* correspondent. It was a classic example of how a politician abroad tries to deal with an embarrassment with international repercussions which has occurred at home. Nonetheless it strikes an odd and unusual note in Gladstone's life, for he was in general a creator rather than a clearer-up of embarrassments. He was not a diplomatic politician. Normally he broke new ground and left it to others to smooth off the jagged edges. That on this occasion he had to go round Vienna – fortunately a very compact city at that time – endeavouring to explain away the gaffes of others indicated how mistakenly low level and ill tailored for him was the task which he had undertaken.

He did not allow the diversion unduly to upset him. He also found time to buy some china during the day, dined with the ambassador, went to the Opera, but found twenty minutes of it enough (a fairly rough dismissal of the offering of the city of Mozart and Haydn from someone who was by no means a musical philistine), finished reading a major work on Corfu, and was off the next morning by the Semmering pass and what he supposed was 'the most beautiful and wonderful railway in the world'.[8]

For his first month in the Ionian Islands Gladstone probably enjoyed himself more than tolerably. He at least half liked the ceremonial aspects of his charge. He held levées with enthusiasm. For 29 November he recorded: 'Ball in the evening. With huge difficulty I got through a quadrille.' His 9 December entry best caught the flavour of his life and attitudes at the time: 'a great dinner when I was dragged out into [*sic*] an Italian speech. Next came a soirée and a ball. We returned to the ship by midnight in stiff rain. I still carry a giddy head. A. Gordon remains unwell. Lacaita is invaluable.'[9] On 18 December he arrived in Athens for a good-neighbour visit. He had never been there before, even though it had been the centre of so much of his thought and study for much of the previous forty years. He was surprised to find the Acropolis covered in snow and reacted almost breathlessly to the unusual scene: 'The view – the ruins – & the sculptures, taken together are almost too much for one day.'[10] He dined two nights with the unpopular King Otho, who forthcomingly agreed that the time was not ripe for *enosis*, but who may, by so doing, have contributed substantially to his own deposition just over three years later. Gladstone was back in Corfu on Christmas Eve. As another side excursion from Corfu he visited Philiates, then in Albania, and stayed a night with the Turkish governor of the province. It was his one experience of Muslim life and he did not like it: 'The whole impression is most saddening: it is all indolence, decay, stagnation: the image of God seems as if it were nowhere.'[11]

In spite of these distractions he had succeeded in putting together a vast despatch, containing his analysis of the situation and his proposals for limited action, which he sent off to the Queen and the London government on 27 December. It defended philhellenism as a noble aspiration, for belief in which Ionians should not be persecuted, but pushed its practical achievement well into the future. 'What would be the position of Corfu, with its great strategical importance, in the hands of a Power so unable as Greece must be to defend it?' He linked the 'small question' of the 'Union of the Seven Islands and the Kingdom of Greece' with the much larger (and certainly much vaguer) one of the 'reconstruction of all political society in South-Eastern Europe'.[12] In the meantime some moderately substantial advances towards 'home rule' under British sovereignty should be made. To this end the Lord High Commissioner (still Young, for Gladstone had the much looser role and title of Commissioner Extraordinary) should be authorized to summon the Ionian Assembly into a special session for the presentation to it of these constitutional proposals. But Young could not present them, being compromised by his leaked and contradictory plan of 1857. He should therefore be recalled, and Gladstone appointed in his place.

This plan was agreed to in a telegram from Lytton dated 11 January 1859. 'The Queen accepts. Your Commission is made out,' it almost exultantly ran. Yet this news, so far from opening Gladstone's way to triumph, led for him to nothing but an ignominious end to his mission. *The Times*, then in the middle of Delane's long editorship, which was marked by general friendliness towards Peel and his relicts, particularly Aberdeen, and later by strong support for Gladstone in his first premiership, nonetheless published a wounding leader on 13 January. It accused Gladstone of breaking Young on the wheel of his personal convenience. He smashed Young, it was alleged, and used the Ionian Islands as stepping-stones to the indulgence of his excessive taste for classical scholarship. Much more serious, however, was the law officers' ruling (perhaps Bethell was getting his own back for Gladstone's tiresomeness on the Divorce Bill) that the lord high commissionship, as opposed to his vague previous appointment, precluded his sitting in Parliament. Not only was his Oxford seat declared vacant, as it would have been had he become a Secretary of State, but he was declared ineligible for re-election, which as a member of the Cabinet he would not have been, so long as he held his Corfu post. It seems amazing that no one had previously thought of this hazard. It was in any event a penalty he was not prepared to accept, and he immediately set about disembarrassing himself of the office which he had been eager to achieve. On 1 February Gladstone resigned the office to which he had been appointed on 11 January. On 13 February he was re-elected for Oxford. The University, which had been somewhat grudging towards him in 1853 and was to be worse than grudging in 1865, treated him on this most vulnerable occasion with generosity and elected him unopposed.

A replacement for Corfu was found in the shape of Sir Henry Storks, who had Mauritian colonial experience and was hastily shipped out to arrive on 16 February. In the meantime, on the 5th, Gladstone had presented his constitutional proposals to the specially summoned Assembly. His legal status was doubtful. He was no longer Lord High Commissioner. This did not affect the force of his Italian oratory, but nor did it render it more persuasive. His proposals were almost unanimously rejected on 16 February, the day of Storks's arrival. He nonetheless handed over with good humour, but was happy to leave three days later. Within six hours he was prostrated by sea-sickness: 'at the lowest depth', he wrote.

To be 'at the lowest depth' was for Gladstone a certain indication of how quickly and forcefully he would begin the ascent. By Pola he was better. By Venice his appetite for sightseeing and other forms of activity had become voracious. It was the first time he had been there since

1832, and he marked his return with a formidable three days of looking at buildings and pictures, buying china, going to the opera, listening to the Austrian band at Florian's café, and dining with the unfortunate Archduke Maximilian, who was to die before a Mexican firing squad within a decade. He then made his way by the cities of the plain to Milan, and was struck by the atmosphere of mounting tension as the Austrians prepared for the war with Piedmont and France which began two months later: 'At Vicenza we had cavalry & artillery by the Station about to march: more cavalry on the road with a van & pickets, some with drawn swords: at Verona regiments in review: at Milan pickets in the streets; as I write I hear the tread of horses patrolling the streets. Dark omens!'[13]

At Turin, four days later, he dined with Cavour, the Piedmontese Prime Minister, from 5.30 to 8.30 and then left by the 9.30 train. The Mont Cenis rail route was not complete and he had to go down the French side in a traineau or sledge ('*most* disagreeable'). He spent a Sunday and Monday in Paris and then crossed overnight getting home to Carlton House Terrace on the morning of 8 March. His mission could not by any standards be regarded as a success. It had two ironic postscripts. In 1863 Palmerston, with the almost unanimous support of the Cabinet, handed all the islands over to Greece. The only clear opposition came from Westbury (formerly Bethell), the Lord Chancellor. Gladstone was more nonplussed than opposed. It was clearly against his 1859 view, but he could hardly be outflanked in both philhellenism and anti-imperialism by Palmerston. At about the same time Gladstone was semi-seriously proposed for the throne of Greece, King Otho having in the meantime been disposed of. The Duke of Edinburgh, Queen Victoria's second son, was the leading suggestion, with both Gladstone and Lord Stanley as alternative British candidates. At Hawarden the rumours were received with amusement tinged with pleasure.

Back in England for that spring of 1859, Gladstone reacted to the Corfu fiasco in what was probably the best possible way for a man of his energy and temperament. He put the problems of the Ionian islanders behind him. The chapter was closed. He refused the grand cross of the orders of both the Bath and of St Michael and St George which the government offered him (how strange and bathetic it would have been if he had spent the remaining thirty-nine years of his life as Sir William Gladstone), and moved his mind first to the more promising prospect of Italian unity, which had engaged it on the way home, and then to the British political scene. The second and much the more productive half of his public life was about to begin. He was quickly to prove the underlying truth of Aberdeen's judgement of him. He was to show himself, if not exactly 'terrible', at least formidable 'in the rebound'.

13

The Hostile Partnership with Palmerston

For his future, and that of British politics, Gladstone's three hours with Cavour were more important than his three months in Corfu. The Italians he had always thought less disappointing as descendants of their classical forebears than he had found the Ionic Greeks, particularly when they rejected out of hand his constitutional proposals. During previous visits he had been sceptical about the uniting of the Italian peninsula, but by the spring of 1859 the combination of the tide of excitement sweeping the north and Cavour's assured persuasiveness not only stilled his doubts but kindled his enthusiasm. The atmosphere which percolated from him through the Gladstone household was well captured by a letter which his then six-year-old son, later to be Campbell-Bannerman's Chief Whip in opposition and Home Secretary in government, wrote to his father in October 1860: 'Mama . . . has been telling me about good Garibaldi. Did you really go down the dungeon? . . . I hope Garibaldi will get Naples, because he is good. And I want the King of Naples to go because he is wicked and shuts up people.'[1]

There were broadly only two subjects on which Gladstone agreed with Palmerston. The first was Italy, and the second was their shared coolness (although differently expressed) to an extension of the franchise. It was the prominence of these two issues, the first still more than the second, in the three months following Gladstone's return from Corfu which made Palmerston temporarily less repugnant to him than was Disraeli and led him to make a choice of direction which had the most momentous permanent effects. But his movement, although decisive, was carried out in a peculiarly crabwise fashion.

His first days in London were marked by a frenzy of mainly political activity. During the day (Tuesday, 8 March 1859) which began with his morning arrival from Paris he had separate meetings with four or five of his Peelite colleagues as well as with the Colonial Secretary and Lacaita, went to the House of Commons for three hours and took the oath (following his re-election for Oxford), read a new Bagehot pamphlet on parliamentary reform, and indulged in several rescue encounters with ladies who had been deprived of his ministrations for several months, although he had managed one or two redeeming attempts (in what language?) in the Corfu streets.

On the next day he had a further range of interviews, signing off (with the Prime Minister among others) from the Ionian Isles and signing on with the British Museum. The great Round Reading Room was then under construction, and Panizzi became as frequent a visitor to Carlton House Terrace as Lacaita (they often came together). Gladstone made a brief parliamentary re-entry speech about the Museum on 18 March, but both his reading and his thoughts were concentrating on what he would say on Disraeli's Representation of the People Bill, which came before the House on the 21st, and was debated in the course of that and six subsequent nights. After listening to Disraeli's opening speech and the first night's debate, Gladstone made a diary entry in a rare form: 'sorely puzzled', he wrote.

This attempt at a second Reform Bill had emerged from the Conservative Cabinet at the end of February after considerable dissension and the resignations of the Home Secretary (Spencer Walpole) and the President of the Board of Trade (Henley). As with all nineteenth-century franchise measures the question of the distribution of constituencies was just as important, in some ways even more so from a party point of view, as was that of who should vote. Even after 1832 the boroughs, particularly the smaller ones, were grossly over-represented in relation to the counties. And the counties maintained their Conservative tradition despite Derby and Disraeli having abandoned protectionism at the beginning of the decade. The affiliations of the boroughs were more mixed, but there was no doubt that a transfer of seats from them to the counties would produce some tilt in the political balance towards the Tories, and might easily more than counteract the effect of a lowering of the property qualification for a vote, about the political effect of which there were in any event greatly varying views.

The bill which eventually emerged from a reluctant Cabinet, and which Disraeli spiritedly commended to the House on 21 March, was a package composed of extending the £10 householder franchise from the boroughs to the counties (that is, widening the electorate there), introducing a new £20 lodger (non-householder) franchise in both, supplementing these provisions with a series of 'fancy franchises', as

John Bright memorably christened them, and taking seventy seats away from the smaller boroughs to give eighteen to the larger boroughs and fifty-two to the counties.

The fancy franchises, which were thought to be a direct product of Disraeli's over-fertile imagination, included votes for those with an income of £10 a year from the funds, or £20 a year from a government pension, or £60 capital in a savings bank account, or (if not otherwise qualified) were doctors of medicine, lawyers, university graduates, ministers of religion or in some categories of schoolmasters. Disraeli's pre-eminent modern biographer has written with brutal honesty about Disraeli's motives on the issue: 'It would be absurd to claim that Disraeli viewed the matter other than first and foremost in the light of party expediency.'[2] But were his motives worse than anyone else's? Apart from the Radicals, who believed straightforwardly in the democratization of the franchise, the general mood among politicians from 1852 to 1867 was that an extension of the electoral base was inevitable, even if not particularly welcome, and that it was legitimate to manoeuvre so that the maximum advantage was achieved both from their party's being the agent of the change and from the form in which it was done. There was no great difference in this respect between Tories and Whigs (becoming Liberals) or indeed Peelites, except that the last did not have a clear enough constituency interest for it to be obvious how they could best benefit themselves.

Disraeli's 1859 bill suffered from over-complication and from failing to satisfy any non-Conservative interest. Russell and Palmerston managed to come together in an amendment against giving a second reading to a bill which failed to make a larger extension of the franchise in the cities and boroughs. The contradiction was that one (Russell) of Queen Victoria's 'two terrible old men' wanted more reform and that the other was glad of an excuse to avoid it altogether, a position which Palmerston brilliantly maintained for the remaining six years of his life. This did not prevent their alliance, supported by the Radicals, resulting in a government defeat by the surprisingly large margin of thirty-nine.

Gladstone's contribution was characteristic of his ambiguities in that spring of rebound. He spoke for an hour and twenty minutes on the penultimate night, his first major intervention for nearly a year. There were two memorable aspects to his speech. The first was an almost lyrical defence of the virtues of small (that is, semi-rotten) boroughs. They had been the nurseries of statesmen, of Pelham, both Pitts, Fox, Canning, Peel and, he might have added, of himself. It was not an obvious way in which either to mark his transition to Liberalism or to support a measure which disfranchised seventy of them. The second was a sustained piece of raillery of Palmerston, whose attitude to the issue was in fact very close to his own and whose long-term Chancellor of the Exchequer he was about to become. He mocked him for having needed war in 1855, peace in 1856, the dissolution of Parliament in 1857 and the dissolution of his government in 1858 to save him from reform. Having thus boxed several compasses, Gladstone proceeded to vote for the bill, with the government, and in a minority. Later, on a separate motion, he voted in a large majority against the introduction of the ballot, thereby conspicuously not paving the way to one of the principal reforms of his own first administration.

Derby decided to dissolve on the defeat, and was justified to the extent that he improved Conservative numbers in the House of Commons by about thirty, their greatest strength since Disraeli's destruction of the Peel government thirteen years before. On the other hand the new figure was still short of a majority and the opposing forces had become more inclined to come together. So the election gains, far from providing the Conservatives with a secure foundation for government, put them out for another seven years and left Derby without office (not that he ever greatly cared about that) for most of the last decade of his life.

Gladstone was crucial to this new anti-Conservative stability, but he did not show this by his behaviour during the election, any more than he had by his vote in the division which had led to the dissolution. He was unopposed at Oxford, for the last time as it turned out, and therefore needed to do nothing on his own behalf. But nor did he campaign for anyone else, not even in Flintshire. Parliament was dissolved between 19 April and 31 May. He made no speech during this period. He visited Oxford from 6 to 13 May, but this was first for the purpose of having his son Stephen confirmed by Bishop Wilberforce at Cuddesdon, second to be installed as one of the first honorary fellows of All Souls following an 1857 change in the statutes (he stayed four nights in the college), and only third to pay the customary round of visits to Heads of Houses to mark his re-election.

For the rest his time was taken up with reading George Eliot's just published *Adam Bede*, entertaining the Duc d'Aumale (Louis-Philippe's fourth and most interesting son), twice visiting the Carlton Club, from which he was on the brink of resignation, and writing a hurried but substantial article for the *Quarterly Review* on the Franco-Piedmontese war against Austria in Italy (which had started at the end of April). He never went outside the Home Counties during this period, and indeed five months passed after his return from Corfu before he visited Hawarden, thus imposing upon himself a total absence of ten months. In London he did a good deal of rescue work, although he did not appear to be obsessively concentrated on any individuals. On 25 May, however, he thought he had transgressed sufficiently, with a lady named Trelawney, to resort to the use of the scourge for the first time for two years, and the last time ever according to his diary records.

Although he himself took no part in the campaign there was one campaigning speech which made a great impact upon him. That was by Palmerston in his Tiverton constituency on 29 April. Palmerston was also unopposed, but in order to achieve this result he made an appearance at a hustings in his Devon borough and there delivered himself of some impromptu remarks which struck a strong chord of response in Gladstone's italophil heart. Palmerston in a half-modern fashion had prepared a hand-out from his speech, although in a way that was far from modern he had himself written it out in his own beautiful hand, and the reporters, also eschewing modern practice, had not taken this hand-out on trust or deserted their posts in Tiverton market-place. The written text merely said that any Conservative attempts to drag Britain into the Italian war on the Austrian side must be resisted. The 'spontaneous' additions included the statement that 'if the consequences of Austrian aggression should be that she should be compelled to withdraw to the north of the Alps and leave Italy free to the Italians . . . every generous mind will feel that sometimes out of evil good may flow and we shall rejoice at the issue . . .'[3]

These words excited Gladstone. Aberdeen, even in the last year of his life, penetratingly understood him and immediately perceived this. He told Graham that Palmerston's 'brilliant stroke' at Tiverton would have 'secured Gladstone' and made him ready 'to act with him, or under him'.[4] Palmerston's words were no doubt the more effective in this respect because, although unscripted, they were not at variance with his premeditated thought. He had written to Granville several months before:

> I am very Austrian north of the Alps but very anti-Austrian south of the Alps. The Austrians have no business in Italy, and they are a public nuisance there. They govern their own provinces ill, and are the props

and encouragers of bad government in all the other states of the Peninsula, except in Piedmont, where fortunately they have no influence.[5]

Gladstone, possibly smarting both from Schwarzenberg's contemptuous dismissal of his Neapolitan pamphlet eight years before and from his more recent experience of having to run around Vienna explaining the leak of Sir John Young's despatch, might not have endorsed Palmerston's enthusiasm for Habsburg power even north of the Alps. Nevertheless he regarded Palmerston's forthrightness towards getting the Austrian white coats out of the Po valley as an immense improvement on Derby–Disraeli respect for the simulacrum of power of the Hofburg and the supine attitude towards it of their weak Foreign Secretary, Lord Malmesbury. When, eight months later, Gladstone had to explain the step of joining Palmerston, he did so with the one word 'Italy'. But he made no reference to the Tiverton speech in his diary, and in the six weeks between it and the formation of the second Palmerston government his method of transition became even more crab-like than hitherto.

On the afternoon of 6 June a meeting took place in Willis's Rooms (formally Almack's and a fine haunt of early nineteenth-century dissipation). Why it was there is a mild mystery. Two hundred and seventy-four MPs were recorded as being present, and they included several Whig magnates who could have accommodated that number in their own London houses, and, in default of that, the Reform Club, palatial, then both sectarian and only sixteen years old, would have been more than adequately welcoming. But it was nonetheless in the faintly rakish surroundings of Willis's that the *accouchement* of the Liberal party is commonly regarded as having taken place. And the equivalent of the first cry of the newly emerged infant was when Palmerston (then aged seventy-five), having mounted the platform first, gave an assisting arm to little but no longer very agile Johnnie Russell (then aged sixty-seven). This gesture of common courtesy was elevated by resounding cheers into the approximate nineteenth-century equivalent of Martin Luther nailing his notice to the church door in Wittenberg or of the embattled farmers by the rood bridge at Lexington firing 'the shot heard round the world'. Both Russell and Palmerston said they would serve under the other. John Bright also spoke and said that he would support such a government, although he had excluded himself from membership of it by the vehemence of his recent speeches against the peers and the upper classes. Nonetheless Manchester rallied to Whiggery, and, flavoured by the Peelite presence of Sidney Herbert and James Graham, produced a new cocktail in the shape of a party of government which was to last for fifty-six years.*

There were to be six Liberal Prime Ministers during this period. The first two, Palmerston and Russell, were the stars of the Willis's meeting. The last three, Rosebery, Campbell-Bannerman and Asquith, were not present for the good reason that they were respectively aged twelve, twenty-three and six at the time. The third in chronology, who was to be incomparably the most dominant of the fifty-six years, was also not present, and for the less good reason that he did not choose to go. This was despite the presence of Herbert and Graham. Gladstone made no excuse. He just stayed away. And he compounded this by voting for the (Conservative) government in the 11 June division on the Whig–Liberal amendment to the Address.

That division, which took place after three nights of debate on a Liberal amendment moved by the then almost juvenile Marquess of Hartington, put the Conservatives out for another seven years. It resulted in the defeat of the government by thirteen and immediate resignation. That result was achieved against the vote of the man who was to be both the greatest beneficiary and the greatest ornament of the new political pattern thus created.

Gladstone's was a controversial but a quiet vote. Almost all the other big parliamentary guns – Palmerston, Disraeli, Russell, Bright, Sidney Herbert, Graham, Roebuck, Cornewall Lewis – fired off during the three nights. Gladstone did not, although abstinence from a major debate was unusual on his part. He merely slipped unobtrusively into the lobby and cast his vote for the Conservative government. The remaining prominent Peelites in the House of Commons, Herbert, Graham, Cardwell, all voted the other way. Gladstone no doubt felt the separation keenly, particularly from Herbert. It was less than sixteen months since they had jointly expressed 'the fervent wish that in public life we might never part'. Gladstone was also subject to some metaphorical jostling. Two days before the vote he recorded that he had seen Mrs Herbert, 'who threatened me'.[6]

In the case of anyone but Gladstone such behaviour would have seemed an almost certain indication that he was preparing rather shamefacedly to slip his old moorings, go back into full communion

* To 1915, when the last purely Liberal government dissolved itself in the Asquith coalition.

with the Conservatives, and thereby hope to solve the problem of his need for office. In his case, however, such an interpretation bore no relation at all to either his motivation or the way in which events turned out. He had rejected all the Derby–Disraeli overtures of 1858, and although he might in the meantime have become more aware of the futility of politics without office, he had also, in his perpetual struggle to find an equilibrium point which enabled him to be anti-Disraeli without being pro-Palmerston (and vice versa), been moved a few notches towards Palmerston. His preferred outcome after the election was a Derby–Palmerston coalition with Disraeli moved away from the leadership of the Commons without being given the Foreign Office as a consolation. But that possibility disappeared at Willis's Rooms and by the time he voted it must have been obvious to him that his vote was unlikely to help the government to survive. So far from trimming for office he was indulging in another bout of Maynooth-style perversity, voting against his interest, against his friends, against his evolving beliefs, all out of some sort of loyalty to the past.

Counterbalancing this was the fortunate fact that Gladstone by this stage in his life did not need to look after his own interests. His force was such that anyone endeavouring to form a stable government wanted him in it. This was perfectly illustrated by the events of the few days after the Commons vote and by the sense of slightly resented inevitability about the way in which Gladstone emerged from them.

When Derby resigned the Queen presaged her foolish attempt twenty-one years later to keep Gladstone out in favour of Hartington by trying to get Granville, then young (only forty-four) as well as benignly unabrasive, instead of either Palmerston or Russell. This attempt to consult her own preference rather than the political realities (it was surprising that the Prince Consort allowed her to do it) would probably have foundered in any event, but it was most firmly blocked, not so much by Palmerston's unwillingness to be number two, as by Russell's determination not to be number three. Up with the number-two position he was prepared to put, but not, as an ex-Prime Minister, with the number-three one. So, by Monday, 13 June, Palmerston was again Prime Minister, and by late that night Gladstone was Chancellor of the Exchequer. He would have accepted no other office.

Russell became Foreign Secretary, Cornewall Lewis, who had hoped to be Chancellor, Home Secretary, and Granville, deprived of his undeserved premiership, Lord President. Among the Peelites, who always did well for office when they could be persuaded to take it, Gladstone was buttressed by Argyll as Lord Privy Seal, Herbert as Secretary of State for War, Newcastle as Secretary of State for the Colonies and Cardwell as Chief Secretary for Ireland. Clarendon, who had been Foreign Secretary in the previous Palmerston administration and was to be so again under Russell and then under Gladstone in the second half of the 1860s, was left out, which may have accounted for the bitterness of his wife's comments on Gladstone's return to the Exchequer. Lady Clarendon complained that Gladstone had forced himself into his old job, thereby producing the effect of a ripple demotion among the Whigs (Lewis slipped to the Home Office and her husband out altogether): 'Why he who voted in the last division with the Derby ministry should not only be asked to join this one, *but be allowed to choose his office*, I cannot conceive or rather, I *can* conceive, for I know that it is his power of speaking. They want his tongue and they dread it in opposition.'[7]

This was no doubt the principal reason why Palmerston wanted Gladstone. If he was not in, he devastated ministries from the outside. There was also a feeling that if the finances of the country were to be decently run Gladstone had to be at the Treasury. He had made himself, despite having held the office only for one great budget, a second indifferent one and a third response to the emergency of war, the indispensable benchmark for all nineteenth-century Chancellors of the Exchequer. At one level the last thing which Palmerston wanted was a moralizing, powerful and cheese-paring Chancellor. He liked to spend money, particularly on extravagant fortifications of the south coast against the French, and he was bored with the economical approach to government. Yet he knew that if he wanted his government to last (which it did for six and a half years and was brought to an end only by his own sudden but not premature death on the threshold of eighty-one) he needed an economic discipline which was as firm as it was tiresome, and that if he was safely to pursue his own foreign and defence policy adventures he needed to be tethered to a post by a cord which, while generous and even flexible, would not break under pressure. The only person capable of providing that post and cord was Gladstone, and the reason why Palmerston was a statesman and not just a mountebank with dyed whiskers was that he had the underlying wisdom to see the need for this irksome discipline.

Palmerston therefore had more than adequate motive for wishing, slightly gloomily, to have Gladstone join him. Why did Gladstone, after all his denunciations of Palmerston's deficiencies and his wholly unsatisfactory brief experience of office under him in the early months of 1855, wish to join the new Prime Minister? He recorded remarkably little in the way of explanation.* When he declined or renounced office, in 1855, in 1857, in 1858, he wrote reams of explanation of his negative behaviour. When he accepted it and had something positive to explain, he kept much more silent. 'Italy', his one-word explanation, was perhaps more aphoristic than comprehensively convincing. If this was his dominating concern it was not clear why he had insisted on being Chancellor or nothing. Foreign Secretary or a less departmentally exhausting portfolio might have better served that interest. His niece by marriage, Lucy Lyttelton, then only seventeen and later as Lady Frederick Cavendish the widow of the Phoenix Park tragedy and later still the eponym of the Cambridge college for mature women students, provided in her diary a fine example of the mixture of loyalty and mystification with which Gladstone fans received the news of his acceptance of office under Palmerston:

> Uncle William has taken office under Ld. Palmerston as Ch. of the Exchequer, thereby raising an uproar in the midst of which we are simmering, [in] view [of] his well-known antipathy to the Premier. What seems clear is that he feels it right to swallow personal feelings for the sake of the country; besides he agrees at present with Lord P.'s foreign policy, also he joins several Peelites. . . . There is this question, however: why, if he can swallow Palmn. couldn't he swallow Dizzy, and in spite of him go in under Lord Derby? I don't pretend to be able to answer this, but one can enough understand things to be much excited and interested. . . .[8]

His Oxford constituents were at least as mystified as was his niece and less inclined to balance their surprise with loyalty. A candidate, in the

* Perhaps the most revealing was in a letter to Sir William Heathcote, his colleague since the 1855 death of Inglis in the representation of Oxford. Although Gladstone claimed to be untroubled by doubt it was nonetheless remarkably defensive in tone. There were two main points at issue: first reform, and second foreign policy. Reform he desired to see settled. Derby had lost all chance of doing this by dissolving. (Why then did he vote for him in the 10 June division?) He ought therefore to 'assist those who may perhaps settle it'. On foreign policy (by which he presumably really meant Italy) he pronounced himself 'in real and close harmony with the new premier, and the new foreign secretary'. 'How could I,' he concluded, 'under these circumstances, say I will have nothing to do with you, and be the one remaining Ishmael [presumably using the word in its rare sense of an outcast] in the House of Commons?' (Quoted in Morley, *Life of Gladstone*, I, pp. 627–8.)

shape of the Marquess of Chandos, heir (if that was the right word) to the near-bankrupt second Duke of Buckingham and himself chairman of the London and North Western Railway, was immediately nominated against him, and ran him fairly but not desperately close in the short contest which followed. On 1 July Gladstone was declared re-elected by 1050 votes to 859.

His resentment that the contest took place at all was however very considerable. It reduced him, in his diary, to almost total incomprehensibility. 'I am sore about the Oxford Election; but I try to keep myself in order: it disorganises and demoralises me, while such are the riddles of *my* "human nature" it also quickens mere devotional sensibility. O that I had wings.[9] More important was the permanent disenchantment with the University as a constituency which followed from this contest. Before 1859, whatever disputes or upheavals were involved, Gladstone was proud to be member for Oxford. After 1859, he wished that he had another, less presumptuous constituency. Palmerston, as in so many matters and despite Gladstone's expression of harmony in his letter to Heathcote, felt the reverse. 'He is a dangerous man,' he said in 1864. 'Keep him in Oxford and he is partially muzzled, but send him elsewhere, and he will run wild.'[10] As with a number of more important matters, Palmerston kept the undesirable at bay for what was effectively his lifetime, but Gladstone's parliamentary divorce from the University seat began in 1859. He visited Oxford only three times in his remaining six years of his tenure as a burgess.

This was not because of an excessive preoccupation with Treasury and Cabinet business. Indeed his summer was much occupied with three distinctly non-governmental pursuits. In June and again in August he gave generous bursts of sittings to G. F. Watts, already at forty-two an eminent and fashionable portrait painter. The result was two pictures, one of which is now in the National Portrait Gallery and the other at Hawarden.

In July Gladstone read Tennyson's *Idylls of the King*, which had just been published, and became fascinated for a time with the works of that great contemporary, one of the few Victorians whose eminence equalled his own. For 18 July, the day on which in a speech lasting one hour and forty minutes he presented a provisional budget, he noted also that he had read Tennyson, 'who has grasped me with a strong hand'.[11] It was a remarkable tribute both to Tennyson's fascination and to Gladstone's eclecticism. There must be few Chancellors of the Exchequer who have been grasped by the hand of a poet on budget day.

Gladstone then read or re-read Tennyson's previous published collections, *Poems* from 1842, *The Princess* from 1842, *In Memoriam* from 1850 (it had taken Tennyson seventeen years after Hallam's death to produce this threnody) and *Maud* from 1855. In mid-August Gladstone wrote to Whitwell Elwin, the editor of the *Quarterly Review*, suggesting that he might do a substantial critical article. 'Will you let me try my hand on a review of Tennyson. . . . I have never been fanatical about him: but his late work has laid hold of me with a power that I have not felt, I ought to say not suffered, for many years.'[12] Elwin having agreed, this became his main holiday task. Penmaenmawr that year became as devoted to Tennyson as to sea-bathing.

The result was a highly readable 15,000-word essay.[13] The style is measured and orotund, with his praise couched in a schoolmasterly mode. But it was less obscure and convoluted than many of his speeches and it bounded along with interest and verve. Tennyson was rebuked for the 'somewhat heavy dreaminess' of *Maud*, 'the least popular, and probably the least worthy of popularity, amongst his more considerable works'. But it was essentially *Maud*'s militarism which offended Gladstone. 'No more shall commerce be all in all, and Peace / Pipe on her pastoral hillock a languid note' was a couplet which struck an unacceptable note for Gladstone, and he set about refuting Tennyson's apparent belief that war was an antidote to mammon-worship with a statistical intensity which would have been more appropriate to a Cobden speech against the Corn Laws than to a piece of literary criticism. Nearly twenty years later Gladstone himself came to see this, and added a footnote apologizing that the 'war-spirit in the outer world' at the time of the article had 'dislocated my frame of mind, and disabled me from dealing even tolerably with the work as a work of imagination'.

In Memoriam got much more approval, for not only was it 'perhaps the richest oblation ever offered by the affection of friendship at the tomb of the departed', but it also contained an advance antidote to *Maud* in the lines 'Ring out the thousand wars of old, / Ring in the thousand years of peace.' *Idylls of the King*, which had provoked the article, did even better. The romance of the Arthurian legend and the character of the King himself, a sort of mixture of Hope-Scott and the Prince Consort (or 'crowned curate' as George Meredith called him), made an instinctive appeal to Gladstone. 'Wherever he [Arthur] appears,' he wrote, 'it is as the great pillar of the moral order, and the resplendent top of human excellence.' Towards Lancelot he was predictably more ambivalent, but the temptation and guilt of Guinevere fascinated him, although also bringing out his schoolmasterly mode. The following passage might almost have been written by one of Gladstone's appointments as Warden of Glenalmond College:

> In any case we have a cheerful hope that, if he continues to advance upon himself as he has advanced heretofore, nay, if he can keep the level he has gained in *Guinevere*, such a work will be the greatest, and by far the greatest poetical creation, that, whether in our own or in foreign poetry, the nineteenth century has produced.

The conclusion of the article was even more glowing: 'Of it [the *Idylls* as a whole] we will say without fear, what we would not dare to say of any other recent work: that of itself it raises the character and the hopes of the age and the country which have produced it, and that its author, by his own single strength, has made a sensible addition to the permanent wealth of mankind.' Even so it is doubtful whether Tennyson, who never forgot and rarely forgave a bad review and was riding very high at the time, Laureate (appointed by Russell) since 1850 and earning much fame and money, regarded the praise for *In Memoriam* and *Idylls* as balancing the attack on *Maud*. It is always the criticism rather than the praise which writers best remember. It was to be another twenty-four years before enough grass had grown for the joint Scandinavian cruise of Prime Minister and Poet Laureate to take place and to lead to Tennyson (who had previously refused a baronetcy from both Gladstone and Disraeli) accepting a peerage from his sailing companion.

The third of Gladstone's non-governmental pursuits of the first summer of his return to office began on 30 July 1859 when he met Marion Summerhayes. His first diary entry described her as 'full in the highest degree both of interest and of beauty'.[14] He then saw her on twelve out of the next nineteen days, having been away from London for three of the blank seven. She was his greatest infatuation since Elizabeth Collins in 1851. It was probably less physically urgent but more romantic than that previous obsession. She became intermingled with his current fascination with Tennyson and the Arthurian legend. He read *The Princess* to her, and began to see her in a heavily charged pre-Raphaelite light. She was an artists' model, as well as a courtesan (not a unique combination), and his suggestion on their eighth day of acquaintance that he would commission a portrait of her by William Dyce was therefore perhaps not as far-fetched as it at first sounds. Both she and Dyce seem to have responded with at least adequate enthusiasm, and the calmly madonna-like result now reposes in the Aberdeen Art

Gallery under the title, at once demure and romantic, of *Lady with the Coronet of Jasmine*.

Gladstone was then away for a month but during a brief return in mid-September there was a fresh burst of Miss Summerhayes, mostly with a richly romantic undertone. On the 16th he read Tennyson with her for no less than four and a half hours, and was 'much and variously moved'. On the 17th there was 'a scene of rebuke [of and by whom?] not to be easily forgotten', and in the evening of the 19th after seeing her from 6.30 to 7.30 he brought her to Downing Street at 11.00 'for 1 hour, espy. to see the pictures'.[15] She remained a frequent subject of encounter throughout the autumn and winter, and continued (having in the meantime become Mrs Duke) to cross his path in varying circumstances until 1867. In July 1861 he wrote: 'Altogether she is no common specimen of womanhood,'[16] a remark well justified both by her appearance in the Aberdeen Art Gallery and by her impact upon him.

Gladstone's summer, his first in office for five years, was obviously not occupied entirely with Tennyson, Watts and Summerhayes. There is nonetheless a strong impression that he treated his return to both Cabinet and Treasury more as though he were conferring a favour upon his colleagues than panting thankfully back to office under a Whig Prime Minister. It may be that the ease with which he had stepped from the support of one government to a key job in its successful adversary (as pointedly expressed by Lady Clarendon) had gone temporarily to his head. The strict Whigs were always an alien group to him. The superficial explanation was that he was not aristocratic enough, either in origin or in manner. But this is contradicted by the fact that, of the three dukes in the government (Somerset at the Admiralty as the third), one (Newcastle) was his oldest political friend and another (Argyll) became his closest Cabinet ally. It was more that he was too serious, too God-fearing and too resolutely nineteenth century to suit the general run of the Whig cousinage who liked to believe that they kept alive the easier-going spirit of the eighteenth century. It is certainly almost impossible to imagine Gladstone in the coloured coats which went out with or before the accession of the Queen. However, in that Cabinet the only members to have been born before 1800 were Campbell, the Lord Chancellor, who balanced it by having also been born the son of the Presbyterian minister in Cupar, Fife, and Russell, who while of impeccable lineage was not exactly a ball of rakish fun. No doubt the spirit of the eighteenth century did not just depend upon date of birth, and was probably epitomized after Palmerston by Granville (born in the year of Waterloo). But here again there is the confusion that, of all the ministers who came to serve under Gladstone, Granville was the one whom he most liked, who could talk to him most persuasively, and who even managed to get Gladstone to write him letters which were almost jaunty rather than architectonic in style.

What is less open to dispute is that the heritage into which Gladstone was entering was a potentially glorious one. He became one of a triumvirate of power, with the first of the other members twenty-five years and the second seventeen years his senior. Palmerston had many reservations about Gladstone, and was in (1864) to say: 'Gladstone will soon have it all his own way; and whenever he gets my place, we shall have strange doings.'[17] Yet by persuading him to accept office in 1859 Palmerston not only gave Gladstone the opportunity to become both the longest continuously serving and most dominant Chancellor of the Exchequer of the century but also threw to him the future leadership of the newly founded Liberal party. There was one unspoken proviso, which Gladstone just, but only just, managed to meet. This was that he should not resign. And although he claimed (as a joke) that he never attended a meeting of the Palmerston Cabinet without the precaution of having a letter of resignation in his wallet, and although Palmerston claimed (as a joke) that he kept the fires of his Broadlands house burning with the fuel of such letters from Gladstone, there is no record of them in the Palmerston archives (perhaps naturally if this was the use which was made of them), and, still more to the point, Gladstone stayed put.

This was in spite of a good deal of provocation from Palmerston. The Prime Minister did not really want Gladstone to go, but he much enjoyed teasing him, and was determined that he should not think himself either indispensable or omnipotent. 'However great the loss to the Government by the retirement of Mr Gladstone,' he wrote during the great fortifications dispute to the Queen, to whom he was consistently disloyal about his Chancellor of the Exchequer, 'it would be better to lose Mr Gladstone than to run the risk of losing Plymouth or Portsmouth.' (To the French rather than to the Tories, although the latter risk may also have been in Palmerston's mind.)

This was good for Gladstone, who under a more nervous Prime Minister might have been inclined to overplay his hand and not to last the course. Their correspondence is interesting not so much for the issues discussed as for the light that it sheds on the balance and interplay of their personalities. Palmerston was much neater in phrase than Gladstone. This applied as much when he wanted to compliment his

Chancellor as when he wanted to controvert him. Thus, after Gladstone's budget of February 1860, he wrote: 'I hope you are none the worse for that triumph on Friday for which the Government is much the better.'[18] It would have taken Gladstone three paragraphs to say this. The seventy-five-year-old Prime Minister was much faster over the ground than was his forty-nine-year-old Chancellor. His jauntiness, which sometimes so irritated Gladstone, expressed itself in an admirable pithiness. Gladstone, however, was a powerful if not a darting correspondent. He was courteous, firm, fearless, and formidable in argument. They were a remarkably dissimilar yet balanced pair, each providing enough weight on the rope to ensure that neither fell into the mud and that the contest, never out of control, lasted long enough to see Palmerston out and to prepare Gladstone for coming to full power.

Gladstone had been right to jump the way that he did in 1859. It was better to have Disraeli as an opponent across the floor of the House than as an enemy on his own side. And it was better to have Palmerston as a chief with whom he could live, partly because he was so old and partly because he and Gladstone were so different that they could not be jealous of each other. It was a hostile partnership, but it worked, or at least it creaked along for six and a half years.

— 14 —

God's Vicar in the Treasury

Just as it was the budget of 1853 which made Gladstone's first chancellorship, so it was that of 1860, and the negotiations for a commercial treaty with France which led up to and determined much of the shape of it, which made his second one. For his first two or three months, as we have seen, he treated Exchequer matters with a curious casualness. His July 1859 budget, which he presented four weeks after taking office, was ostensibly a holding operation, but in reality it was even more an almost insolent reassertion of financial discipline.

Cornewall Lewis, like almost every previous Whig Chancellor of the century, had left the public finances in a fair state of laxity. Expenditure, mainly military, was 25 per cent up on the pre-Crimean War level, but was not covered by a corresponding increase in revenue. Gladstone took over a £5 million deficit. He also inherited an excited military climate. There was a colonial war with China. There was also war in the heart of Europe for the first time since 1815. That latter conflict on the plains of Lombardy was a war which, particularly as Britain was not involved, Gladstone might have had his heart much more than in the Crimea. The battle of Magenta took place on 4 June and the battle of Solférino on the 24th. They were both victories for the French (and the Italians) over the Austrians, as is demonstrated by the presence of these names on the street-maps of Paris and not of Vienna. What was more relevant to Gladstone, however, was that these events provided a smokescreen of excitement behind which his budget passed with surprising ease and scant attention. It invites comparison with Neville Chamberlain's 'hidden' 20 per cent devaluation of sterling in September 1939. There was so much else happening that it was neither widely noticed at the time nor much subsequently remembered.

Equally Gladstone's 1859 budget contained a swingeing rise in taxation by the standards of those days. He put income tax up from fivepence to ninepence in the pound, the highest peacetime rate that had then been experienced. And to compound the impact he stipulated that all the increase should be collected in the first half of the financial year. He did it while protesting that he disliked the tax, which should in general be reserved as an instrument of war. However, its greater use had been made necessary by the laxity with which expenditure had been allowed to grow since he was last at the Exchequer.

This budget went through on what Asquith would have called 'oiled castors'. For Saturday, 16 July, Gladstone recorded: 'Cabinet 2–5½: two hours took my Budget through, *pur et simple*.'[1] The only grumbling appears to have come from Lewis, but as he had as Chancellor in 1855–8 been largely responsible for the build-up of the deficit, and was also manifestly sour at not himself being again in that office, he did not cut much ice. Nor was the House of Commons difficult. There was no great clash with Disraeli, and not even a division.

Whether this easy passage helped Gladstone to settle in to a Cabinet headed by two Whigs is not clear. On Saturday, 6 August, such was the contrast between bursts of strenuousness and long periods of leisure which then made up the pattern of the parliamentary time-table, after attending and speaking in the House of Commons from noon to 1.30 p.m., he spent the afternoon in a Cabinet and wrote, a little dismissively: 'but the Cabinet is now . . . just a place for conversation'.[2]* Four days later, however, at the traditional ministerial Fish Dinner in the Trafalgar Tavern at Greenwich he much moved the audience and even Palmerston himself with the felicity of his sudden toast to the Prime Minister. But by 31 August he was writing a bitter letter of complaint to Argyll (who had missed the last two Cabinets) about the behaviour on the Italian question of Palmerston and even more so of Russell,† ironically in view of his own future handling of this relationship, calling in aid the Foreign Secretary's brusqueness to the Queen 'as a sovereign and a woman':

> When I look over what I have written [he concluded, to Argyll], it does not look very kind towards the two most eminent men in the Govt., one of them particularly. But I am sorry to say first that I believe I confess the general feeling of our Colleagues: secondly that, as I learned, the Queen has undergone very great pain in this matter: thirdly that the conduct

* Gladstone in fact used the one Greek word λέσχη in place of the last five English words.

† The issue was largely procedural. Russell wished to change a despatch, relating to whether an international conference should be proposed, which the Cabinet had approved and the form of which the Queen had accepted. The matter was resolved at a 'holiday' Cabinet on 29 August.

pursued has been hasty, inconsiderate, and eminently *juvenile*: fourthly, one is led to fear that it may have left behind disagreeable recollections.[3]

Nevertheless he had been much occupied before his departure from London on 18 August with moving into 11 Downing Street, and did not therefore seem afflicted with the uncomfortable restlessness which had led him after only a few weeks to resign (in 1855) from the previous Palmerston government. The removal was far from complete. He kept his other No. 11 in Carlton House Terrace, left his London books there, continued to use it as a base for his seven children, and quite often for himself and/or his wife as well. His letters over the next six years were just as likely to be addressed from one as from the other. This was hardly economical. Mid-Victorian prosperity, which as a leading member of the Peel and Aberdeen governments he had done as much as anyone to bring about, was obviously and justly benefiting him. This was in contrast with the years of Oak Farm worry and austerity on the one side and of old-age apprehensiveness and even a combination of stinginess and willingness to sponge which beset him in his years of greatest fame.

His 1859 autumn was marked by two non-Oxford academic honours. On All Saints Day, together with his Cabinet colleague Sir George Grey, his brother-in-law Lyttelton and the ubiquitous Bishop Wilberforce, he received a Cambridge honorary degree. In December he paid a five-day visit to Edinburgh which resulted in his being pre-elected as Rector by the University Court there, although he was not installed or called upon to deliver his rectorial address until the following April. He then spoke on 'The Work of Universities' and survived 'a crowded and kind Assembly' (in the Music Room in George Street) without riot or egg-pelting.

By far his most pregnant encounter of that autumn, however, was Richard Cobden's visit to Hawarden on 12–13 September. Cobden, then aged fifty-five, had been returned, unopposed and in his absence in America, for Rochdale at the spring general election, having been out of the House since he lost his West Riding of Yorkshire seat in the Palmerston triumph of 1857. He was still away for the Willis's Rooms meeting, but he was greeted at Liverpool on 29 June by letters from both Palmerston and Lord John Russell (for whom he had a much higher regard) pressing him to join the new government as President of the Board of Trade. He declined, on the ground that his opposition to Palmerston's policies had been so complete that suddenly to accept office under him would be ridiculous. But his long and good-humoured interview of refusal with Palmerston a day or two later left no bitterness and indeed substantially improved their relations. It also left Cobden with a slight sense of guilt towards the government and of futility about his future purpose in Parliament. Palmerston had shrewdly asked him how he expected to influence foreign policy in particular if he could never join a government.

Cobden had decided to spend the winter of 1859–60 in Paris, partly for reasons of economy, a course few Englishmen would today contemplate for that reason. While there he sought to occupy himself by engaging in commercial discussions with the French. In this way he might assuage his own sense of frustration, give some help to the government from the outside, and promote not only free trade but the relaxation of military tension. To fulfil this role, however, he needed a strong patron within the British government, and Gladstone offered the best prospect. As Chancellor he obviously held a key office. He had a proven record on free trade. Already coming under pressure for heavy armament expenditure against the French, not only from the Prime Minister, but also from his old friend Herbert as Secretary of State for War and from the Duke of Somerset as First Lord of the Admiralty, he had a strong motive for wishing to improve London–Paris relations. And he was also developing an affinity with Radicals. Once he had made his Conservative break, Gladstone was in many ways more at home with the pacifism, the anti-protectionism and the moral-force politics of the left of the Liberal party than he was with the more casual and less ideological outlook of the Whigs. This paradox was of much importance for British politics in the last forty years of the nineteenth century.

Of more immediate impact, however, was the consequence that when Cobden wrote to Gladstone from Manchester on 5 September suggesting that he might 'run over' to Hawarden in the following week and have 'a little talk' about trade with France,[4] Gladstone responded with alacrity. Although he was only four days into his Penmaenmawr holiday he arranged to return to Hawarden and receive Cobden on the following Monday and Tuesday. His diary entries expressed satisfaction with the expenditure of time and the sacrifice of holiday. For the Monday: 'Mr Cobden arrived. Several hours walk and talk with him.' Then later that evening: 'Conv. . . . with Mr C. on Currency.' And on the Tuesday morning, with more commitment: 'Further conv. with Mr Cobden on Tariffs and relations with France. We are closely and warmly agreed.'[5]

Gladstone saw him off at 11.00 and returned that afternoon to Penmaenmawr and a new burst of sea-bathing and work on Tennyson.

Cobden's skill lay in presenting the matter to Gladstone in terms which were by no means exclusively commercial. Obviously the freeing of trade with Britain's most important neighbour was in itself a highly desirable objective. But Cobden also argued for it as a corrective to the mounting fear of war with France (soon to be fortified by Napoleon III's annexation of Savoy and Nice) which was a feature of that autumn, and hence offered some protection for the Chancellor against the clamour from his colleagues for increased expenditure on armaments. The difficult point for both of them was that a bilateral commercial treaty was not wholly compatible with the strict doctrine of generalized free trade. Yet such bilateralism was the only hope of making progress with the *étatiste* French government, even more true to the spirit of Colbert in 1859 than it is today. Gladstone and Cobden agreed that this difficulty could be got round by allowing an asymmetry in the treaty. The British would make their concessions apply to other countries as well as to France, while the French could refrain from benefiting the Eskimos or even the Austrians in order to match a concession to the British. Thus was a British doctrine of non-discrimination maintained in theory, although in practice the concessions were directed towards French needs: it would have been difficult to argue that the heavy cut in wine duties was likely to be of much benefit to Swedes or Canadians, or that fine gloves, on which there was another important reduction, were at that time likely to flood in from Brazil. When the negotiations were complete Cobden felt it necessary to write defensively to Bright on this point: 'I will undertake that there is not a syllable on our side of the treaty which is inconsistent with the soundest principles of free trade.'[6]

In his anti-armament struggle Gladstone needed every help that he could get that autumn. Not only was there an expensive little war going on with China. His greatest friend in the government, Sidney Herbert, who however in the two years before his premature death in 1861 was too much of a victim of the widespread ministerial disease of departmentalitis to be much of a Cabinet ally, wanted to raise battalions of volunteers, fortify Portsmouth and Plymouth, and scatter Martello towers over much of the south of England. Somerset, as First Lord, wanted new 'line of battle' ships as well as the iron-plating of as many existing ones as possible.* And they both of them had the enthusiastic

* Gladstone in reply to this put up a sensible argument against the concept of the vast

and even hectoring support of the Prime Minister, while Gladstone before his 1860 budget did not have quite the prestige that he was to enjoy immediately after it.

On 15 December Gladstone received a formidable letter from Palmerston. 'Sidney Herbert has asked me to summon a Cabinet for tomorrow that we may come to a decision on the Fortification Question,' it menacingly began, 'and I am most anxious that the arrangements which he has proposed should be adopted.' He then proceeded to paint a nightmare scenario.

> One night is enough for the Passage to our Coast, and Twenty Thousand men might be landed at any Point before our Fleet knew that the Enemy was out of Harbour. There could be no security against the simultaneous landing of 20,000 for Portsmouth, 20,000 for Plymouth and 20,000 for Ireland. Our troops would necessarily be scattered about the United Kingdom and with Portsmouth and Plymouth as they now are these two dock yards and all they contain would be entered and burned before Twenty Thousand men could be brought together to defend either of them.

£10 or £11 million, he concluded, needed to be spent on fortifications, but there was no need for this to be a direct burden on the budget. It could be financed by a loan, payable over twenty or thirty years.

'The objection to borrowing for Expenditure is Stronger for Individuals than for a Nation,' he cheerfully continued. But his conclusion was less benign:

> If we do not ourselves propose such a Measure to Parliament it will infallibly be proposed by somebody else & will be carried; not indeed against us, because I for one should vote with the Proposer whoever he might be, but with great Discredit to the Government for allowing a Measure of this Kind involving one may say the Fate of the Empire to be taken out of their Hands.[7]

Not only did this missive show Palmerston as addicted to the emotive use of capital letters as was his Sovereign; it also amounted to as great a

---

battleship, though it required about another hundred years to become acceptable to professional naval opinion. 'Is it really wise', he wrote to Palmerston, 'to continue the present outlay on so great a scale for the building of these maritime castles which we call line of battle ships and which seem to be constructed on the principle precisely opposite to that of all land fortifications, and to aim at presenting as large a surface as possible to the destroying fire of an enemy?' (Guedalla, *Gladstone and Palmerston*, p. 113.)

mixture of siren song and intimidating barrage as has ever been deployed by a Prime Minister against his Chancellor of the Exchequer.

Gladstone, however, was proof against even such a bombardment. The French Emperor might or might not have been able to take Portsmouth or Plymouth but he would have found it much more difficult to overwhelm Gladstone. The Chancellor had the paradoxical advantage that, having been at Hawarden until specially summoned, he had read neither the Prime Minister's letter nor Sidney Herbert's paper on fortifications until he arrived at 10 Downing Street as the Cabinet began. He therefore had a good stalling position. His order of proceedings for the day was to travel up from Chester, to attend the Cabinet from 3.30 to 6.00 p.m., to seek sustenance of various sorts from Lord Aberdeen, the Duke of Newcastle and Marion Summerhayes, to dine with Sidney Herbert, whose paper together with the history of Pitt's aborted plan of 1785–6 for fortifying the dockyards he had belatedly read, and then to go to bed complaining of being 'much oppressed with cough and cold'. The next day he consequently rose late and wrote only fourteen letters, including ones to the Prime Minister, Herbert and Russell, as well as conducting three interviews before departing for Hawarden and arriving there late at night and 'in bitter frost' for two weeks of Christmas holiday.

The delaying tactics were effective. Palmerston in January 1860 never managed again to bring matters to the boil, and on 7 February, three days before his great budget, Gladstone, choosing his time well, wrote a dismissal of Palmerston's December proposal which was as intransigent as Palmerston had been thrusting, and, for once, a good deal more succinct. 'My mind is made up and to propose any loan for Fortifications would be on my part, with the view I entertain, a betrayal of my public duty.'[8] Palmerston was left to cleave for the shore: 'I have received your letter of this Morning. We will let the Question about the Fortifications rest for the present as there will be Room left for them in your Budget.'[9]

This budget had been due on 6 February, the date having been wisely chosen to get through the French treaty, which Cobden had succeeded in negotiating to the point of signature on 23 January, before the rats could get at it. A four-day postponement had, however, been made necessary by Gladstone's ill health. He had been intermittently bronchial since his 16 December complaint of 'cough and cold', thereby once again disproving the view that vast energy (plus, as it turned out, exceptional longevity) is necessarily connected with robust health. He had spent most of New Year's Day in bed, and although he functioned more or less normally during January he was severely stricken down on 3 February. That day was taken up with an almost endless series of special-interest deputations, which were in favour of the French treaty in general and cumulatively against it in almost every particular, and by the next morning (Saturday) he was worse and had to submit to strenuous remedies. 'Sent for Dr Fergusson early who found the right lung somewhat congested: he gave me antimonial wine, James's powder in pills, more mustard plasters, and at night a hot sponge coating round the chest wh proved very powerful.'[10] Even so Gladstone accepted on the Sunday that the budget on the Monday was 'physically impossible'.

It was then arranged by Palmerston (as leader of the House of Commons) that the budget statement should be on the following Friday, and be preceded by a Cabinet on the Thursday, which with apparent consideration was to take place in Gladstone's house. But Gladstone had had enough of pre-budget Cabinets. A week before he had recorded: 'Cabinet 1–4¼: very stiff. I carried my remissions [of customs and excise duties] but the Depts. carried their great Estimates.'[11] And Palmerston, behind his consideration, was clearly anxious for some reopening. 'Some of our Colleagues', he wrote, 'wish to have more discussion and Explanation about the arrangements, and also to endeavour to come to an Understanding about the Fortification Question upon which, like me, they have a very strong Feeling.'[12] Gladstone was not so easily caught. His reply, containing the passage rejecting a fortifications loan which has already been cited, made it clear that Friday was as much as he could manage ('I shall have no strength either of heart or lungs to spare'), and simply allowed the Cabinet to take place in his house but also in his absence. He remained firmly upstairs, even though he had been out for a recuperative drive on the previous day.

The ordeal to which he was about to subject himself was indeed a testing one. It was the third-longest speech that even he ever made in Parliament, and the postponement had inevitably (and perhaps even deliberately) increased the tension. *The Times*, a little mockingly, said that the question of the day had become 'How is Mr Gladstone's throat?' and suggested it was 'just a little ridiculous that all Europe should hold its breath because an English gentleman cannot make an oration in his best manner'. Ridiculous maybe, but also flattering to Gladstone, to the House of Commons and to Britain. It is some time since the chancelleries of Europe hung upon a British budget speech.

Of the fateful day itself Gladstone wrote: 'Secs. and Dr Fergusson as usual. Had to make changes in figures & finished all up. H of C at 4¼.

Spoke 5–9 without great exhaustion: aided by a great stock of egg and wine. Thank God. Home at 11. . . . This was the most arduous operation I had ever had in Parliament.'[13]

The speech filled sixty-one columns of Hansard, as against seventy-two for his 1853 triumph. But the impact was at least as strong, although the speech, in cold print and after nearly a century and a half, is much less impressive. In 1853 he took fiscal themes and beat them into a batter of high oratory, historical continuity and quasi-philosophical coherence. In 1860 he took fiscal themes and, over four hours, presented them, persuasively but often pedestrianly, as fiscal themes. His argument was not bureaucratic. It is difficult to believe that any significant part of the vast speech could have been written by anyone but himself. It was too idiosyncratic and also too ingenuous for any hand but his own to have been seriously at work.

His long panegyric in favour of French wine (in support of his reduction in the duty from five shillings and tenpence to three shillings a gallon), for instance, is a strong example of this. What Treasury official would have written thus for Gladstone?

> There is a notion gone abroad that there is something fixed and unchanging in an Englishman's taste in respect to wine. You find a great number of people in this country who believe, like an article of Christian faith, that an Englishman is not born to drink French wines. Do what you will, they say; argue with him as you will; reduce your duties as you will, endeavour even to pour the French wine down his throat, but still he will reject it. Well, these are most worthy members of the community; but they form their judgement from the narrow circle of their own experience, and will not condescend for any consideration to look beyond this narrow circle. What they maintain is absolutely the reverse of the truth, for nothing is more certain than the taste of English people at one time for French wines.

There came a most affecting passage in which he seemed to be arguing for fine growths as an aid to medicine:

> We hear of the rich man's luxuries; and of contemplated reductions in duty upon articles which the poor man does not consume. Now, I make an appeal to the friends of the poor man. There is a time which comes to all of us – the time, I mean, of sickness – when wine becomes a common necessity. What kind of wine is administered to the poor man in this country? We have got a law which makes it impossible for the poor man when he is sick to obtain the comfort and support derived from good wine, unless he is fortunate enough to live in the immediate neighbour-

> hood of some rich and charitable friend. Consult the medical profession: ask what sort of wine is supplied to boards of guardians in this country; go on board the Queen's ships and see the wine supplied there. . . .

When on some naval visit he had been pressed to sample the wine supplied to a sailor after surgery, 'it was with great difficulty I succeeded in accomplishing the operation'.[14]

In spite of this vinous excursion, and of many other *obiter dicta* ('All those of the labouring classes who are in good circumstances are large consumers of currants,' he suddenly announced), the speech, compared with its famous predecessor, remained lacking in high flights of Gladstonian oratory. Over a third of its mammoth length was devoted to a detailed justification of the commercial treaty with France, and although the general concept of the treaty, 'a great European operation', as he wrote of it to his wife, was noble enough, its individual provisions were not conducive to rhetoric. Nonetheless every point was argued with a mixture of force and simplicity. He loved to prove a point to his own satisfaction with arguments which were sometimes as naive as they were original. He certainly revealed an extraordinary state of strangulated trade between Britain and its nearest and most populous neighbour. In 1858 total British exports of manufactured goods were £130 million, of which no more than £688,000, barely a half of 1 per cent, went to France. And of that £688,000 nearly a third was accounted for by Cashmere shawls – that is, was merely an entrepôt trade from India.

He also laid down a governing principle for his finance which had the advantage that it freed him from a simple 'tea and sugar' approach to fairness towards the poor and which he stated straightforwardly as follows:

> It is a mistake to suppose that the best mode of giving benefit to the labouring classes is simply to operate on the articles consumed by them. If you want to do them the *maximum* of good, you should rather operate on the articles which give them the *maximum* of employment. What is it that has brought about the great bettering in their position of late years? Not the mere fact that you have legislated here and there for the purpose of taking off 1d. or 2d. in the pound from some article consumed by the labouring classes. This is good as far as it goes; but it is not this which has been mainly operative in bettering their condition as it has been bettered during the past ten or fifteen years. It is that you have set more free the general course of trade; it is that you have put in action the emancipating process that gives them the widest field and the highest rate of remuneration for their labour.[15]

The reductions in duty arising from the French treaty amounted to about £1.4 million. On top of these Gladstone proposed a further series of reductions, most of which, apart from timber, were fairly minor, but which had the combined effect of reducing the number of items on which duty was levied from the thousand or so which prevailed at the beginning of the main Peel government and the 419 which were still there in early 1859 to 48, of which only 15 produced significant amounts of revenue. These changes cost nearly another £1 million. All this might, give or take a small amount, have been financed out of a currently occurring fortuitous reduction of debt interest charges, known as the cessation of the long annuities.

Gladstone, however, decided to make two further changes, one in one direction and one in the other. He raised the rate of income tax by another penny, which brought in about £1½ million. And he again did it in an admonitory way. Public expenditure at the time of his 1853 budget was approximately £52 million. In the seven years between this and his second budget it had risen to around £70 million, a rate of increase totally disproportionate to the growth in national wealth, rapid although that had been. If this disproportionate growth had been avoided it would have been possible to have dispensed entirely with the income tax, the hope of which Gladstone had indeed held out in 1853. The fact that this had not happened he regarded as in some sense the collective responsibility of the prosperous classes, and he was right to the extent that they enjoyed the still relatively rare privilege of the vote and were the main formulators of a climate of opinion which had permitted the increase. It was therefore just, even desirable, that they should pay for the laxity which they had encouraged. Income tax went up from ninepence to tenpence in the pound.

The second change, although it was a remission and not an increased imposition, proved much more controversial. This was the repeal of the paper duties, at a cost of about £1 million. Gladstone produced a list of sixty-nine trades, from the manufacture of artificial limbs to shipbuilding, which he claimed would benefit marginally from the change. It would also help rural life, for 'where there are streams, where there are villages, where there is pure and good air and tolerable access, there are the places in which paper manufacture tends to establish itself'. But overwhelmingly the impact of the change would be on the ability to produce cheap newspapers and cheap books. It would amount to the removal of a tax on popular knowledge. And events were unmistakably to show that the change (which was not in fact implemented for another year) had a most powerful effect on the shape of the newspaper market. *The Times* never again held the position of the largest-selling English newspaper. Furthermore there was a substantial (although not permanent) shift from London to the provincial cities as centres of newspaper production. Hitherto there had been little of substance published in England (Scotland had an indigenous press) outside the capital. By 1864 the circulation of the provincials was nearly twice that of the London dailies.

Neither the force of Gladstone's arguments nor the attraction of these likely developments was sufficient to generate anything approaching unanimous Cabinet enthusiasm for the repeal of the paper duties. Gladstone thought that he had with him Russell, Argyll, Milner Gibson (with whom more than anyone else he agreed at this time, although – or because – Gibson was commonly considered the most Radical member), Newcastle, Granville and, maybe, the Lord Chancellor (Campbell). Of a Cabinet total of fifteen, that was hardly a commanding majority. And among the others were not only Gladstone's closest friend Herbert and his other Peelite 'ally' Cardwell, but the Prime Minister as well. Palmerston was a strong minister on his own subjects and a strong personality, but he was not exactly a strong Prime Minister. He went his own way, and allowed others, notably Russell and Gladstone, to go theirs, rather than attempting to co-ordinate the whole work of the government. Gladstone contrasted him with Peel in this respect. In Peel's government a minister always opened an issue with the Prime Minister before he took it to Cabinet. In Palmerston's this was not the habit. Ministers went straight to Cabinet, and, if the Prime Minister did not agree with them, hoped to outflank him there. Nevertheless, not to have the Prime Minister on his side was for a Chancellor making an important and controversial taxation change a grave source of weakness. And, although it was a matter of remission and not of imposition, the change was controversial both because the encouragement of a popular press was regarded by many as dangerously subversive and because many of his colleagues would much rather have spent the £1 million on fortifications and ironclads.

The changes, although announced in a single unified budget, still had to be implemented in separate individual bills. Therefore, despite Gladstone riding temporarily high immediately after the budget, and securing its approval on 24 February after a successful winding-up speech and with a majority of 116, far bigger than the government's normal strength, that was far from being the end of the matter. Palmerston had plenty of opportunities for reopening. At the end of March he began an epistolary bombardment which continued intermittently for several months, and on 5 May Gladstone recorded: 'Cabinet 1¼–4¼. Lord P spoke ¾ hour agt. Paper Duties Bill! I had to reply: Cabinet agt. him except a few.'[16] This last comment of Gladstone's was probably over-sanguine, and the opposition in the Cabinet communicated itself to Parliament. When this bill was taken in the Commons three days later he found himself speaking 'to a very adverse House', and even worse he found that his great majority of 116 had shrunk to one of 9.

This obviously left him and the bill very exposed before the Lords, who were far from enthusiastic about cheap newspapers. The position was made worse by Palmerston writing to the Queen one of the most disloyal letters which can ever have been sent to the Sovereign by a Prime Minister about a proposal of his Chancellor of the Exchequer. The Lords, he informed her, 'would perform a good public service' if they threw out the bill. She, in turn, described such an event to her uncle Leopold of the Belgians as '*as a very good thing*'. These letters were not made public at the time, but the feeling which led to their being written of course communicated itself to the political classes, helped to embolden the Lords to a rejection by 193 to 104, and was confirmed by the unconcealed public joy with which Lady Palmerston, witnessing the Lords' debate, received the news of a defeat for her husband's government. Gladstone then tried ineffectively to secure some strong government reaction to what he described as this *coup d'état* by the Lords. The strength of the phrase stemmed from his belief that the Lords by throwing out a financial measure on second reading had upset a constitutional understanding that had prevailed since the seventeenth century. But the strength of his phrase was not matched by any general strength of Cabinet reaction. Only Russell and Gibson backed him at all fully. Eventually, in early July, some mild resolutions of protest were introduced and carried. Palmerston introduced them and Gladstone spoke later in the debate. As they spoke in almost directly opposite senses this added a considerable element of farce to the proceedings.

Gladstone, however, was not in a mood to enjoy the farce, although his tastes in humour often inclined in that direction. It was altogether a miserable summer for him. His immediate post-budget prestige collapsed much more quickly than it had done in 1853, and he came to be widely regarded in both Cabinet and Parliament as hectoring and rather wild. He was often unwell: at the end of April he was intermittently in bed for five days ('Nipped again by the East Wind on my chest'); in mid-July he had another two days of incapacity with a stomach bug; and at the end of that month he was once again in bed for a day with an unspecified complaint. He was several times on the brink of resignation, against military expenditures, or in favour of paper-duties repeal, or against inactivity in response to the House of Lords. Although on Saturday, 2 June (at Cliveden, where, with the Sutherlands he spent five weekends that summer) he wrote; 'My resignation *all but* settled,' there is an underlying feeling that he had no steady wish to go. His state of mind was perhaps best summed up in a letter which he wrote to Argyll on 6 June, describing to the Duke a meeting which he had just had with Palmerston, during which Palmerston, 'kind and frank' in manner, had stressed his own determination to press ahead with a full programme of fortifications* and warned Gladstone of the 'evils and hazards' which would attend him if he did resign. Gladstone appeared not to resent this warning but concluded:

> I am now sure that Lord P. entertained this purpose [of a major increase in defence expenditure] when he formed the Government; but had I been in the slightest degree aware of it I should certainly but very reluctantly have abstained from joining [the government] and helped as well as I could from another bench its Italian purposes. Still I am far indeed from regretting to have joined it, which is quite another matter.[17]

So Gladstone teetered on the brink. But crucially, from the point of view of his evolution into the heir of Palmerston and Russell, he did not go. He suffered, however, from being thought 'anxious to wound but afraid to strike'. His reputation as a blowhard resigner whose threats need not be taken too seriously stemmed to a large extent from the events of that summer. He also suffered on 20 July from the further indignity of having a Savings Bank Monies Bill defeated in the House of Commons on a thin division by 116 to 78. Small though the figures were, the division entailed the loss of the bill and suggests lack of active support on the part of the government whips. He noted it as 'my *first* defeat on a measure of finance in the H. of C.', but endeavoured to take it in one his St Sebastian moods: 'This ought to be very good for me, & I earnestly wish to make it so.'[18]

The session also dragged on uncomfortably long, and he found

* It was in this conversation that Palmerston made to Gladstone the surprisingly particular statement that he 'had had two great objects always before him in life: one the suppression of the Slave Trade, and the other to put England in a state of defence'. (*Diaries*, V, p. 495.)

himself attempting to deal with his Treasury correspondence ('44 envelopes to open') in the absence of his private secretary as late as 21 August and taking minor debates in the House as late as the 23rd. Eventually he got to Hawarden on the 27th, and then had the full month of September at Penmaenmawr, as well as most of October at Hawarden. He had no major holiday task on hand (although he made an abortive attempt at 'a paraphrastic translation of [Aristotle's] Politics', which never saw the light of day. As a result he had rather too much time to spare, and devoted an excessive amount of it to agitating himself and others about the possible remarriage of his clergyman brother-in-law Henry Glynne to a Miss Rose, who had been governess to the Glynne girls. It would be easy for the uncharitable to think that Gladstone's objection was to any marriage which might produce a Glynne male heir and so upset the Hawarden succession, but Miss Rose was also open to some *ad feminam* objections.* It was, however, another example of Gladstone getting too excited about other people's marriages when he might have been much wiser to let them make their own decisions without his influence.

Altogether the year of 1860 was not an obviously good one for Gladstone. Nonetheless his usual birthday summing-up on 29 December was less breast-beating than had often been his custom. His main concern was the secular and not unusual one of growing older: 'began my 52nd year. I cannot believe it. I feel within me the rebellious unspoken word, I will not be old.' He concluded with an expression of 'the unbounded goodness of God and of [my] own deep deep deep unworthiness',[19] but that for him was no more than par for the course.

Less obviously, however, 1860 had been an important stage in his advance to pre-eminence. Despite the evaporation of his popularity during the summer, he had added another formidable budget to his record of achievement. And, perhaps even more important, he and Palmerston had begun to acquire the habit of living together if not in harmony at least without rupture. They had taken each other's measure, and had survived in the same government. By the end of 1860, therefore, Gladstone was already well on the way to meeting the main provision for his succession to the Liberal leadership, which was that he should not resign.

* Eventually she had to be paid off with the very considerable sum of £5000, which led to Gladstone, who was the intermediary in making the payment, being quite falsely accused in an Irish newspaper of making it to cover up his own immoral activities.

15
The People's William

Gladstone's experiences in the summer of 1860, both with the Tory House of Lords and with his Whig Prime Minister, did much to drive him towards what became in some but not all respects an advanced Liberalism. This process was aided by two parallel developments. First death removed nearly all his close political associates. Aberdeen, the 'tutelary deity' of the Peelites as Gladstone had described him in 1855, subsided in December 1860 at the full age of seventy-six. Then in August 1861, Sidney Herbert, who had been forced by ill health to resign from the War Office in July, died at only fifty. Gladstone was desolated by this, the more so perhaps because of their recent disputes within the Cabinet.

Thus the two politicians with whom he felt the closest emotional links, one of a previous and one of his own generation, had both gone within eight months, and the latter event in particular filled him not only with sadness but with morbidity. When Herbert had come back through London on 31 July, after an unavailing health journey abroad, Gladstone went to look from a window of a neighbouring house in order to watch him as he came and went from his house in Belgrave Square. 'Alas it was a sore sight.'[1] Two days later Herbert died at Wilton, where a week after that Gladstone attended the 'alike sad and soothing' funeral. There is a view that, had Herbert lived, he and not Gladstone would have succeeded to the Liberal leadership after Palmerston had died and Russell had withdrawn. This is hardly more plausible than the view that Oliver Stanley, a somewhat similar figure who died in somewhat similar circumstances in 1952, would have frustrated Harold Macmillan in 1957.

Less than three months later James Graham died unexpectedly at sixty-nine. Gladstone had not been as emotionally close to Graham, a less highly strung character, as to the other two, but he had been the one upon whom he most depended for sensible advice, and Graham's last significant Commons speech, in support of the 1861 budget, had been made in response to a direct appeal from Catherine Gladstone that an intervention from him would make her husband feel less isolated.

Newcastle, Gladstone's contemporary like Herbert, survived only three years after Graham. In June 1862, Charles Canning, another contemporary and the son of Gladstone's first political hero as well as himself a former Governor-General of India, also died, and the Peelites, apart from Gladstone himself and Cardwell, who although able and ambitious, was never central to the group, became collectively extinct. Thereafter Gladstone had no partners with even a claim to equality.

Not only the Peelites were vulnerable in the early 1860s. Within the government, Campbell the Lord Chancellor died in June 1861 and George Cornewall Lewis the Home Secretary in April 1862. Office is normally a preservative, and it was unique for a Cabinet to have a third of its members struck down in office, four of them within a year. It was made the more remarkable by the fact that its chief, healthily imperturbable, sailed on to an age at which nobody had previously contemplated presiding over a government. (Gladstone overtook him when he formed his fourth administration.)

Outside the British government, Cavour went of a fever in June 1861, the Prince Consort of, maybe, another one in December of the same year, and John Neilson Gladstone in February 1863. Of these deaths, that of the Piedmontese statesman who had so kindled Gladstone's Italian enthusiasm in 1859 was affecting ('What a deathbed: what a void'[2] was his characteristic comment on reading an account of Cavour's end) and that of his brother with whom he had first seen Italy thirty-one years before much more so. The attention which he devoted to performing every possible fraternal service at and after the death of J. N. Gladstone was remarkable by any standards, and particularly so for someone carrying Cabinet responsibilities. He went to Bowden Park, near Chippenham, three days before his brother's death and stayed there for ten days, returning to London only after the funeral. He wrote long harrowing accounts of the deathbed scene, the tone of which can be judged from his concluding sentences:

> The chamber of death was cleared: and then the loud weeping went through all the house: but when it had sounded *in* the room it was hushed again; they [his brother's daughters] restrained themselves lest at the solemn moment of his passage to his God, he should be intruded on by human earthly woes. But we are near the break of Saturday's dawn.[3]

Gladstone then spent a week comforting his seven orphaned nieces (and one seven-year-old nephew), arranging the funeral, and clearing up the estate, both legally and physically. His slightly officious sense of family duty, his morbidity and his religious commitment united to make him an exceptional mourner. Tom and Robertson Gladstone were also present at the death and the funeral, as indeed was Helen, but they, although largely unoccupied, neither stayed for long nor took the central responsibility.

It was nonetheless the demise of Prince Albert which not only carried its extraordinary panoply of national mourning but also made the greatest difference to Gladstone's future. He had been staying at Windsor only fifteen days before the Prince's death, and although he was subsequently to pass many long weeks as minister in attendance at Balmoral as well as continuing to make occasional one- or two-day semi-official visits to Windsor, his position as one of the Queen's favourite politicians, his diligence and loyalty as a minister fortified by her interest in and close knowledge of his wife and children, began to decline almost as soon as the Prince became a sacred but frozen memory and not a present adviser. This was well before Disraeli had major opportunities to ingratiate himself and poison the springs of the Queen's relationship with Gladstone.

The papers-duties issue and the antipathy to the Lords which arose out of it gave Gladstone what was, until then, one of his few popular causes. The issues on which he had hitherto fought his strongest parliamentary battles were not calculated to make him a hero of the people. Standing out against anti-papist hysteria, denouncing the excesses of Lord Palmerston's jingoism as in the Don Pacifico debate, resisting an enquiry into the mismanagement of the Crimean War and then advocating an early peace with Russia rather than outright victory, keeping divorce as a wholly exceptional upper-class privilege, defending small boroughs as 'the nurseries of statesmen', and upholding the full rigour of church rates on Dissenting parishioners may all have been appropriate issues for thundering speeches from the member for Oxford University. But they were not likely to win him a mass popular following.

Yet his personality as it was developing in his sixth decade, and above all his vibrant and declamatory speaking style, began to cry out for the stimulus and indulgence of mass popular audiences. The House of Commons was where he had made his reputation and where he exercised his power, but the capacity of the chamber was no more than 500 rather blasé members, a handful of ladies behind a grille and a few hard-scribbling reporters. And Gladstone, just in the way that some runners are better at a mile than a sprint, and some reviewers at 3000 rather than 1000 words, was developing into a natural 5000- or even 15,000-, arena man. The Sheldonian Theatre at Oxford, let alone the London banquets and lectures, at which he increasingly often recorded himself as 'giving thanks for the House of Commons and/or Ministers' or for the quality of the (frequently) episcopal address, could not begin to fill his needs in that respect.

Aided by the affront which his 1859 by-election had inflicted this created a conflict of constituency pulls. In the summer of 1861 he seriously contemplated an immediate withdrawal from Oxford and a transfer to another seat. South Lancashire, which became his destination after his 1865 defeat, was immediately on offer because a third seat was being created there, and deputations waited upon him. This constituency had the advantage for oratory of geographically embracing both Liverpool and Manchester (although not preventing their independent representation in Parliament), and thus holding out the enticing prospect of addressing great assemblies in the St George's and Free Trade Halls. The other possibility was the not very demotic although at that stage safely Liberal one of the City of London, where the Foreign Secretary, one of its four members, had decided, on the threshold of seventy, to become a peer. He thus exchanged the name of Lord John Russell, to which he had given a unique reforming resonance, for the more routine ex-Prime Ministerial earldom, which has nonetheless descended through three generations of exceptional intellectual quality. Eventually, to the considerable relief of the Prime Minister, Gladstone decided to stay where he was until the next general election. Palmerston hoped Oxford would keep him at least half muzzled. Gladstone had to settle for the small step of resigning from the Carlton Club, which he did in March 1860 and which his faithful amanuensis Robert Phillimore thought a considerable mistake, particularly as Phillimore added encouragingly, 'They hate Gladstone more at Brooks's than they do at the Carlton.'.

Relations between Gladstone and the Prime Minister proceeded on a superficially uneven keel. Their correspondence mingled the most crunching and forthright disputes, on matters both of substance and of form (the latter generally the more dangerous between colleagues), with bursts of consideration for each other. Gladstone would be delighted to defer to the Prime Minister on the date of the Whitsun recess and hence when his Finance Bill might start in committee. Palmerston was happy to make the Provost of The Queen's College Bishop of Gloucester, and would Gladstone like to convey 'the news to his constituent'? The Lord Chancellor had unfortunately died and what were Gladstone's views about a replacement and consequent promotions among the Law Officers? They both of them showed a most admirable ability to argue vehemently without personal bitterness. When for the 1861 budget

Gladstone finally got his renewed attempt at removing the paper duties through a Cabinet which the day before appeared to have been almost unanimously against him, he added to his relief his appreciation of 'Ld. P. yielding gracefully'.[4]

Yet some of the disputes were very sharp. In late February 1861, just after the Estimates had been settled, Palmerston sent round a paper demanding an extra £3 million for naval defence. This would be the equivalent, in relation to today's budget size, of a Prime Minister suddenly demanding an extra £10 billion of uncovenanted expenditure, rather comparable with the costs a century and a quarter later of another Prime Minister's commitment to the poll tax. However, Chancellors were more robust in those days. Within an hour or so, Gladstone sent back 'a strong paper of objection, amounting at one point nearly to complaint', and Palmerston's demand evaporated.

Three months after this the Prime Minister was writing what could hardly be regarded as either a friendly or a supportive letter to his Chancellor: 'You must be aware that your Budget is not much liked in the House except by the comparatively small Band of Radicals below the gangway, who are thought to be your Inspirers in financial matters. . . .'[5] And another two months after that Palmerston was complaining that his rights as First Lord of the Treasury were being abrogated. He did not intend to assert them over the Chancellor to the extent that Sir Robert Peel had (a shrewd thrust), but: 'I wish it to be clearly understood between us that I do not intend to be set aside as I have been on this occasion, and to be made without my Knowledge and Consent a virtual Party to Proceedings of which I intirely disapprove.'[6]

This arose out of an obscure dispute about the financing of the new Law Courts in the Strand, which Gladstone for a variety of reasons, mostly but not all associated with the cost of the site, had wanted to be in Lincolns Inn Fields instead. Gladstone had to deal with this letter on the day on which he also gave his final decision to the South Lancashire deputation, conducted the committee stages of his Inland Revenue Bill for four hours, and made another Commons speech in a debate on the Italian situation, which concluded at 1.15 a.m. This did not cause him to delay in his 'second and long letter to Ld. P. in reply to his indictment – [written] after consultation with Sir J. Graham'. The press of events did, however, lead him to write: 'What a day, my brain whirled.'[7]

His reply to Palmerston began as though it were going to be an apology: 'I have read with much regret your letter of today.' But the regret soon turned out to be more associated with Palmerston having written the letter than with Gladstone having provoked it. There next followed a substantial chunk of moderately convincing justification for Gladstone's view that he had not acted discourteously or unreasonably. Then he reached his admonitory but not succinct conclusion:

> At the same time, meaning to speak without reserve, and not being *certain* that your letter has been written in momentary forgetfulness, and under the pressure of events, of the facts I have related, I cannot omit to say that its language appears to me to be of equivocal construction, and suggests the idea that you may have meant by its tone to signify that you thought the time may have come when the official connection between us ought to cease. If such is your intention I beg by this letter to leave the matter entirely at your choice, and I shall feel that at the close of the session, in the present state of our financial affairs, it can be done without any public inconvenience. If you have no intention of this kind, please to consider the last sentence as never having been written. I shall expect to hear from you before any Cabinet is held.[8]

The next Cabinet took place the following afternoon and proceeded normally, without any disruption of the government. Palmerston had presumably assured Gladstone that his admonition was in no way to be interpreted as a desire for a separation. Gladstone had made it clear that he was no man to accept a rather half-baked rebuke. On the other hand he may have been contributing to the impression in Palmerston's mind that he talked about resignation too freely and frequently for there to be much need to take it seriously. Gladstone's pattern, the Prime Minister disparagingly informed the Queen in the following year, was 'ineffectual opposition and ultimate acquiescence'.[9]

What was also the case was that as Gladstone's budgets succeeded each other throughout the first half of the 1860s – he produced a total of seven under Palmerston – and as their financial skill made at least some of Palmerston's extravagances compatible with modest surpluses, and as they also coincided, the severe trade hiccup of the American Civil War apart, with the continuation of mid-Victorian prosperity, so the idea of Gladstone performing his spring rites at the Treasury came almost to assume the status of a national institution. The university boat race in March, a Gladstone budget in April, the opening of the Royal Academy in May were all signs of stability. This gave a growing strength to Gladstone's position, however much he might irritate Palmerston. It is reminiscent of the position in the Federal Republic of Germany a hundred years later when Ludwig Erhard's economic management provided the essential foundation for Adenauer's foreign policy successes, but earned no affection from his chief as a result. Gladstone, however, was a much more formidable political personality than Erhard, who knew how to run an economy but not how to run a government.

Gladstone's growing reputation for probity and indispensability provided his often unstable personality with necessary cushions for its rashness. This rashness, apart from his vertiginous sexual–charitable forays, showed itself in three bewildering political excursions during these last years of Palmerston. The first was his animadversions on the American Civil War, the second his attempt to tax charities, and the third his sudden lurch towards universal (male) suffrage.

In April 1862 he began a new wave of provincial political forays. The first was to Manchester, and was not significantly different in form from the visit which he had paid to the same city nine years before. He stayed for three nights a little off-shore in the Cheshire residence of a rich manufacturer. On one day he inspected the factories of his host and of one or two others. On the first two evenings there were large dinner parties at which Gladstone held forth, or 'conversed' as he put it, on the distress of the cotton trade which was already resulting from the American Civil War. On the third evening he gave a major address, which was the central purpose of the visit and to which he had devoted far more effort of preparation than any House of Commons performance, other than a budget, had ever seemed to call forth. He was at it on the first evening, on the second afternoon, on the third morning, and then, an almost unheard-of practice, 'read it aloud to C[atherine] by way of trial'. It was delivered in the Free Trade Hall 'crowded with a most cordial auditory [*sic*]'. The subjects were the not altogether complementary ones of Prince Albert and the cotton trade. But most interesting was the nature of the audience for which he took such trouble. It was the Association of Lancashire and Cheshire Mechanics Institutes. There was nothing demagogic about what he said. Even the Queen was pleased, and somewhat moved, by his tribute to the late Prince Consort. And on distress in the cotton trade he was naturally as Chancellor rather defensive. But he was nonetheless paying high respect to what was essentially a working men's organization.

The next day he devoted himself to civic festivities: the presentation of an address at the Town Hall with a full-scale Gladstone speech in reply; a special service in the cathedral; a luncheon with more speeches; and then off to Hawarden in the afternoon. It was a visit, except for its more leisurely time-scale, such as any leading politician might have paid to any major provincial city a hundred years later. The difference was that in 1862 very few of them did. Gladstone was breaking new ground, and he did it still more noticeably in the North-east in the following autumn.

The pattern there was similar to Manchester, except that the ship-building rivers of the Tyne, Wear and Tees introduced an element of water pageant, the enthusiasm was greater, and Gladstone was more indiscreet. He and Catherine Gladstone arrived from Carlisle (near where they had been staying with the then eighty-four-year-old Lord Brougham, to whom Gladstone had latterly become a devoted visitor) on Monday, 7 October 1862, and were installed in the considerable establishment (Gladstone wrote of 'the Park and Gardens of this beautiful place') beyond Gateshead of William Hutt, who was then MP for that town. As at Manchester there were large dinner parties for local notables. On the Tuesday morning, as well as a myriad other activities, Gladstone 'reflected further on what I should say about Lancashire [a curious choice of subject for Tyneside] and America'.[10] Then to Newcastle where, after appraising Grey Street as 'I think our best modern street', he addressed at 6.00 p.m. 'a crowded and enthusiastic dinner of near 500' in the Town Hall. He commented that the hall was 'not very easy to fill with the voice'. Nevertheless his words rang only too far and too fast, to London and across the Atlantic. The notorious passage, as it quickly became, was this:

> We know quite well that the people of the Northern States have not yet drunk of the cup and they are still trying to hold it far from their lips – which all the rest of the world see they nevertheless must drink of. We may have our own opinions about slavery; we may be for or against the South, but there is no doubt that Jefferson Davis and other leaders of the South have made an army; they are making, it appears, a navy; and they have made what is more difficult than either, they have made a nation.[11]

It was a major indiscretion, stating that the attempt of the North to uphold the Union by force was lost, and implying strongly that Britain was about to recognize the Confederacy. Charles Adams, son and grandson of Presidents and full of Bostonian virtue and style, who was American minister in London, in fact reacted coolly but nonetheless hinted to Russell that had he not been so restrained he would have asked 'for his passports' (whatever that diplomatic phrase meant; why did an ambassador or a minister not keep them with him, and why did he in any event need more than one?). Russell was considerably embarrassed and had to explain that Gladstone did not intend exactly what he had said. It is to be hoped that he did better in this respect than Gladstone himself did in a letter which he prepared for his secretary to send to complaining correspondents:

> Mr Gladstone desires me to remark that to form opinions upon questions of policy, to announce them to the world, and to take, or to be a party to taking, any of the steps necessary for giving them effect, are matters which, although connected together, are in themselves distinct, and which may be separated by intervals of time, longer or shorter according to the circumstances of the case.[12]

Russell indeed covered up for Gladstone with as much loyalty as could possibly have been expected, but he did write to him saying that 'I think you went beyond the latitude which all speakers must be allowed.' Palmerston probably minded less. He was somewhat more pro-South, would like to have organized a mediation between Union and Confederacy and was never averse to Gladstone getting himself into trouble and thus weakening his Cabinet influence.

Why did Gladstone do it? He was not in fact particularly pro-South. He was much more akin to a man of Massachusetts than to one of South Carolina. And it was not demagogy either, although many of his fellow politicians who were free from temptation in this respect thought that he was making himself drunk with crowds. But the Tyneside crowds would mostly have preferred a more resolute anti-slavery message.

Gladstone at this stage had some anti-American prejudices of a type prevalent in England for the hundred years between the United States beginning to do things on a big scale and the results of this bigness turning the balance in the Second World War. He regarded them as a crude and braggart people. It never occurred to him to visit them at home. Yet he had become a surprisingly close friend of Charles Sumner, the senator–orator from Massachusetts, who had first visited Hawarden in 1857, and who became for Gladstone something of the equivalent of Plantagenet Palliser's Ezekiel Boncassen in *The Duke's Children*. And at the end of his life when he looked back on the Newcastle speech, he was as warm towards the United States as he was critical of himself. 'Strange to say', he wrote in 1896,

> this declaration [that Jefferson Davis had made a nation] most unwarrantable to be made by a minister of the crown with no authority other than his own, was not due to any feeling of partisanship for the South or hostility to the North. Many who wished well to the Northern cause

> despaired of its success.... The friends of the North in England were beginning to advise that it should give way, for the avoidance of further bloodshed and greater calamity.... My offence was indeed only a mistake, but one of incredible grossness, and with such consequences of offence and alarm attached to it, that my failing to perceive them justly exposed me to very severe blame.

He added: 'And strange to say, *post hoc* though perhaps not *propter hoc*, the United States have been that country in the world in which the most signal marks of public honour have been paid me, and in which my name has been the most popular, the only parallels being Italy, Greece, and the Balkan Peninsula.'[13]

This was a handsome apology, but written thirty-four years after the event. The comment of John Bright, already in general a considerable admirer of Gladstone, was fully to the point and more contemporary. Three days after the speech he wrote: 'He [Gladstone] is as unstable as water in some things; he is for union and freedom in Italy and for dissension and bondage in America.'[14]

One thing that Gladstone's blunder did not damage was the success of the remainder of his progress through the North-east. On the following day, the Wednesday, there was a celebratory river expedition, but it was hardly a rural picnic. It proceeded for twenty-two miles past the most industrialized river banks in England, and its purpose was to give an opportunity for public acclaim:

> Reached Gateshead at 12 [the diary account ran], after an Address and reply embarked in the midst of the most striking scene which was prolonged and brightened as we went down the river at the head of a fleet of some 25 steamers amidst the roar of guns and with the banks lined and dotted above and below with great multitudes of people.

There were even said to be men providing a swimming guard of honour in front of the Gladstone boat, a scene recalling Betjeman's poem about 'Captain Webb the swimming man', who made his way endlessly through the murky industrial canals of the West Midlands. 'The expedition ended at six, I had as many speeches as hours,' Gladstone continued. 'Such a pomp I probably shall never again witness: circumstances have brought upon me what I do not in any way deserve.... 'The spectacle was really one for Turner and for no one else.'[15]

On the Thursday they moved from Tyne to Tees, and repeated the steamboat cavalcade from Middlesbrough. It had been prefaced by a public tour of Newcastle, by an address to the Naval Reserve there and by a speech to a large meeting in the Town Hall and another at Sunderland, where he was seized by giddiness and 'had to take hold of the table' before continuing his speech. That day amounted to fifteen hours of continuous activity, concluding with another public banquet. That night he wrote: 'I ought to be thankful: still more ought I to be ashamed. It was vain to think of reading, writing or much reflecting on such a day.'[16] Saturday, with only a luncheon speech in York, must have seemed like a holiday after his exertions.

What did the crowds signify? Most of all the simple undiscriminating fact that Gladstone had become a name which tripped off people's lips, that he had an identifiable appearance which did not betray his fame and his authority, and that when they went home and said they had seen Gladstone that bestowed prestige rather than caused mystification. There was also some feeling that he was on their side, not in the sense of an economic class struggle, for he was never strong on the social condition of the people, but in the sense that he was for seriousness against cynicism, for moral purpose against frivolity, for the achievements of industrial and industrious Britain at a time when it was supreme in these respects, and also in some sense for the solid striving of the northern provincial centres as against the glitter of London and the soft landscape and more traditional society of the South of England.

There was no other ministerial politician who could fill this role. Of the others who could claim to be household names, Russell and Palmerston were very much metropolitan and South of England Whigs, in spite of their both having been (briefly) at Edinburgh University a half-century or more before. Disraeli was too brittle, and Derby, even though he lived in 'a stink of chemicals' on the edge of Liverpool, was essentially a parliamentary politician. The view of Gladstone as an elevated but nonetheless popular politician was neatly captured by the jingle locally composed for the occasion:

> Honour give to sterling worth,
> Genius better is than birth,
> So here's success to Gladstone.

His wife, who had been through all the strenuous Tyne and Tees days without complaint, thought it was the first time he had ever been properly honoured.

For Gladstone's democratic progress William Hutt and the several other local MPs and aldermen who organized visits and attended him on them were important agents. The steamers and the Town Hall banquets had to be provided, and the populace informed where they might see and cheer the great man. For these owners of large and comfortable houses conveniently adjacent to the big provincial cities, and often themselves substantial manufacturers or engineers as well as civic dignitaries, there was a lot to be said for tying the big gun of the Chancellor as firmly as possible into the Liberal party (of which, by no stretch of the imagination, could he be regarded as having been a supporter for more than three years), and in particular to their non-Whiggish and provincial tendency within it.

For Gladstone things were never quite the same again after Newcastle. He may have made a nonsense of his American Civil War speech, but this was more than balanced by the rapture of his reception. He became, to put it vulgarly, hooked on crowds. His diary remark about thankfulness and shame showed a good deal of insight. His quarter-envious, three-quarters disapproving colleagues might have been mildly assuaged by his self-criticism, but not more.

Six months after Newcastle, in the budget of 1863, Gladstone launched his Don Quixote attack on charities. The attack was made the more quixotic by the fact that he had absolutely no need to do it. Despite the adverse trade effects of the American Civil War and severe distress in Lancashire, to the relief of which the Gladstones were forthcoming in their personal capacities although William was cautious in his Exchequer role,* he ended the financial year 1862–3 with a surplus, massive for those days, of £3¾ million. Some concessions were obviously called for and he reduced the rate of income tax from ninepence to sevenpence in the pound, as well as bringing down the tea duty. But he sought to make one move the other way. He proposed to bring in £¼ million by removing the tax exemption which the income of registered charities had hitherto enjoyed. How his rather querulous Cabinet colleagues let him do it is difficult to imagine. There is no record of any stiff Cabinet struggles, such as those he had experienced with his paper-duties concessions in 1860 and 1861. The whole budget was approved in a two-hour sitting on the day before he presented it to the House of Commons. It is impossible to avoid the thought that there must have been some colleagues who were quite willing to see him take a tumble.

* A party of distressed mill operators was provided with shelter and some agricultural work at Hawarden, and Catherine Gladstone actively organized relief schemes in Blackburn and other Lancashire towns.

Gladstone's approach to the issue was based on a tramlines logic which could sometimes take over his mind, and was buttressed by what Palmerston saw as his ability to persuade himself of the rightness of any view which he chose to hold. Here he persuaded himself that tax on the income of charities was not just a fiscal convenience but a moral imperative. If ever a man deliberately poked a stick into a wasps' nest it was he. He supported his action with the following arguments. Most money at the disposal of charities came from legacies. But deathbed bequests were not nearly as laudable as giving away money during a man's lifetime, when he genuinely deprived himself of spending power. In a legacy he merely deprived someone else. (To this precept Gladstone gave considerable practical effect. Throughout his adult lifetime he gave to charity £114,000, the equivalent of £5½ million today, spread surprisingly evenly over the decades.)[17] Lifetime gifts were, however, made out of taxed income and, assuming they went to the revenue accounts of charities, enjoyed no concession. This was perverse, and meant that not only did the existing law on the taxation of charities offend the principle that all money, 'a trust from God', should be taxed alike, but also favoured the less worthy over the more worthy form of giving. To make sure that no wasps in the nest were left undisturbed he added, for good measure, the argument that most charities were inefficiently and even corruptly run.

The furore was considerable. The 'wasps' assembled a most formidable deputation which waited upon Gladstone at 3.30 p.m. on 4 May. It was headed by the Duke of Cambridge (Commander-in-Chief and the Queen's cousin) and made up, *inter alia*, of both Archbishops* and of that Earl of Shaftesbury who epitomized philanthropy. Gladstone

* Longley had recently been translated from York to Canterbury, with Gladstone's strong approval. Thomson, after only a year at Gloucester, had replaced him at York, but against Gladstone's wishes. Gladstone had written a long but good letter to Palmerston urging the claims of Wilberforce. It was vintage Gladstone, urging Wilberforce's appointment on the highest grounds of principle: he was a fine bishop, a great preacher, a unifying influence within the Church, maybe a bit social but how desirable it was to have a prelate who could 'maintain the hold and influence of religion upon the higher circles of civil life'. And then Gladstone's jesuitical side came to the surface, and he slipped in a good fall-back defence: 'But those who think he meddles too much in London would gladly see him removed to a spot where he would no longer be within an hour of the Metropolis.'

It was unavailing. Wilberforce, who had been at Oxford for seventeen years, did not go to York, and Thomson, once his curate and a diocesan for only a year, did. Gladstone might be the most dominating Chancellor of the century, but Palmerston was still Prime Minister, and liked so to remind Gladstone.

received them for forty-five minutes, and then, less than an hour later, got up in the House of Commons and spoke for three hours and ten minutes in defence of his proposals. It was widely thought to have been one of the two or three outstanding parliamentary performances of his life. It was cogent and trenchant and defiant, but it was inevitably defensive, and its artistry and muscular skill lay in the triumph of technique over circumstances. It was the equivalent of a captain's 80 on a bad wicket in a Test match which was in the course of being lost. He put everything he had into it: 'Worked hard on my papers all the morning. Spoke 5.10–8.20 with all my might, such as it was; after such prayer as *I* can make.' But it was a dying fall: 'The feeling grew more favourable to the act of justice we recommended: but we could not fairly ask our friends to divide, and withdrew the Clauses.'[18]

The retreat was complete, redeemed only by the brilliance of the bugle call by which it was ordered. Yet Gladstone took it very much in his stride. Eighteen-sixty-three was altogether a good year for him, much better than 1860 and 1861 when he had experienced heavy strains in living with Palmerston. His position in the government had become secure and powerful. He was in full command of the Treasury, and could run it without undue effort. That summer he spent the whole of August at Hawarden, an almost equally complete September at Penmaenmawr, and then two weeks 'in attendance' at Balmoral. The last does not sound much like a holiday but Gladstone was surprisingly successful in making it so, with long walking expeditions (one of nineteen miles) on his own. The fortnight appeared to involve only two dinners and three audiences with the Queen, who when she had tried to have a fourth had found Gladstone missing in the hills. These limited contacts he found perfectly agreeable, and it was only after a similar tour of duty in the following year that he recorded a little maliciously: 'she weighs I am told 11 stone eight pounds – a secret! Rather much for her height.' And again: 'Mrs Bruce says the Queen was not well: and it seems she drinks her claret strengthened, I should have thought spoiled, with whisky.'[19]

His pleasure in Penmaenmawr was at its peak in those years of the early 1860s. In 1862 he had there enjoyed twenty-seven sea-bathes, the presence of two bishops (Oxford and Gloucester who must have treated each other warily in view of the impending York choice), as well as having two deans within driving distance, and a twenty-four-hour visit from the Dowager Duchess of Sutherland, whose husband, the second Duke, had died in 1861. They had both often entertained Gladstone when the Duke was alive, notably during his enforced twenty-six days at Dunrobin in 1857, but it was with Harriet Sutherland, an intelligent and forceful woman, four years older than himself, that Gladstone's particular friendship lay. During the parliamentary sessions of 1862 and 1863 he spent respectively six and seven weekends at Cliveden, the Sutherland palace on the middle Thames which Barry had built only a decade or so before and which was to pass through the Grosvenors before finding its way to the Astors in 1893. The Dowager Duchess died in 1868 but not before she had played a notable part, at Gladstone's instigation, in entertaining Garibaldi on his somewhat swaggering visit to England in 1864. The hero of the Risorgimento was said to be the only man who had ever smoked a cigar in her private sitting room, as well as requiring carefully placed spittoons.* Duchess Harriet was a considerable source of political solace and advice to Gladstone, and it was a pity that her son, the third duke, became so virulently partisan as to call him a Russian agent in 1878.

In 1863 Penmaenmawr was almost as good as in the preceding year. The Duchess did not come and there was only one bishop in the neighbourhood, but he was a major prelate. Tait, already Bishop of London, later succeeded Longley at Canterbury. There were twenty-one sea-bathes, but some concern about 'my stiffening limbs'. After a walk of twenty-five and three-quarter miles (very precise) on his way across North Wales from Hawarden he feared that his days 'of long stretches' were over. In general, however, he seems to have been less obsessed with growing old than had been the case at the beginning of his fifties. Of the turn of the year 1862–3, when he became fifty-three, he wrote with a satisfaction and an optimism which, while not complacent, would have been unimaginable a dozen years before: 'thus ending well what has been so good a year. We sat, and heard the bells chime in 1863; may its course be blessed to us all.'[20] And a year later, while there was some of the old introspective note about sin, his birthday entry was very calm compared with his previous habit. Two days after that, at the end of that calendar year, there was more of an attempt at high-flown

* This led to a current anti-Gladstone joke which the *Economist*, at that time very pro-Gladstone, recalled and printed when it turned away from him at the time of the Home Rule split. In response to a not very serious suggestion that there would be much to be said for a marriage between General Garibaldi and the Duchess, it was pointed out that the General already had a wife at home. 'Oh, there is no problem,' it was countered, 'Gladstone is here, and we could get him to explain her away.' (Ruth Dudley Edwards, *The Pursuit of Reason: A History of the Economist*, p. 378.)

prose than a repetition of the old breast-beating: 'And so farewell old year. May the next if given fly away with wings unsoiled.'[21]

One almost inevitable disappointment of the period was that, as Willy Gladstone came to the end of his Oxford years, so his failure to emulate his father became manifest. He had got a first in Honour (classical) moderations two years before. But the diary entry for 7 June 1862 read: 'Heard in the morning of Willy's *second* class [in Greats]. The news was chill; but it is easy to see it may be good.'[22] Then it was decided that Willy should go back to Oxford, and read for another honours school in Law and History, and perhaps try for an All Souls fellowship. Six months later, however, there came the even worse result from this: 'A letter from Willy informed us he had only a 3rd Class in the Law and History Schools. Both his virtues & his faculties excellent: it would be very wrong to complain if his energy is not quite on the same scale.'[23] It is with deep sympathy for Willy that one feels the struggle between Gladstone's parental affection and his difficulty in understanding how anyone called William Gladstone could possibly fail to have almost infinite reserves of energy. The All Souls prospect naturally evaporated and it was not clear what Willy was going to do. However, he became MP for Chester three years later (at a cost to his father of £2000), but not to much more purpose than had been achieved by the parliamentary careers of his uncles and grandfather. And in the autumn of 1862 Stephy followed the well-worn path from Eton to Christ Church, and Gladstone had a second horse in the Lit. Hum. stakes. Admirable and dedicated a parson though Stephen Gladstone became, however, he did no better in this race than had his brother.

To balance these disappointments there were two reconciliations across the Anglican–Roman frontier, neither of them complete, but each marking some assuagement of old wounds. His sister Helen had regained an even keel and after 1858 settled for several years, until she again went to live in Germany, in the appropriately named St Helen's Priory in the Isle of Wight. There she was surrounded by a calm if very Catholic atmosphere. She was also close to Osborne, which enabled Gladstone to combine Court visits with calls on his sister. On at least one occasion (in 1859) he even had her over to Osborne House for luncheon with the Household (that is, not with the Queen) after a Privy Council meeting. Ironically it was General Grey, the husband of Caroline Farquhar, who extended the invitation, and the visit, which seems to have gone smoothly, certainly indicated a vast revival in Gladstone's trust in her. On another (1861) occasion he found her entertaining Cardinal Wiseman and his chaplain Dr Vaughan (later himself Cardinal Archbishop of Westminster). So far from upsetting Gladstone this was followed by his travelling back to London with them and having 'much conversation' on the next day.*

It was for Gladstone a year of ebbing suspicion towards Roman Catholics. His theoretical tolerance might have been thought established by his brave opposition to the Ecclesiastical Titles Bill ten years before. But tolerance in matters concerning the action of the state was different from tolerance in matters relating to family or friends. He saw himself as having a special responsibility, in the memorable phrase he had used to (and of) Hope-Scott in 1845, 'as one of the sentinels of the Church of England on the side looking towards the Church of Rome'. Until the spring of 1861 he had interpreted this so rigidly that for ten years he had had no contact with Manning. Then there was a hesitant correspondence, the initiative coming from the future Cardinal, who wanted back the early letters which he had written to Gladstone, in exchange for those which Gladstone had written to him. Then there was a meeting. Manning called on Gladstone on 20 March: 'Saw Manning: a great event: all was smooth: but *quantum mutatus*! Under external smoothness and conscientious kindness there lay a chill indescribable. I hope I on my side did not affect him so. He sat where Kossuth [the Hungarian nationalist leader] sat on Friday: how different!'[24]

It was hardly an emotional reunion but thereafter relations were normal, and in the late 1860s almost back to warmth, even though Gladstone believed (falsely) that Manning had wanted his letters returned in order to destroy them and thus help to obliterate traces of his Anglican past. The appearance of Purcell's reckless and often misleading biography of Manning in 1895, as we have seen, recurdled Gladstone's sour feelings towards Manning, but by then the latter was dead, and the attendant chaplain of Gladstone's 1861 journey from Ryde to Waterloo was Cardinal Archbishop.

Gladstone's third major excursion to the wilder shores of political rashness came in May 1864, a few weeks after he had presented a well-received, relatively brief and uncontroversial budget. Its main provisions were a further income tax reduction from sevenpence to sixpence (it was nearly back to the fivepence with which he had started in 1859, but with

* On the other hand this clear evidence not only of Helen's commitment to the Roman Church, but also of her strong position in it, did nothing to counter his fanatical conviction twenty years later that she must have reverted to her Anglican faith, and to arrange for her burial accordingly.

a surplus instead of a deficit and lower indirect taxes), and some remission also of the sugar and fire insurance duties. The Cabinet had accepted the budget in a single sitting of one and a quarter hours, which was in sharp contrast with the 1860 and 1861 experiences.

On 11 May, a Wednesday and therefore in the habit of the nineteenth century a minor day for parliamentary business (the equivalent of a modern Friday, when the House both sat and adjourned early), Gladstone was dealing for the government with a 'gesture' bill, moved by a Yorkshire Liberal (Baines) and designed to reduce the property qualification for the borough franchise. The debate lasted only from noon until 2.45 p.m. and there was no question of a division.* Gladstone nonetheless turned it into the major sensation of the month, if not of the session. Palmerston had written him a note that morning urging him not to commit himself and the government to any particular sum for the borough franchise. (As this pointed to a degree of apprehension, it is difficult to understand why the Prime Minister did not solve the whole problem by getting the compliant Home Secretary, George Grey, to deal with the matter; it was not an occasion which called for a 'great Gun' as Palmerston flatteringly referred to Gladstone when he wanted him to demolish Disraeli six weeks later.)

Gladstone, it could be said, obeyed the instruction to the letter. He did not concern himself with the minutiae of £6 (or £8 or £10) franchises. He simply took the whole argument up by the roots and set it down upon a new basis. He looked back over the various attempts at franchise reform of the past fifteen years and found it a scandal that there had been no advance from a position in which only one-tenth of those with a vote were 'working men', for the very good reason that only one 'working man' in fifty possessed a vote. His argument was tightly sociological, which is of considerable interest when the question of his motive is looked at. It was not desirable that the upper stratum of the working class was shut out while the lower stratum of the middle class was let in. Then came the sentence which was erected into a sensation: 'I call upon the adversary to show cause, and I venture to say that every man who is not presumably incapacitated by some consideration of personal unfitness or of political danger, is morally entitled to come within the pale of constitution.' Then, in a very Gladstonian way, he immediately qualified his declaration: 'Of course, in giving utterance to

* Although in the following session Baines pressed a similar bill to a vote and was defeated by 248 to 214, with Gladstone voting in the minority.

such a proposition I do not recede from the protest I have previously made against sudden, or violent, or excessive or intoxicating change.'[25]

'Some sensation', Gladstone laconically commented, adding that it was due less to what he had said than to defensive complacency on the part of his hearers. There was a lot of scurrying round the House. Two whips ran off to tell Phillimore of the enormity of what his chief had just said. There was a contrived scene in the chamber when it was suggested that the Prime Minister (who had gout) should be sent for and asked if he agreed with the Chancellor. Palmerston did not agree, and on the next day he wrote the first of a nine-letter correspondence (five from Palmerston, four from Gladstone) which extended over the next week and a half. The Prime Minister's tone was obviously one of determined remonstrance, but it was also remarkably good-humoured, as had been the case in previous exchanges. Gladstone in turn was unrepentant but never sullen.

Palmerston began, 'I have read your speech, and I must frankly say with much regret [that] there is little in it that I can agree with, and much from which I differ.' He added, 'Your speech may win Lancashire for you, though that is doubtful, but I fear will tend to lose England for you.' The use of 'you' rather than the more obvious 'us' as the last word may be taken as an interesting indication that, even in exasperation, Palmerston was assuming that the future lay with a Gladstone leadership.

Gladstone began his first reply: 'It is not easy to take ill anything that proceeds from you,' and continued with some fairly convoluted explanation of the real meaning of his words. Palmerston then moved increasingly on to the point that Gladstone's further and major sin was that, in receiving a delegation of working men, he had urged them to agitate for an extension of the franchise. 'The function of a Government is to calm rather than to excite Agitation,' he comprehensively concluded. Gladstone then gave a superb display of both the irrepressible and the naive sides of his character. The solution, he wrote, obviously was to publish his speech as a pamphlet. Once it was available in full the balance and sense of his words would surely set all doubts at rest. Palmerston wanted no such thing, but he failed to budge Gladstone. 'You are of course the best judge as to your own line,' he concluded with more tolerance than triumph.[26]

This exchange led to no quarrel between Gladstone and Palmerston, but it did lead to a new wave of argumentativeness in their relationship. Gladstone used his long days at Balmoral in October 1864 to fire off two provocative letters to Palmerston. In the first he suddenly reverted to the question of railway nationalization – not of the operations but of the track – an issue which had lain quiescent since his 1844 legislation as President of the Board of Trade, but which had come back into discussion as a result of uncontrolled and unco-ordinated building, quite often undertaken merely to force a bigger adjacent company to buy up the unwanted but possibly competitive track. Palmerston reacted, as might have been expected, with some dismay. 'It is impossible to form a Judgement of your Plan till the Details are made out, but I own it appears on the first Blush a wild and more than doubtful project.'[27] He did, however, eventually concede that there should be a Royal Commission on the subject, which deliberated under the chairmanship of the seventh Duke of Devonshire, and resulted in a negative report.

The second letter was of more serious immediate import and was, it might be thought, a most tendentious piece of aggression against an old Prime Minister, on what turned out, to no one's surprise, to be the threshold of the last year of his life. Gladstone produced a convoluted mixture of prose and figures, running to well over a thousand words, which complained that, over the lifetime of the government, naval and military expenditure had only come down from £30 million to £26 million, whereas, given various special factors such as the ending of the China War, it ought to have done so by more. It was hardly a very obvious abuse, and it got back an even longer but much more enjoyable reply from Palmerston. First he said that he had delayed replying until Gladstone had finished his 'severe but successful Labour in Lancashire' (which was a euphemism for 'another of your demagogic tours'). Then he produced his own piece of counter-aggression: 'I think that any Body who looks carefully at the Signs of the Times Must see that there are at present two strong Feelings in the National Mind, the one a Disinclination to organic Changes in our representative System; the other a steady Determination that the Country shall be placed and kept in an efficient Condition of Defence.'[28]

So much for Gladstone's two pet nostrums of the decade. Having nailed his colours to these hardline masts, Palmerston proceeded to adopt a more modern approach to national budgeting than anything Gladstone was likely to encompass. It all came back to what the Prime Minister called:

> the Fallacy of Joseph Hume who always maintained that the Financial Concerns of a Nation were similar to the Nature of those of a private Individual, whose Income being a fixed and definite Sum, his Expenditure

> ought to be regulated by it: whereas in Fact the Cases are just opposite to each other, and with Regard to a Nation the proper and necessary yearly Expenditure is the fixed Sum, and the Income ought to be adjusted to meet that Expenditure'.[29]

Gladstone complained in his diary that the arrival of this 'pamphlet letter from Lord P. about Defence Estimates holds out a dark prospect'. While it may be thought that Gladstone had somewhat deliberately walked into the dark prospect, there can be no doubt that the exchange marked the beginning of a new phase of greater tension between Prime Minister and Chancellor which persisted, although correspondence continued to flow freely from both sides, until Palmerston's death almost exactly a year later. It also made membership of the Cabinet and of the government much less of a pleasure for Gladstone. On 19 January 1865 he wrote: 'Cabinet 3¾–6½ very stiff indeed, on Estimates. Sky dark.' And on 28 January: 'Last night I could have done almost anything to shut out the thought of the coming battle. This is very weak: but it is the result of the constant recurrence of such things: estimates always settled at dagger's point.' Yet again, on 7 February, the day Parliament reassembled: 'I flinch from the Session.'[30]

The inherent trouble was that he was the aggressor without possessing sufficient forces to sustain the assault. Palmerston was sitting comfortably on interior lines of communication. The national finances were healthy (thanks largely to Gladstone), the Prime Minister and the service ministers were no longer asking for any great new expenditure on armaments, merely for a maintenance of the existing, hardly monstrous level (about £1.6 billion at present-day prices), there was no question of additional taxation, only a moderation of the rate at which reductions could take place, and the Cabinet was perfectly content to sustain this balance. On 19 January Gladstone had been forced to admit: 'In regard to the Navy Estimates I have had no effective or broad support: platoon firing more or less in my sense from Argyll and Gibson.' Such haphazard small-arms fire from only two members was clearly insufficient, and the stark and obvious fact was that Gladstone had only the unappealing choice of defeat or resignation. As he did not want to resign he would have done better to have called off the battles before he had lost them. But that was not his nature, and as a result he inflicted unnecessary humiliations upon himself and pointless strife upon the Cabinet.

It might also have left him freer to make his own taxation dispositions. As it was, Palmerston was courteously teasing him only a day or so before his ninth budget on 27 April 1865. 'If you will allow me to say so,' he wrote, 'some of your best financial arrangements lost much of their deserved popularity by the ingenious Complications with which they were accompanied. It will be as well on this occasion not to fall into the similar mistake. . . .'[31] Gladstone had wanted to levy a tax of fourpence in the pound upon all rateable buildings, and it was this which Palmerston was determined to get him off. Gladstone was nonetheless able to bring income tax down from sixpence to fourpence, tea duty from one shilling to sixpence and further to diminish the fire insurance duty (a curiously pervasive issue of the time).

In June Palmerston graciously tossed an episcopal nomination to Gladstone, and the Regius Professor of Divinity went from Christ Church to Chester. The Prime Minister hoped the choice might help Gladstone with his 'oncoming election'. It did not, or not sufficiently so at any rate. The government gained twenty-six seats throughout the country, but on 17 July 1865 Gladstone was out at Oxford. The size of the University poll was considerably increased by the introduction for the first time of postal voting (thereby improving the relative influence of country clergy as against resident dons). Gladstone's sitting colleague Heathcote polled 3236, the new challenger Gathorne Hardy 1904, and Gladstone himself 1724. 'A dear dream is dispelled,' he wrote. 'God's will be done.'[32]

The quietism lay more in words than in deeds. He had already been nominated for South Lancashire (in those days there was no obstacle to multiple nomination), and the next morning he was off to the north, and in the afternoon addressed 6000 people in Manchester and in the evening 5000 in Liverpool. He was indeed 'unmuzzled' by Oxford, as Palmerston had feared that he would be, and by 20 July had succeeded in being elected for South Lancashire. The meetings were, however, more of a triumph than the result. In a three-member constituency he ran only third to two Tories, although a good thousand ahead of the other two Liberals.

The election made little difference to the balance or direction of the government. Lord Westbury had been forced out by nepotistic scandal at the beginning of July and was replaced by the seventy-five-year-old Cranworth as Lord Chancellor. Otherwise there was no change of personnel. Palmerston's main desire had become that of preventing changes. The Cabinet met once on 24 July. ('All in good humour,' Gladstone recorded, although others reported him as being in a subdued mood), and then shuffled off on holiday. The new Parliament did not meet, even to choose a Speaker, until nearly seven months after its election, which must surely be a record for dilatoriness. Gladstone went to Hawarden on 27 July and did not return to London until 20 October. For the first time for six years he did not go to Penmaenmawr and applied himself heavily to family and estate affairs. In late September he made a ten-day Scottish ducal excursion (Buccleuch and Argyll), but was recalled to Liverpool on account of the death of Robertson Gladstone's wife, the lady against whom he had become so excited in 1839. Over the intervening twenty-six years he had come to value her more, and in middle life he had moved closer to Robertson than to either of his other brothers, and indeed depended substantially on his sponsorship and support for the South Lancashire seat. Once again, as with John Neilson Gladstone's death less than two years before, he devoted more than a week to a Liverpool visit of mourning, support and comfort. From there he went to Clumber, where he had first waited on the old fourth Duke of Newcastle thirty-three years before and where he was currently engaged in the vast and unrewarding task of clearing up as an executor the chaotic family and financial legacy of the fifth Duke.

It was against this sombre and wearing background that Gladstone, on the evening of 18 October, received news of the sudden death of Palmerston. His last letter to Gladstone, courteous in intent and jaunty in tone, had contained no hint of an impending end. 'I do not foresee any reason for calling the Cabinet together till the 10th of November,' he had written on 7 October.[33] Alas, this easeful prospect could not be maintained. The Cabinet next met on 28 October, but under a different Prime Minister. There was no trouble about Russell's succession. There were only two people who could have put in doubt the return of the old Whig to 10 Downing Street – after thirteen years away, the second longest interval ever between two premierships of the same man. The first was the Queen, and she, perhaps because of the looming shadow of Gladstone appeared to have learnt her lesson from her Granville experience in 1859, and made no difficulty. The second was of course Gladstone himself, who had been urged by some, including notably that worldly prelate Wilberforce, to make a pre-emptive strike for the top place. He showed no desire to do so. The flame of ambition was burning relatively low in him at the time. He even betrayed some signs of dismay at the general election victory of the previous July, feeling after more than six years in office that there were attractions in the freedom of opposition. He accepted with at least a show of reluctance the leadership of the Commons which a change from a Lower House to an Upper

House Prime Minister made vacant ('The charge of leading fastened on me'). Also, he positively believed that Russell was entitled to another term and wrote to tell him so within a few hours of getting the Palmerston news. Russell received the commission on the following day.

There was consequently no sense of upheaval. The premiership merely passed from a man who would have been eighty-one to one who was seventy-three. They were the two oldest of those who had ever then held that office. This was indeed perhaps one of Russell's attractions for Gladstone. The only fault with him that Gladstone could immediately find was his inactivity in organizing a proper state funeral for Palmerston. Gladstone stepped in as soon as he got back to London and 'a solemn and touching scene' (taking three and a quarter hours) was arranged in Westminster Abbey for the following Friday. It was an appropriate final act of courtesy in the relationship of Gladstone and Palmerston, who, agreeing on little, behaved with considerable propriety towards each other.

Nonetheless Palmerston's death, in relation to both the achievements and the pyrotechnics of his career, passed surprisingly quietly. The House of Commons, despite his fifty-eight years of membership, was not recalled for tributes. Yet his death did mark the effective end of mid-century politics, even though Russell, like a juggler performing at the end of a play, as was fashionable in Paris theatres of the time, kept the season open for another eight months.

16

Disraeli's Foil

At the turn of the year 1865–6, Gladstone was fifty-six, no longer young but with not a hint of an old man about him either, his hair still black, his face hard and lined, that and his lithe movements giving an (accurate) impression of great power. There was none of the fuzziness of line which became a characteristic of his appearance from the age of about seventy onwards.

Disraeli was sixty-one, old and stiff for his years, but in some ways welcoming this, for, as with Harold Macmillan a hundred years later, an affectation of age became part of his style. The Queen, prematurely dumpy, was still only forty-six, although already the grandmother of both Kaiser Wilhelm II and King George V, as well as of a few others who had less *Kaiserliche und Königliche* futures. Russell, as we have seen, was seventy-three (although with twelve more years ahead of him), and Palmerston was dead. Most of the other mid-century politicians were also dead, and the stars of the end of the century, Salisbury, Joseph Chamberlain, Rosebery, William Harcourt, Randolph Churchill, had not emerged.

Britain was still pre-eminent. Her manufacturing strength was not to be seriously challenged until the American north-east had bounded forward after the Civil War, and the new German Empire had digested its gains of 1866 and 1870. Although on Gladstone's fifth-sixth birthday the horrors of the Prussian siege of Paris and still more the Commune could not be foreseen, the glitter of the Second Empire was already wearing thin, and the French challenge to Britain was finally ceasing to be military, and was moving into a ninety- or hundred-year period when it was cultural and social rather than industrial or commercial. At home the 'respectable' working class was continuing to rise above the abyss and to form itself into mechanics' institutes and friendly societies and craft unions with an ethos which attracted Gladstone's approbation. And Ireland, at once the running sore of the Britannic Isles and the most conveniently placed of all areas of colonial exploitation, was quiet. But quiet in a temporary and deadened way, in the aftermath of the famine and the mass emigration. Gladstone more than almost anyone, although Disraeli once made a brilliantly prescient speech, had the foresight to see this and to see also that Ireland was capable, with a population a quarter of the British total (it had been a third before the famine) as opposed to the 3 per cent in Northern Ireland today, of gravely weakening the whole United Kingdom polity.

However, at the beginning of 1866 the Irish threat was largely either in the past or in the future. Although in fact the threshold of a period of great change, political, industrial and social, the 1860s seemed a time of unusual stability. There were only a few who would have emulated Edmund (later Lord) Hammond, permanent under-secretary of the Foreign Office, who told a new Foreign Secretary (Granville) within days of the outbreak of the Franco-Prussian War in July 1870 that rarely had he seen such a lull in Europe. But Hammond was in tune with a generally confident mood in British political society.

Perhaps because of this wider sense of stability some changes in the pattern of parliamentary and associated social life began to set in, which, once made, broadly persisted at least until 1939, and in many respects until the present day. Gladstone's diaries, with their obsessive parcelling up of time, are an exceptional source book for patterns of life. Every day is recorded and often divided into quarter-hour slots. He was exceptional in the amount that he accomplished, and exceptional too in the waging of his unrelenting battle with time, but the fixed points of his days and his years did not differ greatly from those of other committed and successful contemporary politicians. In the 1860s they still lived under a very different regime, both within a day and within a year, from that which came to prevail in the twentieth century. The pattern of the day changed within a decade or so, the pattern of the year took nearer half a century to do so. In both cases the change was associated with a shift in parliamentary habits.

There is a widespread view that Parliament in the mid-nineteenth century was an undemanding occupation for gentlemen of leisure. So far as its leading members were concerned, this is not true. And even in the case of the larger numbers who saw their duties as being to listen and to vote rather than to speak, their assiduity in providing an attentive audience was much greater than is the habit today. What is the case is that the parliamentary year was then divided much more equally into a six- or seven-month session of intense activity and an almost equally long recess of undisturbed calm. Between 1855 and 1870 there was only one very brief autumn session of Parliament. Prorogation almost invariably took place between the last week of July and the third week in August and both Houses then remained in recess until the last days of January or, more frequently, the first week of February. (This pattern of six months of guaranteed recess became somewhat eroded in the last decades of the nineteenth century and disappeared finally by 1914; 1907 and 1913 were the last years without an autumn session.)

These long intervals of opportunity for non-London life and non-political activity were however balanced by the most strenuous parliamentary demands between February and August. The parliamentary day was slung very late, but it was long, with many of the most crucial hours being those after midnight, and the weekend, a term which has since invaded French but was then many decades short of establishing itself in English, was accorded little protection. Apart from the short Wednesdays (the equivalent of modern Fridays), Mondays, Tuesdays, Thursdays and Fridays were full House of Commons days, which meant beginning at 4.30, mostly adjourning for a brief dinner interval at 7.30, and then continuing with major debates until an average of about 1.30 a.m., but quite often until 2.30 a.m. or even later. Saturday sittings were not regular, but not very exceptional either. Between 1948 and 1987 there were only two occasions when the House of Commons met on a Saturday, one because of the Suez War in 1956 and one on the day following the Argentine invasion of the Falklands in 1982. Gladstone mostly experienced twice as many in the course of a normal session.

In addition, Saturdays, particularly under the long Palmerston premiership, were the normal Cabinet day. And, to compound the insult, as it would seem to someone used to modern indulgences, one o'clock was the normal time of meeting; 3.30 or 4.00 p.m. was the normal time by which the business was completed.

Despite these obstacles, and despite the non-existence of any term for it other than a 'Saturday to Monday' and even that hardly coming into use until a few decades later, weekending was nonetheless becoming something of a habit with Gladstone, and no doubt at least as much with other less vigorous ministers too. He would often go to Cliveden, or less frequently to other Thames Valley, or Surrey, or Kent, or Hertfordshire houses after a Saturday Cabinet. On one occasion indeed he went to Cliveden (then owned by the Sutherlands) after a Saturday evening Buckingham Palace banquet. Such short journeys, done by train to the nearest local station, Taplow for Cliveden for instance, took no significant time longer than they would today. The railways had become reliable and quite swift, although not comfortable for long journeys.

There were a lot of smuts and no dining cars. (The first meal served on an English train was in 1874, in a Pullman car between London and Bedford, but it was the early 1880s before restaurant cars became at all widespread.)

This stage of railway development joined with the habits of official life to make Home Counties retreats essential for weekend entertaining during the session. The great houses of the North and Scotland were reserved for the autumn and early winter, with the visits more on a mid-week than a weekend basis. At these seasons the Gladstones were considerable country-house visitors. To take ducal palaces alone, and to use again the fifteen-year span between 1855 and 1870, they stayed at Albury, Blenheim, Chatsworth, Clumber, Drumlanrig, Dunrobin, Eaton,* Holker, Inverary, Raby, Trentham and Woburn, at most of them more than once, and apart of course from the innumerable Cliveden 'session' weekends already mentioned.

With these and other short excursions the late Saturday arrival was balanced by the return not normally being necessary until late on the Monday morning. Indeed there is an impression throughout the week of light morning work. Breakfast parties were frequent, and were Gladstone's favourite form of entertaining, although he and his wife also gave small dinners, mostly for eight or ten guests, and occasional evening parties, including in June 1865 a ball to which the Prince of Wales came and stayed until half-past two.

The 'breakfasts' were however predominant. Gladstone did not do them on the relentless scale of Monckton Milnes, of whom it was said that his reaction to news of the Second Coming would undoubtedly have been to send the Saviour a card for one of these repasts. Gladstone would probably not have approved of the joke (although his sense of humour was often unpredictable), but he did enjoy Milnes's parties, and his own were by no means entirely different. In late July 1863 he noted, perhaps with relief: 'Eight to breakfast. The twelfth and last [of the session].' A detailed and friendly description of one which took place in June 1866 was given by Charles Adams, American minister in London, a commentator capable of considerable astringency (although not as much as his son Henry Adams, whose satirical novel *Democracy* portrayed the Washington scene of the 1870s in far from flattering terms). Adams wrote after he had received an oral invitation from Mrs Gladstone:

* Not then strictly ducal, for the Marquess of Westminster did not get his 'step' until 1874.

> I decided to go. I found no cause to regret the decision for the company was very pleasant. The Duke and Duchess of Argyll, Lord Lyttelton, Lord Houghton, Lord Frederick Cavendish and his wife, and one of his uncles and several whom I did not know. I forgot Lord Dufferin. We sat at two round tables, thus dividing the company; but Mr. Gladstone took ours, which made all the difference in the world. His characteristic is the most extraordinary facility of conversation on almost any topic with a great command of literary resources, which at once gives it a high tone. Lord Houghton, if put to it, is not without aptness in keeping it up;* whilst the Duke of Argyll was stimulated out of his customary indifference to take his share. Thus we passed from politics, the House of Commons, and Mr. Mill, to English prose as illustrated from the time of Milton and Bacon down to this day, and contrasted with German, which has little of good, and French. . . . After an hour thus spent we rose. . . . this is the pleasantest and most profitable form of English society.[1]

The breakfasts took place in Carlton House Terrace and not in Downing Street, and in this as in other ways were wholly dissimilar from Lloyd George's working and persuasive meals of that name which were held first in 11 and then in 10 Downing Street a half-century later. Gladstone's breakfasts were social as much as political in intent, and did not involve bacon and eggs or toast and marmalade. They comprised meat dishes and wine, spread themselves over most of the morning, say from 10.00 or 10.30 to 11.30 or noon, and might just as well have been called early-luncheon parties. They were comparable with, although less Lucullan than, the 'breakfasts' which in the 1870s Charles Dilke gave for Gambetta and other guests at the Café Anglais in Paris.

These 'breakfasts' obviously precluded much serious morning work being done, either before or after them, particularly as at the latter end Gladstone often went on a picture-viewing or buying expedition. How much could be done before obviously depended on what time he got up, and on this his diaries are curiously uninformative. But it cannot have been very early. Although he could perform short-term feats of endurance, he needed on average a good deal of sleep. At Hawarden, where there was nothing to keep him up at night, he habitually began with church at 8.30. But that implied no more than a 7.30 or 7.45 rousing, and in London with the persistence of nights which began only at 2.00 or 3.00 a.m. it is difficult to believe that he was not later.

* As Monckton Milnes (for this was he after his 1863 ennoblement) was regarded as one of the great nineteenth-century wits, he might not have been too pleased by this qualified accolade.

Once the breakfasts, whether they were social or private, were over, there was no question of any further meal distraction until dinner. The hours between one and three, in complete contrast with, say, Churchill's habits even under the worst stresses of the Second World War, were free for meetings or other business. Apart from the 'luncheon' at the Seaforth Rectory in 1853* and one or two provincial public occasions (as at Burslem, Staffordshire, in October 1863, where the lunch with speeches went on until past seven, and was then followed by a dinner at eight), the first diary mention of a London 'luncheon' was on 13 July 1863 and took place at Lord Granville's house. But it was a Sunday (and therefore not a day of normal pattern), the time was not specified and there was no subsequent use of the word until an occasion, again on a Sunday, at Lord Lothian's in 1867.

If there was no Cabinet or other meeting, the early afternoon up to about 4.30, around which time Gladstone mostly went to the House of Commons, was thus free for Treasury work. But there is little evidence that he did it in any routine office way. He was constantly writing political letters, frequently acquainting himself with official reports and occasionally preparing papers for the Cabinet. But there is little record of his ever going into the old Treasury Chambers between Whitehall and 10 Downing Street. He operated from one or other of his residences, 11 Downing Street or 11 Carlton House Terrace, and this meant that his own private reading and writing was much more intermingled with Treasury business than would otherwise have been so, or would normally be the case today. He spent very little time sitting in the Chancellor's official room, with his officials on call, and working systematically through Treasury papers.

Having gone to the House of Commons at 4.30 or so, he rarely stayed there continuously, even when he was making a major speech. Indeed he claimed towards the end of his sixty-two years of membership that he had only once dined in the House. This must have been more a matter of habit than of gastronomy for although a healthy eater he never showed much interest in the refinements of cuisine. His normal break-time began at 7.30, although it could be a little later, and was sometimes as brief as half an hour. Thursday and Friday, 13 and 14 March 1865 provide a fairly typical pair of House of Commons days. For the first: 'H. of C. 4¾–7½ and 8½–1'; and for the second, when he dined at Lord Russell's, 'H. of C. 4½–7½ and 10½–11'.[2]

* See pp. 179–80, above.

The three hours for dinner which he took on the second day, assuming that the Russell dinner started as soon as the House was suspended (and dinners, while they had receded a lot from six o'clock, which was quite usual in the early part of the century, were still earlier than the 8.30 which became fashionable in the 1880s and 1890s), was generous. Often he would be away from a dinner party within an hour and a half of arriving, thus posing a difficulty of reconciling the great number of courses which were offered and at least sometimes consumed* with the speed with which they must have been served. This was not only to meet the needs of importunate parliamentarians but also because of the press of post-dinner activity in which the *beau monde* then engaged. These were the opera, the theatre, a considerable round of late-evening parties at Cambridge House (Lady Palmerston), Stafford House (Duchess of Sutherland), Derby House (Lady Derby) and many other Mayfair residences, as well as the occasional ball.

The Gladstones participated surprisingly fully; and when it is remembered that he added to these, not only his considerable late-night parliamentary commitments, but also his 'rescue' activities, often involving a couple of nocturnal prowls a week, it is amazing that he got any sleep at all. The six months of a mid-Victorian parliamentary session were sufficiently strenuous that the balancing length of the recess was not so much an indulgence as a need.

The interval of just over three years between the death of Palmerston and the beginning of Gladstone's first premiership was a period of political confusion and paradox. It was also one in which Gladstone did not cover himself with glory. First as leader in the Commons with Russell as Prime Minister in the Lords, and then as a slightly inadept leader of the opposition trying in vain to deal with the weaving manoeuvres of Disraeli, he was not happily placed. He avoided again being leader of the opposition until 1886, when he had become so senior that he could discharge his duties at least as loosely as Churchill did in 1945–51.

The confusion, paradox and opportunism were memorably caricatured in Trollope's *Phineas Redux* (published in 1873–4), in which Mr Daubeny (Disraeli) explained to his bewildered but bewitched party that, in order to maintain the values of conservative England, the true duty

* When the Speaker (Denison) dined with Palmerston in his (Palmerston's) eighty-first year he was much struck by the Prime Minister consuming two plates of turtle soup, a dish of cod with oyster sauce, a paté, two entrées, a plate of mutton, a slice of ham, and a portion of pheasant. (Guedalla, *Gladstone and Palmerston*, p. 453.)

The delicate features of religious intensity:
John Keble, *left*, John Henry Newman, later Cardinal, *right*,
and James Hope Scott, *below*.

Two prelates, also of roughly Gladstone's generation at Oxford who, in widely differing ways, were more worldly.

Left: Bishop Samuel Wilberforce of Oxford and Winchester.

Below: Henry Manning, Anglican Archdeacon of Chichester, later (but only fourteen years so) Roman Catholic Archbishop of Westminster, and then after another ten years, Cardinal.

Facing page: Gladstone in 1858: trim of figure, fierce of eye and smart of dress (in 'Brougham' trousers, white waistcoat and fancy cravat). In reality his career and not merely his tie was then at a loose end.

Above: The fourth Earl of Aberdeen, the most elusive of all post-1832 Prime Ministers but to Gladstone 'the man in public life of all others whom I have loved'.

Left: Lord John Russell, from 1860 first Earl Russell, the quintessential Whig, whom Gladstone did not love but whom he placed, together with Peel (a high tribute) and Disraeli (a less high one) in a triptych of those with outstanding political courage.

Sidney Herbert, Gladstone's friend and short-lived contemporary, a man who aroused his intense affection as did Aberdeen and Hope-Scott and no one else, but with whom he constantly disagreed in Cabinet.

Facing page: Harriet, Duchess of Sutherland, a close friend of Gladstone's from the middle 1850s until her death in 1868 (painted by Winterhalter about 1850).

Right: Lady with the Coronet of Jasmine, the portrait of Maria Summerhayes, one of his 'rescue' cases, which Gladstone commissioned from William Dyce in 1859 and which today reposes in the Aberdeen Art Gallery.

Right: Laura Thistlethwayte, former courtesan who became a proselytizing theosophist as well as a Grosvenor Square and Dorset lady of substance, with whom Gladstone was considerably infatuated during his first premiership.

Palmerston, *above*, and Disraeli, *left*, were Gladstone's only political rivals as post-1850 Victorian stars. He disapproved of them both but wisely although almost accidentally settled in 1859 for a reluctant partnership with Palmerston (who was twenty-five years his senior) and a symbiotic opposition to Disraeli. As a result he eventually outshone them both.

of the party of squire and parson was to ditch the Whigs by disestablishing the Church. Substitute the franchise issue for disestablishment and this was an almost exact description of Disraeli's behaviour in first wrecking both the Reform Bill and the government of Lord Russell, and then carrying through a much more radical Reform Bill of his own. Gladstone was the bewildered (but not bewitched; his opinion of Disraeli was never lower) victim of these kaleidoscopic tactics. He was not nimble enough to deal with Disraeli's opportunistic turn of speed. As a result the good humour of his speeches, on which Dean Stanley had so strikingly commented in 1854, temporarily deserted him and he was judged by many to be blundering and blustering. This applied particularly after the last Derby government, which elided into the first Disraeli government, came in at the beginning of July 1866. Until then Gladstone had his continuing authority as Chancellor, and while not adjudged to be quick-footed as leader of the House was counted as formidable. At the end of April 1866, less than a week before his last budget, he even managed to make, on an amendment to the Russell government's Reform Bill, which had been debated over eight nights, one of the most remembered of all his parliamentary orations. He spoke from one to past three in the morning, but was rewarded only with a government majority of five, well below its nominal strength. Nevertheless, 'it was a famous victory', or at least a famous speech.

It contained his crushing rebuke of Disraeli, who had taunted him with his Oxford Union speech of thirty-five years before,* and also a daring passage on the contrast between Russell's 'warp and woof' Whiggery and his own belated transition from Conservatism. This passage comprises a striking example of how a Latin quotation could then be used for oratorical rather than for pedantic affect:

> My position then, Sir, in regard to the Liberal Party is in all points the opposite of the noble earl, Lord Russell. Lord Russell might have been misled possibly, had he been in this place, into using language which would have been unfit coming from another person. But it could not be the same with me. I am too well aware of the relations which subsist between the party and myself. I have none of the claims he possesses. I came among you an outcast from those with whom I associated, driven from them, I admit, by no arbitrary act, but by the slow and resistless forces of conviction. I came among you, to make use of the legal

* See pp. 23–4, above.

phraseology, *in pauperis formâ*. I had nothing to offer you but faithful and honourable service. You received me, as Dido received the shipwrecked Aeneas –

> *Ejectum littore, egenum*
> *Excepi*
> [an exile on my shore I sheltered].

And I only trust you may not hereafter at any time say

> *Et regni demens in parte locavi*
> [and, fool as I was, I shared with you my realm].

You received me with kindness, indulgence, generosity, and I may even say with some measure of confidence. And the relation between us has assumed such a form that you can never be my debtors, but that I must for ever be in your debt.

The peroration, widely thought to be of compelling if somewhat florid quality, was also notable for depending on another untranslated Latin gobbet to lift him to the culmination of his argument. It was also based on an historical inevitablism, reminiscent of his speech on the so-called Jew Bill nearly twenty years before.

Perhaps the great division of tonight is not the last that must take place in the struggle. At some point of the contest you may possibly succeed. You may drive us from our seats. You may bury the Bill that we have introduced, but we will write upon its gravestone for an epitaph this line, with certain confidence in its fulfilment –

> *Exoriare aliquis nostris ex ossibus ultor*
> [which, *pace* Hartley Shawcross, may be very freely translated as 'We will be the masters soon']

You cannot fight against the future. Time is on our side. The great social forces which move onwards in their might and majesty, and which the tumult of our debates does not for a moment impede or disturb – those great social forces are against you; they are marshalled on our side; and the banner which we now carry in this fight, though perhaps at some moment it may droop over our sinking heads, yet it soon again will float in the eye of heaven, and it will be borne by the firm hands of the united people of the three kingdoms, perhaps not to an easy, but to a certain and to a not distant victory.[3]

The majority of five which was the result of the 'great division' was regarded as humiliating for the government and there was a substantial Cabinet group in favour of resignation or dissolution. The amendment had been moved by Hugh, Earl Grosvenor, son of the Marquess of Westminster and later himself the first Duke, as well as Willy Gladstone's colleague as Liberal member for Chester, and thirty-five nominal Liberals had voted for it. The voice was Grosvenor's voice (which gave it a neighbourly disagreeableness for Gladstone) but the hands were the hands of Robert Lowe, *Times* leader-writer and MP for Calne. Over several months Lowe put up an inspired performance against any advance towards democracy and, thanks to John Bright's gift for a phrase, achieved immortality as the leader of the 'Adullamites' or cave-men. Later he was an unmemorable Chancellor of the Exchequer in Gladstone's first government (perhaps inevitably an unrewarding job under the man who had himself done it so well and for so long), so that when he came to be elevated to the peerage in 1880 Gladstone insisted, against the Queen, that he should have a viscountcy, not on account of his Treasury services, but because of the brilliant effectiveness of his opposition (to Gladstone) in 1866: 'a man who had once soared to heights trodden by so few, ought not to be lost in the common ruck of official barons'.[4] This was a striking example both of Gladstone's generosity and of a certain stiff chivalry, accompanied by a fine sense of gradations of rank, which informed not a few of his actions.

The activities of Lowe and his followers succeeded both in killing the bill and in getting the government out by midsummer. The immediate occasion was an eleven-vote government defeat on a somewhat technical amendment which however Gladstone had made into a vote of confidence. Forty-four Liberals voted with the Conservatives.

That left the alternatives of dissolution or resignation. There was much to be said for dissolution. The basic contradiction was that the country expected reform, that the leaders of the Liberal party in both Houses (Russell by long conviction, Gladstone by recent but vehement conversion) were committed to it, but that many of their parliamentary followers, elected essentially to support Palmerston, who detested reform, were at best unenthusiastic. They provided fertile territory for a Conservative opposition which was anxious to make mischief, was relentlessly opportunistic and above all eager to prevent a Liberal triumph on the issue. A new Parliament, elected on a mandate to extend the franchise, would have cleared the fog and filthy air. But Brand, the Liberal Chief Whip and a future Speaker, was implacably opposed. He was no enthusiast for reform and he had on his side the sound argument that the dissolution of a Parliament barely a year old would be deeply unpopular, if only on grounds of expense, with most members, to which he added the probably unsound supporting argument that it would produce a bad result. Russell and Gladstone allowed themselves to be persuaded.

Resignation, however, was a peculiarly long-drawn-out process. This was partly because it was opposed by the Queen (she was in favour not of dissolution but of acquiescence), who deliberately arrived slowly from Balmoral. A week after the decision Russell and Gladstone went together to Windsor ('we had warm receptions at both stations', was one of Gladstone's comments, which would have caused cynical amusement in those who believed him to be suffering from crowd addiction), but it was another ten days before Gladstone recorded the formal severance from official life in a series of comments each of which had elements of both poignancy and pungency:

> Went to Windsor to take leave. H.M. short but kind. . . . H. of C. on return: took my place on the Oppn. bench: the first time for 15 years. Dined at the Mansion Ho. (King of the Belgians): thanked for the H. of C. Finished in Downing St. Left my keys behind me. Somehow it makes a void.[5]

The Russell government had never seemed deep-rooted. But the Gladstone chancellorship was. He had been at the Treasury for seven years, and the sense of void after such a period of incarceration was wholly understandable. He had been less a prisoner of official life than is a modern minister, but there may nonetheless have been an element of a pit pony blinking its eyes after a long period in the shades. He did not however react to his new freedom by retreating upon Hawarden. On the contrary, he recoiled from that base, normally such an important part of his life, for an even longer period than he had done in 1858–9, when, following his four-month Ionian expedition, he had not gone home until nearly five months after his return to London.

In 1866–7, the position was still more extreme. During the session of 1866, when he was first leader of the House and then leader of the opposition, it was perhaps natural (although unusual for him) that between January and July he did not once travel the 200 familiar miles. But what was not natural was to spend the whole of August and nearly the whole of September visiting South of England houses (Wilton, the Bishop's palace at Salisbury, Woburn and Cliveden among others), before departing for Italy on 28 September. Accompanied by his wife, by his daughters and, for the Christmas holidays, by his three elder sons, he was away for four months, returning to London on 29 January 1867. He then allowed another two and a half months to pass before an Easter visit to Hawarden, which meant that it was the first time he had seen his main house, his main library and his estate for fifteen months. He was then there for two weeks, but did not spend another night there for four months, even going in one day from London to Penmaenmawr in August, and stopping in Flintshire only to pick up clothes. Thereafter a normal Hawarden pattern was resumed. The break was odd, almost inexplicable, and Gladstone, normally so free with explanations and analyses of motives, offered no comment. It was a minor example of his natural extremism. He did not do things by halves. Hawarden was mostly the centre of his post-1850 life. Yet twice he appeared to turn away from it.

The Roman autumn and early winter of 1866–7 was due partly to a desire to get off his feet the dust of British politics, which during the summer of defeat and resignation he had come to find distasteful, and partly to his natural italophil travelling exuberance, which had been suppressed by seven years in office. Save in very exceptional circumstances, ministers did not then go abroad, and it was eight and a half years since he had been on the mainland of Europe, and eighteen years since he had even passed through Rome (on his wild Lady Lincoln chase). Nonetheless it was a cool display of nerve to absent himself from England for four months at a time when he was the most likely but not the certain future leader of his party, and when he had just suffered a bruising rather than successful session in the House of Commons.

He was far from being entirely cut off from British contacts in Rome. Apart from several visiting Anglican clerics, Monsignor Talbot (portrayed by Lytton Strachey as Manning's great channel for Vatican intrigue) and the painter Joseph Severn, who helped to make up Gladstone's Roman circle, there were no fewer than three of his former Cabinet colleagues in Rome for some or all of the time. The Argylls came at the beginning of December, and occupied rooms beneath the Gladstones' spacious lodgings in the Piazza di Spagna. Cardwell and Clarendon were the other two, and the latter wrote to Lady Salisbury (the stepmother not the wife of the future Prime Minister) a mildly mocking account of Gladstone's activities:

> Italian art, archaeology and literature are G's sole occupations. Every morning at 8 he lectures his wife and daughters upon Dante, and requires them to parse and give the root of every verb. He runs about all day to shops, galleries and persons, and only last night he told me that he hadn't time for the reading room, and hadn't seen an English newspaper for three or four days.'[6]

This was to some extent contradicted by a private informant of Morley's who told him 'that Mr Gladstone seemed to care little or not at all about wonders of archaeology alike in Christian and pagan Rome, but never wearied of hearing Italian sermons from priests and preaching friars'. Morley himself endorsed this description: 'He was a collector of ivories, of china, of Wedgwood, but in architecture in all its high historic bearing I never found him very deeply interested. I doubt if he followed the controversies about French, Gothic and Italian, about Byzantine and Romanesque, with any more concern than he had in the controversies of geology.'[7] Although Morley came to know Gladstone much better than Clarendon ever did, the diaries nonetheless bear out the old Whig more than the (then) young Radical.

What seems certain is that whether the alternative attractions were literary, aesthetic or religious they were successful in diverting Gladstone's mind from any obsession with British politics. He appeared detached and relaxed throughout the four months. Foreign (or local) issues occupied him more. On this trip, much more than on any previous journey with the possible exception of his progress across the north of Italy in 1859, he was treated as a grand visiting statesman. He had a private audience of nearly an hour with the Pope (Piux IX) in his second week in Rome. The audience began with a touch of stately farce:

> ... I repaired to the Vatican in household uniform. I found the Pope dressed with great simplicity in white.... When I had bowed and kissed his hand, dropping on one knee as before the Queen (an operation in which he took my hand himself) he motioned, and asked me to sit down on a chair placed over against him. Mr Russell* had told me that it was his wont notwithstanding this invitation to stand: I therefore begged permission to do so as I should if before the Queen. But he said if the Queen ordered you to sit, you would sit. *Allora*, I said, *Santo Padre non mi resta altro che di ubbidare: Roma locuta est*, quoting the famous words of St Augustine.... The Pope smiled, and finished the sentence, *causa finita est*.[8]

They then had a fine *tour d'horizon*, touching on everything from the strict etiquette of the Court of England, through Fenianism (a favourite subject of British politicians when talking to Supreme Pontiffs) to the prospect for the French troops staying in Rome (they were withdrawn four years later and with them went the Pope's temporal power). Gladstone was invited to come again, bringing his family, which more

* Odo Russell, later ambassador in Berlin at the time of the 1878 Congress, who became first Lord Odo Russell when his father became Duke of Bedford and then Lord Ampthill, was in 1866 unofficial British representative at the Vatican.

formal visit of blessing took place six days later. In Rome he also saw a total of twelve cardinals and commented oddly in a letter to the Duchess of Sutherland, 'I observe reserve in conversation, except with such persons as cardinals.'[9]

In Florence, then the seat of government of the nearly united Italy, he called on King Victor Emmanuel I. 'He spoke with an outstanding freedom,' Gladstone wrote, again to his Duchess, although the significance of this comment needs to be adjusted for the nineteenth-century tendency of all interlocutors of crowned heads to regard any remark from them beyond 'good morning' as an expression of extraordinary frankness. At Florence he also saw Bettino Ricasoli, Cavour's successor as chief minister, and was given a banquet at Doney's restaurant by forty-five members of the Italian Parliament, arranged by the grateful Poerio.

In Paris, on the last stage of his journey home, he was treated with equal attention: dinner with the Emperor and Empress in the soon to be burnt Tuileries (where he was 'surprised at the extreme attention and courtesy of both their Majesties with whom I had much interesting conversation'); another evening banquet given by the political economists of France in joint honour of Gladstone and Cardwell, and installation (for Gladstone, not Cardwell) as a foreign associate of the Institut de France, a rare honour.

Back in London on 29 January 1867, a week before the opening of the new session, he faced an uncertain prospect which turned out worse, for the short run at any rate, than anything he could have expected. The session of 1867 was full of complexities, obscurities and sheer *opéra bouffe* blunderings from one side of the stage to the other. The third Derby–Disraeli government had achieved office in the previous July on the basis of uniting with Lowe's 'Adullamites' to defeat, because it was dangerously democratic, a Russell–Gladstone Reform Bill which would have enfranchised an additional 400,000 voters. Of the two previous Conservative governments the first had lasted only ten months and the second only sixteen. Disraeli had thus passed from being forty-one years old, at which age he had destroyed Peel and ended the last previous effective Conservative government, to sixty-one without any secure hold on power. He was increasingly aware of this. 'Power, it has come to me too late,' he was sadly to ruminate even at the height of his post-Congress of Berlin success.[10] His principal aim in the autumn of 1866 therefore became that of keeping the government in office, despite its being nominally in a substantial minority in the House of Commons and there seeming no reason to think that a dissolution would change that. To achieve this result he had to keep the parliamentary initiative, maintain the divisions within the Liberal ranks and weaken Gladstone. These objectives became much more important than any question of defending a particular position on the franchise. As Robert Blake wrote a century later: 'Of Disraeli at this time it could be said as Lord Beaverbrook wrote of Lloyd George: "He did not seem to care which way he travelled providing he was in the driver's seat."'[11] One difference between Gladstone and Disraeli was that Gladstone always believed, sometimes to his own humiliation but also in a way that made him in the last resort a greater man, that he could drive in whatever direction he judged right, whereas Disraeli, although a tactician of genius and (in his own phrase about Salisbury) 'a great master of gibes and flaunts and jeers', was a manoeuvrer rather than a statesman of wide strategy.

So much for Disraeli, but what about Derby, who was head of this government until February 1868, less office-hungry and less opportunistic? It was, however, a Conservative and not a reactionary which Derby had become. He had been a member of the Cabinet which had carried the 1832 Reform Bill, and had become impressed (perhaps over-impressed) by the strength of popular feeling for reform which had manifested itself over the summer of 1866. It had begun, oddly enough, with a demonstration in Carlton House Terrace on 27 June. A large group had surged to Gladstone's house from a meeting in Trafalgar Square. Gladstone was out, dining at Grillion's club, but Mrs Gladstone was at home and, apparently at the request of the police, had gone to the balcony accompanied by two daughters and had bowed and/or waved to the crowd, which, with many shouts of 'Gladstone for ever', had then peaceably dispersed. The Gladstones were nevertheless much criticized for pandering to the mob.

Then, a month later, there were the Hyde Park riots, which sprang out of a reform meeting which Gladstone had been asked to address (but had refused), continued sporadically for three nights, led to a tearing down of railings and reduced to tears the not very effective Home Secretary, Spencer Walpole. It was a gentle *émeute* compared with a revolutionary day in Paris, but it took place on the edge of Mayfair, indeed almost under Disraeli's windows, and created a wave of apprehension. More influential with Derby, however, was the series of large and orderly marches and meetings of respectable citizens which took place in the main provincial towns, many of them addressed by John Bright.

The two principal members of the Conservative government were therefore, for somewhat different reasons, persuaded by the autumn that they should introduce a Reform Bill of their own. But, partly because they faced some trouble within their own Cabinet, they did little about preparing for it until the session was on top of them. The original intention was to proceed by vague resolutions of the House paving the way for a Royal Commission which by a year's deliberation would obviate the need for legislation before the session of 1868. For the government this course would have the advantage both of excusing their procrastination and of imposing it on the opposition. It would be difficult for the Liberals, having failed ignominiously in 1866, to bring in another bill of their own while the Royal Commission was sitting.

The Royal Commission needed some steer on the angle from which they were to consider the vast subject. On 22 December Derby wrote to Disraeli giving his suggestions, and the flippancy of his tone owed less to an early onset of the Christmas spirit than to his interest in delay over substance: 'Of all possible hares to start I do not know a better than the extension of household suffrage, *coupled with plurality of voting*.'[12] 'Plurality of voting' meant that where an elector had multiple qualifications under the again envisaged 'fancy franchises' and, for example, met the property test, was a university graduate as well as a clergyman, had more than £X in the 'funds' and paid more than £Y in direct taxation, he should have votes in the *same* constituency, on each of these grounds. There thus opened the prospect that, by a brilliant sleight of hand, the Liberal leadership could be outflanked by unfurling the banner of household suffrage (although in practice limiting it to those householders who paid rates directly, as opposed to 'compounders' who did it through their landlords), while neutralizing any dangerous political effect, by almost balancing 400,000–500,000 'dangerous' new voters with 300,000–400,000 'safe' additional votes through plurality.

'Household suffrage', however 'cribbed, cabined and confined' (in a subsequent Gladstone phrase), was a most powerful legend, and one which was launched into practical politics by Derby's letter. Gladstone, looking back many years later, first admitted that it outflanked him ('We did not wish to make at once so wide a change as that involved in a genuine household franchise'); and second that it threw him on to the defensive ('But the government, it must be admitted, bowled us over by the force of the phrase').[13] It thus put the government, Disraeli in particular, well on the way to his primary objective of skewering

Gladstone. There were also penalties for the government. Three of the Cabinet of fifteen, Cranborne (soon to be Salisbury), Carnarvon and General Peel, the younger brother of Sir Robert (what was he doing serving under Disraeli?), regarded the term household suffrage as anathema. Two of them might have weakened under Derby's persuasion, but Cranborne, rather like Enoch Powell in the Thorneycroft–Birch–Powell resignations of 1958, implacably drove them on, and on 2 March 1867 they all resigned. The substance of their analysis was absolutely correct. Household suffrage, they said, will live, but the balancing safeguards, plural voting based on fancy franchises and admission to the vote for direct ratepayers only, will die.

They failed to allow, however, for the momentum of manoeuvre, as in a brilliant cavalry action, which had seized the Disraeli-directed if Derby-led government. The resigners were replaced by two fairly obscure dukes (Marlborough and Richmond) and one even more obscure commoner (Lowry Corry) and the charge swept on. On Friday 12 February, quite contrary to the earlier intention, Disraeli, without Cabinet consultation, had committed the government to bring in an immediate bill. On the 25th he introduced, with studied lack of enthusiasm, the so-called 'Ten-Minutes Bill', which provided only for a £6 franchise in the boroughs, a £20 one in the counties, fancy franchises but no plurality. It was so called not because the speeches were limited to ten minutes, as in a certain modern House of Commons procedure, but because it had been agreed upon only ten minutes before it had to be presented, first by Derby to a Conservative party meeting and then by Disraeli to the House. It was designed to show the resigning ministers how out of touch they were, to invite opposition at a Carlton Club meeting and to build up pressure for something stronger. Disraeli withdrew it on 4 March and announced that a fortnight later he would revert to the plan for household franchise for ratepayers plus plurality of voting which had been foreshadowed in Derby's letter of 22 December.

This tergiversation sounds as though the government ought to have been gravely damaged. In fact it was the opposition that suffered. Did this stem from Gladstone's clumsiness, or from the inherent difficulty of dealing with Disraeli at the peak of his opportunistic form, which was as difficult as gathering up a basketful of eels? Curiously, Gladstone apprehended the difficulty in advance, and then failed to profit from his prescience. He had written to Brand, the Liberal Whip, early in his Roman sojourn.

> Now [Disraeli] has made in his lifetime three attempts at legislation – the budget of 1852, the India Bill of 1858, the Reform Bill of 1859. All have been thoroughly tortuous measures. And the Ethiopian will not change his skin. His Reform Bill of 1867 will be tortuous too. But if you have to drive a man out of a wood you must yourself go into the wood to drive him. That is what I am afraid of. . . .[14]

Gladstone may have been afraid of it, as he had every reason to be, for Disraeli was far better than he was at woodcraft, but he was inept at keeping away from the treacherous paths. In particular, he failed to realize that Disraeli's governing tactic was to defeat any amendment from Gladstone, even if it meant accepting a more extreme one from another source. He had to show he was winning, and this meant showing that Gladstone was losing.

This task was made easier by Gladstone commanding at that stage no great resources of loyalty or affection in the ranks of a parliamentary Liberal party which had been elected to support Palmerston. He was respected as a Chancellor and feared as an orator, but not revered or loved as a leader. His strength in that capacity was coming to lie much more among the non-parliamentary masses, who admired but did not know him, than with the members of Parliament, most of whom in fact did not know him either, but thought that they ought to do so. He was beginning to suffer from what Bagehot, in general an admirer, described as not knowing the difference between leading and driving. This was well illustrated by the two meetings of the Liberal parliamentary party which he held during the run-up to his three House of Commons humiliations of the spring. Of the first, held in his own house on 21 March, he recorded: 'Meeting of the party 2½–4. I spoke near an hour: the end as good as I could hope.'[15] And of the second on 5 April: 'Liberal Party's meeting at 2. Spoke at length.'[16]

At both these meetings the alleged purpose was to consult the party. At both it seems more likely that he harangued its members, and considerably exaggerated the degree of acceptance that he achieved. On 25 March the second reading of the bill went through without a division, as had been agreed at the meeting on the 21st, but Gladstone's two-hour speech, exposing in detail the inconsistencies of the bill, was reported as losing the attention of the House. This mild failure was nothing compared with an 11–12 April debate on Gladstone's principal amendment. He both opened and wound up. The amendment provided that a qualified tenant could vote whether or not he paid his own rates. This lost the support of some Whigs. It was, however, predicated upon a £5 qualification and not full household suffrage, and that lost the support of some Radicals. The so-called 'Tea Room Revolt' led to a significant defection from Gladstone. Forty-three Liberals voted with the government and twenty were absent unpaired. Cranborne, Gladstone's old Oxford colleague Heathcote and five other Tories voted for the amendments, but this hardly compensated. The result was that in a House with a nominal Liberal majority of seventy-seven, the principal amendment to the principal bill of the session, moved by the Liberal leader of the opposition, resulted in a majority of twenty-one for the Conservative government. Gladstone's comment of 'A smash perhaps without example'[17] was in the circumstances relatively restrained.

Gladstone went home in chagrin, contemplating retirement to the back benches, and Disraeli went home in triumph, calling in at the Carlton Club on the way and being toasted by Matthew Ridley as 'the man who rode the race, who took the time, who kept the time, and who did the trick'. He was pressed to stay to supper (it was then nearly 3.00 a.m.) but disengaged himself with habitual reserve and went on to Grosvenor Gate, his wife, a Fortnum's pie and a bottle of champagne.[18] Even Bishop Wilberforce, Gladstone's continuing friend, but a cleric who could take a political temperature, wrote a little later: 'The most wonderful thing is the rise of Disraeli. It is not the mere assertion of talent. He has been able to teach the House of Commons almost to ignore Gladstone, and at present lords it over him, and, I am told, says that he will hold him down for twenty years.'[19]*

Gladstone did not flounce out of the leadership (nor is there much indication that he was near to so doing), but he resolved to move no more amendments of his own and indeed became somewhat fitful, for a leader of the opposition, in his Commons attendance, except on the Reform Bill. But on that he had to endure at least two more humiliations and one unvalorous retreat. On 9 May he supported another attempt to deal with the problem of compounding (paying rates through the landlord) and 'Spoke earnestly and long for Comp. Householders: in vain. Beaten by 322:256. Much fatigued by heat and work.'[20] Then in the middle of May there was the most bewildering of all Disraeli's shifts of position. Hodgkinson, whom Gladstone patronizingly described as 'a local solicitor little known in the House' (this form of words may have been occasioned by a stab of jealousy on account of his both being

* A rash prophecy: Disraeli was dead after fourteen years and Gladstone was Prime Minister for nearly twelve of the twenty.

member for Newark and getting away with his amendment), had put down a form of words which simply abolished 'compounding' and therefore the problem of the compounder by providing that within boroughs no rate could be levied which was not individually paid. There was a competing and better-drafted amendment down from H. C. E. Childers, who was regarded as a mouthpiece of Gladstone, and that was sufficient to make the Hodgkinson amendment relatively attractive. So Disraeli, apparently without consultation with Derby or any other member of the Cabinet, simply accepted it. It added nearly half a million voters to the electoral rolls, in other words doubled the effect of the bill. 'Never', Gladstone wrote, 'have I undergone a stronger emotion of surprise than when, as I was entering the House, our Whip met me and stated that Disraeli was about to support Hodgkinson's motion.'[21] The speed and irresponsibility with which Disraeli moved left Gladstone floundering.

Once Hodgkinson's amendment had been accepted (even though its form proved impracticable and had to be replaced by a government redraft) most of the other previous subjects of argument fell away as irrelevant. The fancy franchises, plural voting and the £5 franchise were all transcended. The remaining controversial issues were female suffrage, on which John Stuart Mill's amendment was comfortably defeated by 196 to 73, with Gladstone voting in the majority, and the enfranchisement of lodgers, who were regarded as a dangerous voting group. Eventually, provided they did not move often and occupied rooms of an unfurnished rateable value of £10 (which meant they were fairly lavish) they were allowed in. (By 1869 only 12,000 had met the qualifications, of whom two-thirds were in Westminster or Marylebone, only twenty-eight in Manchester and one in Birmingham.)[22]

Third reading took place on 15 July and extracted from Gladstone an extraordinary confession of the weakness of his position on the bill: 'A remarkable night. Determined at the last moment not to take part in the debate: for fear of doing mischief on our own side.'[23] Without provocation from Gladstone this stage passed without a division (as he had wished). The Lords, under Derby's control, were amenable, thereby showing that their partisanship was more a matter of party than of issues. They made no more than a handful of amendments, of which only one, designed to protect minorities in three-member boroughs (such as Birmingham) by giving each elector only two votes, survived the return to the Commons. The bewildering bill, which enfranchised approximately a million new voters, as opposed to the 400,000 which is all that the too radical Russell–Gladstone bill of the previous session would have done, was safely law by 15 August.

Gladstone had already departed for Penmaenmawr on 10 August. He could not look back on the session with much satisfaction. There was a wave of complaint that as party leader in the Commons he was remote and chilling and would not fraternize. His old friend Sir Thomas Acland wrote, taking as he said 'a great liberty', to tell him a few home truths.

> Well, what is pressed on me is that . . . there is an impression that you are absorbed in questions about Homer and Greek words, about *Ecce Homo*, that you are not reading the newspapers or feeling the pulse of followers . . . and besides that there is so little easy contact with the small fry, as when Palmerston sat in the tea-room, and men were gratified by getting private speech with their leader.[24]

Morley wrote that Gladstone lacked the little civilities and hypocrisies of political society, and Phillimore on one occasion told him that if he would only say something to a particular member, even if it was to abuse his views or tell him that he smelt, instead of ignoring him completely and implying that he knew neither his face nor his name, that member would immediately become his most devoted follower (perhaps a little difficult to believe). What is striking about this catalogue of complaint is that it is so familiar. It has been heard about every political leader from Peel to Churchill, from Balfour to Heath. The only man of whom it was manifestly not true was Baldwin, and although his qualities were somewhat underestimated for half a century after his withdrawal from office, he does not provide the most outstanding example of dynamic leadership or bold statesmanship.

Gladstone therefore had no great need to worry about this shower of nervous, well-intentioned but tiresome advice. In fact, as is often the case, he was being asked to improve his leadership performance by changing the personality which had made him, and not twenty-five or thirty other equally available men, leader in the first place. There is no evidence that the issue worried him at Penmaenmawr, where he remained (with twenty-five sea-bathes that year) for almost a full month before retiring to Hawarden for ten weeks, interrupted only by one night in Liverpool with his brother Robertson and five at Holker (near Carnforth) with the Duke of Devonshire.

There was then a brief autumn session (the first since 1854). It had been called to provide credits for a punitive expedition against King Theodore of Abyssinia. As, however, that particular Lion of Judah was generally held to have behaved very badly by rounding up and holding in chains all available British subjects this did not cause much controversy or take long. The session was over inside two weeks, and by 3 December Gladstone was back at Hawarden for another hardly interrupted two and a half months.

He was again much preoccupied that autumn and winter with Homeric studies, but there is also a sense of detachment from the affairs of day-to-day politics, a gazing at the more distant future rather than a reaction to short-term shifts in the political weather. No doubt this was to some extent a reaction against recent parliamentary buffetings and humiliations. His fifty-eighth birthday, however, passed with only the most cursory of introspective reflection: 'Another year of mercies unworthily received is added to the sum of my days: of wanderings and backslidings: of much varied experience in the world & in private life. I long for the day of rest.'[25]

Tree-felling, then in its tenth year, became a dominant and hazardous Hawarden activity. On 23 December: 'Willy and I felled a good tree. . . . A splinter struck my eye, causing some inflammation: and in the evening Dr Moffatt came and sent me to bed'; and on the 24th: 'In bed and in the dark all day. Much rumination: on imperial concerns – & on Homer – among other matters'; and on Christmas Day, 'Kept to bed till 1am [*sic*]'. However, Gladstone was always a great man for the recuperative effects of bed, and by 27 December he was back at the slaughter in the park: 'Today a tree we were cutting fell with Harry [his third son, then aged fifteen] in it. He showed perfect courage and by God's mercy was not hurt.' A month later he was himself again the victim and had to 'put off letters on account of a finger a little bruised in the chances of woodcutting in the afternoon.'[26] There arises the thought that, in spite of his sparse frame and taut movements, he might have been a little clumsy. From the September day twenty-five years before when he had shot off the forefinger of his left hand (and subsequently always wore a black stall, or occasionally a glove) while reloading one barrel of a gun with the other fully cocked, he had shown some proneness to accidents.

At the end of February 1868 Disraeli became Prime Minister. Derby was sixty-eight, well younger than Palmerston or Russell, but a combination of his gout and his doctor made it impossible for him to carry on, and the last Prime Minister to be born in the eighteenth century disappeared from the scene and died a year later. Disraeli had a genuine affection for Derby, but was nonetheless delighted to have 'climbed to the top of the greasy pole'. In March he gave a grand reception to celebrate the event, and borrowed the new Foreign Office from Derby's son Stanley for the occasion: Mrs Disraeli thought 10 Downing Street 'so dingy and decaying'. The party was a dazzling symbol of Disraeli's rise (although he himself was reported as looking 'impenetrable' and 'low', while his wife looked 'ill and haggard'). There were present princes and princesses, dukes and duchesses, ambassadors and prelates – and the Gladstones. Gladstone did not exactly enthuse over the event: 'Dined at Mr Cardwell's. . . . Mr Disraeli's party and Speaker's Levée at night'[27] was the only mention it got in his diary. But he went, and thereby kept up the *convenances* of mid-Victorian politics. The emphasis should be on *mid*, for it is much more doubtful whether, had a similar celebration taken place nine or ten years later, he would have done so, or would indeed have been welcome.

Five years the elder, Disraeli had thus got to be first minister ten months before Gladstone was to do so. Despite the symbiosis of their relationship in the sixth, seventh and eighth decades of the century, however, there was one event in Gladstone's life in that winter of 1867–8 which was still more important to his future than Disraeli's accession to the foremost place. As he ruminated around the political horizon during the long Hawarden weeks of recess, so the words of his 1845 letter to his wife ('Ireland, Ireland! That cloud in the west, that coming storm, the vehicle of God's retribution . . .') came to have more meaning for him than when he had written them; and when he made his major speech of the 1867 autumn, at Southport on 19 December, it was almost entirely devoted to Irish issues. Thereafter, except during his preoccupation with Bulgarian atrocities and wider aspects of the Eastern Question in 1876–80, his mind was never to be free of Ireland and the Irish.

Part Three

THE FIRST PREMIERSHIP AND THE FIRST RETIREMENT

1868–1876

17

'My Mission is to Pacify Ireland'

In spite of that haunting 1845 phrase, Gladstone for the first fifty-eight years of his life had applied himself very sparingly to Hibernian problems. His principal practical impact upon Ireland had been his 1853 budget decision to bring it within the scope of the income tax, from which it had been spared by both Pitt and Peel. While this unionist approach could be interpreted as a mark of confidence in the metropolitan as opposed to the colonial status of Ireland, it did not exhibit much sensitivity to the difference between the socio-economic structures of the two islands, and it was naturally not popular in the second island. Nor had he ever made a speech as sharply if flippantly penetrating of the paradoxes of Anglo-Irish relations as Disraeli had in 1844.*

In 1867–8 Gladstone had never visited Ireland. He had planned an 1845 visit with Hope-Scott and Philip Pusey, the great Pusey's elder

* Disraeli's House of Commons words of 16 February 1844 were:

'I want to see a public man come forward and say what the Irish question is. One says it is a physical question, another a spiritual. Now it is the absence of the aristocracy. Now it is the absence of railways. It is the Pope one day and potatoes the next. A dense population inhabit an island where there is an established church which is not their church, and a territorial aristocracy, the richest of whom live in a distant capital. Thus they have a starving population, an alien church, and in addition the weakest executive in the world.

Well, what then would gentlemen say if they were reading of a country in that position? They would say at once, 'The remedy is a revolution.' But the Irish could not have a revolution and why? Because Ireland is connected with another and a more powerful country. Then what is the consequence? The connection with England became the cause of the present state of Ireland. If the connection with England prevented a revolution and a revolution was the only remedy, England logically is in the odious position of being the cause of all the misery of Ireland. What then is the duty of an English minister? To effect by his policy all those changes which a revolution would effect by force. That is the Irish question in its integrity.

brother, who was then MP for Berkshire, but almost at the last moment the plan fell through. In this respect, however, he was no worse than Disraeli, who never crossed St George's Channel, or than many other fellow politicians. Gladstone, like Asquith, did go for one proper visit, but this was not until 1877, when he was nearly sixty-eight years old and had already been a Prime Minister much concerned with Irish problems for five years. Also, in 1880, he slipped ashore from a yacht on a Sunday morning, but only to attend a service in the Anglican cathedral of Christ Church. His proper 1877 visit lasted nearly a month, but its impact upon him was limited by its being confined to official and ecclesiastical Dublin together with stays in five 'ascendancy' mansions of the Irish home counties.

It is, however, strange that curiosity had not led him to Ireland earlier. He had so often taken the Irish Mail from Euston as far as Chester, from where after the Britannia bridge was completed in 1850 the next stop was Holyhead. He would have been almost there in the time he frequently devoted to walking from Chester station to Hawarden. Had he never been tempted to remain on the train for this further two hours, to make the short two-and-a-half-hour crossing (admittedly he was a bad sailor), and then to step ashore in a country which was so different from and yet so crucial to the predominant island? Indefatigable a traveller and relentless a sightseer, up and down the Italian peninsula and from Dresden to Athens, though he had proved himself to be, there is no evidence that either the Georgian urbanity of Dublin (not much admired at the time) or the mountains and lakes of the west ever exercised a comparable pull upon him.

Until the late 1860s Gladstone's views on Ireland were largely conditioned by two contrary strands of thought. First, his respect for a judgemental Concert of Europe made him ashamed that the condition of Ireland exposed a flank so damaging to England's reputation. Whenever continental rulers wished to deliver a *tu quoque* against England they had Ireland readily to hand. Schwarzenberg, for instance, had not failed to raise it in his dismissive reply to the remonstrance against Neapolitan gaols which Gladstone had persuaded Aberdeen to send him in 1851. Even more significant was the letter which Gladstone wrote to Guizot, the statesman–savant of France, in 1872. Gladstone was then Prime Minister and Guizot, aged eighty-five, in the last eighteen months of his life and out of office for the past twenty-four years. It was remarkable and typical of Gladstone that he should have taken the trouble to write such a letter 'out of the blue'. Its content, written in the aftermath of Irish Church disestablishment and of the first Land Act was even more revealing.

> It is very unlikely [Gladstone began] that you shall remember a visit I paid you, I think at Passy in the autumn of 1845, with a message from Lord Aberdeen about international copyright. The Maynooth Act had just been passed. Its author, I think, meant it to be final. I had myself regarded it as *seminal.* And you in congratulating me upon it, as I well remember, said we should have the sympathies of Europe in the work of giving Ireland justice – a remark which evidently included more than the measure just passed, and which I have ever after saved and pondered. It helped me on towards what has been since done.[1]

The saving of Britain's Irish reputation in Europe (and indeed America, although there it was more difficult to redeem and the jury was further away from his mind) was for Gladstone as important a motive. as the relief of distress in the congested districts of the west of Ireland.

Second, and somewhat contradictorily, there was what J. L. Hammond in his great book on *Gladstone and the Irish Nation* regarded as the wretched parsimoniousness which sprang from his too many years as a cheese-paring Chancellor of the Exchequer. This made him suspicious of Ireland as a potentially dangerous source of demands upon the Treasury. One of Gladstone's deepest political beliefs, which he inherited from Peel, was his view that the miseries of the English poor (which were manifestly acute between the end of the Napoleonic Wars and his first budgets) stemmed largely from the unnecessary burdens of indirect taxation which the eighteenth-century tradition of rich sinecures for the governing class and other lavish pay-outs imposed upon them. He saw loose public expenditure not as a means of redistribution in favour of the poor but as a discrimination in favour of the undeserving rich. A large part of the moral fervour of his Treasury policies came from this conviction. And it took him a long time to see that Ireland in this respect, as in so many others, was different from the rest of the United Kingdom. Ireland was not going to achieve a stable agrarianism, towards which Gladstone's policies eventually made a major contribution, without new forms of public expenditure. Yet Gladstone's earlier and instinctive attitude is well illustrated in a letter which he wrote to his wife on 9 April 1859, when he was not even in office, but had the previous night attacked Disraeli's handling of the Galway Packet Contract, an issue which assumed temporary prominence. 'The scene [in the House of Commons] was sickening,' he wrote, 'and all the Irish were there most of them vying with each other in eagerness to plunder the public purse.'[2]

One way of reconciling the conflict between guilt and parsimony which raged in his mind was to give priority to the issue of the Anglican Church in Ireland. This, unless it was dealt with by what was called concurrent endowment (that is, maintaining the establishment but giving levelling-up money to the Roman Catholics), to which Gladstone was implacably opposed, did not involve public expenditure. Furthermore, any issue touching on religion, even if in some ways an awkward one for him, as was certainly the case here, also carried an inherent fascination.

On the maintenance of the Anglican establishment in Ireland Gladstone had started from the most intransigent position. In his 1838 *The State in its Relations with the Church* he had wished not merely to maintain the full panoply of the state-supported episcopacy in the thirty-two counties but to exclude from a public service job in Ireland anyone who was not a communicating Anglican. And in the same year he both fulminated and voted against the flicker towards concurrent endowment which was represented by the small Maynooth grant. By 1845, however, when he perversely and on purely historical grounds resigned from the Peel Cabinet on the Maynooth issue, he had considerably shifted his position. Indeed, once he had lost his faith that Church and state could be run by a joint clerisy, he began to move into a somewhat ambivalent position even on the merits of establishment in England. An independent Church might be better than a purely Erastian one owing more to Prime Ministers than to the apostolic succession and the early Christian fathers. These doubts were strengthened by the Gorham judgement of 1850. They were inhibited, however, by his eighteen years as member for 'the God-fearing and God-sustaining University of Oxford' (in his own slightly hyperbolic deathbed phrase). The University, with some famous exceptions who attached more importance to doctrine than to mitres, was devoted to the powers and perquisites of an established Church and to its own special position as both its ornament and its seminary.

Gladstone's 'unmuzzling' as a result of his transference from Oxford to South Lancashire in July 1865 was therefore important to the evolution of his public (perhaps more than his private) position on Irish Church disestablishment. It must however be said that he made his first resonant pronouncement on the issue three months before he ceased to be member for Oxford. He insisted on speaking (although it could hardly be regarded as a responsibility of a Chancellor of the Exchequer who was not then leader of the House of Commons) on a motion from James Dillwyn, Radical MP for Swansea, drawing attention to the deleterious anomaly of an Anglican established Church in Ireland, and calling upon the government to take action. Gladstone once again demonstrated his mixture of naivety and wilfulness by first thinking that he could speak (from the Treasury bench) in a private member's capacity, and then, when Palmerston remonstrated against this course, believing that he had met the objection by assenting to the first part of the motion but not promising any specific government action. The speech not unnaturally attracted a lot of attention, particularly in Oxford, and suggests that Gladstone's mind was already writing off the dreaming spires.

The retreat to South Lancashire in that summer of 1865 and the death of Palmerston in the autumn removed two of the obstacles to action as opposed to abstract condemnation. Nevertheless Gladstone did not attempt to drive the Russell government to legislation. Its energies were concentrated on its unsuccessful Reform Bill. In May 1867, however, when he had no responsibility for the government's programme, he showed his resilience to the buffetings he was receiving from Disraeli, as well as a shrewd sense that if one front was going badly there was much to be said for opening up a different one. He threw into a debate on Irish universities a statement of firm notice that Parliament could not long delay dealing with the Irish Church. This, unlike suffrage reform, had a unifying rather than a divisive affect upon the Liberal party.

The views which he expressed in his December 1867 speech at Southport were therefore not the result of a sudden lurch, but rather the end of a gradual but predictable curve which had started nearly thirty years before and had taken him through almost 180 degrees. What was new and surprising was the prominence which he chose to give to them. Southport placed Irish Church reform and Irish land reform in the centre of the English political battle. The speech was made the more courageous by coming immediately after a wave of Fenian attacks. In the previous year, in an almost Ruritanian act, the Fenians of New York had mounted an invasion of Canada. In September 1867 an armed gang had rescued two Irish prisoners from a police van in Manchester and shot one guard dead. And in December, only a few days before the Southport speech, part of the wall of Clerkenwell Prison was blown up and twelve people killed. Gladstone of course condemned these outrages, and indeed was particularly vehement against the irrationality and injustice of the attack on Canada: 'Canada has inflicted no wrongs on Ireland; Ireland has wrongs; Canada has no power to remedy them.'[3] But he also urged looking behind the outrages to the grievances of the Irish people out of which, even if illegitimately, they sprang. The first of the desirable consequences which he predicted from remedying these grievances was impressively idiosyncratic. When this has been done, 'instead of hearing in every corner of Europe the most painful commentaries on the policy of England towards Ireland we may be able to look our fellow Europeans in the face'.[4]

Just as the speech was made more courageous by the terrorism which immediately preceded it, so it was made more significant by a statement which immediately followed it. Russell announced his intention not again to take office. The titular leadership of the Liberal party thus became vacant, and the succession was wide open to Gladstone, even apart from the dominance of his personality, by virtue of his leadership in the Commons without a senior rival in the Lords. In December 1867, therefore, the majority party, for such it had loosely been in every election since 1847, achieved both a new leader and a new first item for its programme. Gladstone and Irish reform became the new device on the banner. It was not the most obvious combination with which to rally the freshly enlarged but still restricted (to about two and a half million) electorate of England, Scotland and Wales. However, the moral and oratorical force of the one transcended, for a time at any rate, the limited appeal of the other.

The first manifestation of Gladstone's leadership and of his choice of issue on which to exercise it came at the end of March 1868, when he initiated a four-day debate (such time could the leader of the opposition then command) on his intention to bring in three resolutions on the Irish Church. A Conservative amendment to delay their consideration until the next Parliament was handsomely defeated, the old Palmerstonian majority thus reasserting itself after the vicissitudes of the suffrage issue. It was yet another example of Gladstone being 'terrible in the rebound'. Disraeli's triumphs of the previous year did not repeat themselves in his first real test as Prime Minister. Even the curt and cryptic sentences of Gladstone's diary managed to convey a full sense of triumph:

> Spoke 1½ hours after D (who was tipsy) in winding up the Debate. Walked home with Harry and Herbert [his younger sons, then respectively sixteen and fourteen] a crowd at our tail. The divisions each nearly

> sixty [the first gave Gladstone a majority of sixty and the second one of fifty-six] were wonderful. The counts are big: and I, how little.[5]

A month later, the substantive resolutions were put to the vote. The majority on the first was still bigger than the 'wonderful' sixty, and the other two were not opposed. This made the position of the government untenable. As with Russell two years earlier, Disraeli's choice appeared to lie only between resignation and dissolution. However, after so many years of waiting, he had been Prime Minister for only two months. So he hit upon an ingenious compromise. He would dissolve, but not until the autumn. For this course he had both a good excuse and a good ally. The excuse was that the election ought to be fought on a new register based upon the provisions of the 1867 Reform Act. The ally was the Queen, who was already loath to see Disraeli go. He needed her, for there was an important element in his Cabinet, including Gathorne Hardy, his Home Secretary and strongest debating colleague, and his two ducal substitutes, Richmond and Marlborough, who were strongly in favour of immediate resignation. Both his cynical skill at man-management and his jaunty relations with the Queen (so different from those of Gladstone) were well illustrated by the letter which he wrote to her on 8 May indicating how he had circumnavigated the problem with Marlborough (which took the steam out of the other two would-be resigners): 'The Duke of Marlborough seemed a little bilious when Mr Disraeli returned from Osborne so ultimately, acting on Yr Majesty's sanction, Mr Disraeli announced to his Grace that Yr Majesty had been pleased to confer on him the blue ribbon [of the Garter].'[6]

Gladstone followed up his Irish Church resolutions by introducing a bill to suspend any new beneficial appointments in the Church of Ireland and, with a majority of fifty-four on second reading, carried it through the House of Commons at the end of May. The Lords threw it out by the larger majority of ninety-five later in the summer, but it was nonetheless a rumbling warning of what was to come, as well as a display of Gladstone's renewed parliamentary power. Disraeli might be temporarily Prime Minister, but he could extend his term for eight months after the night of Gladstone's triumph over his 'tipsiness' only at the price of sharing parliamentary power with him. During the remainder of that session of 1868, which expired on 28 July, Gladstone spoke with great frequency and on almost every subject under the sun. He spoke on the new Law Courts, on the Navy estimates, on Glasgow electoral arrangements. As his days were full with many other engagements and occupations his diaries give the impression of his blowing in to the House of Commons, sounding off on whatever subject was under discussion, and generally exercising his remarkable facility for being as economical with his own preparation time as he was profligate with House of Commons listening time. What was indisputable was that he had completely regained his parliamentary confidence and authority after the trough of 1867. Gladstone was very much a Prime Minister in waiting during the session of 1868.

He was not pressing. He had a calm summer. In the last week of the parliamentary session, at the strong invitation of Lady Palmerston, he went to Broadlands, where he had never been in Palmerston's day, but only for the shortest possible time; he was back in London by 11.00 the next morning. After ten days at Hawarden and one of speechmaking in Liverpool and St Helens he went to Penmaenmawr on 10 August and remained there, interrupted only by another short Lancashire excursion, for five weeks (twenty-eight sea-bathes). His Hawarden six weeks from mid-September to the beginning of November were then broken by one night in Warrington and two visits of four nights each at his brother's house in Liverpool, all for electioneering purposes. An aspect of his character, at once endearing and incorrigible, was revealed by his diary entries for two successive meetings. On 12 October, at Warrington: 'Spoke over 1½ hours: too long.' On the 14th at Liverpool: 'Meeting in Amphitheatre, 7½–11. Spoke 1¾ hours.'[7] He then retreated to Hawarden and Homer for three weeks, which were interrupted by the death at the age of sixty-three of Harriet Sutherland, a painful loss for him, and a journey to Staffordshire for her funeral at Trentham. He also diverted from Homer to read the two volumes of the twenty-five-year-old Charles Dilke's *Greater Britain* (which he referred to as *Greater World*, but compensated for his inaccuracy by annotating it heavily). Then he returned to Liverpool and another twelve days of electioneering.

South Lancashire had been divided, and Gladstone had become candidate for the new South-west division, which excluded the Manchester area and, with Warrington (now in Cheshire but historically Lancashire) and Preston added, was not very different from that part of the recent Merseyside Metropolitan County which was north of the estuary. H. R. Grenfell, a brother-in-law of the Earl of Sefton, who was a Liverpool grandee almost on the Derby scale, had been adopted as his running mate. Grenfell himself was a man of substance, later to be Governor of the Bank of England, and was thought greatly to strengthen their joint appeal to the Whig elements in the constituency. Gladstone was even led by the choice of Grenfell to write (on 1 August) of 'brilliant prospects' in the constituency.

What in fact occurred was a brilliant campaign followed by a dismal result, as, except in Midlothian, was frequently Gladstone's experience. Morley wrote that 'the breadth, the elevation, the freshness, the power, the measure, the high self-command of these [1868 Lancashire] speeches was never surpassed by any of his performances'.[8] Morley supported the claim by reference to Gladstone's speech at Leigh on 20 October, in which he delivered even-handed blows against both 'constructive' radicalism and constitutional conservatism. On the first point 'he assailed the system of making things pleasant all round, stimulating local cupidity to feed upon the public purse, and scattering grants at the solicitation of individuals and classes'. On the second he responded to the accusation that his Irish proposals would destroy the constitution by mockingly recalling that he had already known it wholly ruined and destroyed seven times, starting in 1828 with the repeal of the Corporation and Test Acts and ending (for the moment) with the Russell government's attempt at suffrage reform. Understandably in the circumstances, he omitted to mention that he had himself been violently opposed to the first three of the seven measures.

The result was declared on 24 November, and put Gladstone in third place (with only two elected), about 300 behind both R. A. Cross (later Disraeli's Home Secretary) who headed the poll and Cross's Conservative colleague. It was not much consolation that Gladstone was 500 votes ahead of Grenfell. It was an extraordinary result. Other party leaders have occasionally lost their own constituencies, Balfour in Manchester in 1906, Asquith in Fife in 1918, MacDonald at Seaham in 1935, but in all these cases it has been when their party was caught in a severe ebb-tide or when the circumstances were otherwise exceptional. But Gladstone in 1868 swept the country. The Liberal expectations, which had been modest in the summer and early autumn, were far exceeded. The conventional figure for the Liberal majority was 112, although there was still room for ambiguity at the edges. Even more striking was the Liberal plurality in votes: 1,355,000 to 883,500. And deeply paradoxical was the fact that the best Conservative performance in the three countries was in Ireland. In Scotland they polled only 16 per cent.

In the midst of this Conservative massacre there were one or two notable Liberal defeats. John Stuart Mill was beaten in Westminster by the stationer–statesman W. H. Smith. But this was small beer compared with the defeat in Lancashire of the Prime Minister-elect of the new (quasi-) democracy. Palmerston's 1864 warning that Gladstone might win Lancashire but lose England was shown to be singularly wide of the mark. What Gladstone did was to win England (and Scotland and Wales and even Ireland) for his party but to lose Lancashire for himself.

This perverse result created remarkably little reaction among the public, and no dismay comparable with that which followed his Oxford defeat in Gladstone himself. The public were used to politicians shuffling constituencies about as quickly as a Mississippi steamboat gambler did a pack of cards and Gladstone had the cushion that, a week before the Lancashire result and almost inadvertently, he had been comfortably but not gloriously elected for Greenwich. It was not glorious because he was 300 votes behind a local alderman, but it was comfortable because he was nearly 2000 ahead of the challenging Tories.

It was ironical, and perhaps a little chastening, that the greatest platform campaigner of his age should, on the threshold of his first and most powerfully reforming ministry, have been rejected in the constituency in which he had orated mightily and elected in one which he had not visited. South-west Lancashire was not easy territory in which to conduct a campaign centred on Irish religion. There was a substantial 'orange' element among those on the electoral register, while the balancing 'greens' were mostly excluded from it. But nor did Greenwich, for different reasons, prove to be easy when the next election came, and the Merseyside setback undoubtedly took a little of the gilt off Gladstone's gingerbread. He had also, as a further mildly exacerbating factor, been defeated for the chancellorship of Edinburgh University three days before.

His diary entry for the day of the Lancashire defeat read:

> Went in at 10.30 to vote – with Robn. [his brother] and Mr Heywood [his running mate in 1865, and his host for much of this 1868 campaign]. Till midday the case looked well. Then we fell back regularly.... Employed myself on Homer at all intervals. Returned to [Heywood's house] with Robn. Finished [Fanny Burney's] Evelina.[9]

The next day he went off on two short Cheshire country-house visits before returning to Hawarden on Saturday, 28 November. The newly created Lord Halifax (formerly Charles Wood) came for that night at his own request, as an unofficial envoy from Windsor. He was an odd choice for such a role, as he was not particularly close to Gladstone, and, although he had been in Palmerston's Cabinet, he was originally unwilling to join Gladstone's, although he came in as Lord Privy Seal in 1870. However, the intelligence which he brought, some of it welcome, some of it less so, was of more than sufficient interest to make up for any inappropriateness as a go-between. He said that Disraeli proposed to resign immediately and not wait to meet Parliament. This was then an unusual course, which made the outgoing Prime Minister wish secrecy maintained until the following Tuesday. Halifax added that the Queen objected to Clarendon as Foreign Secretary and also to one or two possible lords-in-waiting (including one of Gladstone's Cheshire hosts) who had been in the previous Liberal government.

Gladstone was not concerned about the lords-in-waiting, but the Clarendon objection was both surprising and serious. It might have been supposed that the urbane old Whig, who had known the Queen throughout her reign and been in Cabinets since Melbourne's day, would have been very acceptable. However, he was also a mocking old Whig and had taken to referring to the Queen as 'the Missus', a nickname which, when it got back to her, was not popular. (As he also habitually referred to Gladstone as 'Merrypebble' it might have been thought that the honours were even.) Gladstone was however committed to Clarendon, not emotionally (he would have preferred Granville) but because he had given him an undertaking six months earlier. Perhaps because of this detachment and thanks also to the good offices of General Grey, the Queen's private secretary, he managed to handle tactfully this first disagreement, and got her to see that Clarendon could be avoided only at the worse price of letting it be known that he was a victim of royal disfavour.

Grey, who was to be the next significant arrival on the Hawarden stage, carried some embarrassing luggage for his dealings with Disraeli and Gladstone alike. When he had waited upon the former nine months earlier to tell him that he was to be Prime Minister it was thirty-four years since he had beaten him in the High Wycombe election of 1835 (having done so twice before in the two elections of 1832). When he came to Gladstone on the same mission it was thirty-three years since his wife (then Caroline Farquhar) had reacted so dismissively to Gladstone's presumption as a suitor and his unfortunate manner of carrying a bag across the park at Polesden Lacey. Grey, younger son of the Earl Grey of the first Reform Bill, was, however, a skilled and sensible courtier who surmounted with aplomb these hillocks of difficulty. He telegraphed to Gladstone on Tuesday, 1 December, saying that he had a letter from the Queen and asking where he should personally deliver it. He expected Gladstone to come to London, but Gladstone, entering into the spirit of secrecy, said it would attract less attention if Grey came to Hawarden. It also gave Gladstone an extra day of recoil before action.

Grey accordingly took the 9.45 morning train from Windsor (Slough?) 'direct to Chester'. It took until 4.15 to get there, thereby illustrating the pre-1890s joke that GWR stood for 'Great Way Round'. The arrival both of his telegram and of himself led to dramatic legends. Evelyn Ashley, the then thirty-two-year-old younger son of Lord Shaftesbury, formerly private secretary to Palmerston and later his biographer, was staying at Hawarden and was watching Gladstone tree-felling in the park when the telegram was brought out. According to an account which Ashley published in a magazine article thirty years later, Gladstone opened the little buff envelope himself, read the telegram, handed it to Ashley (no excessive secrecy there), saying only 'Very significant' and continued to attack the tree. After a few more blows he rested on his axe and said, 'My mission is to pacify Ireland.' Then he continued his onslaught until the tree was down, after which he went into the house and sent Grey a reply ensuring that the mountain came to Mahomet.[10]

The account of Grey's arrival was provided by the General himself. To his surprise he was met at Chester station by Mrs Gladstone, who insisted that he stayed the night at Hawarden, whereas he had intended to return by the 2.15 a.m. Irish Mail train. At the castle he was 'taken at once by Mrs Gladstone into an almost dark room – the only light being the fire, and the two candles by which Mr Gladstone was working'. He further commented that he 'was received with the most open, frank and cordial manner by Mr G'.[11] He made just as good an impression on Gladstone. 'He [Grey] was very kind and true,' the new Prime Minister wrote.[12] In this mood of mutual respect they travelled together from Chester to Slough on the following day. During the journey they established a *modus vivendi* on Irish Church matters. The Queen would not like disestablishment, but Grey accepted that Gladstone was committed. The Prime Minister would however endeavour to massage her susceptibilities. On the specific issue the limited accord held well.

When the train was specially stopped at Slough (Grey had telegraphed to the station master) Gladstone walked to Eton, saw his son Harry (where was Herbert?) and then continued across the river and up to the Castle, thereby missing a crowd which had assembled to greet him at Windsor station. By then the Queen had returned from her afternoon drive, and he had a full audience of discussion and not merely a formal session of appointment. Indeed he had to ask her whether he ought not to kiss hands: 'she said yes & it was done'.[13] She was mainly concerned with matters of personnel (what she called Lord Clarendon's 'indelicacy' – although this matter was well on the way to resolution – the importance, if Lord Hartington became Viceroy of Ireland, of the Duchess of Manchester, whom he subsequently married, but not until 1892, 'not do[ing] the honours'), and the Irish Church came up only when 'the time for the train was fast approaching'. Altogether it was a signal-box-dominated approach to the premiership.

All went well for the moment. He found the Queen 'kind, cheerful, even playful'.[14] By 6.00 he was formally Prime Minister. By 7.00 he was at Carlton House Terrace and engaged on Cabinet-making. He was a month short of fifty-nine years of age, a member of Parliament of thirty-six years' standing (with a short break) who had been a Cabinet minister (mostly as Chancellor of the Exchequer) for twelve years. Rivalled in previous ministerial service by the heterogeneous mixture of Palmerston, Russell (on his return to Downing Street), Lloyd George (because of the length of his Treasury tenure), Churchill and Callaghan (because of the width of his departmental spread), he was on balance ahead of them all, the most ministerially experienced man ever to become Prime Minister. But there was nothing *réchauffé* about him. In the context of 1868 he was a new man, full of elemental and even dangerous force. He had four premierships of varying success ahead of him. He also had behind him nearly six decades of unusual interest and achievement.

Robert Rhodes James has written a persuasive thesis that Churchill would have been little more than a footnote to history had he died on the threshold of his premiership, when he was sixty-four. This would certainly have been so of Salisbury had he gone in 1886 at the age of fifty-six, or of Macmillan had he done so in 1956 when he was sixty-two. But such obscurity would emphatically not have been the fate of Gladstone had he died instead of becoming Prime Minister in 1868. He would still have been a major nineteenth-century figure. The country would, however, have been deprived of its most quintessential Prime Minister. He was this because he was the one who most dominated the busy junction where executive power, parliamentary command and democratic validity jostle together. His executive power, which he exercised with gusto, was modified by respect for and conflict with the whims of the Sovereign. His parliamentary command was accompanied by endemic revolts against his driving force. His democratic validity also had elements of paradox in that it was based on his ability to rivet great audiences who were held by his flashing eyes while hardly understanding the convolutions of his interminable sentences. No one else however has so mingled the three sources of constitutional power. Lloyd George rivalled his spell-binding oratory, but lacked his personal parliamentary authority. Churchill could not match the spontaneous popular oratory as opposed to the parliamentary setpieces.

In 1868 Gladstone could be held to epitomize the words of Browning's *Rabbi Ben Ezra*:

> Grow old along with me!
> The best is yet to be.

But he also had more pre–Prime Ministerial achievement and interest behind him than any except one of his fellow Prime Ministers, and that one, Wellington, did not achieve much in 10, Downing Street.

18

A Commanding Prime Minister

The early part of Gladstone's first government was as enjoyable for its participants as office can ever be expected to be. The Prime Minister afterwards spoke of that administration as 'one of the best instruments for government that ever was constructed', and did so in a way which made the statement a nostalgic lament rather than a boast of his own skill at Cabinet-making. Of the fourteen gentlemen whom he so assembled, six were peers (then a low proportion), only one a duke (although another was a duke's heir), and of the twelve who survived until 1886 no more than four supported Gladstone in the great Home Rule split of that year. But for the moment there was harmony. Gladstone's diaries for the last weeks of 1868 and the session of 1869 give an impression of contentment, confidence and tolerance, with bursts of almost boyish good humour.

At the two turn-of-the-year milestones, his birthday and New Year's Eve, he wrote with an enthusiasm which nearly suppressed his usual breast-beating. On 29 December: 'This birthday opens my 60th year. I descend the hill of life. It would be a truer figure to say I ascend a steepening path with a burden ever gathering weight. The Almighty seems to sustain and spare me for some purpose of His own deeply unworthy as I know myself to be. Glory be to his name.'[1]

On 31 December his satisfaction was still more evident:

> This month of December has been notable in my life, as follows.
>
> Dec 1809. Born
> 1827. Left Eton
> 1831. [First] Classes at Oxford
> 1832. Elected to Parliament
> 1838. Work on Ch. & State Published
> 1844. Took office: Lord of the Treasury
> 1846. Sec. of State.
> 1853. Chancr. of Exr.
> 1868. First Lord.

He then added a perceptive comment on the restricted and often too reactive life of a minister: 'Swimming for his life, a man does not see much of the country through which the river winds, and I probably know little of these years through which I busily work and live, beyond this, how sin and frailty deface them, and how mercy crowns them.' He ended almost on an exultant note: 'Farewell great year of opening, not of alarming, change: and welcome new year laden with promise and with care.'[2]

Apart from a bizarre expedition to Hatfield in the second week of December, he had exceptionally remained in London over Christmas and until he went to Hagley on 29 December and then to Hawarden. The Hatfield stay, which no doubt fulfilled a prior commitment to the thirty-eight-year-old and recently succeeded Salisbury extended across four days, interrupted by an excursion to Windsor. It was bizarre because it was an uncompromising Tory house from which to complete the making of a Liberal government. It also foreshadowed almost exactly similar behaviour by Asquith thirty-seven years later during the making of the next major reforming government.*

Gladstone spent the first three weeks of 1869 at Hawarden. It was inevitably a working holiday with his attention mainly on preparation for the Irish Church Bill. He had visits from three of his colleagues: Granville (but more as leader of the House of Lords and an easy companion than as Colonial Secretary), Spencer as Irish Viceroy, and Sullivan as Irish Attorney-General. He also entertained an Irish ecclesiastical go-between, Archdeacon Stafford of Meath, and Sir John Acton, on the threshold of ennoblement but sufficiently unworried by his famous aphorism about the corruption of power to be eager to attend upon the new Prime Minister. (Gladstone never gave fashionable general house parties of the sort in which he frequently participated at ducal and other great houses, but he liked visitors, was always willing to have people from Cobden to Parnell for a specific purpose, and often mingled them with young family friends.)

Despite the press of work on his Hawarden days it was a cool thing

* In December 1905, Asquith, who had just become Chancellor of the Exchequer and was already the obvious future Liberal leader, stayed four nights at Hatfield, travelling up to London by train each day and trying to unravel the foolish 'Relugas Compact' under which he and Edwarad Grey and Haldane had agreed that they would not serve unless Campbell-Bannerman retreated to a nominal premiership in the House of Lords. From this distraction he returned each night to various Hatfield festivities including a fancy-dress ball.

for Gladstone to remain so long away from London at such an early stage of his first premiership. His diary entry for 8 January 1869 illustrates the pattern. After church at 8.30, he:

> Wrote to the Lord Chancellor – Lord Granville – Mr H. A. Bruce [Home Secretary] – Mr Hamilton [Treasury permanent secretary] – Lord St. Germans – Bishop of Oxford – M. Bratiano – Dean of Westmr. – Dr Miller – Mr Fortescue – Gen. Grey – Lord Southesk – Mr Happs, Mr Gurden, Mr Reeve – Mr Hammond [Foreign Office permanent under-secretary] – Telegr. to Mr H[ammond], Sir C. Trevelyan – Mr G. O. Trevelyan minutes. *Two* evening messengers from London. Felling a tree in aftn.... Read Giffen on Finance.[3]

The purpose of his operating from 200 miles away rather than in Downing Street or Carlton House Terrace was well captured in a half-sentence of a letter to Clarendon, whom he showered with very courteously expressed foreign policy advice: 'in point of hours it is much the same here and there though [here] the free hours feel much more free which is a great thing'.[4]

Gladstone came to London on 22 January and began a period of intensive 'softening up' on the Irish Church Bill (at Hawarden he had applied himself to its intellectual preparation). He went first, accompanied by his wife, on a two-day visit to the Queen at Osborne. He could not persuade his sovereign to attend the opening of Parliament, which was fixed for 16 February, even though it was a new Parliament, elected on a new franchise, with a new Prime Minister, and turned out to be the beginning of a new political epoch. But he may have succeeded in diminishing her opposition to the Irish Church changes.

However, Gladstone at this stage in their relationship was often over-optimistic about the effect of his explanations and persuasions on the Queen. On the first evening he wrote: 'Saw the Queen on the Irish Church especially and gave H. M. my papers with explanations which appeared to be well taken. She was altogether at ease.'[5] On the second day he did not know what to make of her absolute silence on the subject. That evening at dinner she had Mrs Gladstone and not the Prime Minister to sit next to her. The truth was that she had not made head or tail of Gladstone's 'papers' until Sir Theodore Martin, the Prince Consort's biographer, had been summoned to write a summary. Then she did not much like what she saw, and ten days later Gladstone was recording: 'A letter from H. M. today showed much disturbance: which I tried to soothe.'[6] Nonetheless his talks with her, and perhaps even more with General Grey on the December journey from Chester to Slough, had prepared the ground for her acquiescence in the inevitable, and when there came a crunch with the House of Lords in July she was helpful to the government.

Gladstone also guarded his flank against a predecessor's possible sourness. Five days after his return from Osborne he went to Richmond and spent forty-eight hours at Pembroke Lodge with Russell. 'Much conversation with Lord R. on the Irish Ch. and other matters,' he recorded.[7] During that first year of the government he took a lot of trouble with the old Whig, but gradually the rule that nearly all Prime Ministers are dissatisfied with their successors, perhaps even more so if they come from the same party, asserted itself, and Russell drifted into discontent. Gladstone, when he wished, could be both solicitous and flattering. He was persistently so with John Bright, who was more opinionated than effective as President of the Board of Trade, but whom Gladstone determinedly treated as a great man as well as a great orator. This was partly because of his natural sympathy with what Professor Matthew calls 'the sentimental side of Victorian Radicalism', and was in marked contrast with his total inability, a decade later, to massage the abler but notably unsentimental Joseph Chamberlain.

With the Queen, in a different way, Gladstone was just as unskilled as he was to be with Chamberlain, but with most of the members of his Cabinet he was elaborately courteous and nearly as solicitous as with Bright, certainly so with Clarendon, with Granville, with Argyll (to whom he wrote frequent general political letters while never interfering in his departmental Indian affairs), with Earl de Grey, the Lord President, whom he made Marquess of Ripon. The one whom he handled least well was Hartington, treating him like his much more amenable brother Frederick Cavendish, who after he married Lucy Lyttelton in 1864 became almost a Gladstone family satellite. In 1868 he made Hartington Postmaster-General, which bored him, and in 1870 he forced him to go to Ireland as Chief Secretary. This was a bad preparation for patronizingly handing over the leadership to him in 1875 and then, inevitably but without delicacy, superseding him in 1880. It was not surprising that Gladstone lost Hartington in 1886.

Despite the complaints of his whips and of Phillimore and Acland, however, Gladstone could mostly cajole when he wanted to. He was psychologically incapable of flattery with some people, most notably the Queen, with Chamberlain as a runner-up, although in the latter case it was simple consideration, well short of flattery, which was lacking. Sometimes, with others, his courtesy failed because it was too elaborate and heavy-footed, but mostly his failures in human management were because he had not tried, hardly knew or noticed the person concerned, or just failed to understand that a word from him might make all the difference. But, in general, particularly away from politics, his manners were very good, and his charm, especially when he was not trying to achieve a result, formidable.

In 1869 he was solicitous to keep both his Cabinet and his majority together. Although by the time he left Hawarden he had got his own mind almost completely clear on what he wanted in the Irish Church Bill, he nonetheless allowed time for five Cabinets before the opening of the session, and a long sixth (mostly on the bill) between the Queen's Speech on 16 February and his exposition of the details to the House of Commons on 1 March. All the January and February 1869 Cabinets were early-afternoon occasions, starting at 2.00 or 2.30. As soon as the session began, while he kept to the same time of day, he reverted to Palmerston's Saturday habit.

Given that there was no formal agenda and no secretariat to record the results, Gladstone seems to have handled the meetings in a taut and orderly way. While it is difficult to believe that he emulated Attlee's laconicism there was no suggestion of Churchillian orotundity either. Before each meeting he made out a neat little agenda card for his own use, and ticked each numbered item as he disposed of it. He was indeed in most ways instinctively neat. After he reached middle age this did not apply to his clothes, despite a ludicrous 1870 attempt by the *Tailor and Cutter* to portray him (in a joint representation with his son Willy) as being almost glossy. Photographs show him as carelessly and semi-shabbily dressed in his habitual formal London clothes, worn even for striding over the hills of Wales from Penmaenmawr. Sometimes he allowed the variant of lighter-coloured trousers with an 1840s-style brown stripe down the side.

He had a passion for sorting papers and arranging books. It was one reason why he liked departures and arrivals. On the day before he returned from Hawarden to London for his first testing parliamentary session as Prime Minister he wrote: 'Attempted to re-establish order with a view to departure'. On his second, third and fourth days back in Carlton House Terrace, he wrote variants of 'Arranged books & papers a little.'[8] Still more revealingly, when he arrived back at Hawarden for an autumn three weeks in the following November he recorded:

'Worked 6 hours on my books arranging and re-arranging: the best brain rest I have had (I think) since Decr last.'[9]

As well as giving his Cabinet full rein, if not to disagree on the major thrust, at least to feel that they had been fully consulted on the details, Gladstone in the run-up to the bill also kept in touch with others whom he thought might be useful. He could not expect much help from the bishops, although he maintained an open line to Tait of Canterbury which led to the Primate not voting against the second reading in the Lords (although certainly not voting for it) and reluctantly seeking a settlement rather than preparing for an impasse. Thirlwall of St Davids was the only prelate who went into the lobby for the bill, but Magee of Peterborough, later Archbishop of York, and the perennial Wilberforce of Oxford (who might have been expected to do better in view both of old friendship and of his impending promotion to Winchester) were scouts scurrying between the lines and incurring both the limited gratitude and the dangers of such a role.

Gladstone also kept in close touch with Delane, the editor of *The Times*, and with Manning, already archbishop but not yet cardinal. Hitherto the *Daily Telegraph*, then firmly Liberal, had been Gladstone's principal ally in the press, while Delane had been a little too Palmerstonian for his taste. But Palmerston was dead and Delane was very much a man of the moment. The Prime Minister saw him several times during the spring and summer of 1869, sometimes writing him notes of conspiratorial invitation: 'If you can again find yourself in my little room at the H. of Commons this afternoon at 5, I shall be glad again to exchange a few words with you on the present aspect of the situation.'[10]

Manning was an obvious ally of Gladstone's on the issue, almost too much so to be an interesting one. However, he did have the advantage of fully agreeing with Gladstone, not only on the need for Anglican disestablishment but also on the unacceptability of 'concurrent endowment'. Gladstone was against it for reasons of cost to the British Exchequer, Manning for reasons of threat to Roman authority if Irish prelates and priests became pensioners of the London government. The confluence of these views was powerful and satisfactory. Gladstone also found Manning a useful channel for dealing with Archbishop Cullen of Dublin and the Irish hierarchy, perhaps too convenient if he wished to avoid a colonial approach to Ireland.

This led to a temporary renewal of warmth between Roman Catholic Archbishop and Anglican Prime Minister which would have seemed unimaginable at the time of their chilly 1861 resumption of contact after a ten-year gap. Manning wrote to Gladstone on 24 July 1869: 'But at this time I will only add that I may wish you joy on personal reasons. I could hardly have hoped that you would have so framed, mastered, and carried through the bill from first to last so complete, so unchanged in identity of principle and detail, and let me add with such unwearying and sustained self-control and forbearance.'[11] The momentum of Manning–Gladstone reunion was, however, heavily circumscribed by Manning being about to become the animator and agent of Vatican ultramontanism, which sent Gladstone into his greatest bout of anti-Romanism since Wiseman had ensnared (as he thought) his sister Helen in 1842.

The conduct of the Irish Church Bill through the House of Commons and the command of tactics in the dispute with the Lords which developed in late June and July was almost exclusively handled by the Prime Minister himself. Chichester Fortescue, Lady Waldegrave's fourth husband and *cavaliere servente* at her Strawberry Hill festivities, for whom she did not bother to change her name on marriage, was not a strong Chief Secretary for Ireland. He was allowed more of a role in the following session's Land Bill, although even then provoking more exasperation than admiration from Gladstone. But in 1869 he was kept firmly on the sidelines. It was only in the very last stages of the summer dispute with the Lords that Gladstone, struck down by a severe gastric attack, the intermittent effects of which lasted for four or five weeks, was forced to delegate, and then he did so to Granville and not to Fortescue.

For the main engagements Gladstone was in full and direct command, and discharged his commission with a combination of authority, persuasiveness and sustained energy which produced admiration from the most disparate sources. Of his three-and-a-quarter-hour speech introducing the bill, Disraeli, frequently so scornful of Gladstone's verbosity, said: 'There was not a word wasted.' The future Archbishop (Frederick) Temple (admittedly just about to be given his first bishopric by Gladstone but not normally of his ecclesiastical tendency) wrote that 'The Irish Church bill is the greatest monument of genius that I have yet known from Gladstone; even his marvellous budgets are not so marvellous.'[12] Morley, who was a partisan but not a blind one, and who had a fine eye for discriminating between the relative quality of Gladstone's different performances, wrote that, 'since Pitt, the author of the Act of Union, the author of the Church Act was the only statesman in the roll of the century capable at once of framing such a statute and expounding it with the same lofty and commanding power'.[13]

This power enabled him to carry the second reading after four nights of debate by the striking majority of 118. It was the first time since the beginning of the Peel government, twenty-eight years before, that a major party clash had been resolved so decisively. In the 1850s and most of the 1860s governments had fallen or survived and controversial bills had been carried or defeated by majorities of between five and nineteen. Few things could have more symbolized the change from mid-century political confusion to the relatively clear late-century alternatives of Gladstone and Disraeli or Salisbury than that 118. And Gladstone himself treated it as having an almost mystical significance. 'A notable and historic Division,' he described it in his diary.[14] In a letter to Manning on 3 June, when the bill had gone through its committee stage like a tank brushing aside bushes which stood in its path and when the third reading had been secured by an almost equally impressive majority of 114, he commented with a mixture of pride and ambiguity that 'The House has moved like an army, an army where every private is his own general.'[15] Gladstone was right in attaching importance to the earlier steadiness of the majority which had acted (to continue and maybe to confuse the military simile) like an artillery barrage upon Queen, peers and bishops. If it had not made them surrender it had made them see the advantage of a negotiated peace.

He would also have been right, had he taken satisfaction in his own contribution to that result, which he did not do, for self-congratulation as opposed to a conviction of the rightness of his own case was never part of his conceit. His introductory speech may have been a masterly example of lucid exposition, but it was his one-and-a-quarter-hour winding-up speech on 23 March, a nutshell of succinctness by his standards, which was the debating triumph and was rightly chosen for inclusion in the treasury of Gladstone's orations. This speech had an easy confidence which made comprehensible his otherwise paradoxical (late-life) remark that he was only nervous when opening a debate (presumably with a prepared text) and never when replying and therefore depending upon the inspiration of the moment to turn a pudding into a soufflé. This concluding speech, largely unprepared, is a brilliant example of his best flowing debating style, and is a standing contradiction to any view that he was a pompous, humourless and viscous speaker. His sentences in this speech were, as always, long and elaborate, but perfectly constructed and easy to read. He had some good jokes. He engaged with Gathorne Hardy, who had spoken immediately before him; with Disraeli, who had opened the debate for the opposition; with Lord George Hamilton, who had made a successful maiden speech which presaged a parliamentary career lasting into the Balfour–Asquith epoch; and with Spencer Walpole, the tearful Home Secretary of 1867; and he annihilated Stafford Northcote, his former private secretary who had become Conservative MP for North Devon. The whole speech conveys an exceptional force and mastery over both subject and audience.

It was not only in the setpiece debate that Gladstone demonstrated by his stamina and unflagging patience a Prime Minister's strategic command combined with a detailed knowledge of the intricacies of a bill which few departmental ministers would have been able to rival with a measure of their own. There were thirteen committee days, all concentrated within three weeks, and then, after a short interval, a couple more days for report and third reading. For around seven or eight hours on all of these days Gladstone was continuously on the government bench, always listening, always in charge, intervening on all the most difficult points, invariably with knowledge and conviction, mostly with judgement. The fact that the bill got through the Commons so compactly, the majorities always above a hundred, the debates intensive but never running out of control, the government never having to seek a pause because of some new point which it could not answer or some setback from which it needed a few days to recover, owed much to the Prime Minister's hands-on generalship.

Over the Lords he could obviously exercise no such control, both because of the absence of a Liberal majority and because he could not there participate, even though he sat listening upon the steps of the throne for some significant part of the proceedings. Second reading was carried by 179 to 146, a very large vote in the then under 500-strong House. Canterbury and York (as well as the already mentioned Winchester and Peterborough and most other bishops) abstained, and thirty-six Conservative peers headed by the Marquess of Salisbury (the Hatfield visit perhaps justifying itself) voted for the bill. It was only the second time in a generation that the Conservative leadership in the Lords had been defeated in a division.

This promising start did not prevent the Lords mauling the bill at committee stage. They concerned themselves very much with the temporalities rather than the spiritualities. As Morley succinctly put it: 'The general result of the operations of the Lords was to leave disestablishment complete, and the legal framework of the bill undisturbed. Disendowment on the other hand was reduced to a shadow.'[16] This at least had the advantage of reducing the dispute between the two Houses to a haggle about money, which was perhaps more manageable, even if less elevating, than a clash of religious principles. However, Church money, and in particular Church stipends, were more than capable of raising passions. The controversy was further fuelled by the Lords twice insisting on an alteration to the preamble of the bill. This alteration, while it did not have direct practical effect, predicated the whole exercise on a 'concurrent endowment' approach which was as repugnant to Gladstone as he believed (probably rightly) it was to almost all Irish opinion.

The loss between the two Houses of the only major bill of the first session of a government commanding the biggest majority for more than a generation would have been a grave constitutional affront, and an appropriate atmosphere of crisis lay on official London throughout the two middle weeks of July. Despite the result of the second reading division, the opponents of the bill had a secure Lords majority for amendments which were unacceptable to the government, and in a game of shuttlecock between the two Houses twice voted for them. On the other hand there was nervousness as well as defiance among the opponents of the government and the bill. Disraeli's general strategy was to let the government run into exhaustion and unpopularity rather than to engage it in mortal combat during its youthful vigour. Cairns, the once and future Lord Chancellor and the new Conservative leader in the Lords, had nothing like Derby's confidence and was more concerned to balance on his recently acquired bicycle than to ride it towards a constitutional revolution.

Nor were many of the bishops enthusiastic for a quarrel *à outrance* with, on any showing, the first committed churchman to be Prime Minister since Peel and by some criteria the only dedicated Anglican ever to occupy 10 Downing Street. Nor did they wish to risk their position in the House of Lords in a defence of their somewhat shadowy brethren from Offaly or Meath. Their interest was to avoid the weakness of the Irish Church damaging the establishment in England, and it was by no means clear whether discretion or valour best served that end. The ambiguity of the two Primates had already shown itself in their abstention on second reading.

The underlying forces working for a settlement were therefore strong, and when Gladstone on 12 July persuaded the Queen, without supporting the bill or urging a particular settlement, to impress on Archbishop Tait the dangers of a major clash with the government, the cards were stacked for a victory. Gladstone's final contribution was to fall ill on 22 July. No one else could have marshalled the forces for the bill as well as he had done, but Granville, without passion or indignation, was the man to make the final small concessions and negotiate the settlement with Tait and Cairns. Gladstone then presented the argument to the Commons in a speech which, according to Phillimore, was 'universally praised'. It was one of his accomplishments, springing out of his taste for constructive solutions, that he could use his oratory to defend a compromise as well as to denounce an iniquity. On this occasion, however, it required a fierce effort to perform at all. He was somewhat unhinged by the strains of his illness and the crisis with the House of Lords. On the day of the settlement he wrote: 'The favourable issue left me almost unmanned, in the reaction from a sharp and stern tension of mind.'[17] And on the next day: 'Dr Clark came in the morning & made me up for the House [it sounds almost like a scene from Waugh's *The Loved One*] whither I went 2–5 p.m. to propose concurrence in the Lords Amendments. Up to the moment I felt very weak but this all vanished when I spoke, and while the debate lasted. Then I went back to bed.'[18]

The result gave him one of the greatest satisfactions of his political life. The element of compromise was small. Gladstone had got his first major bill through almost unscathed. He had frightened the House of Lords more than they had frightened him. Despite the hesitant recovery of his health, he was exultant as the session came to an end. He made his last appearance of the year in the House of Commons on 5 August, applied himself to working a small ecclesiastical measure, the Bishops' Resignation Bill, through its committee stage (a task which not even Asquith or Baldwin, let alone a later Prime Minister, would have thought of undertaking), and went that evening to see *Cox and Box*, the new Sullivan and Burnand operetta (Gilbert was not yet on the scene). The following day he had his final Cabinet until late October, with no very momentous agenda items, except for a preliminary discussion of the next session's programme. After that he was on a semi-convalescent holiday, keeping to his bed a certain amount, reading *Pride and Prejudice* and then George Eliot's *Romola*, applying himself to the bestowal of honours, which fascinated him almost as much as did the making of bishops, and on 10 August removing himself for nearly a month to Walmer Castle.

Walmer went with the wardenship of the Cinque Ports, in which office Granville had succeeded Palmerston in 1865, but Gladstone went there more as to a rented holiday house (without, however, any rent) than as a guest. 'We prowled about,'[19] he noted when he arrived, and Granville came only for one night during the whole stay. Gladstone had some walks along the coast, over and under the white cliffs, and some drives around south-east Kent, but he did not bathe, probably because of the intermittent persistence of his complaint. In the last week of August he was back in bed, although saying that this relapse was 'caused I fear by a high wing of grouse yesterday'.[20] He did, however, manage several games of what he described as 'cricket round the hat with my four sons'.[21] He had some family visitors, including his brother Robertson. Bishop Wilberforce came for three days, and Archbishop Tait drove the fourteen miles from Canterbury for dinner and 'much conversation'. Tait wrote a curious account of the visit, which suggests that the grouse had done more harm than the cricket had done good. 'Reached Walmer Castle about 6.30,' he recorded. 'Found Gladstone lying in blankets on the ramparts eating his dinner, looking still very ill. . . . He joined us at night full of intelligence. His fierce vigour all the better for being a little tempered. . . .'[22]

From Walmer Gladstone made his way via London (two nights), Raby Castle in Durham as the guest of the Duke of Cleveland (four nights), and the London and North Eastern and Caledonian Railways (one night) to Balmoral. There he stayed for two weeks as minister in attendance. Full vigour seemed to have returned, although on 7 September at Raby he was complaining that 'there is a weakness of the organs not yet overcome'. By Saturday the 11th, however, having arrived at Balmoral at 6.00 that morning, he had a visit from his clergyman son Stephen accompanied by the two younger boys and walked fourteen and a half miles with them in the afternoon and then another four miles home on his own. 'Met the Queen out: and dined with her,' he laconically recorded.

On the next day he had reluctantly to accept 'Crathie (Presbyterian) Ch. with H. M. at 12.' He had had his fingers burnt by a royal complaint during one of his Chancellor's visits in the early 1860s that he had taken a Household carriage twenty-eight miles to escape from the austerities of Presbyterianism into the lusher ritual of Episcopalianism. He was still attempting to fight back in 1869 but was defeated by Scottish weather: 'A plan for meeting S. and the boys to have service in the wood half way to Braemar was stopped by ceaseless rain.'[23] When he left Balmoral on 25 September, he did so even more heroically, abandoning all mechanical or horse-drawn transport at Banchory to walk fifteen miles over the Cairnmount, which brought him into Fasque for a brief fraternal weekend by, as it were, the back door. (What, it is tempting to ask, happened to his luggage, and indeed the considerable quantity of working papers – he complained that on the previous day he had had to dispose of sixty-two letters – by which he must have been accompanied? He had no private secretary with him, but there was presumably a servant who conducted his bags by train or carriage.)

While at Balmoral Gladstone settled no less than four episcopal appointments* as well as a list of forty-seven to whom lay honours were to be accorded. 'I take it there are few among them whom it would not be creditable to appoint,' he cautiously wrote to Clarendon. The composition of this list had been broadly settled at a 'conclave' of ministers just before the holidays. Gladstone had approached the task in an ecumenical mood, and had proposed a Jew,† two Roman Catholics (the one a Liberal MP and Norfolk younger son who became Howard of Glossop, and the other Acton, already mentioned), as well as seeking a Nonconformist peerage, about the candidates for which he consulted John Bright. He also offered a Garter to the current Duke of Norfolk. But Norfolk was a less good Liberal than his MP younger brother and

* Wilberforce to Winchester; Mackerness (a staunch Liberal) to Oxford in his place; Lord Arthur Hervey (a younger son of the first Marquess of Bristol – the Herveys were then a more devout family than subsequently) to Bath and Wells; and Temple to Exeter (an appointment which proved very controversial because of a combination of the high apostolic and anti-Erastian tradition of the diocese and of Temple's having contributed to the 1860 *Essays and Reviews*, which some regarded as semi-heretical).

† This recommendation, which was for Sir Lionel de Rothschild, who had eventually won his battle over the parliamentary oath which had kept him, although a several times elected member, out of the House of Common, was however blocked by the Queen; and her objection, despite a long and powerfully argued letter from Gladstone, was persisted in. In the course of resisting the arguments of the government (Granville was also involved, although in a more light-footed way than Gladstone) she permitted herself several animadversions. 'But she *cannot* consent to a Jew being made a Peer – tho' she will not object to a *Jew* baronet – and she is quite certain that it wld do the Govt. harm rather than good,' she wrote on 24 August. And on 1 November, for the argument was long drawn out: 'she cannot think one who owes his great wealth to contracts with Foreign Govts for Loans, or to successful speculations on the Stock Exchange can fairly claim a British Peerage. However high Sr L. Rothschild may stand personally in Public Estimation, this seems to her not the less a species of gambling, because it is on a gigantic scale – & far removed from that legitimate trading wh she *delights* to *honour*. . . .' (Guedalla, *The Queen and Mr Gladstone*, pp. 249 and 254.) Lionel de Rothschild died without his peerage. His son Nathan Meyer Rothschild became the first Lord Rothschild (and the first Jewish peer) in 1885, again on the recommendation of Gladstone.

turned it down on the ground that it might commit him to support the government. The Duke of Leinster also refused one of the Garters which had been made available by the deaths of Derby and Westminster, and they eventually went to de Grey, who was a serving member of the government, and to Stratford de Redcliffe, the most eminent living ex-ambassador, whose diplomatic skill was such that he had almost single-handedly caused the Crimean War. Stratford was not, however, a landed grandee of the sort that Gladstone had originally wished to honour. This experience, buttressed by the lord lieutenancy of Staffordshire having to be offered three times before it was accepted, pointed to some separation of the territorial aristocracy from Liberalism well before 1886.

Despite these occasional setbacks, Gladstone enjoyed patronage. He liked sending little notes such as that to the Speaker (Denison) on 12 August: 'I wrote a few days ago to your Chaplain to offer him the Chair of Modern History at Cambridge.'[24] He was alleged to have said, echoing Melbourne, that he thought bishops died only to vex him with the problems of appointing their successors. And he did in fact write in the autumn: 'In consequence of the death of the Bp of Carlisle, a perturbed Sunday.'[25] In reality, however, he loved shuffling the ecclesiastical pack, and although he did so with care and concern for fairness in liturgical balance, he was by no means immune from expecting some political return for religious preferment. He wrote to each of the four bishops whose promotion he had secured during his 1869 Balmoral visit urging them to vote for the following session's Irish Land Bill. His conviction of the virtues of his own policies stilled any doubts which he might have had about twisting episcopal and other arms in order to put them through. Norfolk was probably wise to refuse a Garter if he wished to remain independent of the government.

Gladstone's respect for rank also made him enjoy adjusting the higher grades of the peerage. When he made de Grey Marquess of Ripon in 1870 it was a rare elevation without such special reason as service as a viceroy (which Ripon did later, but that was hardly relevant at the time), and when he made Westminster a duke in his resignation honours of 1874 it was positively the last creation of a non-royal dukedom. Gladstone himself was one of the only four post-1865 Prime Ministers who never accepted 'a ribband to stick in his coat' (the others were the odd trio of Bonar Law, Ramsay MacDonald and Neville Chamberlain), but he enjoyed sticking them in the coats of others.

After his return from Balmoral and Fasque at the end of September,

Gladstone divided that autumn of run-up to his sixtieth birthday between Hawarden and London. He spent October at Hawarden. Then he had three and a half weeks in London, with intervals of three nights at Windsor and two with Clarendon ('a delightful hospitality') near a still unsuburbanized Watford. The main purpose of this London period was the holding of no less than five Cabinets of preparation for the 1870 session, with the shape of an Irish Land Bill, a heavier cloud from the west than the Church Bill, providing the central issue of contention. Then he had another two and a half weeks at Hawarden before an Advent two weeks in London and another five Cabinets trying to get Whig magnates to reconcile their (mildly) reforming instincts with their passionate belief in the supremacy of property rights, above all in land.

During the first of the Hawarden chunks of time he was much occupied with the purchase of the adjacent Aston Hall estate, including two collieries (which however seemed to be more productive of embarrassing industrial disputes than of any flow of profits). He paid £57,000 (nearly £3 million at present values) for the acquisition, £12,000 of which was raised by a mortgage, and wrote the distinctly unradical comment: 'If I have an ambition, it is to make an Estate for my children.'[26] On the first day of his second Hawarden interlude he more mundanely recorded: 'Moved my clothes & c. into my new (old age) dressing room on the first floor. Worked a little on my books. Cut down a stump.'[27] He always liked advancing to meet the end of his mortal life, book arrangement was his best mental relaxation, and tree-cutting his best physical exercise.

Gladstone's major preoccupation during that autumn was, however, Mrs Thistlethwayte. Laura Thistlethwayte was a splendidly indeterminate figure sitting on the crossroads between respectability and the *demi-monde*, geisha-like malleability and opinionated pontificating. In social origins she was not unlike the 'Jersey Lily' who came along a generation later. Lillie Langtry was the daughter of a Channel Islands canon, Laura Bell (as Mrs Thistlethwayte was born) of a minor member of the Ulster gentry, Captain Bell of Bellbrook, County Antrim, which coincidence of names gave him perhaps more of an air of territorial substance than he deserved. Miss Bell had undoubtedly been an available London courtesan in her youth, but in 1852 she had succeeded in marrying a gentleman of wealth and connection even if not of much discernible interest or achievement. A. F. Thistlethwayte had a house in Grosvenor Square and, later, another in east Dorset. The marriage transformed her social position more than it filled her emotional needs. It also set her free to embrace some half-baked theosophical ideas, which would have been anathema to Gladstone had they not come from her.

He appears to have first met her riding in the park in 1864, the year of the death of the Duke of Newcastle, of whom she had become a considerable friend. Arthur Kinnaird, MP for Perth and last encountered as Gladstone's Italian travelling companion on his 1838 Catherine Glynne courtship tour, also played some intermediary role. Mrs Thistlethwayte's relationship with Gladstone did not however much ripen until after he had become Prime Minister. This might be interpreted as an indication of her worldly ambition, although Gladstone was a very good worldly catch at any time in the 1860s or even before; in addition Mrs Thistlethwayte always remained noticeably reticent about exploiting her relationship with him for gain or prestige.

What is much more probable is that it required the death of the Duchess of Sutherland (in October 1868) to create a vacancy in one half of the slot which Mrs Thistlethwayte came to fill. This does not mean that Gladstone saw Laura Thistlethwayte as remotely the equal of Harriet Sutherland. He greatly admired the Duchess's intellect and judgement and there was only a latent sexual element in their relationship. There is no evidence that he admired Mrs Thistlethwayte's intellect and judgement. It would indeed have been a grave matter had he done so. He once attended one of her religious lectures at the London Polytechnic and wrote of the experience: 'I would not much want to repeat it.' When she was bombarding him with twenty-three separate packages of her fortunately unpublished autobiography in September–October 1869 he recorded: 'A fresh supply of Mrs T's MS: XI–XIII. The tale is told with great modesty, & its aspect is truthful though not quite coherent.'[28]

With Laura Thistlethwayte there was for him a strong element of physical infatuation. Yet she was not the equivalent of one of his 'rescue' cases, even though he often wrote the culpatory × symbol (but not the ʎ one, which he had last inscribed in 1859) after an encounter with her. She had more than rescued herself. It would not have been much good telling her that she ought to give up Grosvenor Square and the Dorset manor in order to improve herself at the Clewer House of Mercy, which he had helped to establish at Windsor. Yet Gladstone's near obsession with her in the autumn of 1869 required the absence of any other woman outside his family whose interest he wished particularly to arouse and in whom he wished to confide. Hence the importance to the Thistlethwayte relationship of the death of the Duchess of Sutherland.

It also required an effective cessation of his general 'rescue' activities, which indeed was markedly so in that autumn of 1869.

Yet in the phrase 'near obsession' at least equal weight needs to be put upon the qualifying adjective as upon the noun. When he returned to Hawarden from Balmoral he began to write to her intensively, and did so eleven times that October. In the course of the correspondence she appears deliberately to have heightened the emotional atmosphere, provoking a semi-quarrel, the resolution of which produced a tighter sense of mutual commitment. 'The letter of yesterday from Mrs Th. caused me to ruminate in a maze,' he wrote on 19 October. And on the 20th: 'A letter from Mrs T. much wounded [and] disturbed me. I have a horror of giving inner pain to a woman.'[29] The last phrase sounded distinctly impersonal, but this was misleading for from this time he (unfortunately) began his letters to her 'Dear Spirit', although ending them no more committingly than 'Ever yours, W. E. G.' He also took to wearing an engraved ring which she had given him.

When he returned to London she was away and the letters continued to pour from him – six in the next ten days. Then she returned, and Gladstone took to calling on her in Grosvenor Square. He was there eight times in the next ten days, in addition to an occasion when he dined with 'the Thistlethwaytes', and one call which she made at Carlton House Terrace. The Grosvenor Square calls were sometimes in the early evening, sometimes after dinner and mostly lasted for one and a half to two hours. They were snatched with great determination. 'Cabinet 2–4. Saw Mrs Th. 5¼–7¼' (10 November),[30] and 'Mrs Thistlethwayte on the way to G. W. R. Off to Windsor at 5. We dined with H. M. and a party of 13' (16 November).[31] Gladstone seemed relatively immune from guilt after these encounters, although he had recorded on 28 October: 'Wrote to Mrs Thistlethwayte: in great gravity of spirit. Duty and evil temptation are there before me, on the right and left. But I firmly believe in her words "holy" and "pure", & in her cleaving to God.'[32]

When he went back to Hawarden for his late-November visit a similar pattern of letter-writing was resumed, as was a pattern of visiting when he returned to London for a cluster of Cabinets on 6 December. Attention was increasingly concentrated on the Saturday to Monday visit which Gladstone had arranged to pay to the Thistlethwaytes' Dorset house on 11–13 December. It was an engagement which he had not only arranged but was resolved to fulfil. It coincided with the most crucial period in the difficult Cabinet discussions on the Irish Land Bill.

There had been a Cabinet on the Thursday afternoon, a 'conclave' (on the subject) on the Friday morning and the determining Cabinet was due on the day after his return from the Thistlethwayte weekend. But nothing was going to divert him from Boveridge (the Dorset house). 'On Monday till evening I shall be out of town,' he firmly informed the colleagues with whom he was locked in discussion. And so for the Saturday morning he was able to record: 'Off at 10.30 with A. K[innaird MP, who appeared to be constantly on hand in the relationship, performing either a procuring or chaperoning role] to join Mrs Th. and her party at Waterloo. We reached Boveridge in heavy rain between 2 & 3. Saw the fine *stud*. And walked a little about the place. Saw Mrs Th. several times.'

The Sunday, however, appeared to be the more highly charged day. It began naturally enough with a service at the local church, which was Cranborne, but continued strangely, there being no service in the afternoon, with Mr Thistlethwayte 'reading a Sermon of over an hour'. There was also a walk with Mrs Thistlethwayte, in addition to which she 'came to my rooms aft. and at night'. Then the lushness of Tennysonian romanticism took over, which was always a bad sign with Gladstone: 'Miss Fawcett [a maid or a guest, and whose hair?] let down her hair: it is a robe. So Godiva "the rippled ringlets to the knee".'[33]

On the Monday he drove to and from a meet of foxhounds with his hostess, before she saw him and Arthur Kinnaird off at Fordingbridge station. He was back at Waterloo at 7.15 p.m., in time for dinner with his Chief Whip, which comprised '3 hours with Fortescue [Irish Secretary] and Sullivan [Irish Attorney-General] on Irish land'. The next day he satisfactorily surmounted a three-and-a-half-hour Cabinet (three hours of it on Irish land) and got the main provisions of the bill agreed. He had emulated Drake in completing his game of bowls before engaging with the Spaniards.

Moreover his Boveridge expedition had on the whole been emotionally calming rather than disruptive. He had obviously got himself far into what he had described a little earlier as 'deep matters' and he wrote on his return of 'how far [he] was at first from understanding her history or even her character'. However, that Dorset weekend, with whatever intimacies which did or did not take place, appeared in retrospect to have been the high-water mark rather than an instigation to further emotional plunges in their relationship. Letters continued to flow. Gladstone wrote to her nine times during the Christmas and New Year month that he spent away from London. But there was no mounting frenzy. Following a pattern familiar from some of his 'rescue' cases, and one which obviously exposed him to a charge of hypocrisy, Gladstone had decided that it was his duty to urge the restoration of full relations with her husband, but this did not prevent the continuation, although on a gradually diminishing scale, of correspondence and meetings. There could, however, be bursts of resurgence, as in the early summer of 1871, when he lunched with her (without a party) in Grosvenor Square on seven occasions within six weeks. She lived until 1894, latterly in somewhat straitened circumstances and sharing a Hampstead 'cottage' with a sister of General Ponsonby, Grey's successor as the Queen's secretary. Gladstone, mostly then accompanied by his wife, used occasionally to take a long afternoon's drive from Downing Street during his last government, with a call upon her providing the destination. He did not however attend her funeral, and there was a sense that he felt some relief at her departure.

Three questions remain. First, how much did she divert Gladstone's attention and energies from affairs of state during this crucial early period of his first premiership? Professor Matthew, whose judgement on any matter relating to Gladstone must always be given first consideration, puts his preoccupation with her lower than that of Asquith with Venetia Stanley. Gladstone never got near to Asquith's occasional outpourings of four letters a day. Nor did he write them during Cabinet meetings. On the other hand the tone of Asquith's Stanley epistles was consistently lighter than anything which emanated from Gladstone. Asquith provided social and political gossip, laced with amusing and somewhat cynical comment upon his colleagues. Gladstone by contrast was often peering into the dark places of the soul. What was also true, however, was that in both cases they were bicycling towards the edge of the cliff without much risk or intention of going over it, or, apart from a brief wobble on Asquith's part in May 1915, of allowing their capacity for the transaction of public business to be affected by their infatuations.

The second question is to what extent was Gladstone's reputation, and therefore his authority, damaged by inner-circle knowledge of his temptations. A comment which the newly succeeded fifteenth Earl of Derby, then a Tory but later to serve as Colonial Secretary under Gladstone in the 1880 government, wrote in his diary for 11 December 1869 is a good indication of the mixture of knowledge, amusement and mildly mocking tolerance which characterized the attitude of the political class:

> Strange story of Gladstone frequenting the company of a Mrs Thistlethwaite [*sic*], a kept woman in her youth, who induced a foolish person with a large fortune to marry her. She has since her marriage taken to religion, and preaches or lectures. This, with her beauty, is her attraction to G and it is characteristic of him to be indifferent to scandal. But I can scarcely believe the report that he is going to pass a week with her and her husband at their country house – she not being visited or received in society.[34]

The third question is that of how far this extravagance with Mrs Thistlethwayte damaged Gladstone's relations with his wife. The answer to this must be 'somewhat'. Catherine Gladstone can hardly fail to have been at least half aware of some of his peregrinations. She had, for instance, arrived in Carlton House Terrace from Hawarden shortly before his return from Boveridge on 13 December. However, she was used to him, and there was no evidence of any approach to crisis in their relations. The year ended with the Gladstones apparently in good shape mentally, although less so physically. Mrs Gladstone was laid up with the family complaint of erysipelas from Christmas Day onwards, and Gladstone took to his bed, this time with some sort of bronchial infection, for a few days over the period of his sixtieth birthday on 29 December. But he greeted that milestone, which was certainly then regarded as the entry to old age, with aplomb.

> My sixtieth birthday. Three score years! And two score of them at least have been full years. My retrospect brings one conclusion. 'Mercy Good Lord is all I seek' for the past; for the future grace to be Thine instrument if scarcely Thy child.
>
> My review this year includes as a prominent object L. T. the extraordinary history, the conflicting appeal, the singular avowal.[35]

Two days later, on New Year's Eve, he wrote:

> At midnight listened to the bells which closed this for me notable year. Its private experience, in the case mentioned on Wed., has been scarcely less singular than its public. May both be ruled for good. Certainly my first 12 months as Minister have passed with circumstances of favour far beyond what I had dared to anticipate. Thanks to God.[36]

19

Irish Land and European War

Eighteen-seventy was a less rewarding session than that of 1869. Irish land proved more intractable than the Irish Church. The French and the Prussians fought each other, and the British government became preoccupied with maintaining its neutrality. The legislative haul was again considerable, but several of the measures did not arouse the enthusiasm of the Prime Minister. Nevertheless, the year as a whole was one in which he and the government maintained their zest.

The Irish Church Bill settled the issue to which it was directed, and its passage united the Cabinet and the Liberal party. The Irish Land Bill signally failed to settle the Irish agrarian issue. Such a settlement was indeed almost impossible within a United Kingdom in which any attempt to deal with the largely different problems of Irish rural society was vitiated by the fear of the English (and Scottish) governing class that making life tolerable for the Irish tenantry would feed back across St George's Channel and undermine the much less oppressive landlord system in Great Britain.* Furthermore, the Land Bill of 1870, so far from solidifying the majority, came near to breaking up the Cabinet and was always at risk from Liberal defections. It did however pave the way to the more effective Irish land legislation of Gladstone's second government.

The paradoxes surrounding Gladstone in his first years as Prime Minister were manifold. The force of his personality, both public and private, and the authority of his parliamentary command were essential to the holding together of the government and the carrying through of the many and disparate measures of reform which it initiated. His position as first minister was therefore unassailable, partly for this reason and partly because, exceptionally, there was no one who wished to assail it. Although it was a strong government (Morley thought, possibly with

* The essential difference was that in Britain it was in general the landowner who made capital improvements, whereas in Ireland, with its multiplicity of holdings, it was mostly the tenants who had effected such drainage, fencing, making of farm-roads and construction of farm buildings as had taken place.

a touch of exaggeration, that it was the strongest Cabinet that was ever assembled), it contained no future Prime Ministers. This was unusual. To take three quick historical cuts, Peel's main government contained Derby, Aberdeen and Gladstone himself. Gladstone's last government, in contrast with his first, contained Rosebery, Campbell-Bannerman and Asquith. And Asquith's government contained Lloyd George and Churchill. Perhaps more important from the point of view of Gladstone's impregnability, it contained no one who urgently *wanted* to be Prime Minister.

This was as well, for Gladstone, although personally pre-eminent, held views which in a spread of ways were at variance with those of both his colleagues and his followers. Whereas in the last years of Palmerston he had appeared, although a recent convert to Liberalism, to be embracing advanced Radical positions, some aspects of his old Conservatism perversely reasserted themselves when he was himself in the supreme position and had no Prime Minister above him to needle. He was cool on the Elementary Education Bill of 1870, on the University Tests Bill of 1871 (which removed the Anglican monopoly from the governing of the two universities; that on their admissions policy had already gone) and on the Ballot Bill, which finally became law in 1872.

Even on the issues where Gladstone was at one with his party he was mostly so for subtly different reasons. On Ireland, which he made his central purpose, he was unusual both in being willing to admit that Fenian outrages were what concentrated the otherwise complacent English mind upon the problem, and in regarding its damage to Britain's reputation in Europe as a determining factor. And on continental problems, epitomized by the Franco-Prussian War, his attitude was neither that of the old Whigs, who believed in a mixture of Palmerston's bluster and Russell's pragmatic diplomacy, nor that of the Cobden–Bright tradition of keeping out of foreign quarrels at almost any cost. Gladstone believed in the Concert of Europe, the settling of disputes by the consensual authority of the great powers, and was as willing to bear burdens and risks on its behalf as he was unwilling to pursue chauvinist aims.

His Cabinet may or may not have been the strongest which was ever assembled but it was not one which was easily led. His closest colleague ought in theory to have been Edward Cardwell, who was the only old Peelite Commons minister left. (There was also Argyll in the Lords.) But Cardwell, an able, self-confident, opinionated departmental minister, as strong on intellectual certainty as he was weak on oratory and easy-going charm, was more consistently in disagreement with the Prime Minister in Cabinet than was almost anyone else. At the War Office Cardwell carried through major army reforms, but also inevitably found himself at odds with the Prime Minister's instinctive military parsimony. It was not only departmentally, however, that he and Gladstone were on opposite sides. They were so on Irish land, on English school education, on the final abolition of university tests and on the ballot.

Lowe, who had been generously made Chancellor of the Exchequer in spite of his wrecking Gladstone's leadership of the Commons in 1866, was expected to be awkward, and was. He did, however, have the advantage of being determinedly in favour of ending patronage in the civil service, and from his Treasury vantage point was able to bring to completion for all departments except the Foreign Office the reforms which Gladstone had initiated in 1853–5. Eventually and accidentally he was to do Gladstone a second grave disservice. In 1873, when the government was staggering and the Prime Minister was already exhausted to a point which impaired his judgement, Lowe was thought to have disqualified himself from continuing to hold the Exchequer by some irregularity in telegraph accounting for which the Postmaster-General and the First Commissioner of Works were more to blame. Gladstone dispensed with the two lesser ministers and transferred Lowe to the Home Office. Then, reverting to old fascinations, he could not resist adding the Exchequer to his own already excessive burdens. The outcome was not good for the final phase of the government.

In addition to these two difficult colleagues, Gladstone, particularly on Irish land, was always vulnerable to the nervousness of the Whig magnates about any threat to landlords' rights. Granville wrote to him on 25 September 1869, at the beginning of the preparation for the Land Bill, of 'those who will take a purely landlord view' and naming in this category 'Lowe, Argyll, Clarendon, Cardwell, and very moderately so Hartington'.[1] Granville himself was central to the Whig cousinage, but he had the advantage from this point of view of not being a magnate. For a nineteenth-century earl he had very little property. Indeed when he died in 1891 his estate was found to be bankrupt.* Furthermore he gave every sign of having reached a conscious and sensible decision to exploit his greatest political asset, which was a unique ability to ease his and others' relations with Gladstone. He could lead the Prime Minister

* See p. 594, below.

on a light rein, always accepting his basic positions but getting him to see men and events in a calmer perspective than he might otherwise have done. This role owed more to Granville's personality than to his office, but it was nonetheless somewhat enhanced when Clarendon died in June 1870 and Granville moved from the Colonial Office to the more central position of Foreign Secretary. He was a vital ball-bearing of the government, performing an important emollient role, particularly between Gladstone and the old Whigs but to some extent between the Prime Minister and all his colleagues.

John Bright ought to have performed the same function between Gladstone and the Nonconformist Radicals, although they unlike the Whigs were on the back benches and prominent in the provincial cities rather than in the Cabinet. But Bright was both unwell and opinionated, so that he was often absent and when he was there generally had some pet scheme of his own, which he was more interested in pushing than in giving support to Gladstone's contiguous but not identical positions. Gladstone was more pre-eminent than predominant in his first Cabinet, and on no issue were the hazards for him sharper than on the Irish Land Bill, which was intended to be for the 1870 session the great follow-up to the Irish Church Bill of 1869. But the issue was more tangled and, in addition, Gladstone for the 1870 session ignored Graham's 1853 maxim about the avoidance of 'overlapping business', that is the danger of trying to run two major bills through Parliament at the same time. The second reading of the Elementary Education Bill came only a week after that of the Irish Land Bill.

As has been touched on in the context of Mrs Thistlethwayte, Gladstone pursued a policy of intensive consultation in preparation for the session of 1870 and the Irish Land Bill in particular. There were ten Cabinets between 26 October and Christmas and another eight between 21 January and the Queen's Speech (once again delivered by Commission and not in person) on 8 February. They were not exclusively concerned with the Land Bill, but most of the time of most of them was so directed. The issue was how far between the minimum and the maximum approach should the government go. The minimum approach was that the Irish tenant should, if evicted, be entitled to compensation for his own improvements to the property. This was not seriously contested. The maximum approach was what came to be called the 'Three Fs' – fixity of tenure, fair rent and freedom of sale (of the accrued rights of the tenant). This maximum, which was to be enacted eleven years later in the second Gladstone government, and which like all delayed concessions would have been much better done earlier, was regarded as beyond the bounds of practicality in 1870. As Gladstone wrote on 12 March 1870 to Manning, who had passed on the critical although constructive reactions of the Irish Catholic bishops to the bill: '. . . I am bound in frankness to say that the paper enclosed in your former letter proposes changes in the Bill, which neither the nation, nor the Parliament, nor the Cabinet, could adopt. We might as well propose the repeal of the Union. . . . Not one man has ventured to argue in the House of Commons for these changes.'[2]

What Gladstone endeavoured to do was to build on the minimum to the greatest extent that was compatible with holding his Cabinet together. He avoided its disruption only by a narrow margin, and J. L. Hammond was probably correct in writing that 'although he gained the consent of his colleagues, he did not gain their conviction'.[3] When on 25 January he finally got the bill through the Cabinet his diary entry ran: 'The *great* difficulties of I.L. Bill *there* are now over, Thank God.'[4]

Gladstone's original instrument for building on the minimum was to take an ancient convention known as Ulster Tenant Right, to extend it to the other three provinces of Ireland and to turn it from a convention into a law. This right enabled the tenant to bestow or sell the title to occupancy. This concept of creating a form of property in the right of occupancy made it essential that the tenant should be protected from eviction, or at least compensated for it if it took place. There could be no property in a 'right' which could be terminated at the whim of the landlord. What the Irish tenants wanted was statutory protection from eviction, but the most that Gladstone could persuade his weak but stubborn Chief Secretary for Ireland, let alone the rest of the Cabinet, to give them was the right to compensation when it had taken place. To make even this right effective there had to be some public intervention in the rent-fixing process. If a tenant simply did not pay a manifestly fair rent his landlord could hardly be made to pay compensation for evicting him without making a mockery of the whole concept of land ownership. And that was about as likely to be accepted by a Whig Cabinet as was Church disestablishment by a Tory one. On the other hand if the landlord could fix any rent he liked and then freely get rid of those who did not pay it that would make compensation for disturbance meaningless.

So some provision for resort to the courts on what was and what was not a fair rent was inevitable. Gladstone was inclined to make it as elaborate as possible because he liked complicated schemes. The Cabinet accepted any regulation with reluctance. The Tories, who did not divide against the second reading of the bill, fought hard against the relevant clause. The Lords amended it by substituting an 'exorbitant rent' for an 'excessive rent' as the trigger which set off the process. Gladstone, under pressure from Granville as the leader of the Lords, accepted with reluctance the apparently minor change. Although the only dictionary difference between the two words is that 'excessive' means to exceed the proper amount and that 'exorbitant' means to do so grossly, the difference nonetheless enabled the courts to interpret the protection narrowly enough to render it almost a dead letter.

For the rest the bill contained an obeisance to a scheme of tenant land purchase with some Treasury assistance, which was Bright's favoured solution but which was a very pale forerunner of the effective Conservative measures for peasant proprietorship which were taken around the turn of the century thirty years later. Altogether the Land Bill of 1870 assaulted some shibboleths and pointed a way for the future much more effectively than it changed the reality of agrarian life in Ireland. Unlike the Church Bill it did not settle the issue to which it was directed. It raised questions rather than disposed of them. To the end of his first government, however, but not much longer, Gladstone persisted in the over-sanguine belief that he had dealt with Irish land as effectively as he had with the Irish Church. He thought that if he could add the third achievement of a bill dealing with Irish university education (as he tried to do in 1873) he would have achieved a triple crown and gone far towards fulfilling his proclaimed mission 'to pacify Ireland'. And beyond that, as he genuinely believed, lay the hope of an honourable retirement from politics as soon as his government (he thought of it not as his first but as his only one) was over. He could then devote 'an interval between parliament and the grave',[5] not exactly to repose but to God and Homer and his other religious and intellectual interests. As he wrote to the Queen in March 1873 (using the habitual third person), 'he has the strongest opinion against spending his old age under the strain of that perpetual contention which is inseparable from his present position'.[6]

Hammond believed there were two central reasons why Gladstone did not get Irish land as right as he got the Irish Church. The first was that he had not adequately prepared influential opinion or provided himself and others with a background of more or less incontrovertible facts. In an age of 'blue books', which had proved particularly effective on factory reform and public health, he ought to have fortified himself and indoctrinated others by setting up a quickly reporting Royal Commission or other enquiring body as soon as the government came into power. This enquiry could have investigated and deliberated during 1869 and greatly strengthened the Prime Minister's hand in 1870.

Second, Hammond thought that while Gladstone had immersed himself in Irish history, he was not well informed about the realities of mid-Victorian life in 'John Bull's other island'. He had never been there, and he was curiously inhibited about talking to those who knew well the situation on the ground. Unionist sentiment, which at that time was not challenged in the Liberal party, was dedicated to maintaining the United Kingdom of Great Britain and Ireland, even though at that stage its sixty-nine-year-old history was both brief and dismal and its future fifty-two years were to contain little but searing trouble. The union was sacrosanct to establishment opinion in Britain, but the instinctive reaction of such opinion was to treat talking to and being influenced by the indigenous Irish as almost the equivalent of 'nigger loving'.

Gladstone was on the threshold of devoting the last third of his life to Ireland, yet he was not immune from this approach. The fifth Earl of Bessborough tried hard to persuade Gladstone to consult Sir John Gray about the Bill. Gray was the proprietor and editor of the *Freeman's Journal*, which was pre-eminently the paper of Irish tenant farmers. He was also MP for Kilkenny and had been knighted by the Palmerston government. Furthermore, Gladstone had been warned by O'Hagan, his Irish Lord Chancellor, that 'the success of the Land Bill depends on the *Freeman's Journal*; if it says, We accept this as a fixity of tenure, every priest will say the same, and *vice versa*.'[7] Yet Gladstone would not see Gray. Instinctively he approached the problem of Irish government almost in a Colonial or Indian spirit. He became prepared to sacrifice the unity and future of the Liberal party to trying to right the wrongs of Ireland, but he made it, in Morley's phrase, 'almost a point of honour . . . for British cabinets to make Irish laws out of their own heads'.[8]

In the same way he used Manning as effectively his sole channel of communication with the Catholic Church in Ireland. This was odder in 1870 than it had been in 1869 with the Irish Disestablishment Bill. Manning knew something about both the Anglican and the Roman Churches in Ireland, but he knew next to nothing about Irish land tenure. And an ill-informed conduit is always a potentially misleading one. Further more any renewal of relations of trust and friendship with Manning, which had seemed possible the previous year, had been shattered by Gladstone's deep disapproval of the Archbishop's role in urging Pope

Pius IX forward to what for Gladstone were the excesses of ultramontanism and the pernicious, divisive and unhistorical doctrine of papal infallibility. Manning's activities in this direction were at their height in the spring and summer of 1870, and Gladstone's anti-Roman feeling became incandescent. It was a minor and lucky miracle that he waited five years to compose and publish his pamphlet entitled *The Vatican Decrees and their Bearing on Civil Allegiance: A Political Expostulation* rather than dashing it off immediately and publishing it, maybe under an easily pierced veil of anonymity, while he was still Prime Minister.

Such partial knowledge and imperfect channels meant that Gladstone's bill strained the loyalty of the Whigs without achieving much of a response in Ireland. This double-barrelled coolness was perhaps inevitable, but it was nonetheless marked. Gray himself voted against the second reading, the bishops said that it could not be regarded as a settlement of the question, and the Dublin Municipal Council passed a resolution of inadequacy. Nor was the passage through Parliament nearly as solidly assured as had been that of the Church Bill. Then the Tories could be depended upon to oppose, and the Liberal majority to support. With the Land Bill the Tory opposition was more sporadic and therefore more dangerous, because it helped to make unanimous Liberal support less reliable. Indeed the most damaging enemy of the bill in the Commons was Roundell Palmer, who had been Attorney-General in the Palmerston and Russell governments and Gladstone's adjutant in several past parliamentary struggles. However, Gladstone, with that mixture of simple generosity and willingness to stoop to conquer which were equally persistent parts of his character (and which he had previously shown to Lowe) made him Lord Chancellor when Hatherley resigned in 1872 and employed him in the same capacity (as well as advancing him to the earldom of Selborne) in 1880–5.

Despite these hazards the Land Bill got through the Commons by Whitsun. Gladstone celebrated by allowing himself to be taken by Granville to Epsom for the Derby. His reaction again illustrated his mixture of naivety and enthusiasm ('no one of such great simplicity had ever before been found in so exalted a station', Jowett, the Master who made the Balliol of good jobs for the well-qualified boys, said of him when he became Prime Minister). Gladstone's diary entry read:

> Went off at 11.45 to the Derby by the S.E. Railway, with Granville, who most kindly arranged everything, including two drives through beautiful country. I was immensely interested in the scene, and the race. Conver-

sation with P. of Wales – Admiral Rous [the public handicapper, a fine title] – and many more. The race gave me a tremor. We reached Walmer at 7¾....[9]

The measure then survived the Lords and a little shuttle between the two Houses, including the acceptance by the Commons of the unfortunate 'exorbitant' for 'excessive', to become law by the end of July. Gladstone had two associated disappointments. First he was forced to accompany the Land Bill with a Coercion Bill (the curiously brutal name commonly used in the late nineteenth century for Irish bills giving special powers to courts and police against politically motivated crime). He was very loath to do this, but a combination of Fenian activities on the ground and the pressure of his colleagues forced him into it. This combination also postponed for a year the implementation of his desire, as an assuaging measure, to release another batch of Fenian prisoners beyond the forty whom the government had freed (with beneficial results according to the Viceroy) in early 1869. When this second batch were eventually let out it was with the short sighted provision that they should be banished from both Britain and Ireland itself; so they went to the United States and acted as dedicated agents of terrorist recruitment and fund-raising.

The other disappointment was that his desire, embraced even more strongly by Hartington as Irish Chief Secretary, to improve the infrastructure of the Irish economy by nationalizing and extending its railway system, ran into the sand of Cabinet opposition and postponement. Gladstone did not push this as hard as he ought to have done, but he was nonetheless always somewhat predisposed towards railway nationalization for England, both when he was President of the Board of Trade in the 1840s and in the Palmerston government in the early 1860s, and for Ireland a decade later.

By the spring of 1870 Gladstone's attention was increasingly engrossed by English education, both lower and higher. The middle or secondary range was, unfortunately for national purposes, left to look after itself, that is confined to the public schools and to a few haphazardly placed ancient grammar schools. This persisted until Balfour grasped the nettle in 1902 and thereby, such can be the perversity of political rewards, helped to produce the Conservative electoral débâcle of 1906. In 1870, however, it was the need for an *elementary* education bill which was regarded as urgent, as was that for removing the remaining Oxford and Cambridge religious tests. Legislation on elementary education was eagerly sought within the government by de Grey (Ripon) and W. E. Forster. As Lord President and Vice-President of the Council, these two carried the ministerial responsibility for education, such as it then was. This eagerness was shared by many of the Liberal party's most prominent provincial supporters, as well as by several other Cabinet members (notably Bruce, the Home Secretary), but not by the Prime Minister.

Gladstone was never very interested in popular education. He was half willing to go along with a fashionable view that the crushing of France by Germany in 1870 owed a great deal to the Prussian system of state education. However, he was far from giving the highest priority to military victories and his mind was set much more on Eton than on the Technischen Hochschulen of Bismarck's Berlin. He was an unashamed elitist. To him education meant the rigours of traditional classical scholarship. Although it was of course manifestly impractical to provide this sort of instruction for more than a tiny minority, he did not easily embrace the utility of more humble forms of teaching. He could not, however, contest the inevitability of a major measure of reform.

The existing position, in which of 4.3 million children of school age (in England and Wales), only 1.3 million were in state-aided schools, 1.0 million in purely voluntary (and often very inefficient) schools, and 2.0 million outside any educational provision, was not defensible. Confronted with this reality Gladstone's own preference was for increasing the grant to the existing Anglican (and Roman Catholic) schools, and filling the gap with new state schools – Board Schools as, because they were administered by local education boards, they came to be called – which would provide only secular education on the rates, while allowing the priests or ministers of the various denominations to come in at their own expense and provide full doctrinal instruction for the children of their own adherents. This, he wrote to Bright, provided the only prospect of 'solid and stable ground'.

His approach to the education of the 'uneducated' classes was at least as much that of a churchman as of a reformer. He no longer believed that Anglicanism should be imposed upon everybody, but he was most unwilling to see the existing Church of England schools absorbed into a secular national system. To illustrate the matter with particularity, he would have been horrified if at Hawarden his brother-in-law Henry Glynne, or his son Stephen Gladstone when he succeeded Glynne as rector in 1872, had been inhibited from religious instruction, and instruction which embraced the Anglican 'formularies', in the Church school there. Simple education should be for piety as much as for knowledge, and piety (for Anglicans at any rate) involved some understanding of the dogma and structure of the apostolic Church. A religion based solely on Bible teaching intermingled with some vague ethical principles would always be for Gladstone a poor and sterile thing.

His only solid ground was not however ground which he was able to hold. Hardly anyone except himself was in favour of the position. It did not satisfy the Anglican lobby, which was less tolerant of 'lesser breeds without the law' than Gladstone had become; it did not satisfy the Dissenters, who wanted simple Bible teaching on the rates; and it did not satisfy the mostly Erastian members of the Cabinet who wanted a more politically attractive solution. This was provided nearly three months after the introduction of the bill into the House of Commons by the Cabinet's decision on 14 June to accept what became the famous Cowper-Temple amendment. Cowper-Temple was the Whig member for South Hampshire who had been intermittently a junior minister for the quarter-century from 1841 to 1866 but whom Gladstone had not included in 1868, although with another touch of magnanimity he was to make him a peer in 1880. Cowper-Temple's amendment provided for basic or Nonconformist religion, that is the Bible and a few hymns, on the rates. It went through the House of Commons on 16 June, for which day Gladstone's diary entry included the stoical entry: 'Explained the plans of the Govt in modification of the Bill to an eager and agitated House. . . . Exhausting Siroccolike heat.'[10]

Gladstone was half self-willed ideologue and half parliamentary old trouper who would expound with vehemence to the House of Commons a decision of his government even when he had accepted it with the utmost reluctance. His reluctance on this occasion was so great that it probably contributed to the exhaustion at least as much as did the humidity of the weather. Matthew describes the Cabinet decision as 'a major personal blow for Gladstone' and his acceptance of it as 'a concession which rankled more deeply' than any other obeisance he made to hold his government together.[11]

The concession made, the Education Bill ground on through the Commons until it completed its course amid the opening distractions of the Franco-Prussian War. It was not seriously contested by the Conservative opposition (although they modified it as soon as they came to power in 1874 in a way that Gladstone regarded as constitutionally improper),*

* He took the view, much at variance with more recent practice, that incoming governments should accept the legislation of their predecessor.

and as a result it was not seriously interfered with by the House of Lords. In several of the many divisions Tory votes were an essential contribution to the government majority. Thus on 30 June an amendment moved by Jacob Bright, John Bright's younger brother, which proclaimed the doctrine that religious teaching in state schools should not be in favour of, or opposed to, the tenets of any denomination, was defeated by 251 votes to 130. The 130 were all Liberals. The majority was effectively provided by over a hundred Conservatives. It was not a happy dependence or one which was good for the cohesion of the government party.

Matters were made worse by the insertion in the bill of a provision which became the much denounced and therefore famous Section 25 and enabled school boards to pay to denominational schools the fees of poor children. This led to an excited Nonconformist conference of opposition at Manchester in 1872, and to an agitation in which Joseph Chamberlain first came to national prominence. Chamberlain did not win his battle – the ground for which he chose to fight was in fact ludicrously narrow, for very few school boards contemplated doing any such thing – but he made life very uncomfortable for a High Anglican leader of the Liberal party, and also set a depressing pattern, which persisted until terminated by the Butler Act of 1944, of making British education policy more a battleground for denominational and social dispute than a basis for improving the instruction of children.

Gladstone did not therefore set the schools issue to rest by his reluctant swallowing of Cowper-Temple. And no sooner had he imbibed this disagreeable medicine than he was confronted with a second nauseous potion in the form of the University Tests Bill. More than fifteen years previously Gladstone had been converted to the admission of non-Anglicans to the University and to its bachelors' degrees. (There were of course two universities involved, but he found it very difficult not to believe that the intellectual life of the universe centred on Carfax, or that even the greater Trinity in the Fens could hold a candle to Christ Church.) But he was still loath to allow non-Anglicans any place in Oxford's controlling institutions, including the membership of Convocation which would follow from their being allowed to take masters' degrees. Admission to headships of houses, professorships and membership of the governing bodies of colleges through fellowships he recoiled from still more strongly. In 1865, when Goschen, then a backbench Liberal MP for the City of London, had brought this matter to the fore by an (unsuccessful) private member's bill, Gladstone had somewhat extremely written to a Nonconformist correspondent: 'I would rather see Oxford level with the ground, than its religion regulated in the manner which would please Bishop Colenso.'[12]* By 1870 the matter had advanced to the stage of Coleridge, later Chief Justice and at the time Gladstone's Solicitor-General, being allowed to make another attempt to end the tests, provided he brought forward the bill in his private capacity and not as a law officer of the Crown.

This halfway house closely matched Gladstone's own evolving attitude. He was coming to accept the inevitable but his reluctance persisted. '... I am almost tempted to say,' he wrote to Coleridge with a characteristically fine if convoluted shade of meaning, 'it would be impossible, after my long connection with Oxford, to go into a new controversy on the basis of what will be taken and alleged to be an absolute secularisation of the colleges.... I incline to think that this work is for others not for me.'[13] This bill got much further than Goschen's had done, but foundered between the two Houses in July. Gladstone, further evolving, then agreed to its being made a government measure for the following session. And then, with his curious capacity once he had decided to bite a bullet to bite it hard, himself introduced the measure on 10 February 1871. In April and May he resisted with considerable indignation attempts by Salisbury substantially to amend it in the Lords. Eventually, on a second consideration, the Lords voted Salisbury down by 129 to 89, and all academic appointments at Oxford and at Cambridge (which had already been a little more liberal), with the exception of those with a specific religious function such as the deanship of Christ Church and the theological professorships, became open to those of all beliefs or none.

The immediate effects should not be exaggerated. Roman Catholics by their own abstention remained for some decades almost entirely absent from Oxford, despite Newman's first fleeting return visit in 1878. Those of non-Christian faiths, except for a few home-grown eccentrics and (later) maharajahs, nawabs or their equivalent, were hardly envisaged, and even the Nonconformists remained peripheral to the University. They made their own Oxford encampments (Mansfield College, founded in 1886, and Manchester College, founded in 1889), as well as gradually becoming strong in colleges such as Queen's with a large

* Bishop Colenso of Natal (although of Cambridge provenance) then occupied a position in the Church roughly equivalent to that of Bishop Jenkins of Durham in his high days.

northern intake. Jews, epitomized by Herbert Samuel and L. B. Namier at Oxford and Edwin Montagu at Cambridge, were probably the greatest early beneficiaries. But until well into the twentieth century the majority of Heads of Houses were in Anglican orders, college chapels were regarded as obligatory until a new wave of post-1945 colleges dispensed with them, the University church of St Mary's continued to be both Anglican and geographically central to Oxford, if not as doctrinally so as in the days of Keble's Assize Sermon and Newman's incumbency, and Christ Church remained the only college in Christendom which contained the cathedral church of a diocese within its purlieus. Gladstone could claim without remotely straining his well-known capacity for sophistical argument that he had avoided 'an absolute secularisation of the colleges'.

Nevertheless the passages of the Elementary Education Act of 1870 and of the University Tests Act of 1871 were far from exhilarating experiences for him. They exemplified the burdens rather than the pleasures of office, and they also demonstrated the difficulties which flowed from the contradictions between his past and his present, his beliefs and his followers, his emotions and his intellect. There was, however, an important difference between the two issues: the University Tests boil, once lanced, subsided satisfactorily; the Elementary Education issue, once raised, reverberated on to weaken the government and to exacerbate Gladstone's relations with his party.

Compared with these lacerating if parochial issues (but at a time when the British parish was the most famous and observed one in the world), the problems of the Franco-Prussian War must have been almost a relief for Gladstone. It started on 19 July 1870 within a fortnight of the appointment of Granville as Foreign Secretary following the death of Clarendon, and therefore involved the Prime Minister more than might otherwise have been the case in those days of departmental devolution and the prerogatives of secretaries of state. It came, even more than 1914 and incomparably more than 1939, out of a clear blue sky. It was not only Edmund Hammond, permanent undersecretary of the Foreign Office, who totally misjudged the prospect in his initial report to Granville. Bismarck, five months before, was equally unprescient. 'The political horizon as seen from Berlin', he had informed the King of Roumania in the February of 1870, 'appears at present so unclouded that there is nothing of interest to report. . . .' Hammond, however, was merely a weather forecaster, whereas Bismarck was a rain king. If he found 'nothing of interest to report' he had the power to fill the gap and according to popular retrospective judgement he proceeded so to do.

At the time, however, British opinion started strongly pro-Prussian, and regarded the French Emperor as having behaved like one of his imperial bees and killed himself as a result of delivering an unprovoked sting. Queen Victoria, for instance, who admittedly had strong family reasons for partisanship, wrote to Gladstone on 19 July: 'It is not a question of *Prussia* agst France but of *United Germany* most *unjustifiably attacked*, fighting for hearth & Home – so *no one* can help feeling warmly for them.'* Again on 3 August she assured him that 'Germany as a real & natural ally would always be safe – never aggressive.' And on 2 October, with the French army crushed, Napoleon III a prisoner, his Empress a refugee in England and Paris invaded by Prussian troops, she was still animadverting: 'What a dreadful exhibition of falsehood and boastfulness the French continue to make! It shows a corruption wh is the cause of the Country's downfall – & one of the most disgraceful exhibitions is the way in wh all turn agst the Emperor and Empress & *all* about them!'[14] Meanwhile, from the other end of the political spectrum, the young Sir Charles Dilke, who was just about to mount his British republican campaign but before doing so was rushing around the battlefields as well as witnessing the proclamation of the Third Republic in Paris, was also full of vague feelings of nordic solidarity with the Germans.[15] It was one of the few issues on which he agreed with the Queen.

Gladstone took a more restrained position. 'On the face of the facts France is wrong,' he informed Brand, his former Chief Whip, 'but as to personal trustworthiness the two moving spirits on the respective sides, Napoleon and Bismarck, are nearly on a par.'[16] Gladstone, with this view, had three objectives in relation to the war. First, he wished to keep Britain out. In retrospect this does not sound too difficult. It is indeed not easy to see on which side Britain might have intervened. To have supported Prussia could have been a work of supererogation, and to have supported France would in the decisive days between July and September have been so unpopular as to be impossible. But at the time there was great concern that Britain would in some way or other be drawn in, accompanied by calls, mainly from those who were so

* These emotions did not however weigh with the Prince of Wales, who preferred the glitter of *la ville lumière* to German hearths and homes, and was regarded by his mother as dangerously pro-French.

predisposed, for a substantial increase in British military capacity. Gladstone was equally concerned to resist this.

The danger point was Belgium. Both on grounds of strategic interest and of sentiment an invasion of that somewhat ramshackle kingdom by either belligerent would have transfixed any British government. The matter was dramatized by *The Times* on 25 July (six days after the French declaration of war) publishing the text of a secret Franco-Prussian treaty of 1867 or 1869 (there was some dispute about the date) which included a provision that Prussia would not object to France swallowing Belgium and Luxembourg. The Prussians admitted to Granville that there had at any rate been such a draft, done they said in the hand of Benedetti, the somewhat over-active French ambassador to Berlin. The matter was complicated by the fact that the text as published by *The Times* was in less than the perfect French which it was difficult to believe that Benedetti, in spite of his Italian name and his German immersion, would have produced. This pointed to Prussian origin (Bismarck's Chancery while respecting the language of diplomacy was less immaculately francophone than the court of Frederick the Great a hundred years earlier).

With France at war with Prussia, however, it was difficult to see that the treaty, whether of draft or stronger status, of French or Prussian origin, had any continuing relevance. The more present danger was that the Prussian generals, as were their descendants forty-four and seventy years later, would be attracted by an axis of advance up the Meuse valley and past the forbidding fortresses of Namur and Dinant. This sufficiently worried Gladstone that he modified his anti-militarism and urgently encouraged the War Office to study means of sending 20,000 troops to Antwerp. Also, on 30 July, he persuaded the Cabinet to propose to France and Prussia a treaty by which, if either of them violated the neutrality of Belgium, Britain would co-operate with the other for its defence. This might have been regarded as a classic example of an initiative taken too late, but oddly it worked. Prussia accepted immediately. Moltke's war plans, unlike those of Schlieffen and Rundstedt in the two world wars, did not involve Belgium. And France hesitated only until the battle of Wörth had been lost, and then signed on 9 August. Gladstone thus achieved the second of his objectives.

The third was more elusive, partly because it was another issue on which he failed to carry his Cabinet. When the French had lost the war (and when public sympathy in England had substantially swung back to their side) Gladstone wanted to rally the neutral powers of Europe against the German annexation of Alsace and half of Lorraine on the ground that no such change should be made without the consent of the population. This differed from the basis on which the French government was objecting. It took its stand on the inviolability of established frontiers, particularly if they involved French soil. This was a hazardous position in view of the French annexation, little more than a decade before, of both Nice and Savoy. But it was also a position preferred by some members of the British Cabinet, while others dissented from Gladstone on the ground of traditional Whig realism. Protests were not going to make Bismarck give up the opportunity to annex two of the richest provinces of Europe. Why, therefore, invite failure by ineffective intervention? As a result Gladstone had an unusually humiliating Cabinet on Friday, 30 September: 'Cabinet 2¼–6. I failed in my two objects 1. an effort to speak with the other neutral powers against the transfer of A. & L. without reference to the populations. 2. (Immediate) release of the Fenian prisoners.'[17]

Gladstone was far from all-powerful as Prime Minister. He had, nonetheless, attained two of his three objects in relation to the war. He had also done a couple of very odd things, which between them illustrate some of the contradictions of his bewildering character. When war became virtually certain on 14–15 July, British government stocks including Consols fell heavily. At a long Cabinet on Saturday the 16th reports were received and dispositions made which caused Gladstone, as he informed the Queen by letter, to be more confident that France would respect the neutrality of Belgium and that Britain, partly in consequence, would be able to keep out of the conflict. These of course were both bull points for Consols, and on the Monday Gladstone calmly bought for his own account £2500 of them at the temporarily depressed price of 90. It was a shrewd speculation, and it is unlikely that it ever occurred to him, through his carapace of innocence and faith in his own motives, that he was doing anything remotely improper. He made no effort at concealment.

His second action was utterly different but equally surprising. That year, as in the previous one, he did not go to Hawarden when (on 10 August) he had disposed for the session of both Parliament and Cabinets, but went as in 1869 to 'Granville's hospitable abode at Walmer'. There he remained, with a short London interlude, until 6 September. On 23 August he began to read a recently published work of Emile de Laveleye, a Belgian savant who then enjoyed considerable international fame, entitled *La Prusse et l'Autriche depuis Sadowa*. On the 26th he wrote to

Reeve, the editor of the *Edinburgh Review*, to ask whether he would like a substantial anonymous review of this book for his October number. Reeve accepted on the 29th (who would not in the circumstances?), and on 1 September Gladstone began to write, although he did not finish reading Laveleye until the 6th, and continued through and beyond his Walmer holiday. He was still sending 'revises' to Reeve from Hawarden as late as 7 October.

The result was an 18,000-word article which used Laveleye's book only as a launching pad and was indeed rightly entitled *Germany, France and England*, rather than *Prussia and Austria*, with which latter country it had relatively little to do. It surveyed with great frankness, and equal orotundity the behaviour of France and Prussia before and during hostilities, and did so in a way which was sufficiently pro-Prussian and anti-French as to meet even the exacting standards in this respect of Queen Victoria. There was, however, one exception, and that was the rumoured (at that stage) Prussian intention to annex Alsace-Lorraine. That was castigated as 'harsh, almost brutal'. He concluded with a survey of England's position in the shaken-up world which followed from France's loss of 'ten great battles running' culminating in Sedan and the capture and overthrow of the Emperor. Here he attempted to ride two very different and difficult circus horses. The first was one of simple rejoicing at the good luck (not the moral superiority, he was quick to add) which flowed from his own country's geographical position. 'Happy England!', he actually wrote, and attributed this happiness, without eschewing even the most hackneyed of clichés, to 'that streak of silver sea'.

The second horse was his devotion to the Concert of Europe. By a supreme irony, in that summer when the ultramontanism of Piux IX drove Gladstone's anti-Roman Catholic feeling to its peak, he concluded by citing St Augustine's already quoted maxim '*Securus judicat orbis terrarum*'. Gladstone used it in the context that 'the general judgement of civilized mankind ... has censured the aggression of France; it will censure, if need arise, the greed of Germany'.

What was most striking about this article, however, was not its content, but the fact that he wrote it, and also his desire and belief that it might remain anonymous. The inversion of the habits of modern politicians is almost complete. Rare are the speeches without speech-writers, and rare too are the memoirs without ghost-writers, even when the putative author has the leisure of semi-retirement. And then it is hoped that the surrogates will so capture the style of the principal that their intervention may be concealed. Gladstone, on the contrary, had both the energy and the intellectual grasp to pour out the words from his own pen, but wished to suggest, for reasons of tact and diplomacy, that they were written by someone else. When he republished the essay, eight years later and then under his own name, he added the footnote: 'This article is the only one ever written by me, which was meant, for the time, to be in substance, as well as in form, anonymous. Motives of public duty, which appeared to be of sufficient weight, both led to its composition, and also prohibited me from divulging the authorship.'[18]

Once again, Gladstone's naivety had reared it head. There was probably not much chance in any event of the anonymity holding. The temptations for Reeve, the editor, to drop delicate hints that he had a most notable contributor must have been considerable. Apart from this, Gladstone chose to write his 'anonymous' article in his most recognizable style. Even read today, it is impossible not to imagine him declaiming it in the House of Commons. The slightly prolix courtesy, the elaborate constructions, the Latin (and one Greek) quotations occurring at just the appropriate intervals are all there. But above all it is instinctively predicated on the assumption that the statements were in a sense *ex cathedra*, interesting because of who was making them. The secret of the authorship lasted at most for forty-eight hours. It was a characteristic Gladstone enterprise: born of surplus energy, intellectually interesting without being of the highest quality, simple in apparently believing in a utopian secrecy, yet sufficiently shrewd that nothing which came out was beyond what he really wanted to say.

In spite of the war and its repercussions Gladstone's 1870 autumn was calmer than those of the two previous years. He avoided Balmoral, although superficially his relations with the Queen were in quieter waters than in either 1869 or 1871, in both of which years he spent a substantial period there. He also had fewer Cabinets in preparation for the session of 1871 than in the two previous years. Although he did not get to Hawarden until late in September he nonetheless spent a total of sixty-eight nights there between 1 October and 12 January. He should have returned to London invigorated, but in fact he came back to observe the beginning of the decline of his government. It was a slow process, for the government still had another three years to run. Coincidentally, for neither was the cause of the other, there also began a deep disenchantment in Gladstone's relations with the Queen, and *vice versa*. And that, once it took place, was irrevocable.

20

Sovereign and Prime Minister

A salient fact of late-nineteenth-century Britain was that the two figures who most symbolized the nation and the age, Queen Victoria and Gladstone, did not get on. This had by no means always been so. While Prince Albert was alive Gladstone had been a Court favourite. And in the early years of the Queen's widowhood, while she was withdrawn from all politicians, he was considerably preferred not only to 'those two dreadful old men' Palmerston and Russell, but also to Disraeli who, although he had progressed a good deal from being 'that detestable Mr D'Israeli' of 1846, was still regarded as a little exotic for full trust.

The deterioration began during Gladstone's first premiership, and was underpinned by Disraeli's successful flattery and constitutional impropriety in deliberately turning the Queen's mind against Gladstone in the six years after 1874. By 1880 she was a partisan Tory imbued with a deep dislike of the leading Liberal statesman, whom she nonetheless had to endure as her first minister for a longer cumulative period than any of the other nine who served her in this capacity. It was not Disraeli's finest service to his monarch or his country.

It would however be ludicrous to put the whole blame upon Disraeli. He was unrestrained in exploiting an opportunity, but the opportunity had first to be there. How and why did Gladstone, possessing as he did a great, even excessive, respect for the institution of the monarchy, and starting from his very strong Court position in the 1850s and his perfectly adequate one in the 1860s, allow it to arise? He undoubtedly changed more during the course of his long career than do most public figures. It is difficult to reconcile the neat and primly good-looking young Church and state High Tory of the 1830s with the somewhat wild eyes and flying locks of the People's William of the 1870s, 1880s and 1890s. The Queen could have claimed that the sober and earnest young statesman whom she and her husband had found so much in tune with what they saw as the needs of mid-century Britain was very different from the towering leader (as his supporters saw him) or the destructive demagogue (as she and most members of the South of England prosperous classes saw him) of the last twenty-five years of his life. His first premiership caught him almost at the end of the transition and on the threshold of this last phase.

But, if Gladstone changed to a bewildering extent, so too did Queen Victoria, perhaps even more so, and mostly in a diametrically opposite direction to that in which Gladstone was proceeding. Philip Guedalla, a largely forgotten non-academic historian of the inter-war years, and, insofar as he is remembered, underestimated – because of his straining after epigram and over-dramatic imagery – produced a penetrating *jeu d'esprit* in his introduction to the correspondence of the *The Queen and Mr Gladstone*. He amused himself and some others by claiming that the long reign of Victoria was a myth. There were really three Victorias:

> The youngest of the three was Queen Victoria I, who succeeded to King William IV. Her reign, by far the shortest of the three, was distinguished by a romping sort of innocence. It was a girlish Regency, appropriately housed at Brighton, where she rode out with aged beaux, her ministers, and listened with admiring eyes to Lord Melbourne's explanations of everything. . . . She was succeeded shortly after marriage by Victoria II, a widely different type. This queen, no less impressionable than her cheerful predecessor, bore the unmistakable impress of her married life. A gifted husband . . . transformed her views; there was a change of manners, since the royal nurseries transformed her way of life; and it is interesting to observe the shock sustained by former intimates of Victoria I, when they found themselves in the more austere presence of Victoria II. Lord Palmerston, a lively feature of the former Court, who . . . had been 'the one with whom I communicate oftenest after Lord Melbourne', was quite unnerved by his experience.[1]

Just as Melbourne and Palmerston were the political favourites of the reign of Victoria I, so Peel and Aberdeen and Gladstone were those of that of Victoria II, when material progress, earnest endeavour and liberal thoughts mingled together to produce a Court atmosphere from which Melbourne was lucky to be spared by death, which would have oppressed Palmerston had he not had the brazen assurance to be indifferent to it, and in which Disraeli was regarded as a flamboyant parvenu. But the reign of Victoria III was still to come. It was essentially a Disraeli creation and therefore began only in 1874. But it was casting its shadow before it in the early 1870s, when the guiding presence of Albert was becoming less immanent and Gladstone's moral imperatives were coming to grate.

> After the long, dreary years of her retirement [to quote Guedalla again], it was a new sensation. For a touch of novelty was needed, if the melancholy charm of her eternal mourning was ever to be broken; and a skilful minister applied the magic touch. He even found her a new title. Monarchs have often raised their ministers a step in the peerage; but what minister before Disraeli bestowed a step in the monarchy upon his sovereign. The Queen became Queen-Empress; and a deeper change came with the change of style. For now she learned to recognise herself in a fresh character; and the modest outlines of V. R. soon vanished in the new magnificence of V. R. I.
>
> The change was more than titular, since it marked the Queen's transition to her third and final manner.... Disraeli's Queen reigned on, ageing a little with the years, until the roaring streets acclaimed her jubilee and, in a few years more, a silent gun carriage passed by under the grey light of 1901. But almost to the end her loyalties remained the loyalties of 1878 – her throne, her empire, the fighting services, a spirited foreign policy, and a strong distaste for Radicals.[2]

If this thesis is even half accepted, Gladstone around 1870 had to deal with a Queen who had run her race as Victoria II, and was at least becoming ready for the Prince Charming who, somewhat arthritic and asthmatic although Disraeli had become, was to transform her into Victoria III. And at the same time Gladstone himself was in firm transit in the other direction, increasingly finding crowds more attractive than Courts, and with a growing conviction of his own righteousness. The contrary movement of two such formidable objects was a guarantee of the turbulence of the water around them.

When Gladstone became Prime Minister Queen Victoria was forty-nine and a half years old (a little under ten years his junior), with nine children of her own, the oldest twenty-eight and the youngest eleven, was already eight times a grandmother, and was just completing her seventh year of widowhood. During these seven years she had hardly been seen in public, although she had once opened Parliament, at the beginning of the session of 1866, but had done so with waxen visage, responding to neither the populace outside nor the peers inside. London and Windsor had become almost equally distasteful to her. Only Osborne on the Isle of Wight and Balmoral in Aberdeenshire, neither convenient for the transaction of official business, were congenial or, she insisted, good for her delicate health. Nevertheless she worked quite hard at papers and correspondence, although complaining to far busier ministers that her burdens were unique. She had in General Grey an unobsequious private secretary with a Whig background who firmly believed that she ought to pull herself together and undertake more public engagements, and a doctor in William Jenner (not to be confused with his more eminent but unrelated namesake who had invented vaccination) who was professionally reputable but who encouraged her valetudinarianism. When Grey died in 1870 he was succeeded by Henry Ponsonby, who was at first referred to as Colonel Ponsonby, but when he settled into the job became General Ponsonby, rather like a housekeeper receiving the honorary title of 'Mrs'.* Ponsonby, whatever his rank, was a man of firm Liberal views (indeed his son became a Labour MP and his grandson Labour Whip in the House of Lords, although that of course was not necessarily proof of his own radicalism).

The Queen was not therefore surrounded by reactionary influences, although Jenner encouraged her resistance to greater visibility, which would also in a sense have made her more democratic. There was in addition John Brown, 'the Queen's highland servant' as he had become officially designated in 1865, although ceasing at the same time to be confined to Balmoral and allowed to operate at Osborne as well. His political views are not known. He came from a Liberal part of the country, but was probably not naturally of a reforming turn of mind. Then there was Disraeli, who had had a nine-month run with the Queen for most of 1868. He had made the most of it, referring to 'we authors, Ma'am' when her *Highland Journal* was published, and had received his first offering of royal primroses. But he had not captivated or prejudiced her mind in the way that he was so effectively to do during his second and long government.

At the November 1868 general election she would almost certainly, had she possessed a vote, have used it for the Conservatives rather than for the Liberals. But it is also true to say that in all the previous six general elections of her reign she would have voted for the incumbent government, whether it was Tory or Whig. She had hitherto been loyal rather than partisan. Eighteen sixty-eight was the break-point. At all the subsequent six she would undoubtedly have voted Conservative. In 1868, however, her preference was clear (although she had just had a strong argument with Disraeli about whether Bishop Tait of London should become the new Archbishop of Canterbury; at the end of it, however, Disraeli

* Surprisingly, Gladstone himself bestowed this description upon his very definitely unmarried sister Helen. He so described her in a 22 July 1870 letter to the Prussian minister in London requesting on the outbreak of the war a *laissez-passer* from Cologne, and did so again at the time of her death.

deferred to her, which on a matter he would have regarded as of such importance Gladstone would not have done), but her preference was not obsessive. She was disappointed but not dismayed by the election result.

It never occurred to her for instance that she might have played with trying to get a Whig peer to accept the premiership and have confined Gladstone to his old stamping ground of the Exchequer combined with the leadership of the House of Commons. She despatched General Grey to Hawarden with perfect propriety, and the initial attitude of both Queen to new Prime Minister and of Prime Minister to Queen was probably well expressed, allowing a little for the natural flattery of persuasive correspondence, in an exchange of letters between Gladstone and his old Eton and Christ Church contemporary Dean Wellesley of Windsor. Wellesley was as close to the Queen as any Anglican dignitary ever was (she preferred Scots Presbyterians, without ever being over-keen on 'men of God', north or south of the border). He wrote to Gladstone on 27 November 1868:

> 1st. I know that the Queen has a great regard for you, and believes you to be attached to her & anxious to consult her wishes & comfort, as far as is possible, so that you need have no fear but that you will be received *at the outset* [my italics] with the greatest cordiality personally. . . .
>
> 4. Everything depends upon your manner of approaching the Queen. Her nervous susceptibility has much increased since you had to do with her before & you cannot show too much regard, gentleness, I might even say tenderness, towards Her – Where you differ it might be best not at first to try and reason her over to your side but to pass the matter lightly over with expression of respectful regret, & reserve it – for there is no one with whom more is gained by getting her into the habit of intercourse with you. Put off, till she has become accustomed to see you, all discussions which are not absolutely necessary for the day. . . .

The advice was precise and perceptive, and the opening encouragement was the more convincing for being realistically qualified by assuring Gladstone only that the Queen would not be *initially* hostile to him. After that it was up to him. He took Wellesley's letter well and replied on 29 November:

> Every motive of duty, feeling and interest that can touch a man should bid me to study to the best of my small power the manner of my relations with H. M. She is a woman, a widow, a lover of truth, a Sovereign, a benefactress to her country. What titles! I should be ashamed even to add to them the recollection of much kindness received.
>
> On the other hand I have plenty of besetting infirmities. Among others

> I am a man so eager upon things as not enough to remember always what is due to persons – and I have another great fault in the unrestrained or too little restrained manifestation of first impressions, which I well know is quite a different thing from the virtue of mental transparency. The height is among friends to find those who will frankly warn me against those and other errors. . . . But indeed few things would be more painful to me than the thought in retrospect that I could at any time cause H. M. one moment of gratuitous pain or trouble.

In other words Gladstone saw and was grateful for the force of Wellesley's advice but, much though he desired to serve and be appreciated by his Sovereign, was very doubtful whether his temperament would enable him to live up to it. The recipes which Wellesley laid down were those which Gladstone was quite incapable of following. He had an immense respect for the Queen, both as an institution and as an individual – probably more than Disraeli did – but the chances of his being able to turn this into gentleness, tenderness and restraint in pursuing his point when he was convinced that he was right, and that his views were in accordance with the best interests of the monarchy and the country, were quite negligible. Thus, even before he kissed hands as Prime Minister, this exchange of letters illuminated with a harsh clarity (insofar as that word could ever be applied to Gladstone's opaque phrases) the bleakness of the future landscape.

Such full bleakness took some time to be attained, and for the earlier half of the life of his first government relations were, in diplomatic terms, 'normal' or even a little warmer. It was in 1871–2 that the real freeze-up began, although even after that there could be intervals of hesitant thaw. What was, however, always the case, in the bad periods and the better ones alike, was the huge amount of Prime Ministerial time that was devoted to relations with the Sovereign. It was qualitatively different from any recent practice. Not only were there the frequent extended autumn visits to Balmoral (two weeks in 1869, good-tempered release in 1870, a week in 1871, rather huffy release in 1872, and ten days in 1873), the often inconvenient journeys to Osborne, the full letter after each meeting of the Cabinet, and the daily letter of description of proceedings in Parliament (a task now long since delegated to a whip). All this was in a sense routine, and was to be matched by at least an equal effort (although more skilfully conducted and more copiously rewarded) by Disraeli in 1874–80. What were special to Gladstone were the long and often argumentative audiences (conducted standing, for it was only in the subsequent government that she accorded Disraeli the surreptitious privilege of sitting – surreptitious because he removed the chair before leaving in order that no Court servant should be aware of how familiar he had been) and the long and equally argumentative letters which Gladstone chose to address to her on specific matters of policy or appointments. These exchanges, both oral and written, were of doubtful utility. Neither fitted in with Wellesley's advice. The former led to her complaining that Gladstone addressed her like a public meeting (she might have done better to get him, too, to sit down), and the latter, encouraged it must be said by almost equally long royal replies, led more often to an impasse rather than to a resolution. She could not effectively answer Gladstone's over-meticulous arguments, which made her irritable, and she found it easier to say no on paper than face to face.

Of Gladstone's near contemporaries as Prime Minister, Disraeli as we have seen was equally Queen-obsessed, although in a totally different and much more productive way. Palmerston, Russell and later Salisbury remained more detached. Even they necessarily had more Court duties than is the almost minimal practice today, but they did not get emotionally involved. Palmerston sailed jauntily through all disagreements. Russell had the true Whig's approach to the monarchy as a convenience rather than an institution for reverence. And Salisbury, while in the Golden and Diamond Jubilees of 1887 and 1897 he built on the Disraeli practice of exalting and even exploiting the Queen–Emperor as a symbol of Empire, patriotism and unionism, wisely got on with his own business and left the Queen to get on with hers.

Examples of Gladstone's less relaxed and more interventionist style abounded from the beginning of the government. On a day in his first week of office on which he wrote a total of thirty letters, five of them were to the Queen and two to her private secretary. The first small storm blew up before he had even begun to hold regular Cabinets and concerned an election indiscretion of G. O. Trevelyan, the father of both the historian G. M Trevelyan and the Labour Minister of Education Sir Charles Trevelyan. G. O. Trevelyan was then a young junior minister at the Admiralty and had been rash enough to say that the Court and the Duke of Cambridge (the Queen's first cousin) as Commander-in-Chief were obstacles to army reform. Gladstone responded with horror and with two letters, each of which must have taken him half an hour to write, in hand of course. The indiscretions were 'extraordinary and unaccountable'. 'Mr Gladstone cannot but humbly subscribe to Your Majesty's judgement that an error of this nature even raises the question whether, if it was in Mr Trevelyan's mind to point to Your Majesty in the expressions he used, he can be allowed to continue in the office which he holds.'[3] Then, three days later, after a thunderbolt to Trevelyan and a propitiatory reply, Gladstone wrote again with continued contrition but also a glint of optimism: 'Mr Gladstone has a very strong sense of the offence committed, but it appears to him that the confession is frank and manly, and he feels confident that the gentleman, who is really a gentleman of high character, ability, and promise, has received a lesson for life. With this preface, Mr Gladstone desires to take Your Majesty's pleasure.'[4]

The Queen's pleasure was that the apology should be accepted, although with an additional one to the Duke of Cambridge, and Trevelyan remained a member of successive Gladstone administrations until in 1886 he temporarily broke with his chief on Home Rule, thereby incurring the Queen's equally temporary approval, for he changed his mind on the issue in 1887. The main impression left by the incident and the correspondence is that Gladstone took it a great deal too portentously. The wise equivalent of Disraeli's 'We authors, Ma'am' would have been to say 'These inexperienced junior ministers, Ma'am. . . . I'll see he doesn't do it again,' and leave it there. But that was not his way.

The next issue which gave rise to reams of correspondence was the Queen's recoiling from a public suggestion that she might open the parliamentary session on 16 February. She did so on the just acceptable grounds of health and the unacceptable and unconstitutional one of her dislike of the Irish Church Bill. She had come to treat a state opening of Parliament as a health hazard comparable with a visit to a fever camp. It was too cold outside and too hot inside. Moreover riding backwards in a carriage upset her. Gladstone accepted the decision with obsequious resignation:

> Mr Gladstone prays to be allowed to assure Your Majesty that he is deeply and habitually sensible how great are the burdens entailed by Your Majesty's exalted station, and by her manifold, weighty and incessant obligations. . . . In the present instance he will not only obey Your Majesty's desire but will do so in the spirit of humble and earnest co-operation and concurrence.[5]

Then in May 1869 there was a most laborious but amicable exchange on the question what should be done about an uninvited visit from the Viceroy of Egypt, and in June another on the question whether the

Queen should open the new Blackfriars Bridge and also take in an inspection of the equally new (Victoria) Embankment, the Farringdon Viaduct and the Metropolitan Railway ('of which the construction is most curious', Gladstone wrote, presumably intending to be enticing). This produced an outburst of horror from the Queen: 'The fatigue and the excitement would be *far too* great,' quite apart from the well-known intolerable heat of London in June. Eventually, after heavy pressure from Gladstone and the City of London authorities and with General Grey, as always, in favour of less neurasthenia and more activity, she did it in November, and was delighted with the occasion: 'Nothing cld go better or more satisfactorily in *every possible way* than the ceremony and long progress thro', the Queen must think – nearly a million of people today.'[6]

This more than outweighed the summer dispute about peerages, of which Sir Lionel de Rothschild was the only casualty. The Queen, although grumbling about the substance, had been helpful to the government in the crisis of the late summer with the Lords about the Irish Church Bill. She decided that she would prefer the sacrifice of a few Leinster bishops and deans to a major clash between the Lords and the Commons in the first year of a strongly supported government. So on balance the first year of the government did not pass at all badly between them, and a pre-Christmas letter which the Queen wrote as soon as she got to Osborne on 18 December was more of a budget of chat than a letter of business to her Prime Minister:

> The Queen hopes Mr Gladstone's cold is much better? Here we have a dreadful gale but the Queen had a good passage.
>
> The accts of the dear D^ss^ of Argyll are a *little* better.
>
> Still it is a most anxious state – the Queen's heart bleeds for the dear Duke! –
>
> P^ce^ Leopold is quite well again.[7]

Moreover she displayed during that Christmas recess two of her rare shafts of liberalism, both on ecclesiastical matters. In December she wrote that 'the exhibition of illiberality in the Church towards Dr Temple* is a disgrace and shows how ignorance & bigotry blind people and destroy all real spiritual religion wh is quite lost sight of'.[8] And in January 1869, when a new bishop for St Asaph was under consideration, she laid down the simple principle that 'The Queen believes that a

* The future Archbishop of Canterbury, whom Gladstone had just nominated to Exeter (see p. 305n, above).

Welshman is almost necessary for a Welsh see on acct of the language.'[9] As Gladstone was moving towards appointing Dr Joshua Hughes, who was an indisputably Welsh Welshman who did a good deal for the promotion of Welsh language and education, this was welcome if original doctrine. From Llandaff to Bangor and from St Asaph to St David's most recent prelates had been ignorant of the language of eisteddfods.

The Queen's next touch of liberalism, and as it turned out of sound political sense, came before the budget of 1871. Lowe introduced a tax on matches. The Queen wrote expressing great doubt about its fairness between rich and poor.

> Above all it seems *certain* that this tax will seriously affect the manufacture and sale of matches wh is said to be the *sole* means of support of a vast number of the very poorest people & *little* children, especially in London, so that this tax wh it is intended shld press on all equally, will in fact be only severely felt by the poor, wh wld be *vy wrong* – & most impolitic at the present moment. – The Queen trusts that the Govt will reconsider this proposal, & try & substitute some other wh will not press upon the poor.[10]

Three days later the Queen's remonstrances, aided by those of East End match girls, induced the Cabinet to make the Chancellor give way and substitute twopence on the income tax for the match duty.

The Queen also showed signs in May 1872 of being a moderate on the *Alabama* arbitration issue* and loath to see any chauvinistic break with the United States on this vexed question. These fairly isolated manifestations apart, she was, whether agreeing or disagreeing with Gladstone, replete with nearly all the conventional English prejudices. She hardly ever had a good word to say for the Irish. The French were a 'nation wh, with but few exceptions seems to be entirely devoid of *truth*, & to live upon vanity, deception, amusement and self-glorification'.[11] John Stuart Mill's 1870 revival of a female franchise bill led her 'to call Mr Gladstone's attention to the mad and utterly demoralizing movement of the present day to place women in the same position as to professions – as *men*'. She was particularly horrified with the thought that they should be medical students. 'But to tear away all the barriers wh surround a woman, & to propose that they shld study with *men* – things wh cld not be named before them – certainly not in a *mixed*

* See pp. 356–60, below.

audience – wd be to introduce a total disregard of what must be considered as belonging to the rules and principles of morality.'[12]

Predictably she was wholly opposed to the release of Fenian political prisoners, which Gladstone was anxious to push through in 1870–1, and, less predictably and not very attractively, she was almost obsessively vindictive towards a half-demented youth called Arthur O'Connor who made a mock assassination attempt against her in February 1872. He had no weapon more offensive than an unloaded imitation pistol, and John Brown was able to cover himself with glory and earn a £25 annuity for life by seizing it from him. It was about as serious as the 1983 invasion of Buckingham Palace by an amiable lunatic which discomfited Home Secretary Whitelaw but did not greatly excite Queen Elizabeth II. Queen Victoria, on the other hand, besieged Gladstone with letters complaining about her special exposure, the state of the law, the leniency of the sentence and the general weakness of the judge who, finding O'Connor an inadequate, gave him only a year's imprisonment just as, according to the Queen, he had recently given only three months to a man 'who [had] pushed his wife under a Dray Cart'. She demanded that O'Connor be deported, and eventually he agreed to go abroad voluntarily, provided, as he shrewdly negotiated, thereby raising doubt about his degree of mental deficiency, that it should be to a healthy climate.

There had also been a depressing little incident in February 1870 when the Gladstones had the Waleses (the Prince then aged twenty-eight, but already looking immensely self-indulgent, although benignly so) dining with them at 11 Carlton House Terrace, and the Prime Minister very circumspectly wrote to the Queen to ask whether they might be permitted also to ask Princess Louise, her fourth and eldest unmarried daughter, then aged twenty-one. The Queen's reply, maybe occasioned by slight resistance to the thought of a direct relationship between the heir to the throne and the Prime Minister, was at best unequivocal and at worst slightly snubbing: 'It is very kind of Mr and Mrs Gladstone to ask Pnss Louise – but she never dines out except at Marlborough House.'[13] It is impossible not to append the comment that if the poor girl had been allowed to range a little more widely she might not have made such a disastrously unhappy marriage as that which she contracted in the following year with Argyll's heir, the Marquess of Lorne.

On balance, however, relations jogged along tolerably if exhaustingly until the summer of 1871. Then what might have been expected to remain a minor dispute suddenly sent out ripples of resentment and left lasting grievances on both sides. The contentious political issue towards the end of that session was an Army Regulation Bill, which Gladstone would have liked to be a more far-reaching measure of reorganization and reform but which was largely confined to the abolition of the purchase of commissions (and also of promotions), with provision for the compensation of officers who lost presumed property rights. (The militia was also brought by the bill under more effective War Office control.)

This bill ran into obstructive tactics in the House of Commons, which made Gladstone, who then had no idea what he was going to experience from the Irish in his next government, as angry as he was surprised. He wrote to the Queen on 14 June: 'at the morning sitting today the House went into Committee for the tenth time on the Army Bill. Much of the same obstruction, which it is difficult to characterize by the epithets it deserves, but of which there is little doubt that it is without precedent in the present generation, was continued.'[14] And on another occasion he complained to her that while he had:

> during his whole parliamentary life ... been accustomed to see class interests of all kinds put themselves on their defence under the supposition of being assailed, he had, he regrets to state, never seen a case where the modes of operation adopted by the professing Champions were calculated to leave such a painful impression on the mind. . . .[15]

It was something that in June he was still hopeful of her sympathy against these tactics. In July they had a slight altercation about the behaviour of the Duke of Cambridge on the issue. The Queen was 'sure that Mr Gladstone & the Govt must feel very grateful to [him] for the support he has given to the Army Bill'. Gladstone in fact thought Cambridge was distinctly equivocal. The best he could do in the House of Lords, after speaking, was to abstain. The Queen herself was never at direct loggerheads with the government over the Army Bill and the abolition of purchase. At first she was in favour of the government's proposals, but probably lost her enthusiasm when she discovered how deep-seated was the latent opposition of the old officer class, from the Commander-in-Chief downwards. She was even more impatient when she realized that the delay would keep Parliament sitting into late August, and her irritation was then about equally directed towards the government for raising the tiresome issue and the opposition for opposing.

She did not however resist the government's tough tactic for circumnavigating the obstruction. When, on top of the Commons delay, the bill foundered in the Lords, the Cabinet simply decided to proceed by prerogative. The purchase of commissions had been made illegal by an Act in 1809, except where it was regulated and the price kept under control by royal warrant. The warrant had merely to be cancelled, and the deed was done. It was a tactic at once daring and clever. It was open to a strong charge of constitutional arrogance because it cocked a snook at the parliamentary process. Legislation being in danger of failing, the government coolly declared it unnecessary, which raised the considerable question why they had started on the process in the first place. On the other hand it was a brilliant manoeuvre for it left the enemy forces not merely frustrated but dangerously outflanked. The abolition could be achieved without the bill, but not the compensation, which was the last result which the officers and their supporters wanted. The Lords were humiliated as well as outraged, for they had no alternative but to turn round like squirrels in a cage and pass the bill.

This masterful display of executive power was a fine sample of Gladstone's ruthlessness when, as was frequently the case, he was convinced of his own rightness. The Queen's acquiescence was perhaps surprising and it may have left her with a certain residue of resentment which contributed to the bitterness of the consequential dispute on the apparently trivial issue of the date of her departure for her 1871 Balmoral autumn. Parliament that year dragged on to 21 August. There had the day before to be a meeting of the Privy Council to approve of the speech which was read on her behalf by the Lord Chancellor to bring the session's proceedings to an end. She was prepared, under great protest, to stay in the south until the 18th, but not a moment longer. If that did not suffice, as it did not, a quorum including at least one Cabinet minister had to be assembled on Deeside, which was what eventually happened.

The Queen and the Prime Minister became locked in mutual misunderstanding. He did not appreciate that she was for once genuinely unwell. He had a good deal of excuse for not doing so. She had cried 'wolf' so often, even at the beginning of 1870 putting forward for not opening Parliament the wonderfully blanket reason that 'It is a very unwholesome year.' In 1871, however, she arrived at Balmoral in a genuinely poor state and suffered two weeks of severe illness, of which the symptoms appeared to be a constriction of the throat, an abscess on the arm and a general state of debility. Jenner took it seriously enough to send for Lister, the founder of antiseptic surgery. Ponsonby, partly because he disagreed with Jenner on almost everything, took a more optimistic view and recorded the hope that she would soon be better, accompanied by the odd thought that 'Here away . . . from all her children she feels comfortable.'[16] There seems no doubt, however, that she was seriously ill for two to three weeks after her arrival at Balmoral, and low for the whole of September.

She, for her part, was even more impervious to the difficulties which Gladstone had to face on *her* behalf. Eighteen-seventy-one was the peak year of mid-Victorian republicanism. Dilke mounted a considerable campaign, and his friend G. O. Trevelyan (by no means as chastened 'for life' as Gladstone had assured the Queen that he was in 1869) had written an anonymous pamphlet entitled *What Does She Do With It?* which was an attack on the Queen's parsimony and hoarding of money. In these unpropitious circumstances Gladstone had in the early summer to defend a marriage dowry of £30,000 (approximately £1.5 million at today's prices) for Princess Louise and an annual allowance of £15,000 (£750,000) for Prince Arthur, later Duke of Connaught, in August. There was widespread impatience with the demands of the brood, exacerbated by the invisibility of the Queen. Had Gladstone been able to point to the Queen's remaining for prorogation it would have eased his task, and it rankled that he could not. But what rankled still more was the way in which the Queen reacted to his well-intentioned and sensible advice.

First she let off on 10 August a dithyramb of complaint and did it to Hatherley, the Lord Chancellor, rather than to the Prime Minister, which was in itself almost a manifesto of no confidence. The burden of her complaint was that ministers, and in particular Gladstone and Granville, apologized for her not performing more public duties instead of saying that it was a miracle that she managed as much as she did:

> She has opened Parliament this year & the fatigue and trouble & agitation of Princess Louise's marriage, held all her Drawing-rooms, Investitures – Councils – received all the Royal Visitors who came, held 2 Reviews, & went to two public breakfasts, besides opening the Albert Hall & St Thomas' Hospital. All these have been done in one year & the Queen would really ask what right anyone has to complain.
>
> They should also plainly state that the Queen cannot undertake any night work in hot rooms & when much talking is required, nor any residence in London beyond 2 or 3 days at a time as the air, noise & excitement made her quite ill, cause violent headaches & great prostration.
>
> It is really abominable that a woman, a Queen, loaded with care &

anxieties, public & domestic which are daily increasing should be unable to make people understand that there are limits to her powers.

What killed her beloved Husband? Overwork & worry – what killed Lord Clarendon? The same. . . .

She concluded with dark hints of abdication:

She must solemnly repeat that unless her ministers support her & state the whole truth she cannot go on & must give her heavy burden up to younger hands.

Perhaps then those discontented people may regret that they broke her down when she might still have been of use.[17]

What was worse was the letter which Ponsonby (despite his position as a firm ally of Gladstone's and – privately – a stern critic of the Queen on all these public engagement matters) wrote to Gladstone on 15 August:

May I venture to observe that it sometimes strikes me The Queen does not fully understand the case. I do not know what the Lord Chancellor said, but I think Her Majesty looks upon the question of her staying for the Prorogation as a very small matter. And one moreover that scarcely affects herself. I mean I think she looks on it as if she were being urged to do this for a political purpose – In order to help the Government. . . .[18]

This drove Gladstone into resentful indignation, which he expressed in his reply to Ponsonby with perhaps some exaggeration springing from exasperation of the moment but also with an underlying bitterness which suggested permanent damage:

I am surprised and sorry, that the Queen should think that we have had really in our minds, during this deplorable business, the benefit of the Government, an idea which I believe has never occurred to any of us. But I am much obliged to you for mentioning it. . . .

Upon the whole I think it has been the most sickening piece of experience which I have had during near forty years of public life.

Worse things may easily be imagined: but smaller and meaner cause for the decay of Thrones cannot be conceived. It is like the worm which bores the bark of a noble tree and so breaks the channel of its life.[19]

Six weeks later Gladstone reached Balmoral for just over a week's stay as minister in attendance. In the interval he had been in lodgings at Whitby in North Yorkshire, where his son Willy had become MP in 1868, for two weeks of sea-bathing and had spent another three weeks at Hawarden. On his way to Balmoral, moreover, he had made a political progress, with warm receptions at Perth and then at the intermediate stations to Aberdeen, where he had spoken three times, once in the main assembly rooms, once to a working men's club, and once at a Lord Provost's luncheon. 'There was much enthusiasm for the Government,' he recorded.[20] His main speech at Aberdeen, where he received the freedom of the city, might in fact have carried the Queen's agreement, for it was one of the most anti-Irish that he ever made, accusing that nation of ingratitude in its lack of response to the two reforming measures of 1869 and 1870, and fifteen years later was singled out by Lord Randolph Churchill as the last anti-Home Rule speech that Gladstone ever made.

Nevertheless this may not have been the most tactful way in which to approach Balmoral, particularly in view of the August interchange with Ponsonby, but there was no suggestion that it was the reason why she let him wait several days after arrival before seeing him. That was due more to her still making the most of her slowly recovering health and perhaps to continuing resentment on her part too. Altogether it is difficult to judge how frosty the atmosphere was during this Balmoral visit. When he eventually saw the Queen his diary entry ran: 'Long interview with H. M. She was very kind: & much better.'[21] And he wrote to his wife on the next day: 'I bade farewell reluctantly to Balmoral, for it is as homelike as any place away from home can be, and wonderfully safe from invasions.'[22]

On the other hand he wrote to Glyn, his Chief Whip, on the Sunday: 'I go from here Wednesday morning, unless invited to stay on a little.' He left on the Wednesday. More significant was a passage in a 1 October letter to Granville, to whom he found it easier to expose a bruise than to either his Whip or his wife: 'Her repellent power which she so well knows how to use has been put in action towards me on this occasion for the first time since the formation of the Government. I have felt myself on a new and different footing with her.'[23] On balance the petty issue of the date of the Queen's 1871 departure for Balmoral probably did mark a significant point in the decline of their relationship. It need not have been an irrevocable decline had the Queen in particular had the will to reverse it, but she did not; and Gladstone was passing into a mood in which he accumulated grievances with a certain grim satisfaction.

This deterioration was underpinned by their next serious argument, which was on a matter of more substance than the Balmoral departure nonsense. At the beginning of November 1871 the Prince of Wales caught typhoid staying at a country house near Scarborough. Lord Chesterfield, a fellow guest, and the Prince's groom, who were also infected, both died. So nearly did the Prince. He was desperately ill at Sandringham for the first two weeks of December, but miraculously rallied on the 14th, the tenth anniversary of his father's death in somewhat similar circumstances. It was very bad luck for Sir Charles Dilke, who was launched on an autumn campaign of republican meetings and found that his movement around the provincial centres, from Newcastle to Bristol to Leeds to Bolton to Birmingham, was punctuated by increasingly alarmist bulletins about the Prince which produced increasingly hostile audiences. The developments might have been regarded as even worse luck for the Prince, although when his fever eventually receded it became apparent that the momentum of the English republican movement had gone with it. His six weeks of illness had done more for the stability of the Throne than had his previous thirty years of life.

The first and lesser impact of the Prince's illness and recovery upon Sovereign–Prime Minister relations was concerned with the place, date and form of the national service of thanksgiving which was generally agreed to be called for. This was not allowed to be easy. St Paul's and 27 February 1872 were settled on without too much difficulty, but there were a lot of other problems to worry about. The service must be short and simple; the Queen could not absolutely commit the Prince or even herself to attend, and if they did should she and the Prince and Princess ride in one carriage as she wanted or in two as they appeared to want? Eventually all was sorted out and the public enthusiasm gave her much gratification. It was Blackfriars Bridge writ large.

She was also in an unusual supplicatory position towards the Prime Minister that winter because she had conceived a great desire to go to Baden-Baden at Easter to see Princess Feodore of Hohenlohe-Leinigen, her twelve-year-senior half-sister, who she rightly thought might be nearing the end of her life. She appeared to accept that she needed the permission of the government for this expedition, and approached securing it in a very submissive tone, rather like a young officer trying to get a week's special leave from his colonel. She first raised it in a letter of 10 January, and after making a very strong case for a last visit to 'her dear Sister' (who did in fact die eight months later) whom she had not seen for six years, she continued:

> What the Queen wld therefore propose to do – wld be to run over to Baden! where her sister lives – at Easter when that Bathing place is quite

> deserted & where she cld get a private house, outside the Town she hears, – taking advantage of the Easter recess to do this. . . . the Queen wld not propose being away longer (*including* the journey there and back) than *under 3 weeks*. . . . The Queen has not mentioned this to a soul beyond her *own* Courier Kanne, till she has mentioned it to Mr Gladstone.[24]

Gladstone replied a little sternly, recognizing the case for the visit but suggesting several reasons, including the need to make dispositions about the future of the Prince of Wales, against the Easter timing. The Queen was determined but not peremptory. She sent him a letter she had just received from Princess Hohenlohe in the hope that the tale of suffering it contained would melt his heart. It did, to the extent of his tacitly withdrawing his opposition provided the plans were kept secret for as long as possible. On 19 February, however, still five weeks before departure, she wrote to say that more or less public plans would now have to be made, and in doing so illustrated a startling contrast between her eager ingenuity when she wanted to do something and her magnification of obstacles when she did not. A three-country journey of 600 miles became much less of a burden than a drive along the Embankment to the City of London.

> She wld wish to go straight *through France* stopping *nowhere* & thus avoiding the fatigue of any visitors on the road – wh wld be difficult in going the other way [presumably through Belgium and Germany]. Besides that the quiet embarkation at Portsmouth & quiet disembarkation in the Dockyard at Cherbourg wld save gt fatigue to herself & prevent all *delay* from *fogs* in the rivers – Thames & Scheldt. She went that way in '68 to Lucerne.
>
> The Queen concludes that there cld be *no political* objection or personal risk in going *thro' France*?[25]

In spite of the sadness of her mission there is a touch of throwback to the spontaneous enthusiasm of Guedalla's Victoria I about her approach to the journey, and she may be thought to come more attractively out of this correspondence than did Gladstone. As he hinted in his first letter, he was limbering up, somewhat laboriously, to use the aftermath of the illness of the Prince of Wales to push through a scheme which had been for some time maturing in his mind. This was intended to fulfil the double objective of providing a pediment for the three columns (the first the Church Bill, the second the Land Bill and the third the University Bill of 1873) of his policy of pacifying Ireland and at the same time providing employment for the Prince.

There was general agreement, embracing certainly the Queen, and up to a point the Prince himself, that such employment was desirable. At the time of his typhoid he was thirty years of age, had been married for eight and a half years, had five children, was a leader of fashion, which he tempered with a mild easy-going liberalism, or at least reaction against his mother's rigidities, but was best known for idleness, self-indulgence and dissipation. However, there was a hope that his long fever and narrow escape had washed away his sins as well as his vitality and that with the rebirth of his innocence there was an opportunity for a new beginning on a life of greater public service. The Queen gave to his elder sister, the Crown Princess of Prussia, an affecting picture of him at Osborne in mid-February: 'It is like a new life – all the trees and flowers give him pleasure, as they never used to do, and he was quite pathetic over his small wheelbarrow and little tools at the Swiss cottage. He is constantly with Alix [the Princess of Wales], and they seem hardly ever apart!!!'[26]

It was a narrow window of opportunity for by May she was back to complaining that he was gadding about too much, and Gladstone may have missed the window by a few weeks, for he submitted his memorandum of serious proposals only on 5 July. But the timing seems unlikely to have been crucial. The proposals united in opposition the Queen and the Prince, which was a deadly although by no means an inevitable alliance. In a long (3000 words) and lucidly argued letter Gladstone first reviewed several canvassed proposals for the special association of the Prince with one or other of several departments of state, the Foreign Office, the India Office or the War Office, and found them unsatisfactory, as he did that for a special fostering role in relation to art, science and philanthropy. He then came to his recommended solution, which was that for the winter season the Prince should reside for several months in Dublin and take over the role of Viceroy, which office would be abolished, thereby releasing to him the salary and other considerable emoluments of that office. (This was a clever bait, for the Prince was finding it difficult to live on his income.) The Chief Secretary would, however, continue in being with responsibility for Irish administration, although the Prince by working closely with him would gain experience in executive government.

For the rest the Prince (and the Princess) should for the London summer season take over from the Queen the (undischarged) responsibility for providing from Buckingham Palace an active Court and the leadership of society. Somewhat curiously he had supported this in a previous letter to Ponsonby by saying: 'I am convinced that society has suffered fearfully in moral tone from the absence of a pure Court.'[27] It was curiously and somewhat tactlessly put because from the Queen it had not had an impure Court (although she could have interpreted his words otherwise) but no Court at all, and from the Prince it was quite likely to get the reverse.

Gladstone summed up his proposals in a way that made them sound a little like a regime of long runs and cold baths prescribed by a *mens sana in corpore sano* schoolmaster: 'Four to five months in Ireland, two or three in London, the Autumn manoeuvres, Norfolk and Scotland, with occasional fractions of time for other purposes, would sufficiently account for the twelve months.'[28] There was no chance of the proposals being accepted. The Prince was filled with no nostalgia for his 1861 escapade at the Curragh (when a young actress had been smuggled into his quarters) and hated the idea of nearly half a year of exile. The Queen (with some justification) thought that there could be constitutional complications about the Prince's position in Ireland, and half tried to sugar the pill for Gladstone by saying that there, 'placed at the head of a smaller and inferior society to that of London . . . he will be surrounded by Gentlemen of the Irish conservative party who will endeavour to attract him to their views'.[29] Her rejection of the Buckingham Palace Court suggestion on the other hand contained no sugar and a smart snub: 'The Queen considers [this] to be a question which more properly concerns herself to settle with the members of her family as occasion may arise.'[30]

Gladstone might have done well to recognize defeat, but this was not his way. Five days after her reply she got another 2000 words. She discouragingly acknowledged 'Mr Gladstone's long letter', again doubted the feasibility but promised to consult the Prince of Wales when he came to Osborne in a few days' time. Two weeks later she reported that his reaction was as adverse as her own and added: 'The Queen therefore trusts that this plan may now be considered as *definitely* abandoned.'[31] Three weeks later Gladstone redeployed the argument in another 2000 words. The Queen replied that she 'thinks it useless to prolong the discussion on this proposal'. Gladstone, in return, 'need hardly say with how much grief he finds his views to be so unequivocally disapproved by Your Majesty on a matter of so much importance, either way, to the interests of the Monarchy. But, having been permitted to explain himself at so much length, and with such freedom, he refrains from further trespass on Your Majesty's patience.'[32]

He ended, a little huffily, by saying that 'as matters now stand' he would assume that he need not that year go to Balmoral (although he had been invited). A week later she renewed her invitation for him to go 'for 2 days . . . but if there is nothing very special to communicate the Queen hardly likes to urge Mr Gladstone to put himself to the inconvenience & fatigue of coming over'. Gladstone did not go, although he circled Balmoral, at three houses and an inn, for three weeks.

In November there was an anti-climactic little exchange in which the Queen may have had her tongue more firmly in her cheek than did Gladstone. Clinging to a very puny raft in place of the proud ship which he had endeavoured to launch, Gladstone wrote from Hawarden: 'It would without doubt be a great object gained if, without reference to any other means, the Prince of Wales could, through your Majesty's influence or otherwise be induced to adopt the habit of reading. The regular application of but a small portion of time would enable him to master many of the able and valuable works which bear upon Royal and Public duty.'[33] The Queen replied after two weeks: 'With respect to an observation in one of Mr Gladstone's letters respecting the Prince of Wales – she has only to say that the P. of Wales has never been fond of reading & that from his earliest years it was *impossible* to get him to do so. Newspapers & *very rarely*, a novel, are all that he ever reads. . . .'[34]

The government lasted just over a year after this depressing ending to an enterprise which Gladstone undoubtedly thought he had started in order to underpin the monarchy, while the Queen and some of her Court no doubt thought it was in order to underpin his Irish policy. The enterprise had by any standards been conducted with determination, powerful arguments and a marked lack of persuasive tact. It was a significant notch in the downward progress of their relations. Gladstone's first and strongest government, while it produced no open rupture, ended with their relations substantially worse than they had been at its beginning.

21

'Ever and Anon the Dark Rumbling of the Sea'

In April 1872, Disraeli went to Manchester and delivered one of the most memorable polemics of the nineteenth century. The Free Trade Hall ought to have been Gladstone territory just as a great provincial meeting was almost a Gladstone patent. But Disraeli was capable of emulating as well as mocking his *vis-à-vis*, although he did it in a very different style, sardonic rather than uplifting, but at least equally generous in amplitude. Disraeli's Manchester speech, almost unbelievably, lasted three and a quarter hours, throughout which he sustained himself with two bottles of very weak brandy and water. Its claim to near immortality, however, was all concentrated in barely two minutes of brilliant imagery. The government, he said, was losing its destructive energy:

> Their paroxysms ended in prostration. Some took refuge in melancholy, and their eminent chief alternated between a menace and a sigh. As I sat opposite the Treasury bench the ministers reminded me of one of those marine landscapes not very uncommon on the coasts of South America. You behold a row of exhausted volcanoes. Not a flame flickers from a single pallid crest. But the situation is still dangerous. There are occasional earthquakes, and ever and anon the dark rumbling of the sea.

That speech, if it did not cause, at least coincided with a political turning-point. Hitherto Disraeli had been a hesitant leader of the opposition, with only nine months of interim premiership behind him. From 1868 it had been very much Gladstone's Parliament, and there had been strong Conservative party murmurings that they might do better under a different leader. Suddenly the situation appeared transformed. Disraeli came to look a future as well as a past Prime Minister, and even ministers began to feel that they should prepare for a *nunc dimittis*. In sharp contrast with the careerist political culture of today when Prime Ministers find it difficult to get rid of their colleagues, nineteenth-century Prime Ministers often had a problem keeping men in their governments. And no one was riveted to the results of the next general election, regarding it as much nearer to an unpredictable act of God than a subject for obsessive political manipulation.

This was as true of Gladstone himself as it was of his subordinates. He was by no means above political manoeuvring, but his eye was also always half-fixed on that desirable interval 'between parliament and the grave', and his morbidity made him doubtful in his sixty-third year of his actuarial chances. Of his fourteen Cabinet colleagues of 1868, Clarendon had died, Bright and Childers had retired because of ill health, and Hatherley was about to do so for the same reason. The survivors and the four (Halifax, W. E. Forster, Stansfield and Selborne) who had joined or were about to join them were beginning to feel the imminence for the government of 'twilight and evening bell'. There remained two of the most notable achievements of the government – the Ballot Bill and the conclusion of the *Alabama* arbitration and settlement with the United States – to be brought to a safe lodging (which was accomplished in July 1872 in the former case and two months later in the latter), and one great failure – the Irish University Bill – to be endured before the government in March 1873 made its first attempt at escape from office. After defeat on the Irish Bill the Cabinet decided on resignation, which Gladstone accordingly tendered to the Queen on 13 March. Disraeli coolly and ruthlessly refused to take office. He would have been in a minority in the House of Commons, but a dissolution would have been open to him as it had been in roughly similar circumstances to Russell in 1846 or to Derby and himself in 1852, and was to be to Campbell-Bannerman in 1905. But he had had enough of minority office and decided that he wanted to see the government get still deeper into the mire. After a week's interregnum he forced them back into office.

The Ballot Bill was not much more welcome to Gladstone than had been the Elementary Education and the University Tests Bills. It was nearly forty years since he had informed the readers of the *Liverpool Standard* that the fall of the Roman Republic was to be attributed to the corruptions of secret voting, and while there were few subjects, except perhaps for the importance of religion in politics and the quality of Dante's poetry, on which his views of the 1830s were within hailing distance of those of the 1870s, he had retained a certain resistance towards the idea that those who deserved the vote also needed the protection of being able to exercise it secretly. His ideal polity was a mass of contradictions. He liked small boroughs with restricted electorates which could nurture statesmen without distracting them from higher things with the squalor of local log-rolling. He also liked the idea of voters as independent gentlemen who strode to the poll with their heads high and the courage to declare their choice without fear or favour. (It must be said that this caricature of Athenian democracy did not bear much relation to his own early experience of Newark.) Yet he had also come to believe in the good moral sense of the masses against the classes. The great democracy of Northern England and Scotland, acting like a vast jury, was the best hope of saving Britain from the brittle values of the metropolitan 'upper ten thousand' and their Home Counties hangers-on, of whom Disraeli had made himself the unesteemed mouthpiece.

Gladstone put these incompatibilities through the mincing machine of his mind and came out at first with a rather bland pâté. In his first speech as Prime Minister, when he went to Greenwich (a very rare experience during the eleven years he was member for that borough) to secure his re-election after taking an office of profit under the Crown, he produced the somewhat delphic statement that 'I have at all times given my vote in favour of open voting, but I have done so before, and I do so now, with an important reservation, namely, that whether by open voting or by whatsoever means, free voting must be secured.' In the 1870 session Hartington, acting not very departmentally as Postmaster-General, brought forward an anti-corrupt-practices bill which would, *inter alia*, have introduced ballot voting. It was a government measure but a low-pressure one. It was not given much priority compared with Elementary Education and Irish Land, the favoured measures of the session. This bill foundered, but another, concentrating on the ballot, was introduced by a private member late in the session. This was a 'gesture' bill rather than a serious attempt at legislation, but it nonetheless marked a decisive stage in the argument. This was partly because the Prime Minister spoke, and for the first time committed himself favourably on the issue, and partly because it secured a favourable vote in a full House of Commons. Gladstone said that many whose occupations made them vulnerable to pressure now had the vote and that these new social circumstances made the protection of their freedom necessary. Necessary more than desirable was the implication, and this was confirmed by his diary entry for 29 June in the following year, when the Ballot Bill was having its third canter round the parliamentary course:

'Spoke on ballot, and voted in 324–230 with mind satisfied & as to feeling a lingering reluctance.'[1]

In this 1871 session broadly the same bill had progressed to being a major government measure. W. E. Forster, nominally only Vice-President of the Council but a seasoned ministerial performer in the House of Commons, who had piloted the Education Bill in the previous session, was in charge. He drove it through an obstructing chamber. Then, after the amazing amplitude for such an apparently simple measure of eighteen days of Commons Committee and forty years of public discussion the Lords threw it out (and did so by the insultingly small vote of 97 to 48) on the ground that it had not been adequately considered. Gladstone reacted with more passion against the Lords than he had hitherto mustered in favour of the ballot. This could be regarded as a typical sign of his imperiousness: once his own mind, however reluctantly, had embraced the need for a change, he was impatient of the obscurantism of those who had not moved with him. In his holiday-interrupting speech in his son's Whitby constituency on 2 September, he denounced the Lords for frustrating the will of the people's House, and said that the next time round the bill would be presented with 'an authoritative knock' on the door of their Lordship's House. In 1872 he threatened first a special autumn session, a rare event, and then, if the Lords still did not give way, a dissolution. Disraeli was not at all keen to risk his future prospects on this issue, and so, as a result of one of those processes of osmosis between the Conservative leader in the Commons and allegedly independent-minded Tory peers, the Lords gave way in early July and the crisis was averted. The first secret-ballot by-election took place as early as 15 August 1872. The last major legislative reform of Gladstone's first government was in place.

To the second achievement of 1872, the resolution of the ten-year-old *Alabama* dispute with the United States, Gladstone's commitment was total and his influence was crucial. Furthermore, the settlement not only was the greatest nineteenth-century triumph of rational internationalism over short-sighted jingoism, but also marked the break-point between the previous hundred years of Anglo-American strain and the subsequent century and more of two world wars fought in alliance, a Cold War conducted by the American-led but partly British-created NATO, and several decades in which at least some people in both Washington and London believed strongly in a special relationship between the two countries.

It was nearly fifty years between the *Alabama* settlement and President

Wilson's philosopher-king descent on the Paris of the 1919 peace treaty and nearly seventy before the 'westward, look, the land is bright' British mood of 1940. There were some nasty disputes on the way, particularly in the trade field but also over Venezuela in 1895–6. It was nonetheless the case that, after 1872, war between Britain and the United States became almost inconceivable, whereas in the previous hundred years it had been twice a reality and several times a possibility. The acceptance of the *Alabama* award therefore left at least as great an imprint upon Britain's future orientation as did Lansdowne's forging of the entente with France in 1904 or Ernest Bevin's determination to commit the United States in Europe in 1947–9. Morley's judgement that Gladstone's 'association with this high act of national policy is one of the things that give its brightest lustre to his fame' was not hyperbolic.

Bright though the lustre and high the act, however, the circumstances out of which it arose were of byzantine complication and a classic example of an oak growing out of an acorn. In July 1862 when pro-Southern feeling was at its height in Britain (Gladstone made his Newcastle speech ten weeks later), a thousand-ton sloop, steam-powered but wooden hulled, set off from the Mersey, where she had been built, on a trial cruise of jollification. She anchored in an Anglesey bay. The celebrants were quickly taken off by tender and replaced by a more determined crew. The sloop then sailed to the Azores where she was equipped by supply ships from London and Liverpool with officers, armaments and coal which turned her into a ready-for-action Confederate man-of-war. Thus accoutred, the *Alabama*, as she had also become, proceeded to terrorize Union shipping in the North Atlantic to an extent which would surely have aroused both the admiration and the amazement of German U-boat commanders in the First and Second World Wars. Single-handedly, it was alleged, she had almost cleared the ocean of the Union marine.

That there was some dereliction of Britain's proper discharge of her neutral duty was difficult to deny. Customs officials in Liverpool were dilatory in sending in reports and the Foreign Office, then presided over by Russell, was dilatory in acting upon them when they were received. On the day on which the *Alabama* sailed, Russell, having waited for the opinion of the Law Officers, decided, ineffectively, to detain the ship. Gladstone, as Chancellor at the time, was responsible for the customs agents.

The United States government bore heavy resentment over the activities of the *Alabama* (and of one or two other less devastating marauders originating in British waters, one from Australia) and wanted compensation. Towards the end of the 1860s, with the war won, there were two new factors compared with 1862. First, British opinion had swung away from the South and towards the victorious North. Second, it was obvious that the unsundered United States was on the road to becoming a major commercial force, and maybe a world power as well. These considerations, fortified by some appropriate guilt on the part of Palmerston's surviving colleagues, predisposed the 1868 Gladstone government towards a settlement. By good fortune its short-lived Disraeli predecessor had also committed itself in the same direction. That government had agreed to a convention by which a mixed Anglo-American commission should decide upon the settlement of all outstanding claims between the two countries, and had further agreed that, in the event of failure to agree, the *Alabama* claims in particular should be referred for arbitration to the head of a friendly state. (In 1871 the King of Prussia, newly elevated to be German Emperor, performed the role in relation to a minor related dispute.)

As a result the *Alabama* settlement, which could so easily have been demagogically opposed, never became a matter of bitter inter-party dispute. At one stage, indeed, the far from blameless Russell threatened to cause more trouble in the Lords than Disraeli ever did in the Commons. The 1868 convention foundered because the US Senate, mainly for internal political reasons, failed to ratify it. But when a new and similar plan was launched in early 1871 Disraeli agreed that Stafford Northcote should be one of the five British commissioners who under the presidency of Lord de Grey (soon to be Ripon) went to Washington to try to negotiate a framework treaty under which an arbitration could take place. Northcote's presence and his good relations with de Grey effectively hobbled the opposition in the House of Commons. And in June of the following year Gladstone, writing to the Queen, referred to 'the signal prudence of Mr Disraeli during the anxious period of the Controversy with the United States and the value of the example he had set . . .'.[2]

Such restraint was very desirable, for the Americans, while apparently wanting a settlement, advanced, or at least talked about, the most fantastical claims. The nigger in the woodpile, if this phrase may be used about such a vehement and distinguished opponent of slavery, was Gladstone's old friend Charles Sumner, Senator from Massachusetts and chairman of the Senate Foreign Relations Committee from 1861 to 1871. His 1857 visit to Hawarden seemed to have done peculiarly little good in improving his disposition towards Britain or Gladstone. He was the leading advocate of the so-called 'indirect claims', which could be crudely defined as blaming the *Alabama* for the North taking longer to win the Civil War and charging Britain accordingly. In one speech in the Senate he suggested a figure of £400 million, which was approximately six times the size of total British annual public expenditure at the time. On another occasion he proposed that a cession of Canada to the United States might act as an assuagement. These could have been dismissed as 'noises off' had not Hamilton Fish, the founder of a famous Hudson Valley foreign policy dynasty and President Grant's Secretary of State, been very apprehensive of Sumner; he was frightened to negotiate far away from Sumner's extravagant imperatives.

In these circumstances it required nerve, first on the part of the British Commissioners to get the Washington treaty signed and then on the part of the British Cabinet, in view of the continued American muttering about the indirect claims, to let the matter go to the five specified arbitrators – nominees of Great Britain, the United States, Italy, Switzerland and Brazil – who met in Geneva. There the day was saved by a combination of Charles Adams, the American nominee, and Chief Justice Cockburn, the British nominee.

Adams had been minister in London at the time of the escape of the wretched ship, but far from being full of personal resentment was the only man on the American side who had the cool statesmanship to jettison the wilder claims. Cockburn's behaviour was even more of an unexpected bonus, for he was a natural illiberal British chauvinist. Great though was the trouble caused by his famous and long-lasting definition of obscenity, he seemed to have been sufficiently relaxed by 'abroad' to make unanimous the decision that Britain was responsible for the acts of the *Alabama*. The other arbitrators fluctuated between these two poles on the different counts, and ended up by deciding on a total British liability of £3¼ million. This was at once a vast sum by Victorian standards, directly equivalent only to about £160 million today, but in relation to national income more like £4 billion, and in relation to the size of the budget (to which it added approximately 5 per cent) the equivalent of a modern £150 billion. Yet it was barely a third of what the Americans had demanded, even when the indirect claims were set aside. It was also the equivalent, in 1870s terms, of fivepence on the income tax, although the government, quite rightly, treated it as a once-for-all item rather than a normal revenue outgoing, and made no attempt to cover it by taxation in a single year. Far transcending the importance of the sum, however, was the fact that the government, in the plenitude of Britain's power, accepted the principle of the liability.

The autumn of 1872, once the *Alabama* affair had been settled, was one of relative calm for Gladstone, indeed of almost unbelievable calm, so far at least as external circumstances were concerned, by modern Prime Ministerial standards. There was no parliament from 9 August until 6 February 1873. There was no party conference. It never occurred to him to visit his constituency. In October 1871 he had addressed a large open-air meeting on Blackheath, and that he judged was enough until the general election of 1874. He never went there in the interval. The Queen in the spring of 1872, maybe as a thanks-offering for being allowed to go to Baden-Baden, or maybe as a rather good royal tease (although it does not sound exactly her style), had offered him a grace-and-favour house in Greenwich in order to ease the discharge of his constituency duties. He firmly and courteously refused 'for reasons purely domestic and personal to himself, with which it is quite unnecessary to trouble Your Majesty'.[3]

He was continuously at Hawarden from 10 August to 18 September, the late-summer sea-bathing urge seeming for once to have deserted him. Then he went on a three-week Scottish tour, which with neither Balmoral nor speeches was singularly free of political duty. His last Highland port of call, after six days with the Liberal Marjoribanks (later Tweedmouth) at Guisachan, was at Strathcarron, an Easter Ross property of the then only twenty-four-year-old Arthur Balfour, by whom Gladstone was temporarily enchanted. 'I really delight in him, no more and no less,' he informed his wife. After six days he reluctantly returned to London for a Cabinet requested by Granville on commercial relations with the French Republican government which had somewhat tentatively followed the fall of Napoleon III. A constant feature of Gladstone's country-house visits was that he never suffered from travel fever and prolonged his recreation well into the day of departure and indeed up to the moment of the train leaving. Long and often roundabout walks to the stations were his habit. On this occasion he rather overdid it. He had gone on an expedition with his host which involved crossing a little loch to get to the station of Achanalt. Balfour recorded fifty-eight years later that the wind was so strong and the boatman so old that as they approached the bank 'I saw our train approaching with ill-timed punctuality.' A combination of wading ashore and waving to the engine-driver enabled the train to be caught. 'As the train ran slowly out of the station,' he continued, 'I saw with intense thankfulness a pair of wet socks hanging out of the window to dry.'[4] Gladstone's account is remarkably compatible. His diary entry was a shade stately: 'The lake nearly caused my missing the train but by effort we gained it.'[5] To his wife he was more detailed and confirmatory of Balfour: 'I took off my feet (the Scotch say change your feet) when I got into the train and effected a partial and considerable drying by dancing my socks in the air and putting my shoes in the sun.'[6]

He then noted that he had 'a journey of 650 miles without break. . . . the Highland line very fine from Aviemore to Dunkeld'. He added that 'Bruce got in at Granton & we discussed various things.'[7] This conveys a vivid picture of both the efficiency and the intimacy of Victorian railway travel. It was remarkable that, less than forty years after Peel took nearly a month to get from Rome to London, his political heir should be able to wade in a remote North of Scotland loch one morning and preside over a Cabinet at 2.00 the next afternoon. And it was in a different way equally remarkable that the Prime Minister, travelling alone, should not be particularly surprised when the Home Secretary casually joined him at another wayside station. Bruce wrote to his wife: 'He [Gladstone] was very friendly and communicative, and I saw more of him than I ever did before.'[8] It is curiously easy to imagine these two Victorian statesmen, soberly rather than glossily clad (although Gladstone had presumably regained his socks and shoes by then), sitting opposite each other in the buttoned upholstery of corner seats and engaged in earnest conversation as the train meandered through Scotland before gaining momentum in England. To avoid early-railway romanticism, however, it is necessary to note that Gladstone recorded it as being '1¼ h. late' at Euston. Even more remarkable was the Highland cavorting of a sixty-three-year-old moralizing Liberal leader with a twenty-four-year-old future Conservative Prime Minister who came to be the epitome of elegant realism and deflating wit.

Once in London Gladstone used the opportunity to hold not one but three long Cabinets (sitting in aggregate for fourteen hours), to dine with Mrs Thistlethwayte ('stayed late X') on the first night, as well as on the third, and to see many other people before returning to Hawarden for another unbroken month on 18 October.

Then in mid-November he paid his first visit to Oxford since his defeat as member for the University in 1865 and stayed a couple of nights with Warden Talbot and his Lyttelton wife in the newly erected multichrome splendour which Butterfield had just provided for Keble College. There followed a month in London, interspersed with two short weekends at Sandringham (the Prince of Wales) and Hatfield (Salisbury – 'there are no kinder hosts than here')[9] and a 'dine and sleep' at Windsor, which he approached very much as a duty and not a pleasure. During the month he held no fewer than ten Cabinets, supplemented by another six early in the new year of 1873 between 22 January and the opening of the parliamentary session on 6 February. In the meantime there had been another six weeks of Hawarden calm, save only for a forty-eight-hour expedition to his brother Robertson, then alone and declining towards his 1875 death. William Gladstone combined this with a controversial philosophical–theological address to Liverpool College. He thus had over a hundred nights at Hawarden – more than in any year since his asylum from politics in 1857–8 – and another thirty-two at other destinations away from London during that long recess.

Paradoxically, the number of recess Cabinets was also a record. They were mainly concerned with preparations for the new session, and as time went on they became increasingly concentrated on the Irish University Bill. The Prime Minister's own mind was overwhelmingly so directed. He regarded the reform and expansion of university education in Ireland as an essential third leg to the programme of pacification to which he had already contributed Church disestablishment and the Land Bill. And the Queen's destruction of his plan to overarch the three by employing the Prince of Wales to give Ireland a new status in relation to the Crown made him the more anxious to complete the tripod. Furthermore, his tastes, his interests and his experience made him only too anxious to engage obsessively with the issue, bristling with difficulties and with a history strewn with failure though it was. He made himself a great theoretical expert on the subject. He read voluminously around it, thus occupying many hours of his Hawarden autumn. The result was that his 13 February speech introducing the bill, for all that it lasted three hours, was the most fascinating and ingenious lecture, showing an amazing command over the facts of the history of higher education in Ireland and an equally impressive ability to construct his own theory out of them. He delivered a disquisition on the nominal suzerainty of the ancient but shadowy University of Dublin over its sole constituent college, Trinity, which he described as 'perhaps the wealthiest college ... in Christendom', far superior in that respect to his own humble *alma mater* of Christ Church. He was equally compelling and original on the paucity of modern non-vocational university training in Ireland: a total of only 784 arts students, he managed to demonstrate, of whom no more than an eighth came from the Roman Catholic three-quarters of the population. This compared with a Scottish figure of 4000 arts students, in a country with barely a half of the Irish population.

The whole speech is a wonderful example of Gladstone's expository style, compelling, daring (there are a lot of attacks on venerable institutions and practices), with the figures never boring because, if not exactly made up for the purpose, they are selectively presented so as at once to surprise the listener and to carry him along with the argument. They are manifestly all his own work. No official would ever have contrived to present them so tendentiously.* Despite the sonorousness the pace is fast, and there is always a tension about what he is going to say next. The 20,000-word speech is easy and rewarding to read today, and goes far to explain how a full House of Commons, whether in agreement or disagreement, could listen to him over such broad acres of time.

Unfortunately, however, while Gladstone's scheme was an elegantly constructed castle in the air, and while his speech advocating it was magnificent, the bill suffered from one fatal flaw, which was that no one except himself really wanted it. This applied to his Cabinet, which was the reason that he had to have so many meetings to get it through, and it applied particularly to the most departmentally concerned member of it. Hartington, having gone reluctantly to Ireland at the end of 1870, became enough engaged with its problems that he was offended when Gladstone in the summer of 1873, with that maladroitness which frequently afflicted their relations, responded to a false rumour that Hartington wanted a change by offering him a return to his old position as Postmaster-General.

Hartington was sceptical about the form of the University Bill, but even more did he believe that there were two other measures of Irish reform which should be given priority over it. The first was public ownership of the railways and the second was local government reorganization. The object of the latter was to get away from the haphazard rule, at once inefficient and undemocratic, of Dublin Castle. The Castle was not corrupt but it was remote and relied on favourites who were almost by definition unrepresentative 'Castle Catholics', the Irish equivalent of Uncle Toms. And beneath it there was only the archaic structure

* Eight and a half years later Edward Hamilton, one of his most devoted private secretaries and later joint permanent secretary of the Treasury, after listening to him before the Leeds Chamber of Commerce, wrote in admiration of 'the unrivalled style in which he manipulates figures and dresses them up in a wholly new light'. (Bahlmann (ed.), *The Diary of Sir Edward Walter Hamilton 1880–1885*, I, p. 174.)

of grand juries. Hartington could not much interest Gladstone in either issue. The Prime Minister's mind was all on raising the number of students of the humanities in Ireland from 784 to perhaps 1500, or at most 2000. It was, to say the least, a disproportionate concentration of attention.

Furthermore, in order to give his higher education scheme even a chance of success he had to hobble the very meaning of the word 'university' and limit the studies of those arts undergraduates to an extent which meant that they might almost as well have been studying dentistry or one of the other vocational courses about which he was so disparaging. The saddest passage in his otherwise magnificent speech was that in which he described the restrictions which would have to be placed upon the university:

> It can have no chair in theology; and we have arrived at the conclusion that the most safe and prudent course we can adopt is to preclude the university from the establishment of chairs in two other subjects, which, however important in themselves in an educational point of view, would be likely to give rise to hopeless contention. . . . The two subjects to which I refer are philosophy and modern history. [Laughter.][10]

It was curious that he should have got himself impaled, from the other direction as it were, upon the same stakes which had speared Newman in his Dublin lectures twenty years before. In one of the uneasiest passages in *The Idea of a University* Newman endeavours to reconcile his view that 'the very name of University is inconsistent with restrictions [on the range of its teachings] of any kind' with his reluctant acceptance of the Pope's view that the university he had been asked to set up in Dublin must be a purely Catholic one. Newman tied himself in knots to try to resolve this contradiction, yet Gladstone, who was always very well up in Newmaniana, seemed to have learnt little from it. He exposed himself to the derision contained in that bracketed 'Laughter', yet failed to win over the Irish hierarchy. Cardinal Cullen was a very hardline Archbishop of Dublin, whose mission was to impose the will of Rome upon the Irish Catholic Church, which on his appointment in 1852 he had found almost as Gallican as the French Church of those days. The Irish Church obviously did not have the prestige of being the 'eldest daughter', but it had the alternative advantage of remoteness coupled with devout adherents.

Cullen and his bishops, contrary to the hopes and expectations of Manning, on whom, in spite of his ultramontane excesses at the Vatican

Council, Gladstone still depended too much, killed the bill. They wanted no system of education which mingled the religious and the secular power. But Gladstone had already made too many concessions to them for the bill to arouse any advanced Liberal enthusiasm. And the vested interests, in the shape primarily of Trinity, which he proposed to federate with Maynooth, Magee (a Presbyterian) College and two of the three existing Queen's Colleges, were obviously opposed. So was the third Queen's College at Galway, which he proposed to wind up on the ground that its main product were lawyers trained at too high a public cost. The bill therefore had plenty of enemies and hardly more than one friend, although powerful and dedicated in his solitariness.

The bill perished soon after 2.00 a.m. on the night of 11–12 March. Gladstone had moved the second reading in another long expository speech on the 3rd, and then, after four nights of debate, wound up immediately before the fatal division. As he described it to the Queen, 'Mr Disraeli rose at half past ten, and spoke amidst wrapt attention until midnight [despite deep underlying disapproval Gladstone was nearly always much more gracious about Disraeli's speeches than vice versa]. Mr Gladstone followed in a speech of two hours.'[11] The bill was then defeated by 287 votes to 284. The margin was narrow, but as this was in a House with a normal Liberal majority (even after a few bye-election losses) of eighty-five, and as Gladstone had described the bill as 'vital to the honour and existence of the government', the effect was nonetheless shattering.

Gladstone's winding-up speech won more praise than votes. Speaker Brand described it as 'a magnificent speech, generous, high-minded, and without a taint of bitterness, although he was sorely tried, especially by false friends'.[12] But its effect was less than that of the sullenly hostile pastoral letter which Cardinal Cullen caused to be read in all the Catholic churches of Ireland two days before the vote. It was the defection of Irish members which provided the seismic shift against the bill, and it was the prospect of this opened up by Cullen's broadside which encouraged Disraeli to alert his whips, sharpen his words and thus provide a solid Conservative vote. Only this could make the shift decisive. Morley was both neat and justified in writing that 'the measure that had been much reviled as a dark concordat between Mr. Gladstone and the pope, was now rejected by a concordat between the pope's men and Mr. Disraeli'.[13]

Forty-three Liberals voted against the bill, but only eight of them were English or Scottish members. The other thirty-five were from

Ireland, twenty-five of them Catholics. On an alternative basis of classification, the unsuccessful 'aye' lobby was made up of 222 English members, 47 Scottish and only 15 Irish. The 'no' lobby contained 209 English, 10 Scottish and no less than 68 Irish members. This was the reverse of the pattern which was subsequently to become a feature of all measures of Irish reform over the thirty years when Gladstone and then Asquith tried to carry Home Rule in time to prevent the rise of Sinn Fein republicanism and the move to complete separation. In 1886, 1893 and 1912 (as in the subsequent re-runs of 1913 and 1914 made necessary by the Parliament Act) there was never an English majority for a Home Rule Bill. The majority, when it existed, was provided by an overwhelming preponderance of Irish members and strong support from the Scots, this last feature being the only one which was present in 1873.

Despite more widespread unease on his own benches, Gladstone would have got his second reading, and maybe sustained the whole bill more or less intact, had it not been for Cullen and his supporting bishops. He was probably justified when he wrote bitterly to Manning on 13 March: 'Your Irish Brethren have received in the late vote of Parliament the most extravagant compliment ever paid them. They have destroyed the measure; which otherwise was safe enough.'[14]

Until a late stage Gladstone was unaware of the danger. 'No apprehension is at present entertained,' he wrote to the Queen on 5 March. Four days later he had changed his mind and when the defeat occurred he recorded that it 'was believed to cause more surprise to the opposite side than it did to me'. He then acted with all deliberate speed. He adjourned the House of Commons for thirty-six hours and promised them a statement of the government's intentions at the end of that interval. He caused the Queen to be immediately informed, despite it then being 2.45 a.m. And he summoned the Cabinet for 1.00 p.m. on what had become the same day. There was a complication because, although contrary to his frequent practice he does not record himself as being ill, he was engaged in intensive medical consultation. He wrote to his doctor – Andrew Clark – on the day which concluded with his winding-up speech and the great defeat; he went to see him at 11.30 on the following morning immediately before visiting the Queen, and did so again on the morning after that, which was the day when he formally tendered his resignation. For the last occasion he recorded that Clark 'completed his examination and gave me his careful judgement'.[15] Twenty-one years later he reminiscently but obscurely wrote that 'Clark . . . would give me on medical grounds no encouragement whatsoever.'[16]

Gladstone's complaint appears to have been general exhaustion, from which he suffered during the remainder of the session of 1873 and indeed through to the end of the government, rather than anything more specific and immediately menacing. He nonetheless obviously gave a high priority to his visits to Clark, which added to the commitments of a peculiarly burdensome week. It may also have turned his mind towards resignation rather than dissolution. These were the alternatives (as opposed to ignoring the defeat, revising the bill or going for a vote of confidence) to which the Cabinet quickly narrowed their options. Resignation would give him the 'temporary rest', about the need for which he recorded himself as 'strongly advised'. Dissolution would do the reverse. It also offered little prospect of a Liberal victory.

The Cabinet being satisfactorily amenable – Gladstone had written a few days before of it as being 'most harmonious, at this critical time' – resignation was the course determined upon, and he formally presented it to the Queen thirty-six hours after the defeat. An hour and a half later he announced it to the House of Commons. Disraeli then proceeded to throw his spanner into the works. The deadlock was complete, and Gladstone was furious, as he often was, with Disraeli's manoeuvres. The latter's motive was of course tactical. Although the Conservatives had gained thirteen by-election seats from the Liberals in the previous two years, Disraeli did not believe that the prospect for a decisive Conservative victory was yet secure. And the Parliament, under the Septennial Act, still had a possible two years and ten months of life. Gladstone insisted that when the opposition deliberately set out to inflict a major defeat on a government, as it had done with its heavy whipping for 11 March, there was a special obligation on it to provide an alternative.

The only person who might have resolved the impasse in the way Gladstone wanted was the Queen. But she chose not to do so. This was perhaps her first act of gross favouritism towards Disraeli. Undoubtedly by that stage she would have welcomed a change of government, and she might have been right from a national point of view. The Liberal administration was running down, as all its principal members had the sense and the public spirit to see. March 1873 would have been the right time for a change. But if Disraeli counselled otherwise she accepted his judgement, in a way that she would not have done without protest with Gladstone. And she accepted the price, which was that she had to soldier on for another eleven months (it could have been longer) with an unloved Prime Minister.

Late on the Sunday evening, 16 March, she requested Gladstone to resume his office. He was staying with a large party at Cliveden, where he had not been since the death of his old friend the Duchess of Sutherland in 1868 and the consequent change of generation in the house. It was another remarkable example of his reluctance ever to put off a visit and his liking for country-house gatherings, the pleasures of which, however, hardly diminished the flow of his writing and reading. Already during that day he had compiled a memorandum on the whole course of the crisis before sitting down at 10.45 p.m. to write a substantial response to the Queen's request. The note was one of resigned acquiescence. He would 'repair to London' the following morning, would see 'some of the most experienced members of the late Government', and would endeavour to prevail upon them to join with him in picking up the unwanted burden. But the position had been sufficiently 'unhinged' that he doubted whether the government or the Parliament 'can again be what they were'.[17]

These commitments he faithfully discharged, but with no great sense of urgency and still less of zest. It was 10.15 the next morning before his 'adieu to our *most* kind hosts' (Gladstone's hosts were almost invariably given a high accolade) and it must therefore have been nearly noon before he started on his consultations, beginning with Granville. The reluctance to do any effective business in the morning was a persistent feature of mid-Victorian political life. However, the results of the consultations were unenthusiastically positive and at a Cabinet on the following day the formal decision to resume office and to try to keep the Parliament going into 1874 was taken. Gladstone did not get the rest which he and Dr Clark thought he needed, and while the new and unexhilarating goal of keeping the Parliament alive into the next year was narrowly achieved, these ten months in which borrowed time was thrust upon the government brought little advantage to the Liberal party or the country. Gladstone, his judgement maybe impaired by exhaustion, made a whole series of mistakes, most in themselves small but leading to a cumulative impression of a government in decay. And one of those mistakes, which was himself to take over the Exchequer in August 1873, was both crassly foolish for a Prime Minister at the limit of his reserves and singularly unfortunate for the direction in which it set the government's programme for the 1874 general election.

—— 22 ——

Defeat and Retirement

Gladstone's small but damaging mistakes began in the year before the defeat of March 1873. In the late winter of 1872 he had been arraigned before the House of Commons for two displays of arrogant corner-cutting. In the first case he wished to appoint Sir Robert Collier to a vacancy on the Judicial Committee of the Privy Council. Collier, who later became Lord Monkswell and founded an interesting dynasty, was a fine lawyer, whose personal qualifications were never challenged. Nor was there anything unusual about propelling the Law Officers into high judicial office. Indeed, when a few years later the Chief Justice of the Common Pleas was transformed into the Lord Chief Justice of England the office became known as the 'Attorney-General's pillow', so frequently did political Law Officers go direct to that position. But there was a specific provision that a judicial appointment to the Privy Council had to have served as a High Court judge in either England or India. Scotland or Ireland would not do.

Gladstone solved the problem by appointing Collier to the puisne bench for a two-day spell. It was efficacious but arrogant, and was resented by the judicial bench, whose members protested strongly through Chief Justice Cockburn. Motions of criticism were pressed in both Houses. In the Commons Gladstone had a majority of twenty-seven, not glorious for a government with a nominal majority of nearly a hundred, and in the Lords, which mattered less, one of two. Collier was embarrassed and Gladstone had used up credit. It was a maladroit affair.

The second imbroglio was even less necessary. The village of Ewelme, near Wallingford, had and has a peculiar connection with the University of Oxford. Today it provides a grace-and-favour residence for the Regius Professor of Medicine. Until 1871 the rectorship of the parish had been a subsidiary benefice for one of the University's professors of divinity. As a compensation for the severance of that link, which followed from the semi-secularization of the University, it was provided that the rector of Ewelme, while no longer a professor of divinity, must continue to be an Oxford MA. This could hardly be regarded as an onerous restriction upon Gladstone. In general he was loath to accept the appropriateness of anyone who was not a graduate of one of the two old universities as suitable for Anglican orders, and within this category he often had difficulty in keeping to the unwritten rule that an Oxonian bishop should next time be balanced by a Cantabrigian one.

This made his handling of the Ewelme issue bizarre to the point of inexplicability. First he offered the living to W. E. Jelf of Christ Church, a Tory and an Evangelical, which meant that it was doubly broad-minded on Gladstone's part. Unfortunately Jelf declined and Gladstone then became fixed on W. W. Harvey, another Tory, a scholar of moderate note and a fellow of King's College, Cambridge. The only thing that he and Gladstone had in common was that they had been Eton contemporaries in the 1820s. It was perverse, to say the least, to choose a Cambridge man for this not particularly rewarding but Oxford-restricted appointment. And it was at once provocative and disdainful to believe that, having done so, he could obviate the problem by the method which he chose. He prevailed upon Oriel College to accept Harvey as a member and, after the statutory forty-two days, to get him admitted to 'M. A. status' and hence to Convocation. It was a curiously similar device to that which he had used with Collier, and it produced a not dissimilar reaction. There was no vote on this occasion, but he had a very rough debate only two and a half weeks after the Collier one.

Both these incidents were widely regarded as showing that exhaustion combined with an imperious nature were leading Gladstone away from judgement and proportion towards a petulant authoritarianism. They damaged him both inside and outside the government. The next incident was hardly Gladstone's fault, except insofar as it conveyed an impression, half justified, of remoteness from those aspects of the business of his own government with which he was not obsessively absorbed. He was very much an 'all or nothing' man. In the instance of the 'scandals', as he came himself rather damningly to call them, he reacted with a determined heavy-handedness, but allowed an unforeseen consequence of his solution of the problem to lead him into what was almost a new version of Collier or Ewelme.

The 'scandals' were the misallocation (but not misappropriation) of public money to the telegraph service* which touched the Chancellor of the Exchequer (Lowe), two other ministers, the Postmaster-General

* See p. 315, above.

and the First Commissioner of Works, who were not at the time in the Cabinet but whose predecessors and successors quite often were so included, and two others in the Treasury, one political and one official. The matter began to break in early July 1873. As the facts emerged, Gladstone took the view that all concerned must cease to hold their current posts. He did not, however, feel that they should incur the full penalty of exclusion from office. In the case of Lowe this was right, for his responsibility was remote and Gladstone admired him as a notable if difficult man, while having reservations about his performance as Chancellor.

In the case of Monsell, the Postmaster-General, the fault was more direct, and he did leave the government, although compensated with a peerage in the following year's honours. Ayrton, the First Commissioner of Works, appeared to be the most to blame and compounded his fault on 30 July by attempting such an exculpatory and limited definition of ministerial responsibility in the House of Commons that Gladstone felt it necessary to get up after him and disavow what he had said. It must have been one of the most devastating of public Prime Ministerial rebukes. Nonetheless Gladstone thought that Ayrton ought to be given a compensating office. It was another example of his addiction to some private scale which mingled hierarchy and justice and often caused him considerable inconvenience. This was certainly so here, for the post which Gladstone was determined to offer Ayrton was that of Judge Advocate-General, which normally involved presenting the result of courts martial personally to the Queen; and the Queen, while in general sympathetic to Gladstone over these troubles, was determined never to have to see Ayrton. After several letters and telegrams it was agreed that Ayrton should have the job with the humiliating condition that all his communications must be made in writing.

There were wider ministerial repercussions. A new senior office had to be found for Lowe and a new Chancellor as his replacement. Furthermore Ripon was anxious to resign as Lord President, partly because he was on the brink of a sharp transition from being Grand Master of the Freemasons of England to admission into the Roman Catholic Church. This half eased and half complicated the position. Eventually Gladstone settled Lowe by ennobling Bruce as Lord Aberdare, transferring him to the Lord Presidency of the Council, and thus vacating the Home Office. For Chancellor there were several possible candidates, but Gladstone felt under heavy pressure to take the job himself, and the conventional wisdom is that he was forced into it by his

Cabinet colleagues. But by which of them? There is a singular lack of documentary support and the impression persists that he was more tempted than coerced. In any event he received for the fifth time the Chancellor's seals of office on 9 August, and within forty-eight hours descended on the probably disappointed Cardwell – for he was one of the candidates – at the War Office and disclosed to him a fiscal strategy which must have been germinating in the Prime Minister's mind well before he was 'drafted' to the Exchequer: 'I told [him] in deep secrecy my ideas on the *possible* finance of next year, based upon abolition of Income Tax & Sugar Duties with partial compensation from Spirits and Death duties. This only might give us a chance.'[1]

The last sentence presumably referred to electoral prospects, although the dominating impression conveyed is not that of political opportunism but of eagerness to put his hands back upon the fiscal levers. The state of overstrain in which he approached the end of the session (prorogation took place on 5 August) should have made him more cautious. On 23, 26 and 27 July he was in bed for most of the time. On 6 August he wrote to the Queen: 'The labours of the last few days have been incessant and the peculiarly invidious character of those labours has not unnaturally increased the strain; but Mr Gladstone has been well-tended, and hopes to come through without breaking down. . . .'[2] It was not exactly the best foundation on which to add the heaviest department to a Prime Minister's normal burdens of co-ordination and leadership.

Gladstone's metabolism enabled him to move with bewildering rapidity from disturbingly frequent bouts of prostration to displays of almost manic energy. Within five days of his apprehensive letter to the Queen he was outlining his fiscal programme to Cardwell before leaving in the late evening for a 3.30 a.m. arrival at Hawarden. 'Off at 8.50,' he wrote, 'with a more buoyant spirit and greater sense of relief than I have experienced for many years on this which is the only pleasant act of moving to me in the circuit of the year. This gush is in proportion to the measure of the late troubles and anxieties.'[3]* A still more extreme

* These had embraced not only the purge of the government but the tragic and dramatic death of Bishop Wilberforce, with whom Gladstone's life had been closely intertwined for forty-five years. After a Cabinet on Saturday, 19 July, Gladstone had gone to Holmbury, near Dorking, to stay with Lord Edward Leveson-Gower. Granville and the 'great diocesan' (to give him at the end his more favourable sobriquet), were due to join them there. 'We were enjoying that beautiful spot,' Gladstone wrote, 'when the Groom arrived with a message that the Bp. had had a bad fall.' He had been riding up to the house from Leatherhead station with the Foreign Secretary. One and a half hours

example of his alternations was provided a couple of weeks later. As soon as he arrived at Balmoral he excused himself from dining with the Queen and took to his bed with a gastric attack. Within a week he did a day's walk of thirty-three miles over very rough Highland ground, which took him to what he kindly described as 'a good hotel at Kingussie', where, however, he was 'sorely disturbed with rats'.

There was a hidden hazard in Gladstone's taking over the Treasury which, had he apprehended it, might have made him hesitate more than did his mercurial attitude to his own health. This was the clear rule that MPs accepting ministerial office were held to have vacated their seats and had to seek re-election by their constituencies. The position about those adding one office to another was more complicated, although there were precedents associated with Lord North, Spencer Perceval and Canning which suggested that in these circumstances no re-election was necessary. But these were not strictly relevant, for the 1867 Representation of the People Act had redefined the rules. The intention was to make them less strict. But the outcome was an unsatisfactory ambiguity of language which had not since been tested, and which left plenty of room for argument about whether Gladstone, once he had taken the seals of the Exchequer, was entitled to sit as member for Greenwich. The point was not academic, for in the event of the seat being vacated the Conservatives would contest it, and the expectation was that Gladstone would lose.

Gladstone became aware of the problem on the day he took office, and a week later wrote to his old Whip Brand, who had succeeded as Speaker and in whose hands the matter would ultimately lie, saying that he was taking no resignation initiative but was seeking the best legal advice. Speaker Brand wrote back reserving his judgement but saying that he was sure Gladstone was right to take such advice. This might

---

later Granville arrived to say that Wilberforce was dead. After his notable quarter-century as Bishop of Oxford he had enjoyed the lusher pastures of Winchester, Gladstone's compensation to him for having missed York and Canterbury, for only three years. Both the loss and its circumstances were a heavy blow to the Prime Minister and a bad preparation for the next testing three weeks. But what an extraordinary vignette of Victorian life is provided by this confluence of events. The country's most eminent bishop (and episcopal eminence then counted for much more) had been killed on a Saturday evening riding up a country lane from a railway station with the Foreign Secretary to dine with the Prime Minister. Even late-twentieth-century Sunday newspapers might have felt compelled to give the tragedy priority over their pet scandal of the week.

have been helpful had the best legal advice not been hopelessly divided. Coleridge and Jessel, two of the most eminent lawyers ever to hold the posts, were respectively Attorney and Solicitor, and took the view that Gladstone was safe. But within a month Jessel became Master of the Rolls and two months after that Coleridge became Chief Justice (Gladstone not being in the least put off his preferment by the Collier case). In the meantime there had been an unhelpful intervention from Selborne, the Lord Chancellor, who took a contrary view and was supported in it by the Lord Advocate (whose *locus* in the matter was far from clear).

This kept the issue open so that the incoming English Law Officers had to be asked to endorse or contradict the opinion of their predecessors. They were Henry James and William Harcourt, whose jurisprudential distinction did not match that of Coleridge and Jessel, but who were both (particularly Harcourt) to achieve high political importance. On this early test, however, they showed little of either political acumen or legal decisiveness. After consulting Charles Bowen, then Junior Counsel to the Treasury,* and widely regarded as the most subtle and acute of nineteenth-century legal minds, they reported on 1 December that there were very strong arguments both for and against the view that the seat had been vacated. It might have been better had they had more of the spirit of Jessel, who is reputed to have said of himself: 'I may be wrong, and sometimes I am; but I have never any doubts.'

The issue hung over Gladstone throughout the autumn of 1873. It was not currently critical, for with Parliament in recess there was no question of his incurring penalties by sitting illegally. With the opening of the new session in February 1874 it would, however, become so. On 18 January Gladstone wrote: 'On this day I thought of dissolution. Told Bright of it. In evening at dinner told Granville and Wolverton [formerly Chief Whip Glyn]. All seemed to approve. My first thought of it was as an escape from a difficulty. I soon saw on reflection that it was the best thing in itself.'[4] Then, ironically, he received on the 20th, when he was once again bed-bound, a memorandum from Sir Erskine May, the most famous of all clerks of the House of Commons, which would no doubt have been decisive with the Speaker, opining firmly that the Greenwich seat was not vacant.

* Two years later Bowen became Asquith's pupil master. It is perhaps worth noting that when in the spring of 1914, following the Curragh 'mutiny', Asquith as Prime Minister took over the War Office, he assumed his exclusion from the House of Commons until he had been to East Fife for re-election.

The problem had been a running sore over the last five months of the Parliament's life, increasing the sense of a government whose time was exhausted, and it was an important factor in determining the date of a disastrous general election. But there is no evidence that the Liberals would have done better at any other practicable date. A bigger influence on the shape and result of the campaign was the unfortunate budgetary strategy which Gladstone formulated.

J. L. Hammond, as we have seen, was the foremost proponent of the view that the Treasury spirit was Gladstone's poison. Set him free from it and he became an imaginative statesman, upholding the Concert of Europe and international arbitration, sensitive to the agrarian as well as to the political wrongs of Ireland, even capable of measures of constructive reform at home. Imprison him in its toils, and he became a penny-pinching miser, elevating the reduction or abolition of particular taxes to the status of an ultimate achievement, and willing to trample on all sorts of other desiderata on the way.

Gladstone believed that the bold fiscal scheme which he had outlined to Cardwell, particularly as he had resolved to supplement it by a considerable remission of local property taxation, would have at least three advantages. First, as a dashing and outflanking manoeuvre, it would enable the government to seize the political initiative, which it had manifestly lost, at least since the defeat of the Irish University Bill, and dictate the agenda on which the general election, whether it came before or after the budget, would be fought. Here he ought to have remembered that such manoeuvres, as in 1867, were more in Disraeli's style than in his own. Second, he hoped that it would reconcile to the government the non-political men of moderate property, the ordinary run of the middle classes who cared more about the solid comfort of their domestic lives than about political or social or even religious ideology. But this again was not Gladstonian. His natural appeal was moralizing rather than materialistic, and he had fulminated too often against the politics of the pork barrel for it to be sensible to rest on a short-term financial enticement to defeat a growing longer-term affinity of these groups with the suburban respectability flavoured by imperial excitement of the new Conservative party.

Third, Gladstone believed that the reproclamation of fiscal austerity and the minimalist state, which the abolition of the income tax would symbolize, was the best available formula for uniting the Liberal party. While there is room for argument about his judgement on the first two propositions there can be no doubt that on this third one he was profoundly mistaken. Joseph Chamberlain, for example, then only the Mayor of Birmingham, but soon to be one of that city's MPs and by the time of Gladstone's next government the leader of the Radical wing of the party, described (admittedly after the election had been lost) the election address in which Gladstone presented his proposals as 'the meanest public document that had ever, in like circumstances, proceeded from a statesman of the first rank. His manifesto was simply an appeal to the selfishness of the middle classes.'[5] Chamberlain was by no means alone. The *Economist* under Bagehot, and the *Bee Hive*, an important Radical journal in spite of its teashop-like title, were both vehemently opposed. An article in the latter complained that 'Mr Gladstone has sacrificed the lower classes, who worshipped him, to the richer classes, who disliked him.'[6]

Beyond the affront to the constructive Radicals, Gladstone's budgetary plans were also potentially disruptive within the Cabinet. Whatever else he was, Gladstone was not an irresponsible financier. He would not sacrifice a balanced budget even to get rid of the income tax. This meant that despite the £5 million surplus with which he started the year and the £2 million of new revenue which he proposed to raise from spirits and death duties, he needed at least another £600,000 to cover the abolition of the income tax, the remission of the sugar duties and some relief of local taxation. This money he saw as coming from a reduction in the service estimates, with the emphasis on the naval ones. This was strongly resisted by Goschen, the First Lord of the Admiralty, and also by Cardwell, the War Secretary. Neither of them had been extravagant ministers and had been steadily if marginally squeezed throughout the life of the government. They felt they could do no more and an unresolved Cabinet crisis was the background to Gladstone's 18 January decision to dissolve. The dissolution was as much against the Admiralty and the War Office as it was against the Tories.

The other objection to Gladstone's 1874 fiscal programme was that it was manifestly against the tide of history. When eight years before he had concluded his electoral reform oration with the ringing message (at least to those who understood it) of: '*Excoriare aliquis nostris ex ossibus ultor*. You cannot fight against the future. Time is on our side. The great social forces which move onwards in their might and majesty . . . are against you,' there was not only force but validity in what he said. But in 1874 he was in the reverse position. His fiscal programme failed to deflect the Conservative tide at the election. It was also manifestly the last shot of an old war rather than a harbinger of the future. From its reintroduction in 1842 to 1874 the abolition of the income tax had been a flickering flame of hope, never achieved and mainly kept alive by Gladstone himself fanning it away from extinction. After 1874 it ceased either to flicker or to be even a contingent hope. At that election it was a desperate ploy by a beleaguered government, and did not work. At no subsequent general election could it even have been thrown into the arena by any serious party.

Gladstone's decision to play this card, and to do so in the cause of Liberal unity, points both to his very imperfect knowledge of the party of which he had become the leader after only eight years of adherence, and to the extent to which 'the People's William' had gone into retreat during his first prime ministership. In contrast with his building up of his position against Palmerston by the force of his popular appearances and appeal, Gladstone effectively abandoned public meetings and speeches between 1868 and 1873. In a period of a little over five years he addressed only three popular audiences, and all these occasions were concentrated within eight weeks in the autumn of 1871. The first was in the small North Yorkshire fishing town of Whitby, where his eldest son was member. The second was at Aberdeen, when he received the freedom of the city on his way to Balmoral. And the third was to an enormous open-air assembly on Blackheath in his own constituency. It was effectively his only visit to Greenwich in the course of that Parliament. When the election came, however, he spoke there three times, once in Greenwich itself, once in Woolwich and once at New Cross. They were all open-air afternoon occasions, the Greenwich one in pouring rain, with audiences of between 5000 and 15,000. But he spoke nowhere else. There was no nationwide campaign, and the government went down to heavy defeat without deployment of its greatest battering-ram. That was in accordance with the habit of the time, and Disraeli spoke no more frequently or widely.

Gladstone's very different pattern in the run-up to 1880 was therefore to be the bigger shock. But it cast no shadow before it in 1874, and accompanied by his demagogic abstinence in 1868–73 meant that he had reverted to being a politician very much confined (as were most others) to Westminster, Whitehall, the Court and his favoured country houses. Greenwich was a thoroughly unfortunate constituency for him. It aroused neither his affection nor his interest. On the widely separated occasions when he went there it was only for an afternoon, and it gave him no additional angle of sight outside the metropolis. South Lancashire, even Oxford, which provided a special dimension to his life, had been better. Midlothian, when it came, was the best of the lot, although even there he was distinctly sparing in his visits.

His attitude to Greenwich, and still more his retreat from provincial speaking, made the end of his first government a period when he was more cut off from his natural reservoirs of support than at any time since 1859, maybe even since he first became Chancellor in 1853. And this, combined with his too enthusiastic embrace of Treasury negativism, helped to set him off on his chase for a Britain without income tax which proved as electorally ineffective as it was programmatically sterile for the Liberal party. Hammond may have exaggerated, but he got hold of a piece of essential truth when he saw that Gladstone, once he had become party leader, was much better away from the Exchequer.

The most interesting letter which Gladstone wrote during the campaign was to Lord Fermoy on 28 January. Fermoy, who appeared to have written one of those tiresomely tentative letters which combine a general inclination to support with a need for reassurance on a particular issue, was told: 'With respect to Home Rule I have not yet heard an authoritative or binding definition of the phrase, which appears to be used by different persons in different senses. Until the phrase comes to have a definite and certain meaning, I have not thought myself justified in referring to it. . . .'[7] The reply was a remarkable paving exercise for his 1886 conversion: nothing he wrote to Fermoy was inconsistent with the attitude he took twelve years later.

Whether Gladstone believed the election would be won is not certain. He wrote to Bright on 27 January that 'the feeling of our friends is excellent', which could be regarded as cheerfulness in the bunker. Michael Foot might have said it during the 1983 campaign. On the next day, however, after his first Greenwich expedition, he wrote: 'An enthusiastic meeting. But the general prospects are far from clear.' And a week later, when the results, with his own coming early, were beginning to trickle out, he was more disenchanted than usual with Greenwich and recognized the certainty of national defeat: 'The general prospect was first indifferent, then bad. My own election for Greenwich, after Boord the distiller, is more like a defeat than a victory, though it places me in Parliament again.'* Two days after that he concluded the

* Boord, then a thirty-five-year-old Tory gin-maker got first place with 6193 votes. Gladstone came next with 5968. The second Tory was 400 votes behind that, and the second Liberal another 300 votes short. It was easy to see why Gladstone did not feel triumphant.

tale of declining hopes with: 'The issue of the Elections is now irrevocably bad.'[8] It was by far the worst Whig–Liberal result since 1841.

What Gladstone greatly minded was not so much the loss of office as the sense of rejection. This was exacerbated by his persistent belief in the meretriciousness of Disraeli. On the whole he was clear-headed about the causes and consequences of the defeat. But the one raft of unreality to which he clung was the conviction that Disraeli's government would be quickly seen through. '... I am confident that the Conservative Party will never arrive at a stable superiority while Disraeli is at their head,' he wrote to the Lord Advocate at about that time.* He was somewhat self-exculpating, as is almost inevitable, about the reasons for defeat. 'We have been swept away, literally, by a torrent of beer and gin,' he wrote to Spencer, his Irish Viceroy. 'Next to this comes Education: that has denuded us on both sides for reasons dramatically opposite; with the Nonconformists, and with the Irish voters.'[9]

He had three competing preoccupations to prevent his brooding excessively on the ingratitude of the electors, although none of them, except perhaps for the last, provided him with much comfort. The first was the question of whether he would await defeat in Parliament before resigning or whether he would accept dismissal direct from the electorate. Precedent was in favour of the former course, although not overwhelmingly so. Disraeli had gone precipitately in 1868. But Gladstone was never much in favour of following Disraeli. 'The leaning of my mind is in favour of the old constitutional course,' he wrote on 9 February. The Queen leant otherwise. 'I had a letter from the Queen which seemed to me to be of scant kindness,'[10] he noted five days later. Its central message was clear. 'She thinks', so she wrote in the third person, 'that whatever advantages there may be in adhering to usage & precedent, that it is counterbalanced by the disadvantages of nearly 3 weeks delay, for the Country and the public Service.'

Furthermore Gladstone had perpetrated the insensitivity of not remembering that the meeting of Parliament would coincide with the

* The new government's life of over six years was as long a span as that achieved by any Prime Minister between the death of Liverpool and 1895. But it did not win a second general election, which feat was not to be performed by a Conservative until Salisbury (Disraeli's successor in the leadership of the Conservative party) was greatly aided by the disruptive effect on the Liberal party of Gladstone's final years. In a sense therefore Gladstone was formally correct, although wrong in spirit, in his dismissive 1874 judgement.

return of her second son the Duke of Edinburgh from his St Petersburg marriage to a daughter of the Tsar. 'The Fêtes etc' would make it physically impossible for the Queen to contemplate a change of government at the same time. 'People are apt to forget as she told Mr Gladstone the other day, that the Queen is a *woman* who has far more on her hands & far more to try mind & body than is good *for anyone* of her sex & age.'[11] Once she was off on this line she was potentially unstoppable, and on 20 February Gladstone wisely went to Windsor and resigned. 'H. M. very kind: the topics of conversation were of course rather limited,'[12] he ambiguously recorded. But she acknowledged his loyalty to the Crown, and offered him a peerage, which he emphatically did not want and the acceptance of which would have been much more in her interest than in his.*After 1874 there were to be three Prime Ministers in the House of Lords, but it was not a forum which would have suited Gladstone. As Lord (or even Earl of) Hawarden he would have been hobbled.

The second preoccupation arose from his conviction that, out of office, he must give up 11 Carlton House Terrace. As was so often the case with Gladstone, it was the reverse of the normal pattern. Most Prime Ministers, if they do not already have one, acquire a London house when they are deprived of 10 Downing Street. Gladstone never greatly used the official residence, extravagantly kept up his 'Carltons' base (in which highly patrician quarter he had lived for thirty-five years) when he did not much need it, and then decided, when he did need it, that it had become far beyond his means. His means were indeed heavily diminished, partly because of over-investment in building up the Hawarden estate for his descendants, partly because of the mismanagement of his Seaforth property by his brother Robertson, and partly because, like all sound curators of the public finances from Pitt through Asquith to Baldwin and Neville Chamberlain, he had no golden fingers for the conduct of his own affairs.

A few months later he worked out with pessimistic precision his financial position. It showed that the affluence of the previous twenty years, since the recovery from the Oak Farm débâcle, had been allowed almost completely to dissipate itself. While admitting that he was still rich in mostly unrealizable assets he arrived at a depressing income

* There is no record that at this stage she suggested an earldom, which in spite of the Russell precedent and the shortly-to-follow Disraeli example was then much less part of the automatic Prime Ministerial rations than became the twentieth-century habit, from Balfour to Eden, until life peerages somewhat queered the pitch.

position following the loss of his £5000 official salary, 'which supplied the greater part of my expenditure'. His total income for the future he estimated at £6050, of which the Flintshire estates provided £4900. But against this had to be set debt interest amounting to £2250. Then he put 'necessary allowances' for his wife and five children (two were presumably excluded because marriage settlements had been made) at the modest sum of £1530. He next subtracted £670 as the minimum amount which he could give to 'Charity and Religion' and £600 for keeping up the house and policies at Hawarden, which led to a residue 'for all general expenditure whatsoever, in which is included everything relating to myself' of £1000. He could increase this to £2500 by letting Carlton House Terrace for the season, and he did indeed proceed to do this in 1874, but to do it regularly 'would be like publicly advertising need'. On the other hand, if he sold the house and its furniture and at least part of his collections of porcelain and paintings, he estimated that he would realize £50,000 (or approximately £2½ million at today's values). His estimate was close, for he did in fact raise £48,000 by various sales over the following couple of years. This would enable him to put his income back to over £6000, which would be perfectly tolerable, although he would have to provide for some sort of London residence out of it.

This more or less forced change of circumstance became intertwined in his mind with the third preoccupation, which was his desire to give up the leadership of the Liberal party and to withdraw into being (more or less) a private member of Parliament. They were both part of the 'winding out of the coil', as he obscurely but dramatically put it. Catherine Gladstone was not initially enthusiastic about either, but she came to see the need for the change of house more quickly than the desirability of withdrawal from the leadership. 'Conversation with C. G. on the probable changes in our position and consequent measures,' Gladstone wrote for 7 February; 'at first she was startled.'[13] Then a month later he recorded: 'Conversation with C. on the situation: she is sadly reluctant to my receding into the shade.'[14] His own reasoning was cogently summed up in a memorandum which he wrote, only it appears as a mind-clearing exercise for himself, on Saturday, 7 March. That day he breakfasted at Grillion's, the political dining club, which also then assembled for Saturday breakfasts, a double indication of how different official London patterns still were in 1874 from those of this century. He read part of Disraeli's early novel *Vivian Grey*, which when he had finished it he categorized as 'the first quarter extremely clever, the rest trash'. He saw and discussed the question of the leadership with a mystifyingly diverse (and mostly irrelevant) collection of people. And he wrote the following sketch:

> (1) To engage now, is to engage for the term of Opposition, & the succeeding term of a Liberal Government. . . .
>
> This is not consistent with my views for the close of my life.
>
> (2) Failure of 1866–8 [that is, his realistic appraisal of his lack of success as either leader of the House of Commons in a government of which he was not Prime Minister or as leader of the opposition].
>
> (3) My views on the question of Education in particular are I fear irreconcilable with those of a considerable proportion of [the Liberal party].
>
> (4) In no case has the head of a Govt. considerable in character & duration, on receiving what may be called an emphatic dismissal, become Leader of Opposition.
>
> (5) The condition of the Liberal party requires consideration.
>
> a. It has no present public *cause* upon which it is agreed.
>
> b. It has serious & conscientious divisions of opinion, which are also pressing, e.g. on Education.
>
> c. The habit of making a career by & upon constant active opposition to the bulk of the party, & its leaders, has acquired a dangerous predominance among a portion of its members. This habit is not checked by the action of the great majority, who do not indulge or approve it: & it has become dangerous to the credit & efficiency of the party.[15]

Upon the basis of these thoughts, reinforced by one additional issue separating him from the bulk of the Liberal party which came to the fore in the summer of 1874, Gladstone shaped and maintained his determination to disengage. His colleagues resisted. It would have been insulting had they not done so. But their dismay was more than formal, although not perhaps as strong as that of the Liberal adherents in the country. It was, however, nearly another year before he could get the shadow Cabinet to accept his resolve and settle upon Hartington as the replacement leader. Gladstone was therefore nominally still leader throughout the session of 1874 and up to the threshold of that of 1875. Nevertheless his effective disengagement began at Easter 1874.

He performed his routine duties at the opening of the session and spoke twice. 'I am tempted to say, I wish it were the last,' he wrote of his first speech in the new Parliament. Then on Good Friday, 3 April, he 'wound up [Carlton House Terrace] with a good deal of labour:* and closed my door, perhaps hardly now mine, behind me.' He left for

* Apart from anything else, there were 3500 books to deal with.

Hawarden that afternoon and in the remaining nine months of that year spent only thirty-nine nights in London, most of them staying with the Frederick Cavendishes in 21 Carlton House Terrace, a familiar neighbourhood. Until midsummer he was largely at Hawarden. Then Stephen Glynne died suddenly in London (he had been searching for antiquities in Shoreditch High Street). There was a great local funeral at which the estate and the neighbours said farewell to the last Glynne to preside over Hawarden. The nominal ownership passed at once to Willy Gladstone, but that was more a fiction than a fact. He was to predecease his parents, and from 1874 until their deaths around a quarter of a century later, William and Catherine Gladstone were the undisputed squire and chatelaine of Hawarden. Their second son, Stephen, whose own son was eventually to become the third-generation Gladstone heir and the route by which the property has since descended, was already rector of the parish.

Although Glynne's death bound the Gladstones even more closely to Hawarden in the medium run, it made the 'dear place too *sore*' for Catherine Gladstone in the short run, and they were not there much between the funeral and the autumn. In the final month of the session, despite it being a record-breakingly hot July, Gladstone engaged for the first time with the new House of Commons. Two out of three of the subjects on which he chose to do so were divisive rather than unifying within the Liberal party, and even on the third his motives were not those of the mass of his followers. The first was the Scottish Patronage Bill, on which he 'spoke (long)' on 6 July. The issue of how ministers of the Presbyterian Church of Scotland should be appointed was, to say the least, a remote one to call forth the first speech for nearly four months of the leader of the opposition. The second was the Public Worship Bill, an anti-ritualist measure, which Archbishop Tait had promoted in the Lords and which came to the Commons, with Disraeli's rather ill-informed support, only at the end of the session. Gladstone intervened, as Robert Blake put it, 'like a thunder clap and moved six portentous resolutions'[16] outlining the proper liturgical position of the Church of England but designed primarily to undermine the Archbishop's bill, which, discreditably popular though it was with the Queen, the Prime Minister and the majority of both Houses, was later widely agreed to have been foolish and divisive for the Church.

Divisive within political parties it certainly also was. Disraeli, who would have been wise to have kept a decent silence on Anglican disputes, denounced ritualism as 'mass in masquerade' and quarrelled on this issue with Salisbury, his Indian Secretary, whom he also denounced as 'a great master of flouts and jeers'. Gladstone, whose primary feeling was against the Church and its liturgy being made a parliamentary football, went so far as to warn both Archbishops that if they persisted in supporting a particular amendment (against which Gladstone spoke on 5 August) he would regard himself as 'altogether discharged from maintaining any longer the establishment of the Church'. This was not as extreme a lurch as it might at first sight have appeared, for Gladstone, at least since the Gorham judgement of 1851, had been distinctly conditional in his attitude to establishment. It was Erastianism, the subordination of Church to state, to which he was most opposed, and he regarded these debates as being a very bad example of parliamentary interference in matters with which legislators had no business. However, the most extreme Erastians were to be found among his Whig colleagues. Sir William Harcourt, whom he had recently made Solicitor-General and who was to be first Home Secretary and then Chancellor of the Exchequer in subsequent Gladstone governments, was insolently so. He liked to refer to what was to Gladstone the divine vehicle of apostolic religion as 'the parliamentary church'. Sir Andrew Lusk, Liberal MP for Finsbury, went even further in saying that it was 'a department of the state for the management of which the House is responsible'.[17] When this sentiment on the opposition benches was joined to the opportunist populism of Disraeli's support for the bill, Gladstone was in a hopeless minority and had eventually to withdraw his resolutions. However, he got considerable satisfaction out of his rebuke of the rumbustious Harcourt on 5 August: 'it had become needful'. Needful it may have been, but it was hardly a contribution to rallying the Liberal party.

On the third issue, Disraeli's Endowed Schools Bill, which was designed to redress the balance of the 1871 settlement, Gladstone's opposition was in accord with his party, although the grounds for his objection, primarily that it violated the duty of a government to accept the legislation of its predecessor in the previous Parliament, and secondarily that it was an attack on the endowed schools commissioners, of whom Lord Lyttelton was one, had a certain particularity about them. Altogether Gladstone's month in London did little to reconcile him to parliamentary life, and on 7 August he set off for a Penmaenmawr holiday, his first there for six years, with relief. He lunched that day in Grosvenor Square with Mrs Thistlethwayte, with whom relations had been active during this London interlude, and she drove him to Willesden Junction to pick up the five o'clock express from Euston.

In North Wales he managed only fifteen sea-bathes that year, suspending the operation for a week from 11 August 'on sanitary grounds'. (This presumably meant his own health rather than general pollution, for he spent half the next two days in bed and full of 'physic'; though it did not prevent his being fairly boisterous during the half days when he was out of his bed: 'we went up Moel Ynion: were wet to the skin: forded the stream knee deep: excellent tea in the cottage above Aber 9d a head'.)[18] His main intellectual activity was writing for the October number of the *Contemporary Review* a 10,000-word article on 'The Church of England and Ritualism', which put into literary form many of the thoughts he had developed and the points he had made in the July–August debates. He was also casting his mind forward to the visit that he was to pay to Ignaz von Döllinger in Munich in the following month, to the intense theological discussions he was to have there, and to the anti-ultramontane pamphlet, descriptively entitled *The Vatican Decrees in their Bearing on Civil Allegiance: A Political Expostulation*, which he was to launch upon the world in November, and which was to sell nearly 150,000 copies.

His German journey lasted from 7 to 25 September, and was his first escape from Britain since 1866–7 and his first visit to Döllinger since 1845. He took two of his children – Willy and Helen (the future vice-principal of Newnham College, Cambridge) – with him to Bavaria, but not his wife, despite her temporary distaste for Hawarden.

His first stop was Cologne, where he briefly saw his sister. He reached Munich on the evening of the second day, was put up and generally looked after by the British minister to Bavaria, Robert Morier (later a notable ambassador to St Petersburg) and then plunged into an orgy of discussion with Döllinger. On the next day he talked with him continuously from 10.30 a.m. to 6.00 p.m. The day after that they put in another six and a half hours. On Gladstone's third and fourth days in Munich they had long afternoon walks (and talks) together. On one of them they encountered the Archbishop of Munich, who three years before had excommunicated Döllinger for his opposition to the Vatican decrees. Döllinger's position had then become that of an Old Catholic, believing that Pius IX was doing immense harm to the ancient faith. This position Gladstone found both sympathetic and sustaining. It inspired him to write his expostulatory pamphlet on his return to England, and it caused him to make on the spot a significant addition to his ritualism article and to send it off for last-minute inclusion. As part of his argument that ritualistic practices in some Anglican churches carried no threat of the Romanization of England he added the following passage:

> At no time since the sanguinary reign of Mary has such a scheme [for Romanization] been possible. But if it had been possible in the seventeenth or eighteenth centuries, it would still have become impossible in the nineteenth; when Rome has substituted for the proud boast of *semper eadem* a policy of violence and change in faith, when she has refurbished and paraded anew every rusty tool she was fondly thought to have disused; when no one can become her convert without renouncing his moral and mental freedom, and placing his civil loyalty and duty at the mercy of another; and when she has equally repudiated modern thought and ancient history.[19]

This was obviously a profoundly anti-Catholic statement, casting doubt as it did on the civil allegiance of British converts or adherents of the Church of Rome, and Gladstone, when republishing the article four years later, appended a footnote of convoluted half-denial that this was what he meant. It was a classic example of Gladstone embracing one cause and argument with such enthusiasm that he did not pause to consider its repercussion on other causes and arguments which over a period were equally or more important to him. And here he obviously ran grave risks to his ability to lead a party with many Roman Catholic supporters, and in particular to pursue a policy of Anglo-Irish reconciliation. For the moment, however, he gave his religious enthusiasms priority over his political ones, and was inclined to welcome any personal disqualification which strengthened his case for shedding the Liberal leadership. By 1878, on the other hand, when Bulgarian atrocities had replaced Vatican aggressions in the centre of his mind, and Midlothian and the return to full political commitment was only just over the horizon, his priorities were different. Hence the footnote.

These matters for the moment disposed of (and Döllinger having gone to Bonn for an anti-ultramontane conference), Gladstone took himself and his son and daughter on a four-day tour of the Bavarian and Austrian Alps. It was strenuous (his daughter was commended for being able to keep up with the nearly sixty-five-year-old ex-Prime Minister over twenty-nine miles of far from level terrain), the scenery aroused his profound admiration, as did one or two other local attractions ('Saw the Obersee – Bartholomäus Haus – (& the singularly beautiful waitress)', was a surprising shaft in the diary) and so, without the future casting a shadow, did a 'beautiful river walk' to Berchtesgaden 'with a Führer . . . who was a charming specimen of these bold hardy active South Bavarians'.[20] Then he went to Nuremberg and saw a lot of painted churches before returning to Cologne, where over two days, having got into the habit of talking subjects to destruction, he had thirteen hours of conversation with his sister, which discussions (one wonders what was the balance of listening and talking on the two sides) must have formed much of the basis for his determined conviction at the time of her 1880 death that she was on the brink of return to her Anglican faith.

On Gladstone's return to England he based himself at Hawarden for the remainder of the year. He paid four country-house visits, all of them only a night or two except for a full week at Whittinghame with Arthur Balfour (still aged only twenty-six, but 'how eminently he is *del miglior luto*' – of more than common clay – Gladstone wrote), for which he made a special eleven-hour journey from Hawarden. He was deep in religious controversy, his *Vatican Decrees* pamphlet appearing on 7 November and provoking a rash of rejoinders, including responses from Newman and Manning. Lest there be any danger of the pot ceasing to simmer he wrote a major and stringent review of *The Discourses of Pius IX* for the January 1875 number of the *Quarterly*. He finished the year reading George Eliot's *Middlemarch* ('it is an extraordinary, and to me a very jarring book') over seventeen days. It had been published three years before, so what with that and with *Vivian Grey*, which was over thirty years old, he was less up to date in 1874 with his novel reading than was his general habit.

Dominating all this was the imminence of formal escape from the leadership. For all practical purposes he had renounced the obligation nearly a year before, but it was nonetheless a considerable relief and help towards 'the winding out of the coil' when, on 3 February 1875, Hartington, with a reluctance wholly appropriate to the empty vessel which he was offered, took over the role. Gladstone at sixty-five saw himself as having a last five years or so of life in which to make peace with his God and war against his religious enemies, whether they be presumptuous Roman pontiffs or Erastian low churchmen. He underestimated his longevity as much as he overestimated his ability to remain politically quiescent.

23

THE TEMPORARY WITHDRAWAL

WHEN GLADSTONE CAME BACK to London from Hawarden on February 12 1875 he was freer of parliamentary and other political obligations than at any other time since he had joined the Palmerston government in June 1859. He nonetheless continued to observe the pattern of the parliamentary year, more so indeed than in 1874, when he had expressed his chafing at the wheel of duty through long absences during the session. In 1875, by contrast, he did not return to Hawarden, except for a Whitsun week, until 7 August. In London, however, he was both unsettled in his residence and undiligent in his attendance at the House of Commons.

Within two weeks he (or his agent) had found a purchaser for 11 Carlton House Terrace in the shape of Sir Arthur Guinness, grandson of the first brewer of the black gold of Ireland and himself then head of the family business and Conservative MP for Dublin City until he was made a peer in 1880. Gladstone's view that the Terrace had become suitable only for men much richer than himself was amply underpinned by the status of his purchaser. The transaction was completed on 15 April, when the Crown lease was assigned to Guinness for £35,000. Gladstone wrote of the departure as being 'like a *little* death. . . . I had *grown* to the House, having lived more time in it than in any other since I was born.'[1] He did not, however, react against the 'usurpers', Tory and plutocratic though they were. In the summer of 1876 he recorded: 'Tea at No 11 C.H.T. – Lady O. [Olivia Guinness was the daughter of the Earl of Bantry] kind & simple. Went over the altered rooms.'[2] Most of the furniture had been disposed of in an on-site sale, but some of it was taken over by Guinness, a great supporter of the Anglican Church in Ireland, which aroused an ironic but not unfriendly reflection from Gladstone: 'Sir A. G. has the chairs & sofa on which we sat when we resolved on the disestablishment of the Irish Church in 1868.'[3]

Later that spring Christie's held a four-day sale of the paintings, porcelain and *objets* which had been collected over nearly forty years. The receipts were £9351. One Italian picture (Bonifazio's *Virgin*) made

£483 and the next best price was £430 for Dyce's Marion Summerhayes portrait, *Lady with the Coronet of Jasmine*, which was thus propelled on its journey to the Aberdeen Art Gallery. A picture which Gladstone had bought as a Giorgione made only £85 and an equally doubtful Murillo only eleven guineas. Nonetheless Gladstone's cash and income position was substantially retrieved. The leasehold house had provided the equivalent of nearly £1¾ million in today's money, and the decorative sale came to nearly £500,000 on the same basis. When his London books, less a substantial number removed to Hawarden, had been valued a few weeks earlier Sotheby's put the Hansards at £150 (how delighted would be most modern MPs to get the equivalent £7500 for their accumulation of those freely issued pale-blue volumes) and the rest at £670 (£33,000). They all appear to have been acquired by Lord Wolverton, formerly his Chief Whip George Glyn, presumably at valuation price.

For the remainder of the parliamentary session of 1875 the Gladstones rented another but much smaller Carlton House Terrace house fifty yards from their previous one. This (No. 23) he described as 'our new and humble nest', although they were quickly giving breakfast and dinner parties there for around ten guests. For his few autumn nights in London he was in Arthur Balfour's house at 4 Carlton Gardens, and for the winter three months at the beginning of 1876 he rented that for £300, again a substantial sum by Victorian standards.* During February he had settled on 73 Harley Street, then regarded as a relatively modest and remote residence, as a more permanent establishment, and bought a thirty-year lease. It was mid-May before they could move in, and after Easter he was back in the 'Carltons', staying with the Frederick Cavendishes at 21 Carlton House Terrace, and even in the following September when he came to London unexpectedly (and excitedly) he stayed with Granville at No. 18. There is no doubt that, even though he thought it inappropriate to the modesty of his wealth, Gladstone regarded that strip of semi-palatial London as his metropolitan village. When his tenure of the Balfour house came to an end he wrote that it was 'a departure from a *neighbourhood* where I have lived for forty years,

* Balfour was away on a six-month world tour before which he had been brought even closer to Gladstone by his behaviour when May Lyttelton, Gladstone's niece and perhaps the only real love of Balfour's life, died at the age of twenty-four. The amount of the rent for 4 Carlton Gardens nonetheless suggests an arm's-length transaction and rather belies Gladstone's later reputation for borrowing houses rather than paying for them.

& where I am the "oldest inhabitant"'.[4] For the Harley Street house he never showed much affection. In spite of the thirty-year lease he gave it up soon after he again became Prime Minister in 1880. In this second premiership 10 Downing Street had to serve as a residence as well as an unregarded office. And when he was again in opposition, first in the second half of 1885 and then for five and a half years until 1892, he spent much of his London time in the sylvan but suburban remoteness of Dollis Hill, an Aberdeen-owned villa between Willesden and Neasden. This was commemorated by the telephone exchange between there and West Hampstead bearing until 1971 the appellation of GLAdstone.

After Hartington took over as leader for the session of 1875, Gladstone continued to sit on the front bench, which, he said, was what both Hartington and Granville (the leader in the Lords, and the senior of the two) desired. 'I . . . took my seat nearly in the same spot as last year, finding Bright my neighbour, with which I was well pleased,' he wrote to his wife on 18 February.[5] His attendance was far from regular, however, and even more noticeable was the absence of the long and late hours in the House which had previously been his habit. 'H. of C. 4.30–6.00.' became a regular entry. Quite frequently he would intervene, often on an unexpected subject, during one of these brief parliamentary forays. Thus on 15 March (although he then went back to the House after dinner) he spoke on the Regimental Exchange Bill in a way which produced an unforgettable account from Disraeli to the Queen. 'Mr Gladstone not only appeared but rushed into the debate . . .' he wrote. 'The new Members trembled and fluttered like small birds when a hawk is in the air.'[6] His front-bench colleagues were even less enthusiastic about these sudden depredations than were the fluttering new members or the new Prime Minister, who was, however, well schooled in preserving in such circumstances a sardonic calm.

Partly to underline the severance of his political ties and partly to economize, Gladstone kept no secretary during the second half of the 1870s. This meant that he spent much of his time grappling with and complaining about the 'chaos' created by his incoming correspondence. Particularly after the Bulgarian and other aspects of the Eastern Question brought him back into the mainstream of political controversy in the autumn of 1876, the volume of his mail would have been crushing to almost anyone else who tried to handle it with his meticulousness. When he returned to either Hawarden or Harley Street he was typically confronted with about 300 unopened items, and the daily intake was a substantial proportion of this. The only assistance on which he called was that of available children – Mary, Helen, Herbert and even Willy, although the last was then a member of Parliament in his late thirties. (But as Gladstone himself when not merely an MP but a Privy Councillor and an ex-Cabinet minister had been called upon at almost exactly the same age to perform the same function for his own father, there was an element of poetic justice about this.)

For the most part, however, Gladstone hacked through the correspondence himself, although this involved him in writing letters of a type with which the pens of few subsequent ex-Prime Ministers can have engaged. The superintendent of the Lost Property Office at Euston Station got a missive in early June 1875, and the stationmaster at Chester as well as the manager of the bookstall there was a constant recipient of letters which would presumably produce a substantial price today. Perhaps because of these burdens Gladstone had one of the earliest telephones installed at Hawarden. It was there from 1880. But evidence of use is missing. There were indeed few others with whom he could have communicated. He referred to it as being 'most unearthly', and it is indeed easy to imagine that anyone – Granville seems the most likely target – assaulted down 200 miles of cable by Gladstone's unmistakable tones would have found the experience extra-terrestrial and unnerving.

Throughout 1875 and most of 1876 Gladstone's life was active in the production of pamphlets but quiet in his engagement with politics. The white heat of his opposition to ultramontanism produced not only his *Expostulation* of November 1874 but a follow-up entitled *Vaticanism: An Answer to Reproofs and Replies* which was published in February 1875. He had carefully collected the various ripostes, including a paper of 200 pages from Manning, which his first pamphlet had attracted, and set himself to refute them. Although this second instalment was more violent in tone than the first (the Roman Church he described as 'an Asian monarchy: nothing but one giddy height of despotism and one dead level of religious subservience'), it made less impact and the sales were barely a quarter those of the first. Nonetheless the two together earned him substantial sums, and Granville wrote optimistically from Italy that the 'enormous profits' from his pen might render unnecessary the sale of 11 Carlton House Terrace. This was probably prompted by the fact that the royalties were about the only aspect of the pamphlets of which Granville's unpolemical mind approved.

His slightly weary 'why-does-he-make-such-a-fuss' disapproval was, however, mild compared with that of Cardinal Cullen, who in 1874 ordered prayers that Gladstone might see the error of his ways to be said in every Catholic church in Ireland, and three years later was still sufficiently resentful that when Gladstone called upon him in Dublin he managed a cool rebuff which few other than the Queen could have achieved: 'You know Mr Gladstone we could have given you a warmer reception had it not been for certain pamphlets which we in Ireland did not like very well.'[7] But nor of course did Gladstone like Cullen, remembering too clearly his part in the death of the Irish University Bill.

By the time of that Irish visit in the autumn of 1877 the iniquities of the Pope in Rome and the Vatican Council had been largely superseded in Gladstone's mind, and this process was reinforced by the death of Piux IX three months later and the election of Leo XIII, who, while hardly ecumenical (he proclaimed the invalidity of Anglican orders, although he also laid the foundations of Christian Democracy with the encyclical *Rerum Novarum*), was markedly less ultramontane, and made Newman a cardinal four years after Manning had been elevated by Pio Nono.

Gladstone turned from what he called 'my polemical period' in a variety of directions. Over the summer and autumn of 1875 he was unusually free of any sustained intellectual task, although as there was always work to progress on one or other of his eccentric Homeric monographs the threat of idleness was kept at a far distance. But over much of that year's recess his effort was more physical than mental. He was preoccupied with getting the thousands of the Carlton House Terrace books which he had not sold into an orderly amalgamation with his previous Hawarden ones. Thus for 6 September he wrote: '3½ hours work on books, carrying and arranging. 2¼ hard work on getting my tree down. Rather overtired,' he not surprisingly concluded.'[8]

In the spring of 1876 the appearance of G. O. Trevelyan's life of Macaulay provoked him to a major appraisal of the then sixteen-years-dead Whig historian and poet who had coined the most memorable (and mocking) of all the phrases about Gladstone's early career. But there was neither rancour nor sycophancy about Gladstone's review, and it remains one of his best literary pieces and a remarkably balanced judgement of Macaulay – and balance was not normally Gladstone's foremost quality.

In that summer he turned to the content rather than to the frontier battles of his religion and worked on the outline of a never completed book on Future Punishment (that is, Hell). This produced a clutch of papers on which, when putting them aside, he wrote: 'From this I was called away to write on Bulgaria.'[9] And with that call there began another chapter which led to Midlothian, to his return to the premiership and the leadership, and eventually to the Irish crusade of his last active decade.

The withdrawal from politics was therefore short-lived, at most from Easter 1874 until the return began in the closing months of 1876 and gathered momentum during 1877. But while it lasted it was genuine enough both in interest and in the change in his pattern of life. Apart from his concentration on mainly religious writing, he was also much preoccupied with family affairs: deaths, marriages, even a birth, and settlements. Robertson Gladstone, the brother to whom he had latterly been closest, died in Liverpool in September 1875, and with his death the extent of the mismanagement of the Seaforth property, and indeed of the other remaining family interests in Liverpool became even clearer. Robertson had several sons, all of whom died unmarried and fairly unprosperous too, so that 1875 was effectively the end of the strong Gladstone mercantile presence in Liverpool, which John Gladstone had started eighty-eight years before. Then, in April 1876, George Lyttelton threw himself into the staircase well of his Marylebone house and died without regaining consciousness. There were another twenty-two years of married life still ahead for the Gladstones, but the other couple in the Hawarden double wedding of the summer of 1839 were both dead, the one at forty-three, the other at fifty-eight.

In the spring of 1875 William and Catherine Gladstone had become grandparents for the first time. Agnes Wickham, as she had become in 1873, was the mother. Five of the other six Gladstone children were then still unmarried, and Willy, at the age of thirty-five, and nine years after he had become an MP, had only recently married Gertrude Stuart, daughter of Lord Blantyre and granddaughter of Harriet, Duchess of Sutherland, at St George's, Hanover Square. The London celebrations, at an unfashionable time of year, were muted, but when the couple came to Hawarden a few weeks later there were fantastic estate junketings. On two successive nights there were dinners of 400 and 450 people with balls afterwards. 'Carving and speaking' was how Gladstone described his role. On the fourth night he recorded: 'A servant's ball this evening closed at length our part of the marriage festivities. Our guests have been nearly 2500: one third children.'[10] These events were also in the train of the Hawarden wedding of Gertrude Glynne, the orphaned daughter of the former rector, with the heir to Lord Penrhyn, and grandson of the creator of the massive granite fort of Penrhyn Castle, fifty miles further along the North Wales coast.

The central purpose of the celebrations, however, was to authenticate Willy Gladstone as squire of Hawarden and heir to the Glynnes. Yet, in his generation, it never worked. It was not the spirit of the Glynnes which obstructed him. Much more inhibiting was the omnipresence of his father, anxious that the property should be firmly in the hands of his son, yet quite incapable of not dominating it, him, his new wife and everything else within sight. For his remaining fourteen years of life there is no evidence that Willy Gladstone exercised an independent squirearchical role. He lived at least as much in the shadow of the 'great people' as had Sir Stephen Glynne.

In the same year, however, a Gladstone son – Herbert, the youngest – did at last achieve some academic distinction. He had broken with the rigid Christ Church tradition of his father and his elder brothers and gone from Eton to University College, Oxford. But the change had not made him do other than follow his brothers in not getting a first in Classics (Willy and Stephen had both got seconds; Herbert did worse and got a third). But he then switched to History and was placed in the first class for that school, followed by a teaching post at the new Keble College. The School of Modern History was no doubt not quite the equivalent of Literae Humaniores in his father's eyes, and the Warden of Keble was admittedly his cousin by marriage, but it was nonetheless an achievement on the part of the future Liberal Chief Whip, Home Secretary and Governor-General of South Africa, which made it the best Gladstone academic performance since his father's triumphs of 1831.

Another feature of Gladstone's life during these few years of semi-withdrawal was his perennial interest in seeing different parts of Britain and the careful foresight with which he planned visits to this end.* This was always an underlying feature of his life, but it was one which was able to come more to the surface in these few years of relative freedom. A spectacularly concentrated and illustrative day was Tuesday, 5 October 1875. It was the end of a four-day visit to the eighty-five-year-old Lord Bathurst at Cirencester, where Mrs Thistlethwayte was also a guest. He set off in the morning to return to Hawarden, a mildly

* See p. 621n, below, for an estimate of the remarkably few areas of England, Scotland and Wales which Gladstone had not visited by the time that the infirmity of age made him abandon travel except in search of health.

difficult cross-country journey by twentieth-century standards. The interest was the number of cameos which he hung upon the necklace of his journey: 'Expedition to Gloucester and Worcester Cathedrals. After 50 years! Both most interesting – Worcester sumptuous. . . . At Gloucester we had most of the service and saw Canon Harvey. At Chester went to the Theatre for a spell – short but long enough.'[11] Having regained Hawarden (the journeys apart from perhaps the Cirencester–Kemble and Chester–Hawarden stages were of course all done by train), he finished one book and read parts of another two before going to bed.

A month or so later he went for a stay of no less than eight days to Chatsworth, where the seventh Duke of Devonshire had two of his sons, Lord Frederick Cavendish and Hartington, who in differing ways were to impact so sharply upon Gladstone in 1882 and 1886, to help entertain him. Then he went on for a few days to Hickleton, the Halifax house in the Yorkshire coalfield. On the last day at Chatsworth he heard the news of Disraeli's capture for the British government of the controlling interest in the French-built Suez Canal, and reacted strongly, with Whig approval both there and at Hickleton, against what he regarded as this showy, vulgar and internationally disruptive *coup de théâtre*.

Between September 1876 and November 1877 he made three major tours within the British Isles, each lasting around three to four weeks. The first was to Yorkshire, Durham, Northumberland and the Scottish Borders. He stayed at Raby Castle, the Deanery in Durham Close, Ford Castle at Coldstream, Alnwick, Jervaulx Abbey and Castle Howard. Then in January 1877 he went to the near West Country, staying at Longleat, the Bishop's palace at Wells, Dunster Castle, Orchard Neville near Glastonbury, Bowden Park near Chippenham (with his nephew) and Savernake near Marlborough.*

* The Ailesbury house at Savernake latterly became the home of Hawtrey's preparatory school until its rather scandalous demise in 1994. But it was with other schools that Gladstone had trouble when staying there. He went into Marlborough and addressed the boys of the then thirty-year-old College, making there almost the only anti-Etonian remarks of his life. He developed a theme, similar to that of Trollope's *The Way We Live Now* (1875), critical of the impact upon Eton of the rampantly plutocratic standards of the 1870s, which new standards many, including the Queen, found offensive. He referred to 'The constant influx of the wealthy, and the tendency of wealth and large money indulgences amongst boys . . . to corrupt and lower the tone of the school' (*Diaries*, IX, p. 191n). This led to a defensive–offensive reply in the *Eton Chronicle*, and to a few years of shadow over his habitual relationship of excessive devotion to the school. No doubt the heightened political tension of the period contributed to the reaction.

In the autumn of that year he made his sole sojourn in Ireland. He was there nearly a month, but he did not venture beyond counties Wicklow, Dublin and Kildare. He stayed at the great houses of Kilruderry, Coolattin, Powerscourt, Calton, Abbeyleix and Woodlands. But it was Glendalough, the ancient and pastoral Christian site in the Glenealo valley, which made the deepest impression upon him. 'The harmony of the scenery with the remains is perfect,' he wrote.[12]

Wherever Gladstone was, England or Ireland, Hawarden or London, touring Europe or visiting a country house, and whatever he was doing, unless absorbed in reading or writing, whether he was felling a tree* or walking through an urban street or across a tract of countryside, he was intensely alert, not always to human atmosphere, but to whatever caught his eye, to light, to buildings, to scenery. And he could come out with most unexpected observations. Just as, on the Obersee in September 1874, he noticed 'the singularly beautiful waitress', so in July 1876: 'I was greatly struck, returning Holborn way, with the now really great beauty of the City [of London] as well as its astounding stir.'[13] It was not a commonplace reaction to the great wen at the peak of its coal-smut-filled sky and its horse manure-covered streets. But Gladstone, whatever else he was, was not a commonplace man. In the next phase of his career, which began eight weeks to the day after his Holborn *aperçu*, he was seen by some as an increasingly demented and irresponsible old man (he was nearly sixty-seven at the time), by others as the most inspirational of Victorian statesmen. What is indisputable, however, is that 1876 began the reforging and reinforcement of his position as the uniquely powerful oratorical communicator of the century.

* This in the 1870s became an almost obsessive form of recreation. The Hawarden park must have been considerably denuded, and visiting deputations of supporters expected to be able to take souvenir chips away with them. But it was not only at Hawarden that he performed arboreal slaughter. He was liable to practise his skill on other people's grounds; and it would have been a rash act for anyone who did not have substantial parkland with a few redundant trees to invite Gladstone to stay.

Part Four

THE REBOUND INTO THE SECOND PREMIERSHIP

1876–1885

— 24 —

'Of All the Bulgarian Horrors Perhaps the Greatest'

For 28 August 1876 at Hawarden Gladstone's diary entry comprised: 'Worked on a beginning for a possible pamphlet on the Turkish question: I stupidly brought on again my lumbago by physical exertion.'[1] The next four days he spent mostly in bed. His entry for Thursday the 31st captured the flavour of the week: 'Kept my bed till four & made tolerable play in writing on Bulgarian Horrors: my back is less strained in bed, where I write against the legs.'[2] On the Friday he 'sent off more than half to the printer'. On the Sunday he rose in time for church at 11.00 (and again at 6.30), and then left at 10.15 p.m. to catch the 'Limited Mail' train to London, where he descended upon Granville's house at 18 Carlton House Terrace at 5.00 a.m. His homing instinct for Carlton House Terrace was as strong as that of any pigeon. What was wrong with 73 Harley Street? What made him think that he would be a welcome guest in someone else's house at five in the morning (where he immediately went to bed until nine), or indeed at Granville's at any time of the night or day in view of the mission on which he had come, which was to disturb the peace of the Granville–Hartington-led Liberal party?

Yet, such was the strength of his personality and the quality of Granville's affection, that he almost certainly was, even in these circumstances, wholly welcome. And his employment of the fourteen or fifteen hours after his second awakening was remarkable even by his own standards. He wrote two letters and conducted five interviews, his visitors including the editor of *The Times* (Delane), Panizzi of the British Museum and the American minister (Pierrepont). Then: 'In six or seven hours, principally at the B. Museum I completed my MS making all the needful searches of Papers and Journals: also worked on proof sheets. Granville had a small very pleasant dinner party,'[3] he graciously concluded.

The next day he 'Finished the correction of the revises before one: discussing the text with Ld G. & making various alterations of phrase which he recommended. At seven I received complete copies.' Then occurred one of the most remarkable minor incidents in Victorian politics. Gladstone, Hartington and Granville went together to the Haymarket Theatre to see a farce entitled *The Heir at Law*. The rest of the audience was, not surprisingly, somewhat stunned.

Later that night Gladstone sent a complimentary copy of his hurriedly conceived, written and printed effusion to, among others, the new Earl of Beaconsfield. Disraeli, with typical dramatic effort, had spoken for the last time in the House of Commons, of which he had been a member for thirty-nine years, on 11 August, had walked to the bar of the House, gazed upon it, regained the normal ministerial exit behind the Speaker's chair, and walked out upon the arm of his faithful secretary Monty Corry (later Lord Rowton), pulling on his gloves and encompassed in a long white overcoat (which might have been thought over-wintry, not merely in colour but in weight, for even a London August). The next day it was announced that he had become Earl of Beaconsfield, which he pronounced *Bee*consfield, and which followed the elevation of his wife (five years dead at this time) to the viscountcy of the same name at the end of his first premiership.

The complimentary copy did not assuage the new earl. Writing to his Foreign Secretary on 8 September, Disraeli described the pamphlet as 'vindictive and ill-written – that of course. Indeed in that respect of all the Bulgarian horrors perhaps the greatest.'[4] And he took enough pleasure in the typically derisory phrase with which he endeavoured to puncture Gladstone's indignation that he repeated it with a slight variation in a speech at Aylesbury on the eve of the poll in the Buckinghamshire by-election which followed from his elevation. Gladstone meanwhile, having seen the original 2000 print of his pamphlet supplemented within two days by a second instalment of 22,000 and then grow to a total sale of 200,000, was so swept away by the cause as to take the extreme step of visiting his Greenwich constituency, where on the afternoon of Saturday, 9 September, he addressed an audience of 10,000 who assembled on Blackheath in spite of the heavy rain. This clash between him and Disraeli, in the words of Robert Blake, 'injected a bitterness into British politics which had not been seen since the Corn Law debates'.[5] With their utterly conflicting styles, Gladstone's pulsating moral indignation and Disraeli's sardonic cynicism, they each infuriated the other, and increased the mutual hostility. They were both somewhat out of touch with their colleagues on the issue, for Derby and Salisbury on the Conservative side and Hartington and Granville on the

Liberal one were all clustered on some fairly moderate ground in the middle.

Nonetheless Gladstone and Disraeli staged between them the greatest setpiece drama of Victorian politics. Protagonist and antagonist exaggerated their styles and roles as though they had been coached by Henry Irving. The previous contender for the dramatic accolade – the Don Pacifico debate of 1850 – was outpaced not because any single occasion in 1876–80 was more memorable, but because the Pacifico clash was all over in a few days and was played out almost entirely within the parliamentary dimension. The Eastern Question was on the contrary a full three-act drama, and it was not primarily parliamentary, let alone exclusively so. It embraced Gladstone's pamphlets, his denunciatory meetings up and down the country culminating in the Midlothian campaign, balanced by Disraeli's mordant and provocative flippancies as well as his sole but spectacular appearance at an international diplomatic conference. Moreover it left a permanent imprint on the line of the divide in British politics. It separated the North from the South, the classes from the masses, and high moral tone from an appeal to self-interest flavoured with music-hall patriotism and mocking wit. The Whigs of the age first of Melbourne and then of Palmerston could hardly be regarded as more earnest than the Conservative party of Peel. But there was no comparison between the earnestness of the Liberal party under Gladstone's second leadership and that of Disraeli or even Salisbury.

The genesis of Gladstone's fervour on the issue is difficult to analyse. Was he, perhaps semi-consciously, looking for a cause for which, with a clap of thunder and a whiff of smoke, he could re-emerge as the dominating central figure of politics after a fairly boring two and a half years during which he had been trying to persuade himself that he wished to concentrate on theology? Or was he spontaneously seized with a passionate sympathy for the sufferings of the Balkan Christian communities which left him no alternative but to erupt with his full and extraordinary force? Arguments in favour of both propositions can be effectively deployed, and no doubt the most likely answer is that there were elements of both in his motivation.

In favour of the more cynical explanation is the consideration that he was not much good at theology, or at any abstract or speculative subject, and probably knew it. He was always much more at ease with the historical and organizational aspects of religion than with its philosophical content. He did not have an absolutely first-class analytical mind. He had a very good mind, which he nurtured throughout his long life with an exceptional intake of diversified information. It would never have been appropriate to say of him, as Oliver Wendell Holmes said of Franklin Roosevelt: 'a second-class intellect, but a first-rate temperament'. Gladstone had a mind which fully deserved his two Oxford firsts and which then retained the full vigour of its curiosity for nearly seventy years. He was well in the half dozen cleverest Prime Ministers, although he did not have quite Peel's orderliness or Asquith's smooth-purring if conventional machine of a mind, or Rosebery's gifts as a delicate stylist, or Churchill's as a sonorous one. What made him pre-eminent were his physical rather than his intellectual gifts, formidable by normal standards though the latter were: his energy and the commanding force with which he delivered his not always limpid words.

All this meant that when he inscribed on the docket of his papers on Future Punishment the pregnant phrase, 'From this I was called away to write on Bulgaria', he was turning from a task he did indifferently to one which he did spectacularly well. It did not follow that what he did was contrived for his own convenience. He was driven on Bulgaria by the same sort of elemental force which had seized him at the time of his Neapolitan pamphlets twenty-five years before. But there were two balancing paradoxes. The first was that he knew incomparably more about Naples in 1851 than he knew about Bulgaria in 1876. In 1851 he had spent a winter on the spot. He had visited the gaols. He had met some of the victims. From the point of view not only of knowledge but also of reasons for direct sympathy there was no comparison between the two involvements. In 1876 he had never been nearer to the violated provinces than Vienna or his one night in the hills above the Albanian coast, both in 1858. At the end of July 1876, he had admittedly delivered a two-hour House of Commons oration against the government's policy towards Turkey, but he had concentrated very much on the responsibilities which flowed from Britain being a signatory to the Treaty of Paris which had ended the Crimean War, and had deliberately eschewed raising the question of the alleged atrocities. Furthermore, as there are many examples to demonstrate, such a speech required from Gladstone no concentration of preparation.

During the Hawarden month which intervened between then and his sudden outburst of bedridden pamphlet-writing there was no indication of any special reading on the subject, although he no doubt closely followed the various reports which indicated that as many as 12,000 Bulgarians may have been massacred by the Turks. The *Daily News* carried reports from J. A. MacGahan, that newspaper's special correspondent in Batak as well as its publication of an explosive despatch from the United States consul-general Eugene Schuyler. W. T. Stead also sent to Hawarden copies of his Darlington *Northern Echo*, in which from early August onwards that crusading editor was whipping up a great campaign. Nonetheless Gladstone's knowledge of Bulgaria was far from profound. Yet, when he began to write, the phrases poured out of him, not only with passion, but with at any rate a superficial grasp of local terminology which produced one of the most famous examples of nineteenth-century polemics:

> Let the Turks now carry away their abuses in the only possible manner, namely by carrying off themselves. Their Zaptiehs and their Mudits, their Bimbashis and their Yuzbashis, their Kaimakams and their Pashas, one and all, bag and baggage, shall I hope clear out from the province they have desolated and profaned. This thorough riddance, this most blessed deliverance, is the only reparation we can make to the memory of those heaps on heaps of dead; to the violated purity alike of matron, maiden, and of child. . . .

Other, less famous, passages were even more highly charged:

> There is not a cannibal in the South Sea Islands, whose indignation would not arise and overboil at the recital of that which has been done, which has too late been examined, but which remains unavenged: which has left behind all the foul and all the fierce passions that produced it, and which may again spring up in another murderous harvest from the soil soaked and reeking with blood, and in the air tainted with every imaginable deed of crime and shame. . . . No Government ever has so sinned; none has proved itself so incorrigible or, which is the same, so impotent for reformation.

The Turks had indulged in 'abominable and bestial lusts' and were responsible for scenes 'at which Hell itself might almost blush'. At Blackheath on the Saturday after publication Gladstone balanced his use of somewhat less emotional language by the effect of his physical presence and his half-terrifying, half-inspiriting gaze. Morley caught brilliantly his oratorical technique and impact when he wrote of Gladstone addressing himself 'in slow sentences to imaginary Ottomans, whom he seemed to hold before his visual eye'.[6] Gladstone was always addicted to what may be called the second-person argumentative case, and he used it both sonorously and memorably on that damp Saturday afternoon in south-east London at a time when oratory was more popular than football:

> You shall receive your regular tribute, you shall retain your titular sovereignty, your empire shall not be invaded, but never again as the years roll in their course, so far as it is in our power to determine, never again shall the hand of violence be raised by you, never again shall the flood-gates of lust be open to you, never again shall the dire refinements of cruelty be devised by you for the sake of making mankind miserable.

In the course of this speech he also probably went further in a pro-Russian direction than in any of his other pronouncements and did so in terms which now sound curiously reminiscent of Churchill's June 1941 offer of alliance to Stalin: 'I, for one, for the purposes of justice, am ready as an individual to give the right hand of friendship to Russia when the objects are just and righteous, and to say, in the name of God, "Go on and prosper!"'[7]

Gladstone was stronger on the rhetoric of indignation than on detailed knowledge of what was happening in the Balkans, and Disraeli's desire to burst the bloated bladder of expostulation with a sharp pin of mocking deflation is understandable. Disraeli's danger was that he might prick not only the monstrous engine of Gladstone's indignation but also his own repute with serious-minded middle opinion. His remark on 10 July that he was sceptical whether 'torture had been practised on a great scale amongst an oriental people who ... generally terminate their connection with culprits in a more expeditious manner'[8] was thought to show more wit than heart. So was his dismissal three weeks later as 'coffee-house babble' of the claims (which turned out to be more or less accurate) that 12,000 had been massacred. The same applied to his September quip that Gladstone's pamphlet was the greatest of the Bulgarian atrocities. They were both near to the style of Bishop Wilberforce's 1860 request to T. H. Huxley to tell him and the audience which of his grandparents he regarded as most closely descended from an ape. They were more provocative than persuasive.

Equally Disraeli's violent private attacks on Gladstone belied the view that his calm was unruffled while Gladstone went over several tops. Disraeli was recorded as saying in October 1876 to Lady Derby: 'Posterity will do justice to that unprincipled maniac Gladstone – extraordinary mixture of envy, vindictiveness, hypocrisy and superstition; and with one commanding characteristic – whether preaching, praying, speechifying, or scribbling – never a gentleman!'[9] Then in the summer of 1878, after Gladstone had exaggeratedly condemned the annexation of Cyprus, Disraeli produced the second most memorable of his anti-Gladstone aphorisms, which ranks only just behind those 'exhausted but still menacing volcanoes on the coast of South America' because it was more contrived and ended with a dying fall instead of a swish. On 27 July the Prime Minister told a Saturday-evening banquet in the Knightsbridge Riding School (the venue could hardly have been better chosen to epitomize Gladstone's denunciation of the West End of London as being increasingly unsound in its political values)* that his antagonist was 'a sophistical rhetorician inebriated with the exuberance of his own verbosity, and gifted with an egotistical imagination that can at all times command an interminable and inconsistent series of arguments to malign an opponent and to glorify himself'.[10]

Behind this clash of persons and of styles there was a profound difference of approach to the problems of a Britain moving out of that secure, prosperous, yet unostentatious third quarter of the nineteenth century, for which Peel had laid the foundations, helped by Gladstone, hindered by Disraeli. It had been a period somewhat analogous to the forty years of the Federal Republic of Germany and its quiet bourgeois successes. Those German successes were achieved under the threat of the Soviet Union in its days of apparent strength. Mid-Victorian England only had the challenge of the somewhat tinselly Second French Empire, whereas late-Victorian England faced the much more solidly based economic rivalry leading to superiority of the United States and Germany.

Gladstone and Disraeli fought their battle of the late 1870s on the hinge between these two periods. Disraeli reacted by putting on the show of a dawn raid on the shares of the Suez Canal Company; of proclaiming the Queen Empress of India; of threatening to go to war to keep the Russians out of Constantinople (even if this involved treating Turkish oppression of Christian provinces as inventions prompted by Liberal lack of patriotism masquerading as conscience); of himself theatrically dominating the Congress of Berlin, though hobbling across the scene rather than bestriding it ('*der alte Jude, das ist der Mann*', as Bismarck was alleged to have said); of annexing Cyprus; and of waging two blatantly imperialist wars, one against the Zulus and the other in Afghanistan.

Gladstone's reaction was to play the 'moral force' card and to reforge

* See p. 411, below.

his links with popular Radicalism and mass audiences, which links had been largely in abeyance since the beginning of his previous government. First, he saw with singular clarity that relative decline was inevitable for Britain. The United States in particular would 'probably become what we are now, the head servant in the great household of the World, the employer of all employed'.[11] For an 1878 article, even though written for an American audience, this was remarkably prescient, particularly for one who never crossed the Atlantic and therefore never fell under the almost electric spell of the New World. And, in these circumstances, his thought continued, nothing could be more dangerous than to extend an empire which was already somewhat beyond the sustaining force of the metropolitan country. This was a recipe for overstrain, conflict and eventual disorderly defeat.

It also led to the debauching of the public finances. Between 1874 and 1880 the Disraeli government turned an inherited surplus of £6 million into a deficit of £8 million. Just as Gladstone as a young Peelite in the 1840s abhorred the laxity of Whig finance, so in the 1870s as an old (in years not in party commitment) Liberal he denounced the budgetary consequence of Tory imperial adventures. Conservative profligacy played almost as large a part as Conservative aggression in the thundering denunciations of the Midlothian campaign.

Gladstone also decided that he had to rouse 'the masses against the classes' and the provinces against the metropolis. This was not an easy or a natural decision for him, for his cast of mind was instinctively hierarchical. He respected rank. He strained his own finances by building up the Hawarden estate for his heirs. He liked filling his Cabinets with grandees. When the Duke of Sutherland denounced him as a Russian agent in 1878 (which gave particular pain because of his friendship with the Duke's dead mother) his greatest solace was that the Duke of Westminster drove over to Hawarden to signify his support, and (privately) rebuked Sutherland from the platform of an even better endowed if more recent dukedom. Gladstone maintained the slightly ludicrous view that he was not rich enough to be a peer (which was one-third an excuse which suited him well, one-third an expression of modesty, and one-third a disdainful gesture). In his four premierships he made 101 peers, an experience which made him loath to include himself in the mêlée.

At first he moved cautiously in form if not in language on the Turkish question. He believed that writing pamphlets was more restrained than making speeches, and that if a speech were made at all it was different doing so in one's own constituency from doing so on a barnstorming tour. Hence the Blackheath afternoon on 9 September, despite his having already decided (although not announced) that, whatever else the future might hold, he was not again going to contest the unesteemed and ungrateful Greenwich. During that late summer and early autumn there were nearly 500 meetings up and down the country, mostly organized by the Eastern Question Association, which was non-party and indeed largely non-political in the sense that it was inspired and run not by parliamentarians but by men of letters and clerics: Carlyle, Ruskin, Burne-Jones, the historians E. A. Freeman and J. A. Froude, the Bishop of Manchester and Canon H. P. Liddon. Typically they passed resolutions abhorring the atrocities and condemning the moral detachment of the government. This detachment had been well summed up by Disraeli's August statement that 'our duty at this critical moment is to maintain the Empire of England':[12] in other words to be pro-Turkish and anti-Russian.

Gladstone spoke at none of these autumn demonstrations other than at Blackheath. His nearest to public visibility was when on his September–October tour of North-eastern country houses he was greeted by welcoming crowds at the railway junctions or the castle gates and delivered himself of some brief polemics. Alnwick was a striking example of this, which cannot greatly have pleased his firmly Tory host, the Duke of Northumberland. On 8 December he 'spoke (I fear) 1½ hours, with some exertion, far from wholly to my satisfaction' to the culminating London convention of the campaign. This was in the St James's Hall, and was intended as a riposte to what Gladstone regarded as some grossly provocative remarks by Disraeli at the Lord Mayor's Banquet a month before. The convention was a gathering of intellectual leaders presided over by grandees, thereby rather contradicting the demotic and (allegedly) demagogic nature of the campaign. The Duke of Westminster took the chair at one session, and the Earl of Shaftesbury at the other. Anthony Trollope spoke (as did, *inter alia*, James Bryce, Henry Richard, G. O. Trevelyan, the Bishop of Oxford, and Henry Fawcett). Thomas Hardy, aged thirty-six and in the audience, noted with amusement the vain efforts of chairman Westminster to get Trollope to bring his remarks to an end. Gladstone even tried (unsuccessfully) to get the not quite empurpled Newman to come down from Birmingham and participate. It was to this audience that Gladstone with perhaps unconscious irony chose to denounce the 'upper ten thousand'. When did they 'ever lead the attack in the name of humanity'?

In this early phase of the four-year clash, Gladstone could not justifiably be regarded as having either unduly savaged his country's government or rocked the boat of the Granville–Hartington-led Liberal party. Nevertheless there was a lot of criticism against him for crashing in like a rogue elephant. Hartington required much massage from Granville, Spencer and other Whig figures to prevent him resentfully throwing in his hand, and Lady Frederick Cavendish, often the unhappy cushion between her revered uncle and her respected brother-in-law, had a worried time. Uncle William, she allowed was too 'headstrong', but she was sure that he was moved by 'love of justice and mercy' and not by ambition. The Court, poisoned by Disraeli and by a somewhat narrow concept of patriotism, thought otherwise. At a levee on 12 March 1877 Gladstone noted that 'the Queen smiled: but had not a word'.[13] A year later it was worse: 'Went to the Levee. The Prince [of Wales], for the first time, received me drily: the Duke of Cambridge, black as thunder, did not even hold out his hand. *Prince* Xtn. [of Schleswig-Holstein, the impecunious husband of the Queen's third daughter] could not but follow suit. This is not very hard to bear.'[14]

In fact he minded it a good deal, although without the slightest thought that it might deflect him from his righteous course. And when, just over another year later, at the Royal Academy Banquet of 1879, he found that the frost had thawed and that 'the P. of W. was just as of old', it was difficult to know whether it was this or 'Lord B[eaconsfield] *not* [being] warmly received by the general Company'[15] which gave him greater pleasure. It should, however, also be recorded that, three weeks after that, he derived equal satisfaction, for he was generous as well as righteous, from the following incident: 'Went by invitation to afternoon tea with Lady Derby. Found myself face to face with Lord Beaconsfield; & this put all right socially between us, to my great satisfaction.'[16]

Gladstone's social life embraced a wider dimension than these royalties, Lady Derby or even Lord Beaconsfield. On 10–12 March 1877, he spent a remarkable Saturday to Monday at the house of Sir John Lubbock near Farnborough, Kent. Lubbock, later the first Lord Avebury, was at that time Liberal MP for Maidstone, a fellow of the Royal Society and formidable as a promoter of reforming and philanthropic causes as he was successful as a banker. Among his other guests he had Sir Lyon Playfair, another FRS who was also MP for St Andrews and Edinburgh universities, T. H. Huxley and John Morley. It was the first time that Gladstone had met Morley, then aged thirty-nine and editor of the *Fortnightly Review*. Morley was to be not only his official biographer, but also the most devoted colleague of his last decade. After this initial encounter Gladstone wrote: 'I cannot help liking Mr J. Morley.'[17] (The touch of surprised reluctance presumably arose from Morley's well-known agnosticism.) To add to this intellectual feast they walked on the Sunday afternoon to call on Charles Darwin in a neighbouring village. Darwin, according to Morley, was dazzled that 'such a gentleman' should have visited him. Huxley, using with Morley their mutual saving of time while Gladstone was at church, said of him: 'why, put him in the middle of a moor, with nothing in the world but his shirt, and you could not prevent him from being anything he liked.'[18]

Over the turn of the year 1876–7 there had been a European conference at Constantinople. This was much in accordance with Gladstone's desires, for he believed above all in the Concert of Europe asserting itself. Such a view potentially separated him from his Radical allies, for they rightly saw the Concert as an essentially conservative concept, owing more to Castlereagh than to Cobden. However, the conference failed. The Turks rejected its demands, and there was no united will to impose them. Not only Britain, although Derby as British Foreign Secretary was a main instigator of the conference, but Austria and France were weak in their support, while Germany was mainly concerned to try to avoid too rough a rupture between Austria and Russia, which would destroy the *Dreikaiserbund*, united in favour of emperors but not of much else.

As the hope of a concerted solution receded, so the two sharp swords of the Balkan Christian communities reacted in different but typical ways. Gladstone devoted himself to writing another pamphlet, this time on the sufferings of Montenegro. On 19 April he 'finished, corrected and sent off my article on Montenegro which from the intense interest of the subject has kept me warm, even hot, all the time I have been writing it'.[19] But it did not heat the British public. It sold only 8000 copies and was something of an anti-climax after the *Bulgarian Horrors*. Meanwhile the Tsar moved towards war, which he declared against Turkey on 24 April, five days after Gladstone had completed his Montenegrin pamphlet and three days before he took his next important step, which was to put down five resolutions (on the Eastern Question) for debate and division in the House of Commons.

Typically Gladstone made up his mind during a day which he spent entirely in bed, with one of his sudden bouts of stomach upset and two visits from his physician: 'This day I took my decision: a severe one, in face of my not having a single approval in the *Upper* official circle. But had I in the first days of September asked the same body whether I ought to write my [Bulgarian] pamphlet I believe the unanimous verdict would have been no.'[20]*

The resolutions declared that the Porte (that is, the seat and entity of Turkish government) had offended against humanity; that, in the absence of adequate guarantees for the future, the Porte had accordingly lost all claim to moral or material support from the other powers; that British influences should be deployed in favour of local liberty and devolved government in the desecrated provinces; that the European Concert should reassert itself and exact all necessary changes from the government of the Sultan; and (in a wrapping-up procedural address to the Crown) that British policy should henceforth be based on these principles. Gladstone announced the exact form of the resolutions to the House of Commons three days later, saying: 'I make this motion on my own responsibility, and not as the organ of any party or section of a party.'

This disclaimer was hardly enough to prevent the motion being a deeply embarrassing one for the hesitant Liberal leadership. They were nervous of getting into a russophil position, but they were even more nervous of being assailed by the force of Gladstone's oratory. And they would, of course, have to decide whether or not to vote with him, either course presenting grave disadvantages. As was usual, Gladstone and Hartington moved stiffly at arm's length from each other while the more supple Granville attempted a compromise. 'Puss' Granville was lucky (although probably also cunning) in his timing, and caught Gladstone for a meeting with himself, Hartington and Wolverton (the former Whip) immediately after the Royal Academy dinner on Saturday, 5 May. About this dinner Gladstone struck an almost exultant note: 'spoke for "Literature!" My *reception* surprised me, it was so good.'[21] In this euphoric mood, post-applause as well as post-prandial, he was remarkably conciliatory. 'What they ask of me is really, from my point of view, little more than nominal.' He was wrong. His agreement to modify the second resolution and move only that and the first, although ranging over all five in his speech, produced a sense of let-down among both the hardline parliamentary Radicals such as Dilke and Chamberlain and the more utopian outside enthusiasts. It did however produce a

* The contribution to the Bulgarian pamphlet of Granville, the colleague most naturally disposed to support Gladstone, was to suggest the excision of 'bag and baggage' from the key paragraph, thereby illustrating the capacity of advisers, unless overruled, to destroy all the most resonant passages.

more or less united Liberal division lobby, although a weak one for the key vote resulted in defeat by 354 to 223, a majority far in excess of the nominal Conservative preponderance.

It also led to a memorable, even if not notably vote-winning, oration from Gladstone. He had to make it in unfavourable circumstances, for his deal with Granville exposed him to a multitude of points of order and procedural wrangles, which occupied the House almost until dinner time. When he eventually came to his main speech the House was emptying and those who remained were an impatient audience. He addressed them for his habitual two and a half hours. 'The House gradually came round . . .,' he recorded. His performance escaped by an even wider margin than usual any danger of being woodenly text-bound for he forgot his 'eyeglass', and could not read such limited notes as he had prepared.* It was in this speech that he launched his denunciation of the false values of the West End of London. Arthur Balfour, who as leader of the House at the time of Gladstone's death, twenty-one years later, had to pronounce the first panegyric, reverted to this 1877 occasion: 'I shall never forget the effect which this speech left on my mind. As a mere feat of physical endurance it was almost unsurpassed; as a feat of parliamentary courage, parliamentary skill, parliamentary endurance and parliamentary eloquence, I believe it will always be unequalled.'[22]

After the disposal of Gladstone's resolutions there was a lull in the British debate while the Russians moved into position and then successfully fought the Turks. The next act of the British political drama had to await the Russo-Turkish armistice, the Treaty of San Stefano and the height of London war fever, all in the early months of 1878. Then the music-halls (or at least one of them) rang to the chorus of:

> We don't want to fight, but by Jingo if we do,
> We've got the ships, we've got the men, we've got the money too.

This could be regarded as an anti-Gladstone hymn, for it neatly encapsulated everything he was most against, fighting an unjust war,

* Although Gladstone was so sparing in the amount of time he devoted to the preparation of even his greatest (and longest) speeches, he compensated by often taking pains subsequently to correct and edit them into a publishable state (there was a strong demand for them as pamphlets). He always found this an irritating burden, neither relaxing nor intellectually constructive. Thus, twelve days after this occasion, he wrote: 'Began the ever odious task of correcting my Speeches as made in the late Debate'. (*Diaries*, IX, p. 220.)

'jingoism', a term which it put into the language, maintaining an over-large fleet of vulnerable ironclads, sending troops unnecessarily to die, and, perhaps even worse, wasting public money and upsetting the probity of the budget. He had become a keen, almost obsessive theatre-goer, with the music-hall by no means excluded from his patronage. Stage histrionics and pulpit thunderings almost equally engaged his interest, and the former if anything had the edge at this stage in his life. Nevertheless these controversies marked a certain extrusion of his influence from the metropolis and its Home Counties. He chose to attack the West End. The West End of 'stage-door johnnies' and even of more modestly pleasure-seeking members of the middle class chose to mock him. Immediately his great clash with Beaconsfield was the prelude to the strong (but somewhat sterile) Liberal victory of 1880, but it also sowed the first seeds of the Liberal retreat to the bastions of the West Country, the Pennines and the Celtic fringes.

The conurbation on which Gladstone advanced within three weeks of his 'resolutions' debate was, however, the least remote, mountainous or Celtic in the whole of Britain, that of Joseph Chamberlain's Birmingham. On 31 May 1877 he went from Hawarden, where he had spent a Whitsun fortnight, to speak at the inaugural meeting of the National Liberal Federation. He stayed with Chamberlain, then an MP of not quite a year's standing. Radical Joe was not then in the full splendour of his gabled Italian gothic Highbury mansion, which was built only in 1880, but in a more modest but still substantial villa on the fringe of Edgbaston. It was nonetheless an exuberant day. Gladstone was hauled in triumph the couple of miles from the station to Chamberlain's house for an early dinner with many guests.

The meeting, in Bingley Hall, was from 7.00 to 9.30. The venue was itself a challenge. Bingley Hall was a big hangar-like exhibition hall with no seats for the multitude but an elastic standing capacity. Gladstone, when told there were likely to be more than 10,000 present, was uncharacteristically doubtful about his ability to command the cavernous space, but was persuaded that if Bright could do it so could he. In fact the audience far exceeded the estimate. Gladstone put it at 25,000 and Chamberlain at 30,000. There was speculation about whether so many had ever before assembled under one roof. Gladstone's one-and-a-quarter-hour speech contained no memorable passages, but did not disappoint. He always gave good value.

There was a number of quirks surrounding the visit. In bringing together the National Liberal Federation, which was made up of a hundred or more lesser caucuses clustered around the Birmingham core, Chamberlain was seeking a broader-based successor to the National Education League. In the early 1870s he had tried to use this as a vehicle to rally provincial Nonconformists against Gladstone's education policy and to launch himself into national politics, but had found it narrow for the latter purpose. It was thus odd that he should want Gladstone at the Federation's inaugural meeting and perhaps even odder that Gladstone should have made it his major engagement of the spring. The explanation on Chamberlain's side was that, although equivocal about Gladstone's anti-Turkish crusade, he wished to draw him back, for a short time at least, into the Liberal leadership to counteract the baleful Whiggery of Hartington and Granville. The irony was that the sixty-seven-year-old former Premier, once drawn back, stayed more than long enough to drive Chamberlain not only out of Liberal communion but out of his own caucus as well.

Gladstone for his part had an equally compelling reason for going to Birmingham. He wanted the support of the National Liberal Federation for his Eastern policy. And once in Birmingham he of course swept the faithful along with his eloquence. He also temporarily embraced his host in the compass of his enthusiasm. On the next day too he did Chamberlain proud. He performed at a breakfast party, visited a factory of the Birmingham Small Arms Company, lunched at a Birmingham board school, received a municipal address at the Town Hall and spoke at a final dinner before retreating to Hagley for the night. He also arranged one of the most maladroit visits of his sometimes maladroit life. In the late afternoon he took Chamberlain with him to see Newman at the Birmingham Oratory. A Gladstone–Newman rendezvous, particularly with Gladstone anxious to push Newman into supporting his Bulgarian agitation, would in itself have been an uneasy occasion. It was made positively absurd by adding to the mix Chamberlain, whose whole cast of mind and religion, such as the latter was, was as different as it is possible to imagine from that of Newman, and indeed of Gladstone. It is not surprising that the result was a tense twenty minutes of stilted conversation.

There was indeed an undercurrent of tenseness to the whole Birmingham visit. Gladstone had been gracious but reserved. Chamberlain had been welcoming but undazzled. Perhaps the most spontaneous warmth was in Gladstone recording that he 'saw Mr. Chamberlain's very pleasing children'.[23] As these would certainly have included Neville (then aged eight) and maybe Austen (then thirteen) this presence of two future leaders of the Conservative party introduced a final twist of irony to the proceedings. Although the visit served the different purposes of both Gladstone and Chamberlain, it left no residue of affection or mutual understanding.

It was Gladstone's only political excursion for some months except for some almost accidental July speeches. These were to spontaneous crowds in Plymouth and Exeter, where he went ashore from a four-day English Channel cruise in the yacht of Donald Currie, the founder of the Castle (later Union Castle) shipping line. Gladstone went infrequently to the House of Commons, and left London for Hawarden on 28 July, an early retreat by the standards of Victorian parliamentary sessions. He stayed at Hawarden almost uninterruptedly from then until the beginning of his only Irish tour in mid-October. During that long static period he developed, again almost by accident, a novel form of semi-passive political campaigning, one which has never since been repeated except perhaps by one or two American presidential candidates who fought from their 'front porches'. On 4 August he wrote: 'A party of 1400 came from Bolton! We were nearly killed with kindness. I began with W[illy] the cutting of a tree; and had to speak to them, but not on politics.'[24] Two days later *The Times* reported that 'the very splinters which flew from his axe were picked up and treasured as relics'.

Two weeks after that about 3000 came from Salford and Darwen, and Gladstone seemed to be warming to the attention. They were 'very well managed', he wrote. Two days after that there were 2000 from Bacup who were 'very hearty and enjoyed themselves much'. It seems as though the momentum was growing and no self-respecting Lancashire industrial town would be allowed to escape sending a contingent. In fact, however, the end of the holiday season and peculiarly dismal weather brought the expeditions to an end. There were 600 from Leigh and Rossendale on 1 September, and that was that. These activities aroused some London cynicism, with other politicians, who would have been appalled but also amazed and flattered to have been pursued to their country estates by enthusiastic crowds, affecting to believe that there was more contrivance than spontaneity about the excursions and that Gladstone had arranged it all as a massage for his own demagogic ego. Whether the 'invasions' were planned or impulsive, welcome or burdensome, there could be no doubt that they showed how Gladstone's denunciation of Disraeli's pro-Turkish imperialist showmanship had reknit the alliance between himself and provincial democracy.

25

Midlothian Beckons

In the early stages of the Russo-Turkish War the campaign favoured the Russians, and Disraeli, egged on by the Queen, came very close in July 1877 to advocating British intervention on the Turkish side. Fortunately he had a reluctant Cabinet and a more than reluctant Foreign Secretary in the shape of Derby, who pointed out that Britain would have no allies. Disraeli replied that the British needed none other than the Turks who, soldier for soldier, were worth twenty Spaniards – he was drawing an analogy with Wellington's Peninsular campaign. The Turks proceeded to give some force to his argument by their resolute defence of Plevna, which kept the Russians 250 miles or so from Constantinople for five months. As it was the fear of Tsarist troops on the Golden Horn and the Bosphorus which most excited English bellicosity, this produced an autumn lull. But when on 9 December Plevna at last fell, and the Russian armies advanced to spend their Christmas almost within sight of the minarets of Stamboul, the most virulent phase of the British political battle began.

In January 1878 a British fleet was despatched to the Dardanelles. Lord Carnarvon, the Colonial Secretary, resigned from Disraeli's Cabinet, and there was a Russo-Turkish armistice, which at least removed the imminent threat of the Tsar bestriding the Bosphorus. It also led on to the March Treaty of San Stefano, with the creation of a huge Bulgaria and the effective throwing out of the Turks from Europe except for a tiny Constantinople hinterland. At the end of January Gladstone used the improbable ambience of a six-hour dinner of the Palmerston Club at Oxford to deliver his strongest denunciation of 'Beaconsfieldism'. On 24 February, and again two weeks later, there were London Sunday afternoon demonstrations against Gladstone. On the first Sunday his Harley Street windows were smashed. On the second he and his wife had to seek refuge in the Cavendish Square house of his doctor, and then escape in a cab escorted by four mounted constables. In most of the Northern or either of the great Scottish cities he would by contrast have been carried shoulder-high. In the previous November he had crushingly defeated Stafford Northcote for the rectorship of Glasgow University* and in March he both announced publicly that he would not stand again for Greenwich and received a strong invitation to become a candidate for Leeds, as safe a Liberal seat as it was populous an electorate (49,000). Gladstone gave a stalling answer at that stage. Two months later the first flicker of a Midlothian possibility came over the horizon.

In the meantime, the Treaty of San Stefano had been signed at the beginning of March and at the end of the month Derby had resigned (after hesitating too long to make his going effective) against the warlike steps of ordering Indian troops into the Mediterranean and calling up British reserves. On 9 April Gladstone voted in a small minority of sixty-four against the latter step, which well illustrated the limited parliamentary strength of hard-core anti-'Beaconsfieldism' as opposed to those, like Hartington, who thought it wise from time to time to assuage Gladstone rather than to expose themselves to the blast of his oratory. This combination of Liberal disunity and lukewarmness gave House of Commons protection even to a government front bench as weak as that which had been left by Disraeli's departure to the Lords.

The country was a different matter, particularly in the North and Scotland, and it was on this dimension that Gladstone's attention became increasingly concentrated. In the summer of the Congress of Berlin he made only one major speech in Parliament, and that, on 30 July, was notable more for its length (his almost statutory two and a half hours for an important debate) than for its content. His own version of the occasion was realistic. He had been suffering over the weekend from the 'depressing and sharp pain of a gumboil'.[1] On the Monday of his speech his face was less distorted, although: 'I was in body much below par but put on the steam perforce. It ought to have been *far* better.'[2]

'Putting on the steam perforce' was a vividly truthful rather than a flattering phrase for a great orator to write about himself after an indifferent day and fitted in with some other almost devastatingly self-critical remarks which he made around this time. When his letters to Samuel Wilberforce were sent to him in 1879 by the Bishop's biographer with a request for their free use, Gladstone acceded but added the

* To defeat one's former private secretary was not perhaps the most glorious of political big-game hunts. It was also the case that in the same autumn the Duke of Buccleuch had been elected Chancellor by the graduates of Glasgow; only undergraduates voted in the rectorship election.

private comment: 'They are curiously illustrative of a peculiar and second-rate nature.'[3]

Such surprising shafts, accompanied by a certain inherently comic quality about his persona and his reaction to some events, made Gladstone a much more sympathetic character than his moralizing and didactic personality might at first sight lead one to suppose. Thus for 14 June 1879 he remarked: '6–11. Attended the dinner of the Savage Club. Too long and the clouds of tobacco were fearful. In other respects most interesting. It was impossible to speak ill of so quick and sympathetic an audience. I returned thanks for Literature & was (like the *ensemble*) too long; but nothing could exhaust their patience.'[4] The audience would have been composed of 'literary gents' and some actors. Gladstone loved any audience with histrionic affiliations. This fitted in with his April 1878 reaction to an address of an hour which he gave to 'a remarkable meeting' of Nonconformist Ministers in the Farringdon Street Memorial Hall, where, twenty-two years later, the Labour party was to be founded. 'Never did I address a better audience,'[5] he wrote. They were, of course, themselves mostly performers and this gave them something of the same quality which, a decade and more later, he attributed to what he described as the best audience of his whole life – a congress of actors, because they were the ones who best understood what he was trying to do.

On the Sunday morning following the four hours of tobacco-clouded (and no doubt liberally wine-supplied) Savage Club jollification, Gladstone recorded himself as being 'laid up with deranged liver & bowels'. Dr Clark came, prescribed castor oil and tactfully laid 'the blame on eight hours of heat [the length of the celebration seemed to have grown overnight] & on preserved peas'.[6] An alternative if less tactful explanation would have been that Gladstone was suffering from a good old-fashioned hangover. There is some inconclusive evidence from the pattern of his quite frequent sick headaches, which kept him in bed for half a day or so, that he may have been subject to this form of retribution after occasional over-indulgence. On the one occasion (in 1885) when he dined alone at Grillion's, for by accident no one else came, he entered himself in the club book as having consumed a single bottle of champagne, which was quite moderate, particularly as he might not have finished it. While there is no evidence that his consumption, unlike that of Asquith, ever rendered him unsteady, he liked wine throughout his life, and, as with most people, probably drank more under stimulus of animated conversation than in solitary state.

Over the summer and then the recess of 1878 Gladstone was politically quiet. Private obligations filled some of the slack. In May at a dinner party of the Frederick Cavendishes he sat down next to the Duchess of Argyll, who immediately had a stroke and died within a few hours. Whether because of the proximity or for more general reasons of respect for the Duke and his family, Gladstone went to the funeral near Helensburgh, travelling all night from St Pancras 'in a Pullman bed with rest but no (continuous) sleep'.[7] After the interment he went to Glasgow, and looked at a 'highly interesting' exhibition of pictures. Glasgow, with no Kelvingrove Gallery for another twenty years, let alone a Burrell Collection, was nevertheless foreshadowing its twentieth-century reputation as a centre of both indigenous and imported art.

Then he took an evening train to Sheffield, on his way to Clumber, the Newcastle house where he had first waited on the fourth Duke in 1832, and where he was still laboriously trying, fourteen years after the death of his friend the fifth Duke, to discharge his thankless duties as a trustee of the embarrassed estate with its degenerate heirs. (A year later the task was made even more onerous by the house being badly burnt.) On this visit he devoted two and a half days mainly to trying to sort the letters of the fifth Duke, an obligation which it might be thought a once and future Prime Minister could have delegated.

This Clumber visit, and Gladstone's continuing efforts to make some sense out of the financial chaos of the Newcastle affairs, prompts a comparison between the way in which he and Disraeli discharged their earlier-incurred ducal obligations. They both liked a duke, but had different ways of showing it. Disraeli had benefited greatly from his 1840s association with Lord George Bentinck and had also been assisted by Bentinck family money in the purchase of Hughenden. In 1880, in the last year of his life, Disraeli summoned the head of the Bentinck family, a twenty-two-year-old Coldstream Guards subaltern who had recently succeeded as sixth Duke of Portland, to visit him there. No one else was present other than Montagu Corry. Nevertheless Disraeli came down to dinner in the blue riband of the Garter, but regarded this as a substitute for conversational effort. The meal passed in barely broken silence, but all too slowly for the mystified and uneasy young nobleman. Then Disraeli rose to his feet, said, 'My Lord Duke, I come from a race which never forgives an injury, nor forgets a benefit,' and bizarrely announced that he proposed to make the Duke's stepmother (his closest relation, for both his parents were dead and he had made a cousinly succession) a peeress in her own right. (She became Lady Bolsover.) He then closed the evening, sweeping aside the Duke's attempt to reply and retired to his red boxes.[8] Disraeli paid his debts with theatre, mainly devised for his own amusement, Gladstone with a heavy-footed almost interfering devotion.

It was one of the paradoxes of Gladstone's life at this time that, as his denunciations of the 'upper ten thousand' and 'the West End of London' became more shrill, so his own social life became if anything more elevated. In the autumn of 1878, despite his habit of not giving grand house parties, he had two dukes (Bedford* and Argyll), as well as another duchess (Westminster) and the marquisal Baths, to stay at Hawarden. His own excursions that autumn included an early October semi-walking, semi-speechmaking tour of the Isle of Man (eight speeches in six days, which was prodigal particularly as the Manxmen had no United Kingdom votes) with his son Stephen. Then, after two weeks at home, he progressed via Bedfordshire to Cambridge. He stayed with the Bedfords at Woburn and with the Cowpers (he became Gladstone's Irish Viceroy in 1880) at Wrest Park. In Cambridge, he stayed with the Sidgwicks, she Balfour's sister and founder of Newnham, he the foremost exponent of Millite philosophy in the University and a vigorous educational reformer. Gladstone's Sunday there comprised Trinity chapel at 10.30, a sermon from the Bishop of Ely in the University church at 2.00, King's College Chapel at 3.30, and dinner in Trinity for the first time since he had stayed in that Master's Lodge in 1831.

In 1879 he was more adventurous than in the previous year. Not only did he go in the spring to two great south Midland houses for the first time, but he spent five early-autumn weeks on what was half a return pilgrimage to Dr Döllinger and the Bavarian Alps and half a descent into Venice for the penultimate (the last was in 1889) of his nine Italian

* With Bedford (the ninth Duke, 1819–91), whom he described as '*most* worthy', he acted in a very firm and, for Gladstone, surprisingly Whiggish way. Disraeli had offered a peerage to the Duke's younger brother, Lord Odo Russell, for his special services as ambassador in Berlin at the time of the Congress. Russell accepted with enthusiasm, but was then warned off by his brother acting as Gladstone's agent. 'Great was therefore my surprise,' Russell wrote to Gladstone, 'when the Duke told me that in your opinion by accepting this peerage I was virtually repudiating the political principles of my family and of my party, and that you held that I should defer the acceptance of the Queen's offer until our party was once again in power.' (*Diaries*, IX, p. 346.) Nevertheless he reluctantly accepted the ukase, and the Ampthill title did not come into existence until 1881 – even after the change of government Gladstone made Lord Odo wait another year.

visits. The country-house visits of the spring were both significant harbingers of his remaining fifteen years in politics. The first was to Althorp, where his host was the fifth Earl Spencer, the 'red earl', as he was known on account of his beard rather than his politics. When the Home Rule split came in 1886, Spencer, perhaps because of his experience as Irish Viceroy in 1882–5, was to be the most faithful to Liberalism of the grand old Whigs, although also, as First Lord of the Admiralty in 1894, the most jagged of the rocks on which Gladstone impaled himself during the last sad months of his fourth premiership.

The second was to Mentmore (built 1852–4), one of the great Rothschild piles of the Vale of Aylesbury which had come to the fifth Earl of Rosebery through his marriage to Hannah de Rothschild, the only child of Baron Meyer and thus the principal Rothschild heiress of her generation. The marriage brought more wealth than happiness to Rosebery. But nothing, not even winning the two Derbys which were run during his sixteen months of undeserved and unrewarding premiership, brought him contentment. Rosebery's interest for Gladstone in 1879, apart from the shafts of charm and wit which shone through his spoilt and misanthropic character, exemplifying themselves in his qualities as a writer and powerful if florid orator, sprang from the other Rosebery territorial base at Dalmeny, which looked north across the then bridgeless Firth of Forth and south over the city of Edinburgh.

From the first mention of Midlothian in his diaries, which was in the entry for 16 May 1878, Gladstone had been increasingly attracted by the prospect of standing at the next election in that Scottish county, for which Edinburghshire was the alternative name. The constituency was geographically centred on the capital city, although extending beyond it and including on its electoral register only those inhabitants, whether of the city or of the hinterland, who qualified for the very restricted pre-1886 Scottish county franchise. Rosebery was regarded by Gladstone as the key to the seat, and indeed he acted as Gladstone's host and sponsor during the two phases of the immortal Midlothian campaign, as during two of the three less dramatic subsequent general elections which Gladstone fought in the constituency.

Why was Gladstone attracted to Midlothian rather than to Leeds? The answer is far from obvious. It cannot have been a simple Scottish pietistic loyalty, for from Newark through the most Anglican of university seats to Lancashire to metropolitan Greenwich he could hardly have been less affected by this sentiment over the previous forty-seven years of his parliamentary life. Nor was it the desire for democratic validity.

Gladstone family photograph taken on the west side of Hawarden Castle *circa* 1868. Catherine Gladstone seated at the table in the centre; back row: Agnes Gladstone, W.E.G., Sir Stephen Glynne (looking very faintly askance at 'the great man') and Lucy Lyttelton (Cavendish); seated: unknown boy, Helen Gladstone, Willy Gladstone, Herbert Gladstone, Henry Gladstone, Lord Frederick Cavendish.

Tree-felling scene at Hawarden, probably in a mid-1880s autumn, although it was not until 1891, after thirty-three years of the pursuit, that Gladstone hung up his axe. Mrs Gladstone is looking unusually diva-like centre-stage. Willy Gladstone is sitting lugubriously on the trunk.

Queen Victoria and the Prince Consort towards the end of Albert's life.
While their marriage lasted (he died in 1862) she approved of Gladstone.

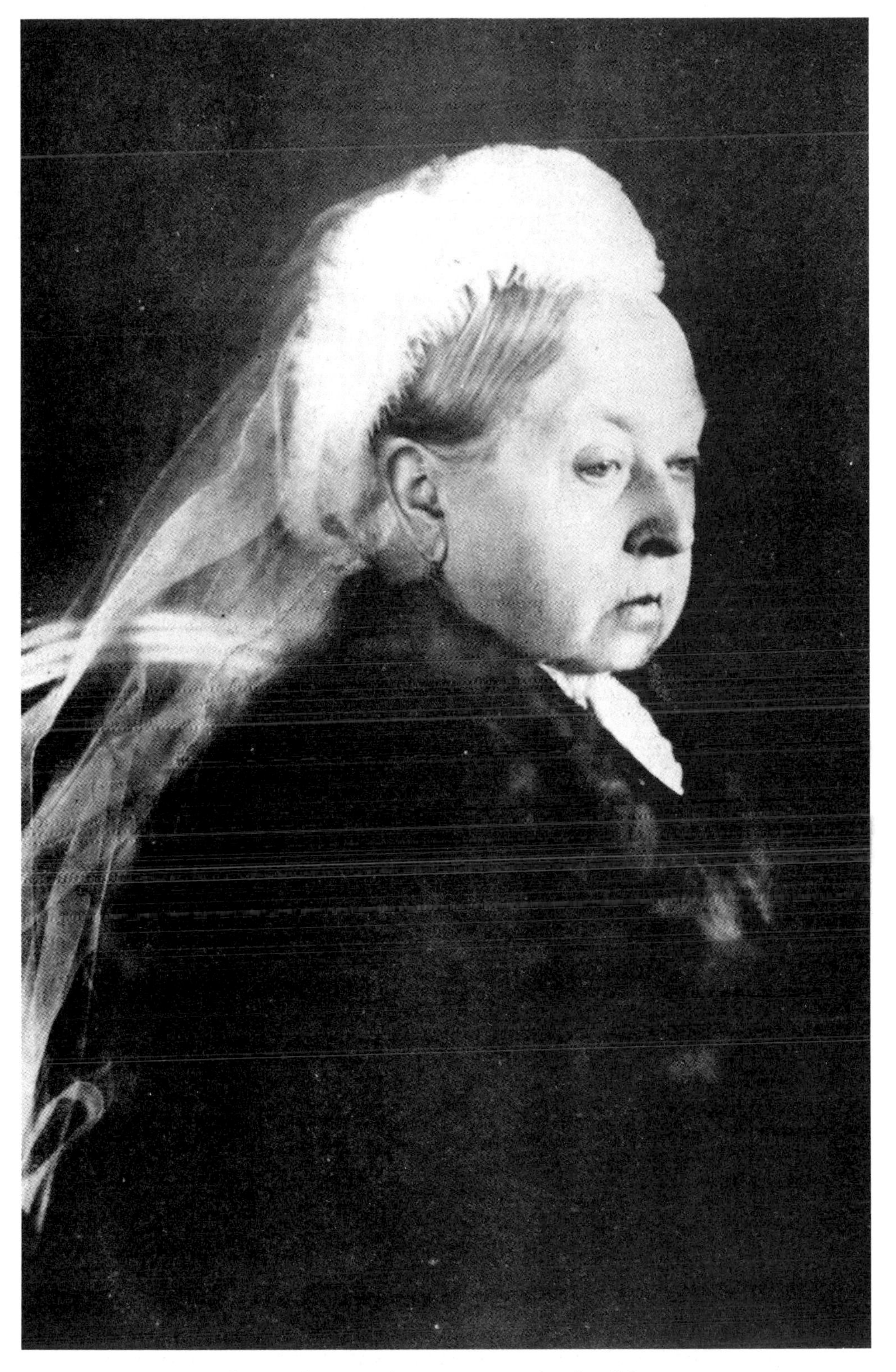

Afterwards, as in this 1890s picture, she did not.

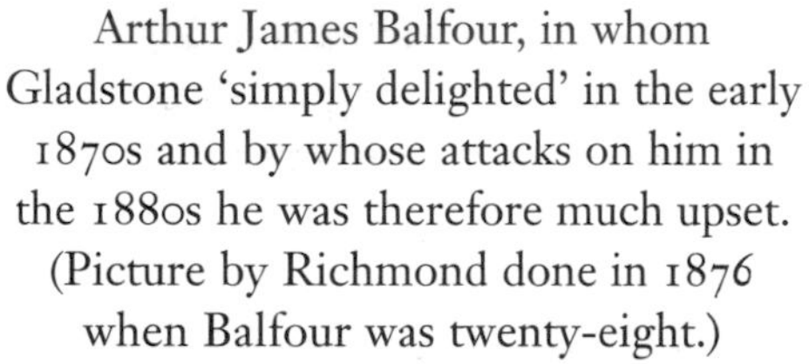

Arthur James Balfour, in whom Gladstone 'simply delighted' in the early 1870s and by whose attacks on him in the 1880s he was therefore much upset. (Picture by Richmond done in 1876 when Balfour was twenty-eight.)

The eighth Duke of Argyll, a close colleague of Gladstone's for a quarter of a century until he resigned over Irish land in 1881.

The Cabinet in 1883 (a contrived picture): from left to right: Dodson, Kimberley, Hartington, Harcourt, Derby, Granville, Gladstone, Selborne, Carlingford, Dilke, Childers, Northbrook, Chamberlain, Spencer.

The Prince of Wales *circa* 1875 looks benignly self-indulgent.

The second Earl Granville, 'a vital ball-bearing' of three Gladstone governments.

The Edinburgh of the Midlothian Campaign.

Two Whigs:
Lord Hartington, later eighth Duke of Devonshire, *left*,
the Red (and fifth) Earl Spencer, *right*, but red in beard rather than in politics,
who however remained faithful to Gladstone on Home Rule.

Two Radicals:
Joseph Chamberlain, *left*, looking glossy and sharp,
Sir Charles Dilke, *right*, looking opulent and sad.

Above: A Gladstone family group at Hawarden in the mid-1880s (see p. 462). Standing from left to right: Mrs Willy Gladstone, Willy Gladstone, Mary Gladstone, W.E.G.; seated: Henry Gladstone, Herbert Gladstone, Agnes (née Gladstone) Wickham with child, Catherine Gladstone, Edward Wickham, Stephen Gladstone, Helen Gladstone.

Right: Belabouring the Egyptian fellahin: an 1882 *Punch* cartoon illustrating the incongruity of Gladstone in 'the most civilian and almost parsonical of habits' indulging in a rare burst of militarism.

GLADSTONE INVADING EGYPT

Gladstone flanked by his official family of private secretaries, *circa* 1883:
Horace Seymour, Spencer Lyttelton, George Leveson Gower and Edward Hamilton.

Leeds, as has been stated, had nearly 50,000 electors. Midlothian had 3620. Nor was Midlothian a risky contest and therefore a greater challenge, with victory in consequence a greater prize. Leeds had a stronger Liberal preponderance, but, with a mass electorate uncontrolled by as efficient a caucus as that which Chamberlain had manufactured in Birmingham, it was not as accurately predictable. The smallness of the Midlothian electorate made those who were voters subject to reliable individual analysis. Such an analysis was carried out in advance by two Edinburgh lawyers who looked after the nuts and bolts of the campaign under Rosebery's command and with his money. In January, 1879, just before Gladstone committed himself to the seat, they reported, through the Liberal Chief Whip, that he could count on a majority of about 200, 'after giving *all* the doubtfuls (251) to the Conservatives'.[9] (It was a remarkably accurate forecast; the actual 1880 majority was 211.)

The Midlothian campaign, while it was magnificent, was not therefore electorally bold. Gladstone indeed explicitly recognized this in his letter of acceptance: 'You have also been kind enough to supply me with evidence which entirely satisfies my mind that the invitation expresses the desire of the majority of the constituency.'[10] Nor was the campaign necessary to win Midlothian. The purposes for which it was necessary were the reimposition of Gladstone's authority on the national political scene, and the sending out of beams of Liberal enthusiasm. Edinburgh from this point of view was as well placed a lighthouse as it is possible to imagine. It was a subsidiary metropolis without being much seduced by either the fashionable jingoism of Mayfair, Belgravia and Kensington or the popular jingoism of the music-halls which made 'Beaconsfieldism' attractive to London and the Home Counties. It was a story which was to repeat itself in minor key just over a hundred years later when Scotland was noticeably cool on the Falklands War.

There was one complication about Midlothian, which was that the sitting Conservative member was Lord Dalkeith, the son of Gladstone's old friend, Cabinet colleague in the Peel government and occasional host at Drumlanrig, the fifth Duke of Buccleuch. This juxtaposition appears to have had no effect, one way or the other, upon Gladstone. He had no desire to do the Buccleuchs down, and indeed opened his campaign in the elegant Edinburgh Assemby Rooms (sometimes called the Music Hall) in George Street with a tribute to their qualities as noblemen and to Buccleuch's (and Dalkeith's) setting 'us all an example in the active and conscientious discharge of his duty, such as he believes it to be'.[11] Equally, however, there is no evidence that he was remotely embarrassed by the virulence of the conflict or by inflicting the territorial defeat. He was on particularly challenging form in the Corn Exchange of the town of Dalkeith, where he set out a programme of all-round devolution for the different parts of the United Kingdom.

The truth was that Gladstone, both because this was made necessary by his having moved so far across the spectrum of politics and because he believed he was serving God's purposes, was ruthless in the subordination of personal to political considerations. He did not quarrel with those with whom he disagreed, but nor did he hesitate when new needs sundered old friendships. Thus in the early 1880s he accepted almost with equanimity the ruptures with Argyll and John Bright, the two members of his first two governments for whom he consistently expressed the highest esteem. The politically much more important 1886 defections of Hartington and Chamberlain were in a different category, for in separate ways he underestimated them both almost as much as he had certainly overesteemed Bright and probably Argyll too. Compared with any of these his personal relations with Buccleuch, largely quiescent for a decade and a half, were barely a molehill in his path.

Although Gladstone committed himself to Midlothian fifteen months before what turned out to be the date of the general election – the Parliament could have run another year after that – he did not say a definite 'no' to Leeds, and he did not visit Edinburgh until ten of those fifteen months had passed. He thus moved into a position curiously comparable with that which he had occupied in 1868, and when the election came was nominated for both constituencies, just as he had previously been with South-west Lancashire and Greenwich. The difference was that in 1868 Gladstone lost the seat in which he campaigned, and had to sit for the one which he had never wanted or sought. The result was the wholly loveless marriage of his eleven years in Greenwich. In 1880, by contrast, he secured the seat which he wanted, and Leeds, which elected him by 24,622 against 13,331 for the leading Conservative, was left waiting at the altar. He passed on the disappointed bride to the youngest and most politically committed of his sons, who had just unsuccessfully fought Middlesex. Herbert Gladstone was returned unopposed for Leeds when his father renounced the seat, and sat there with mutual satisfaction until 1910.

Eighteen-seventy-nine, at least until Gladstone's first Midlothian excursion, which lasted from 24 November to 8 December, was a year of waiting. The two imperial wars against the Zulus and the Afghans, which in Gladstone's view piled Pelion on the Ossa of the vainglories of 'Beaconsfieldism', disfigured the year, but for the rest the weather provoked the most comment. It was a spectacularly cold Christmas and New Year over the turn of 1878–9. Gladstone left London for Hawarden in a thick fog on 20 December, arrived after midnight and worked until nearly 3.00 a.m. on his accumulated mail. Next morning he 'Rose at nine: and saw the sun! Such a treat for a cockney at this season!'[12] Late-Advent high pressure produced intense cold, even in North Wales. By Christmas Eve it was such that he could not chop wood. On Christmas Day 'we worked on clearing the pond for skaters'. On the day after, Granville came for a night, and Gladstone found that his guest's water-drinking (no doubt for his gout) 'has [not] been favourable to his general mental force and especially his initiative'.[13]

By contrast Gladstone, on his sixty-ninth birthday two days after Granville's departure, was exultant about his own vigour. 'And why has my health, my strength, been so peculiarly sustained? All this year and more – I think – I have not been confined to bed for a single day.' This was not remotely true; according to his diary he had spent in bed at least part of fourteen days, scattered over the months of January, February, July and November, as a result of specific if minor ailments. But perhaps the interesting thing was that, stimulated by the continuing good hard weather, he believed it to be so. 'In the great physical and mental effort of speaking to large auditories, I have been as it were upheld in an unusual manner. . . .' He continued: 'Was not all this for a purpose? . . . If I am spared for another birthday God grant that by that time there may have been a great shifting of events and parts & that I may have entered into that period of recollection and penitence which my life much needs before its close.'[14]

The last sentence was bewilderingly contradictory. If there was to be 'a great shifting of events and parts', which could mean nothing but the defeat of the government, this was totally incompatible, given the hand that he was playing, with his retreat into a 'period of recollection and penitence'. It is better perhaps to return to the weather, which was more susceptible to objective verification than were Gladstone's yearnings or musings about his own future. The massive frosts continued until 18 January 1879, and then disappeared abruptly.

They were not balanced by a warm and serene summer. Gladstone, who in general was not greatly interested in or affected by weather, gradually became obsessed by its awfulness. For 12 August he wrote with emphasis, '*Our first pure summer's day for the year*,' and the evening before on a drive to and from Chester he had noted that 'The very faintest tinge of yellowing is just beginning to appear on some of the crops'.[15] On 5 September he attended what he described as a 'service of humiliation for the weather' in Hawarden church. By then most of the faintly yellowing corn had been destroyed; six inches of rain fell on North Wales in two late-August days. It was only after this that he decided that 'all things considered it seem[ed] right to undertake the journey'[16] (to Venice). There fortunately 'the moon [was] full, the weather delightful.... Band played in the Piazza at night: we all sat & *iced* before Florians.'[17] He never saw Venice after that visit.

By the time of the first phase of the Midlothian campaign in late autumn the British weather had been superseded in Gladstone's mind by more exciting subjects for comment, although his two foremost biographers have done their best to make up for this by supplying conflicting colour. Morley wrote of 24 November, the day when Gladstone progressed by train from Liverpool to Edinburgh, with intermediate station speeches at Carlisle (an audience of 500), Hawick (4000) and Galashiels (8000), as 'a bleak winter's day'.[18] Magnus described it as a 'beautiful sunny day'.[19] The *Scotsman*'s 'Meteorological Register' for that day leans towards Morley by recording Edinburgh weather as having been 'overcast, showery, with a maximum temperature of 44°F'. What was certain was that it was a day of enthusiastic progress and of triumphant arrival in his new constituency. It was dark when he reached Edinburgh, but 'the scene even to the West end of the City was extraordinary both from the numbers and the enthusiasm, here and there a solitary groan or howl. We drove off to Dalmeny with Ld Rosebery and were received with fireworks & torches. I have never gone through a more extraordinary day.'[20]

The first week was devoted to strict Midlothian campaigning. He made another nine speeches, of which four, receiving addresses or replying to a toast, were short and to small audiences. The other five were major orations, whether judged by their content and length or by the number of people listening to and indeed held rapt by them. At the Edinburgh Assembly Rooms he addressed 2500, at the Dalkeith Corn Exchange 3500, the same number in the West Calder Assembly Rooms, 5000 in the Edinburgh Corn Exchange and then, on the same Saturday afternoon as the Corn Exchange meeting, 20,000 in the Waverley Market. The venues were local to the constituency, but even the physically present audiences were wider-based – enthusiasts came in from all over Scotland – and the reading audience was fully nationwide. Throughout the kingdom all serious newspapers (and most were so in those days) carried four- or five-column reports of the major speeches. This meant that, although unprepared in detail, each of the speeches had to be different from the others in theme, and sufficiently coherent, even fastidious, in language as not to repel Liberals of light and learning who absorbed the words not in the emotional atmosphere of a mass meeting but in the more critical calm of their breakfast rooms. Gladstone's oratory here, as elsewhere and at other times, was a little turgid, but there could be no ranting.

He did however indulge, to use Morley's oxymoron, in 'intellectual sentimentality'. In this category could be placed his references to the Zulus and to the Afghans, both of whom he saw as the pawns of Disraeli's showy imperialism, which was as cruel to its overseas victims as it was corrupting to the appetites of its home supporters. Of the Zulus 10,000 had been slaughtered 'for no other offence than their attempt to defend against your artillery with their naked bodies, their hearths and home, their wives and families . . . '. Of the Afghans, his audience was called to remember that 'the sanctity of life in the hill villages of Afghanistan, among the winter snows, is as inviolable in the eyes of Almighty God as can be your own'.[21] To balance this there was the immense seriousness of the arguments which he put before his mass audiences. In the Edinburgh Corn Exchange, for instance, he spoke to 5000 for one and a quarter hours on the most intricate and statistical detail of Disraeli's financial profligacy. At West Calder he spoke to almost as many on the details of foreign policy and on why quack remedies (that is, protection) were no answer to the current agricultural depression.

He never pandered or talked down to his audiences. He treated them to the same full rigour of his elevated and erudite if somewhat tendentious style of argument as he deployed before the House of Commons. The flattery lay in assuming their seriousness and judgemental capacity. And given the reverence he excited this increased the self-respect of those who came to his meetings and thereby gave them a satisfying experience. They felt that they had been raised to membership of some mystical tribunal of the nation. To his mass 20,000 standing audience in the Waverley Market (at which he noted that people who had fainted were 'continually handed out over the heads . . . and were as if dead'),[22] few of whom were within miles of the county franchise, he gave the same accolade of dignity. You 'who do not fear to call yourselves the working men of Edinburgh, Leith and the district' were nonetheless part of the great assize of Britain.

In the second week of the campaign Gladstone gave overt expression of the truth that the object was much wider than winning Midlothian and deserted Edinburgh for other Scottish towns and cities. On Monday, 1 December, he made speeches at Inverkeithing, Dunfermline, Aberfeldy and Perth (two, one to a civic gathering of 1500 in the City Hall for the conferment of the Freedom and the other to an open-air meeting of 4000). The Friday was his Glasgow day, beginning with his rectorial address before an audience of 5000. He had devoted far more preparatory attention to this than to any other speech of his Scottish fortnight. It was essentially an attack on the plutocratic values which in the 1870s were widely perceived as having gained as much ground as they were again to do 110 years later in the 1980s.

The anti-plutocratic theme was an interesting and delicate one for Gladstone, for he most certainly was not an egalitarian. Ruskin, staying at Hawarden in January 1878 ('In some respects an unrivalled guest, and those important respects too'),[23] had suggested that Gladstone was in the category of those who believed 'one man [was] as good as another'. 'I am nothing of the sort,' Gladstone was reported as replying. 'I am a firm believer in the aristocratic principle – the rule of the best. I am an out-and-out *inequalitarian*.'[24] He believed that men should have the opportunity to accumulate large fortunes. Some of his strongest provincial supporters, moved by his moral fire although mostly Nonconformist and not sharing his Anglicanism, were engaged at the time in doing precisely that. And he perhaps believed even more strongly in the hereditary principle. But he was against the flaunting of wealth, whether it was old or new. He took this view partly, but only partly, on conservative, social-order grounds. He did not want the poor stirred up by profligacy into an unwillingness to accept their lot.

He also believed that the flaunting of great wealth was morally bad. What he liked best was an austere duke of large fortune (he had had too much trouble with the Newcastles to want poor dukes), public spirit, intellectual interest and Liberal views, living well within his income and ploughing the rest back to secure the future of his estates and his heirs. Trollope's Duke of Omnium (Plantagenet Palliser before he succeeded, not the self-indulgent and corrupting old Duke) was very much to his taste, except that had Trollope lived to write sequels in the late 1880s, they would almost certainly have portrayed Omnium as a Liberal Unionist. What Gladstone liked next best were men like Samuel Morley, a Congregationalist teetotaller who became a Nottingham hosiery magnate. Morley devoted much of his immense fortune to building Dissenting chapels and to general philanthropy, subsidizing both the Liberal *Daily News* (of which he was principal proprietor) and the political career of his son. This son, Arnold Morley, became Gladstone's Home Rule Chief Whip after the Brands and the Glyns and the Grosvenors had defected. What Gladstone liked least was plutocratic display, particularly when it was accompanied by any fondness for Disraeli's imperialism. His least favourite ducal family was probably the Marlboroughs, of whom he harshly said in 1882: 'there never was a Churchill from John of Marlborough down that had either morals or principles.'[25]*

There was no absence of either morals or principles in his Glasgow University address. Apart from his repudiation of luxury and the obsessive pursuit of mammon, he extolled 'the intellectual dignity' of a vocation 'in the Christian ministry', elevated ratiocination to the centre of human experience ('thought is the citadel'), and left his audience with four guides which they should follow in controversy: 'truth, charity, diligence and reverence'. The address lasted one and a half hours and sounds austere fare for the traditionally rumbustious rectorial occasion. 'The blue caps [the Tory students] as well as the red [Liberal] cheered fervently, at the close,' he wrote.[26] The explanation which John Morley gave was that all, even those for whom the topics and the treatment were not particularly sympathetic, were so captivated by the sheer quality of the physical performance that they were sorry, even after ninety minutes, 'when the stream of fascinating melody ceased to flow'.[27] To believe that the students wanted still more is perhaps a tall order, but the indisputable fact remains that, in contrast with some more modern Glasgow rectorial occasions, there were no eggs, no catcalls and sustained applause. And it took place at a time of tense political controversy.

There was then a late luncheon (and another speech) in the second great hall on the University's new (opened in 1870) Gilmore Hall site. After a pause of little more than an hour he was on his way to the St Andrew's Hall, the home of Glasgow music until it was destroyed by fire in 1962, where he addressed 6500 for another one and a half hours.

* By then he had been tormented for a couple of years by Lord Randolph Churchill, particularly on the issue of Bradlaugh's oath. He never knew Winston Churchill. The words, although quoted in Roy Foster's admirable study of Randolph Churchill, do not sound quite authentically Gladstonian.

Then at nine he went on to the City Hall where he spoke, without apparent flagging, to another 2500. 'Did not God in his mercy wonderfully bear me through?'[28] he laconically (for once) mused.

The next day he received the Freedom of Motherwell and Hamilton before spending a Saturday to Monday at Dalzell, the middle Clyde Valley house of a Liberal MP. Then he returned by train to Hawarden, through another series of station demonstrations at Carlisle, Preston, Wigan, Warrington and Chester. These railway crowds brought those whom it was calculated he had addressed (in thirty speeches and over his fifteen-day circuit) to the precise figure of 86,930.[29] As a less friendly observer also calculated that he had delivered himself of 85,840 words during this fortnight, there was a close balance between output and audience.

Gladstone arrived back at Hawarden in high morale. Lucy Cavendish, who was there, recorded in a phrase as vivid as it is dated that, while her aunt took to her bed in a state of exhaustion, Uncle William was 'as fresh as paint'. Moreover, she thought him, for the first time, 'a little *personally* elated'.[30] His mood and behaviour were that of a general after a decisive battle, anxious to pause and write his despatches rather than to be off in hot pursuit and in search of the next engagement. On the first day he stayed in bed until mid-morning 'nursing my throat'. Then he felled a sycamore in the afternoon as well as revising his rectorial address for publication by John Murray, writing to the *Scotsman* to refine some point, and beginning the revision of all his Midlothian speeches, also for publication, which he was surprised, a few days later, to discover amounted to a book of 255 pages. He showed no desire to exploit his triumph by going to London, seeing his colleagues and adding to the turbulence which his thunderous campaign had already created for the official Liberal leadership.

There had been a divisive plan to give Gladstone a London banquet on his return from Midlothian, which would in effect have been an anti-Hartington rally. That had been dropped, wisely if Liberal unity on the threshold of a general election was regarded as desirable. Then there was a proposition, strangely headed by A. J. Mundella, Radical MP for Sheffield and a leading instigator of anti-Turkish indignation in the autumn of 1876, that there should be a banquet of loyalty to Hartington in February. Next, with one of those pieces of elephantine subtlety beloved of whips and other political fixers, it was thought that circles could be squared and the embarrassment of the principals combined with the entertainment of the audience by getting Gladstone to preside over this feast. Two hundred and forty Liberal MPs subscribed to the projected pageant, and Gladstone unenthusiastically consulted Granville about whether he should accept. Fortunately Hartington had the robust good sense to turn it down flat. The 240 MPs got their money back, and Gladstone was saved having to make a speech even more rich than usual in convoluted obscurities and qualifying sub-clauses.

Hartington shared with William Harcourt, and with almost no one else who worked closely with Gladstone, the quality of being undazzled by him. Many of the others were often irritated by and sometimes (behind his back) deeply critical of Gladstone. But they were nonetheless to a greater or lesser extent swept away by the force of his personality. Hartington and Harcourt, although sharply different characters in other respects, who moreover ended up in diametrically opposite political camps, were the only two batsmen who were not intimidated by his fast bowling, Hartington because he just stood there, letting the balls bounce past him, and Harcourt because he hit back with confidence if not always with skill. Hartington's phlegmatic character was brilliantly caught by a description which Derby wrote in his diary after a visit by him to Knowsley in October 1879. Hartington, although in many ways the quintessential Whig aristocrat in politics, never got on particularly well with his fellow landed magnates, neither Derby himself, whom he once dismissed as no more than an owner of Liverpool ground rents, or Salisbury, who was too much of a non-sporting intellectual for Hartington's taste and who, when they were working in close alliance in 1891, retaliated by complaining that 'Hartington is at Newmarket and all political arrangements have to be hung up till some quadruped has run faster than some other quadruped.'[31]

Derby's description of Hartington was:

> He talks of politics sensibly but without animation, and leaves on one's mind the impression of thinking the whole concern a nuisance.... He talks in a slow, drawling way, as if the exertion of opening his mouth were disagreeable; but what he says is sound, hard sense, conveyed in few words. He has some humour and enjoys a joke. I cannot imagine him excited or angry.[32]

This picture of Hartington as an early and cisatlantic exponent of the style of speech practised by some East Coast American gentlemen and known as 'Long Island lockjaw' is a vivid one. Hartington, however, was both more intelligent and more ambitious than conventional wisdom allows. After a shaky start he had come quite to enjoy being Liberal leader and probably thought that his efforts in this role meant that he deserved to be Prime Minister, even though his mixture of realism and negligence made him unwilling to fight for the top job in either 1880 or 1886. Nevertheless he was seriously discussing (with Granville and Forster) as late as October 1879 the possibility that Gladstone might be prepared to serve under him as Chancellor of the Exchequer, and during the 1880 election campaign he bestirred himself to make no less than twenty-four speeches, well in excess of Gladstone's own fifteen. They did not have the same resonance, although their impact was far from negligible and, like Gladstone's, they were subsequently collected into a book. His criticisms of Disraeli were sharp, and there were indications of further measures of Liberal reform, affecting local government, the franchise and even land tenure. He was then forty-six years old, and was undoubtedly trying.

Gladstone stayed at Hawarden over Christmas and ten days into the New Year. His seventieth-birthday thoughts were even more than usually a mixture of exultation at the strength which God personally gave him, somewhat routine self-criticism and an old man's awareness that he must be approaching the end of his life:

> For the last 3½ years I have been passing through a political experience which is I believe without example in our Parliamentary history. I profess . . . to believe it has been an occasion when the battle to be fought was a battle of justice humanity freedom law. . . . If I really believe this then I should regard my having been morally forced into this work as a great and high election of God. And certainly I cannot but believe that He has given me special gifts of strength, on the late occasion especially in Scotland. But alas the poor little garden of my own soul remains uncultivated, unweeded, defaced. . . . Three things I would ask of God over and above all the bounty which surrounds me. This first that I may escape into retirement.* This second that I may speedily be able to divest myself of everything resembling wealth. And the third – if I may – that when God calls me He may call me speedily. To die in Church appears to be a great *euthanasia* [a curious use of the word]: but not [at] a time to disturb worshippers. Such are some of the old man's thoughts, in whom there is still something that consents not to be old.[33]

* This at first sight sounds total hypocrisy in view of his relish for the past and future battles for which he was divinely armed. But an opaque and convoluted previous sentence suggests that what he really had in mind was an early retirement *after* he had won an election, probably formed a government, and corrected the evils of 'Beaconsfieldism'.

Most of the last twenty days of January were taken up with the death and burial of Gladstone's sister Helen. She was reported as dangerously ill on the 10th, and less than thirty-six hours later he and Sir Thomas and Lady Gladstone were on the night boat to Ostend for Cologne. She died four days after they arrived, and they then stayed nearly another week, clearing up and assembling the doubtful evidence for her having reverted to the Anglican faith, or at least rejected post-Vatican Council Roman Catholicism.

There followed a four-day visit to Fasque and Helen's physically safe if doctrinally doubtful funeral and burial in the Episcopalian chapel there. On the Perth train from Euston Gladstone 'made a stage of the journey with Ld Hartington, alone, & conversed on the situation'. It was much the longest of his only three encounters with Hartington between the two phases of his Midlothian campaign, and was another indication (compare the journey with H. A. Bruce in 1871) of the chance intimacies which, much more than today, were a feature of Victorian railway travel.*

Disraeli, encouraged by the false dawn of two favourable by-election results, announced the dissolution of Parliament on 8 March and Gladstone returned to Edinburgh a week later. This time he went from London and was greeted by thousands at all the major stations of the east-coast route. At Grantham the Mayor headed 2000. At York the Lord Mayor brought 6000, and at Newcastle there were too many to count. In Edinburgh 'the wonderful scene of November there was exactly renewed'. Such repetition, which broadly persisted throughout the two subsequent weeks, had the advantage of avoiding any sense of let-down for Gladstone and the disadvantage of leaving little fresh now to describe. Again he stayed for most of the nights at Dalmeny, although Lord Rosebery, who did not believe in promoting a campaign by halves, had also taken a house for Gladstone's use in George Street in the heart of the New Town,† and Gladstone spent five nights there (and,

* This intimacy continued at least to the halfway mark between the Gladstone epoch and today. In the 1930s, when the author's father was a South Wales MP, much of the social coherence between him and neighbouring members revolved around shared railway journeys between Paddington and Newport or Cardiff. Aneurin Bevan, the most notable if not the most popular among them, was always regarded as something of an outsider because he lived in London and did not travel on the normal pattern of 'parliamentary' trains. I think the intimacy ceased when compartments were replaced by open coaches. Greater speed may also have had something to do with it.

† After the contributions which his father made at Newark, Gladstone never spent any significant sum of his own money on election expenses. Oxford was cheap, and after that

typically, three days mostly in bed) as well as using it for the day and evening of the poll and count. He also spent one night at Lord Reay's house near Galashiels.

The speeches were once again splendid on-the-spot successes. But it was a second gallop around the course, as far as both subjects and venues were concerned. The most memorable was his winding-up speech at West Calder, which modest town always seemed to pull out his oratorical stops, on the Friday before the Monday poll. By then, owing to the spread-out nature of the polling days in different constituencies, he knew that the national result would be a Liberal victory. Furthermore he had already been elected for Leeds and was almost certainly going to win Midlothian. So there was no question of his being in a *contra mundum* mood, forced to fall back on the defiant faithful. Yet he chose to sound his most explicit 'masses against the classes', the 'nation against selfish interests' note:

> We have great forces arrayed against us, and apparently we cannot make our appeal to the aristocracy, excepting that which must never be forgotten, the distinguished and enlightened minority of that body of able, energetic, patriotic and liberal-minded men, whose feelings are with those of the people, and who decorate and dignify their rank by their strong sympathy with the entire community. With that exception, I am sorry to say that we cannot reckon upon what is called the landed interest, we cannot reckon upon the clergy of the established church either in England or in Scotland, subject again and always in each case to the most noble exceptions, exceptions, I trust, likely to enlarge and multiply from day to day. On none of these can we place our trust. We cannot reckon on the wealth of the country, nor upon the rank of the country, nor upon the influence which rank and wealth normally bring. In the main these powers are against us, for wherever there is a close corporation, wherever there is a spirit of organized monopoly, wherever there is a sectional and narrow interest apart from that of the country, and desiring to be set up above the interest of the public, there, gentlemen, we, the Liberal party,

---

those who were begging him to stand for this or that constituency were always the *demandeurs* and had to finance the campaign if they wished to have any chance of his accepting. This was in sharp contrast with the position of his father, his brother and his brother-in-law (Stephen Glynne), who had to buy their seats, and often did not get delivery when they had paid. Furthermore, Gladstone had the indifference of a great man (Churchill was another) to being beholden, to Rosebery for a seat, or Donald Currie for providing a yacht for cruises, or Aberdeen (in the late 1880s and 1890s) for lending him the Dollis Hill villa. It never occurred to him that they could expect anything in return except for the pleasure of knowing and serving him.

> have no friendship and no tolerance to expect. Above all these, and behind all these, there is something greater than these – there is the nation itself. This great trial is now proceeding before the nation. The nation is a power hard to rouse, but when roused, harder still and more hopeless to resist. . . . We have none of the forms of a judicial trial. There are no peers in Westminster Hall, there are no judges on the woolsack; but if we concentrate our mind upon the truth of the case as apart from its mere exterior, it is a grander and more august spectacle than was ever exhibited either in Westminster Hall or in the House of Lords. For a nation, called to undertake a great and responsible duty, – a duty which is to tell, as we are informed from high authority, on the peace of Europe and of the destinies of England [he would not get away with that word in Midlothian today], – has found its interests mismanaged, its honour tarnished, and its strength burdened and weakened by needless, mischievous, unauthorised, and unfortifiable engagements and it has resolved that this state of things shall cease, and that right and justice shall be done.[34]

So were the burghers of West Calder asked to rise above any narrow material interests and so were they sent away with the impression that they were morally superior to the plutocracy and had laid upon them a more serious judgemental duty than even the most elevated of bewigged dignitaries. And so ended too the Midlothian campaign.

The result was declared in the early evening of 7 April. Gladstone did not go to the count but remained in the George Street house until Reid, the principal agent and one of the brilliantly accurate conductors of the canvass of January 1879, brought him the figures. Reid could have said 'Here is the result, Mr Gladstone, from which you will see that your two great series of speeches may have changed six votes since the estimate that I gave you before you set foot in the constituency.' But I doubt if Reid did. He was more likely to have been caught up in the enthusiasm of the assembled crowd of 15,000 whom Gladstone, followed by Rosebery, addressed briefly (for him) from a window of the house before returning in a torchlight procession to Dalmeny. Gladstone's mood was not triumphalist. 'Quite satisfactory' was his restrained comment on the result and he distributed some of the credit to others, noting that Rosebery spoke 'excellently well' and that 'wonderful, & nothing less, has been the disposing guiding hand of God in all this matter'.[35]

That night, with his extraordinary capacity for concentration under excitement, he wrote his address of thanks to the electors. The next evening he left Edinburgh by train and with three hours of sleep despite 'frightful unearthly noises at Warrington' reached Hawarden the following morning. He stayed there for twelve days in what can only be described as a mood of elation. His sole complaint was against the volume of incoming mail. And even here there was a mixture of satisfaction and dismay: 'Postal arrivals 140! Horrible!' For the rest his enthusiasm and beneficence was unexampled. He was reading Scott's *Guy Mannering*, '*dear* Guy Mannering', he wrote, and 'that most heavenly man George Herbert'. There were two Lyttelton nephews staying. Neville, later a general, was 'a real fine fellow'. Edward, later headmaster of Eton, was a 'capital fellow', who helped with the mail. The return, first of Herbert and then of Willy Gladstone from their electoral contests, were triumphant occasions of estate loyalty. Samuel Plimsoll (MP for Derby and famous for his 'line'), who was in reality making a good-natured nuisance of himself by his determination to organize a victory parade for Gladstone's entry into London, which could hardly have been less helpful in relation to the Queen, Hartington or Granville, was nonetheless summoned to Hawarden for a night and, although 'overflowing with his own subject of the Mercantile Marine', was found 'an original and childlike man, full of reality and enthusiasm'.[36] John Bright 'came over from Llandudno' and was 'most kind and satisfactory'.[37] There never was a time when Gladstone wrote with such benignity about everybody and everything.

The key visitor was his former Whip, George Glyn, now Lord Wolverton, who could not resist continuing to perform the more interesting half of his old functions. He came for two nights. On the first 'he [threatened] a request from Granville and Hartington' and left Gladstone 'stunned'. On the second night he so persuasively argued 'on the great matter of all' (that is, another Gladstone premiership) that on the third (after his departure) Gladstone wrote out his Cabinet list. On the day after that Gladstone pursued Wolverton to London with a letter of spectacular obscurity of form, even though its substance was almost brutally clear. Everything should be decided 'on the ground of public policy'.[38] That apart, Granville or Hartington should head the government. That apart, Gladstone should seek repose. There was no question of honour or delicacy demanding that the established leaders should give way to him. There was no question of his seeking office for his own sake. It was all a matter of what 'public policy' demanded. Armed with this deadly if (or because) unprecise weapon, buoyed up by his post-Midlothian euphoria, and at seventy, 'not consent[ing] to be old', he set out for London on the afternoon of Monday, 13 April 1880.

26

Victory, Where Are Thy Fruits?

Disraeli received the news of his final defeat – for at seventy-five and in his state of health there was no possibility of revenge – brooding in solitary state at Hatfield, where he was surprisingly installed in Salisbury's absence abroad. From John Morley to Robert Blake there is agreement that he took the crushing result well. 'Dignified imperturbability' was Blake's felicitous phrase for his demeanour. The results were more or less a reverse image of those of 1874, just as those of that year had been of those of 1868. There were party majorities of about a hundred in each of the three cases. This left Gladstone a clear two-to-one victor in the series, and, even though his campaign may not have shifted many votes in Midlothian, it had a considerable 'lighthouse' effect. Conservative representation in Scotland fell from nineteen to seven, a position as weak as that in the late twentieth century. In Wales there were only two surviving Conservatives, and even England produced a non-Conservative majority, which has been a rare phenomenon since the death of Palmerston. Only in Ireland were there more Tories than Liberals (twenty-five against thirteen) but that was balanced by there being sixty-five 'Home Rulers', of whom thirty-five were firmly affiliated to Charles Stewart Parnell, who replaced Isaac Butt as Nationalist leader immediately after the 1880 elections, and thirty wore the label more loosely.

Disraeli, despite his stoicism, did not hasten to resign, or to hurry the Queen back from her Easter holiday in Baden-Baden. Nor did he use his decisive influence to reconcile her to the prospect of a Gladstone government. There was much need for someone, and most of all him, to perform this last role. On 4 April she had written of Gladstone to her private secretary (Ponsonby): 'She will sooner *abdicate* than send for or have any *communication* with *that half mad firebrand* who wd soon ruin everything & be a *Dictator*. Others but herself *may submit* to his democratic rule but *not the Queen*.'[1] On the 7th Disraeli told her that she need not leave Baden for another week. On the 21st he resigned, having advised her to send for Hartington, which may have been constitutionally correct, for the latter was still nominally the leader of the victorious party in the Commons, although it was gratuitous to add the recommendation that he was 'a Conservative at heart [and] a gentleman'.

Hartington's gentlemanliness (for which he may not have felt the need for Disraeli's imprimatur) is widely thought to have embraced an indifference to being Prime Minister. That is modified by a letter which he wrote to his father on 13 April. In this, after saying that he thought Gladstone would need to be pressed to be Prime Minister and that he did not think such pressure likely, he added that in consequence 'it does look a very hopeful prospect for me'.[2] This was already quite unrealistic. Wolverton, after his two-day visit to Hawarden, had reported the central truth to both Hartington and Granville on the 12th: Gladstone was available to be Prime Minister, but would not contemplate serving in any subordinate capacity. Once that was starkly clear neither the Queen's semi-hysterical repugnance nor Hartington's mild ambitions had more hope of survival than small sailing boats in the path of a hurricane.

More so than in 1868, the 1880 Liberal majority appeared to the nation and the world as being a Gladstone-created one. He was summoned, as Morley put it, 'by more direct and personal acclaim' than any predecessor. The Queen had no choice. And by fulminating she struck a blow, not at Gladstone's premiership, but at the Sovereign's role in the choice of chief minister, at least in post-election circumstances. Disraeli, had he been a wiser and less sycophantic friend, would have seen this and advised her accordingly during the several days after his resignation when he remained her crucial confidant.

Instead there occurred the following sequence of events. Hartington was summoned to Windsor on 22 April and asked to form a government. He said that a government could not be formed without Gladstone and that he understood that Gladstone would not take a subordinate position. The Queen, according to her own account, said that 'there was one great difficulty, which was that I could not give Mr Gladstone my confidence'.[3] She then adduced some reasons for this sweeping statement, against which Hartington attempted a qualified defence of Gladstone. The upshot was that he was charged to convey the Queen's views to Gladstone, and to ascertain whether he was adamant that he would not serve under Hartington. Hartington saw Gladstone four hours later in Wolverton's house. Wisely, having consulted Granville, Hartington ignored his instructions and did not repeat the Queen's expression of her inability to give Gladstone her confidence. But he did pose the direct question whether Gladstone would serve under him or anyone else. 'This', he said, according to Gladstone's account, 'is a question which I should not have put to you, except when desired by the Queen.' Gladstone's reply sounds fairly chilling. He affected to approve of the Queen, and therefore of Hartington as for the moment her agent, requiring 'positive information', he noted that he was not asked to give reasons but only to say yes or no, and accordingly reiterated his negative: 'I have only to say I adhere to my reply as you have already conveyed it to the Queen.'

He then added one of the most conditional offers of support ever made. And to add insult to injury he prefaced it by saying that he could not understand why it was to Hartington rather than to Granville that the Queen had applied, since it was to Granville that he had 'resigned his trust' in 1875. Nevertheless, if a government were formed by either, his duty would be to give them all the support in his power. But, alas: 'Promises of this kind . . . stood on slippery ground, and must always be understood with the limits which might be prescribed by conviction.'[4] If Hartington needed any further convincing that Gladstone was inevitable, that sentence alone must have been sufficient to do it. At the end of the following morning he again went to Windsor, this time accompanied by Granville, who, as the Queen herself rather oddly put it, 'came down on the chance of seeing the Queen'. The chance worked, but she saw them separately, and reluctantly accepted from Hartington his refusal of the commission. He admitted that he had not been generously used, but loyally stressed Gladstone's 'great amount of popularity at the present moment amongst the people' (the Queen's words) and also urged her strongly not to begin by saying she had no confidence in him.

She next saw Granville, by whom she was clearly unimpressed on this as on some other occasions. He 'seemed very nervous' and 'much distressed at the painful position I was in'. He 'kissed my hand twice and said he feared he had lost some of my confidence, but hoped to be able to regain it'. The Queen in response was about as unaccommodating as Gladstone had been when he told Hartington that if any other Prime Minister was to be tried it ought to have been Granville and not him. The Queen replied to Granville that 'he certainly had done so [probably by opposing the bill creating her Empress of India], but that I should be very glad if he could regain it'.[5] The gruffness was not wise on her part (no more had it been on Gladstone's) for she was soon endeavouring to deal with the new government as much as possible through Granville because Gladstone was 'not a man of the world', an unattractive catchphrase which she had picked up from Disraeli. Hartington and Granville both endeavoured to console the Queen (and perhaps themselves) with the thought that at his age Gladstone was unlikely to stay long in office. (This was Gladstone's own view at the time; he saw himself as giving the country a quick purge of the evils of 'Beaconsfieldism' and retiring by the end of 1881.) All four – the Queen, Gladstone himself, Hartington and Granville would, in varying degrees and for various reasons, have been horrified to know that there were another fourteen years to go.

Hartington and Granville then returned to London, went immediately to call on Gladstone in Harley Street, and gave him the message that he was summoned to Windsor for 6.30. (There was a lot of shuttling up and down the Great Western line, for it does not seem to have occurred to the Queen that she might save the time of others by going to Buckingham Palace; no doubt they were lucky that she was not at Osborne, or even Balmoral.) Gladstone first sought the assurance of Hartington and Granville that they had unitedly advised the Sovereign that he should be sent for and, having received that assurance, made a half-apology for putting them to the inconvenience of first withdrawing in 1875 and then re-emerging. He had genuinely but mistakenly believed that 'quiet times' lay ahead. He then asked them whether they would both serve under him, and, when they assented, settled immediately that Granville ('but modestly and not as of right') would take the Foreign Office. For Hartington he suggested the India Office, which he claimed, without much convincing reason, was likely to be at that stage the next most important department in the government. Hartington asked for time to consider.

That evening at Windsor Gladstone recorded the Queen as receiving him 'with [the] perfect courtesy from which she never deviates'.[6] That was a familiar Gladstone euphemism, trying to intermingle his strong loyalty to the monarchy with some respect for the truth, for saying that she was fairly chilly. An alternative phrase of his to convey the same meaning was to pay tribute to her 'great frankness'. On this occasion this latter quality showed itself in her desire to know whether he could *undertake* to form a government or merely *endeavour* to form one. She presumably and justifiably thought that the interregnum had gone on long enough, although she put the question in the odd form of saying that she wished to know in order to inform Lord Beaconsfield. Could she still have been playing with the idea of keeping Beaconsfield as

Prime Minister if the Liberals became locked in a Hartington–Gladstone impasse?

Gladstone swept aside any such uncertainty. He *would* form a government. He already had Granville and Hartington on board (the latter was reflecting only on his office, not on his participation), and he told her of some other projected Cabinet dispositions before disclosing that he intended to be his own Chancellor of the Exchequer. The Queen, who informed Disraeli that evening that Gladstone had looked 'very ill and haggard, and his voice feeble', sensibly said that she was amazed by this decision to combine the premiership with the heaviest departmental office. She did not however attempt to resist him. Monarchs have never been much interested in the Treasury. She was much more concerned with who was to be Secretary of State for War, wanting Hartington, but having to be fobbed off with Childers.

She then further illustrated her gift for frankness by telling him that she did not like many of the things he had said during his campaigns. It was the sort of issue with which Gladstone's sophistical convolution made him good at dealing. He said that he had 'used a mode of speech and language different in some degree from what I should have employed had I been the leader of a party or a candidate for office'.[7] She also recorded him as saying that 'he considered all violence and bitterness to belong to the *past*'.[8] What is remarkable is the coincidence of their two accounts, both sharing the advantage of having been written within hours of the interchange, Gladstone's on Windsor paper, implying that it was done either while waiting in the castle for the train or with prudently collected supplies during the journey. This Windsor audience might have been a propitious start in the adverse circumstances had not Disraeli been so immanently there, resigned but always available to poison the mind of 'Madam and Most Beloved Sovereign', as he was writing to her that summer.

That day was a Friday, and between then and the following Wednesday, although not without difficulty, Gladstone assembled a complete Cabinet list. The result struck the Queen as being 'very radical'. It struck almost everybody else as being very Whig. Gladstone took the view that, having got him as Prime Minister, the Radicals ought to be more than satisfied, and be quite happy to see the top half of the Cabinet filled up with the old Whig cousinage. Quite why he expected to be accepted as a paid-up member of the Radical faction is not clear. He was never a Whig, and he had long ceased to be a Conservative, at any rate in the party-label sense of the word. But he was at least equally far from being a Radical in the collectivist, semi-socialist sense which Chamberlain and Dilke had given to the word in the 1870s.

In a Cabinet of only fourteen, Gladstone had six peers plus Hartington, whose membership of the House of Commons until his father died in 1891 hardly made him a commoner rather than a nobleman. Together with Granville and with Kimberley,* who took the Colonial Office after refusing the Indian viceroyalty, Hartington as Secretary of State for India ensured that the three external departments were in the hands of two earls and a marquess. Selborne, soon to be an earl, was Lord Chancellor, Earl Spencer was Lord President, the Duke of Argyll was Lord Privy Seal; and yet another earl, Northbrook, was First Lord of the Admiralty. Of the commoners, Harcourt had Radical friends as well as high Whig connections, but, although a partisan parliamentary bruiser, he was more irascible than ideologically predictable as a Home Secretary. Childers, Secretary of State for War, had spent ten years as a young man in the untraditional atmosphere of Melbourne, Australia, but was said to have grown less radical since his second marriage to the daughter of the Bishop of Chichester. Dodson, of Gladstone's own Eton and Christ Church provenance, was a not very exciting President of the Local Government Board who became a Liberal Unionist in 1886.

John Bright was regarded by Gladstone as a great man as well as a great orator, and exactly what a Radical ought to be, cloudy and moralizing rather than demanding and practical. But precisely for these reasons he had by then come to be seen as a great windbag by his fellow member for Birmingham, Joseph Chamberlain, and by those who thought like Chamberlain. As Chancellor of the Duchy of Lancaster Bright was not however required to deal in actions as opposed to words. W. E. Forster, as Chief Secretary for Ireland, found himself, almost by accident, in charge for the two years before his resignation of the most exposed sector of the government's responsibilities. Forster did not shrink from these for he was a man of force and stubbornness. He was of Radical rather than Whig origins. He was brought up as a Quaker, he had married a sister of Matthew Arnold, and sat for Bradford, which

* Kimberley, although only the first Earl, was not a South African diamond merchant but a member of an old Norfolk family. It is one of the many confusions of British titled nomenclature that while in the case of peerages of metropolitan territorial origin the men were named after the towns (or counties), in the colonies it was the towns which were named after the men, as in Melbourne, Sydney, Wellington, Auckland, Salisbury (Rhodesia) – and Kimberley.

was a town of advanced politics. But both his habits and his views had moved to the right. His favourite pastime had become card-playing and his favourite companion in this pursuit the Duchess of Manchester, later (1892) Duchess of Devonshire. And his conduct of the Education Bill during the previous Gladstone government had brought him into sharp conflict (leaving continuing animosity) with Chamberlain.

Chamberlain was the fourteenth member of the Cabinet and the only representative there of the new-wave Radicalism which had contributed almost as much to the Liberal victory as had Gladstone's Midlothian campaign. Although, ironically, he himself had been elected for Birmingham only in the number-three place, after Bright and Muntz (which should have won him Gladstone's sympathy after his own Lancashire and Greenwich experiences), it was nonetheless the case that the Chamberlain-created National Liberal Federation had been successful in sixty of the sixty-seven seats in which it had engaged. Chamberlain was described by *The Times* as 'the Carnot of the moment', the organizer of victory. Carnot or not, Gladstone thought an under-secretaryship was good enough for him. He attempted to fall back upon what he called 'Peel's rule' of allowing no one into the Cabinet who had not previously served in subordinate office, although it was a rule which was breached by Peel himself in the case of Buccleuch and by Gladstone in his first government in that of Bright. The truth was that Gladstone, in spite of that 1877 night under his Birmingham roof, always wrinkled up his nose at the thought of Chamberlain.

It was Dilke, at least equally well qualified for high office, who made him unwrinkle it. Chamberlain before the election had proposed to Dilke an offensive–defensive alliance by which they would refuse any office unless they were both in the Cabinet. Dilke thought this was over their market price and moderated the compact to demanding that provided one was in the Cabinet the other could accept junior office. Chamberlain accepted this reluctantly, no doubt thinking that it was not merely Dilke pouring water into his wine but also preparing for his own entry into the Cabinet, while leaving Chamberlain to accept lesser office. Exactly the reverse was the outcome. Dilke was sent for first and offered the under-secretaryship at the Foreign Office. He stuck absolutely to the limited compact and said that if this were the offer to him and Chamberlain was not to be in the Cabinet he would refuse. This produced a considerable reaction, both hostile and productive. Gladstone was amazed and affronted. The unctuous side of Granville, who was present as Dilke's putative chief at the Foreign Office, was perfectly captured by Dilke when he later wrote: 'Lord Granville made a disagreeable little speech in his most agreeable way....'[9] Gladstone, however, could not afford to do without both of the Radicals, and he judged that the Queen would probably accept Chamberlain for the Cabinet more easily than Dilke. He conseqently illustrated his remarkable capacity for cloaking in fluent orotundity his recognition of political reality and wrote to Chamberlain on the next morning in the following terms:

> I have made some progress since yesterday afternoon and I may add that there is a small addition to my liberty of choice beyond what I had expected. Accordingly, looking as I seek to do all along to the selection of the fittest, I have real pleasure in proposing to you that you should allow me to submit your name to Her Majesty as President of the Board of Trade.[10]

Thus did a combination of Dilke's loyalty, the Queen's prejudices and Gladstone's flexibility under duress make Chamberlain the junior and much the most Radical member of the largely Whig new Cabinet, and thus too was Gladstone's second government somewhat laboriously assembled. He never referred to it by any phrase approximating to that which he applied to his first Cabinet: 'one of the best instruments for government that ever was constructed'. Nor did it replicate its 1868 predecessor's attribute of containing no one who pressingly wanted to be Prime Minister. With varying degrees of urgency, Chamberlain did (although he later became more interested in power than place); Dilke did; Hartington in a rather sleepy way did, and was understandably mildly resentful about having been passed over; Harcourt was boisterously ambitious; Granville and Spencer, both men who at various times had been or were to be mooted for the premiership, could not be depended upon to say no; and Rosebery (not in the Cabinet until later in the government but the only one who actually got to 10 Downing Street) was always both ambitious and discontented. Nor was that government internally cohesive, as events soon began to show. In the 1886 split no less than seven of the original fourteen of 1880 were to desert Gladstone, and most, but not all, of these defections cast a shadow before them.

The Cabinet of 1880 compared with that of 1868 was therefore a poor vessel for the weathering of storms. The fault for this was almost entirely Gladstone's own. Admittedly the Queen was tiresome in her reaction to his suggested appointments. She objected to Selborne as

Lord Chancellor, Childers as Secretary of State for War, Northbrook as First Lord of the Admiralty (because she would have preferred him in the War Office), and Chamberlain in any senior position. All these objections related to Cabinet appointments. Beyond these she complained about Ripon being made Viceroy of India, about Lord Fife (who subsequently married the Prince of Wales's daughter) becoming Lord Chamberlain (too young), about Dilke (too republican) becoming an under-secretary, about a viscountcy (as opposed to a barony) for Robert Lowe, the excluded former Chancellor, and about Lord Derby (who had deserted Disraeli) being offered a Garter. But these were time-consuming and temper-trying diversions rather than effective ukases. Of the ten points listed she got her way only on the peripheral ones of Fife and Derby. For the rest Gladstone prevailed.

He may have designed the Whig bias partly to reassure the Queen. But it also fitted in well enough with Gladstone's own instincts even if not with his interests. The Queen may as a result of knowing less about him have helped the promotion of Chamberlain over Dilke, but this did not affect the balance of the Cabinet, and where she expressed an individual judgement, even such a sensible one as that Gladstone should not burden himself with the Exchequer, it made no difference.

The real distinction between the government of 1868 and that of 1880 went beyond the relative cohesion of the two Cabinets. The 1868 government, because it had a legislative programme relevant to the dominant issues, was able to make the political weather. The 1880 government not only lacked a structured programme but it also had little idea in advance of the main issues with which it would have to deal. As a result it was always the creature rather than the creator of the circumstances in which it operated. The Prime Minister who had grandly proclaimed in 1868 that 'My mission is to pacify Ireland' had hardly mentioned that unhappy island during the Midlothian campaigns. Yet Irish issues were still more dominant in the Parliament elected in 1880 than they had been in that of 1868. The difference was that the first Gladstone government thrust them before Parliament, whereas the second had them thrust down its own throat by deteriorating circumstances on the ground.

Gladstone's lack of foresight in this respect stemmed largely from his indifference to economic trends beyond purely fiscal and budgetary matters. Governments should not be expected to do anything about fluctuations in the state of trade. Gladstone therefore closed his mind to such issues and set up a rigid 'Chinese wall' between politics and economics. In reality the defeat of the Disraeli government owed at least as much to the economic recession which had set in strongly in 1876–7 as to any political issue; but this could never have been guessed from Gladstone's orations. Equally the swing to budgetary deficit under the Conservatives was due just as much to the consequences of this recession as to imperialist extravagance or a weak hand at the Exchequer; but Gladstone preferred a moralist to a materialist analysis.

The industrial downswing was accompanied by the onset of an agricultural depression which lasted much longer and had more profound causes and consequences. The combination of post-Civil War rebound in America, the completion of the transcontinental railways and the beginning of refrigerated ships gave a great fillip to New World food supplies. In England this produced falling rent-rolls and the first touches of austerity for those rural magnates who were not able to make up by the importation of rich American wives for the adverse effects of wheat and beef from the same source. In Ireland, with its much greater agrarian vulnerability, it meant near catastrophe. Particularly in the congested districts of the western provinces of Connaught and Munster, conditions became worse than at any time since the famine. The majority of Irish landlords made their normal unconstructive contribution, and evictions increased fivefold between 1877 and 1880. In parts of Ireland the degradation of peasant life became unparalleled in Europe west of the Balkans, and the disintegration of civil society a present danger.

Yet such was Gladstone's capacity for concentrating on one train of thought at the expense of all others that he did not particularly notice this. The statesman who in 1868 had given priority to Ireland and who in 1885–94 was to cause the Irish issue to pre-empt his old age, to split the Liberal party and to distort the pattern of British politics for a generation, was in 1879–80 so diverted on to other issues that he even accused Disraeli of raising the side issue of Ireland in order to cloak his iniquities in other parts of the world. Ireland was not the only issue to catch the second Gladstone government unawares. The affair of the oath or affirmation of Bradlaugh, the militantly atheistic new member for Northampton, drained away much of the momentum of the first year. This could not however reasonably have been foreseen.

Again in contrast with 1868, this government had no planned legislative programme to put before Parliament, and it was only after four years that its major non-Irish measure of reform, the extension of household franchise to the counties and hence to the agricultural labourer, got to the statute book. Improvisation was the keynote of the government's performance. Gladstone was fortunately a great improviser as well as a great performer, and many brilliant displays of the qualities which made him both and of his extraordinary parliamentary patience and stamina were needed to keep the government upright in the House of Commons. All of this, particularly during the first two and a half years, when he ludicrously held the Exchequer as well, took a heavy toll of his energies. These, as he himself recognized, were showing some signs of flagging. He wrote to Spencer, whom he had recently made Irish Viceroy, in October 1882, referring to his 'increase of disinclination to work, and disposition (in homely phrase) to scamp it, which I think and know to be a sign of diminished powers. . . . It would be no good to anyone', he continued, 'that I should remain on the stage like a half-exhausted singer, whose notes are flat and everyone perceives it except himself.'[11] He had over eleven years on the stage after that and his notes were rarely flat, except perhaps during the last six months of his fourth premiership. His health was if anything better in his short third and fourth governments than in this long and testing second one. During this 1880 government it was probably worse than that of any subsequent Prime Minister in office, except for Campbell-Bannerman and Bonar Law during their relatively rapid declines to death, until Churchill's second Downing Street spell in 1951–5.

Yet, illness intermissions apart, Gladstone retained his ability to dominate the House of Commons. With Disraeli declining in the House of Lords, Stafford Northcote the Tory leader in the Commons a sheep in sheep's clothing, and Salisbury segregated in the Lords and in any event not a thundering orator, although with a caustic tongue, there was no one in Gladstone's league. Bright was fading. Chamberlain, whose mixture of courage and rancour was to turn him into a master of the whiplash school of oratory, was still a parliamentary tyro, and at this stage never appeared in juxtaposition to Gladstone. Randolph Churchill, in this Parliament at the height of his short-lived powers, deliberately set himself up as an irreverent and irritating mocker of Gladstone. But this role made him more of a mosquito than a fellow eagle able to confront Gladstone beak to beak. Parnell, whose cold, sometimes forceful oratory, with words viscously struggling to get through, diverted the course of this Parliament even more than did Bradlaugh, but he had too small a following before the trebling of the Irish franchise in 1886 and too narrow a beam to be comparable with Gladstone on the floor of the House of Commons.

So Gladstone was unique. He could dominate the House of Commons, not merely on a few setpiece grand occasions, but through night after night of the committee stages of the Irish Land Bill of 1881, the Coercion and Arrears Bill of 1882 and the Franchise Bill of 1884. He did so with a combination of sweep, patience and attention to detail which it is impossible to imagine a Prime Minister exercising today. He could also defend the government against the disasters which befell it with almost too great a power and facility.

From one point of view Gladstone was an ailing Prime Minister presiding over a ramshackle government, within which relations between Whigs and Radicals became increasingly hostile, and staggering reactively from one crisis and one improvisation to another. At the same time he became the only person who could possibly hold the government and the Liberal party together. In the spring of 1880, within the inner circle, his premiership was regarded as more inevitable than welcome. Hartington, as we have seen, was a little miffed. Granville was more loyal than enthusiastic. Chamberlain and Dilke thought they might have done better under a Whig Prime Minister who needed to elevate them to compensate for his own right-of-centre position. Harcourt, always willing to lambast his colleagues in private, would have preferred Hartington, and a lot of the old Whig aristocracy – Bedford and Lansdowne for example – were becoming increasingly unhappy with the social and economic direction of the Liberal party well before Home Rule seriously reared its head.

Yet, as that unproductive and often scourging Parliament ground on, so the desire for Gladstone's early retirement paradoxically evaporated. There was still a general expectation that Hartington would some day come into his political as well as his ducal inheritance, but his own mind was becoming increasingly sceptical about the possibility of his leading a party containing Dilke and Chamberlain, with whom he disagreed on almost every issue which came before the Cabinet. Equally the two Radicals looked forward to a day when they would not need Gladstone, but they did not think they were yet strong enough to confront the Whigs without him. For both wings, therefore, in 1880 to 1885, the alternatives appeared to be Gladstone or split. The prospect of a split grew in the minds of both sides, but the idea that when it came, in 1886, it would be because of rather than in spite of Gladstone, and that it would find Hartington and Chamberlain uniting with each other against him, would have seemed preposterous at any stage in the life of the 1880 government.

Gladstone's position was thus doubly paradoxical. He was oratorically towering in Parliament, yet for a Prime Minister with a majority of a hundred his frequent weakness in the division lobbies was surprising. His Cabinet was increasingly anxious for his continuance in office, yet unwilling to pay the price of submission to his judgement. Not only on a host of minor matters but on several crucial issues, on Ireland, on Egypt, he allowed himself to be overruled. The Queen's picture of him as 'a Dictator', whether or not 'half-mad', was far wide of the mark, and sadly so, for subsequent developments, particularly in Ireland, suggested that he had wiser judgement than his colleagues. Granville's typically jaunty 1886 comment was more to the point. 'I think you too often counted noses in your last Cabinet,' he told Gladstone.[12] The result was a disappointing government, and one which brought more frustration than satisfaction for its ageing but still often high-spirited Prime Minister.

The first summer was particularly wearing, and ended with Gladstone more severely ill than at any time since his erysipelas in the north of Scotland twenty-seven years before. Gladstone first met the new Parliament on 20 May. He noticed 'a great and fervent crowd in Palace Yard; and much feeling in the House'.[13] It was his last exultant note of the summer. First there was a sense of let-down on the Liberal benches at the news that neither Bartle Frere in South Africa nor Henry Layard in Constantinople, both regarded as symbols of Disraeli's imperialism (despite Layard having previously been a Liberal minister), was to be ostentatiously recalled. In fact Layard was quickly sent on a leave from which he never returned and was replaced by Goschen, while Frere was recalled within a few months. So it was only gesture politics which was lacking. But it was enough to create a bad atmosphere and to pave the way to a series of government defeats on peripheral issues. In June the House carried by 229 to 203 a motion from Sir Wilfred Lawson, the dedicated temperance reformer, in favour of local option, against which the Prime Minister had not only voted but had spoken as well. In mid-July there was an even more ignominious rejection of a government-supported proposal to install in Westminster Abbey a monument to the Prince Imperial, Napoleon III's heir, who had been killed fighting with British troops in the Zulu War. The Cabinet had acquiesced out of deference to the Queen, but few of them carried their deference to the extent of attending and voting in the House of Commons. The Prime Minister (and Hartington) voted in a largely Tory lobby with only eight other Liberals. Gladstone not unnaturally described it as a 'weary day', but blithely added: 'Our defeat however on the Monument was on the whole a public good.'[14] And then at the end of that month there was even trouble on a Hares and Rabbits Bill.

None of these issues was of inherent importance (the local-option motion was an expression of parliamentary opinion not an enactment), but they imprinted the image of a government whose authority did not match its majority. As tests of Gladstone's patience, moreover, they did not begin to rival his other two trials of that summer, the Bradlaugh issue and the (Irish) Compensation for Disturbance Bill. They were interspersed around one highly successful event, which, however, was a further addition to the burdens of those few months. On 10 June Gladstone introduced what was at once his twelfth budget and also his first for fourteen years. He did it very much like a veteran stylist coming back to give an apparently effortless performance at the crease or on the tennis court. He did it in two hours, which was a miracle of compression by his standards. It was a largely alcoholic budget. He replaced the malt tax by an agriculturally much more acceptable beer duty, reduced the excise on table wines, tidied up the duties on alcoholic sales, and balanced off the picture by putting a penny on income tax, a tax towards which Gladstone was highly flexible, frequently denouncing it but no less frequently raising it when he wanted to combine sound finance with other fiscal remissions.

The easy demise of the malt tax, over which Stafford Northcote had stumbled throughout the whole of the 1874 government, aroused feelings of envy, irritation and admiration in about equal proportions among Conservatives. Why could Gladstone achieve in two months the great benefit for *their* rural supporters which had eluded Northcote for six years? There could be no question of their opposing the change, and indeed the whole budget went easily through and considerably raised the spirits of the ministerial party. Nevertheless the plain fact was that Gladstone ought not to have been performing such a departmental task at all, but ought to have been concentrating on the overall direction of the government and endeavouring to anticipate events, particularly in Ireland, rather than merely reacting to them.

The discreditable Bradlaugh saga blew up even before the beginning of the session. Bradlaugh had written to the Speaker in advance of the meeting of Parliament, claiming the right to affirm rather than take the oath of allegiance on the ground that the latter would have no meaning for him. Speaker Brand's legal advisers were against allowing such a claim, and he accepted their view, suggesting to Gladstone (and to Northcote) that a select committee should be appointed to deliberate quickly upon the matter. A strong committee resulted. From the government side there were Henry James and Farrer Herschell, the former a most urbane politician, the latter to be twice Lord Chancellor, as well as John Bright. They all supported Bradlaugh's claim to affirm, as from outside the Committee did Selborne, the current Lord Chancellor and a churchman who was as devout as Gladstone himself, although a good deal more conservative. The forces of intolerance on the Committee had a most formidable champion in Hardinge Giffard, Disraeli's Solicitor-General, who went on to become the first Earl of Halsbury, to be Salisbury's (and Balfour's) Lord Chancellor for fourteen years, to lead the 'diehards' against the 1911 Parliament Bill at the age of eighty-eight, and to survive for another ten years after that. The chairman was Spencer Walpole, the lachrymose Home Secretary of the 1866 Hyde Park riot, and Giffard, aided by one or two Liberal defections, gave him both the opportunity and the nerve to exercise his casting vote against Bradlaugh.

This was the situation which confronted Gladstone when the new Parliament met. On 19 May he attended a conclave in the Speaker's library, with a panoply of advisers on both sides. By this time Bradlaugh had announced that if he could not affirm he was prepared to swear. The Speaker claimed that if Bradlaugh had said this in the first instance he would have allowed no interference. But Bradlaugh's public declaration that the oath could mean nothing to him made the matter more difficult. The Speaker then urged that, when an attempt was made to prevent Bradlaugh swearing, Gladstone should move the previous question. The Liberal Whip then said there was no chance of this being carried. It was therefore decided that the least bad course was to go for another select committee, this time to consider not whether Bradlaugh was entitled to affirm, but whether he was entitled to swear. That was accepted by the House without hazard although not without a bitter debate.

That second Select Committee advanced matters little. When the issue came back before the House at midsummer all the old battle lines were reoccupied. Henry Labouchère, Bradlaugh's colleague in the representation of Northampton (or at least in their intention to be so represented) moved that he be allowed to affirm. Giffard, never one to hedge his intransigence, moved a counter-motion that he be permitted neither to affirm nor to swear. This raised in most brutal form the direct issue of whether the acceptability of a member lay with his constituents or with the House of Commons.

Gladstone saw clearly that this was dangerous ground, and said so forthrightly in an hour's speech on the second night. He was also beginning, typically, to develop a more theological, idiosyncratic and probably less persuasive line of argument which, in the various debates on the issue, he came with increasing passion to deploy. This was the rejection of the view that an indiscriminate theism rendered a man acceptable, while its absence put him outside the pale. This crudity he regarded as a negation of nearly 1900 years of Christian thought and doctrine. 'You know, Mr Speaker,' Charles Newdegate MP called out with what might now be regarded as a jaunty saloon-bar camaraderie, 'we all of us believe in a God of some sort or another.' This to Gladstone was the worst sort of apostasy. Better an honest if benighted atheist than a man who believed that he had answered the spiritual needs of mankind by such a threadbare doctrine.

Gladstone's speech was not persuasive. A House with a nominal Liberal majority of over a hundred voted by 275 to 230 against allowing Bradlaugh either to affirm or to attest, and thus forbade him to represent his constituents. Worse still, as Gladstone wrote to the Queen, who was a doubtfully sympathetic audience in view of Bradlaugh's republicanism and advocacy of birth control, both of which she minded more than his atheism, that the House received the result in 'an ecstatic transport, [which] exceeded anything which Mr Gladstone remembers to have witnessed'.[15]

On the next day Bradlaugh presented himself at the bar of the House and claimed to take the oath. The Speaker read to him the resolution of the House which forbade this. Thereupon he asked to be heard and this was allowed. Gladstone described his performance from the bar – a nightmare position from which to address the House – as 'that of a consummate speaker'. Bradlaugh was then requested to withdraw, and putting up some resistance to this got involved in a semi-scuffle with the deputy serjeant-at-arms. This was Gladstone's moment of weakness. As leader of the House he failed to lead, one way or the other, and, sympathizing with Bradlaugh, left it to Northcote to move the two disciplinary motions, the second, after the scuffle, committing Bradlaugh to custody. But, believing also in upholding the collective authority of the House, Gladstone somewhat sheepishly voted for both the motions.

However, Gladstone soon rallied and on 1 July proposed and carried (by 303 votes to 249) a resolution permitting Bradlaugh to affirm. But there was a catch in the tail. He was permitted to do so only on his own responsibility and 'subject to any liability by statute', which meant that he was at risk in the courts. The next day he affirmed, took his place on the Liberal benches and voted in a division. The legality of his action was immediately contested at law, with Hardinge Giffard purporting to represent the outraged conscience of England. Bradlaugh lost and was unseated. He was re-elected in April 1881, but was persuaded to stay away while the government tried to get an Affirmation Bill on the statute book. The session came to an end before they had succeeded. When the next session opened in February 1882, Bradlaugh decided that he had exercised enough patience. He reappeared, advanced up the floor to the table, pulling a piece of paper out of his pocket, and proceeded to administer the oath himself. The next day he was expelled. Ten days after that he was elected for the second time at Northampton.

The unsavoury farce then moved for a year from the Commons to the law courts. At one stage there were four legal actions pending. Bradlaugh's opponents were endeavouring to impose bankrupting penalties upon him for his allegedly illegal vote; he was suing the deputy serjeant-at-arms for assault; his supporters were challenging (at law) the right of the House to exclude him; and he was being prosecuted for blasphemy. In April 1883 the government made a second and more determined attempt to carry an Affirmation Bill and cut through this legal jungle.

This produced another memorable Gladstone speech in which he developed his subtle 1880 thought that there were worse things than atheism into an argument at once sublime and remote. The House, he said with more hope than truth, would be familiar with 'the majestic and noble lines of Lucretius' There then followed a six-line quotation (in Latin of course) in which pagan gods were described as 'far withdrawn from all concerns of ours: free from our pains, free from our perils, strong in resources of their own, needing nought from us, no favour wins them, no anger moves them'. This, he said, was the real evil of the age, far worse than blank atheism, the proclamation of the total detachment of man from God, of God from man.

Morley, then in his very first days as an MP and sharing Gladstone's classicism although not his faith, was twenty years later to write of the House sitting:

> as I well remember, with reverential stillness, hearkening from this born master of moving cadence and high sustained modulation to the rise and long roll of the hexameter, – to the plangent lines that have come down across the night of time to us from great Rome. But all these impressions of sublime feeling and strong reasoning were soon effaced by honest bigotry, by narrow and selfish calculation, by flat cowardice.[16]

In other words, Gladstone lost his bill, although by a majority of only three.

Yet again Bradlaugh presented himself at the bar and yet again he was excluded, although apparently without on this occasion the seat being declared vacant. That, however, occurred once more in the following February (1884), and in what had become an equally routine way he was once more returned for Northampton. Perhaps out of boredom, he did not again trouble the House until July 1885, when in the dying days of that Parliament and with a new Conservative government on the Treasury bench he put the matter to a somewhat *pro forma* further test and was again excluded.

At the general election of November 1885 he was re-elected for the fourth time and at the meeting of the new Parliament in January 1886, the whole charade of the previous Parliament was simply cut into shreds by the firmness of the new (1884) Speaker, Arthur Wellesley Peel, the youngest son of Gladstone's old mentor, who in spite of his names was a Liberal MP. Peel absolutely refused to hear any objections to the taking of the oath by Bradlaugh (who wisely avoided any affirmation complications at that stage). Without debate he was swept in with the others.

The House of Commons then proceeded to coat its previous prejudice and hysteria with a sentimental surface which made its overall performance no more attractive. Bradlaugh became, in the words of his *Dictionary of National Biography* chronicler (who, intriguingly, was Ramsay MacDonald), 'very popular with the House of Commons'. He got a Tory Parliament to pass an Affirmation Bill in 1888, and in 1891, when he lay dying, it unanimously expunged from its records the motion of 22 June 1880, which had been carried in an 'ecstatic transport'.

Whether or not this consoled Bradlaugh, it could not possibly undo the damage which the twists and turns of the affair inflicted upon the authority and momentum of Gladstone in his second government. The Prime Minister could not command the House of Commons on the issue, and his embarrassments were brilliantly and shamelessly exploited by Lord Randolph Churchill with his little group of *francs-tireurs*, commonly called the Fourth Party, who sat below the gangway on the opposition side. Churchill behaved as though Gladstone's support for Bradlaugh's rights meant that he had suddenly become converted to atheism, republicanism and contraception, but did so with such wit and impudence that this preposterous claim both amused and inflicted damage. Churchill's object was to humiliate Northcote, the leader of his own party, as well as to bait Gladstone, and it was an important factor in the equation that Northcote never had the authority to stand up to his own party and lance the Bradlaugh boil, which he would probably have liked to do. Apart from its weakening of the Prime Minister's prestige, the Bradlaugh issue, particularly in the summer of 1880, was a heavy drain on Gladstone's energy and patience, and a contributory factor to his severe pneumonia (as it turned out to be) at the end of July.

On 19 July he wrote: 'H of C 4¼–8¼ & 8–3am: much exhausted.'[17] On the 23rd: 'A severe week & rather overdone.' On the 24th: 'Abandoned through fatigue the Trinity House Dinner: and went off at 6 to Littleburys.'[18]* Then, on the 30th, he was struck down, less violently at first than in the second wave of the attack. 'Seized with chill & nausea' was his initial comment. 'Better when warmer.' He then slept for ten hours 'and got up at 11 seemingly well'.

He saw three ministers and 'got all ready for the Cabinet at 2. Meantime I had been for ¾ of an hour not shivering but shaking as a house is shaking in an earthquake. I had a fire lighted, & put on a thick coat & proceeded with my work.'[19] By 2.00 p.m., however, the Cabinet was forbidden and he was ordered to bed. His amalgamated diary entries for the next four days (31 July–3 August) read:

> Close confinement to bed, strong and prolonged perspirations, poulticing, hot drinks & medicines. Temperature fell from 103 to 101 at night, to 100 Sunday morning but rose again to 103 by the evening. No reading, writing or business; only thoughts. I did not suffer. On Sunday I thought of the end – in case the movement had continued – coming nearer to it by a little than I had done before: but not as in expectation of it. C[atherine] read me the service. Monday the temperature had fallen I think to 101–2 but it was thought well to call in Sir W. Jenner [Dr Andrew Clark was already treating him on an almost hourly basis] whom I greatly liked in his *clinical* character. He was very strict about the economies, e.g. of speech and effort. On Tues. however I saw Godley [his principal secretary, later Lord Kilbracken] & dictated a letter respecting tomorrow's Cabinet. In the evg. the temperature had gone down & Dr C. was delighted: thought the battle won.[20]

The optimistic thought was justified. Thereafter he progressed steadily, getting up on the Saturday a week after he had been stricken, although it required a full month's convalescence, including a ten-day

* Littleburys was an Aberdeen-owned house at Mill Hill where Gladstone spent several weekends that summer.

round-Britain cruise on one of Donald Currie's ships, before he was fully recovered. He had been seriously ill. His congestion of the lungs had been severe, his temperature had been high, and bulletins had been issued every few hours to an apprehensive public. During a miserable summer for himself and his government he had strained himself to and beyond the limit of his capacity. Yet that government had nearly another five years of sometimes productive life ahead, and its seventy-year-old head nearly another fourteen in active politics.

27

Gladstone Becomes the Grand Old Man

Gladstone's fundamental weakness in the 1880 government was that he was trying to hold together too wide a coalition. His social conservatism had become in uncomfortable conflict with his political radicalism. Although his taste for rhetoric and large audiences led him to an abstract respect for the masses against the classes, when it came to the choice of colleagues for a government, or to the organization of the Hawarden estate, or to the houses in which he stayed, he liked the style and values of the old landed ruling class, perhaps indeed attaching more importance to them than did some who had been more completely brought up therein.

He was willing to make a great effort to keep the traditional Whig families within the Liberal tabernacle. He believed that their departure would be bad for the tone and balance of politics. The trouble was that, as the issues of the 1880s evolved, even before Home Rule appeared like a dividing spear, there had ceased to be any significant disputes on which men like Hartington and Argyll were instinctively on the progressive side of the watershed. Trying to keep the old mould was a constant trial for them and an incubus for a Liberal government.

Gladstone had one other bias which rivalled what Dilke once called 'his Scotch toadyism to the aristocracy',[1] and that was the importance which shared classical knowledge played in his personal relations. As a link, although he would have been horrified to admit it, it was really more important than shared religious belief. Thus all the men to whom he was close, from his school and Oxford friends, through Hope-Scott and Manning, Peel and Aberdeen in his middle life, to John Morley and Rosebery in his old age, could confidently and happily exchange Latin and Greek quotations with him. In Morley's case this ability outweighed his agnosticism. Unfortunately, however, neither of the two Liberal politicians whose support on Ireland was vital to Gladstone were classicists. Chamberlain, although surprisingly cultivated for a screw manufacturer who had left school at sixteen – he spoke French adequately and was quite widely read – did not include the dead languages in his intellectual armoury. And Hartington preferred quadrupeds to hexameters.

Gladstone could do without one man but not without both. He would probably have done better to have cultivated Chamberlain and, if necessary, to have let Hartington go before 1886. But he could not bring himself to appreciate Chamberlain. Hartington at least had the advantage of being indisputably partrician, even if he did not know his Virgil. But there was no instinctive rapport between Gladstone and either of these crucial figures. Nonetheless, given the sulphurous state of their mutual relations throughout the 1880–5 government, it was a remarkable feat of man-mismanagement to drive them into each other's arms by 1886–7.

This reversal of alliances was however still well in the future in the early days of Gladstone's second government. Once he had recovered from his pneumonia, he had a relatively tranquil 1880 autumn, although he knew that the shadow of Ireland lay heavily over the prospects for the 1881 session. In his seventy-first birthday thoughts on 29 December 1880, he referred to a 'disturbed' anniversary after which he 'must wait for a calmer session before I trust myself to say what a year it has been, and why'.[2]

On the third day of the new year of 1881 a figure from the remote past re-entered Gladstone's life. Lady Lincoln (restyled Lady Susan Opdebeck by virtue of her Scottish ducal parentage, and her terminated Belgian second marriage) called on him in Downing Street. He had not seen her since his ludicrous Italian pursuit of her in 1849. His diary entry read: 'after some 32 or 33 years I felt something & could say much.' Could he easily relate her to that figure whom he had first described as 'once the dream of dreams', and whose escapade had later so excited his prurience as well as engaging him in twenty-seven days of expensive wild-goose chase? His immediate reaction to the visit was to go to the Lyceum Theatre in order 'to unbend after the strain'.[3] More constructively and with typical concern, he then wrote to her no less than four times in the next fortnight and made continuing strenuous efforts to get the Newcastle estate, itself hardly affluent, to provide some money to relieve her poverty. To this end he stayed on for another year as a Newcastle trustee, an obligation from which after decades of devoted service he had not unnaturally become eager to retire, and also enlisted, somewhat mysteriously, the services of Mrs Thistlethwayte, herself by this time in financial difficulty, as an advocate of Lady Susan's claim on the Newcastle estate. The rationale of this appeared to be that it was through the late Duke (formerly Lincoln and Lady Susan's husband) that Gladstone had first met Laura Thistlethwayte in 1864.

Gladstone's reaction to this twitch upon the thread was symptomatic: already by this second government an important part of his life had come to be lived in the past. As his seventies wore on he became isolated, in the sense that most of his contemporaries had died, much more than, in the same decade of his life, he would be today. And, while in some ways he was young for his age, in at least as many others he was old. In spite of his frequent retreats to a sickbed, he remained physically hard, sparse and energetic. Staying two days at Balmoral (for the first time for thirteen years) in the autumn of 1884, he climbed Ben Macdui, at 4300 feet the highest point in the Cairngorms, taking seven hours forty minutes to do the twenty-mile round trip. He confessed to 'some effort' but it may also have been thought some achievement at the age of nearly seventy-five.

He contrasted that day of mountaineering with life in the House of Commons, where his assiduity remained exceptional. He could sit on the Treasury bench for rather similar periods – seven or so hours – with only the shortest breaks, and without any recorded tendency to go to sleep. He spent more time in the Palace of Westminster than any subsequent Prime Minister with the exception of Baldwin. But he devoted his long hours there to the chamber, always listening, often intervening, whereas Baldwin was much more in the corridors, dining room and smoking room, alien territories to Gladstone, gossiping and absorbing atmosphere rather than directing business. Gladstone also continued his voracious general reading, his night walks in London, perhaps once a week, his tree-felling at Hawarden, and his extraordinary capacity, however heavy the press of official burdens, to get on with postponable tasks, such as the arrangement of books and papers, the keeping of his own accounts, and the writing of family or eleemosynary letters, like those to Lady Susan Opdebeck.

On the other hand he had indisputably come to look an old man. The change set in during the late seventies of the century and the late sixties of his life. Until the end of his first premiership he still looked middle-aged. Then, for the mid-1870s, there is a paucity of photographs. They were the years of his withdrawal, and the photographers were perhaps taking him at his word, although likenesses in those days were a product more of visits to studios than of enterprise and intrusion. By

1878, when Millais painted his first Gladstone portrait (there was a second in 1884–5), and still more by 1879, when he was both photographed and (more flatteringly) painted by Franz von Lehnbach in Munich, he had passed over the divide. His hair had become white and wilder, his clothes more dishevelled and his general air slightly disordered.

Soon afterwards he began to suffer from an old man's chronic ailments as opposed to the sudden onset of illnesses from which he quickly bounced back. His eyesight weakened. He had several bouts of insomnia (although not as bad as those of his wife), and at Hawarden he sometimes alternated between sleeping in the castle and sleeping in the rectory in a somewhat illogical search for the more reposeful bedroom. He was not as bad in this respect as his Midlothian patron and Prime Ministerial successor Rosebery, nearly forty years his junior, who refurbished Barnbougle, a ruined tower on a Forthside promontory in the park at Dalmeny in the vain hope that it might provide a haven against sleeplessness. Gladstone also had trouble with his teeth and, more seriously, with his voice, which was the equivalent of a great pianist being threatened with a stiffening of the fingers.

In spite of these infirmities he remained a most formidable beast of the political forest, a target for lesser animals who wished to earn prowess by taking a nip out of his haunches. He was unmatched in authority or experience by any of his colleagues or opponents, the more so since Disraeli's death in the spring of 1881. Beaconsfield, to give him at the end his designation of the last five years, expired on 19 April in the Curzon Street house on which he had recently taken a seven-year lease, and to which he was confined for four weeks of bronchial decline. Before that he had been about and even active in his waxen way, 'an assiduous mummy' in Lytton Strachey's terrible phrase, moving 'from dinner party to dinner party'. He had last spoken in the Lords on 15 March, and he had last seen the Queen, at Windsor, two weeks before that. Gladstone had twice called at Curzon Street to enquire about the patient but (as he expected) had seen only a secretary (Lord Barrington) and a doctor.

When the end came he was at Hawarden for Easter. He re-acted strongly, as his diary shows, although the language he chose was careful and not hypocritical:

> At 8 a.m. I was much shocked on opening a telegram to find it announced the death of Ld Beaconsfield, 3½ hours before. The accounts 24 hours

ago were so good. It is a telling, touching event. There is no more extraordinary a man surviving him in England, perhaps none in Europe. I must not say much, in presence as it were of his Urn.

I immediately sent to tender a public funeral. The event will also entail upon me *one* great difficulty.[4]

The 'great difficulty' was the encomium he would have to deliver in the House of Commons. The 'public funeral' (by which was meant a Westminster Abbey or St Paul's occasion, for the obsequies which took place at Hughenden were hardly private) was refused in accordance with Disraeli's clear instructions. He wished to be buried in the Hughenden churchyard alongside his wife.

Gladstone's reactions to these arrangements were mixed. To his son in India he wrote at the time that there was something 'very touching' about Disraeli's determination to be buried with his wife. But he later complained to Edward Hamilton that the mock modesty was typical of Disraeli's play-acting: 'As he lived, so he died – all display, without reality or genuineness.' But this was after he had himself been greatly criticized for not going to the 'private' funeral – Hartington, Harcourt and Rosebery did, as well as the Prince of Wales, all but one of Disraeli's former Cabinet and a vast crowd of onlookers – and also for mishandling the timing of the House of Commons tributes. Although the House was adjourned over the hours of the funeral, these were not paid until 9 May, three weeks after the death. Gladstone claimed that he strictly followed the Palmerston precedents (but Palmerston died during a recess) and acted in full agreement with Northcote, the Conservative leader.

When the tributes eventually came, which was on a motion to erect a public monument (against which Labouchère and fifty-five others divided), Gladstone performed with skill and good feeling, satisfying even the Queen, who wrote of 'his fine speech abounding greatly to his honour'. Contemplating it beforehand had made him ill, and he had spent two days in bed with one of his frequent stomach upsets. It was symptomatic of his fundamentally uneasy relationship with Disraeli, based, as he was probably right in stressing, on 'something totally different from personal hatred', but not much on respect either, except for Disraeli's political courage. This he put on a level with that of Peel and Russell and of no one else. But in Disraeli's case he would instinctively have qualified it by regarding the courage as impudent – a gambler's nerve – rather than principled. Above all, however, it was incomprehension which characterized his attitude to Disraeli.

It was also Henry Labouchère, the leader of the revolt against Disraeli's monument, who in that same April of his death fastened on Gladstone one of the most famous catchphrases of the nineteenth century. Half by accident and encased in an implausible passage, he coined the phrase the 'Grand Old Man', which stuck for the rest of Gladstone's life. (There was a touch of mockery as well as affection about its use, particularly after 1885 when GOM could be transposed into MOG for Murderer of Gordon.) Labouchère was Bradlaugh's fellow member for Northampton and was speaking for him in the first of the by-elections which the intolerance of the House of Commons forced Bradlaugh to fight. In these circumstances Labouchère imaginatively described the blessing which Gladstone had given him on his departure from London: 'And, men of Northampton, that grand old man said to me, as he patted me on the shoulder, "Henry, my boy, bring him back, bring him back!"'[5] It is impossible to imagine Gladstone calling Labouchère either 'Henry' or 'my boy' or indeed using the phrase 'bring him back, bring him back'. Nonetheless Labouchère had invented one of the great sobriquets of the nineteenth century. Then, a few years later, Gladstone used of himself the phrase 'an old parliamentary hand', and that too stuck.

To balance Gladstone's real but not excessive infirmities there was the cosseting with which, in the 1880s, he came increasingly to be surrounded. In that second premiership his family and his secretaries melded into an interlocking protective cocoon which was different from anything which had prevailed during his previous periods of office, whether in 10 or 11 Downing Street. There is a remarkable picture of him, *circa* 1883, bearing a somewhat quizzical expression and surrounded by his four private secretaries, the two smaller but senior ones (Seymour and Hamilton) looking eager, the two junior but taller ones (Lyttelton and Leveson-Gower) a little more detached. Catherine Gladstone gave up her substantial periods of absence, either at Hawarden or at Hagley when Gladstone was in London, or occasionally in London when Gladstone was at Hawarden, and became immanently protective of her husband's health and welfare. But she never urged him to retire. She probably sensed that responsibility was a better shield to his body than was rest. The children were also mobilized as part of the protective penumbra.

All the Gladstone children remained close to their parents and all, with the possible exception of Willy, the heir and at least the nominal squire of Hawarden, were totally dedicated to their father's beliefs and interests. Not only Willy as squire but Stephen as rector was based at Hawarden, as was Mary, the second living daughter who remained wholly at home until she married in 1886, at the age of thirty-nine, and even then could hardly have contracted a more solidifying alliance. After romantic flickers with Lord Lorne and Arthur Balfour, and apparently arousing flirtatious feelings (but hardly thoughts of marriage) in Ruskin and Tennyson, she settled for the handsome Hawarden curate, Harry Drew. It is difficult to avoid the feeling that the advantages of his location, which enabled her to go on acting as her father's domestic secretary and the organizer of the household, must have been as powerful a factor as Drew's good looks. She was known in family and adjacent circles, with a mixture of affection and irony, as von Moltke. She was indefatigable on her father's behalf.

Agnes, her senior by five years, was more detached with her Wellington headmaster husband and five children, but was nonetheless quite often at Hawarden. Helen, the youngest daughter, was an early female don, absent at Newnham for the short Cambridge terms, but unwilling to accept the principalship of Royal Holloway College because she thought it would keep her away from Hawarden too much. Lucy Cavendish was also almost a supernumerary daughter, often at Hawarden, sometimes providing London lodging for her aunt and uncle by marriage in the grand house at 21 Carlton House Terrace which she maintained until her forty-three years of widowhood came to an end in 1925.

Of the two younger Gladstone boys, Henry (or Harry) was in Calcutta laying the foundations of a substantial fortune from March 1880 to April 1884, when he came home for two years before returning to his crock of gold. Although he was more money-orientated than any Gladstone since Sir John he was not as a result cut off from communion with his father. During his four early-1880s years of absence, the GOM wrote him letters in which he often revealed his inmost political thoughts more completely than anything he wrote for home consumption, thereby not only providing documents of inherent interest but also showing a close affinity between himself and Harry. Herbert was the most political of the boys, MP for Leeds from 1880, and an eagerly beavering Liberal. He was always available to help his father, and occasionally to embarrass him.

Willy Gladstone, unlike Herbert, was not a natural politician, and his semi-detachment stemmed partly from this. His main interest was in the tunes and words of hymns, and his main skill was at Eton fives (for which he built a rare court at Hawarden). He was parliamentarily unhappy, and he did not stand at the 1885 general election, which was perhaps as well for he did not agree with his father on Home Rule. It would have been terrible had he voted against the bill in June 1886. Also, his position as owner of the estate was distinctly anomalous. The house was run for his parents. Gladstone summoned guests to it at will, and his occasional flitting to the rectory in search of sleep was a sign that he was lord of the whole demesne and not that he was always a guest in one house or the other. Indeed Lord Blantyre, Willy's father-in-law, found the arrangements unsatisfactory for his daughter and thought that the Willy Gladstones ought to have a house of their own, which was achieved with the completion and occupation of the Red House (in the park) in 1884. Hawarden Castle, whether Stephen Glynne or Willy Gladstone was the nominal owner, was always essentially the house of the 'great people' from the 1850s onwards.

Nor did Willy Gladstone survive to inherit fully. He died in 1891 of a brain tumour, which may have affected him for some time previously. But he looked healthy in a striking Hawarden family photograph, which is attributed to the early 1880s and must have been taken either before Henry's departure for India at the beginning of 1880 or after his return four years later. Here everyone appears exactly as they ought to: Willy the broadening forty-year-old squire with his handsome rather than animated peer's daughter of a wife; Stephen, the fine-profiled and wavy-haired clergyman, contrasting with the bald intellectual head of Wickham the headmaster (also a clergyman of course) and his maternal wife Agnes; Harry and Herbert looking like favoured young men, Harry more confident, Herbert more eager. Of the Gladstone women, Mary looked pert, Helen satisfied with her academic life, but white- rather than blue-stockinged. Catherine Gladstone looked adequately matriarchal, but also disengaged and well content that Mary should have taken over much of the household authority from her. Gladstone himself has an air of trying hard not to dominate. It is altogether a remarkable and informative picture.

For most of the life of the 1880 government the luck, both personal and political, ran heavily against Gladstone. There were the two great traumas in the life of the government: the May 1882 Fenian hacking to death of Lord Frederick Cavendish in Phoenix Park within twelve hours of his arrival in Dublin as Chief Secretary; and the immolation of General Gordon in the Governor-General's palace at Khartoum after 320 days of siege. The loss of Cavendish, whom he regarded almost as a son, was a much more severe personal blow to Gladstone than that of Gordon, whom he regarded as an insubordinate and erratic junior general. But the latter was a much more severe political blow to the government. Both left indelible stains.

Yet Gladstone maintained verve and zest. Edward Hamilton, son of the High Churchman whom Gladstone had persuaded Aberdeen to appoint Bishop of Salisbury in 1854, came to work for him in 1880 and succeeded Godley as the principal private secretary in 1882. Hamilton was as dedicated a diarist as Gladstone himself, although with a more flowing and less cryptic style, and his first two volumes, published in 1972, sixty-four years after his death, provide a balancing but on the whole confirmatory account, seen from the other side of the private secretaries' green-baize door, of Downing Street life in 1880–5.

Hamilton, who although far from being an extreme Liberal became a devoted Gladstonian, was struck by the persistent high spirits of his chief. Gladstone could have occasional brief periods of gloom, but for the most part the more dire the events from Majuba Hill to Maamtrasna,* the more he was beset by the recalcitrance of his colleagues, or obstruction in the House of Commons, or the constant time-consuming complaints and advice of the Queen, the more he retained his equanimity. And not only his equanimity: undimmed was his quest for new solutions, and above all his ability, even on the darkest days, to throw himself into enthusiastic conversation or concentrated reading on totally detached subjects. Hamilton at Hawarden was impressed above all by his animation at unhurried breakfasts and by his willingness to deploy the force of his conversational enthusiasm not just before important guests but before whoever was at his table, family and private secretaries receiving as full a treatment as secretaries of state and bishops. 'At dinner,' Hamilton added, 'though in a general way he perhaps hardly lays himself out as much as at breakfast, he is never silent and always bright.'[6]

On the other hand H. C. G. Matthew thinks that by this stage in his life there was becoming something contrived about Gladstone's conversational performances, and that 'performances' was indeed the right word for them. 'In this period, it was almost certain that one of the guests would note his conversation or mood in a letter or a diary.'

* The internecine Connemara murder of a family of five in August 1882 led to the hanging of three men and the deportation of five others. The guilt of one of the three hanged men was open to serious doubt. The case became a long-reverberating cause of dispute and bitterness between the Irish executive and the indigenous population.

Matthew referred to his flow of erudite conversation on a vast range of subjects as something that 'at first almost always charmed', and cited the accounts which Lord Derby wrote of two Gladstone visits to Knowsley as an example of the wearing-off effect.[7] Derby, as his already quoted comment on a Hartington visit has shown, was a sharp-eyed as well as a large-scale host. During Gladstone's first visit, which was in late October 1881, Derby, who had already moved into Liberal communion but was unwilling to join the government because of the recentness of his conversion, wrote:

> The general impression seems to be, & certainly it is that left on my mind, that he is more agreeable, more light & easy in conversation, than would be expected from his manner in public: no subject comes amiss to him, he is ready to discourse on any; great or small, & that with the same copiousness & abundance of detail which characterises his speaking. He has no humour, rarely jokes, & his jokes are poor when he makes them. There is something odd in the intense earnestness with which he takes up every topic. I heard him yesterday deliver a sort of lecture on the various different ways of mending roads, suggested by some remark about the L[iver]pool streets. He described several different processes minutely, & as if he had been getting up the subject for an examination. . . . Since the days of Lord Brougham, I have heard nothing like his eager and restless volubility: he never ceases to talk, and to talk well. Nobody would have thought he had cares on his mind, or work to do. His face is very haggard, his eye wild. . . .[8]

By the time of the second visit, two years later, Derby had become Colonial Secretary, but the impact of Gladstone's many-faceted talk continued to be a source of wonder to him in spite of their frequent Cabinet encounters. This time he wrote that he had 'heard nothing like it since Macaulay', and continued:

> Talk with the Premier in his room, and later out of doors: he began by saying that he wished to discuss some pending questions with me: but after the first five minutes he seemed to forget them & wandered off into a general dissertation on politics, interesting in parts, less so in others, but curious as beginning out of nothing in particular, & leading up to no conclusion. For the first time, a suspicion crossed my mind that there is something beyond what is quite healthy in this perpetual flow of words – a beginning perhaps of old age. . . . He left us at 3 for Hawarden: at the last moment there was a scramble & bustle about missing or forgotten luggage, & in the end he went off with a greatcoat of mine, his own being lost. I imagine his & Mrs Gladstone's domestic arrangements to be incoherent.[9]

From this and other evidence Matthew has created an interesting and plausible theory: 'It is more likely that it was not old age in the sense of senility but a calculated attempt to keep old age at bay which in the case of the Knowsley visit was taken too far. . . . Much is made of Gladstone's lack of self-consciousness. . . . It may well be that, by the 1880s, Gladstone's lack of self-consciousness was being consciously cultivated.'[10]

Whether his moods were contrived or spontaneous Gladstone needed reserves of optimism to bounce through the trials of the 1880 government. The steady run of luck against the administration embraced Parliament, Ireland, South Africa, Egypt and then the Sudan. In addition there were the Prime Minister's troubles with his health, with his colleagues and with the Queen, all accompanied by a mood of almost unparalleled bitterness between parties. Following his severe 1880 summer illness and his four-day relapse in October, he had another three days in bed, this time with tonsillitis, in mid-January 1881. Then on 23 February, ill chance combining with a period of severe weather, when he was returning late to Downing Street from dining with the Waleses at Marlborough House, he:

> slipt off my heels in the powdered snow by the garden door, fell backwards, & struck my head most violently (I was hatless) against the edge of the stone step. A wound of 1¾ inch was cut open, which bled profusely. [It was also deep, according to Hamilton.] All the household were soon most kindly busy: a neighbouring doctor came and bound it up perfectly well. C[atherine] G. arrived and soon Dr. Clarke. I got to bed with very uncomfortable feelings *inside* the skull, as it appeared to me, and some difficulty in placing the head: but thank God had an excellent night.[11]

His recovery was fairly quick, achieved by sleeping for half the time over the first few days and nights, but it was a singularly disagreeable accident for a man of seventy-one who often worried about the physical exhaustion of his brain. It was six days before he could leave his room and nine before he could return to the House of Commons. His recovery was not assisted by the arrival from South Africa of the news of the defeat by the Boers at Majuba Hill and the death of General Colley and of ninety-five other officers and men.

For the next couple of years Gladstone's ailments were mostly confined to his normal short bouts of lumbago, diarrhoea or tonsillitis, but requiring a day or two or three at least half time in bed, to which he always took so easily. Then, after he got to Hawarden on 16 December for his 1882–3 Christmas and New Year holiday, insomnia struck. Paradoxically it was just after he had at last relieved himself of the burden of the Exchequer and when he ought to have been less oppressed than for some years past. But the transition to relaxation was often a dangerous moment for him. Thus in July 1881, as he moved into sight of the completion of the Irish Land Bill, which he had carried almost single-handed and which had involved thirty-two nights of committee stage, the longest since the great Reform Bill, he wrote with more apprehension than triumph of: 'A sharp and long continued labour . . . the heaviest I have ever had: it will I think be followed by a severe fit of lassitude.'[12]

Over Christmas 1882 the semi-sleeplessness began to lower his morale but did not become an obsession until the first week of January. By the standards of some he did not do badly. His best night in that week was six hours, his worst two hours. But by his own high standards of long and undisturbed nights it was devastating. Dr Clark was summoned from London on the 7th and Gladstone agreed both to postpone the visit to Midlothian (his first in the nearly three years since the general election) which he had promised for later in the month, and to accept the need for six weeks of rest cure in the South of France. Lord Wolverton's villa at Cannes was made available as were Wolverton himself and Lord Acton for company, as well as the family party of Mrs Gladstone, daughter Mary, son Stephen and nephew Spencer Lyttelton, who was one of his private secretaries. Apart from Lyttelton, they all set off from Charing Cross on the morning of 17 January. The frequently curmudgeonly Home Secretary (Harcourt) earned good marks by coming unexpectedly to see them off. They crossed to Calais and Paris during the day and then proceeded overnight in a *fauteuil coupée* (a sort of separated Pullman armchair), 'for which the fine [fare?] was I think £11'.[13] If so, and for Gladstone alone, it must have been one of the most expensive railway supplements ever exacted, the equivalent of over £500 today.

The Cannes visit was a success. Gladstone was delighted with the half-developed Riviera in winter, quickly recovered his sleep (although his wife did not), and fretted little at being away from Cabinets, his colleagues and his Sovereign over the start of the new session. Gladstone's colleagues tried him more by resignation than by dissent. He never doubted their right to disagree, and it would not have occurred to him to sack a minister for his views. He regarded a Secretary of State (or the equivalent), once appointed, as inviolate, as much so as a member of the college of cardinals. Such a minister was a servant of the Queen, as he was himself, and as entitled to his own opinion. Gladstone was also good at treating disagreement with courtesy, always trying to pare it down, and not to denounce it. The limpet-like quality of modern ministers had not then developed. Gladstone's problem (as had been Disraeli's) was preventing unwelcome resignations rather than getting rid of colleagues he would rather be without.*

At the end of 1882 when Gladstone was engaged in a delicate Cabinet reconstruction his troubles – and particularly his royal ones – were added to by there being a simultaneous vacancy in the see of Canterbury. Archbishop Tait had died on 3 December. Gladstone, who had needless to say given a lot of thought to the matter, had come to the conclusion that the choice lay between Bishop Browne of Winchester and Bishop Benson of Truro. (Benson had been the founding headmaster of Wellington before becoming the first bishop of the new diocese of Truro.) Gladstone thought that the edge was with Benson, who, although perhaps a little too young at fifty-three, was better in respect of age than Browne who was too old at seventy-one. The Queen, however, thought there should at least be an offer to Winchester and, worse, confused matters by frivolously throwing in the name of the Bishop of Durham at a late stage. Gladstone, who had allowed her to do what she liked about a new Dean of Windsor (Dean Wellesley, almost their only mutual friend since the death of the Duchess of Sutherland, had also died that autumn), was determined to exercise his full constitutional rights in relation to the appointment of a new Primate. He regarded it as one of the most important decisions of his second premiership. It was not that he wished to make a partisan nomination. Benson and Browne were both Conservative rather than Liberal and Broad rather than High Church. But Benson, in Gladstone's view, more than outweighed these disadvantages by being a great pastoral bishop. Fortunately the Queen gave way before

* A striking exception was provided by Lord Carlingford (as Chichester Fortescue, the unesteemed Irish Chief Secretary in Gladstone's first Cabinet). On Argyll's resignation Gladstone brought him back into the Cabinet as Lord Privy Seal. By the autumn of 1884, however, the Prime Minister was anxious to be rid of Carlingford both because of his lack of serious contribution and because he wanted to bring in Rosebery without upsetting the balance between peers and commoners. Despite strong hints, and even the offer of the Constantinople embassy, Carlingford simply sat tight, and Gladstone doubted his right to dismiss him. By exhibiting what Hamilton called 'skin . . . made of buffalo hide', he survived until the end of the government, reluctantly yielding up the Privy Seal in March 1885, when Rosebery at last joined, but continuing as Lord President.

the Prime Minister could mount too high a constitutional horse and utter the threats of resignation which the issue was raising in his mind.*

It was by no means only on appointments that the Queen added to Gladstone's burdens. The fact that their relationship recommenced in 1880 on a much more arm's-length basis than in 1868 did not bring all the compensations which might have been expected. It largely freed him from Balmoral, which he visited only once during the five years of his second premiership; and that 1884 visit was only a matter of two days. In addition there were occasional nights at Windsor and three visits to Osborne.

It was optimistically believed by Ponsonby and Hamilton that the Sovereign and the Prime Minister got on better in conversation than in correspondence, but Gladstone's diary entry for 30 November 1881, a day when he was summoned to Windsor, did not suggest that there was anything extravagant about the greater ease when they were in the same room: 'Received with much civility, had a long audience, but I am always outside an iron ring: and without any desire, had I the power, to break it through.'[14]

It was, however, in the correspondence that the wearisomeness of her constant nagging advice and complaint found its full expression. Her declared 1880 intention to have as little as possible to do with Gladstone and use the (to her) inoffensive even if unadmired Granville as her main channel of relations with the government might at least have avoided this sterile exercise in mutual irritation. In contrast with the first years of the 1868 government the monarch and her first minister expected little of each other. The Queen had long since given up believing that there was anything to look forward to from Gladstone except for his surrender of office, an event which he always kept on the horizon, but which was never reached. Gladstone had receded from his hope of a decade before that the Queen might come to appreciate his loyalty and worth, and was perfectly realistic about this. '. . . I am convinced, from a hundred tokens,' he wrote to Dilke as the latter took up his new office, 'that she looks forward to the day of my retirement as a day if not of jubilee yet of relief.'[15] And he expressed his own accumulated exasperation by telling Rosebery that 'the Queen alone is enough to kill any man'.[16]

* Benson was a successful archbishop for just under fourteen years before dying suddenly and with dramatic irony at morning service in Gladstone's pew in Hawarden church. It was almost exactly the death which Gladstone, still alive at the time of Benson's death but with only eighteen declining months to go, had wished for himself three years before Benson's appointment. (See p. 430 above.)

Yet the Sovereign and the Prime Minister could not leave each other alone. If their relationship was without affection or hope, at least it might have been coolly detached. But the Queen could not resist pouring out her advice and complaints. And Gladstone could not resist replying with a mixture of elaborate courtesy and pedagogic determination to put her right. Frequently, despite the speed of late-Victorian mails, a second issue of complaint would have arisen before the first could be replied to, so that the correspondence was interleaved in such a way that, particularly when she was at Balmoral or Osborne, he was never free of at least one pending censorious letter. And the tone and assumption nearly always was that if Gladstone had only behaved with patriotic firmness, abandoned his Liberal prejudices and pursued good sound Tory policies, the troubles of the country would have been miraculously cured. If he had given more thought to coercion and less to Irish land reform, atrocities would have been avoided. If he had let the military have their head and pursued a more forward imperial policy defeats would not have occurred. If he had locked up more Irish MPs for longer intervals there would have been less obstruction in the House of Commons. If he had either silenced or dismissed Chamberlain (and maybe Dilke as well) the Lords would have been more amenable, or at any rate they would have had less to be intransigent about.

The Queen also sent him messages of warning, as though he was the most inexperienced of ministers, before his projected forays to public meetings. Thus in October 1881: 'I see you are to attend a great banquet at Leeds. Let me express a hope that you will be very cautious not to say anything which could bind you to any particular measures.'[17] And in January 1883, when he was proposing the not very extreme step of addressing his Midlothian constituents for the first time in three years:

> The Queen is sure that Mr Gladstone will not misunderstand her when she expresses her earnest hope that he will be very guarded in his language when he goes to Scotland shortly. . . . Mr Gladstone will remember that when she first saw him in 80 – when she asked him to form a Govt – she expressed her regret at some of his speeches in Midlothian, & he replied that he did *not then* think himself a responsible person.[18]

And so it went on. Hamilton calculated that, during the five years of this government, the Prime Minister had to write to her over a thousand times, and his letters were frequently in reply to hers.* But she, of course,

* Figures given by Herbert Gladstone in his engaging and, as its title implies, still almost wholly filial memoir, *After Thirty Years*, published in 1928, puts a more precise

had much less to do, while to him the correspondence was a heavy supplementary burden. The compensation was that he minded her disapproval, because it was so predictable, much less than he had done in 1868–74. Indeed, slightly led by Hamilton, Gladstone came to the view that the Queen's hostility was partly due to jealousy, which was not the most respectful explanation. Hamilton wrote on 27 September 1883:

> She feels, as he [Gladstone] puts it, aggrieved at the undue reverence shown to an old man of whom the public are being constantly reminded, and who goes on working for them beyond the allotted time, while H. M. is, owing to the life she leads, withdrawn from view. . . . What he wraps up in guarded and considerate language is (to put it bluntly) *jealousy*. She can't bear to see the large type which heads the columns of newspapers by 'Mr Gladstone's movements', while down below is in small type the Court Circular. . . . Due allowance ought certainly to be made for this feeling, especially as it is only in the later days of her reign that She finds Herself with a Prime Minister whose position in this country is unique and unlike that of anyone else of whom She has had experience, or of whom indeed any of Her predecessors had experience.[19]

The reverence which Gladstone excited was real and widespread, but it was far from being universal. The exceptions were particularly and obviously to be found among the Tory political classes. The wildest rumours about him were there likely to spread fast. When his insomnia drove him to the South of France it was widely believed that he had gone mad and was being kept away to conceal this embarrassing fact. While such fantasies were no doubt rejected by those of cooler temperament and more sophisticated information, there was plenty of venom forthcoming from such sources, even when they had in the not too distant past been in close and friendly relationship with Gladstone. Salisbury in 1882 attributed every step in his opponent's Irish policy since 1869 to a greed for votes and office, which as a personal and not merely a political attack was much resented by Gladstone who had several times been Salisbury's house guest and on whose kindness as a host he had commented extravagantly. What he found still more wounding, however, was the virulence of Salisbury's nephew, Arthur Balfour, in whom he had so 'delighted' and with whom he had enjoyed the closest relations barely half a decade earlier.

---

gloss on Hamilton. Gladstone wrote 1017 letters to the Queen, excluding those relating to honours or the formation of the government, in 1880–5. The Queen sent him 207 letters and 170 telegrams.

On 16 May of that same year, only ten days after Gladstone had received the crushing blow of Cavendish's death, Balfour denounced the so-called 'Kilmainham Treaty' for the release of Parnell from gaol and Gladstone's part in it in terms which were in both intent and effect as offensive as it is possible to imagine. 'I do not think', Balfour said, 'any such transaction can be quoted from the annals of our political history. It stands alone in its infamy. . . . They have negotiated in secret with treason. . . .'[20] Balfour never apologized, although he said privately that he regretted that in the heat of the moment he had used such an emotive word as 'infamy', which although objectively justified was better avoided in debate. In fact it was less a matter of heat than an early example of the 'cool ruthlessness', as Churchill described it in *Great Contemporaries*, which enabled Balfour to cross a muddy street 'like a powerful graceful cat walking delicately and unsoiled'.

The depth of Gladstone's feeling was expressed in a letter which he wrote to his daughter Helen in Cambridge: 'I cannot refrain from writing to tell you how vexed, I might also say cut to the heart, I am about Mr Balfour's exhibition yesterday. . . .' There was then a routine and unconvincing denial that he was 'personally wounded' or 'sorry for the Government'.

> But I am concerned, and also perplexed, for him – are his notions of conduct & social laws turned inside out [*sic*] since the days when I knew him, enjoyed his hospitality, viewed him with esteem and regard, nay was wont to mate him with the incomparable F. Cavendish, now lost to our eyes but not to our hearts, as the flower of rising manhood in the land? To see a man *like this* given over to the almost raving licence of an unbridled tongue does grieve me, and I cannot make light of it & do not wish I could, any more than I should if I saw someone rend the Madonna di San Sisto from top to bottom.
>
> You may ask me what is the use of this. It is simply that I would ask you to say as much (or as little) of this as you can, or think proper, either to his sister [Eleanor Sidgwick, the principal of Newnham], or to Mr Sidgwick – they will at least know that it cannot possibly be sincere.[21]

It was not perhaps a wise or wholly dignified letter for Gladstone to write, but it gave startling evidence that the wound was at least as deep as that in his head fifteen months before and also of his epistolatory energy. Many might have half composed such a letter in their heads during a night when grievance predominated over sleep, but few, even if they were not carrying a Prime Minister's burdens, would have put it on paper the next morning. Sloth can have its advantages.

Those hostile to Gladstone were not confined to his professional parliamentary opponents. Hamilton recorded an experience two months later, on 20 July:

> Dined last night with the Cavendish Bentincks. We were 28, and I think . . . I was the solitary Liberal. I am sure that if I had been a Tory all my life the bitterness and narrow-mindedness of my friends would have converted me to Radicalism. It is all indiscriminate abuse. Everything that Mr. G. does must be wrong and wicked, and everything wrong and wicked that happens must be attributable to Mr. G. He has created all the difficulties in Egypt and Ireland. His one object is to ruin landlords, plunder bondholders, and to destroy, in short, the country.[22]

The Queen's antipathy no doubt somewhat encouraged this hostility in the fashionable world, but it could not be regarded as a decisive cause of it. In the first place the Queen was not fashionable, and her pattern of life remained sufficiently withdrawn, even if not quite so obsessively so as in the 1860s and early 1870s, that few except for former Conservative ministers, whom she entertained with unusual frequency, were in contact with her views. And both her private secretary, Ponsonby, and her heir (who *was* a leader of fashion) maintained a much more friendly attitude towards Gladstone, the secretary because of a general Liberal disposition and because he knew better than anyone else with how much Gladstone had to put up, and the future King Edward VII because of an inherent tendency on the part of crown princes to provide a counterbalance to their parents and sovereigns, tinged in his case with a certain natural benevolence provided there was no conflict with his own pleasures and indulgences.

Nor were Gladstone's critics to be found only among Conservatives. In October 1884 Chamberlain, rebuked by the Prime Minister at the instigation of the Queen for using provocative language about Lord Salisbury, responded by bursting out (about Gladstone) to Dilke: 'I *don't* like him, really. I hate him.'[23]* Dilke could also make more detached

* Chamberlain's median attitude to Gladstone was perhaps better represented not by this display of petulance but by a rather good piece of doggerel, which he composed during a Cabinet meeting in May 1884 and tossed across the table to Dilke:

> Here lies Mr G., who has left us repining,
> While he is, no doubt, still engaged in refining;
> And explaining distinctions to Peter and Paul,
> Who faintly protest that distinctions so small
> Were never submitted to saints to perplex them,
> Until the Prime Minister came up to vex them.

but fairly sceptical comments about Gladstone. After Granville in 1882 had urged him and Chamberlain to remember who the GOM was and not to push him too hard in discussion, he commented: 'In other words told [us] to remember [we] were dealing with a magnificent lunatic.'[24] Harcourt could also mingle his occasional acts of tribute, such as attending at Charing Cross station, with highly acerbic comments when he disagreed with Gladstone, as over the control of the Metropolitan police. Yet, whatever their occasional exasperations, all his colleagues, including Hartington, the displaced person of 1880, agreed by this middle phase of the government that Gladstone's continuation in office was essential. There was no impatience during his 1883 six weeks in Cannes. They would much rather he had stayed away for another month over Easter than that he resigned and left them to schism. A cynical explanation could be that they needed him as a figurehead, but quite enjoyed his being an absent one. His being away did not however promote the orderly conduct of business, as was the case when Attlee presided over the 1940–5 War Cabinet in the absence of Churchill. Few effective decisions about the government's programme for the 1883 session (which opened on 15 February) had been taken by the time that Gladstone returned in early March. He was then by no means successful in lancing all the festering boils, but at least the Cabinet and the country felt that the most famous statesman in the world – Bismarck was the only possible rival – was back in charge.

It was largely due to his fame and popular authority that this government, divided and luckless although it mostly was, maintained at least until the beginning of 1885 a fair degree of public support. London drawing rooms might be hostile, but Gladstone's public appearances rarely failed to attract enthusiastic crowds, and the Liberal record in bye-elections (of which there were then about twenty-five a year), while patchy, was far from one of uniform retreat. There were even occasional gains above the 1880 tide-mark. Particularly if the proposed measure for the extension of the county franchise were carried, the Liberals looked set to be the natural majority party. It was only the danger of a post-Gladstone split which threatened this prospect. The idea that Gladstone's leadership could itself provoke a twenty-year Tory hegemony was remote from the conventional wisdom of 1883.

28

The Cloud in the West Darkens

Although Gladstone came into office in 1880 with his mind much further away from Ireland than in 1868 it was quickly wrenched in that direction by the scale of the agrarian distress and the threat to civil order which went with it. The number of evictions for non-payment of agricultural rent had risen from 483 in 1877 to 1238 in 1879, with the rate doubling again in the first six months of 1880. In most cases non-payment followed inexorably from the collapse of his income leaving the rural tenant without any available resources. The Land League had been set up by Parnell and Michael Davitt in October 1877, and its doctrine of the 'boycott' (although the name did not come into use until a little later when Captain Boycott, Lord Erne's agent, became an early target), by which anyone concerned with taking the land of an evicted tenant should be treated like a leper, was proclaimed by John Dillon and Thomas Brennan. Although these leaders were against violence there was also a mounting wave of agrarian crime (or 'outrages' as they were normally then called), particularly in Connaught.

Within eight weeks of taking office the Cabinet reluctantly decided to introduce a Compensation for Disturbance Bill, which not very strong measure of protection for tenants was nonetheless strong enough to frighten three peers – Lansdowne, Listowel and Zetland – into resignation from junior posts, and nearly to drive Argyll out of the Cabinet. Only determined cosseting from Gladstone kept the Duke. All four of them need not have worried unduly for the bill lost its momentum through a considerable Liberal revolt. In the Commons it secured a second reading by a majority of seventy-eight, but this was essentially a majority provided by the Irish (which English arrogance always regarded as making it slightly spurious, particularly on an Irish issue), for twenty Liberals went into the Conservative lobby and another fifty abstained. This left the bill a sitting target for the Lords, who proceeded to throw it out almost contemptuously by a vote of 281 to 51. This outcome could not even be presented as an exercise in Tory obscurantism, for if the whole of the opposition had abstained the defection of Liberal peers would in itself have been sufficient to defeat the government.

This was a severe setback both for Gladstone and for his Irish Secretary, W. E. Forster. Forster was a much more formidable figure than Chichester Fortescue, who had occupied this office in the 1868 government. And the effect on this stubborn man of losing his ameliorative bill was the somewhat paradoxical one of making him see coercion as the only alternative way of governing Ireland. From the autumn of 1880 Forster became a hardline man on Ireland. He settled into an intransigent groove which led to his resignation eighteen months later. In the interval, however, he got a lot of Cabinet support, which made matters awkward for Gladstone, whose instincts were all against Crime Bills and special powers. Morley (not then even an MP, let alone a minister, but already a favoured Gladstone familiar) captured the anguish which Forster's views and the strength of his support imposed on Gladstone by writing to Chamberlain in Birmingham an account of a New Year's Eve (1880–1) dinner in Downing Street at which Granville and Frederick Cavendish were also present:

> Gladstone was interesting as usual; talked about Dante, Innocent the Third, house property in London, the true theory of the Church, the enormity and monstrous absurdity of our keeping Ascension Island, etc., etc., etc. Then after dinner he took me into a corner and revealed his Coercion [scheme] much as a man might say (in confidence) that he found himself under the painful necessity of slaying his mother – it was downright piteous – his wrung features, his strained gesture, all the other signs of mental perturbation in an intense nature. I walked away in a horribly gloomy state. . . .'[1]

To balance this misfortune Gladstone reaped considerable benefit from his wisdom in giving himself a second string to the Compensation for Disturbance Bill by setting up in the summer of 1880 the Bessborough commission of enquiry into Irish land tenure. Bessborough (the sixth earl) was one of the most enlightened of the landowners with large Irish holdings. He was quick as well as enlightened and produced his report by January 1881. It provided a more solid basis on which to get a land bill through both Cabinet and Parliament, and this was successfully achieved in the session of 1881. But it had to be run in double harness with coercion, which indeed was given first legislative priority, with land coming only second. This was the most which was acceptable to the Cabinet. But it was not a happy combination, for while the Cabinet would accept land reform only if it was accompanied by coercion, the Irish party would not try to make it work if it was.

The 1881 Land Act therefore, while a considerable measure with far-reaching and beneficial long-term effects, could not hope, because of its companion, to produce a dramatic relaxation of tension and a new mood in Anglo-Irish relations. The Act broadly conceded the famous Three Fs, Fair Rent, Fixity of Tenure and Free Sale (of tenant right). There were some limitations, particularly those which excluded leaseholders and tenants who were already in arrears with their rent, and several further amending measures were required before the Act reached its full effect. It was also subject to some fluctuation of judicial interpretation, although the specially created Irish Land Commission, with the status of a High Court, established a good general reputation for consistent justice. The Act eventually affected tenure in 65 per cent of the land of Ireland and therein permanently destroyed both the absolute power of the landlord and the doctrine of free contract in rents. Although its provisions for tenant proprietorship (raising the proportion of the purchase price which the state could advance from two-thirds to three-quarters) had little direct effect, the indirect effect over a period was considerable. The restrictions on rent-fixing and evictions made many estate owners eager to divest themselves of their land, and the new mood of withdrawal encouraged the Conservative party towards land-purchase schemes for Ireland which started with the Ashbourne Act of 1885 and continued during its twenty-year post-1886 hegemony.

The 1881 Act was both positively and negatively seminal. Positively it sowed the slow-ripening seeds of a prosperous peasant agriculture in Ireland, although ninety years and Ireland's enthusiastic entry into the European Community were required before that could fully mature. Negatively the Act marked the beginning of the end of the Peelite–Whig Liberal party which Palmerston and Russell had created in 1859. The 1881 Act made a perforation along which it was easy for the Home Rule issue to tear in 1886. In no way, however, could that Act be regarded as a minor or ephemeral piece of legislation.

Despite its far-reaching nature this 1881 measure had a happier parliamentary experience than its 1880 predecessor. This was partly because of the Bessborough report and partly because it was much more Gladstone's measure, whereas the other had been more Forster's. The Prime Minister fought the bill through an unenthusiastic Cabinet, and then steered it with a mixture of patience, courtesy, command of detail and unflagging energy through thirty-two days (many of them extending deep into the night) of committee stage. It would have been an unusual feat of knowledge and stamina for a young Cabinet minister trying to make his name with a piece of departmental legislation on which he was paid to be an expert. What was unique was for a Prime Minister aged seventy-one to display a mixture of towering authority and grinding application to detail. Although endless objections had been repetitiously deployed during this committee marathon, the third reading was carried virtually by default on 29 July. Only 14 voted against (and 220 for). This weak adverse vote, taking the sting out of the opposition, was a powerful factor in getting the bill through the Lords on 16 August.

Had this measure been accompanied, as Gladstone had proposed in the autumn of 1880, by some opening towards greater Irish control over Irish affairs, it might have met with more Irish response. It is unlikely that the particular scheme then advocated by Gladstone, which provided for the devolution to Grand Committees of the House of Commons of most purely domestic legislation, not only for Ireland but also for Scotland and England, would have satisfied Irish aspirations. It might have been more successful in reducing filibustering on the floor of the House (which the Parnellites were then developing into an art form) than in taking the edge off their nationalism. But at least it would have been a more hopeful companion for the Land Act than the two Irish Crimes Acts which were the other main legislative hauls of the session. Gladstone, however, allowed the devolution scheme to be killed in the Cabinet. Chamberlain, a counter-productive advocate, had been his only enthusiastic supporter. It was not the greatest tribute to the Prime Minister's foresight or boldness in Cabinet-making.

As it was, the unfortunate juxtaposition between reform and the taking of arbitrary powers was underlined by the government deciding, within eight weeks of the Land Act becoming law, to lock up Parnell and two other recalcitrant Nationalist MPs in Kilmainham Gaol. No charge or process of law was involved, merely a unilateral decision of the Irish executive. The arrest in these circumstances of the leader of a parliamentary group of more than forty members (soon to be one of more than eighty) who was rapidly becoming, to put it at its lowest, one of the half-dozen dominating House of Commons personalities of the century was a strenuous step for any government to take, particularly as it was based on little more than the hope that it might reduce agrarian crime.

Furthermore the next ten years, from that autumn of 1881 to Parnell's death in October 1891, although this prospect was only dimly perceivable at the beginning, were to make Gladstone's relations with the Irish leader still more important to his political successes or failures than had been those with Peel in the 1840s, with Aberdeen in the 1850s, with Palmerston in the 1860s and with Disraeli in the 1870s. With Parnell however the relations were much more personally distant, and followed a more fluctuating course, than with any of these four statesmen. Peel and Aberdeen, despite occasional hiccups, were always admired chiefs to Gladstone. With Palmerston the partnership, as has been described,* was mostly a hostile one, although remarkably free from venom in the circumstances. With Disraeli there was never either alliance or much mutual admiration, although plenty of symbiosis.

With Parnell there was little intimate contact. Even in the late 1880s, when the 'union of hearts' became the phrase which for a time epitomized the relations between the Liberals and the Irish Nationalists, direct encounters were limited to three or four long business meetings, a dinner with the Gladstones in London and, at the apex, a twenty-hour Parnell visit to Hawarden. But that was well in the future in 1881–2. At this period Gladstone's encounters with Parnell were effectively confined to seeing him across the floor of the House of Commons and engaging in parliamentary exchanges, mostly unfriendly, with him. In his great Leeds oratorical jamboree of October 1881, Gladstone spoke more hostilely of Parnell than he was to do on any other occasion. 'He desires to arrest the operation of the Land Act,' the Prime Minister said; 'to stand as Moses stood between the living and the dead; to stand there, not as Moses stood, to arrest, but to spread the plague.' And he continued:

> If it shall appear that there is still to be fought a final conflict in Ireland between law on the one side and sheer lawlessness upon the other, if the law purged from defect and from any taint of injustice is still to be repelled and refused, and the first conditions of political society to remain unfulfilled, then I say, without hesitation, the resources of civilization against its enemies are not yet exhausted.[2]

Parnell replied at Wexford with an equally memorable phrase, denouncing Gladstone as 'this masquerading knight errant, this pretending champion of the rights of every nation except those of the Irish nation'. A week later, on the recommendation of Forster, but with Gladstone's full approval, Parnell was arrested in his bedroom at Morrison's Hotel, Dublin, and held in protective custody for the next

* See pp. 199–214 above.

six months. His conditions of imprisonment were not severe. Kilmainham Gaol, on the Phoenix Park edge of central Dublin, was convenient for visitors, and he had plenty of them, as well as books, writing material, no prison work (as indeed would have been wholly inappropriate for an uncharged and unconvicted prisoner), and a sitting room with two armchairs and a good fire. Nonetheless the six months of incarceration were a heavy deprivation for Parnell, for he was in the early stages of his famous passion for Katherine O'Shea.

He had first met her in July 1880 and they appear to have become lovers in October of the same year. He was thirty-four at the time, nearly forty years Gladstone's junior, and she was thirty-five. In the previous May, he had been elected chairman of the then loose-knit Irish Home Rule party, displacing William Shaw, the previous chairman, by a vote of twenty-three to eighteen. Possibly after an earlier miscarriage, Mrs O'Shea was by the time of Parnell's arrest pregnant by him, and this child, who lived only a couple of months, was born in February 1882.

At the time of the death Parnell was present at Eltham, Mrs O'Shea's house on the south-eastern edge of London. He was on his way back from a parole visit to Paris to attend his nephew's funeral, but he had to return almost immediately to Dublin to fulfil the conditions of his parole, which he scrupulously did. (Mrs O'Shea's child was not of course acknowledged as his, not even by Captain O'Shea, so that he gained no further privilege by this second death.)

The strength and constancy of Parnell's commitment to Mrs O'Shea was never in doubt from 1880 until his death eleven years later. In the spring of 1882 his desire for freedom was therefore intense. To add to his emotional involvements, he could see the control of events in Ireland slipping away from him and into less disciplined and more violent hands. The Ribbonmen and other secret societies were gaining ground and 'Captain Moonlight' (an evocative portmanteau name, probably Parnell's invention, for the organizers of agrarian crime) stalked the countryside. Gladstone also came increasingly to desire Parnell's release. The Irish leader had been put in prison, not as the result of a judicial decision, but because of executive judgement that his being there would reduce agrarian crime. It did nothing of the sort. The reverse happened. And there was evidence that Parnell had moved to a position in which he was prepared both to advocate giving the Land Act (of 1881) a trial and to denounce violence. The main conduit through which this (broadly accurate) information came was the unfortunate one of Captain

O'Shea, the detached but nonetheless intermittently conjugal husband of Katherine.

William O'Shea, who was at that time MP for County Clare, was a classically unsatisfactory figure. He believed, without any foundation, other than that of having held a commission in the Hussars, he was too much of a gentleman for the Irish parliamentary party, and he was as shifty and self-seeking as he was vain, always looking to exaggerate his own importance and to gain benefits for himself. In other words he was the worst possible go-between. Parnell, perhaps for obvious reasons, was well aware of this and tried to replace him with Justin McCarthy as negotiator. Gladstone was less suspicious,* but it was Chamberlain who at this stage reposed most faith in O'Shea. And Chamberlain was important, because Gladstone in the run-up to that year's budget on 24 April (again the albatross of carrying the Exchequer as well as the premiership) left most of the discussions to him.

The bungling of these intermediaries may have led to the missing of one of the great opportunities in Anglo-Irish history. J. L. Hammond thought that a major settlement between Parnell and the British government might have been achieved if O'Shea had not been so officiously self-promoting and Chamberlain less brash. Whether or not such a utopian outcome was a real possibility, it did not happen. But the Cabinet, on 2 May, did decide that Parnell (and two other prisoners) should be released. He was out of Kilmainham that afternoon and on the following day Forster, who had been the sole opponent of release in the Cabinet, was out of the government. The former Irish Secretary was making his damaging resignation statement in the House of Commons on the Thursday afternoon (4 May) when Parnell arrived, separated a small crowd of members at the bar of the House and strode impassively to his seat.

From Forster's resignation there followed the tragedy of Lord Frederick Cavendish. Gladstone caused surprise by appointing his amiable nephew by marriage to the vacant place. Cavendish made his first journey as Chief Secretary to Dublin overnight on Friday, 5 May and was assassinated in Phoenix Park on the evening of Saturday, 6 May,

* Of O'Shea's general good faith. How early he knew of his position in the triangle is another matter. Parnell was subject to close police surveillance. Harcourt as Home Secretary was fascinated by police reports (particularly on Irish matters, to deal with which he set up the Special Branch in March 1883), was prurient and a natural gossip. It is inconceivable that he was not told of Parnell's irregular arrangements and unlikely that, having been told, he did not pass on the information to his senior colleagues.

only three days after Parnell's release. Parnell denounced the outrage with conviction, dismay and, according to Chamberlain and Dilke, vivid fear for his own life – as a result of the unleashing of a general bloodbath. Despite these protestations the juxtaposition was clearly fatal for any early development of a 'union of hearts' atmosphere.

Gladstone–Parnell relations then entered a three-year period in which they were better than at the time of the Leeds–Wexford exchange of imprecations while remaining well short of the warmth which came in the late 1880s and 1890. What did Gladstone think of Parnell during this relatively calm midstream interlude? In June 1883, Hamilton (always a very good source) reported him as saying that he found the Irish leader 'still a sphinx who probably works for and with the law as far as he dare, and who possibly does not in his heart of hearts hate the Government'. By February of the next year he had retrogressed to the extent of stating that 'he felt towards Sir S. Northcote much the same as he did towards Parnell. Neither of them were really big men or pleasant antagonists; but their places might be taken by worse men, and therefore he preferred keeping them.' In October 1884 he was back to expressing a 'sneaking likeness [*sic*]' for Parnell, to which Hamilton added 'as frequently happens with him when he had an opportunity'.[3]

All this was well short of Gladstone's 1897 remark: 'I cannot tell you how much I think of him, and what an interest I take in everything concerning him. A marvellous man, a terrible fall.'[4] This was of course well after Gladstone in what he saw as the best interests of Home Rule had ensured that the fall was indeed terrible and had himself suffered heavily from it. Nonetheless it is easier to write with dramatic appreciation of those on whom the gates of history have slammed shut than of those with whom one has day-to-day dealings. However, Gladstone's panegyric has to be considered in relation to another statement of his that 'Parnell was the most remarkable man he had ever met';[5] to a judgement of the notably cool Asquith that he was 'one of the three or four men of the nineteenth century';[6] and to R. B. Haldane's opinion that he was the strongest man the House of Commons had seen in 150 years.[7]

What was Parnell's special quality which evoked such extravagant (although admittedly posthumous) tributes from a variety of discriminating judges? A large part of his power of leadership stemmed from his disdainful imperiousness. He added a special ingredient of authority to the natural arrogance of the Anglo-Irish landowners. In his youth he had been something of an upper-class lout, rusticated from Magdalene

College, Cambridge, after a drunken fracas in the Station Road with a manure merchant, and brought to court in his local market town of Rathdrum after another disturbance in the hotel at Glendalough. At this stage in his life he was equally indifferent to his Co. Wicklow squirearchical responsibilities and to the holiness of the Glendalough early Christian site.

Later his arrogance took more dignified even if still ungracious forms. In 1883 his financial affairs had become sufficiently embarrassed that the sale of his house and estate at Avondale in Co. Wicklow seemed the only way out. This was avoided by the raising of a public subscription which by the end of that year had produced £37,000 (not much less than £2 million at today's values). At Morrison's Hotel (a locale which played a chequered part in Parnell's life) the Lord Mayor of Dublin, in the presence of about twenty Nationalist MPs, conducted a small ceremony and handed over the cheque. According to most accounts Parnell cut short the Lord Mayor's encomium, merely asked him whether the cheque was 'made payable to order and crossed', tucked it into his pocket and brought the ceremony to an end. At the banquet that evening Parnell spoke powerfully about the state of Ireland, but confined any reference to the munificent subvention to two cold sentences.

Another example of Parnell's capacity for detachment was later provided during sittings of the 1888–9 Special Commission of Enquiry (into Irish agrarian crime and the allegations of *The Times* about his own involvement), the deliberations of which were vital to Parnell's repute and future. His star counsel, Sir Charles Russell (later Lord Chief Justice), was irritated by Parnell's fitful attendance and threatened through Michael Davitt to throw up his brief if Parnell did not attend the next day's hearing. Parnell dismissed this as a *prima donna*'s tantrum, but did attend at the Law Courts on the following morning. He brought with him a small brown-paper parcel, to the unwrapping of which, before a mystified Davitt, who was beside him, and an exasperated Russell, he completely devoted himself. It contained a tiny particle of gold, which he had assayed from a lump of stone, sent to him by his agent in Avondale. 'After fourteen years' search,' he triumphantly told Davitt, whom he expected to be as excited as he was himself. The incident illustrated many aspects of Parnell's unusual and contradictory character: his interest in rather simple scientific experiments, his proprietorial optimism accompanied by some financial naivety, his self-absorption, and his imperviousness to the reactions of others.

After the Phoenix Park murders the Parnellites were too thrown back on their heels to muster their previous virulence against coercion, and at the same time any British optimism about an early solution was stilled. Government and Nationalists went into a relationship of stand-off, the old parliamentary bitterness somewhat diminished but with no lively constructive hopes, which lasted for two to three years. The dead-sea fruits of this flaccid period were memorably summed up by Dilke when he stayed in Viceregal Lodge, Dublin, at the very end of the government's life:

> Early in the morning of Sunday, the 23rd [May 1885] I attended church with Spencer, and in the afternoon took him for the only walk which he had enjoyed for a long time. We passed the spot where Lord Frederick Cavendish was killed, and accompanied by a single aide-de-camp, but watched at a distance by two policemen in plain clothes, and met at every street corner by two others, walked to the strawberry gardens, and on our return, it being a lovely Sunday when the Wicklow Mountains were at their best and the hawthorn in bloom, met thousands of Dublin people driving out to the strawberry gardens on cars. In the course of the whole long walk but one man lifted his hat to Spencer, who was universally recognised. At his dinner party on the Sunday evening Spencer told us that a Roman Catholic priest who was present . . . was the only priest in Ireland who would enter his walls, while the Castle was boycotted by every Archbishop and Bishop. On Monday morning . . . I paid a visit to the Mansion House at the request of the Lord Mayor of Dublin, taking by Spencer's leave the Viceregal carriages there, where they had in his second Viceroyalty not been before. . . .

In a separate letter Dilke added the comment, directed as much against the whole government's policy as against the Viceroy: 'What a life is Spencer's – cut off from nearly the whole people – good and bad! What sense of duty, what high-mindedness, and what stupidity!'[8]

Dilke's devastating description of the position of the British Governor-General in Ireland within a few weeks of the end of five years of Liberal power showed how far that government was from having settled the problem of Ireland, although on the land issue it had made one important step forward. Ireland was nearer to having settled the fate of the government. Of the ten out of sixteen Cabinet members who at that disintegrating time had submitted tentative resignations, over half of the threats were on the Irish issue. Any early successor administration, Conservative or Liberal, looked likely to be dominated by Irish policy. It was also already clear that the issue was a fissiparous one for the

Liberal party, although the lines of potential division were confused, Chamberlain (and Dilke) then demanding a greater devolution of power than Gladstone, under Whig pressure, was prepared for the moment to push through.

29
THE THIRD REFORM BILL

DURING THE RUN-UP to the 1883 session when Gladstone was recovering from his insomnia at Cannes, his mind and those of the Radicals were turning towards franchise reform. It had always been part of his strategy that the extension of household suffrage from the towns to the countryside should be the major task for the government in the second half of its life. By 1883 his administration was already three years old, and despite the Septennial Act there was no example between 1832 and 1914 of a parliament lasting for more than six years. However, in Gladstone's absence, the Cabinet preferred procrastination to the dangers of disruption with the Whigs which this extension of the franchise might involve. The Radicals were compensated with the inclusion of bills in the Queen's Speech for the reform both of London government and of local government in England generally. The first foundered on the departmental intransigence of Harcourt, who half counted as a Radical, and the second got blocked in its wake.

Harcourt, then aged forty-five, was a brilliant academic lawyer and a fierce parliamentary controversialist whose party loyalties were more fixed than his views. His confidence was that of a Whig patrician, his style that of a partisan Liberal bruiser and his temper that of a mixture of the irascible, the boorish and the wittily charming. By the end of his life he had earned (among the Liberal faithful) the sobriquet of 'the great gladiator'. There were strong elements of Hugh Dalton in him, as well as a touch of Willie Whitelaw's ability to attract affectionate mockery. He would have been more disliked by his often injured opponents had he not been a natural figure of fun.

However, in the following year it was his colleagues and not his opponents whom Harcourt succeeded in bruising. The proposed scheme for London local government was not markedly different in its destination from that which was enacted under Salisbury in 1888. It was to set up a unified (although two-tier) local government for that part of the capital which was already solidly urban, in other words the four-million core which, with its twenty-eight metropolitan boroughs, became for three-quarters of a century the area of the London County Council. But the routes were sharply different. The Liberals proposed to do it by extending (and democratizing) the City of London Corporation. The Conservatives eventually did it by leaving the City as a fine anomaly set in aspic and providing for the serious although not the ceremonial representation of London over its head and around its narrow boundaries.

The key practical difference related to the control of the police. The City controlled its own force through a municipal committee, like any provincial borough. In the rest of the metropolis the constabulary, as remains so today, was directly responsible to the Home Secretary and under no local control. The majority of Gladstone's colleagues, and particularly those who had interest in or knowledge of local government, regarded it as inconceivable that the contribution of a Liberal government to democracy in London should involve the removal from an expanded City Corporation of any power over its own police force. Harcourt, on the other hand, obsessed as he was with the Fenian threat and fancying himself as a Fouché, was equally resolute and a good deal more vehement against any surrender of Home Office prerogatives. Showing an imperfect grasp of the difference between operational and administrative control, he tried to frighten his colleagues with nightmare scenarios of committees and sub-committees having to be summoned before there could be any response to an explosives threat.

The result was impasse. A strong even if sometimes risible Home Secretary is difficult to shift on his own ground, and the outcome was the foundering for that session and indeed for the lifetime of the government of the London bill. And the wider local government measure became rather like a train which is blocked, not because of its own failure, but because the one ahead of it on the line has lost its power. During the early stages of these disputes Gladstone was recovering at Cannes, but failed to resolve them on his return. To a large extent he allowed such issues to pass over his head. They were not for him the essence of politics. It was nevertheless a failure of generalship and produced the second unnecessarily barren session. Moveover it left the government well into the fourth year of its life with remarkably little domestic result to show for its efforts.

This was belatedly but substantially corrected in 1884. Gladstone spent the two middle weeks of September 1883 on a northern-waters cruise in another of Donald Currie's ships, this time the *Pembroke Castle*. Currie's invitation had been for a week around the Hebrides. Once aboard, however, if youth was not exclusively on the prow, pleasure, aided by almost perfect weather, quickly took over at the helm. The party included Tennyson and Mrs Gladstone as well as the GOM, with a middle-aged leavening of Currie himself, Sir Arthur Gordon, who had progressed from ADC in the Ionian Isles to Governor of New Zealand, and Sir William Harcourt, who appropriately for the Home Secretary was present in British waters only, as well as a younger contingent of Mary Gladstone, Hallam Tennyson, Lewis ('Lulu') Harcourt and Laura Tennant, Margot Asquith's short-lived elder sister. Gladstone's uninhibited ability to enjoy such a jollification, and to infuse others into his own sense of enjoyment, was one of his striking and attractive qualities. As a result the cruise, with Currie's happy concurrence, extended from the Hebrides to Orkney, Oslo (then Christiania) and Copenhagen. In the Danish capital there were great junketings with the Danish, Russian and Greek sovereigns, as well as the Princess of Wales, who were all assembled there. There was a Danish royal dinner at the palace of Fredensborg and a return luncheon on the ship, after which Tennyson read 'The Bugle Song' and 'The Grandmother', absent-mindedly beating out his rhythm on the thigh of the Tsarina, whom he mistook (shades of Palmerston?) for a maid of honour.[1]

Queen Victoria was not at all pleased when she heard of these proceedings, ostensibly on the ground that Gladstone had omitted to give her prior notice of his stepping on to a foreign shore and meeting her fellow sovereigns, but possibly also on the ground of simple jealousy that they had made so much fuss of him. He brushed off her complaints with a mixture of equanimity and restrained irritation, and, fortified by Tennyson's acceptance of a peerage, returned to London on 21 September in better spirits for an autumn of legislation preparation than in either of the two previous years.

Between the end of September and Christmas Gladstone was in London almost as much as at Hawarden and held four or five Cabinets. Perhaps more important, however, was the fact that for once he applied himself with foresight and persuasive skill to the conciliation of Hartington, whose continued presence in the government had become essential to the enactment of a Franchise Bill. And such an enactment was in turn essential to determine whether the 1880 government would or would not stand as an administration with major reform to its credit. The 1884 Reform Bill, when eventually enacted, increased the size of the electorate from three to five million. Absolutely it produced the biggest increase in the numbers entitled to vote of the three nineteenth-century franchise measures, but it was not the biggest proportional increase. Ironically it was the 'great Reform Bill' of 1832 which did least from either point of view. In England and Wales that bill added 217,000 to an electorate of 435,000. The 1867 bill, after Disraeli's committee-stage lurch to democracy, nearly doubled an electorate which had over the previous thirty-five years grown to a million. The 1884 bill, in comparison with these increases of just under 50 per cent and just under 90 per cent respectively, produced an overall growth of a little less than 60 per cent. Its effect, however, was qualitative as well as quantitative. It extended the limited town democracy of 1867 to the countryside, which was more of a shock to the remains of English feudalism than anything which had gone before, and the effect was magnified by the bill's running-mate, a Redistribution of Seats Bill, giving the counties for the first time more seats than the boroughs. The coal miners, who mostly lived in industrially scarred countryside rather than in towns, were also brought within the franchise, thereby opening the way to much the largest group of working men representatives in Parliament.

Furthermore the effect of the bill on Ireland was more dramatic than its effect on Great Britain. Since 1829 the impact of Catholic emancipation had been deliberately reduced by keeping Ireland on a more restricted franchise than England. When the 1884 reform ended this, it was therefore the redress of more than half a century of discrimination. As a result, like the release of a dam, it had a greater relative effect. As against the overall 60 per cent increase there was in Ireland an addition of 230 per cent to the electorate. Gladstone and his supporters did this with their eyes open and rather nobly. They apprehended that it would mean more than doubling the size of the Parnellite parliamentary party and also the virtual elimination of Liberal MPs (of whom there were thirty-five in 1880) from Ireland. Both of these apprehensions proved justified. The latter consideration was expected to be more than outweighed by Liberal gains in Great Britain (which supposition was never exactly put to the test in neutral circumstances, always an elusive electoral concept). The embracing of equality for Ireland was a good test of the traditional Whig hallmark of accepting the inevitable with generosity and even enthusiasm. It was a pity that the confidence of the Whig rump, as represented by Hartington, was in the 1880s so low that they did so only growlingly. Their predecessors, from Fox to Russell, had put up a better show.

With the 1884 bill the second Gladstone administration gave itself some claim to look the government of 1830 in the face. Without a franchise bill it might have been remembered for little more than invading Egypt, sending Gordon to his death and being dominated by, but not resolving, the Irish problem.

Gladstone's strategy of holding back franchise reform until towards the end of the Parliament was rational. A substantial change in the size and nature of the electorate undermined the validity of the House of Commons which carried it through. Once there was a new basis for an election it was difficult for long to avoid having one. It would hardly have been acceptable to carry franchise reform in, say, 1881 and then to expect a House elected on a superseded basis to carry moral authority into 1884 and 1885. This would have been particularly so in relation to the representation of Ireland, to the shape of which reform was expected to, and did, make a seismic difference. To enact a Reform Bill early would have been to throw away, like a bee which only had one sting in it, the great Liberal majority of 1880.

But if such a strategy was rational it was also risky. By the start of the 1884 session the government, although barely four years old, was beginning to look fragile. It could not afford calmly to sit out yet another of the periods of political foul weather which, partly because of sheer ill luck and partly because of its lack of inner coherence, had mostly been its lot. Dilke summed it up by writing that 'The Tory game is to delay the franchise bill until they have upset us upon Egypt. . . .'[2] One thing which would have greatly increased the fragility would have been the defection of Hartington and of the faction in both Commons and Lords which looked to his lead. But Hartington had by this time lost all enthusiasm for extending the franchise or indeed for any significant measure of reform.

He was not naturally illiberal. In his first twenty years in the House of Commons he had effectively propounded a number of advanced measures, and in the last phase of his political life as a member of the Salisbury and Balfour Cabinets he was a focus of liberally inclined moderation compared with the clanging imperialism and harsh partisanship which Joseph Chamberlain had by then adopted. But towards the mid-1880s he had come to feel unconfident, unhappy and bunkered in a Liberal Cabinet in which Chamberlain and Dilke made so much of the argumentative running. He was reluctant to hand over to them the post-Gladstone future of the Liberal party, but he did not enjoy serving with them and he no longer felt that he could lead a party which struck a keynote of 'constructive' Radicalism. Harcourt had informed Dilke in January 1884 that if Gladstone went and Hartington took over as Prime

Minister he intended to compensate for his own Whiggery by putting Dilke in the Foreign Office and Chamberlain at the Exchequer. That is exactly the sort of flattering gossip with which politicians when they are in a good mood like to regale each other. Such principal lieutenants would however have been a nightmare for Hartington, and in fact by 1884 Harcourt himself had become at least as likely a successor to Gladstone as Hartington (which was perhaps the reason why his mood was so benign).

This created an interesting new nexus between Gladstone and Hartington. The Prime Minister might upset Hartington with his intermittent adventurousness on Ireland and with his lack of dependable imperial feeling abroad. But he had the great advantage that he was no more of a 'constructive' Radical (defined as one desiring increasingly to use the apparatus of the state to redress social inequality) than was Hartington himself. When at the beginning of the following year (1885) Chamberlain launched the 'unauthorized programme' (his own Radical agenda without blessing from leader or whips) and gave it a fierce cutting edge with the use of the memorable and provocative phrase 'and what ransom will property pay?', he ruffled the feathers of Gladstone almost as much as he did those of Hartington. Furthermore, although Hartington was relatively undazzled by Gladstone, the GOM nonetheless had even for him the unique venerability of being the Prime Minister under whom he had served his whole ministerial career. He was used to him. If Hartington, increasingly sceptical about his own ability to lead the new Liberal party, was to continue in a Liberal government (which he half wanted to do), then he preferred that it should be under Gladstone rather than under anyone else. He did not want a franchise bill and in particular he did not want one without a redistribution of constituencies. This was mainly because he saw the enfranchisement of agricultural labourers unaccompanied by redistribution (to which the Tories were strongly attached) as leading straight to a disruptive conflict with the House of Lords. He was also dismayed by a scenario in which Gladstone got the franchise bill through, used the achievement as a suitable moment for retirement and left him (Hartington) to deal with redistribution and see the Whig interest trampled upon by Dilke and Chamberlain.

Gladstone on the other hand wanted the franchise bill and judged that he could not get it through without Hartington. This was his view without foreseeing the Gordon débâcle. Hartington played an inglorious part in this, but his withdrawal from the government would nonetheless have made more dangerous Dilke's perception of 'the Tory plan to upset us upon Egypt'. Gladstone was willing to countenance redistribution (although he never felt much enthusiasm for destroying old constituency patterns), but he had far too much political sense to put it in the same bill with franchise enlargement. This would be to walk into a quagmire. He might as well try to cross the sands of Dee from Hawarden to the Wirral. The detail would be immense. If the opposition could block franchise extension as well as redistribution they would have no incentive to get on with the latter. And Gladstone had had more than enough experience of failed bills in the previous two sessions. There was no opportunity for compromise with Hartington here. The franchise measure had to be kept separate.

Gladstone was indeed half looking for a favourable plateau upon which to retire, and seemed likely to regard the achievement of the third Reform Act of the century, without regard to whether it was accompanied by redistribution, as providing such a piece of level ground. Much of his own talk and apparent thoughts was directed to looking forward to the moment of release. And its early arrival was the assumption of those closest to him. On 9 November 1883, for example, Edward Hamilton wrote: 'Went this evening to Lord Mayor's dinner. One thought it was any odds that last year's dinner would be Mr. G's last; but here we are again. But this must be his final one.'[3] So Hartington's fears were not ill founded, and his reaction to them was sufficiently strong that in the first half of December the general ministerial assumption was that he would do a pre-emptive resignation before the Queen's Speech in February, fatal although such a Hartington withdrawal might prove to the government.

Fortunately, however, there was one possible avenue of compromise, and this was a postponement of the date of Gladstone's retirement, an issue on which the GOM was always disposed to be flexible. And so, just after Christmas, the knot was untied. Gladstone went to London on New Year's Eve and had a two-and-a-half-hour *tête-à-tête* with Hartington, a remarkably long-drawn-out occasion given Hartington's taciturnity and Gladstone's need to persuade and not just to harangue. However, it worked. Franchise reform would be the main measure for 1884, redistribution for 1885, and Gladstone would remain in the leadership to see through the latter as well as the former. On this basis Hartington would also stay for the time being, although by no means committing himself for the duration.

The franchise bill had a relatively easy Commons passage. Gladstone moved its second reading on 28 February in a speech which the devoted but not always uncritical Hamilton described as being unsurpassed 'for lucidity of exposition, for lightness in touch, for beauty of arrangement, for wealth of language, and for vigour and power'.[4] What was of more interest, however, was Hamilton's description of Gladstone's 1880s approach – rather different from his earlier habits – to a major parliamentary speech:

> Mr G. saw the Attorney General early this morning and for about two hours devoted himself to arranging the materials for his Reform speech. His notes for an expounding speech of this kind are quite a sight – so clear and tidy. It is remarkable that he can always tell how long a speech will be.* I asked him this morning what the length would be, and he said an hour and 40 minutes; and it was within 5 minutes of that time. He went out for a little after luncheon. It is in walking that he thinks out his speeches, and I have no doubt that in taking his turn this afternoon, he rehearsed the plan of his speech and the words of his peroration. Half an hour before he went down to the House he was calmly reading a book (Mrs Roundell's: *Family of Cowdray*, which is interesting him) – and sipping a cup of tea.[5]

The result of the division which followed that debate was a solid majority of 340 to 210. There were then twelve committee nights, modest by some experiences of the time, with no serious upsets or narrow shaves. What for many, particularly Hartington, was the most controversial corner, the equal treatment of Ireland, was rounded by the even more massive majority of 332 to 137.

On issues other than the Irish franchise Gladstone took a conservative, or it could be argued a non-diversionary, approach. He refused the enticements of proportional representation. And on women's suffrage, which at one stage threatened to run strongly, he employed overkill. He authorized his Chief Whip to tell Liberal MPs that if the votes-for-women amendment were carried the bill would be dropped and the government would resign. Gladstone's statement continued: 'This does not imply any judgement on the merits of the proposal, but only on its introduction into the Bill. I am myself not strongly opposed to every form and degree of the proposal, but I think that if put into the Bill it would give the House of Lords a case for "postponing" it and I know not how to incur such a risk.'[6] Eventually the dreaded amendment was

* Not really; an experienced speaker can nearly always get it right within a very few minutes.

defeated by a majority of over a hundred, although with three members of the government (including Dilke from within the Cabinet) abstaining. On third reading on 26 June the opposition did not divide the House: true to the tradition of 1867 the Conservatives were hesitant about recording themselves in direct hostility to franchise enlargement.

Gladstone, who had already made a speech which even Hamilton described as 'more rattling perhaps than judicious',[7] immediately insisted that the Journals of the House should most unusually note the *nemine contradicente* result. This quick-footedness was due as much to tactics as to triumphalism. The next move lay with the House of Lords, and Gladstone wished to subject them to as effective as possible a preliminary barrage. This was not because he wished to provoke a conflict between the two Houses. Others, most notably Chamberlain, welcomed such a prospect, but Gladstone both feared a dispute which could endanger the hereditary principle and wanted the bill on the statute book as soon as possible. He made the most strenuous efforts to maximize government support in the Lords. He even brought it home to Tennyson that there is no such thing as a free peerage. The Laureate, who eventually repaid him with a chiding poem ('Steersman, be not precipitate in thine act') was at first loath to pay his debts with the harder currency of a vote. Eventually, however, after two Gladstone letters to himself, as well as one to his son and another to his wife, he gave way 'despite gout'.

The bishops, on whom Gladstone was equally pressing, were less trouble. After consultation with Benson of Canterbury he wrote to twelve of them, mainly those who had been his own nominees to the bench, and was gratified that all but Stubbs of Chester (and of medieval charters) sent friendly replies within two days. In fact ten of the twelve, plus another two (Thomson of York and Temple of Exeter, later of Canterbury) whom Gladstone had not approached, voted for the bill. Only one bishop (Ellicott of the then united see of Gloucester and Bristol) voted against. Altogether it was much more favourable an episcopal performance than anything which Asquith was able to achieve in the disputes between the two Houses of a generation later. Gladstone, of course, did not attempt to crack a party whip over their mitres, but concentrated, with different letters tailor-made for each bishop, on the high constitutional issues and the dangers to the House of Lords which were involved.

There was also a good turnout of Liberal peers, effectively for the last time. There was never subsequently any major party vote in the House of Lords before life peerages came in seventy-four years later in which the Conservative majority was not overwhelming. It was an end-of-term speech day for the old Liberal–Whig party in which those participating did not realize that it was not merely the term which was ending but the school which in its existing form was to be shut down. Nevertheless the Tories had a majority of 205 to 146 for Salisbury's motion of outright rejection. However, quite a few of the 205 thought that Salisbury's 'leap in the dark' had been rash and were muttering that they were not prepared to vote for a second rejection. This was moreover likely to be a matter of early practical import, for the government's plan, announced by Gladstone two days after the Lords vote, was to bring Parliament back in late October, to re-present the franchise bill, and to follow it with a redistribution of seats bill provided there was a scheme sufficiently agreed between the two sides to offer the prospect of reasonable parliamentary progress.

Compromise was therefore lurking in the background right from the moment of the Lords' intransigence. But before this could come to the surface a noisy overture of denunciation and counter-denunciation between the politicians had to be played out. And while this was going on in public a still more intensive and at the beginning equally implacable exchange was taking place in private between the Queen and Gladstone. The doubts of some of the more moderate Tory peers about the wisdom of Salisbury's lead were in no way shared by their Sovereign. The Queen thought that the Lords had every right to reject the bill, opined that they represented 'the true feeling of the country' better than did the Commons, and acceded only reluctantly to the proposal for an autumn session, saying that she thought '*a more fair & judicious* course' would have been to seek the opinion of the country by dissolution, thereby provoking Gladstone to remark to Hamilton that the logic of her argument really led to the abolition of the House of Commons.

Moreover the Queen settled down to a summer in which she appeared to read obsessively every speech made by a member of the government, senior or junior, and many by backbenchers as well, and write and complain to Gladstone about them. Between 10 July and the end of August he had to write to her no less than sixteen letters, amounting to a total of nearly 4000 words, wearily explaining, excusing, and occasionally half apologizing for what she regarded as the excesses of his colleagues.

Mainly it was Chamberlain who was to blame, but Dilke and even Herbert Gladstone, the GOM's thirty-year-old son, attracted a share of the opprobrium. The Prime Minister on the whole showed admirable restraint under this burden, but he did permit himself a late-July expostulation that: 'Your Majesty will readily believe that he [Mr Gladstone] has neither the time nor the eyesight to make himself acquainted by careful perusal with all the speeches of his colleagues. . . .'[8] Nor was he himself spared her partisan criticism. When he made a few speeches in Scotland in mid-September, some of them admittedly a little close to Balmoral, she wrote to her private secretary, '. . . the Queen is *utterly* disgusted with his *stump* oratory so unworthy of his position – almost under her very nose'.[9] Fortunately the emollient – and Liberal – Ponsonby, so far from passing this on, wrote to Gladstone wishing him rest 'after your most successful visit to the North'.[10]

Despite or perhaps half because of these trials and burdens Gladstone found time in mid-August to write a most formidable memorandum for the Queen. He heralded its importance by referring to it in a covering note as 'a paper which goes beyond the ordinary limits of his official submissions'. The core was contained in the following paragraphs:

> 21. The House of Lords has for a long period been the habitual and vigilant enemy of every Liberal Government. . . .
>
> 22. It cannot be supposed that to any Liberal this is a satisfactory subject of contemplation.
>
> 23. Nevertheless some Liberals, of whom I am one, would rather choose to bear all this for the future as it has been borne in the past, than raise the question of an organic reform of the House of Lords. The interest of the party seems to be in favour of such an alteration: but it should, in my judgement, give way to a higher interest, which is national and imperial: the interest of preserving the hereditary power as it is, if only it will be content to act in such a manner as will render the preservation endurable.
>
> 24. I do not speak of this question as one in which I can have a personal interest or share. Age, and political aversion, alike forbid it. Nevertheless, if the Lords continue to reject the Franchise Bill, it will come. . . .
>
> 26. I wish [an hereditary House of Lords] to continue, for the avoidance of greater evils. These evils are not only long and acrimonious controversy, difficulty in devising any satisfactory mode of reform, and delay in the general business of the country, but other and more permanent mischiefs. I desire the hereditary principle, notwithstanding its defects, to be maintained, for I think it in certain respects an element of good, a barrier against mischief. But it is not strong enough for direct conflict with the representative power, and will only come out of the conflict sorely bruised and maimed. Further; organic change of this kind

> in the House of Lords may strip and lay bare, and in laying bare may weaken, the foundations even of the Throne.[11]

Sir Henry Ponsonby's letter of acknowledgement indicated that this powerful document may have had some favourable effect upon the Queen. October produced a spate of oratory. Salisbury was uncompromising in Glasgow. The appearance of Randolph Churchill and Stafford Northcote in Birmingham provoked a riot (from the organization of which Chamberlain was not far distant). Hartington, Harcourt and Mundella addressed a reform demonstration 'under the windows' at Chatsworth (that was perhaps even more the finale of the Whig–Liberal party than the July vote in the House of Lords). Hartington's speech there was robust, although it neither incurred the censure of the Queen nor rivalled Chamberlain's provocations about 'the insolent pretensions of an hereditary caste'. It was John Morley, however, not then a member of the government but a rising backbencher, who coined the neatest of the anti-peers slogans. 'Mend them or end them,' he said, must be the policy, thereby going far beyond Gladstone's attempt to confine the controversy to the enormity of the Lords' actions and to avoid raising issues of their composition or powers.

Then, almost suddenly, at the end of the month the mood changed. Even the Queen (whether or not influenced by Gladstone's memorandum) became eager for an accommodation, and somewhat critical of Salisbury's intransigence. 'The atmosphere is full of compromise,' Edward Hamilton wrote on 30 October. Gladstone himself was determined to get his bill, but he became less and less attracted by an upending of the House of Lords. He recoiled from the threat (and still more the reality) of a mass creation of peers such as King William IV had been forced to agree to in the 1830–2 struggle, and he disliked equally the idea of a root-and-branch reform to make a more rational second chamber. The Conservatives were also doubtful whether they could hold their forces for a second rejection. The result was some rather fumbling negotiations on the form of a redistribution scheme between Hicks Beach (soon to be leader of the House of Commons and Chancellor of the Exchequer) and Hartington. They were fumbling because it was never clear to what extent Hicks Beach spoke with Salisbury's authority and because Hartington (and maybe Beach too) had a far from perfect understanding of the intricacies of redistribution.

The relevant figure who did have such an understanding was the President of the Local Government Board, Charles Dilke. It was his finest hour. With ambitious forethought he had begun working on a scheme in early July. He brought its heads before the Cabinet on 9 August and got a general blessing subject to the recess supervision of a Cabinet committee of six, of which he was appointed chairman. With typical but not ill-founded Dilke arrogance he then commented: 'I soon got rid of the committee and went on by myself with Lambert.' (Sir John Lambert had been an authoritative permanent secretary of the Local Government Board until he retired in 1882; Dilke brought him back for this special service.) As a result he was able to send Gladstone a detailed plan on 20 September. This was less radical in several respects than Dilke would have liked. He felt he had to pay regard to Gladstone's instinctive conservatism on the one hand and on the other to Hartington's concern for Whig electoral interests (which broadly meant that Whigs should not be overwhelmed by Radicals in the choice of Liberal candidates).

On the first ground he did not dare to touch university representation or other forms of plural voting. On the second ground two-member constituencies (a great Whig attachment) were to be maintained in the counties, except for Yorkshire and Lancashire which were curiously regarded as urban throughout. The other counties were to be divided for the first time. Fifty-six boroughs of under 10,000 were to lose their separate representation, and thirty of under 40,000 their second member. The seats made available by this culling of the remaining semi-rotten boroughs were to be distributed partly to London (which was advanced from twenty-two to fifty-five seats), partly to the under-represented industrial boroughs, and partly to the counties, which for the first time were to exceed the strength of the borough representation. Ireland, Scotland and Wales were to continue to be somewhat over-represented, but within that over-representation were to have a pattern of seats roughly the same as in England.

With his scheme on the table and a mastery of the subject in his head, Dilke was dominant, both within the government and with the Tories in the negotiations of the autumn. 'Chamberlain and I and Mr Gladstone were the only three who understood the subject, so that the others were unable to fight except in the form known as swearing at large,'[12] he wrote in September. He was for once modest in listing Gladstone and Chamberlain, both of whose knowledge was sketchy, as equal experts with himself. And he had another fortuitous bonus which they did not at the time share, which was that he had established a good relationship with Salisbury, who was always a mixture of sour and sweet, through membership of the star-studded Royal Commission on the Housing of the Working Classes (it included the Prince of Wales and Cardinal Manning as well as Salisbury), over which Dilke as the departmental minister surprisingly presided.

The three key meetings between government and opposition were in late November, by which time the House of Commons had re-passed the franchise bill and the House of Lords had acknowledged the new atmosphere by letting it through on second reading, although retaining the power to maul it at later stages if the talks went wrong. They did not. Although the negotiating cast changed somewhat from meeting to meeting, the main business was done by a quintet of Gladstone, Hartington and Dilke on the government side and Salisbury and Northcote from the opposition. There were a number of modifications to Dilke's September scheme. Towns up to 15,000 (rather than 10,000) were merged into their counties; the Tories at one stage, with a Disraelian swoop, proposed going to 25,000.

Furthermore the counties and the big towns were all divided into single-member districts. This was the real gain for the Tories. It laid the foundation of 'villa Conservatism' and the safe Tory seats of the Home Counties and the prosperous suburbs in and around the big provincial cities. On this basis, subject to a few loose ends which he and Dilke subsequently tied up, Salisbury was willing to settle and carried Northcote along with him. There were at least compensating benefits, taking the two bills together, for Gladstone and Dilke. Hartington's position was less happy, for the effective end of the two-member constituency meant the end also of the habit of running a Whig and a Radical in double harness. The Whig interest, which was thought to be dependent upon this tradition (for if a choice had to be made the Radical was likely to be preferred by the selection committee) was only lightly compensated by a last-minute arrangement for about twenty boroughs outside London. If they had previously possessed and were to retain two members, they were allowed to remain as undivided constituencies. However, Hartington was in no position to stand out. Having urged the linkage of redistribution with franchise extension, and representing the forces of mild and aristocratic Liberalism, it would have been quite ridiculous for him to have opposed agreement and insisted on continuing the struggle against the peers. He may have been out-manoeuvred, and the perforation along which the 1886 tear was to occur may have been given a few more holes, but he had no option.

Gladstone on the other hand was delighted by the outcome, which made up for some of the vicissitudes, deserved and undeserved, which constantly beset that government. Mary Gladstone recorded that after the final meeting of the quintet on 27 November he was 'splitting and chuckling'. His pleasure was at the early and suddenly secure prospect of getting the franchise bill on to the statute book. He never took particular pride in the seats bill, regarding it as little more than a key to unlock the door to franchise enlargement. It was nonetheless itself a major measure and as near to a final settlement as is ever possible amid the impermanence of politics. It decisively redrew the electoral map of Britain. There was no further redistribution (or pressure for it) until 1918, and even with the changes of that year and the subsequent and more frequent ones which started in 1950, today's constituency pattern is recognizably based on that of 1884–5, and on no earlier arrangement. The modern single-member county constituency and the modern divided borough are both creations of Dilke under Gladstone.

The autumn session was wound up on 6 December, with the franchise bill on the statute book, although not to come into operation until redistribution was through, and the seats bill past its House of Commons second reading. 'Mr G. went off to Hawarden with Herbert [Gladstone],' Hamilton wrote. 'He never quitted London in greater personal triumph. No one could have achieved what he has done, and at the same time kept his party completely in hand.'[13]

30

MURDERER OF GORDON?

THE IMPERIAL AND FOREIGN policy of the government of 1880, the latter being in those days almost a subsidiary of the former, never achieved any moment of substantial triumph remotely comparable with the home policy success described at the end of the last chapter. In a sense this was in accordance with deserts for that government never achieved an external policy based on any firm ground which brought together principle and practice. Gladstone had both the unconventional vision to see that the British Empire was already over-extended in relation to the metropolitan country's economic strength and the fastidiousness to dislike the tinsel of jingoistic adventures. But he also had a sense of British dignity, perhaps even a subconscious one of the superiority of white Anglo-Saxon men, although his vast writings and innumerable speeches are, for the period, remarkably free of any racist expressions. More oppressively he had the Queen, who believed that she had a special position in matters touching her generals and her proconsuls, as well as half of his own Cabinet and party, and the whole of the opposition in favour of a forward expansionist policy. The almost inevitable result was a mishmash of an imperial policy, withdrawing from the Transvaal, bombarding Alexandria, taking over Egypt, sending out Gordon, taking terrible flak for his insubordinate death and for the wise refusal to avenge it, getting very near to war over the Pendjeh affair in 1885, when the Russians defeated an Afghan force and appeared to threaten the North-west Frontier of India.

Sometimes Gladstone would bring off a minor coup, as when in the first autumn of the government he got the Turks to cede without hostilities the barren little port of Dulcigno to the Montenegrins – always one of his favourite peoples. (Granville announced the news by dancing with joy around Gladstone's room; the Prime Minister received it at once more portentously and more prosaically. 'God Almighty be praised,' he said. 'I shall go to Hawarden by the 2.45 train.'[1]) Equally, at the very end of the government, the conclusion without war of the Pendjeh incident had the spin-off effect of diverting attention and troops from Egypt to Afghanistan and thus turned even the mind of the Queen away from a punitive expedition – in theory limited to avenging Gordon but in practice only too likely to end up with the annexation of the whole of Sudan.

More frequently, however, Gladstone was ducking and weaving to try to preserve the standards of mid-Victorian restraint in the much more imperialist climate of the 1880s. No one became more extreme a jingo than the Queen herself, so that the Prime Minister's view of April 1885 that her judgement had become 'quite worthless' would not have been seriously dissented from by her Foreign Secretary Granville, or her Colonial Secretary Derby (who admittedly was a pretty useless minister himself), or her War Secretary Hartington, or even her own private secretary Ponsonby. Nevertheless Gladstone was constantly compromising between imperialist pressures and his own instincts, which were a mixture of Little Englander caution and Concert of Europe idealism. Neither pointed to the expansion of territory or colonial wars, which were nonetheless a frequent feature of the life of that government. They were mostly backed into without enthusiasm. This reluctance was a good recipe for getting the worst of both worlds, and by no stretch of the imagination could foreign and colonial policy in 1880–5 be called a resounding success. It consumed a lot of the Prime Minister's time, but the highest claim that could be made for it was that, in a somewhat hand-to-mouth way, worse excesses were avoided.

From the beginning a government elected on a largely anti-imperialist platform found itself uncomfortably squelching in too many imperial quagmires. Within the first two years British forces were engaged in battle at either end of Africa and in central Asia. In 1880 there was renewed Afghan trouble, with the defeat of General Burrows at Maiwand followed by the victory of General Roberts after a brilliant 300-mile march to Kandahar. In 1881, General Colley was defeated and killed by the Boers at Majuba Hill. Neither of these campaigns struck at the heart of British power. But they were equally far from being recreational shooting parties. Burrows, for instance, lost nearly a thousand men killed at Maiwand, a casualty rate which, a century later, would have been regarded as unacceptable in either the Falklands or the Gulf wars. And the proportion of defeats made it more difficult to disengage without humiliation, although this was eventually achieved in the Transvaal (for a decade) and Afghanistan.

In 1882 there was the more serious affair of the bombardment of Alexandria, followed by the victory of Wolseley at Tel-el-Kebir and the occupation of Egypt. This embroilment led on through a chapter of mistakes and accidents to the despatch and death in Khartoum of General Gordon, which *dégringolade* overshadowed the last year of the government and gravely weakened Gladstone. Egypt at the beginning of the 1880s was still nominally a Turkish province of which the strategic importance had been much increased by the completion of the French-inspired and French-financed Suez Canal in 1869. This enterprise, on top of the role which France had played through the early campaigns of Napoleon and the cryptology of Champollion in opening Egypt to the modern world, made French influence powerful in Cairo. Their predominance was somewhat redressed by Disraeli's 1875 raid on the shares of the Suez Canal Company. This coup had, however, been strongly opposed by Gladstone, who regarded it as a showy and dangerous example of forward diplomacy, carrying in its train over-extended future entanglement. Such fears proved abundantly true, with the main burden of the over-extension falling upon Gladstone himself, who accepted it with a curious mixture of reluctance and bravado.

Egypt's impact on Europe stemmed not only from its permanent position as the hinge of Africa and Asia fortified by its new function as the conduit to India and beyond. Nor even was the drawing power of an ancient civilization with unique surviving artefacts under a benign winter climate the only or even the main supporting factor. There was a more material one, which was the enormous size of the Egyptian national debt and the wide distribution of its bonds, partly through an indirect formula, among the propertied classes of Vienna, Paris and London and a habit of active trading in the bonds on the bourses of Europe. The size of the debt is indicated by interest upon it consuming two-thirds of the total revenues of Egypt in 1880. Its indirectness arose from much of it being Turkish government stock, issued on behalf of Egypt and underpinned by a so-called annual Egyptian Tribute to Constantinople designed to cover the servicing. Throughout Europe many prosperous investors kept moderate holdings in their portfolios. Gladstone, however, allowed his investment policy to be quite remarkably concentrated upon them. The details of his holdings, together with an attempt at an appraisal of their significance, will be given later.

Inevitably the burden of this huge debt resulted in hesitations in Egyptian government payments and resentment in Egyptian popular opinion. Ismail Pasha, the effectively independent (of Constantinople) Khedive was extravagant and financially ill organized. In 1879 the Anglo-French (so called) Dual Control deposed him in favour of his son

Tewfik Pasha, who was an appropriate precursor of King Farouk. And to balance him there arose in 1881 an equally appropriate precursor of Gamal Abdel Nasser. Arabi was a colonel and an indigenous Egyptian, not a Turk or a Circassian or an indeterminate Levantine like most of those who surrounded the Khedive. 'Egypt for the Egyptians' was the core of his message and the main vehicle for its achievement was to be a fourfold increase in the size of the Egyptian regular army, which was moreover to be paid on time, an experience which had hitherto eluded it – thus setting it at variance with the more promptly serviced bondholders. It was a classic colonels' revolt, half nationalist, half anti-privilege, except for that of the army. Arabi carried out a sort of half-coup in the autumn of 1881, not deposing the Khedive, but forcing him to dismiss his ministers and rendering him semi-impotent.

Gladstone, partly under the influence of the notable Arabist and great *coureur* Wilfrid Scawen Blunt, was at first well disposed towards Arabi, whom he was prepared to see as a latter-day Garibaldi. But in the winter and spring of 1882 he swung away from Blunt* to the more conventional advice of the two British consuls on the spot, Malet and Colvin. (The quintessential proconsular figure, Evelyn Baring, later Cromer, was not in Egypt at the time; he had been there from 1877 to 1879 as debt controller, but was in Calcutta as Finance Minister of the Viceroy's Council before returning to Cairo in 1883 and remaining there until 1907 as the effective ruler of the country.) Partly under their influence Gladstone delivered to the House of Commons in mid-June a most conservative statement of the aims of British policy: 'they are well known to consist in the general maintenance of all established rights in Egypt, whether they be those of the Sultan, those of the Khedive, those of the people of Egypt, or those of the foreign bondholders.'[2] That was three days after Arabi-inspired anti-foreign riots had broken out in Alexandria and had led to the death of fifty and the injuring of another sixty, including the British consul. Arabi then began to fortify the harbour at Alexandria, which activity, it was a little implausibly claimed, threatened

* Blunt got his own back in 1885 by writing a fairly derisory (and maybe imaginary) account of Gladstone's calls upon Catherine Walters ('Skittles'), a *grande horizontale* who captivated, among others, the Prince of Wales and Hartington, in her well-placed *nid d'amour* in South Street, Mayfair. 'Nothing improper seems to have happened,' Blunt wrote of Gladstone's visits. He portrayed him as being archly amatory, congratulating Miss Walters on the smallness of her waist and suggesting that he might manually measure its size. (Elizabeth Longford, *Pilgrimage of Passion*, pp. 217–18.) There is, however, no mention of visits to Miss Walters in the Gladstone diaries, and he concealed few secrets from them.

the safety of the British fleet which was lying offshore. What it more evidently threatened was the European view of Alexandria as a port open to all nations, a gateway which by its architecture and its ethnic mix proclaimed Egypt's status as the eastern outpost of the West rather than as the leader of the Arab world.

When Gladstone reluctantly became convinced that in the interests of 'order' some action against Arabi was necessary his natural preference was for a Concert of Europe intervention, and an ineffective conference was called at Constantinople to explore this possibility. It failed, mainly because Bismarck, who was the pivotal statesman, was indifferent. Let the British and the French do what they judged necessary was his shoulder-shrugging view, and, if they got into a weakening entanglement, so much the better. But the French, only twelve years after the defeats of Sedan and Metz and obsessed with Germany, were cautious, particularly as the more robust Gambetta government had fallen at the end of 1881. The French fleet, which had also been anchored off Alexandria, simply steamed away. So it was the British on their own or nothing. Gladstone was still reluctant to take military action – not surprisingly in view of his past attitude to Egypt and to Disraeli's adventures in general. But he was at variance with the majority of his colleagues, was preoccupied with Ireland, and was additionally worn down by the burdens of the Exchequer. In the Cabinet he was isolated except for Bright and Harcourt. The line of Bright, who eventually resigned on the issue, was close to absolute pacifism, which was never Gladstone's position. Harcourt was far too quarrelsome to be a pacifist, but worked off his aggressiveness by denouncing imperial illusions. *Per contra* all the 'imperial' ministers, the Secretaries of State for India, Colonies, War, Foreign Affairs, and the First Lord of the Admiralty, were firm for action. Chamberlain, much influenced by Dilke's 'Greater Britain' *realpolitik*, was showing his first signs of jingoism. So the line-up was overwhelming, and Gladstone's ability to resist was weakened by his tiredness. For 1 July, after a continuous sitting on the Irish Crimes Bill from the Friday afternoon to 8.00 on the Saturday evening, he wrote: 'My share of the sitting I take at nineteen hours. Anxious Cabinet on Egypt behind the [Speaker's] Chair 4–5.'[3] And four days later: 'My brain is *very* weary.'[4]

It could be said that he was too tired to resign. Resignation, certainly of a Prime Minister from his own Cabinet, would be an energy-demanding process, and Gladstone for once was at the limit of his reserves. So he acquiesced. Admiral Beauchamp Seymour was authorized to send Arabi an ultimatum. If he did not desist from strengthening his forts, a bombardment would commence. Arabi sent no reply, and on 11 July British naval guns pounded the Alexandria waterfront for ten and a half hours. There were not vast casualties (although when Arabi then withdrew from the city there followed substantial death and destruction from rioting), but the action was rough, and was widely seen to be so, both at home and abroad. Bright said in private that it 'was simply damnable – worse than anything ever perpetrated by Dizzie', but his resignation statement on 18 July was moderately couched, so that Gladstone was able to go on referring to him as 'dear old John Bright' and describing him as 'sound as a roach' (a curious comparison). This was in sharp contrast with Gladstone's attitude to Bright when they separated on Home Rule in 1886.* The difference was that on Home Rule Gladstone was passionately convinced of his own rightness, but shared much of Bright's hostility to the bombardment of Alexandria.

Once the Egyptian intervention was launched, however, Gladstone accepted it with mounting enthusiasm. On 11 July he made a heavy-hearted statement in the House of Commons and did not enjoy being baited by his old love, the politically (at least) heartless Arthur Balfour. By the 25th, when he moved a vote of credit to deal with the financial consequences of sending out a land expedition to back up the bombardment, he was on much more certain form. It was a full-scale operation which was to be mounted, with 15,000 men to be sent from England and another 10,000 from India, and Sir Garnet Wolseley, the premier general, to be put in charge. The costs were correspondingly large. Gladstone's vote of credit provided for £2.3 million, paid for by raising income tax from fivepence to eightpence for half the current financial year. The whole undertaking was treated as a proper war (although without a declaration) and not as a colonial expedition engaging only the locally available regular troops. The Prince of Wales, for instance, in his early forties, wished to offer himself as an already somewhat corpulent volunteer officer. (Gladstone and the Queen were agreed – for once – that he should not go.)

Unlike nearly every other British military enterprise between Waterloo and 1914, the Wolseley expedition was a neat, quick and resounding success. He met the Arabi army at Tel-el-Kebir, fifty or so miles to the north-east of Cairo, on 13 September and gained a complete victory with few casualties. Arabi was captured and exiled to Ceylon, and Tewfik

* See p. 558, below.

was maintained as Khedive, but as a client of the British agent-general (soon to be Baring). Within two months, only half by intention, Britain had put a lid on Egyptian nationalism, which was to be kept down for more or less seventy years, extruded French political and military if not linguistic and cultural influence, and assumed responsibility for the most populous and sophisticated country in Africa.

Gladstone was full of immediate satisfaction with the victory. Hamilton, having dined with him (and Sir Reginald Welby of the Treasury and Granville) at the Garrick Club and then gone on to Gilbert and Sullivan's *Patience* at the Savoy Theatre, recorded: 'I never remember seeing him in higher spirits.' He noted that Gladstone had been cheered on both entering and leaving the Savoy and that it was noteworthy that 'any popular signs should be manifested in his favour in a London theatre of all places, where the audience is certainly not much given to Gladstonianism'.[5] Gladstone also ensured that the Secretary of State for War organized major Saturday salutes in the London parks ('I hope the guns will crash all the windows')[6] and rallied the senior prelates (Canterbury being ill, he wrote to York and London) to suggest suitable church thanksgivings on the Sunday. It was a curiously exact forerunner of Churchill's commemoration almost precisely sixty years later of another battle which took place only 150 miles to the west of Tel-el-Kebir.

Yet there were important differences. No one could doubt Churchill's total commitment to the North African campaign, in which the battle of El Alamein was the turning-point, as well as being one, even if the lesser (the other being Stalingrad), of the two 1942 hinges of fate in the Second World War. Tel-el-Kebir by comparison was a minor event. Furthermore Gladstone's enthusiasm might have been regarded as opportunistic and even hypocritical: he embraced the campaign when it was won.

Judgement here must turn somewhat on exactly what in his own mind he was celebrating. Was it that British casualties had been so small? Was it that at any rate the first phase of what might have been an immensely messy undertaking had ended so cleanly? Was it relief rather than triumphalism? Positive answers to these questions, combined with his natural naive enthusiasms, could provide a respectable explanation of his *volte face*. But the probability is that no simple interpretation of motives is satisfactory. Egypt in 1882 occasioned almost as deep and turbulent a struggle between Gladstone's anti-militarist conscience and his belief in the imposition of international authority (preferably by a concert but, if not, by the most responsible power) as did that between his intense sexuality and his pervading sense of sin in his more virile decades. The clashing contradictions of his style and behaviour are brilliantly portrayed by a contemporary cartoon showing him, dressed in the most civilian and almost parsonical of habits, belabouring a wretched Egyptian fellah with his umbrella.

Then there is the issue of his disproportionate holdings of Egyptian bonds. Did these affect his conduct in a way that today might be regarded as corrupt? About the remarkable size of the holdings there can be no doubt, as careful and original research by H. C. G. Matthew has recently made clear. At the end of 1881, when the Arabi crisis began to erupt, he owned a nominal amount of £51,500 of Egyptian Tribute loan, divided in the proportion of about two to one between the issue of 1854 and that of 1871. He had acquired about half of this stock by the end of 1875, and bought the rest in the late 1870s. In his meticulous annual accounts he entered the combined real as opposed to the face value of his two holdings as £40,567 on 31 December 1881. This was equivalent to about £2 million at today's values. It was a very substantial sum for one who had as recently as when he left office in 1874 been complaining about his poverty, and acting upon it to the extent of selling his house (11 Carlton House Terrace), pictures, porcelain and some books. Indeed his going into Egyptians was occasioned by a combination of available funds arising from these sales and of his need for high-yielding stocks in order to correct his low (1874) ratio of income to assets. Nonetheless it was an extraordinary decision to place 37 per cent of his total portfolio (for such it was) at double risk from political instability in Cairo and Constantinople.

Gladstone, however, was rarely a cautious investor. He seemed to have learnt little from his own trouble in clearing up the result of the Glynne family's Oak Farm disaster thirty years before. And although his Egyptian investments turned out satisfactorily (partly as a result of his own political actions) they were at least balanced by heavy losses, realized in 1884, on an equally excessive holding of Metropolitan District Railway stock. Through what he then described as 'one heavy mistake in buying largely into the District R. before it was in a paying condition',[7] he lost about £25,000 (or £1¼ million if the factor of fifty is applied).

While the lower Nile Valley paradoxically proved a safer investment haven than the Inner Circle and its offshoots, the Egyptian loans were nonetheless a volatile stock, with their movements closely following politico-military events. When Gladstone bought the 1871 bonds they stood at 42. By 1881 they had risen to 62, but had fallen to 57 when in the early summer of 1882 first the Concert of Europe failed to work and then even the Anglo-French Dual Control fell apart. But by the end of that year, with Alexandria bombarded, Wolseley victorious at Tel-el-Kebir, and the territory of the pharaohs a British protectorate, they had risen to 82. On the 1871 stock alone Gladstone thus made a capital gain (unrealized however until a few years later) of £7500 (£375,000) over the period of the hostilities.[8]

Superficially this looks a clear case of improper financial interest. By modern standards and with modern press attention, without even intrusive investigation, for his holdings were never concealed, his position would have been wholly untenable. Yet I do not believe for a moment that his primary or even his significantly supporting motivation sprang from financial self-interest. Any contrary view can be refuted both objectively and subjectively. Objectively there was the fact that, with the exception of Bright and Harcourt, Gladstone was the most reluctant of the fourteen members of the Cabinet to accept the need for intervention. Furthermore, when over the next couple of years he had occasion to influence the interests of bondholders, he threw his weight against them, so far as both their coupon return and their priority of security were concerned. He believed strongly that, in the interests of future lending, foreign debts should be honoured, but not elevated above their station.

More important were the subjective considerations. Gladstone's blend of innocence and grandeur transcended the possibility of corruption. It was all of a piece with his purchase and sale of Consols during the Franco-Prussian War; with his rash rescue operations with prostitutes, particularly late in life when his carnal flame had burnt down but the desire of his political opponents to traduce him was stronger than ever; and with his willingness to borrow houses from rich friends and take holidays at their expense without it ever occurring to him that they could expect any return except for the pleasure of his company. In his own mind at least, and to some substantial extent in reality, his purposes were too high for petty corruption to be a possibility. Knight of the Garter although he never aspired to be – it was an honour for the more patrician of his adjutants, not for himself – there was no one for whom the order's motto of 'Honi soit qui mal y pense' was more instinctively appropriate.

For a year or so after the excitements of the summer and early autumn of 1882 Egypt receded from a central position on the London

Cabinet agenda. This quiescence was something of an illusion, for behind only the thinnest of screens there was building up a combination of circumstances which gave striking support to the view that one commitment always leads to another. In the middle and upper Nile Valley there lay a vast territory which was then known as the Egyptian Soudan. Insofar as it was governed at all it was ill governed from Cairo. A self-proclaimed Mahdi or Messiah, who had some experience as both a slave-trader and a middle-rank Egyptian official, raised a banner of rebellion in 1881 and implanted it in soil which was fertile for revolt if not for crops. In 1883 the Khedive's government attempted to put him down. They employed an English commander and 10,000 Egyptian troops. The expedition ought to have been vetoed by the British government, and probably would have been had Baring already been long enough in control. The result was almost an annihilation. Baker Pasha, to give him the title, at once commanding and self-indulgent, by which most Englishmen (but not Gordon, who was too fanatical to be a pasha) in Egyptian service were known, together with his army, was cut to pieces in November 1883. This defeat produced an edgy mood in London and led on, within two and a half months, to the disastrous despatch of Gordon to Egypt and the Sudan.

After turning a difficult corner with Hartington on franchise reform over the New Year of 1884 Gladstone went back to Hawarden for two and a half weeks, no doubt feeling he had earned a further respite. During this period 'Chinese' Gordon (as General Charles Gordon, a fifty-year-old major-general of engineers, was at the time generally known, because of his remarkable exploits on behalf of the Emperor of China during the Taiping rebellion of 1863–4) appeared briefly and, as it turned out, for the last time in England. After service in Egypt and the Sudan in the 1870s and in India (incongruously as private secretary to Ripon as Viceroy, but lasting in that post only for a few weeks), China again, then Mauritius and South Africa in the early 1880s, Gordon had spent 1883 in semi-retirement interspersed with biblical researches in Palestine. From there he committed himself to King Leopold II of the Belgians to take over from H. M. Stanley as administrator in the Congo. Granville and Hartington were asked for their approval and refused to give it. The telegram was drafted as saying that the Secretary of State *declines* to sanction the arrangement. It was transmitted as saying that he *decides* to sanction it. This was by no means the last of the confusions which clouded the final stages of the Gordon saga.

To atone for the mistake the official British objections were withdrawn and Gordon accepted Leopold's commission on 2 January 1884 and then returned to London five days later. He went immediately to stay with his sister in Southampton and was there pursued by W. T. Stead, Morley's successor as the editor of the *Pall Mall Gazette* and the inventor of the so-called 'new journalism'. Stead's interview with Gordon, published first in his own paper and then in *The Times*, dramatically indicated the power of journalism, new or old. Although Gordon dissociated himself in it from the British government's decision to withdraw from Khartoum and the eastern Sudan, the interview nonetheless created a clamour that he should be appointed to carry out the policy of which he had publicly disapproved. 'Gordon for the Sudan' became a catchphrase and also a brand which ignited a forest fire. The result was that, by 18 January, this crazy appointment had been decided upon.

It was crazy because Gordon was temperamentally unsuited to be the agent of a cautious policy. He was the prototype of a *Boy's Own Paper* hero, with an additional capacity to seize the attention and attract the admiration of many who had long passed the age of boyhood. He also saw himself as the hand of God's purpose to an extent which rivalled Gladstone, although they seemed to have been revealed differing versions of that purpose. Furthermore, Gordon, whether or not subject to lost weekends of alcoholism (for which there is some evidence, but which his 1993 biographer contests),[9] was undoubtedly a person of unstable mood who could plunge from bursts of almost manic activity into troughs of withdrawal and inertia. And on top of everything else – this the fault of ministers and not of Gordon – the instructions he was given were far from precise.

Gladstone had little to do with the appointment of Gordon. In mid-December, with public opinion already febrile on the issue as a result of the massacre by the Mahdi of a British-officered army under General Hicks, he delegated Sudanese affairs to a Cabinet committee composed of Hartington, Granville, Northbrook, Dilke and Carlingford. Dilke said that it was 'in order that Mr. G. might avoid writing to the Queen about the matter and get Hartington to tell her verbally'.[10] Cowardice was not one of Gladstone's faults in dealing with the Queen, but he may nonetheless well have wisely thought that a few inarticulate sentences from Hartington might provoke less royal extravagance of opinion than one of his own over-meticulous and over-argumentative letters. This was the origin of the committee which, minus Carlingford, on 18 January commissioned Gordon. It did so in a hurry, pressurized by

Wolseley, the victor of Tel-el-Kebir and increasingly the panjandrum of the whole army, and rather against the initial reactions of Baring, who ought to have been taken more notice of in view of his central responsibility for British policy in the Nile Valley. Gladstone was equivocal. Two days before he had very sensibly written to Granville about Gordon: 'While his opinion on the Soudan may be of great value, must we not be very careful in any instruction we give, that he does not shift the centre of gravity as to political and military responsibility for that country? In brief if he reports what should be done, he should not be the judge of *who* should do it. . . .'[11] Equally Hamilton, who in general closely reflected Gladstonian opinion, wrote on 23 January: '[Gordon] seems to be a half cracked fatalist; and what can one expect from such a man?'[12]

On the other hand Gladstone did not attempt to hold up the appointment. Indeed he wrote apologetically to Granville on the 19th: 'I telegraphed last night my concurrence in your proceedings about Gordon: but Chester [telegraph office] would not awake & the message only went on this morning.'[13] It would have made no difference whether it went late on the 18th or early on the 19th, for Gordon with the over-excited and half-ludicrous urgency which characterized the circumstances of his appointment and despatch, had already left London, *en route* for Brindisi and Alexandria, at eight o'clock on the evening of the 18th, within a few hours of his appointment. At Charing Cross station he had a send-off party at once magnificent and incongruous. Granville (presumably with Foreign Office funds) bought his ticket. General Wolseley performed an equally necessary and more eccentric service. Discovering as the departure whistle was blowing that Gordon had no money on him, he both emptied his own pockets and handed over his gold watch. Hartington and the Duke of Cambridge (still Commander-in-Chief) were also present, but confined to decorative roles.

Three hundred and seventy-four days later Gordon was killed at Khartoum, where he had been under siege for 320 of them. A relief expedition under Wolseley reached the city two days later. The field for recrimination could hardly have been more wide open. Gordon ought not to have been in Khartoum at all. He was sent to advise on the evacuation of the Sudan, not to occupy it. Furthermore, his communications from there were of a highly erratic nature. Dilke, who was one of those responsible for his employment and on Gordon's side to the extent of believing that an early expedition ought to be sent for his rescue, wrote in March: 'Twelve telegrams from Gordon of the most extraordinary nature. . . . We [are] obviously dealing with a wild man under the influence of that climate of Central Africa which acts even upon the sanest men like strong drink.'[14] And he added in September: 'A telegram from Gordon which shows he's quite mad.'[15] The ludicrousness of the whole enterprise was well illustrated by the fact that within eight weeks of the despatch of a specially chosen agent of evacuation the Cabinet was racked by whether or not to send a major force to extricate him and then to perform the role which he had wilfully failed to do.

Over this decision ministers hesitated long enough to ensure the worst of both worlds. Gladstone, supported by Granville and about half the Cabinet, thought that once Gordon had broken his orders he should be left to his fate. Hartington was strong, or at least stubborn, the other way. Dilke and Chamberlain had a position of their own, which was in favour of a small, quick expedition which would get Gordon out and the whole British presence with him. Hartington by contrast wanted a major offensive leading to a prolonged occupation, and Dilke took the view that had Hartington (and Northbrook) not held out for this Gordon might well have been saved.

The issue consumed much of the government's time and energies throughout that franchise bill summer of 1884. In July it provoked yet another of Hartington's threatened resignations and on 2 August Gladstone wrote: 'This day for the first time in my recollection there were three *crises* for us all running high tide at once: Egypt [debt problems], Gordon & franchise.'[16]

The position was complicated in two other ways. First, Gordon would not accept that he needed a rescue expedition. He regarded it as a derogation from his role as a Christian imperialist who could subdue primitive races by a mixture of bravery and empathy. When, on 9 September, Wolseley arrived in Cairo to lead the so-called Gordon Relief Expedition, Gordon was furious at its title. 'I altogether *decline* the imputation that the projected expedition has come to relieve me. It has come to *save our national* honour in extricating the garrisons. As for myself I could make good my retreat at any moment. . . . I am not the *rescued lamb*, and I will not be.'[17] Second, one of Gladstone's most dangerous blind spots was that he could not comprehend the force of Gordon's appeal to the British public and hence his capacity to damage the government. Gladstone was the least pedestrian of Prime Ministers. He could ignite an audience and could endow a cause with an enthusiasm which passed well beyond rationalism. But he did not have the imagination to see how others might do this too, and for ends of which he disapproved. Gordon quickly became for him an ill-disciplined and rather junior general, whose showy and unsubtle Christianity did not compensate for his insubordination.

The news of Gordon's death reached England early on 5 February 1885. Edward Hamilton, awakened at 2.30 in the morning by Brett, Hartington's secretary, who later as Lord Esher was the quintessential Edwardian courtier with a finger in many pies, reacted starkly by saying that it was 'the blackest day since the horrible Phoenix Park murders'.[18] Gladstone was staying with the Duke of Devonshire at Holker in North Lancashire, one of the Duke's subsidiary residences, which looked in one direction to the fells of the Lake District and in the other across the sands of Morecambe Bay. Whether a mainline Cavendish possession or diverted to a cadet branch as it has been for the past 100 years, Holker has long been said to exercise a peculiar charm of view and ambience. It is doubtful, however, if the charm was strong enough to keep high the spirits of either Gladstone or Hartington, who was also there and whose responsibility (but not his exposure) was at least as great as that of Gladstone, when they received the news eight hours after Hamilton.

They left at once for London, and at Carnforth Junction another and well-known scene in the drama was played out. Gladstone was there handed by the stationmaster a telegram which the Queen had sent without use of the habitual cipher. Its terms were more explosive than grammatical: 'These news from Khartoum are frightful and to think that all this might have been prevented and many precious lives saved by earlier action is too fearful.'[19] Low though his royal expectations had become, Gladstone was not pleased by this signal and semi-public mark of disfavour. Dilke, cynical but well informed, said that the Prime Minister's immediate reaction was to enquire what were the politics of the Carnforth stationmaster and what therefore was the probability of the contents of the telegram leaking. Whatever the answer, the question was irrelevant, for there were more than enough other hands through whom the telegram would necessarily have passed to make certain, as was no doubt the royal intention, its position in the public domain.

Nevertheless Gladstone when he arrived in Downing Street at 8.15 was, according to Hamilton, 'calm and collected. He always rises to great occasions; and the greater is the crisis, the more coolly does he keep his head.'[20] That same evening – Gladstone's lack of procrastination in replying to difficult communications was consistently remarkable – he wrote to the Queen with frigid dignity:

Mr Gladstone has had the honour this day to receive Your Majesty's Telegram *en clair*, relating to the deplorable intelligence received this day from Lord Wolseley, and stating that it is too fearful to consider that the fall of Khartoum might have been prevented and many precious lives saved by earlier action.

Mr Gladstone does not presume to estimate the means of judgement possessed by Your Majesty, but so far as his information and recollection at the moment go, he is not altogether able to follow the conclusion which Your Majesty has been pleased thus to announce.

Mr Gladstone is under the impression that Lord Wolseley's force might have been sufficiently advanced to save Khartoum had not a large portion of it been delayed by a circuitous route along the river, upon the express application of General Gordon. . . .[21]

That day was a Thursday. On the following Tuesday Gladstone dined with Lord and Lady Dalhousie, a respectable if Liberal couple, and then went with them to the Criterion Theatre to see a contemporary success called *The Candidate*. Gladstone, as was his way and his strength, recorded the event calmly, merely noting that the play was 'capitally acted'. Hamilton reproved himself bitterly for having allowed Gladstone to go. The occasion was regarded by Tory opinion as the final brick in his reputation as the heartless murderer of Gordon. Unfortunately Gladstone stooped to giving a bad excuse. It was not certain, he said, that Gordon was dead; he might be a prisoner. This incident, in itself unimportant, although insensitive, did a lot of harm. It more than outweighed any benefit which the government derived from Rosebery's quixotic decision, without for once making any difficulties, to become the First Commissioner of Works (in the Cabinet) on 8 February.

After the Gordon débâcle the second Gladstone government was always a holed hull. It was mainly a question of how long it could keep afloat, with a subsidiary one of how long its chief wanted it to do so. In the train from Carnforth he wrote with resignation and almost with relief: 'The circumstances are sad and trying: it is one of the least points about them, that they may put an end to this Govt.'[22] And two weeks later Hamilton recorded:

Mr. G. retains his equanimity marvellously. It is due no doubt mainly to having a clear conscience; but in part to a faint hope that he may be released from the cares of office. A vote of censure is to be moved; and he evidently cannot help secretly cherishing a hope that it may be carried. He even admits that a change of government might be best for the country. . . .[23]

Yet running counter to this was Gladstone's view that a government should not scuttle, particularly in response to unjust charges. When the vote of censure came on a few days later he at least made a far better case than Northcote. But the government's majority fell to fourteen, compared with a margin of forty-four on a similar motion nine months before.

Most of the Cabinet were in favour of resignation on this vote. But Gladstone decided to rally them. His hope of a favourable plateau for his own retirement following the deal with Salisbury on the seats bill had been destroyed. But he did not wish to go out in the depths of the grand canyon into which Gordon had plunged him. So he kept the government going for nearly another four months. But it no longer had either external strength or even such internal cohesion as it had hitherto possessed. Its only achievements during this period were to make progress with the seats bill and to divert the atavistic desire for avenging Gordon by obfuscating the Mahdi and his followers by the more important Pendjeh conflict with the Russians in Afghanistan, which was itself settled without war, so that two conflicts were effectively avoided.

Within the government itself, however, conditions quickly became something between a farce and a shambles. By mid-May Hamilton calculated that at least ten of the sixteen ministers in the Cabinet had hinted at or threatened or in several cases actually proffered resignations. Dilke and Chamberlain, supported by Shaw-Lefevre and probably by Trevelyan too, were threatening to go as a result of the blocking by all the peers in the Cabinet, except for Granville, of a Chamberlain scheme for Irish local government reform embracing a central board, which was supported by all the commoners, including the Prime Minister, except for Hartington. Hartington himself as usual was ready with several reasons why he ought to leave the government, and Rosebery, even with only three months' membership behind him, was never behindhand in finding reasons for escaping office.

Childers, the Chancellor, had also threatened resignation by walking out of the room after he was blocked first on his proposal to increase the beer duty, and again when he proposed to use the wine duty as a half-alternative. Childers was persuaded to come back, but not for long. It was on the beer-duty issue that, on the morning of 9 June, the government was defeated, unexpectedly, by 264 to 252. It was an early result of tentative moves towards an alliance between Parnell and the Conservatives. Thirty-nine members of the Irish party voted against the government. So did six Liberals, and another seventy of them, mostly Radicals, abstained. Thus did the great majority of 1880 run into the sand. Ten hours later there was no dispute in the Cabinet that this time resignation was both inevitable and desirable. Gladstone took it all calmly. 'A quiet evening,' he concluded that day's diary entry. 'Worked on books and papers.'[24]

The Queen was at Balmoral and showed as little initial disposal to come south (she eventually arrived on 17 June) as Gladstone did to travel to Aberdeenshire. On the 13th, however, she wrote and offered him an earldom (as opposed to the unspecified peerage of 1874) and did so in markedly gracious terms. He declined at once, also in generous terms. Such future small services as he could render would be better done from the Commons. The Queen was disappointed. By accepting the earldom Gladstone would of course have done her much more of a favour than he would have done himself. But they had both behaved with high propriety, and his farewell visit to Windsor on the 24th also passed off well. 'Audience of H. M.,' he recorded, '& kissed hands in farewell after half an hour of kindly conversation. . . . Got to the 3pm service at St George's. . . .'[25]

Salisbury began the first and shortest of his three governments that same day, and Gladstone removed himself from 10 Downing Street but only a few yards across Whitehall to 1 Richmond Terrace, a house temporarily provided by Stuart Rendel, then MP for Montgomeryshire and for the next decade and in several locations a most generous host to Gladstone.* At this stage, however, Gladstone did not for long trouble him. He was much away from London during the summer, he spent nearly the whole of the autumn at Hawarden, and he was back in office and 10 Downing Street within eight months.

* See p. 579, below.

Part Five

IRELAND DOMINATES AND AGE WITHERS

1885–1898

31

Slow Road to Damascus

The mood in which Gladstone left office in 1885, at the age of 75, was paradoxically different from that in which he had done so in 1874, when he was more than eleven years younger. On the former occasion he had presided over a notably successful administration except for its declining final phase (but which government is free of such a dying fall?). Yet he was resentful, not so much of his loss of office as of his rejection by the electorate. He was then still short, even by Victorian standards, of being an old man. Yet his talk was of 'winding out the coil' of his life and of seeking 'an interval between parliamentary and the grave' in which to devote himself to theological studies, to which he was ill suited.

By 1885 he had become a still more dominating national figure, and a still more famous international one, but his second government, staggering as has been seen from Bradlaugh to Gordon, was at best a series of improvisations against disaster. Yet at the end of it he was neither resentful nor determinedly seeking a *nunc dimittis.* He no longer believed that he might serve his God and his age better by being a second-rate theologian than a first-rate politician. In a sense he genuinely wanted retirement, but he wanted it with honour, and he had an almost infinite capacity to persuade himself that he was more likely to find this around the next corner than where he currently was. His post-resignation attitude was perhaps best summed up by a letter which he wrote to his only surviving brother, Sir Thomas Gladstone, on 19 June 1885 (an odd and Tory recipient of such a confidence after many decades of coolness): 'My profound desire is retirement, and nothing has prevented or will prevent my giving effect to that desire, unless there should appear to be something in which there may be a prospect of my doing what could not be as well done without me.'[1] The weight, of course, was contained in the second half of the sentence, expressing his willingness to be prised away from withdrawal by some high purpose.

Such a cause – in the shape of Irish Home Rule – was easily forthcoming in 1885, although Gladstone was for a few months hesitant about whether he wished to embrace it, or indeed whether his doing so was necessary by the strict criterion which he had laid down in his letter to his brother. Up to and over the general election of that November (the very satisfactory Midlothian poll was on the 28th, and the national result – 333 Liberals, 251 Conservatives and 86 Parnellites – was also clear by then), he gave priority to the holding together of his party, which he rightly saw as in direct conflict with providing an Irish solution, and also cherished the hope that the Conservatives might grasp the Home Rule nettle. As a result he gave little guidance to the Liberal party or the nation over that summer and autumn, and little encouragement to Parnell to prepare for a Liberal alliance. His mind was nonetheless deep into Ireland, or, it would perhaps be more accurate to say, into the acquiring of factual and academic knowledge about that country. But he spoke little. This was at least partly because his voice was giving him serious trouble. He was diagnosed as suffering from chronic laryngeal catarrh, 'a condition common enough', in Matthew's words, 'amongst elderly actors',[2] and had to undergo twenty-one daily and unpleasant treatments between 17 July and 8 August. How effective they were is not clear, although they at least staved off the real danger of his becoming a tone-deaf Mozart or a castrated Casanova. In the November Midlothian campaign he was able to make six major speeches to large audiences, although the faithful Hamilton found them rather hollow shells compared with the great performances to which he had been used, with Gladstone undergoing the almost unheard-of experience of being upstaged by Rosebery, to whom Hamilton referred as 'being nearly as much the uncrowned King of Scotland as Parnell is the uncrowned King of Ireland'.[3]

Despite this potentially crippling vicissitude Gladstone in 1885 showed little of his 1874 desire to have done with politics. He stayed in or about London for the whole of July and early August and did not go to Hawarden until nearly three months after his resignation. Most of his 'about London' visits that summer were either to Dollis Hill, the Aberdeen villa in what is now NW2, or to Combe Wood, a Wolverton house in an almost equally suburban location on the Wimbledon Common side of Kingston. He also spent a weekend at Keble College, Oxford, with his Lyttelton niece and her Warden husband, the future Bishop of Rochester, next Southwark, and finally Winchester, and at Waddesdon, the then three-year-old Rothschild extravaganza beyond Aylesbury which inspired him to the lapidary comment: 'a remarkable construction, no commonplace [a] host'.[4]

On 8 August he left for a Norwegian cruise of no less than three and a half weeks as the guest of Sir Thomas Brassey, son of a major railway contractor and himself a junior minister in the 1880 government, who subsequently accumulated honours as a fly-paper accumulates flies. He was made a baron by Gladstone in 1886 and an earl by Asquith in 1911. Campbell-Bannerman, not to be left out, made him a GCB in 1906 and Oxford an honorary DCL in the year of his earldom. In 1885 he contributed the yacht, *Sunbeam* (in which, he eccentrically informed *Who's Who* readers, he had travelled 400,000 knots before giving it to the government of India as a hospital ship in 1916), and Gladstone contributed the company. They included his wife, his daughter Mary, his doctor, the man he was soon to appoint his Chief Whip (Arnold Morley), George Leveson Gower, who had been one of his private secretaries from 1880 and who, amazingly, managed to live until 1951, and 'Lulu' Harcourt, the engaging twenty-three-year-old son of 'the great [but sometimes curmudgeonly] gladiator', who met a sticky end in 1922. Lady Brassey and the wife of an admiral were also allowed aboard.

Gladstone always liked the look (even if not the motion) of a rugged Atlantic-influenced sea, whether it was at Penmaenmawr or Brighton or Biarritz; the Mediterranean by contrast, in spite of his enthusiasm for the lands of Italy and of Greece, made little appeal to him until his ninth decade. That August he was prostrate during the two passages across the North Sea, but highly content during the long sojourn in Norwegian coastal waters. Despite frequent treatments by Sir Andrew Clark, he was doubtful whether the 'soft air' was doing his throat much good but he pronounced that his general health was excellent. One day he walked eighteen miles on very rough ground. On another he started to learn Norwegian, which at the age of nearly seventy-six perhaps pointed more to surplus energy than to a careful husbanding of time. He was delighted with his high recognition factor around the fjords and the warmth of the reception.

On 1 September he disembarked at Fort George at the mouth of Inverness Firth and went to Fasque, where he had not been for more than ten years, for a week's visit and the celebration of his brother's golden wedding. Once back at Hawarden, he stayed there, apart from a twenty-four-hour medical visit to London, until he went to Edinburgh (Dalmeny) on 9 November for nearly three weeks of electioneering. Most there thought (wrongly) that it was to be his last campaign, but he did not skimp it. Then he had another uninterrupted six weeks at

Hawarden, going to London only on the day the new Parliament met (11 January 1886) for the re-election of the Speaker.

During this six weeks, which was the key period for the resolution of his mind on Ireland, he had half a dozen political visitors to Hawarden. Lord Richard Grosvenor, still his Chief Whip, came on 30 November and stayed a couple of nights. On one of the two Gladstone spoke for him in his Flintshire election, where polling day was a week later than in Midlothian. On the other he had a long conversation with him 'on men and things'. Gladstone at this stage could not be faulted on the trouble he took with his Whip. He had written to him frequently during his Norwegian cruise and throughout the autumn. And Grosvenor again came to Hawarden for the inside of a day on 21 December. But it was unavailing. The Whig and family pressure on Grosvenor was too strong. After this second visit Gladstone wrote: 'Three hours conversation friendly but with differences.'[5] Grosvenor became what J. L. Hammond described as 'a bitter Liberal Unionist' in 1886.

The other political visitors were more loyal or the exchanges with them more fruitful. Granville was there on 5–6 December and Gladstone noted with satisfaction that 'we are already in promising harmony'. Granville then went as an envoy to Chatsworth, where he found Spencer as well as Hartington, but decided not to report back in person to Hawarden as this 'would give rise to some foolish talk'.[6] Granville remained wholly loyal to Gladstone until his death six years later, but his powers, always supple rather than rugged, were visibly weakening by this time.

Spencer was more of an independent force and one with a deep knowledge of Ireland. He arrived at Hawarden on 8 December and lived up to Granville's encouraging anticipatory report from Chatsworth: 'You will find Spencer as usual very pleasant to discuss with.'[7] Rosebery was there for the first night of Spencer's visit, and might easily have imported a more querulous note into the discussions. Unlike Spencer, who was to be a dedicated and vital ally for Gladstone on this subject, he was never a steady enthusiast for Home Rule. Nor was he a man to miss many opportunities to make difficulty. But on this occasion he was amenable. Gladstone wrote back to Granville on 9 December: 'I think my conversations with Rosebery and Spencer have also been satisfactory. What I expect is a healthful slow fermentation of many minds, working towards the final product.'[8]

The final two political visitors were less mainstream. They were Lord Wolverton, Gladstone's former Chief Whip and ever amenable host and companion from Cannes to Kingston-upon-Thames, and Sir Thomas Dyke Acland, his Christ Church contemporary (and the only one of his early friends who lasted the distance with him, being born in the year of Gladstone's birth and dying in the year of his death). Acland in 1885 was a Privy Councillor and still a West Country MP, although he had never been a seeker after office. He was more independent than Wolverton, but in the last resort neither of them was likely to gainsay Gladstone.

A curious clerical go-between, Malcolm MacColl, whom Gladstone had made a canon of Ripon in 1884, was also at Hawarden for the night of 13 December, and with Lord Salisbury by the evening of the next day. For communication with his successor as Prime Minister Gladstone also used a more eminent emissary. On the 15th he went to Eaton Hall, the Westminster house eight or ten miles from Hawarden, for a 'beautiful morning service' and a luncheon. Arthur Balfour, who had so delighted him in the early 1870s and so offended him in 1882, currently President of the Local Government Board (outside the Cabinet but with the special access which came from being Salisbury's nephew), was staying there, and Gladstone took the opportunity to pour out to him a political message with the expectation that 'he will probably repeat it in London'.[9] To make sure that he did so, Gladstone followed up his words with a letter, but after a five-day interval, curiously long in view both of the importance of the issue and of Gladstone's normal promptness in correspondence. Although it was encased in a typical Gladstonian penumbra of opaqueness its meaning was nonetheless clear enough:

> On reflection I think that what I said to you in our conversation at Eaton may have amounted to the conveyance of a hope that the Government would take a strong and early decision on the Irish question. For I spoke of the stir in men's minds, & of the urgency of the matter, to both of which every day's post brings me new testimony.
>
> This being so, I wish, under the very peculiar circumstances of the case, to go a step further and say that I think it will be a public calamity if this great subject should fall into the lines of party conflict.
>
> I feel sure the question can only be dealt with by a Government, & I desire specially on grounds of public policy that it should be dealt with by the *present* Government. If therefore they bring in a proposal for settling the whole question of the future Government of Ireland my desire will be, reserving of course necessary freedom, to treat it in the same spirit in which I have endeavoured to proceed with respect to Afghanistan & with

> respect to the Balkan peninsula. You are at liberty if you think it desirable to mention this to Lord Salisbury. . . . I am writing however for myself and without consultation.[10]

To some extent the verbal overture, and still more the letter, were counter-productive. Gladstone's message was received with almost complete cynicism by the Tory leaders. The virulence of party hatreds at the time was such that they were incapable of believing him to be activated by any motive other than that of greed for office. To this they saw him as now adding the sin of a nauseating hypocrisy. They were wrong, and the narrowness of their spirit gave them a heavy responsibility for throwing away an unusual opportunity for constructive statesmanship.

A tentative Irish flirtation with the Conservatives had begun in the late spring of 1885, and its first fruits had been seen in the Nationalist votes against Childers's budget, which had played a significant part in the defeat and consequent resignation of the government. Then a few weeks into the life of the Salisbury government Parnell had a secret and melodramatic meeting in a dust-sheeted Mayfair house with Carnarvon, the new Irish Viceroy. For the four or five months after that meeting, which period spanned the November general election, Parnell thought that he had at least as good a chance of getting Home Rule from the Tories as from the Liberal party. And Gladstone assisted him in this belief, even accepting the consequence of the diversion to the Conservatives of the Irish vote in the English towns. There was no period at which Gladstone held Parnell more rigidly at arm's length. When the Irish leader applied to Gladstone in October for guidance on the development of his thought he got a distinct brush-off, delivered through Mrs O'Shea, who in this interchange had replaced her husband as go-between. Gladstone resolutely refused to enter into any competition with the Conservatives on the question of how far he would go in the direction of self-rule. His advice to Parnell was to seek a settlement with the party actually in office, that is the Conservatives.

This sounded disdainful, but in fact it was high-minded on Gladstone's part and in total contradiction of the view, so sedulously held in Conservative circles, that his Irish policy was nothing but a self-seeking search for votes and office by a power-drunk old man. Gladstone was already well down the road to his conviction that nothing short of a separate parliament (although one subordinate to the imperial connection) would settle Ireland. He was prepared, as was proved by future events, to devote another eight years of his ebbing life to trying to achieve Home Rule. But in 1885 he thought that it would be better done by a Conservative government.

The idea that the Conservatives might perform this role was optimistic, but not ludicrous. Carnarvon was in favour. Randolph Churchill was a loose cannon which might go off in any direction. Hicks Beach and W. H. Smith did not seem totally opposed. And the rationale for wishing the Conservatives to do the job was clear. The implementation of Home Rule would manifestly be difficult and divisive, even if there were few of its supporters who would have expected a delay of thirty-seven years, during which the hope of doing it within a continuing British entity would be destroyed.

Even without knowledge of this dismal perspective the attractions of being able to do it on the run were great. There is a well-known political rule that difficult and necessary measures are best accepted from the party or the leader least expected to do them. This was General de Gaulle's strength in relation to withdrawal from Algeria. It was nearly that of the 1964–70 Labour government in relation to trades union reform. Furthermore the Conservative party in late-nineteenth- (and indeed most of twentieth-) century Britain carried the additional advantage that what was proposed by its leaders was almost invariably accepted by the House of Lords. A solution could have been achieved so much more quickly and smoothly without the sterile struggles with the second chamber of 1893 and 1912–14.

It was therefore a clear shaft of perception which made Gladstone see the national benefit of a Conservative-proposed (and Gladstone-supported) Home Rule commitment in the autumn of 1885, and an act of statesmanship which made him tolerant of the pursuit of such an alliance by Parnell. As is always the case a more cynical explanation was possible. Home Rule was one of the most powerfully fissiparous issues of the politics of the past two centuries. It was liable to split any party which touched it. There were obvious attractions to a Liberal in the Conservative party taking the first brunt of the nuclear explosion. Yet as Gladstone's primary motive this is unsustainable. Whatever else characterized his handling of the Home Rule issue it was not the tactics of party manoeuvre.

Conservative incomprehension of Gladstone's high-mindedness was fortified by two accidents of timing, the second a deeply unfortunate one. In the first place Gladstone intervened too late. On the day before he spoke to Balfour the Conservative Cabinet had met and had decided, in the words of Salisbury's letter to the Queen, 'that it was not possible for the Conservative Party to tamper with Home Rule'.[11] In other words the Carnarvon initiative was dead. (Balfour would not necessarily have known of this before the Eaton Hall conversation.) By the time that Gladstone's dilatory letter arrived and was passed around, the circumstances which had given it relevance were more than a week downwind. This heightened the artificiality with which ministers wished to endow it.

It had also been superseded by an apparently contradictory initiative known as the 'Hawarden kite'. Herbert Gladstone, still not quite thirty-two, unmarried and often acting as a private secretary to his father, but an MP of five years' standing, had spent most of the first half of December at Hawarden. He was close to his father, but did not always merely echo his views. He had for instance been known as a declared Home Ruler at least since the previous July. During the autumn he had wished his father would take a more forward line, not keep Parnell so much at arm's length, and look to an early return to Liberal government and not to a Conservative conversion to deal with the Irish problem. On top of this, Herbert Gladstone received a disturbing appeal from a disturbing source (particularly for him, as a member of Leeds) at the beginning of this same over-animated week when the Conservative Cabinet was meeting and Gladstone was talking to Balfour. The source was Wemyss Reid, the editor of the *Leeds Mercury* and in general an important as well as a moderate Liberal who might equally easily follow Hartington as Gladstone. He complained that the Gladstonian case was being allowed to go by default, and that, unless the serious Liberal press were given some guidance, all the running was left to be made by Chamberlain, who, it was thought, had his own reasons for being against an early Liberal return to office.

Herbert Gladstone decided to respond by going to London and seeing Reid on 15 December. The next day he also gave an interview to the editor of the National Press Agency, which supplied material to about 170 local newspapers. He saw his father before he went, but there is no evidence that they substantially discussed Reid's letter or Herbert's mission. Nonetheless the son was of course privy to his father's developing thought and the general drift of his conversations with Granville, Rosebery and others. This knowledge formed the basis of the very hard briefing which he gave to Reid and to the representatives of the National Press Agency. It was the latter which caused the main trouble when its result started to appear in the evening papers of

17 December. The *Pall Mall Gazette* began its long, politically sensational and personally tendentious story on a note of authority.

> Mr Gladstone has definitely adopted the policy of Home Rule for Ireland and there are well-founded hopes that he will win over the chief representatives of the moderate section of the party to his views. Lord Spencer is practically convinced that no other policy is possible, and his authority as the Minister who has governed Ireland during a most troubled time is unimpeachable.

The article then added authenticity by giving some detail about the scheme in Gladstone's mind, in particular saying that Irish members would not be excluded from the House of Commons, but would continue to share in deliberations 'in Imperial affairs'. Still more tendentiously the article concluded:

> Mr Gladstone is sanguine that the policy of settling the Irish question once for all will commend itself to the majority of his party and to the English people, when it is clearly understood that no other course can bring real peace. If he is enabled to eject the Government on this issue, he will have a large majority in the House of Commons for his Irish bill, and he believes that the House of Lords, weighing the gravity of the situation, will not reject it. Should there be a sufficient rejection by moderate Liberals to encourage the Lords to throw out the bill a dissolution would be inevitable, but except in the event of any serious explosion in Ireland that would have the effect of exasperating the popular feeling in England against the Irish the country would in all probability endorse Mr Gladstone's policy and give him an unmistakable mandate to carry it into law. There is reasonable expectation that both Lord Hartington and Mr Goschen will come round to Mr Gladstone's view, and Mr Chamberlain and Sir Charles Dilke, in spite of their present attitude, could not consistently oppose it.[12]

The article was at once deadly accurate and designed to produce an adverse reaction on the part of every person or group of persons mentioned. Spencer was the first to be affronted. His support of the Gladstonian line was as described and he was not diverted from it, but he nonetheless abhorred the form of the disclosure. 'I never was so disgusted in my life', he wrote to Rosebery at the end of the month, 'as I was by the *Standard* and the *Pall Mall*, not to say Leeds revelations.'[13] Then the views of the majority of Liberals as well as of 'the English people' were pre-empted, and any recalcitrant 'moderate Liberals' as well as the House of Lords were threatened with a punitive dissolution if they stood out against a Home Rule bill. Hartington and Goschen (the latter had hardly been in Liberal communion on any issue since 1874 and was to be Chancellor of the Exchequer in a Conservative government within a year) were roughly informed of their expected duty – but counter-productively so, for they both voted against the 1886 bill. And finally Chamberlain and Dilke were sharply given their marching orders.

What did Herbert Gladstone think he was up to? He was not a wholly foolish and in no way a malevolent young man. He claimed that he expected his briefing to be treated as background rather than as a verbatim expression of view, and also as though he were giving his own opinions rather than those of his father. The first hope was naive, the second silly. The idea that his own off-the-record opinions on what exact shape of the bill, or on what Hartington or the House of Lords would do to it, would themselves have commanded vast newspaper space was presumptuous and misplaced. And Herbert Gladstone, whatever else he was, which included being an innovative Home Secretary nearly a quarter of a century later, was not presumptuous. Perhaps for this reason the GOM took his intervention with exemplary parental calm. Herbert was his youngest son, the most politically committed and the most frequently at his father's service of the four. These were all marks of credit or grounds for affection in Gladstone's eyes.

Nonetheless he must have been sorely tried. The 'kite', unfurled in a way that was at once crude and with a touch of subterfuge, not only upset his Liberal colleagues and negated the delicacy with which he had hitherto been endeavouring to bring them along, but also provided fuel for Tory leaders who wished to see his Balfour overture as typical hypocrisy. The first fluttering of the kite was indeed the reason why Gladstone delayed from 15 to 20 December sending the confirmatory letter to Balfour. He in fact wrote it on the 16th, but by that day the preliminary ripples from Herbert's London visit began to reach Hawarden, and he delayed sending it. His relevant diary entries for the 16th read: 'A day of anxious & very important correspondence [he lists, *inter alia*, letters to Mrs O'Shea, Hartington and Balfour]. . . . Matters of today required meditation. After dealing with the knottiest point, I resumed Huxley.* We felled a good ash. Read Burke – Dicey. Suspended the Balfour letter.'[14]

* He was engaged in writing for the *Nineteenth Century* a courteous but highly convoluted and argumentative riposte to an article of T. H. Huxley on the relationship

The next day Gladstone issued a limited and unconvincing denial of the validity of the leak: 'The statement is not an accurate representation of my views, but is, I presume, a speculation upon them. It is not published with my knowledge or authority, nor is any other beyond my own public declarations.'[15] The denial was of course unavailing. What had been published was near enough to the truth to make any disavowal highly conditional, and the damage had been done. Hartington, to whom Gladstone had written a defensive letter* on the same day that he issued the denial, well summed up the new position when he wrote back on the 18th:

> When you say that you are determined to have no intentions at present I understand that you do not desire to take or prepare any action before the [Conservative] Government have had an opportunity of acting. But the fact that you have formed the opinion that an effort should be made by the Government to meet the Irish demand, and that this opinion has been allowed to be made known and cannot be contradicted amounts in my view to action of enormous importance.[16]

The second sentence was tantamount to a polite indication from Hartington that he was about to *prendre congé*. Two days later, although Gladstone had written to him again on the 19th, and was to do so yet again on the 20th, and again on the 23rd, he wrote to his constituency chairman to tell him that he would not move from the position he had taken up in the November election, that is to say he would not sail again under a Gladstonian flag. The strong probability is that Hartington would have broken on Home Rule in any event. But the maladroitness of the kite gave him an excuse for cutting the knot more quickly and therefore more easily, because it meant that he could settle his position before he had to expose himself to the pressure of Gladstone's presence, more formidable than his letters, in the new year.

Could Herbert Gladstone possibly have supposed that he was aiding either his father or the cause of Home Rule by his actions? The first

---

of the Book of Genesis to modern scientific knowledge. The fact that, on a day of agitation, irritation and potential crisis, he was able to turn his mind back to what were, frankly, some rather nitpicking points was at once a tribute to his intellectual (and emotional) discipline and a reflection on his sense of proportion.

* 'The whole stream of public excitement is now turned against me,' it began, 'and I am pestered with incessant telegrams which there is no defence against but either suicide or Parnell's method of self-concealment. The truth is I have more or less of opinions and ideas but no intention or negotiations.' (*Diaries*, XI, p. 451.)

would be plausible only on the assumption that his father had tipped him the wink to go ahead, while no doubt warning him, with what Tories and some Whigs would regard as typical machiavellianism, that the kite would have to be disavowed. There is no evidence for this other than a hypothetical passage in Hamilton's diaries. Hamilton, in spite of his personal loyalty to and friendship for the whole Gladstone family, was very sceptical about Home Rule and critical (to his diary at least) of Gladstone's handling of the matter, which he regarded as precipitate in substance and dissimulating in form. He did however have the 'horse's mouth' advantage of dining with Herbert Gladstone on the evening after his arrival from Hawarden (15 December). And on the 23rd he recorded the version of events at which he had arrived.

> The story of the leakage has now been made pretty clear to me. The Provincial Press ... kept on bombarding Hawarden with application for a lead on the Irish question. Mr. G. declined to commit himself; but he winked at the dropping of hints. Thereupon Herbert G. puts himself into the train; and on arriving in London goes off to the National Press Agency, gives a filial version of paternal views and talks freely with whomever he meets.[17]

Gladstone's reactions on 16 and 17 December were relatively calm, because he was too experienced in political nonsenses and confusions to overreact to them and because, as Hamilton had written after the Gordon débâcle, 'the greater is the crisis, the more coolly does he keep his head'. But there was no sense that he had lit the fuse and was waiting with a mixture of expectation and apprehension for the explosion. Nor was there any doubt that he was discommoded. Herbert Gladstone (rather a bold step in the circumstances) went back to Hawarden by the Irish mail train late on the evening of 16 December. So he would have been there on the morning of the 17th when Gladstone was writing defensively to Hartington and issuing his unconvincing denial.

Herbert Gladstone wrote in his diary for that day the odd comment that 'Father was quite *compos*.' This fairly common abbreviation of *compos mentis* (literal translation: 'sane, of sound mind') appears from the context to have been used by him in the sense of 'calm and composed' as opposed to the more frequent modern meaning of 'in full possession of his faculties, not senile'. Any of the three meanings might in the circumstances have been regarded as distinctly patronizing. It was Herbert Gladstone who needed his father's forbearance at the time, rather than the GOM requiring the son's assurance that he was balanced and of sound mind. And this forbearance was on the whole forthcoming. There is a slight impression that Gladstone might for the moment have preferred the company of his other sons. It was a vigorous tree-cutting season with some noble trunk falling almost every day between then and Christmas. But the woodcraft was recorded as being with Willy or Harry rather than with Herbert. By Christmas Eve, however, he was taking pleasure in the completeness of the family party 'young and old'.

The more plausible explanation of the kite is that Herbert Gladstone brashly believed that his father needed a little push and Liberal opinion a considerable steer in order to bring the two into constructive harmony with each other, and that he himself was a necessary catalyst. This at any rate was the explanation on which he had settled by 31 December when he wrote a long letter (no doubt also intended as a record for himself and others) to his cousin Lucy Cavendish, in which he set out, defensively, defiantly and sometimes a little contradictorily, his version of all the events surrounding the flight of the kite. He defended his own right to speak 'on his own responsibility' as he had done for the previous five years. He specifically denied any collusion with his father: 'With all these matters [that is, his own decision to go to London and the briefings there] my Father had no more connection than the man in the moon, and until each event occurred he knew . . . no more of it than the man in the street.'

He then delivered what may be thought the less than convincing core of his self-justification: 'in regard to my general action I have nothing to conceal and no apology to make. If I had not acted we should have got into hopeless confusion. It may be true that influential men are now all at variance on the question. On the other hand the Liberal Press is for the most part working smoothly and well on certain given lines.' He then concluded a little sententiously but no doubt his words were heartfelt: 'May the end of this great question be good; I can only pray that your great loss may tend more and more to bring ultimate peace to Ireland.'[18] Lucy Cavendish showed this letter to her brother-in-law Hartington, but it is unlikely that it was written for that purpose or had much effect with him. It should have convinced Hartington that the GOM had not contrived the revelation, but this did not affect his central point that, once it had been made, it could not be satisfactorily contradicted because it truly represented Gladstone's state of mind.

What was more to the point was whether Gladstone needed the filial push. This raises the anterior questions of when and how firmly he made up his mind on Home Rule. To dispose of the second of these questions first, the push, insofar as it had any effect on the firmness of Gladstone's commitment, was counter-productive. In the first half of December he gave every impression of moving steadily through the quiet conversion of his colleagues, except that, as so frequently in the past, he saw Chamberlain and Hartington at the end and not at the beginning of the line as he ought to have done – in neither case until after he had returned to London on 11 January 1886.* Insofar as he was thought to have a period of hesitation, such disparate sources as Hamilton, Chamberlain, Harcourt and Hartington thought (wrongly) that lack of support (partly caused by the kite) was giving him pause, and that his mind was swinging back towards retirement.

If a date for the settling of Gladstone's mind on Ireland is sought, the best answer is that it was probably when he committed himself to paper at Dalmeny on Saturday, 14 November 1885, a third of the way through his electioneering in Midlothian. It was an example of Gladstone's still pulsating energy that at the age of nearly seventy-six in the midst of the preoccupations of a campaign and without breaking his normal letter-writing and reading pattern (on that day he read parts of Greville's *Diaries*, of Lotze's *Microcosmus* and of the *Annual Register* for 1819), he should find time to outline a detailed Home Rule scheme, which was not merely unnecessary for the campaign but which it was essential should be kept secret for weeks to come. He did not disclose his draft scheme to Rosebery, in whose house he was staying, although he did outline its main points in a letter which he wrote on the same day to his son Herbert, who was campaigning in Leeds.

Among the circumstances in which he wrote this outline a salient one was that he had two weeks before received from Parnell via Mrs O'Shea an at least equally detailed – and conservative – 'Proposed Constitution for Ireland'. The two papers were different in style and intellectual premiss (as was not surprising) but they rarely contradicted each other, although the one was sometimes precise where the other was vague, and vice versa. Gladstone, for instance, was at this stage firm that 'Irish representation in Imperial Houses [should] remain, for Imperial purposes only,'[19]†

* Gladstone could, however, have deployed good excuses. Chamberlain had been to Hawarden on 7–8 October with 'three hours of stiff conversation' but that was before the election. And Hartington had been invited for an early post-election visit, but had declined on the ground that he was engaged to meet the Prince of Wales in Lincolnshire; no alternative meeting was suggested from either side.

† This qualification opened a large can of worms. Was a vote of censure against a government on, say, Welsh Church disestablishment or excise duties in Great Britain (the Irish ones being different) an imperial question, or was it not?

whereas Parnell said that it 'might be retained or might be given up'.[20] Conversely Parnell was precise on the size and duration between elections of the Irish Chamber, whereas Gladstone was vague. But there was no question at this stage of Gladstone deliberately cleaving close to Parnell. He was still in the phase of being anxious that the latter should make a deal with the Conservative government. He had consequently returned a fairly chilly answer to Mrs O'Shea, even though it had been ironically somewhat warmed up on the advice of Lord Richard Grosvenor, who, despite his incipient Unionism, was too much of a whip to like the idea of losing even Irish votes.

The votes were however to some substantial extent already lost, particularly in the Lancashire boroughs where the Irish were strong, and still more damagingly for the future a gulf of bitterness was opened between many Liberal candidates and Parnell and his party. The Nationalists had issued a manifesto calling upon Irishmen in England to vote against Liberals as 'the men who coerced Ireland, deluged Egypt in blood, menace religious liberty in the school, the freedom of speech in Parliament, and promise to the country generally a repetition of the crimes and follies of the last [1880–5] Liberal Administration'. Sir Henry James, for example, former Attorney-General and a ball-bearing of influence whom Gladstone tried hard to persuade to be Lord Chancellor in his 1886 government, was probably pushed into Liberal Unionism by the virulence with which the Irish attacked him in Bury. It is dangerous to allow parties which may be destined to work together after a campaign to abuse each other too vehemently during its course.

Nevertheless Gladstone's action, somewhat instigated by Parnell's similar exercise, in setting down his own views on the shape of a possible Home Rule measure may well have been decisive in the evolution of his own commitment. No doubt he did not intend this Dalmeny outline to be committing. He merely thought it would be useful to clarify his thoughts and to have a scheme by him if he came to think it right to implement one. But by so doing he immediately moved his mind forward. The act of tentative drafting was a catalyst even more than it was a fall-back. It is a well-known syndrome. The man who has a draft to hand has a powerful weapon with which to overcome those with whom he is arguing. But a draft is a prison as well as a weapon. Having invested intellectual capital he becomes most anxious to use it. Gladstone's Saturday-morning work at Dalmeny, half by accident and half because it captured, as a flash of lightning illuminates a landscape, the way in which his mind was moving, may well have been the few hours in which the last major orientation of his life was fixed. The proposition has the advantages and the disadvantages of being as irrefutable as it is unprovable.

At whatever precise moment it occurred, Gladstone's shift of position to Home Rule,* although it convulsed British politics in a way that in the past 200 years only Peel's conversion to free trade and Lloyd George's adaptation to a Tory coalition have done, was by no means an astonishing *volte face*. He had given remarkably few hostages to fortune in the shape of pledges to maintain the Union in all circumstances. Deep though was the aversion which Gladstone's political genius evoked among his opponents, and profound though was their conviction that he boxed every compass for reasons of most blatant self-interest, it was impossible for them to produce clear examples of his pledging himself against Dublin autonomy. When, seventeen years before, he had launched his first government on the keynote of 'My mission is to pacify Ireland' he had hoped to do it within the framework of Pitt's Union. But he did not exclude an alternative framework, and by the end of that government, in the already cited letter to Lord Fermoy,† he declined to comment one way or the other on Home Rule because of the imprecision with which the phrase was used and the many different meanings which it could bear.

However, Gladstone's freedom from having to eat many of his own words was far from decisive. On the one hand he was widely regarded as the greatest master of explaining away his own statements who had ever bestridden the political stage. And on the other no absence of embarrassing pledges could soften the violence of the shock to which he subjected his party. Throughout the election campaign he had reserved his counsel and said nothing in public which made untenable the position of Hartington, Grosvenor and the other Unionist Whigs. His main speech on the subject had been delivered in the Edinburgh Albert Hall ('to an audience of very manageable size and excellent temper')[21] on the evening of his arrival in the city. The maintenance of the unity of the Empire accompanied by more local self-government for Ireland (it had practically none) had been the twin desiderata, and the route to them which he asked the electorate to open was through a Liberal

* He denied that it was a 'conversion' in the sense that he had undergone one on Irish Church disestablishment. It was more an evolution of mind. (See Matthew, *Gladstone, 1875–1898*, pp. 211–12.)

† See p. 378, above.

majority large enough to give a future government independence of both Tories and Nationalists.

That Gladstone did not achieve, although the Liberals did remarkably well for the end of five years of bumpy Liberal government. There was no revulsion as in 1874. In Great Britain the Liberals had a hundred more seats than the Conservatives. Had Ireland already gone, it would have been one of the only six great anti-Tory majorities of the past 130 years. But Ireland had not gone, did not do so for another thirty-seven years, and under Gladstone's scheme would in any event have continued to affect the strategic shape of the House of Commons. What had gone was the Liberal vote in Ireland. Whereas in 1880 Ireland had returned thirteen Liberal MPs, the 1885 result allowed them not a single representative. The Conservatives on the other hand retained (mostly in Ulster) nineteen of the twenty-six seats which they had held under the much more restricted franchise of that previous election. This differential rate of retreat robbed the Liberals of their overall majority, which would in any case have been more nominal than real, for it was difficult to think of any issue (and certainly not the dominant one of Ireland itself) on which all 333 Liberals could have been got into the same division lobby.

Far more significant than this squabbling over the remnants of Tory or Liberal representation in Ireland, however, was the extent of the Parnellite victory. This was qualitative as well as quantitative. They won 85 seats out of 103 in Ireland (and one in Liverpool), and they won them by overwhelming majorities. In the two divisions of Kilkenny, for instance, a relatively prosperous and urbane Irish county, the Nationalist candidates each polled over 4000 votes, with their Tory opponents getting only 170 for one seat and 220 for the other. In the few Ulster seats which the Nationalists contested, on the other hand, even in ultra-Protestant Antrim, they ran the Tory very close.

This overwhelming expression of Irish opinion made a profound impression upon Gladstone. It did not strike him like a thunderclap when the results came out because the anticipation of such a development had affected his thinking at least since the early autumn. But expectation was one thing and the reality of counted votes another, and the clarity with which the Irish constituencies had spoken was unmistakable. The solidity was such as to create a fear that virtually all the Irish MPs from the three southern and western provinces together with a sizeable minority from Ulster might withdraw from Westminster and set up their own assembly in Dublin. Home Rule might be achieved by secession without the constitutional covering of an imperial Act of Parliament which preserved the theory of Westminster sovereignty. The choice, devastating for the fundamental tenets of Gladstonian Liberalism, would then have lain between military reconquest or the acceptance of an illegal and revolutionary break-up of the United Kingdom.

That Gladstone's thoughts had been much on the delicate hinge between law and popular demand is shown by the pattern of his reading that autumn. In October he read a lot of Irish eighteenth- and nineteenth-century history, contrasting the situation before and after what he had come to see as the 'gigantic though excusable mistake' of Pitt's Act of Union. In November and early December he was into Burke's thoughts on the treatment of the American colonies and A. V. Dicey's just published *Law of the Constitution*. Dicey was to be an unyielding opponent of Home Rule, but his interest for Gladstone lay in his theory of the unfettered supremacy of Parliament and its right both to delegate to and to override subordinate institutions.

Less theoretically Gladstone also studied the two Acts (of the Imperial Parliament) by which Canada led the way to what came to be called Dominion status. Here, however, part of the interest lay in his method of procuring copies of the two Acts. On 9 October he wrote from Hawarden to ask Lord Richard Grosvenor if he would obtain for him the Canada Acts of 1840 and of 1867. Grosvenor complied, although it was hardly a normal part of his Chief Whiply functions. Nor was Gladstone habitually without self-reliance in obtaining his vast intake of books and papers, parliamentary and other. It is difficult to believe that this was not a coded message, effectively informing Grosvenor, to whom he was very attentive at the time, as not only his Whip but also the ambassador of the Whigs to his court, that he was prepared to let Ireland follow where Canada had led. He ended this letter by saying: 'I have been working on Ireland: & have got a speech in me, if I dare speak it.'[22]

Although he was for the moment moving slowly and cautiously, Gladstone did not doubt that Ireland was in a potentially explosive state with a constitutional crisis overlaying yet another rent crisis. One of the attractions of both Parnell's and Gladstone's own Home Rule schemes was that they would leave the new indigenous government to deal with rent and collect the interest and repayments due on land purchase advances. Ethnic stresses would thus cease to compound agrarian ones. But all Gladstone's private sources, from James Bryce, then Regius Professor of Civil Law at Oxford, as well as Liberal MP for Aberdeen and a constitutional expert of world repute, to E. G. Jenkinson, who as head of the Special Branch in Dublin had a more worm's-eye view, agreed upon the extreme fragility of the social and political fabric in Ireland. Gladstone knew that he was only in slack water so long as he was waiting to see if the Tories, with his encouragement and promise of support, were willing to grasp an Irish solution. As soon as it became clear that they would not do so, he did not doubt his own urgent responsibility.

There was another major consideration which weighed with him. Just as in his approach to his first government he was influenced by the thought, unusual for a British politician of the period, that justice to Ireland was necessary for England's European reputation, so after the experience of his second government and on the threshold of his third, he was powerfully influenced by an equally unusual and sophisticated consideration. He thought that Irish violence and English reaction to it was corrupting the whole polity. The most analogous recent situation was *la sale guerre* in Algeria of the late 1950s and its effect upon metropolitan France. Harcourt may have liked emulating Bonaparte's Fouché, but Gladstone had hated being the first Prime Minister since the post-Napoleonic Wars unrest to have a police bodyguard forced upon him. On a broader point he disliked having to introduce the closure and the guillotine into the House of Commons in order to protect its proceedings from depredations of the disaffected Irish. He found he could not overcome Harcourt's determination to use the Fenian threat to keep local democratic control away from the Metropolitan Police. And he had to sponsor coercion bill after coercion bill which between them piled arbitrary powers upon the Viceroy and, even with as reputable a figure as Spencer in charge, led to very messy cases like the Maamtrasna hangings.

Gladstone saw that the maintenance of the liberal state was incompatible with holding within its centralized grip a large disaffected community of settled mind. The result of the 1885 election convinced him that the Irish mind was settled. The turn of the year convinced him that the Tories would do nothing. They preferred party unity to national interest. Up to this point at least Gladstone acted with a rare statesmanship. His overwhelming desire was a quick settlement of the Irish question, which he had come to see, perhaps belatedly but with a strategic instinct which far outweighed that of Salisbury or Chamberlain or Hartington, as an endemic poison to state and society. His only doubt was whether he had the continuing energy to carry through the new policy. Such thoughts could give him moments of discouragement. But essentially he preferred action – even with exhaustion – to repose, and he could always persuade himself that he should attempt one more stage of the perilous ascent which, as in Browning's *Grammarian's Funeral*, he saw as his life's duty.

Unfortunately, at least from the end of 1885 onwards, while his presence and his rhetoric remained magnificent, he was far from sure-footed. Like Peel he broke his party for a cause which was greatly in the national interest. Unlike Peel, however, he failed to carry the cause. He paid the fee, but he missed the reward. What vast benefit for Britain would have followed from an Irish settlement in the 1880s, thirty years before the Easter Rising. And how right – and generous – Gladstone was to see that the best chance of achieving it quickly was from a Conservative government with his playing the not very exciting role of a Russell to Salisbury's Peel. But Salisbury, who was a cynical pessimist as well as a skilled statesman, was not a Peel. The opportunity passed to Gladstone, who had not sought it, and who responded with courage and passion but without a tactical dexterity to match his strategic vision.

—— 32 ——

Schism and Failure

Gladstone came to London from Hawarden on 11 January 1886, ten days before the opening of the new Parliament and the need for him to make a public pronouncement in response to the Queen's Speech. The unusual amplitude of the cushion of time indicated his sense of both the difficulty and the importance of pending moves. His habit, to the dismay of his whips and loyal lieutenants, had long been to arrive only at the last moment.

Even in that year of impending schism, however, he declined to summon an early meeting of the shadow Cabinet, or 'conclave' as he preferred to call it, and even more firmly dismissed Lord Richard Grosvenor's suggestion of his giving an eve-of-session dinner. He had never given such a dinner in opposition (as he had hardly previously been leader of the opposition this was of doubtful relevance), and never, going back to the time of Peel, attended one, '*except* at Hartington's'. Whenever, at this stage of his life, Gladstone's memory went back to Peel it was a certain indication that he was pulling rank or at least age. What he wanted to do, of course, was to deal with his colleagues one by one, and thus exclude the real possibility, given how many of them were disposed to defect, that he might find himself corralled. Thus, on the evening of his arrival in London, he saw Dilke, Granville, Grosvenor and Harcourt – all separately – and on the following day he saw Spencer, Chamberlain, Bright and Mundella, and Granville, Harcourt and Grosvenor for the second time. And on the two subsequent days he introduced Kimberley, Derby, Ripon and Rosebery into the circle of consultation, as well as having a second go at Bright and Mundella, and both a second and a third go at Hartington.

Although he was becoming exasperated with some of his former colleagues, notably Selborne, who on 28 December had written a 'very able but I think deplorable paper' slamming the door on his support for Home Rule, and Hartington, whom he accused to Granville of becoming an agent of chaos by making it impossible in differing ways for either of them (Gladstone or Hartington) to lead the Liberal party, his own public position remained tentative and conciliatory during the mid-January weeks. In reality of course his mind was made up, and therefore his apparent hesitation was no more than the gliding of an eagle waiting to swoop. But he had more than enough wing power to enable him to choose his time. And, while there was a good deal of churning within the Conservative government, he preferred to await the outcome. The agents of the rejected policy of Irish conciliation resigned, first Hart Dyke the Chief Secretary and then Carnarvon the Viceroy. Dyke was replaced by W. H. Smith, the great newsagent who, five and a half years later and ironically in view of his 1886 role, was to share a day of death with Parnell, and to find himself obituarily upstaged. Smith had the honest clarity to see that the only alternative to conciliation was more coercion, and during his brief inaugural visit to Dublin, from 24 to 26 January, successfully recommended a new bill to the Cabinet. They accepted his recommendation, which had the effect of turning his inaugural into a farewell. By the time that he stepped ashore at Holyhead on the 27th the first Salisbury government had been defeated.

In the first days of the debate on the Queen's Speech both sides held off from a direct engagement on Ireland, and Parnell, even though he had by then abandoned his hopes of Home Rule from Salisbury, was equally disinclined to force the issue by putting down and voting on his own amendment. Gladstone's 'waiting' speech, delivered on 21 January, was the one in which he referred to himself as 'an old parliamentary hand', and on this basis advised his supporters to follow him in keeping their own counsel and to await for a little while the development of events. In the retrospective fragment which he wrote in the autumn of 1897, only six months before his death, Gladstone explained his hesitancy on the ground that to have provoked an early division on Home Rule in a House of many new Liberal members might well have resulted in it attracting the support of no more than 200 (as opposed to the 311 who eventually voted for the bill) and killing the issue for the Parliament.

He did not however allow the 'little while' to cover more than a few days, although still avoiding any vote which was nominally on Ireland. When, on the 28th, it became known that three days later the Irish Secretary would bring in a Coercion Bill, he decided to treat that as a *casus belli* and turn off the life machine which until then he had provided for the minority Conservative government. In one sense his indignation could be regarded as synthetic, for there was no member of the House who had been responsible for as many Irish coercion bills as Gladstone himself. But in another sense he was fully justified in seeing this as the final and public rejection of 'Carnarvonism' (Carnarvon's own resignation, decided upon before Christmas, had been made public on 16 January) and thus destroying the basis for Gladstone's tolerance of Salisbury's retention of office. Gladstone's own retrospective description of his reaction was as follows:

> Not perhaps in mere logic, but practicably it was now plain that Ireland had no hope from the Tories. This being so, my rule of action was changed at once: and I determined on taking any and every legitimate opportunity to remove the existing Government from office.... Immediately on making up my mind about the rejection of the government I went to call on Sir William Harcourt and informed him as to my intentions and the grounds of them. He said 'What, are you prepared to go forward without either Hartington or Chamberlain?' I answered, 'Yes'. I believe it was in my mind to say, if I did not actually say it, that I was prepared to go forward without any body. That is to say without any known and positive assurance of support. This was one of the great imperial occasions which call for such resolutions.[1]

The instrument which Gladstone found most conveniently to hand was hardly in the great imperial category. Jesse Collings, then member for the Bordesley division of Birmingham and as complete a Chamberlain henchman as it is possible to imagine, had on the order paper an amendment regretting the omission from the Queen's Speech of any measures benefiting the rural labourer. It took up the smallholdings theme which had been part of Chamberlain's 'unauthorized programme' of 1884, and is commonly referred to as the 'three acres and a cow' amendment. Without Gladstone's swoop to attack, it would have been left to languish as a gesture amendment. Suddenly, however, it was underpinned by the whole weight of the official opposition, it was brought forward for a few hours of debate, Gladstone himself spoke, there was a vote soon after midnight, and the Conservatives were out. There is no more symbolic a test of whether or not a government commands the general confidence of the House of Commons than its ability to carry the Address unamended. The Salisbury government failed that test by a margin of seventy-nine.

No one saw the issue as primarily bucolic. Collings had his few hours of glory, but the speeches were not confined to the cows and their three acres, nor were the votes so cast. Goschen voted with the Conservatives, but he had become used to doing that. What was more serious was that Hartington and Henry James did so too. And neither of them, not Hartington, the too-long-awaiting heir apparent, for whom like several in that position the cards had not fallen right, nor James, the putative Lord Chancellor and epitome of an amenable but respected lawyer politician, split from the party within which they had advanced so near to the differing summits of their ambition on any argument about whether cows should have two or three acres. They and most of the House of Commons realized that what they were voting about was whether Gladstone should form a Home Rule government. Two hundred and fifty-seven Liberals and seventy-four Irish Nationalists voted that he should. Two hundred and thirty-four Conservatives and eighteen Whigs, elected as Liberals, voted that he should not. And, more menacingly, seventy-six Liberals (including John Bright) were absent or present and abstaining.

That division was the beginning of the volvulus which knotted British politics for the next thirty years. The Liberals, having embraced Home Rule, could command no clear majority without the Irish, save in the exceptional circumstances of 1906, for which election they had in any event placed Home Rule on the back burner. Yet their policy was dedicated to getting rid of this parliamentary segment which alone made them, again with the exception of 1906, an intermittent party of government. The Conservatives, on the other hand, who increasingly came to be called Unionists, and whose success largely depended upon the Liberals keeping prominent in their shop window the Home Rule cause, which was unpopular in England, were two or three times deprived of office (in 1886, in 1892–5 and arguably 1910–15) by the Irish, whom they were determined to keep within the British polity, yet whose influence there they deeply resented. It was a fine recipe for stasis in the government of an already challenged empire and led to the efforts of Lloyd George and a varying number of Conservatives to resolve it by coalition in 1910, 1916 and 1919–22.

In January 1886, however, there were shorter-term and clearer-cut consequences. Late at night on Friday the 29th, three days after the vote, the Queen's secretary, Ponsonby, called upon Gladstone at Lady Frederick Cavendish's house, where (as often) he was temporarily installed, and gave him the Queen's commission, 'which I at once accepted'.[2] On the Monday, 1 February, he kissed hands at Osborne, where the Queen, to the astonishment of, *inter alia*, the Prince of Wales, insisted on remaining through the change of government. This did not mean that she allowed the change to go through easily. If anything, she behaved worse than in 1880 because she then had some justifiable even if unrealistic basis for believing that she might turn the tables and get

Hartington. In 1886 she was mildly and improperly obstructive without hope or purpose. Her ploy was to write most indiscreet letters to Goschen and to summon him to Osborne with hints that he might form a coalition government. Goschen, bereft of Liberal loyalty though he was by this time, nonetheless had a sense of constitutional propriety and declined to go, saying that his presence would cause public misunderstanding, and that she had better get on with it and send for Gladstone.

Salisbury behaved somewhat but not much better than Disraeli in 1880. He refused with style the Queen's offer of a dukedom ('His fortune would not be equal to such a dignity. . . . The kind words in which your Majesty has expressed approval of his conduct are very far more precious to him than any sort of title.'),[3] but he encouraged her foolish view that the main mistake of his government was to be dilatory in introducing Irish coercion, although that move became its death rattle. They clucked together over the weaknesses of Carnarvon ('He never could be entrusted with any post of importance again.')[4] and of Hicks Beach (Randolph Churchill would be a much better Commons leader than the latter, Salisbury opined, a view which, within a year, he would violently have repudiated). But he never attempted to tell the Queen that her duty, and her interest, was to give Gladstone's Irish policy a fair if sceptical trial.

What was that policy as Gladstone announced it for the purpose of getting colleagues to join his new government? He sought to ease the process by putting a thin coating of tentativeness over his proposals, but his import was clear enough:

> I propose to examine whether it is or is not practicable to comply with the desire widely prevalent in Ireland, and testified by the return of 85 out of 103 representatives, for the establishment, by Statute, of a legislative body, to sit in Dublin, and to deal with Irish as distinguished from Imperial affairs; in such a manner, as would be just to each of the three Kingdoms, equitable with reference to every class of the people of Ireland, conducive to the social order and harmony of that country, and calculated to support and consolidate the unity of the Empire on the combined basis of Imperial authority and mutual attachment.[5]

On this foundation there was put together a government which included nine – Spencer, Granville, Kimberley, Ripon, Rosebery, Harcourt, Childers, Chamberlain and Trevelyan – who had previously served in a Gladstone Cabinet. But Hartington, Derby, Northbrook, Selborne, Dodson and Carlingford were all part of the Whig withdrawal.

Bright, from a different angle, refused to serve and Dilke was regarded as not available (reluctantly by Gladstone, hysterically so by the Queen) because of his sensational divorce case, which first erupted in July 1885 and led to the effective end of his career. Furthermore two of the first nine, Chamberlain and Trevelyan, joined most hesitantly and lasted in the government for less than two months.*

The Queen added her own quota of difficulties. She was determined neither to have Granville back at the Foreign Office, nor to have Kimberley as a replacement. She wanted either Rosebery (still under forty) or Spencer (although she was much shocked by his conversion to Home Rule), and she got Rosebery. This discrimination against Granville may not have been wholly at variance with Gladstone's own feelings, for Granville was over the hill, although nonetheless an essential ambassador from Gladstone to such Whigs as remained open to persuasion. So it was awkward to move him, and he had to be accommodated with whatever other high-ranking post he found most acceptable. This was the Colonial Office, and from that there followed a notorious piece of maladroitness.

Chamberlain was clearly the marginal adherent, and if he was to be put in the government at all (Gladstone told the Queen that he thought it 'best to take in Mr Chamberlain',[6] a statement well short of enthusiasm) it must have made sense to give him an office from which he would be loath to resign. The bold step would have been to offer him the Exchequer, to which Harcourt, who went there, had at this stage no prescriptive right; he could have been contained at the Home Office for at least a further short Parliament. But Gladstone put Childers in that senior secretaryship of state. Gladstone's attachment to Childers, never a figure of great popularity or charm, was curious. There was no intimacy between them; Childers was never, it seems, at Hawarden. Yet Gladstone allowed him to be several times in the way, with Hartington in 1882, and now (at one remove) with Chamberlain in 1886. Nonetheless these were the dispositions, adverse to Chamberlain's desires, which Gladstone had in mind while he carried on the laborious negotiations for Chamberlain's entry into the government. Distracting him throughout was the fact that he had not yet secured Granville's acceptance of dislodgement from the Foreign Office. In reality Chamberlain's adherence was more important to the success of a Home Rule government than

* Trevelyan, unlike Chamberlain, changed his mind in 1887, accepted Home Rule and moved back into the Gladstonian communion.

was Granville's, but that was not how Gladstone, who had served with the old Whig in six different Cabinets, saw him in relation to the screw manufacturer.

First Chamberlain insisted on having a letter of contract such as might have been drawn up between two business partners. The opening paragraph, written by Chamberlain, stipulated that he should 'retain unlimited liberty of judgment and rejection on any scheme that may ultimately be proposed'. The second, inserted at Gladstone's request, testified to Chamberlain's willingness 'to give an unprejudiced consider-ation to any more extensive proposals which may be made'.[7] The value of these vague avowals was more than neutralized by Gladstone's distaste for the whole concept of such a distrustful letter. However, it having been agreed, he proceeded to offer Chamberlain the Admiralty. The first-lordship scored relatively high in prestige but wildly low in relation to Chamberlain's interests. Birmingham was hardly a great naval city, but more important was the hopelessness of Admiralty House as a base from which to mount a campaign for domestic Radicalism, which still appeared to be Chamberlain's main concern. Had there been mutual trust, such a campaign might also have suited Gladstone's interest. It could have guarded one flank of his concentration upon Ireland.

Chamberlain appears to have seen Gladstone again on the day of the letter of contract (Saturday, 30 January) and a third time on the Sunday after his written refusal of the Admiralty. The slight imprecision derives from these meetings, most unusually, not being specified in Gladstone's diary and from Chamberlain not being a diarist. At the Sunday meeting Gladstone asked Chamberlain what office, in lieu of the Admiralty, he would prefer and was told that it was the Colonies. This of course touched a sensitive nerve in relation to Gladstone's unconcluded nego-tiations with Granville. But it did not excuse his response, which was to look up in surprise and say, 'Oh! a Secretary of State,' thereby implying that such a grand rank – there were only five of them in those days – was a bit over the odds for Chamberlain, whom he saw as a natural occupant of one of the more workaday posts in the second half of the Cabinet. This impression he confirmed by suggesting that Chamberlain might like to go back to his old job as President of the Board of Trade, to which the reply was that he would not like it but would if necessary accept.

The single source for Gladstone's devastatingly revealing reply to Chamberlain is the Dilke papers. It is there further recorded that Chamberlain, after the exchange, was 'furious and will never forgive this slight'.[8] On this reasonably secure but narrow foundation the snub has found its way into at least two lives of Dilke, two of Joseph Chamberlain and three of Gladstone, as well as into Hammond's study of *Gladstone and the Irish Nation*. It is a formidable burgeoning from such a small source, uncorroborated from the Gladstone side, although there seems no reason to doubt that something very similar was said, particularly as it entirely fits in with Gladstone's general attitude to Chamberlain. But the exact words are not wholly verifiable.

Two days later Chamberlain agreed to join as President of the Local Government Board, preferring this to a return to the Board of Trade. He was number eleven in the hierarchy in a Cabinet of fourteen. Having got this far with securing but not elevating Chamberlain, Gladstone might surely have been expected to give him every assuagement which was compatible with the somewhat lowly status but potentially interesting content of his office. He did the reverse. First, in one of his fits of penny-pinching economy, he tried to reduce (from £1500 to £1200) the salary of Chamberlain's junior minister, the temporarily ubiquitous Jesse Collings, who if anything deserved a bonus for having his amendment so conveniently available to bring down the Conservative government. Chamberlain successfully resisted the salary cut, but the argument, which it was almost incredible that Gladstone had ever raised, had driven yet another nail into the coffin of their relations.

Then, on a second issue, and one of more substance, Gladstone managed to behave with equal insensitivity and even greater lack of tactical sense. Chamberlain was still a strong domestic Radical, although becoming implacable on Ireland partly because his view of Parnell had been poisoned by using O'Shea as an unsatisfactory intermediary and partly because his imagination on Ireland was limited almost to a municipal horizon. His broodings on 'the illimitable veldt' came much later and in a different context. In the middle 1880s he was still primarily a 'gas and water' man who could embrace schemes of town councils and county councils and land purchase and drainage and harbour developments for Ireland, though not the more elusive but also more emotive concept of nationhood. This limitation, however, in no way disqualified him from being the agent of utilitarian advance in England. Measures for local government reform and land schemes along the lines of the Collings amendment were part of the Liberal programme. Furthermore they became much easier to get through a Liberal Cabinet as a result of the departure of Hartington and several others who had clashed with Chamberlain in the 1880 government.

In these circumstances Gladstone's tactical plan might be thought almost to have written itself. He needed to keep the gulf between Chamberlain and Hartington as wide as possible, and he needed to get Chamberlain so engrossed in and satisfied with his departmental work that he became reluctant to leave the government. On this basis Gladstone might have been the Emperor of the West, dealing with Ireland more or less as he wished, and Chamberlain, if not the Emperor, at least the semi-independent Viceroy of the East, pursuing reform in England. Such a dual approach would also have had the advantage of keeping Liberals – both MPs and active supporters – a good deal happier. Out of respect for Gladstone provincial Nonconformists embraced the cause of Catholic Ireland with remarkable enthusiasm, but they did not want all their eggs in that basket.

Gladstone, however, was perhaps the greatest concentrator of eggs in the history of politics. Once a cause had fought its way to the front of his mind, whether it was Neapolitan gaols, budgetary economy, the tribulations of the Bulgarians or the urgent need for an Irish Parliament, it engaged his whole force and took priority over everything else. So, at the beginning of March 1866, he took away the parliamentary draughtsman who was working with Chamberlain on a local government bill and redeployed him on Irish work. It is difficult to imagine a more wanton gesture. Once he had done it, Chamberlain's departure from the government, perhaps always more likely than not, became a racing certainty. It is difficult to avoid the view that, so far as Chamberlain at least was concerned, Gladstone in the terms of his January conversation with Harcourt was not merely prepared to go ahead without him, but almost preferred to do so. Yet, once Chamberlain had resigned on the issue and had added a Radical defection to a Whig one, the chances of getting a Home Rule bill through the Commons, let alone the Lords, became slim.

For the preparation of the bill Gladstone took central and detailed responsibility. He used John Morley, in office for the first time as Irish Secretary, as an assistant, but Morley, distinguished man of letters although he was and senior if querulous statesman although he was to become, had no legislative or administrative experience. The Prime Minister did not much consult with other colleagues, except on broad issues with Spencer, and in particular not with Chamberlain. It was rather the same as his reason for not seriously considering him for the Exchequer: he might too easily resign and it was therefore desirable first to minimize the impact of his going (by not giving him too prominent an office) and second to limit the amount of inside knowledge that he might take with him (by not consulting him about the form of the Home Rule Bill). The disadvantage of these protections against severance was that they made it more likely. Ironically it was Harcourt who in late February nearly resigned well in advance of Chamberlain, but on a question of his budgetary prerogative and not on policy. Harcourt was just as hostile to Home Rule and the Irish as was Chamberlain, but even more strongly did he believe in political partisanship, our side against theirs. His internal rows were more about defending his own area of authority than about policy. But it was nonetheless an indication of how fragile was Gladstone's base at this stage that he nearly lost his Chancellor, who was cynical about the main thrust of the government, before he even came to the crunch with his two 'conditional' ministers, Chamberlain and Trevelyan.

When the outline of a Home Rule bill was disclosed to the Cabinet in March Chamberlain took exception to four main points. He was against the exclusion of Irish members from Westminster, and he was against the handing over to Dublin of control over Irish customs and excise. In a sense these two points were linked, although they looked out in very different directions, because the ghost of the Boston tea party would have been raised by reserving such indirect taxes to London without Irish members in the Imperial Parliament. Thirdly Chamberlain wanted to keep the appointment of Irish judges and magistrates in British hands. And fourthly he took an interesting but somewhat theoretical federal–confederal point. He wanted an Irish authority only to be able to do such things as it was delegated to do and not, as provided by Gladstone, everything which was not specifically reserved to London. Trevelyan added that he objected to a putative Irish government being given control of its own police force. The form of self-government which would have emerged had all these objections been allowed would of course have been extremely attenuated. The result would have been a county council without control of revenue, the bench or the constabulary, and only exercising such powers as were graciously sent down to it. This would clearly have neither satisfied the Irish nor justified the upheaval in the Liberal party. Chamberlain's objections were wrecking, as was no doubt the intention.

The issue which Chamberlain at this stage chose to make central, the presence or absence of Irish members at Westminster, was a tangled one, although not that which had most occupied Gladstone in the

General Charles Gordon, the prototype of a *Boy's Own Paper* hero, whose grip on public opinion Gladstone gravely underestimated.

Dinner at Haddo House in September, 1884. The hosts are the seventh Earl (later first Marquess) of Aberdeen, the grandson of Gladstone's old chief, and his wife. Lady Aberdeen has Gladstone on her right and Rosebery on her left. (Pamting by A. E. Emslie, now in the National Portrait Gallery.)

Gladstone and Döllinger photographed by Lehnbach in Bavaria, September 1886. Lord Acton (far right) and Helen Gladstone (seated at the table in white) are also in the picture.

A constant but fatal attraction:

Charles Stewart Parnell

Katherine O'Shea

Gladstone reading in the Temple of Peace, his Hawarden library (probably late 1880s).

And writing, with great difficulty, seven or so years later. Sight was one 'door of the senses' which was indeed closing.

Tennyson in 1890, six years after accepting Gladstone's peerage offer, two years before his death.

The fifth Earl of Rosebery, Gladstone's sponsor in Midlothian and (unchosen) successor as Prime Minister: sometimes an ally, but often a tiresome one, and always prickly and self-regarding.

Sir William Harcourt, an effective parliamentary bruiser, sometimes called 'the great gladiator', but a difficult colleague.

John Morley, the author-statesman who, while not without his own brand of prickliness, was a more loyal prop of Gladstone in his fourth and last government than either Harcourt or Rosebery.

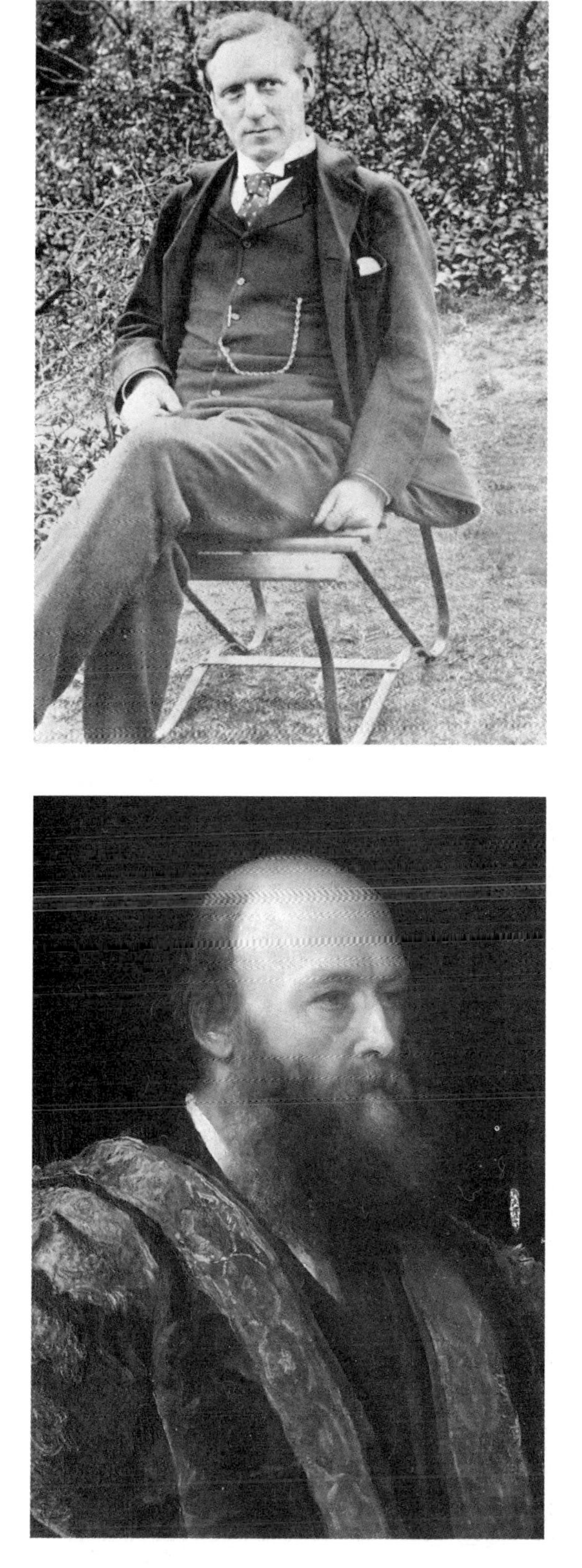

H. H. Asquith as a young Home Secretary in 1894. While not intimate with the Prime Minister, he was the most successful 'new man' in this fourth government and, when Liberalism recovered in 1906, Gladstone's effective long-term heir.

The third Marquess of Salisbury, who three times succeeded Gladstone as Prime Minister. He was a skilled and often partisan opponent, the founder of 'villa', (or suburban) Conservatism, but he and Gladstone did not much engage. They were like ships which passed (and re-passed) in the night.

The Gladstones on one of their last drives.

preceding weeks. This had been Irish finance, both the general arrangements for a semi-separation and the specific ones for financing the buying out, if they so wished, of Protestant Ascendancy landowners by a British government loan of £50 million – a vast sum by the standards of the day, the equivalent of half the annual budget.

One reason for the entanglement which surrounded the question of whether or not Irish MPs should, post-Home Rule, sit at Westminster was that it led on to very treacherous constitutional ground. If answered negatively, as in the bill, it blocked the way to the Dublin Parliament being the first wing of a federal structure in which Scotland, Wales and maybe even England could later be brought into the same design. It also pointed towards Home Rule being a step towards full independence, rather than a final settlement under which the Irish would be content to have at least foreign and defence policy run from London.

If, on the other hand, the answer was positive, then what nearly a hundred years later and in the Scottish context became known as the 'West Lothian question' reared its awkward head. Why should Irish members have the right to vote on, say, an education bill for England and Wales, when English and Welsh members had surrendered all rights over such matters in Ireland? And if an attempt were made to get round this problem by providing that Irish members could vote only on issues which affected all parts of the Kingdom, might not the result be, apart from the difficulty of drawing a satisfactory border line, that one party might command a majority on one set of issues and the other on a second set? Which then should form the government? Furthermore the retention of the Irish members would remove what was almost the sole attraction of Home Rule for some of its more cynical supporters, represented in the heart of the Cabinet by the all too solid flesh of the Chancellor of the Exchequer. Harcourt never made any bones about his indifference if not hostility to Home Rule except insofar as it meant seeing the back of the Irish.

Another reason for the surrounding entanglement was that the 'to retain or not to retain' (the Irish members) question, strong passions though it aroused, was also one, perhaps because there was no really satisfactory answer, on which the crucial individuals were constantly changing their minds. In November 1885, as we have seen, Gladstone's Dalmeny outline of a Home Rule scheme provided for the retention of Irish members 'for Imperial purposes only'. (Parnell's memorandum of two weeks before treated the question indifferently, although by the following May he had become 'stiff against retention'.) Yet by the time of the formation of his third government Gladstone had moved to their exclusion. 'I scarcely see how a Cabinet could have been formed, if the inclusion of the Irish members had been insisted upon,' he retrospectively wrote to Granville on 30 April.[9] It was certainly true that all the Whig peers who retained their Gladstonian allegiance, as well as Harcourt, attached great importance to the exclusion of the Irish. Almost inevitably therefore the bill was so drafted. And Gladstone, as was his way, embraced the new position with an excessive enthusiasm. By the end of May, however, he was back to accepting inclusion and envisaged a complete recasting of the relevant Clause 24. And, seven years later, when it came to the drafting of the second Home Rule Bill, the provision from the beginning was for the retention of eighty Irish members who were, however, to be excluded from voting on purely English or Scottish questions. That exclusion in turn proved indefensible, and with Gladstone's acquiescence the limitation was removed during the 1893 committee stage.

Chamberlain's position on the issue was as unstable as Gladstone's, but his progression from the autumn of 1885 to the spring of 1886, probably by intention, was in diametrically the opposite direction. On 3 January 1886, he wrote to Labouchère that 'the worst of all plans would be one which kept the Irishmen at Westminster while they had their own Parliament in Dublin'.[10] Yet when he resigned in March he made the opposite position the first of his reasons, and between then and his vote against the second reading of the bill on 6–7 June he kept the issue of Irish exclusion in the forefront of his objections. What was his essential motive? Had he come to feel with genuine strength on a point on which his position had been the direct opposite only a few months before, or was he tactically pressing on the weakest point in the Gladstonian lines? Probably the latter. Thirteen years later Barry O'Brien closely questioned Chamberlain for his *Life of Parnell* and in particular pressed him about why he had concentrated on that issue. Chamberlain replied with a splendid harshness: 'I wanted to kill the Bill.' And when O'Brien followed with 'And you used the exclusion of the Irish members for that purpose?', Chamberlain said: 'I did. . . .'[11]

Chamberlain always knew how to find an opponent's solar plexus. Once he had lost his desire to stay in the government, although he nominally retained an open mind about his vote, he was in reality eager to find reasons for casting it against. His killer instinct fastened on the point to which there could be no wholly satisfactory answer and he was further attracted to it by the fact that, although insoluble, it was on the surface an issue easy to grasp. There were none of the intricacies of the financial settlement or of the abstractions of whether powers had to be specifically reserved or specifically devolved. Just as, until he had lost him from the government, Gladstone did not appreciate the implacable force of Chamberlain's debating powers, so he did not understand his ruthless search for the weak point. Gladstone paid heavily for these underestimates and incomprehensions, but there was probably no way in which he could have out-manoeuvred Chamberlain on retention or exclusion. Once 'battling Joe' was lost to the government, the bill was at his mercy. And the indictment of Gladstone's tactical handling is not what he did or did not do in the run-up to the fatal second reading in June but that he did not make it worth Chamberlain's while in February–March to stay in the government.

Gladstone's oratorical performance on the first Home Rule Bill was uneven, but far from uneventful. His high point was on 8 April when he moved the first reading, a parliamentary stage now fallen into desuetude, but which then gave an opportunity for exposition without decision, for the practice was not to oppose in the division lobby a motion of leave to bring in a bill, even when it was as controversial as this one. But no decision in this instance was far from meaning no tension. Edward Hamilton described a commotion which makes a modern House of Commons day sound a sad anti-climax.

> Yesterday was indeed a notable day – the most notable day probably in the annals of the present Houses of Parliament [that is, since the completion of the rebuilding in 1852].... There being rumours that Members were going to appropriate the seats set aside for Strangers, I went down to the House [early].... The scene in the lobby was a lively one. Princes, Ambassadors, Peers, and distinguished strangers were jostling one another and besieging the doorways, ready to rush in the moment entrance was permitted. The Speaker took the Chair at 3.50; and then came the rush without respect to persons.... The scene in the Chamber was not less extraordinary than the scene outside. Every seat had been bespoken hours before; and up the floor of the House were ranged rows of chairs... Mr. G. arrived punctually at 4.30; and his arrival was greeted with a perfect storm of applause – a reception which visibly told upon him. Members stood up, waved their hats and literally shouted. No one dared to put a Question; and in five minutes time ... Mr. G. rose, his rising being the signal for renewed shouts. He spoke for 3 hours and 25 minutes; and held the rapt attention of the House throughout. I have often been more carried away and moved by speeches of his; but as a masterly exposition, as a piece of rhetorical construction, and as a *tour*

de force the speech will always mark among his finest efforts. The old Parliamentary hand had certainly not yet lost its cunning.[12]

Gladstone himself who, among several other of the necessary requisites of a great orator, had the ability to rate with a deadly accuracy the varying quality of his performances, wrote with some satisfaction of the day:

Finally settled my figures with Welby & Hamilton* – on other points with Spencer and Morley. Reflected much. Took a short drive.

H of C 4½–8¼. Extraordinary scenes outside the House & in. My speech, which I sometimes have thought could never end, lasted nearly 3½ hours. Voice & strength & freedom were granted to me in a degree beyond what I could have hoped. But many a prayer had gone up for me & not I believe in vain. Came home, & went early to bed: of course much tired. My legs felt as after a great amount of muscular motion, not with the weariness of standing.[13]

Gladstone's vast speech was never again to be equalled in length or in expository quality by any of his subsequent efforts. In terms of Hansard columns it had, however, often been exceeded in his elastic middle age. By this criterion it ranked only twelfth of his Commons orations. It was only a little longer than his Don Pacifico debate speech delivered thirty-six years earlier. There has been no one else with the possible exception of Churchill (and one may doubt if he exactly commanded before 1914, in spite of his high offices) who has commanded the House of Commons over such a span.

In content as opposed to length the speech was remarkable for its expository detail and for its peroration. The latter extended over perhaps ten minutes, yet never gave the impression that, like Mahler's sixth symphony or Ramsay MacDonald in his last phase, it could not stop because a conclusion proved elusive. Gladstone recalled Grattan's aphorism in his speech of opposition to Pitt's Act: 'The channel forbids union; the ocean forbids separation.'† Then he dealt in high terms with two separate but related issues. First, were the Irish capable of civic

* Sir Reginald (later Lord) Welby was permanent secretary of the Treasury 1885–94 and, a surprising progression, chairman of the London County Council in 1900. Hamilton is already a familiar. It was before the second reading debate a month later that, despite his high mandarin quality, Hamilton's figures turned out to be one of those rare cock-ups which bring forth the profuse apologies of civil servants and the (fairly) gracious tolerance of ministers.

† Which Morley, in an uncharacteristic lapse, cites the wrong way round: (*Life of Gladstone*, III, pp. 313–14.)

virtue? This question, the posing of which may sound insulting, was more than justified within a few weeks by a rasping speech of Salisbury. On 15 May, in the St James's Hall, Piccadilly, he pronounced with a typically Cecilian mixture of originality and arrogance that democracy was suited only to those of Teutonic race (this would have appeared an even odder choice of nomenclature fifty years later), which category he certainly did not see as embracing the Irish, who he thought were in this respect more akin to Hottentots or Hindus. He added that the best use for public money in Ireland was in promoting emigration. These gracious comments added a good deal of fuel to the flames of the controversy.

Gladstone on the other hand totally rejected the widespread English view that the Irish had no taste for justice, common sense, moderation or national prosperity and looked only to perpetual strife and dissension. If an Irishman's loyalty had been checked in its development it was because 'the laws by which he is governed do not present themselves to him, as they do to us in England and Scotland, with a native and congenial aspect'. Where the Irish voluntarily took on an obligation, as when they joined the British army or the Irish constabulary, their loyalty and bravery fully matched that of their 'Scotch and English comrades'. The related question to which Gladstone also applied himself was that of the reconciliation of local patriotism, 'which, in itself, is not bad, but good', with a wider commitment to the cause of the Empire and indeed of mankind. The two he brought together with a fervour and a conviction which would in the late twentieth century be of inestimable service in presenting the full compatibility of the high European case with a strong attachment to national cultures and to regional roots. In Ireland 'misfortune and calamity have wedded her sons to the soil', but this need not close their minds to wider concepts. His final words were:

> I ask that we should apply to Ireland that happy experience which we have gained in England and Scotland, where the course of generations has now taught us, not as a dream or a theory, but as practice and as life, that the best and surest foundation we can find to build upon is the foundation afforded by the affections, the convictions and the will of the nation; and it is there, by the decree of the Almighty, that we may be enabled to secure at once the social peace, the fame, the power and the permanence of the Empire.[14]

This speech was a considerable success, its reception leaving such an experienced observer as Hamilton with the impression that the bill would be carried on second reading, even though it would probably be 'scotched and killed in Committee or undergo most radical amendment'.[15] Gladstone was optimistic, hoping for a majority of well over twenty. He needed such buoyancy for the parliamentary pressures upon him were formidable. On the day after it he had an uncomfortable procedural entanglement with Chamberlain (over the latter's desire to refer in his resignation speech to the details of the Irish Land Bill, discussed in Cabinet but not already presented to Parliament). In the following week he had on the Monday to listen to the opposition of Hartington expressed in what was generally thought to be the most cogent and powerful speech of his life. (Opposing Gladstone instead of living on the same side under his great shadow seems to have had a stimulating effect on oratorical prowess, as Chamberlain's development also showed.) Then he wound up the first reading debate in a speech of one and a quarter hours after midnight at the end of the Tuesday sitting. On the Thursday he had to pay a tribute appropriate to the retirement of that legendary clerk Sir Erskine May as well as sustain Harcourt's first budget. And on the Friday he moved the first reading of the Irish Land Bill in a speech of more than two hours. For the principal performers at least the idea of nineteenth-century parliamentary life as a leisurely pursuit is untenable.

Moreover there was an uneasy feeling abroad that the movement of events was not favourable. This undercurrent surfaced disagreeably when Gladstone moved the second reading of the bill on 10 May. Like all great performers, Gladstone was never one to miss the reaction of the audience. 'Spoke 1¾ hours,' he wrote. 'The reception decidedly inferior to that of the Introduction [that is, the speech of 9 April].'[16] Hamilton was equally honest and more specific:

> It is clear that the speech will do little to improve the prospects of the measure. The concessions in the line of giving Ireland partial representation at Westminster will not satisfy Chamberlain & Co; and the concessions, such as they were, were not clearly explained. His voice was in bad order. At times he was nearly inaudible; though there were bursts of rhetoric occasionally when his animation and passion got the better of his huskiness I do not see now how defeat is to be avoided.[17]

It was not. The second-reading debate was an extraordinarily strung-out affair, even by the standards of the time. Twelve parliamentary days were devoted to this stage, but even more remarkable was the fact that they were spread out over a full lunar month. The vote on the motion which Gladstone had proposed on the first Monday in May came only during the sitting on the first Monday in June, and as was then usual barely before the next day's dawn. There had been a spiral of hope after 27 May when he had summoned and addressed for an hour in notably conciliatory terms a Liberal party meeting in the Foreign Office. If the bill were given a second reading, he almost pleaded, it would be withdrawn and reintroduced in the autumn with substantial concessions, particularly in relation to Irish representation at Westminster. Then, the next day in the House of Commons, Hicks Beach successfully provoked him into a hardening which confined the concessions to Clause 24 (Irish representation) points. He was also led into stressing (accurately but impolitically) that a vote for the bill was a vote for the bill and not just a vague aspiration towards a solution of the Irish problem. Probably this fencing did not matter. The die was already cast.

Gladstone of course wound up on the last night. He never delegated the crucial occasions, whether they were pregnant with defeat or triumph. He spoke of Ireland standing 'at your bar, expectant, hopeful, almost suppliant . . .', and the words might have applied to himself, except that he was not by that stage hopeful. The result was clear-cut. The bill was rejected by 341 to 311. Of the losing 311, 84 were Irish Nationalists, so that of the 333 members who had been elected as Liberals six months before only 229, including two tellers, went with Gladstone into the division lobby. Of the missing 103, a remarkably high proportion cast positive votes the other way. Only 10 were absent or abstained. All the notables, Chamberlain, Hartington, Trevelyan, Bright, Goschen, James, Collings, marched firmly into the Tory lobby.* It was one of the biggest divisions, physically as well as symbolically, in the history of Parliament. Of a total membership of 670, only 18 failed to vote. A curiosity was that a significantly higher proportion of Scottish than of English Liberal members – 37 per cent as against 19 per cent – failed to support Gladstone.

In whatever way it was made up the defection was horrifyingly large. It can, however, be argued that what was more surprising than the number of those who went the other way was that so many remained faithful, given the magnitude of the change and the abruptness with which the new policy was introduced, so soon after an election in which it had not figured either in the Liberal programme or in any of

* Dilke, however, gave what turned out to be his last vote for six years to the government, thereby marking the end of his partnership with Chamberlain.

Gladstone's own speeches. In whichever direction lay the reason for surprise there was no doubt that the vote had brought a phase of the government's life to an end. The possibilities were only resignation or dissolution. Gladstone was firmly for the latter, and had no difficulty in carrying his Cabinet with him. 'Dissolve *nem. con.*,' he minuted the decision at a noon meeting on the day after the vote. How sanguine he was about the result of an election is another matter. He ended a twelve-clause memorandum which he had quickly drawn up for his own use with the words: 'My conclusion is: a Dissolution is formidable but resignation would mean, for the present juncture, abandonment of *the cause*.'[18]

He had no trouble with the Queen on his request for a dissolution, young though the Parliament was. There were at least two reasons which would have weighed with her against the possibility of refusing. The first was that the leader of the Conservative party had already made his attempt to live with the 1885 House of Commons and had failed. The second was that she probably had a shrewd instinct for what the outcome of an election would be. There was unlikely to be any need for her to strain constitutional propriety and play around with the possibility of a Hartington-led and Conservative-supported government in order to get rid of Gladstone. And the electorate did indeed perform its loyal duty, producing an anti-Home Rule majority still more decisive than the House of Commons had done. But, unlike the House of Commons, which registered an almost uniquely full participation, the electorate did it largely by abstention.

On the surface at least the collapse of the vote between November–December 1885 and June–July 1886 was a psephological phenomenon without parallel. In the former general election nearly four million went to the polls. In the latter barely two and a half million did so. Boredom leading to abstention is always liable to be a factor when one general election quickly follows another. Between the two 1910 elections the turnout fell by about a sixth. But this was much less of a collapse than between 1885 and 1886, and between the two mass plebiscites of 1950 and 1951 there was hardly any decline. In 1886, however, there was a substantial countervailing factor, which was the exceptional number of unopposed returns. To some extent these could be regarded as a product of boredom. They were also influenced by the cleverly opportunistic Conservative willingness to withdraw candidates against Liberals, whether of the Hartington or Chamberlain persuasion, who voted against the bill. In Birmingham for instance, the five seats of Chamberlain's fief were all without a contest. In total 152 seats, as opposed to 23 in 1885, were in this category. If in just over 500 seats two and a half million voted, it may be roughly assumed that in the 129 seats which were fought in 1885 but not in 1886 another 600,000 might have done so. Even so, the decline in the participation between the two elections was striking. And it was concentrated on the collapse in the Liberal vote in the counties. In the boroughs the Liberals more or less held their own; they polled a few thousand more than the combined Unionist forces. But in the counties their vote, almost unbelievably, fell from 1,113,693 to 534,508. Even adjusting for the uncontested seats, this was a devastating price which Gladstone paid for first picking up Collings's amendment as a useful tactical instrument and then doing absolutely nothing about it, neither himself deflecting his eye from Ireland nor encouraging Chamberlain to pursue a parallel policy on behalf of the rural labourer. The casting of a Liberal vote in squirearchical villages, except on the great Whig estates, where the allegiance of the proprietor had in any event typically just changed, required some courage. Unfanned by attention, this mostly did not survive for a second go.

The collapse of the Liberal agricultural vote was the central element in the massive Liberal defeat. The Gladstonians retained only 193 seats, a result comparable with the Conservative massacres of 1906 and 1945 and with little else except when Liberal and Labour or Labour and the Liberal–Social Democrat Alliance were struggling over which should be the official opposition in modern British politics. Gladstone himself was a beneficiary of the smaller but not negligible number of unopposed Home Rule returns (forty-two); on 2 July he was elected without a contest,* but after a vigorous five-day visit to the constituency two weeks before. Exceptionally he stayed at the Royal Hotel in Princes Street and not at Dalmeny, but this appears to have been due to Rosebery's absorption in the Foreign Office rather than to any estrangement. Gladstone addressed his usual round of meetings, including a speech of one and a half hours in the Music Hall. Edinburghshire apart,

* He was also elected on the same day and equally unopposed for the separate constituency of Leith. This was a surprising but not inadvertent development. It was done with Gladstone's full if sudden concurrence. Suspicion developed that the intended Liberal candidate (Jacks) was lurching towards Unionism. Gladstone colluded with a few prominent local Liberals to elbow Jacks out of the way by allowing his own name to be put forward. After the election he opted for his normal seat of Midlothian, which led to an August bye-election in Leith. By that time, however, a satisfactory Home Rule candidate in the shape of Ronald Munro-Ferguson (later Lord Novar) had been procured, so that the manoeuvre served its purpose.

however, he spoke only in Glasgow, and in the following week in Manchester and Liverpool. Even these three occasions excited the Queen enough to cause her to remonstrate against the indignity of Prime Ministers taking part in elections.

After these few excursions Gladstone retired to Hawarden and stayed there (at first semi-solitarily, for his wife was in London) for sixteen days while the increasingly bad electoral news came in. On 3 July he thought only that 'the chances now are slightly against us',[19] but by the 8th he wrote starkly: 'The defeat is a smash.'[20] He read and wrote during the day, and then, evening after evening as the outlook became steadily worse, he walked across to the rectory to dine and play backgammon with his son Stephen. His outpouring of letters was even more voluminous than was his habit. He was still Prime Minister of course, although cut off from the machinery of government by 200 miles, except for the postal service supplemented by occasional telegrams. At one level he took his defeat with a resigned calm ('The Elections perturb me somewhat; but One ever sitteth above'),[21] reflecting that he would be as glad to end his painful relations with the Queen as she would to end hers with him. But at another level he became resentfully argumentative. He wrote two bitter letters of complaint to John Bright on 2 July. They were provoked by a speech of Bright's which Gladstone thought attacked his honour and his conduct and not merely his policy, and were remarkable for containing none of the expressions of personal esteem with which Gladstone normally cloaked his political disagreements, and for referring to their past association with more reproach than nostalgia.[22]

Then on 14 July he put on an imitation of the Queen and wrote to the Duke of Westminster,[23] ticking him off for electioneering, on the Unionist side of course. There was then a loose convention that the corollary of peers having no vote was that they should not attempt directly to influence the votes of others, and Salisbury had indeed subscribed to it to the extent of spending most of the campaign in the French spa of Royat. Gladstone no doubt thought that he had a special position *vis-à-vis* Westminster, whom he accused of having struck 'a fresh blow at the aristocracy', by virtue of having made him a duke twelve years before. But his action pointed to tetchiness as well as bossiness. And then, after he had returned to London, he suddenly wrote to Hartington peremptorily demanding chapter and verse for some statements in a speech which the latter had delivered no less than seven weeks earlier.

Gladstone's reactions to losing, as he certainly claimed, were genuinely based on considerations of public policy (his conviction of the urgency of the Irish issue and of his own solution having become the only viable one) rather than of personal convenience. He nonetheless reacted to it with some clear and engaging displays of human pique. What was less clear was how and when he ought to resign. Although he had indisputably lost, and lost heavily, the paradox was that Salisbury was not so indisputably the victor. He had 316 seats in a House of Commons with a membership of 670. Gladstonians and Irish Nationalists together constituted 278/280. (There were always one or two loose cards in any nineteenth-century party count, so that as often as lists were compiled so they produced very slightly varying totals.) Liberal Unionists (or 'seceding Liberals' as Gladstone preferred to call them) were mostly put at seventy-two or seventy-three, of whom around sixty were Hartington Whigs and around twelve Chamberlain Radicals. None of these wanted at this stage to enter a Conservative government, although Goschen (who was not, however, among the sixty Whigs, for he had been defeated in July) was to break ranks by becoming Chancellor of the Exchequer within a few months. No one indeed knew how far these Liberal Unionists would sustain Salisbury on anything other than Ireland. There was frequent talk of Liberal reunion over the next eighteen months, and the uncertainty was bizarrely illuminated by the fact that the essential component of the government's majority sat for the next six years on the opposition side of the House, Hartington and Chamberlain cheek by jowl with Gladstone and Harcourt on the same front bench. They rose to excoriate each other, and the leaders of the smaller group to give crucial support to the party opposite, from the same despatch box.

Despite the confusion the collective mind of the defeated Cabinet moved steadily towards an early resignation rather than waiting to meet the new Parliament. Those, notably Rosebery, who were less dedicated to Home Rule were always predisposed towards resignation, almost as the Spanish Falangists of the 1930s made 'Long live death' into a perverse slogan. And those, like Gladstone, Morley and Spencer, who had become so dedicated, recoiled from the only basis on which they could possibly live with the Parliament, which was that of an Irish policy (or lack of policy) acceptable to Hartington. Gladstone at last came to London on Wednesday, 14 July, held a Cabinet dinner on Saturday the 17th and a final Cabinet on the Tuesday the 20th, when the decision was unanimous, and the resignation was sent to the Queen that afternoon. She was at Osborne, and as had become usual during changes of ministry showed not the slightest disposition to come to London or even to Windsor.

Nor did she express a single word of regret (which might have been hypocritical) about Gladstone's departure, or of thanks for his third period of service as her first minister. She accepted the resignation at once, only reflecting that it might incommode Lord Salisbury by bringing him back two or three days early from his cure.

Even with his French sojourn so foreshortened it was 25 July before the new Prime Minister formally kissed hands. And it was another five days after that before Gladstone was summoned to the Isle of Wight for his farewell audience. The Queen found him 'pale and nervous' and complaining of his train being late. She had made no attempt to assuage the inconvenience of the day trip by offering him luncheon. He found her 'in good spirits' with 'her manners altogether pleasant'. He also noticed that during what he thought (falsely) might be his last audience after fifty-five years in political life and 'a good quarter of a century's service to her in office',[24] she was unwilling to discuss with him any matter of public substance except for civil list allowances for her grandchildren. The next day, however, she wrote him a letter which can be not unfairly summarized as rubbing in the point that she had always thought that his Irish policy was bound to fail, that she had been proved right in this, and that a period of silence from him on the issue would now be most welcome, as well as his clear patriotic duty.[25]

As Gladstone made his early-evening way back across the Solent after that ungrateful audience he was too absorbed in Robert Louis Stevenson's *Kidnapped*, which had just been published and which he read through complete in the day, to be obsessed with grievance. Nor was he really in a valedictory mood, however much, partly for the purposes of pointing up its barren thinness, he might suggest that the audience could be final. His seventy-seventh birthday was approaching but he did not regard himself as beaten on Ireland. One of the reasons that he gave (to Spencer on 4 July) for an early resignation was that 'if there is to be an anti-Irish Government the sooner it begins the sooner it will end'.[26] Even before the defeat was certain, his power of recovery was already enabling him to look to the next government but one. Nor was he any longer saying that the next battle must be fought by other and younger generals. The truth was that he trusted neither their judgement nor their martial determination. For himself, on the other hand, the twelve years which had gone by since his withdrawal of 1874 had increased rather than diminished his appetite for the fray. He set out his game plan for himself with great clarity in a letter to his Calcutta son on 16 July: 'What I think possible is that . . . I should obtain a dispensation from ordinary and habitual attendance in Parliament but should not lay down the leadership so as to force them to chose another leader; and should take an active part when occasion seemed to require it, especially on the Irish question.'[27]

To the implementation of this prescription he proceeded forthwith. He moved out of 10 Downing Street by the end of July. This was much easier for him than on the previous occasion when he had the accumulation of five years' residence. This time he had merely to pack a few crates of books and despatch them to the ever hospitable Lucy Cavendish at 21 Carlton House Terrace (he found it very difficult to keep away from one house or another on that old stamping ground), which he made his not greatly used base until the following spring when he effectively retreated to the Aberdeen-owned villa at Dollis Hill. In early August, however, he was mostly in the near countryside, first with Wolverton outside Kingston, then near Guildford with Sir Algernon West, his private secretary of the prosperous early years of his first government, whom he had made chairman of the Board of Inland Revenue in 1881, and finally outside Chislehurst with Charles Morley, the determinedly Liberal younger son of the Nottingham textile magnate. Gladstone was becoming increasingly fond, more so than of broad-acred ducal palaces, of well-appointed Home Counties residences of more comfort than fame in which the life of the house and the services of the household revolved around himself.

From these various bases he descended upon the House of Commons for three leader's speeches. He seconded the re-election of Speaker Peel, he spoke on the first day of the debate on the Address, and five days later he made a further intervention, this time for fifty minutes, on Irish land, and involving some altercation with the Speaker, whom he had so recently supported. Then he disappeared to Bavaria and Austria for three and a half weeks, although the unusually timed session of Parliament continued throughout this period and up to the last week of September. Lord Acton, but not Catherine Gladstone, was with him. Theological conversations with the now aged Dr Döllinger (eighty-seven) were once again the principal object of the visit, although the scenery of the Traunsee and the Halstattersee attracted much admiration. Lehnbach, the portraitist of 1879, had also survived and on this visit did a double portrait of Döllinger and Gladstone which until recently hung in the German Embassy in London.

Gladstone regained London on Sunday, 19 September, and on the following day gave qualified support to an Irish Tenants Relief Bill which Parnell had introduced. On the Tuesday, he voted for it in a division of 202 against 297, which figures neatly illustrated the balance of the Parliament, an unassailable but not overwhelming anti-Irish majority. On the Wednesday afternoon he went to Hawarden, and stayed there for 125 consecutive nights, the longest continuous period that he ever spent under the Hawarden roof, or for that matter any other roof, between his marriage in 1839 and his death in 1898. He was not giving up, but he was husbanding his energies, which he recognized to be in decline. The question was whether, in Aberdeen's immortal phrase, he was once again capable of being 'terrible in the rebound'.

33

'The Union – and Disunion – of Hearts'

GLADSTONE'S HOPE THAT if an 'anti-Irish' government were allowed quickly in it could be got quickly out proved ill founded. The second Salisbury administration, despite its unclear majority, lasted with authority for six years. This was principally due to the mounting implacability of the Liberal Unionists towards Home Rule and therefore towards the prospect of a fourth Gladstone government. At the beginning of 1887 Chamberlain flirted with the possibility of Liberal reunion, and there was a round-table conference at which Harcourt performed as an eager rather than a neat bridge-builder. Gladstone gave him some discretion, but not too much, for he did not really want Chamberlain back. As a result the enterprise achieved little except for the return of Trevelyan, which might have happened in any event.

Chamberlain, who was a naturally implacable man, then moved hard in the other direction. Hartington stood back from these negotiations at least as much as did Gladstone, and gave the impression that he was glad to be free of the Liberal cage, although this was paradoxical given that he had fled from it in company with Chamberlain, the man principally responsible for making its confines intolerable to him. Hartington was, however, highly susceptible to that anti-Irish *furia* which infected many otherwise calm Englishmen of his and the next generation. When Parnell was ruined by the O'Shea divorce case he told the Queen with an uncharacteristic lack of generosity, particularly in view of his own domestic arrangements with the Duchess of Manchester (not regularized until two years later), that 'I never thought anything in politics could give me as much pleasure as this does.'[1]

The Conservative government also gained authority through a successful ministerial performance. Randolph Churchill as Chancellor blew himself up within five months and Hicks Beach retired hurt from the Irish Office three months later. But their replacements were successful ministers: first Goschen, that nominally cross-party figure of weight and talent, a forerunner of Milner and Waverley (John Anderson); and second Arthur Balfour, who so ruthlessly demonstrated his languid steel in Ireland that his sobriquet changed from 'Pretty Fanny' to 'Bloody Balfour'. Also successful was W. H. Smith, who at the same time moved from the War Office to the leadership of the House of Commons with the grand title of First Lord of the Treasury, which Gladstone thought improper for Salisbury to separate from the premiership. Together they constituted a formidable House of Commons trio.

Balfour was the key figure of the three. He was the agent of Salisbury's perception, in contrast with Gladstone's, that Ireland could be governed from London for another generation. Gladstone's long-term view was both more clear-sighted and more imaginative than Salisbury's. He saw that quick Home Rule offered the only prospect of keeping Ireland permanently within the British connection. But Salisbury's short- to medium-term judgement was cooler. Gladstone convinced himself in 1885–6 that civic order was about to dissolve in Ireland. That conviction, together with his age, made him in a hurry.* Salisbury thought that Gladstone's imagination had become fevered, that the resources of coercion were not yet exhausted, and that it was mostly a question of nerve. And in Balfour, literally nepotistic though his appointment was, Salisbury found the ideal instrument of unsentimental repression, combined with the intelligence to mingle a little reform with the iron fist. Balfour's determination both secured his own passport to the premiership and strengthened the evolving alliance with Hartington and Chamberlain, the key to the twenty years of Unionist hegemony which began in 1886.

Despite these adverse underlying political currents Gladstone's morale was on the whole high during the first four years of that Salisbury government. By the end of this period he was aged nearly eighty-one, and with this advance there undoubtedly went some failing of powers. Both his hearing and his eyesight deteriorated, the former to such an extent that he found theatre-going, which had played a great part in his life for the previous twenty years, had become pointless. This was after an intermediate phase when he tried by a special dispensation the device of sitting on a corner of the stage. In the same way poor vision caused him somewhat to restrict his reading (although not as much as in his fourth government), and was one of the reasons for his growing addiction to backgammon, which consumed after-dinner hours when in

* Lord Randolph Churchill, a master of anti-Gladstone jibes, had in his June 1886 election address bestowed upon him the unforgettable epithet of 'an old man in a hurry'.

earlier years he might have read. His memory, particularly for names but also for recent events, although not for more distant ones, showed signs of fading. From the spring of 1887 there began to be occasional gaps in his diary entries because when he came to write them up in the evening he simply could not remember the names of some to whom he had written in the morning.

On the other hand his physical stamina remained formidable. He felled his last tree a few weeks before his eighty-second birthday, but for a couple of years before that final event he had begun to substitute for arboreal activity the almost equally strenuous one of first sorting and then moving (mostly by wheelbarrow) large quantities of books to St Deiniol's Library in Hawarden village. This institution for residential scholars he founded as a sort of advance memorial in 1889; unlike American presidential libraries however it was not a shell for Gladstone memorabilia but a serious theological and historical research library.

He continued to walk well and to be physically agile. When earlier in that same year of 1889 he was knocked down in London by a passing cab, he got up, pursued the errant driver and held him until the police came. His stamina also showed in his ability to address large audiences for long periods, although this had become almost a reflex action on his part. In the autumn of 1888, on a return National Liberal Federation visit to Bingley Hall in Birmingham, although in contrast with 1877 without Chamberlain as master of ceremonies or even in the audience, he had addressed 20,000 for one and three-quarter hours.

The essence of his good morale during these years was that he was of settled mind so far as his own political future was concerned. He would remain leader of the Liberal party so long as he could see the prospect of settling the Irish question. He had one more river to cross, and that, if not the river Jordan, was a mixture of the Liffey and the Thames, for it was not simply justice in isolation for Ireland, but the reconciliation of Ireland to Britain which inspired him. From his own point of view the advantage was that it gave a continuing but not time-fixed purpose to his life in his late seventies and early eighties. The frequent menace of old age is that it imprisons its victim in a departure lounge of life,* awaiting with a mixture of apprehension and impatience the announcement that the aircraft is ready. Gladstone's sense that he had 'one fight more, the best and the last' (in the words of Browning's *Prospice*) was a tremendous prophylactic against senile futility. While he had a cause,

* The starkly memorable phrase is Sir Robin Day's.

the future lay before him, unbounded except by the prospect of a final success. His energies might be running out but his life was not running down. For the 1890 session he even rented a London house of his own, 10 St James's Square, now the Royal Institute of International Affairs, which had been previously lived in by two other Prime Ministers, Chatham and Derby.

On this basis of expectation he was content to spend long autumns at Hawarden, followed over the turn of the years 1887–8 and 1888–9 with six- to eight-week excursions to Florence on the first occasion and Naples on the second. Each trip was rounded off with a few days in Cannes, which under Rendel and Acton auspices was becoming a favourite resort. At home his country-house visiting, particularly to the very grand establishments, became less frequent. There were many fewer Whig magnates whom he wished to visit or who would have enjoyed entertaining him. He did, however, make a twelve-day West Country Whitsun tour in 1889, which included visits to four houses as well as five nights on the yacht of a Rothschild daughter and several speeches. He was '*delighted*' with the still incomplete Truro Cathedral and regarded Sir William Harcourt's equally new example of the style sometimes known as Parliamentary Tudor, appropriately set in the New Forest, as 'a marvellous creation'.[2] He paid only one constituency visit between the general elections of 1886 and 1892, but that was a substantial one, lasting a week in the autumn of 1890. Lady Rosebery, still a young woman, was dying at Dalmeny, so he stayed with the Dean of the Faculty of Advocates in the Edinburgh New Town. He made four major speeches, two minor ones and visited the newly opened Forth railway bridge.

In general his non-parliamentary speech-making was active during those years. He addressed the annual meetings of the National Liberal Federation not only on the already mentioned Birmingham occasion in 1888, but also at Nottingham in 1887, and Manchester in 1889. He had previously decided to miss the Sheffield gathering in 1890, which was lucky as it fell in the immediate shadow of the Parnell divorce case, to the considerable embarrassment of Harcourt and Morley, who had to perform in his absence. At Newcastle in 1891, to cast forward a little, he was again present and orating, but more mechanically, more floridly and less magisterially than usual. Despite his often imperious attitude to constituencies and followers, he was the first party leader to make a fixture of party conferences. He also addressed major provincial meetings at Swansea, Cardiff, Plymouth and Dundee.

Neither his advancing years nor his concentration upon, almost his obsession with, a single political objective produced any marked diminution in his intellectual activity. Despite his increasing eyesight problem, he was still reading voraciously. His count of books and pamphlets read in 1890, his eighty-first year, for instance, gave the almost incredible figure of 419, supplemented by 39 periodical articles. And his writing also remained prolific. In that same turn-of-the-decade year he earned from articles and reviews a sum of just over £1915,[3] the rough equivalent of £95,000 today.

Gladstone's contemporaries, and some who were younger, began to drop around him almost like flies. Phillimore, probably his oldest friend had gone in 1885; in 1889 Bright went in March, as did Gladstone's sole surviving brother, Sir Thomas; in 1890 Döllinger and Newman died; in 1891 Granville, his oldest political collaborator; and in 1892 Manning and Tennyson. Gladstone took all these deaths with fortitude. This may have been partly because of the strength of his Christian faith. But it also owed much to his sense of his mission and responsibilities as a great commander who, when he heard painful news of illustrious casualties, whether on his own side or the other, could not be distracted from his duties and his strategy. He may indeed have been more affected by the deaths, a couple of years later, of his doctor, (Sir) Andrew Clark, and his valet, Zadok Outram, who after many years in Gladstone's service became an alcoholic and then drowned himself in the Thames. They were operational staff, necessary for the conduct of the campaign.

That strategy, which particularly in the two years from the second half of 1888 to late 1890 (when twelve seats changed from Conservative to Liberal at by-elections) showed strong signs of working well, depended crucially on the partnership with Parnell. This prospered and then festered with an heroic reversal of fortune more akin to the heights and depths of Greek tragedy than to the normally mild landscape of Victorian England. This final phase of Gladstone's relations with Parnell revolved around two of the most famous lawsuits of the late nineteenth century, which was the classical age of not only parliamentary politics but also of great trials with gladiatorial advocates and dramatic denouements. The librettos of Sir W. S. Gilbert were the house ballads of both the Palace of Westminster and the Royal Courts of Justice. These two legal processes were separated from each other by little more than eighteen months, but produced violent fluctuations in Parnell's reputation and hence, perhaps more inevitably than admirably, in Gladstone's attitude to him. In April 1887 *The Times* produced a damaging and, as was demonstrated nearly two years later, entirely unfounded libel of Parnell. They published forged letters in which Parnell appeared to apologize to some of his nationalist supporters for his 'tactical' denunciation of the Phoenix Park atrocity. He hesitated to sue because of suspicion about the prejudices of a propertied London jury. Eventually, however, the government set up a most unfavourable form of enquiry, which was a Special Commission of one lord justice of appeal and two puisne judges, Unionists to a man, who, moreover, were set to investigate every alleged Fenian crime of the previous ten years or more. In spite of this penumbra of obfuscation the Special Commission could not avoid, on its fiftieth sitting day, 21 February 1889, getting to the gravamen. Pigott, the purveyor of the letters, was then so mauled by Parnell's counsel, Sir Charles Russell, that he fled to Madrid rather than face another day's cross-examination, and there committed suicide. Asquith, at the time only a junior barrister standing in for an exhausted Russell, completed the rout by exposing the prejudiced irresponsibility of Macdonald, the manager of *The Times*.

Parnell next experienced a brief period when he was almost beatified in Liberal circles, while his Unionist enemies, from the Attorney-General (Sir Richard Webster), who had been pressurized by the Prime Minister ingloriously to appear for *The Times*, to Joseph Chamberlain, who had become Parnell's dedicated foe and had done much to push the government into setting up the prejudiced enquiry, were temporarily too demoralized to stand against the tide. A week after his vindication (and at just about the hour, as it happened, that Pigott was blowing his brains out at the Hotel Embajadores in Madrid) Parnell went to the House of Commons to make a speech in the general debate at the opening of the new session. He was greeted with an extraordinary standing ovation from the Liberal and Irish benches, led by Gladstone. Edward Hamilton described it as 'unprecedented' and 'rather overstepping the bounds of decorum'.

A month later Parnell dined with the Gladstones in a party of ten. Gladstone described the occasion as 'a Parnell entertainment'[4] and was reported as being 'much pleased' with him. This led on to the apogee of the partnership, which was Parnell's overnight visit to Hawarden on 18 December. He and Gladstone had four hours' solid bilateral conversation, partly that evening and partly the next morning. In addition to that and the normal meals, he was taken round the ruined castle by Gladstone and accompanied the two younger sons on a shooting expedition. He could hardly have made a more favourable impression, political and social. Gladstone wrote: 'He is certainly one of the very best people to deal with that I have ever known. . . . He seems to notice and appreciate everything.'[5] So, it might cynically be commented, do the needs of political alliance, if not frustrated by antipathy, cast a roseate glow over even the most experienced of politicians. Parnell, for his part, went from Hawarden to Liverpool after luncheon on the 19th and there commented, in public, and with almost equal enthusiasm on the talks.

What was just as exceptional as the House of Commons ovation was the complete indifference with which Parnell treated it. He sat impassively until it subsided, and then rose and made a run-of-the-mill speech without any reference to the demonstration. His cold composure made a particular impression across the House on the Tory Solicitor-General, Sir Edward Clarke. Clarke thought the scene 'might have disturbed the balance of mind of a smaller man'.[6] His admiration for Parnell's stature did not, however, cause him to pull any punches when, twenty months later, he appeared as counsel for O'Shea in his divorce suit against his wife and led the Captain through the most damaging and often untrue but uncontradicted allegations against Parnell as co-respondent.

They were uncontradicted because Parnell, after assuring both his own followers and John Morley as the principal Liberal liaison officer that nothing damaging would come out, seemed to have become indifferent to everything except Mrs O'Shea's freedom to become his wife, and he did not take the trouble to be represented by counsel or to instruct Mrs O'Shea's QC to cross-examine her husband on any of his allegations, several of which could easily have been disproved or at least severely shaken. On the day of the hearing Parnell remained at Brighton with Mrs O'Shea, simply saying, when she urged him to go to London and the Law Courts: 'What's the use, we want the divorce. . . .'[7] The case moved to a conclusion with the extraordinary spectacle of one of the jurors expressing his disquietude at this absence of cross-examination, asking for O'Shea to be recalled, and himself attempting to do the job in an amateur and unprepared way.

This quietism in the face of the charges terminated Parnell's prospects of constructive statesmanship. Until the second trial he seemed set upon a classic path: an organizer of intransigence who, after a qualifying period in gaol, became a moderate, even a conservative founder of a new polity, a Nelson Mandela of a hundred years earlier. When the divorce-court verdict was given, on 18 November 1890, it did not exactly destroy his influence, for that remained immanent in Irish politics for many decades after both his 'disgrace' and his death eleven months later. Henceforward however he became a divisive rather than the unifying factor which he had hitherto been.

It was the ridicule to which he allowed O'Shea and Clarke to expose him, even more than the alleged moral turpitude, which was destructive. He was suddenly changed from the remote leader who had stalked with equal and godlike indifference through the corridors of the House of Commons and the market towns of Ireland into the co-respondent who, when O'Shea had unexpectedly arrived, had shinned down the fire-escape of a Brighton lodgings in order that he might deceptively re-present himself at the front door a few minutes later.

In fact the 'fire escape' evidence was doubtful and could have been largely destroyed by any competent cross-examination of the uncorroborated servant who gave it. But as Parnell did not take the trouble to do this, it damagingly stuck. It was however in no way the decisive factor which led Gladstone to repudiate him, and by so doing to stultify the end of his own political life as well as to turn Parnell from a (superficially at least) disciplined and dedicated ally into a wildly destructive force.

Did Gladstone have any practical alternative? He never moralized about the case. Indeed he declined to do so in the most explicit terms. He was recorded by Morley (who when writing of this stage of Gladstone's life did so as his closest parliamentary colleague as well as his biographer) as saying: 'What, because a man is called leader of a party, does that constitute him a censor and a judge of faith and morals? I will not accept it. It would make life intolerable.'[8] Gladstone could often be self-righteous and sometimes priggish, but he was not a hypocrite, and he had seen too much of life and enjoyed the company of too many women whose virtue was not perfect for a straightforward even if long-standing case of adultery to cause him moral revulsion. Furthermore, he must have been uneasily aware of how often he had heard rumour or more of Parnell's relationship with Mrs O'Shea without it causing him either to decline dealings with the Irish leader or to avoid Mrs O'Shea herself as an occasional go-between.* As soon as the outcome of the divorce case was known, Gladstone took his stand on the likely political consequences and not on morals. And to this position he stuck.

The nearest he ever got to making a moral as opposed to a tactical

* He saw her three times in 1882, and in the subsequent six years wrote her twenty-five letters.

judgement was when he wrote to Morley on the eve of the annual meeting of the National Liberal Federation, which took place at Sheffield on 20–21 November. Morley had written asking for guidance on what he should say. Gladstone replied that 'abstractly it was for the Irish to decide whether or not Parnell remained their leader'. Then he referred to Parnell's 'enormous services – he has done for Home Rule something like what Cobden did for free trade, set the argument on its legs'. He concluded, however, that although the Liberal leaders must for the moment 'be passive, must wait and watch', he could not avoid saying to himself 'I mean in the interior and silent forum, "It'll na dee."'[9]

He was more disposed to be tolerant than either of his principal lieutenants, partly because of his instinctive liking for Parnell, which was there before they broke, and which resurfaced, despite the virulence of Parnell's 'rat-in-the-corner' attacks upon him, after the latter's death in October 1891. Morley, in spite of his commitment to Gladstone and to Home Rule, never fully appreciated Parnell's quality of non-intellectual grandeur, and Harcourt simply did not like him, as indeed he disliked the Irish as a whole, even if they were Protestant and landed.

There were, however, plenty of Liberal supporters who were disposed to make up for any eschewal of moralizing by Gladstone, and to go far beyond Morley or Harcourt. Gladstone's problem must be seen against the background of the immensely difficult feat of political engineering to which he had set his hand, which was to concentrate the main political energies of the heavily Nonconformist Liberal party on the handing over of Ireland to a régime which would be dominantly Catholic and might result in a confessional state. This delicate alliance was peculiarly liable to be upset by any issue of sexual morality which could set both sides off on a 'holier-than-thou' competition.

Thus the Irish prelates, after a momentary pause for breath, turned solidly against the leader. Dr Croke of Cashel, the most nationalist of the four Catholic archbishops, threw out a bust of Parnell from his palace. Dr Walsh of Dublin demanded his resignation. The Bishop of Ardagh said that no man false to God and friendship could be true to his country, 'especially that country being Catholic Ireland'.[10] From London Cardinal Manning lobbied Gladstone, the Pope and the Irish hierarchy against Parnell.

Despite this, the barrage from the other side of the religious divide contained plenty of anti-Catholic feeling. *The Times*, hardly a Nonconformist organ but certainly a Protestant one and with a heavy anti-Parnell score to pay off, managed a comment which was as skilful in mobilizing favourite British anti-French prejudices as it was inapposite to what had by any standards been one of the most dominating and persistent love affairs ever to impinge on British political history. It described the Parnell–Mrs O'Shea relationship as 'a story of dull ignoble infidelity, untouched, so far as can be seen, by a single ray of sentiment, a single flash of passion, and comparable only to the dreary monotony of French middle-class vice, over which M. Zola's scalpel so lovingly lingers'.

The Nonconformist divines did not allow themselves to be out-thundered by 'The Thunderer'. The Revd Hugh Price Hughes of the West London Methodist Mission produced some of the most extreme anti-Irish invective. 'We do not hesitate to say', he wrote:

> that if the Irish race deliberately select as their recognized representative an adulterer of Mr Parnell's type they are as incapable of self-government as their bitterest enemies have asserted. So obscene a race in those circumstances they would prove themselves to be would obviously be unfit for anything except a military despotism.[11]

A week later, lest anyone had found his previous meaning too delicate to be fully grasped, and worried by any sullying of the innocence of his seventy-one-year-old sovereign, he told a St James's Hall meeting that 'it would be an infamous thing for any Englishman to compel his chaste and virtuous Queen to receive as her first Irish Prime Minister an adulterer of this type'. Dr John Clifford of the Praed Street Baptist Church, and so unflagging a Nonconformist controversialist that he survived first to figure in 'Chuck it Smith', Chesterton's immortal 1912 poetic satire, and then to be made a Companion of Honour by Lloyd George in 1921, was not disposed to lag behind the Methodists, and added to the spate of denunciation. There was also a strong barrage from the Liberal press, although it was by no means unanimous.

Could and should Gladstone have resisted the Nonconformist clamour? J. L. Hammond, who remains the most penetrating historian of Gladstone's relations with Ireland, thought that he could not. When he had last ignored Nonconformist opinion over the Education Bill of 1870 this had led to the disastrous general election of 1874. A repeat of that experience would be a roadblock insurmountable in Gladstone's lifetime. Given the certain hostility of the House of Lords the only hope of carrying Home Rule lay in securing a massive Liberal majority at the next general election which, with the support of over eighty Irish MPs, could steamroller the remaining Unionist members and intimidate the

Unionist peers. Before the Parnell divorce trial the by-elections suggested that such a result was likely. But if the Nonconformists stood off there was no hope in achieving it.

On the other hand there is in the view of Francis Birrell,* whose 1933 biographical essay on the Grand Old Man is one of the best things in the whole enormous Gladstone bibliography. It was highly praised by Hammond, even though they differed in conclusion on this point. Birrell thought it a tragedy that, among the triumvirate composed of the Anglo-Catholic Gladstone, the Erastian Harcourt and the agnostic Morley, there was no one with any inside knowledge of Nonconformity. As a result they took its fulminations too seriously. A Lloyd George, even a Bright, 'might have taken the bluster at its proper value'.[12]

Birrell puts the main blame on Morley and Harcourt, and Hammond agrees with him to the extent of writing: 'Harcourt's influence at this time was a calamity.'[13] Between them Morley and Harcourt played a key role in getting Gladstone to write his unfortunate, even disastrous letter of 24 November 1890. This was addressed to Morley, although since much of it was written by Morley himself this was a convoluted exercise. Gladstone's letter was designed to prevent the continuation of Parnell as Irish leader. Its key phrase, a Morley insertion (although with Gladstone's reluctant approval) was that 'the continuance I speak of [that is, Parnell at the head of the Irish party] ... would render my retention of the leadership of the Liberal party, based as it has been mainly upon the prosecution of the Irish cause, almost a nullity'.[14]

The purpose of the letter was for Morley to show it to Parnell before the meeting of the Irish parliamentary party fixed for 25 November. Such a tactic ignored Parnell's well-known elusiveness. His capacity for going to ground was formidable. For years previously, at least since 1883 or 1884, his colleagues had often been out of contact with him for months at a time. And at this crucial phase he had no intention of making himself available to unwelcome influence. The nearest that anyone got to him before the meeting was his deputy, Justin McCarthy, cultivated and amiable but hardly forceful, who was briefed by Morley and who caught up with Parnell at the House of Commons post office where he was collecting his mail before proceeding to the meeting. McCarthy then trotted beside him to the upstairs committee room but

* Francis Birrell was the son of Augustine Birrell, the famous wit who was Chief Secretary for Ireland from 1908 to 1916, but whose *bons mots* were inadequate to stop the birth of 'a terrible beauty' in the Easter Rebellion.

failed to divert his attention from the opening of letters, which included nothing from Gladstone or Morley. The meeting, still rather in a trance like an equally supine one in the Leinster Hall in Dublin five days earlier, and ignorant of Gladstone's letter, proceeded to re-elect him as leader with only one semi-dissentient.

As Parnell walked away from this scene of superficial endorsement, Morley at last fell in with him and read him Gladstone's letter. Parnell took it with some equanimity, being able to inform Morley in return of his re-election and thus hardly needing to say that the letter had become otiose. So as an appeal it had, but not as an excommunication, into which the triumvirate proceeded to turn it. Within an hour or so it was given to the press and became the major political sensation of the next few days. There was, perhaps inevitably, some dispute about who among the three cried forward and who cried back.

What is more certain is that publication turned Parnell from a disciplined auxiliary of Gladstone into a bitter enemy (within a fortnight he was referring to him as 'an unrivalled sophist', and denouncing the unsatisfactory form of Home Rule which, Parnell suddenly claimed, was all that he had been offered during the Hawarden visit). He also set himself up as henceforward the firm foe of any British political alliance. Anglo-Irish trust was dead. The virulence of Parnell's reaction was no doubt made the greater by the highly unbalanced state to which his ill health (he was to be dead within a year) and his other vicissitudes, all playing on an inherently unstable personality, had reduced him.

There may also have been a more subtle factor at work. F. S. L. Lyons thought that by 1890, independently of the divorce case and indeed before its impact, Parnell's position 'in his own country and even in his own party had begun ... to exhibit ominous signs of deterioration'.[15] His absorption with Mrs O'Shea (and maybe other features of his character) had led to his taking for granted both his nation and his colleagues. It was, amazingly, five years since he had made a speech in Ireland, and at least two years since he had played any effective role in Parliament. He had stood back completely from the Plan of Campaign which Dillon and William O'Brien had launched in the autumn of 1886 and which for the closing years of the decade had been the main form of on-the-ground protest in Ireland. The effect of this disdainful neglect produced only a gradual and tentative alienation. On a person of Parnell's temperament, however, any slow recognition of this was likely to make him more and not less imperious, and his judgement worse and not better.

The publication of the Gladstone–Morley letter also had the effect of throwing a burning brand into the tinder box of the Irish parliamentary party. They had been bounced into agreeing to Parnell's re-election, but they were far from willing to follow him in a repudiation of the Liberal alliance which had brought them almost within sight of the promised land. It was Parnell himself who had taught them that the constitutional route was the correct one, and the wrench at the last stage of falling back on the violence of the 'hillside men' was more than most of them could contemplate, agonizing though was the conflict of loyalties. They were also no doubt influenced, to greater or lesser extents according to their individual positions, by the solidifying of the Catholic hierarchy against Parnell.

These various tensions were poured into the cauldron of the unparalleled, sometimes bitter, immensely long-drawn-out Committee Room 15 debates of 1–6 December. From a Monday to a Saturday in gothic gloom at the end of the upstairs corridor of the House of Commons, the Irish parliamentary party thrashed out the issue. There were mostly about seventy members present. One session lasted eleven hours. Parnell presided throughout and added a farcical touch by some procedural rulings straight out of *Alice in Wonderland*. But there was always more drama than boredom in the proceedings. Timothy Healy's Saturday taunt – 'and who is to be mistress of the party?' – in reply to John Redmond's complaint that Gladstone was 'the master of the party' was as unforgettable as it was unforgivable, but it was no more than the culmination of a series of memorable and increasingly vicious exchanges.

The only other party since the building of the present Palace of Westminster which it is possible to contemplate indulging in such a feat of self-absorbed yet semi-inspired navel-gazing is the 1950s Labour party, and even those stalwarts of brotherly distrust would not have had this degree of stamina. The immediate result was that the Irish split nearly two to one against Parnell and henceforward sat in the chamber as two parties, their relations characterized by a bewildering mixture of intense hostility and occasional rather dream-like acts of mutual courtesy and friendliness.

Parnell set off to put to the proof his thesis that Ireland was with him even if its craven representatives were not. Dublin remained enthusiastic for its 'uncrowned king'. Cork, his own constituency, was more equivocal. By the stringent test of by-elections, however, he met defeat after defeat. Kilkenny North before Christmas, North Sligo in April 1891 (his best result) and Carlow in the early summer.* He consumed his small remaining reserves of strength in these and other campaigns. He married Mrs O'Shea in June. He was dead aged forty-six in October.

Gladstone retained the leadership of the Liberal party, for the majority of the Irish parliamentary party had acted as he had asked them to do. But his leadership had nonetheless become 'almost a nullity'. The golden prospect of a large Home Rule majority depended upon the fervent atmosphere of the 'union of hearts' holding Irish Catholicism and British Nonconformity in improbable alliance. And the 'union of hearts' depended upon two commanding if utterly different leaders, Gladstone and Parnell, working together in amity. Could more have been saved from the wreck if Gladstone had preserved the goodwill of Parnell by taking the risk of extending the hand of tolerance towards him and genuinely leaving it to the Irish to decide untrammelled? Gladstone would no doubt have had to face a barrage of protest, but his authority was great and he was too old to be frightened.

Nor was he without supporters who thought that, in a fraught situation, this might be a wiser course. Morley might cluck and Harcourt might glower, but Spencer who after nearly nine years as Viceroy knew more about Ireland than either of them, and Asquith, who was to be the most effective member of the weak 1892 government and the first (and last) major leader of the Liberal party after Gladstone, both thought that this would have been the wiser course. It would not necessarily have saved Parnell. The influence of the hierarchy might have disposed of him in any event. But it might have avoided the death throes (politically as well as almost literally) of Parnell being turned against the English connection, and his consequently leaving a legacy which over thirty years proved fatal to the solution of the Irish problem within a British context.

* These defeats (the victors were the candidates put up by Healy and McCarthy as the acting leaders of the majority of the Irish parliamentary party) accurately presaged the result in Ireland of the 1892 general election, when the anti-Parnellites won seventy-one seats and the supporters of the dead leader only nine.

34
The Leaden Victory

After the Parnell débâcle and the smash-up of the Irish party Gladstone became a half-broken man. His optimism before these events had perhaps been excessive. On the basis of twelve by-election victories he regarded a massive Liberal majority at an 1891 or 1892 general election as a virtual certainty. This majority allied to a solid and moderate Nationalist phalanx under Parnell's firm command would intimidate the House of Lords so that a Home Rule Bill could be quickly enacted. With this crowning pediment placed upon his life's work Gladstone could then hand over the premiership (to whom, had he been allowed to exercise his preference, was never consistently clear) and devote such years as remained for him to a quiet communing with his God. He no longer saw himself as writing great works of theology, but he did see the need to settle his soul after the secular buffetings of sixty years in politics. This prospect led him into a series of remarkably benign end-year musings. The self-flagellation (metaphorical as well as literal) of *circa* 1850 was far behind him. On his eightieth birthday at the end of 1889 he wrote: 'Excellent sermons All things smile.' And two days later: 'And so the year has rolled into the great bosom of the Past. We had a grand dinner of 12 at the Rectory. S[tephen] & I played backgammon. The Castle topsy turvy as usual at Xmas: but many are made innocently happy. *Benedictus benedicat*.'[1]

His mood a year later was transformed, and very much for the worse. The new sombreness, however, took a little time to settle. It required evidence both from Ireland of Parnell's destructive fighting strength on the ground and from England of a decisive change in the electoral trend. The latter turned on the Bassetlaw by-election, in which polling took place in mid-December. Gladstone if anything invested it with too much importance, as he had perhaps done with the favourable results of the previous two years. On 11 December he went there himself and addressed meetings in Retford and Worksop, the two principal towns of the somewhat amorphous and uninformatively named Nottinghamshire constituency. It was familiar ground for him with Clumber Park, where he had begun his political career by waiting on the Duke of Newcastle fifty-six years before, almost in the suburbs of Worksop. But it was far from a familiar gesture from a party leader, particularly one who had been three times Prime Minister. Even in the third quarter of the twentieth century party leaders stood back from bye-elections, and in the last quarter of the nineteenth century such an intervention was wholly unprecedented. Nor did it work. Bassetlaw, which in 1885 had produced a narrow Tory majority of 295 (in 1886 the seat was uncontested), dramatically broke the previous trend and put the Tory majority up to 725.

Gladstone, who was at Hawarden,* at first received the news, even in the privacy of his diary, with a superficial 'looking on the bright side' worthy of a modern party spokesman: 'Bassetlaw defeat. A lesson: but the reading of it not yet clear.'[2] On the next day, however, Morley, calling for a morning and luncheon visit on his way from Dublin to London, found him looking like 'some strange Ancient of Days: so different from the man I had seen off at King's Cross [for Retford] less than a week before'. Morley then recorded Gladstone as saying: 'Bassetlaw looks as if we were going back to 1886. For me that is notice to quit. Another five years' agitation at my age would be impossible – *ludicrous* (with much emphasis).'[3]

This was not exactly the way in which he saw the prospect in his year-end summing up of 1890. The horizon had certainly darkened, and most oppressively so: 'We may if things do not go decisively well in Ireland lose hold of that margin which in the constituencies spans the space between victory and defeat. Home Rule *may* be postponed for another period of five or six years. The struggle in that case must survive me, cannot be survived by me.' But he still saw himself as a conscript – even if the commander-in-chief – in the army of justice for Ireland. It was his hopes for a furlough before the end which was the certain casualty, not necessarily the Irish goal or even his own part in securing it:

> O! 'tis a burden, Cromwell, 'tis a burden
> Too heavy for a man that hopes for heaven.[4]

'Undoubtedly it is a new and aggravated condition of my life', he continued, 'if I am finally to resign all hope of anything resembling a brief rest on this side the grave.'[5] Gladstone did not succumb. By this

* He had gone there direct from Worksop, accomplishing the whole swing from London via Retford in seven hours, a tribute to the railway system of 1890 and, for once, his restraint in the length of his speeches.

stage he was almost constitutionally incapable of giving up. But the new and gloomier prospect lowered his spirits and took some of the zest out of even his sanguine temperament.

Between December 1890 and the date which Salisbury chose for the 1892 election (about a year before the statutory limit on the life of the Parliament) there was an interval of eighteen months. During this period Gladstone continued to hope for but hardly to expect an adequate victory, and there is a feeling that his life was on a lower key than had ever previously been the case. It would, for instance, have been difficult to imagine his repeating in February 1891 or 1892 the visit, lasting no less than eight days, which he paid to All Souls College, Oxford, in that month of 1890. There he charmed everybody, and particularly the most die-hard Tories, of which All Souls had a fair quota, by his courtesy, his innocence and the range of his reminiscent conversations. The pleasure was mutual and he wrote to his wife: 'I am reading the Lessons and all sorts of things – such pranks!',[6] while to his diary he gave an impression of unrelenting entertainment and enjoyment: '9–11¾. Breakfast at Magdalen: a gigantic dissipation. Luncheon at Exeter (Prof. Pelham). Dinner at the Vice Chancellor's (St. John's) with the Club [a still extant Oxford institution, not to be confused with Dr Johnson's foundation, The Club, in London]. Read Shakespeare – Tracts on Oxford. Residue of time filled with conversations.'[7]

In 1891 there were no comparable nostalgic excitements, although he spent a short weekend at Eton in March and gave a lecture on the Greek goddess Artemis. Most of that winter he alternated between London, where he stayed mostly at 1 Carlton Gardens in the house of Stuart Rendel, MP for Montgomeryshire until he became a peer in Gladstone's 1894 resignation honours list, and Dollis Hill, the Aberdeen villa. So his housing needs were well and economically looked after. Rendel was an Etonian engineer, who had been a partner of Sir William Armstrong, from 1887 Lord Armstrong of Cragside, the Newcastle shipbuilder and armaments manufacturer, from which association Rendel had clearly made a lot of money. But by the age of little over fifty his chief pleasure and even purpose in life seemed to have become that of entertaining Gladstone, which he did not only in Carlton Gardens but also at Hatchlands, his Surrey mansion, and the Château Thorenc at Cannes.

As a purveyor of hospitality he was closely rivalled by George Armitstead, ten years his senior and intermittently Liberal MP for Dundee until 1885. He came of a more exotic background. He gave his education as 'Wiesbaden, Heidelberg, etc' and his occupation as 'Russia merchant'. This activity must have been as remunerative as Rendel's engineering for in cash terms Armitstead was an even more generous host to the Gladstones. Although he had fine houses in London and Perthshire, he mostly entertained them in hotels. At Easter 1891, they were his guests first at the Victoria Hotel at St Leonards and then at the newly opened Metropole Hotel ('what an abode of luxurious comfort,' Gladstone wrote) in Brighton. Then in September 1891, when Armitstead was staying at Hawarden (so the entertaining was not entirely one way) and when the Gladstones were unusually low in the aftermath of Willy's death, he suddenly performed a major feat of spirit-lifting. 'Mr Armitstead in the morning opened the subject of his giant treat to us,' Gladstone wrote.[8]

And so indeed it was. He proposed to take three Gladstones (Helen as well as Catherine) for a ten-week Christmas and New Year holiday in Biarritz and back via Pau, Toulouse, St Raphaël, Nice and Paris. John Morley and Sir Algernon West were also of the party for some of the time, although whether they were encompassed in Armitstead's generosity was not clear. The Biarritz visit was a clear success. Gladstone loved the turbulent but mild Atlantic weather. 'The sea continued grand and terrible,' he wrote on 30 December. Biarritz with its Basque coast and hinterland was henceforward a favourite destination of Gladstone's. He went back for two subsequent long visits, Armitstead acting as a combination of courier, conversation–backgammon partner and bill-payer on all three occasions. Like Rendel he did eventually get a peerage but it did not come from Gladstone; he had to wait until his eighty-second year, 1906, and the new Campbell-Bannerman government.

For the rest 1891 had few uplifts. It was either flat or worse. In May Gladstone had had a severe attack of influenza with nine days of fever which even involved a break in his diary-writing, the first since his 1880 pneumonia, and kept him away from his regular early church for three weeks. At the beginning of July his eldest son Willy had died after desperate surgery. Gladstone, still convalescent after his 'flu, had been staying near Lowestoft accompanied by his wife until she went to London for the attempt at salvation by operation, and by his daughter Mary, complemented by a three-night visit from John Morley. His host at the house which he had never previously visited was J. J. Colman, the Norwich mustard manufacturer, who welcomed him and his party, without much obtruding. When the dread news came it was at first kept from Gladstone. The penultimate day he wrote of as 'a day of illusion'. Then on the final day Mary Gladstone wrote: 'At 6 [in the morning] I went in to Papa and told him gradually of the alarming news, tho' keeping the worst from him till we were within half an hour of London. He was terribly shocked and broken down, and at Liverpool Street the little note from Helen reached us telling us of the end at 5.30."[9]

Twelve days later after the funeral at Hawarden he went back to Lowestoft for the second half of July. The Clyffe there was the epitome of a semi-anonymous reposeful house of comfort. Such houses, rather than those of historic note, even when accompanied by the 'overflowing kindness' of the hosts, were what he now liked. He did however occasionally venture on to ground which, while mostly loyal and always friendly, was less tailored for his own needs. In February he went to Lord Rothschild's Tring Park for a Saturday to Monday, and commented on the 'extreme kindness' but (not surprisingly) found the Sunday 'very unsabbatical';[10] in September he spent a week at Fasque, his first visit under the reign of the new baronet his nephew, and his last visit ever to that family house in which he had spent long autumns during his periods of greatest emotional turbulence between thirty-nine and fifty-seven years before. And in December he divided four days between visits to Spencer at Althorp and Rosebery at Mentmore. Both of these visits were, however, essentially political, Spencer's party being almost a shadow Cabinet in the country.

His main speech-making excursion of 1891 was to Newcastle for the October annual meeting of the National Liberal Federation. It was his first overnight visit to the Tyne since his unfortunate praise there of Jefferson Davis in 1862. This second visit, for quite different reasons, was not much happier. While his only real interest now lay in Ireland he realized that there had to be some sort of general Liberal platform. So he allowed Harcourt, Morley and others to cobble together the so-called 'Newcastle Programme', which was a capacious ragbag but weak on theme. Home Rule was of course at the head, but it was buttressed by proposals for Church disestablishment in Scotland as well as Wales, for triennial parliaments, for a further measure of franchise reform simply embracing 'one man (but not one woman), one vote', for local vetoes on drink sales, for the establishing of parish and district councils, for employers' liability in industrial accidents and, a little more tentatively, the payment of MPs and restrictions on the hours of work (not of them but of the manual labour force, or at least some parts of it). And brooding over the whole manifesto were heavy warnings to the House of Lords about the consequence for their shape and powers if they resisted the items in this catalogue.

A number of these items were positively distasteful to Gladstone. Most of the others failed to excite his appetite. But he did not have the time or the energy to argue about them in detail. So he decided that the only way to get enough of them down was to abandon his well-known habit of over-mastication and swallow them whole. It was a necessary price for keeping the Liberal faithful enthusiastic for Home Rule. The result was a flailing speech delivered with more vehemence than conviction. It lasted an hour and twenty minutes in the rococo and many-tiered Theatre Royal and was best remembered for the extravagance of his oratorical movements. Sometimes his arms rose high above his head in indignation, sometimes his knees sagged almost to the ground in supplication. When taken in conjunction with the recordings of Gladstone's voice which were made in 1890 and are still extant, with their undulating cadences, slight northern accent and hint of retribution, it is difficult not to recall the opening words of the old American 'Wobbly' song: 'Long haired preachers come out every night / Try to tell you what's wrong and what's right.' But Newcastle was an off day, with Gladstone in his own memorable phrase of thirteen years earlier, 'putting on the steam perforce' in an unusually mechanical way. On more favourable occasions his voice could still have a wonderful vibrancy and his arguments a massive momentum.

The morning after the Theatre Royal speech he received the freedom of Newcastle in the City Hall with a speech of twenty-five minutes and an audience of 2500. Then he retired quickly to Hawarden and wrote: 'Deo gratias for having finished a work heavy at near 82.'[11] With that he endeavoured to put Newcastle out of his mind. He was still a very good judge of the quality of his own performances.

For two months after his return from Newcastle Gladstone slept every night at Hawarden. He made no speech other than on a one-day swoop to Port Sunlight at the end of November when he addressed the Wirral Liberals, and he had no specifically political visitors except for Rosebery, who was typically playing hard to get as a member of a future Liberal government, Arnold Morley, his current Chief Whip, and Edward Marjoribanks, who was to succeed to that office in 1892. He cut down a few of his last trees (it was he who was becoming exhausted, not the arboreal resources of Hawarden), he worked on the text and then the proofs of two long articles on Olympian religion which he wrote for the New York publication *North American Review*. But above all he worked on sorting books in the Temple of Peace, then transporting and installing them in his new memorial library. 'Worked on books here and at St. Deiniols' became a constant daily refrain. In mid-December he left for his 'great treat' at Biarritz and in Provence.

It cannot be said that when he returned ten weeks later he was like a giant refreshed. But he had enjoyed himself and he was at least in a calm mood as he approached the great test of what must surely be his last general election and the determinant of whether or not his life's work was crowned with success. He awaited it more like a gambler with good nerve watching the slowing revolutions of a roulette wheel than like an athlete making a desperate effort in the last lap. There was no attempt at a repeat of the first Midlothian campaign. He remained in London for six weeks after his return and made about a speech a week in the House of Commons, but none of them of much note or even length. Then he went to Hawarden for an Easter fortnight, and began a run of physical ill luck with a not very serious carriage accident on the way to Euston. This was followed by another couple of months in London, although with May spent mostly at Dollis Hill. For the whole of that spring there comes through an unprecedented sense that he was marking time, waiting upon events, and experiencing a perceptible, but steady rather than dramatic, diminution of powers.

The 1892 election began in late June. Gladstone wrote his election address on the 22nd and left London for the campaign on the 25th. He went first to Chester for one of his very few speeches outside Midlothian (the others were whistle-stops on the way to Edinburgh and a big Saturday-afternoon meeting in a Glasgow theatre). At Chester he suffered a nasty eye injury and missed only by a narrow margin having effective blindness inflicted upon him. As he drove in an open carriage from the station to the Liberal Club 'a middle aged bony woman' (he was very precise in his description) threw at him 'with great force and skill'[12] a small missile from a distance of about two yards. The missile sounds innocuous. It was a hard-baked piece of gingerbread about one and a half inches across. But it inflicted considerable damage. It cut the skin of the nose and, much worse, lacerated the pupil of his only serviceable eye. Gladstone felt a heavy blow on the eye and sank back with a curiously measured comment to a companion in the carriage. 'It was a cruel thing to do,' he said. Later he told a doctor that he had never seen 'a woman throw with such spite and energy'.[13] She was not only spiteful and energetic but agile as well. She disappeared into the crowd and was never identified.

Gladstone's reaction was robust. 'After a few minutes of rest & assurance from two casual doctors I went on & made my speech, short of an hour, only reading when needful with the utmost difficulty.'[14] Then he had the eye bound up at the Chester Infirmary and retired to three days of bed and darkness at Hawarden. On the fourth day he went to Edinburgh (Dalmeny again this time) in dark spectacles – which mafia- or Garbo-like accoutrement seems peculiarly inappropriate to Gladstone – and on the seventh day, after his major Glasgow speech, he recorded that 'I thought small thin flat scales were descending upon me: & afterwards observed with some discomfort that there was a fluffy object floating in the fluid of my serviceable eye.'[15] He then decided that he had to give up all reading that was not strictly and officially necessary (a great sacrifice), and even two months later abstained throughout a whole journey from London to Hawarden. Some but not much improvement resulted from this abstinence.

His expectations of the election had also improved, almost inevitably as a natural reaction from the deep gloom following the Parnell smash. When Hamilton saw him on 15 June and again on the 24th he found him 'very sanguine about the result of the fight'.[16] Nor did Gladstone appear to pick up the adverse signs on the ground, even in his own constituency. His campaign from the opening meeting in the Edinburgh Music Hall to a final one at Penycuik and a cavalcade through eighteen villages was in accordance with pattern, as were most of his comments. The only exception was that after the Penycuik day he wrote: 'Thank God all this is over.' And so it was. He never campaigned again.

The early results came in on 4 July and were deceptively good. 'At first they were even too rosy,' Gladstone wrote; 'afterwards toned down but the general result satisfactory, pointing to a gain in G Britain of 80 seats. This may be exceeded.' But the next day it was a different story: 'Election returns unsatisfactory,' he bleakly wrote. And on Wednesday the 6th: 'The returns of tonight were a little improved: but the burden on me personally is serious: a small Liberal majority being the heaviest weight I can well be called to bear. But all is with God. His blessed will be done.'[17]

The overall result was that the Liberals had 273 seats (or 274 if Keir Hardie be included) against the Conservatives' 269. The 269 were firmly buttressed by 46 Liberal Unionists, who by this time had become both more reliable and more comfortable allies for them than were the 81 Home Rulers, still divided by the Parnell schism, for the Liberals. There was therefore a majority of forty for a Liberal rather than a Conservative government and, somewhat less enthusiastically, for Home Rule. But this majority was inadequate in size for intimidating the House of Lords and deficient in coherence for giving a Liberal Cabinet a firm command over its legislative priorities.

Within this disappointing national result, Gladstone's own strength in Midlothian collapsed dramatically. In the 1885 general election (the first on the extended franchise) Gladstone had a majority of 7879 to 3248. In 1886 he was unopposed. In 1892 he was returned only by 5845 votes to 5155. Gladstone dismissed this as 'a small matter', compared that is with the disappointment of the overall result. He explained it in a letter to Harcourt: 'Two thousand voters seem to have gone over from me in a mass. It is simply due to the question of Scotch Disestablishment.'[18] No doubt that vexed question did play a significant and adverse role. But is is difficult to believe that it could have been exclusively responsible for a result so sharply at variance with the general trend. There must surely also have been a feeling that Gladstone was both over the hill and obsessed with Ireland.

He was of course over the hill and in one sense knew this perfectly well himself. The day after his letter to Harcourt he confided to his diary: 'Frankly from the condition (*now*) of my senses, I am no longer fit for public life: yet bidden to walk in it. "Lead thou me on."'[19] Others took an even harsher view of Gladstone's condition. When Harcourt saw him for two hours on 27 July he was reported by his son as 'much shocked at the physical and mental change for the worse in Mr. G. since he left the H. of C. in June. He thinks him confused and feeble.'[20] On the other hand, Sir Andrew Clark, though he had not seen Gladstone since his eye accident, took a more optimistic medical view about his patient's capacity for office, if not about its likely effect upon his longevity. Clark, from the closest knowledge over nearly twenty-five years, was a great admirer of Gladstone's physique and resilience. He had told Granville ten years before that 'Gladstone was not only sound from head to toes, but built in the most beautiful proportion he had ever seen of all parts of the human body to each other – head, legs, arms, and trunk, all without a flaw, like some ancient Greek statue of the ideal man. He added that of all the persons he had treated, Gladstone . . . had the best chance of living to be a hundred.'[21]

On 12 July 1892 Clark gave to Edward Hamilton, not in casual gossip but in a formal statement, his physician's judgement:

> He could see no sign of mental deterioration. Mr. G.'s powers of argument and construction were as great as ever. His powers of hearing and sight were not what they were, no doubt; and he would probably feel

> the strain of worry; but sometimes even worry braced people up instead of breaking them down. He therefore could see no reason why, if necessary, Mr. G. should not embark again on office life. It might hasten his end; but in any case that could not be very distant. He was constitutionally unfit to stand aside.[22]

Apart from his retreat from the view that Gladstone might live to be a hundred this was a favourable prognosis,* more sanguine probably than Gladstone's view of his own capacity during the period between the election result and the meeting of the new Parliament, for which the Queen's Speech was on 9 August. Yet, despite his frailties and his disappointment at the weakness of the victory, he never appeared to waver in his determination to form and preside over a government. The explanation, it is easy to assume, must have lain in his sense of Irish mission and his fear that no alternative Liberal Prime Minister would give Home Rule an adequate priority and momentum. But the amazing paradox was that, while he did not contemplate stepping aside, what he most certainly did contemplate was relegating Irish business to a lower order of priority. From the disappointing election result he drew the almost Chamberlain-like conclusion that not enough attention had been given to 'British questions'.

Consequently, on 20 July and when staying as Armitstead's guest at Fisher's Hotel, Pitlochry ('capital Inn: lovely place'), he drew up 'a *first* view of the possibilities of 1893'. 'It aims', he wrote, 'at obtaining a judgment upon the great Irish question without spending the bulk of the Session upon its particulars (viewing the unlikelihood as far as can now be seen of their at once passing into law): and obtaining a good or fair Sessional result for the various portions of the country. . . .'[23] In other words he proposed to carry a resolution in favour of Home Rule, but to let the bill wait and to get on in the first session with a series of domestic reforms. This memorandum he circulated to a few of his shadow Cabinet colleagues. Spencer, the ex-Viceroy of Ireland, and

* There was an irony about Clark's view that Gladstone could not in any event live long which was reminiscent of the macabre joke about that egregious doctor, Lord Moran, at the time of Churchill's long-drawn-out death in 1965. Moran was in the habit of appearing outside the house in Hyde Park Gate each morning and giving lugubrious bulletins on the patient to the waiting press. Simple pleasure was given by the invention that one morning Churchill himself appeared in apparently restored vigour and said: 'Gentlemen, I have very sad news for you. Lord Moran died during the night.' Clark died, aged sixty-seven, in the year after he gave his appraisal to Hamilton, whereas Gladstone, nineteen years his senior, survived for another six.

John Morley, the putative Chief Irish Secretary, both thought it a major mistake. Spencer said it would look 'faint hearted' and asked what would the Irish say, the answer to which was that they would probably have rendered the issue of legislative priority academic by declining on such a basis to support a Liberal government. By the time that he saw Spencer and Morley on the 27th, the day of his arrival in London from Hawarden, Gladstone was moving to second thoughts.

The trouble was that Harcourt, who was to be Chancellor and the effective leader in the Commons, very much liked his first thoughts, and tried hard to bully him into sticking to them. During the previous ten days Gladstone had written unusually warm letters to Harcourt, who had responded with appropriate friendliness. But as soon as they were both in London, relations deteriorated. Harcourt, with his usual truculence, was probably concerned to establish his defensible space at the Treasury as well as with the Irish point. After their first meeting (of one and three-quarter hours) Gladstone wrote: 'Formidable especially at my age';[24] and a couple of weeks later: 'Conclave 3–5. A storm. I am sorry to record that Harcourt has used me in such a way since my return to town that the addition of another Harcourt would have gone far to make my task impossible.' But he added: 'All however is *well*: it comes ἄνωθεν [from above].'[25]

By all being well Gladstone meant that Harcourt had reluctantly acquiesced in his second and dramatically different draft which he had written on 1 August and which put a Government of Ireland Bill at the very top of the list. The logic of the situation pointed irresistibly in this direction. Apart from the government's dependence upon the Irish, it would have made no sense for a nearly eighty-three-year-old Prime Minister, kept in politics only by a dedication to the Irish cause, to have postponed dealing with it for the first eighteen months of what showed every sign of being a short-lived government. The surprise is that Gladstone's intention flickered in this direction for a couple of weeks of post-election sag. It is also surprising that Spencer, having been an upright but unimaginative Viceroy in 1882–5, should have become such a resolute supporter of the policy which had driven nearly all his fellow Whigs out of the Liberal party.

Nevertheless the upset with Harcourt occasioned by Gladstone's temporary wobble gave an unpleasant twist to the business of cabinet-making. This was accentuated by the behaviour of Rosebery, who was even more tiresome than usual. That spoilt Scottish earl and (through his deceased wife) Home Counties plutocrat, who had spent most of the first half of the 1880s agitating that he was not in the Cabinet by the age of thirty-six and had struck Dilke (no mean judge) as 'the most ambitious man he had ever met', now that he had achieved a certain indispensability as Foreign Secretary in a weak government, decided that he had a temperamental unsuitability for public office and would play very hard to get. His natural misanthropy had been increased by the Gladstones' election stay at Dalmeny having apparently not gone well. Hamilton, whose loyalty to Gladstone was becoming tempered by his dazzlement by Rosebery, recorded on 11 July: 'Evidently things have been very unpleasant at Dalmeny. R. says he has had a terrible week of it. It is evident that Mr. and Mrs. G. have got on his nerves, which are not in the best of conditions, and they have been apparently more than usually tactless.'[26]

On 31 July Rosebery wrote to Gladstone declining office. 'I am the best judge of my unfitness for public life,' he started with a combination of sententiousness and mock modesty. He then disappeared to Dalmeny, followed by a flurry of appealing letters culminating in a visit of supplication from John Morley, who had come by the overnight train, on the morning of 5 August. Together they travelled back to London, but Rosebery then found it necessary to retreat for a weekend in Paris to 'clear the cobwebs out of his brain'. After his return, with or without cobwebs, he withdrew to his house near Epsom for further communion with his conscience and then contradicted Morley's view that he had come round, and told Gladstone in a 'very trying and rather sad' (Gladstone's words) interview on 11 August that he could not join. Then he went to Mentmore, his great Rothschild pile near Leighton Buzzard,* which was conveniently placed for receiving further representations. These were abundantly forthcoming, most influentially, it appeared, from the Prince of Wales, Buckle (the vehemently anti-Gladstone editor of *The Times*), and Henry Primrose (Rosebery's cousin).

Gladstone wisely abstained from further appeals until 15 August, the day he went to Osborne to accept office. Then, under pressure from his private secretaries, he wrote Rosebery a rather cool note saying that the Queen wished him to be Foreign Secretary and that the office was still open. Gladstone, unlike the courtiers and the private secretaries, and even the Harcourts and the Morleys, who had persuaded themselves

* It was almost as though he had to touch all his possessions in order to assure himself what a favour he would be conferring on a Liberal government if he agreed to join it. For the facts (not the judgements, with which he would not agree) see Robert Rhodes James, *Rosebery*, pp. 242–5.

that Rosebery was essential, sensibly thought that Spencer as leader of the House of Lords and Kimberley as Foreign Secretary would do more or less as well as Rosebery filling both posts.

Rosebery's response to that final cool offer was an insufferably self-regarding telegram. 'So be it. Mentmore' was the message he sent to Gladstone at Osborne. The substance was redolent with the conferring of a benefit rather than a commitment to co-operation. And the signature was at once arch and arrogant. Rosebery was an *allumeur* (if the word can be used in the masculine) on a scale which Gladstone had hardly encountered since Arthur Hallam died over sixty years before. And he was not even a very good Foreign Secretary. By September he had got the government in its first but considerable mess with his unilateral and jingoist handling of Uganda, which Rosebery, against the views of Gladstone, Harcourt and most of the rest of the Cabinet, was determined to turn into a permanent British possession.

The Queen, for once, caused relatively little trouble over Gladstone's return to office. Admittedly she wrote of her contemplation of it 'with utter disgust'.[27] She publicly accepted Salisbury's resignation 'with much regret', which was unusual and improper but insignificant. She momentarily flirted with the idea of trying to get Rosebery instead, but made no serious diversionary attempt in this or any other direction. On 11 August the Salisbury government was defeated on an amendment to the address by 350 votes to 310, and by the 15th Gladstone had kissed hands (in fact omitting to do so) and the new government was in being.

The rest of his Cabinet-making went somewhat more easily, although Gladstone claimed that it was the most difficult of his four experiences in this field, and Labouchère made a public fuss about being left out. For this Gladstone gallantly took the blame, rather than allowing Labouchère to put it on the Queen. In reality both factors were at work. Labouchère was distasteful to the Queen and somewhat brash for the Prime Minister's taste, although Gladstone would have been content for him to achieve his second major ambition, which was the Washington Legation (raised to an embassy only in 1893), had this not been vetoed by Rosebery.

The Cabinet contained only two members whom Gladstone did not know well. They were Herbert Henry Asquith and Henry Hartley Fowler. Asquith became the youngest member of the Cabinet, appointed at thirty-nine to the senior secretaryship of state. He had been chosen by Gladstone as the most appropriate backbencher to move the amendment which brought down the Salisbury government, and did so with a most accomplished debating speech. Subsequently he proved the outstanding success of the government, 'the best Home Secretary of the [nineteenth] century', was Magnus's somewhat sweeping judgement, and by so being laid the foundation of his brilliant career. He was also, despite being a 'new man' from a Yorkshire Nonconformist background who had been in the House of Commons for only six years, highly congenial to Gladstone. Here again, as with Morley, the essential link was Asquith's classical erudition. Balliol had comfortably overcome Batley and put Asquith, in Gladstone's eyes, in a quite different category from Chamberlain. His position was further (although later) buttressed by Gladstone's fondness for his second wife, Margot Tennant. She was exactly the sort of pert young woman, flattering and unintimidated, whom he liked. She was several times bidden to Hawarden, and on the occasion of her first visit in 1889 he had written her a four-stanzaed piece of verse, of which the first ran:

When Parliament ceases and comes the recess,
And we seek in the country rest after distress,
As a rule upon visitors place an embargo,
But make an exception in favour of Margot.*

In December 1890 Gladstone went for a five-day visit to the Tennant Scottish house near Peebles, and when the Asquith marriage took place in May 1894 (even though it was one of his last engagements before a doubtfully successful cataract operation which effectively closed down seventy years of diary-keeping) he attended and signed the register together with Rosebery and Balfour.

Fowler, the solicitor from Wolverhampton, and twenty-two years' Asquith's senior, could not compete in these fashionable stakes. In 1892, however, he was also a successful minister and effective debater, who carried the Parish Councils Bill, the major legislative achievement of that government. For the rest the ministry was a familiar Gladstonian one, with Herschell again Lord Chancellor, the secretaryships of state apart from the already mentioned Home and Foreign ones filled by Kimberley, Ripon and Campbell-Bannerman, with Spencer at the Admiralty, Mundella at the Board of Trade, and G. O. Trevelyan at the

* The rhyme with 'embargo' stressing the silence of the final t and supplemented in subsequent stanzas with 'cargo', 'argot' (with its French silent *t*) and 'far go', recalls the famous exchange many decades later of Lady Oxford (as Margot Tennant had then become) with the 'blonde bombshell' Jean Harlow, who persistently addressed her as 'Margotte', until told: 'The *t* is silent in my name, Miss Harlow, as I presume in yours.'

Scottish Office. A. H. D. Acland, the son of Gladstone's Christ Church contemporary, Shaw-Lefevre and Arnold Morley brought up the rear of the Cabinet. There was also James Bryce, in ministerial office for the first time as Chancellor of the Duchy of Lancaster with that office's scarcity of administrative duties enabling him to act as a general constitutional adviser.

Although Gladstone could still gear himself up for formidable feats of endurance, particularly if they involved declaiming on his legs before an audience, the normal conduct of a Prime Minister's business had become just beyond his capacity. Rightly if he was to retain adequate authority, he had cursorily dismissed a scheme canvassed by Hamilton and others that he might ask someone else (perhaps Spencer) to become Prime Minister while himself accepting one of the grand honorific offices with the specific role of drawing up and conducting the Irish Bill. (The only vestige of this which survived was the perverse one that he took the office of Lord Privy Seal as well as that of First Lord of the Treasury, which he had done in his 1886 administration but not in his two previous and major ones.) Nor did he act upon an alternative Hamilton suggestion that at 'conclaves', the informal precursors of modern Cabinet committees, he should nominate on an *ad hoc* basis a presiding colleague who could actually hear what was being said.

What he did do as a recognition of his deafness was to take the more iconoclastic step of changing the locale and physical shape of Cabinet meetings. He rationalized this by pretending that the new arrangement was inherently better. Hamilton wrote on 19 August:

> Mr G. has just discovered, after many years of Cabinet holding, that it is not right for Ministers to sit round a large table with blotting books and paper before them and with the consequent temptation to write things down unnecessarily and to draw pictures of nothing and nobody. He proposes now that he alone should sit at a writing table (with Rosebery on his right hand) and that the others should sit round as closely as they can. This arrangement will partly get over the difficulties of his deafness: and the discovery is opportune.[28]

Then, on 27 October, he continued: 'Mr. G. held his first autumnal Cabinet today. They met in his own room – the corner room on first floor (over the old Cabinet room) – in No. 10 Downing Street.'[29]

Amazingly, however, and once again illustrating Gladstone's unique capacity to be larger than life, but not wholly rationally so, he responded to the challenge of taking on for the fourth time a burden which was just beyond the perimeter of his capacity by an absolute refusal to concentrate all his energies upon it. He continued with four other tasks, all of which any normal man would have abandoned, postponed or at least neglected when struggling on the frontiers of his strength to be Prime Minister at an older age than any other man before or since. The first was to complete a long article for the *North American Review* designed to refute an attack in the same periodical by his old but separated friend the Duke of Argyll on the principle of Home Rule. On his first three days in London after the election he worked hard on this abstract argument for a recondite journal.

Second, he was intent on doing a new translation of the Odes of Horace. He conceived the idea in the Fife Arms Hotel at Braemar in the immediate aftermath of the election and made a start within a week. On his journey to London from Hawarden on 27 July for his immediately pending 'formidable' interview with Harcourt he worked the whole way on the Odes. No doubt the searching for appropriate English renderings was easier on his eyes than continuous reading. He was at them again as soon as he had sent off his anti-Argyll article to the *North American Review*, and then, a good deal more intermittently, during the autumn. He returned to more serious Horatian work during his Biarritz Christmas holiday. The translations were eventually published by John Murray in 1894.

One reason why his application to Horace became spasmodic during the early autumn was that he had agreed to deliver on 24 October the first Romanes lecture in the Sheldonian Theatre at Oxford, and proceeded to devote the most disproportionate amount of time to its preparation. He started on 31 August, which was two days after the third and the most dangerous but also the most farcical of his three accidents of that summer. After an afternoon drive with his wife he 'walked & came unawares in the quietest corner of the park on a dangerous cow which knocked me down and might have done serious damage'.[30] There are slightly more dramatic versions, including Magnus's statement that he had to lie down, feigning to be dead, until the cow's attention was distracted and he could escape first behind a tree and then back to the Castle. The malfeasant beast was apparently not part of a dairy herd but a wild heifer which had intruded into the park and was subsequently shot. It was compensated by the tributes of having its head permanently displayed at the Glynne Arms in Hawarden village, and of evoking an elaborate wreath despatched with a card inscribed 'to the memory of the patriotic cow which sacrificed its life in an attempt to save Ireland from Home Rule'.[31] Gladstone, although he had walked home and sat down calmly at dinner, suffered a few weeks of mild ill effect, which was not surprising at nearly eighty-three.

The incident did not much distract him from the preparation of his Oxford lecture. Between the end of August and mid-October he spent substantial portions of fifteen separate days working upon it. During this period he surprisingly pleaded this preoccupation in a letter to the poet's son, as a reason for not agreeing to act as a pall-bearer at Tennyson's Westminster Abbey funeral. Then he recorded on 17 October: 'Finished at last writing my interminable lecture.'[32] But he still devoted parts of another three days to touching it up, including an occasion when he assembled an audience of half a dozen or so at Hawarden (not all family, for one, James Stuart, MP for Hoxton, was a former fellow of Trinity College, Cambridge) and read it to them for an hour and twenty minutes. His approach to the actual performance was equally respectful. He engaged in correspondence with the eponymous Professor Romanes (not a venerable Oxford don but a forty-four-year-old Canadian-born, Cambridge-educated scientist, who had held a chair of physiology at the Royal Institution) on the question whether he should wear a red or a black gown, and he arrived in Oxford and was installed in the Christ Church Deanery two days in advance.

Altogether it was a remarkably disproportionate elaboration, particularly from the man who with no indication of more than half a morning's preparation had delivered some of the greatest (and longest) of nineteenth-century parliamentary orations. It can only be interpreted as an old man's act of Oxford pietism, a gesture of thanksgiving for sixty-three years of connection with the University, which has at least had the lasting effect of giving the Romanes series a unique prestige among all Oxford lectures. Fortunately, in the circumstances, the occasion was a success. Gladstone pronounced the 'audience excellent'. *The Times*, not then his most enthusiastic supporter, reported: 'He was in excellent voice, and each word and intonation was fully appreciated by every person in the crowded theatre.'[33] This was despite the fact that the lecture's title, 'An Academic Sketch', hardly lived up to the preparations. It was in fact an erudite survey of the history and spirit of the University, with some sidelong glances at Cambridge which made him anxious to be assured by the former fellow of Trinity that these were fair. The crowning irony was that, having devoted all this attention to a private excursion to Oxford, he stubbornly declined to deliver the obligatory Prime Minister's speech at the Lord Mayor's Banquet which took place two weeks later. Andrew Clark was encouraged to provide a medical prohibition. Two Cabinet meetings had to consider who should be the substitute, until it was devolved through Ripon to Kimberley.

Gladstone's fourth preoccupation was with the affairs of the Granville estate. Granville, as we have seen,* had never been a broad-acred as opposed to a many-cousined earl, but it was not realized until after his death in April 1891 that he was effectively bankrupt. This may have been the principal reason why he had refused the marquessate which Gladstone offered him at the end of the 1886 government.† When it became clear that there was a substantial deficit on the estate Gladstone occupied himself in the matter with all the relentless dedication which he had shown in dealing with the Oak Farm débâcle or the embarrassed affairs of the fifth Duke of Newcastle. Following a sombre report from Waterhouse, the great accountant, he set himself to raise gifts of £10,000 each (£500,000 today) from magnates who had been Granville's associates. It was a club with a stiff entrance fee and for membership of which social and political cachet was also required. The prospective list makes interesting reading. Ten appear at first to have been approached: Westminster, Devonshire, Spencer, Lansdowne, Rothschild, Brassey, Northbrook, Sefton (Derby's rival as an owner of Liverpool ground rents), Derby himself and Burton (originally Bass, the brewer). Later Gladstone added Currie the shipowner, Aberdeen, Rosebery and Northbourne. They responded with varying degrees of generosity. Westminster declined absolutely. Devonshire on the other hand, despite the political separation, 'behaved right ducally'. The others dribbled out differing (in fact rather substantial) amounts so that £18,000 (£900,000) had been subscribed by the end of 1892 and Gladstone was able with a final modest subvention from himself and the skilled services of Mr Waterhouse to avoid any technical state of bankruptcy.

With these preoccupations, as well as semi-blindness and semi-deafness, it is amazing that Gladstone had any time at all to spare for the premiership. Yet, although he managed to avoid London between 16 August and 28 September, and again for most of October, he nonetheless showed almost surplus energy in his pouring out of memoranda to his Foreign Secretary (of whose forward policy in Uganda he was deeply critical), his India Secretary (on bimetallism), his Chancellor

* See p. 315.

† Wolverton also refused the similarly proffered step to a viscountcy, giving the very respectable reason that it would look too much of a reward for hospitality given to Gladstone, and would bring discredit to both of them.

of the Exchequer and his Home Secretary, his Lord Chancellor and his Irish Secretary on a variety of topics, but above all, in one great effusion, to the Queen. For the middle ten days of September he went from Hawarden for a North Wales holiday, partly at the Beddgelert 'chalet' of Sir Edward William Watkin MP, who had become a Liberal Unionist in 1886 but who was nonetheless interesting to Gladstone as the leading advocate of the Channel Tunnel, and partly at the Marine Hotel, Barmouth. Watkin believed in elevated as well as subterranean routes and had just made a road to the summit of Snowdon, which he persuaded Gladstone to open before a crowd of 2000 and from a platform on a boulder which has since been known as Gladstone's Rock. He also provided David Lloyd George, then aged twenty-nine and an MP of just over a year's standing, as a guest at dinner in the chalet. On the last day of that holiday Gladstone began to write a major memorandum for the Queen and continued to play around with it (although giving priority to his Romanes lecture) until it was eventually submitted five weeks later.

It was a strange document to have sent to an unsympathetic and not very subtle sovereign. The premisses were a lament for what Gladstone regarded as recent deteriorations in the politico-social structure. This part was written with a stark force and honesty, but, so far from being likely to move the Queen's mind, was almost perfectly crafted to elicit from her a murmured 'Whose fault do you think that is?' or 'I told you so' at the end of each paragraph. His central theme was the dangerous degree of class confrontation introduced into politics by the alienation of property from the Liberal party:

> The leading fact, to which he [Mr Gladstone] would point, is in his judgment a very painful one: it is the widening of that gap, or chasm, in opinion, which more largely than heretofore separates the upper and more powerful from the more numerous classes of the community. Such an estrangement he regards as a very serious mischief. This evil has been aggravated largely by the prolongation and intensity of the Irish controversy.
>
> But it began to operate years before the present Irish controversy began in 1885–6. There were at least six ducal houses of great wealth and influence, which Mr Gladstone had known to be reckoned in the Liberal party at former times, and which had completely severed themselves from it before Home Rule had come to be in any way associated with the popular conception of Liberalism.

After 1886, however, this division 'widened and hardened':

> Such was the character of this movement of Liberal dissent, that the supporters of the present Government in the House of Lords cannot be estimated at more than one tenth or one twelfth of that assembly. As regards landed property, Mr Gladstone doubts whether Liberals now hold more than one acre in fifty, taking the three kingdoms together. In the upper and propertied classes generally, the majority against them, though not so enormous, is still manifold.
>
> Yet, for the first time in our history, we have seen in the recent election . . . a majority of the House of Commons, not indeed a very large, but also not a very small one, returned against the sense of nearly the entire Peerage and landed gentry, and the vast majority of the upper and leisured classes. . . . The moderate Liberal (and by moderate Liberal Mr Gladstone means such a person as Lord Granville and Lord John Russell) has not quite become, but is becoming, a thing of the past.

From here he proceeded to argue that the effect of this was to make the Liberal party more radical and democratic (a development which he implicitly regretted), and that the history of at any rate the past sixty years showed that in the direction in which the Liberal party moved so sooner or later did the country. His remedy was to dispose (favourably) of the Home Rule question as quickly as possible. This he referred to as 'eminently Conservative [deliberately using a capital and not a small c] in the highest sense of the term'. Such a quick cut offered the best hope of halting the two processes of property deserting the Liberals and that party consequently being pushed to the left. But he was not very sanguine of achieving the remedy, and perhaps not of the desired result following if he did. '. . . Mr. Gladstone therefore, well aware that his own time is short, does not confidently count upon success in bringing the great controversy to an early issue at a definite time.'[34]

The Queen caused Ponsonby to send only a brief acknowledgement, which was courteous to the extent of saying that she 'fully appreciates the motives which have led to his laying his views before her'. In her own journal she wrote on the fourth day after it had been despatched to Balmoral: 'Reading a long memorandum from Mr. Gladstone about the political situation, which is very curious.'[35] And that was that.

Much of the work of the Cabinet (which met seven times between 27 October and 21 November) was concerned with the preparation of the Irish Bill, which it had been painfully agreed should be the priority for the session of 1893. It was difficult work. The old unanswerable questions of whether there should be Irish members at Westminster (this time the inclination was to say yes), and if so, how many, and what should they vote on, quickly reared their ugly heads. And their ugliness was fully matched by that of the moods of the Chancellor of the Exchequer. On 11 November Gladstone wrote that 'Harcourt came early and poured out antiIrish opinions, declaring himself pledged to them'; and later that day: 'Cabinet 2½–5. One person outrageous.'[36] And again, on 23 November: 'Cabinet 2½–4. Something of a scene with Harcourt at the close.'[37] It was a relief when the Prime Minister got further consideration of the Irish Bill delegated to a Cabinet committee composed, as he wrote, of 'WEG; Spencer; Chancellor; Morley; Bryce; and Bannerman'; and an even greater relief that 'Chancellor' in this shorthand meant Lord Chancellor Herschell and not Mr Chancellor of the Exchequer Harcourt.

Gladstone then retreated to Hawarden for three weeks, where he had acrimonious correspondence with Rosebery and worked with Morley on the bill, the committee apparently having been conveniently forgotten. Morley he found 'so genial and effective', as well as 'a great stay in Rosebery troubles'.[38] Morley unfortunately was less complimentary about Gladstone's working habits at this stage, and also about some of his other attributes. His diary painted a much less noble picture of the Grand Old Man in decline than that which he chose to give, nearly ten years later, in the last chapters of his resonant biography. Altogether the government of 1892, even by the somewhat low standards of collegiality which are more the rule than the exception in British Cabinets of at least the last hundred years, cannot have been a happy one in which to serve or over which to preside.

Nor was the interlocking support by a combination of Gladstone's family and his private office as much of an assuagement as it had been in the government of 1880. Hamilton was no longer available, having been promoted too high to be a secretary, even to the Prime Minister. He was effectively the second man in the Treasury, and although he maintained close contact with Gladstone and was a ubiquitous figure on the Whitehall and social scene, it was not the same as being full-time in his service. Furthermore he owed departmental loyalty to Harcourt, and his old and close friendship with Rosebery became more difficult to combine with devotion to Gladstone as Rosebery became an independent political power and Gladstone's likely (but by no means chosen) successor.

As a substitute for Hamilton Gladstone paradoxically moved to a still more senior official. Sir Algernon West, who had been Gladstone's private secretary in 1868–72, was due to retire as chairman of the Board of Inland Revenue, and in the run-up to the change of government Gladstone had persuaded him to do special post-retirement service as head of his private office. (Spencer Lyttelton came back to assist West.) But West was sixty in 1892, whereas Hamilton had been thirty-three, much nearer to the optimum private secretary age, in 1880. Moreover, and partly no doubt as a result, West was less skilled at melding official life with the idiosyncrasies of Gladstone's household pattern. Maybe the family, Mrs Gladstone and the daughters, had become more difficult to deal with in the meantime. On 2 August Hamilton, possibly by this time a slightly malicious source, enjoying while sympathizing with the difficulties of his successor, had written:

> I fear more than the usual amount of confusion and fuss reigning in Carlton Gardens [Rendel's house, where the Gladstones were not unusually installed] – Mrs. G. and Helen waylaying everybody, scheming this and scheming that, intercepting letters and almost listening at keyholes. I pity poor Algy West, who naturally complains with some bitterness. I advised his *insisting* on having everything in his own hands.[39]

And on 9 December, when that year's Biarritz expedition was under discussion: 'Algy West is much put out about the whole thing. The family decline to listen to anything he has to say.'[40] Wherever the fault lay, that happily 'interlocking protective cocoon' of family and secretaries of the 1880s was not in equal harmony in the 1890s or able to provide an adequate compensation for the truculence of Harcourt, the self-centredness of Rosebery and the occasional behind-the-arras vinegar of Morley.

The truth probably was that Gladstone by this stage was not much good at working on the intricacies of legislation. (He was still brilliant at sustaining a bill in the House of Commons once its details had been determined, but that was a matter for 1893 and not for 1892.) What he did however do well in that autumn of waiting for the final joust was to set a good shape for the general legislative programme of the government. Despite his age, his small majority and his preoccupation with Ireland, this was incomparably better planned than that for the 1880 government, when the circumstances were more propitious. As a result the last Gladstone government had a very respectable record, creating district and parish councils, raising the school-leaving age, limiting the hours of railwaymen, accompanied by important administrative advances, Mundella creating the labour department of the Board of Trade, and Asquith putting new strength into the factory inspectorate.

Even Rosebery, arbitrating more successfully at home than abroad, earned trade union gratitude by settling the coal dispute of 1893.

But in early December 1892 all of this was in the future and the intricate problems of drafting the second Home Rule Bill, as well as the intractable behaviour of some of his colleagues, were weighing heavily on Gladstone. He had a few nights of sleeping badly, encouraged Clark to say that another Biarritz sojourn would do him good, mobilized the ever available Armitstead to perform the functions of a Thomas Cook's man who presented no bills, and on 20 December he was off, getting to Folkestone in time to attend an afternoon service in the 'beautiful church' and to Biarritz thirty-six hours later. He was away until 10 January. He returned to face his final parliamentary lap – 'one fight more, the best and the last'. It was certainly the last, and in the quality of his own performance, although not in the results achieved, almost the best.

35
Last Exit to Hawarden

Two days after his return, on 12 January 1893, Gladstone reported to his physician: 'Biarritz has been very kind to me and the sleep has been completely restored.'[1] He celebrated this happy result and marked his general gratitude to Clark by sending him a copy of a Gladstone bust made in Rome in 1868, which was very close to the time when Clark began to treat his illustrious patient. Nevertheless Gladstone approached his final circuit around the hazardous course of the Great Home Rule Handicap with an unusual and almost pathological nervousness. On the eve of the session he wrote: 'Official dinner & evening party. 8–11. I feel, what? much troubled & tossed about; in marked contrast with the inner attitude on former like occasions.'[2] The next day he spoke for fifty minutes in sharp reply to Balfour in the debate on the Address, and pronounced himself 'much tired'. And on the day after that: 'Did not rise until 10.30. Now that I have taken the plunge I feel slightly more at home'[3] – which was an understandable but nonetheless odd expression to use for someone who had experienced nearer sixty to fifty debates on the Address, and dominatingly participated in most of them.

Nor did his neurosis remain permanently at bay once his plunge had taken him into the water. On 5 February, returning from a Sunday-morning service at the Chapel Royal he felt 'both depression & worry'. On the 13th before he made his last marathon oration on the motion for leave to bring in (or first reading) of the Government of Ireland Bill, he 'felt very weak having heard every hour (or all but one) strike in the night.* I seemed to lie at the foot of the Cross, and to get my arm around it. The House was most kind, and I was borne through. The later evening I spent on the sofa.'[4] Seven weeks later when the bill came to its second reading, however, he seemed to have got back to normal to

* He did not, however, anticipate the much later attempt of his fellow Carltonian, George Nathaniel Curzon, to get the night chimes of Big Ben silenced because of their interference with his sleeping.

the extent of merely recording that he worked on papers for the debate in the morning and spoke for one and a half hours in the afternoon.

Despite this hesitant approach to the early fences, Gladstone's conduct of the Government of Ireland Bill throughout that punishing session became a feat of sustained parliamentary resource which has rarely if ever been equalled before or since by any Prime Minister, let alone one aged eighty-three. It was made the more remarkable by the high likelihood that he throughout appreciated that his skills and his energy would be in vain. Nor was he much assisted by a sustaining Cabinet, apart from Morley and Spencer. Rosebery's commitment to Home Rule was always skin-deep, and he quickly peeled it off as soon as Gladstone was out of the way. Within eight years it had become the foremost of the 'fly-blown phylacteries', a phrase of which the resonance exceeded the meaning, which he urged the Liberal party to discard. Harcourt was always unpleasantly hostile.

The two difficult issues which remained to be decided after Gladstone's return from Biarritz were first the old basically unanswerable question of Irish representation at Westminster, and secondly the financial settlement, particularly in relation to customs and excise. The first was temporarily resolved on the basis that there should be an Irish representation reduced from 103 to 80 to bring it in line with population, and that these numbers should 'in general terms' (that is, if a satisfactory dividing line could be devised, which was not so far the case) be excluded from voting on purely British questions. This was agreed on 13 January, with an overruled minority of Harcourt, Asquith, Fowler and Acland, who, in differing ways and activated by different reasons, were a disturbing quadrilateral of dissent, and one which proved itself to be right, at least to the extent that their scepticism about a satisfactory dividing line proved incontrovertible. In July the government gave up the attempt to find one and amended the crucial Clause 9 of the bill so as to give Irish representatives unrestricted rights of participation in all business.

Although less inherently difficult, the financial provisions proved even more of a quagmire. This was partly because of the anti-Irish ill will of Harcourt (tempered only by his equally rumbustious anti-Toryism), who was of course in a key position to cause financial trouble, and partly by a malevolent voodoo which seemed to sit on British official calculations in relation to Irish finance. In 1886 Welby (permanent secretary to the Treasury) and Hamilton (more directly to blame) had made an embarrassing error. In 1893 an at least equally serious mistake was made, with the major blame resting on that normally impeccable prodigy Alfred Milner, then aged only thirty-eight but already West's successor as chairman of the Board of Inland Revenue. In 1892 Welby again and the Dublin Castle administration were also involved. The result was to muddy the financial issues to an extent which now makes it difficult and doubtfully worthwhile to disentangle them. It is perhaps sufficient to say that the financial clauses had to be largely recast after the second reading of the bill, and that Gladstone was always dealing with them heavily on the defensive.

The circumstances surrounding the presentation of the second Home Rule Bill to Parliament were therefore remarkably unfavourable. The majority was thin, although, such as it was, more cohesive than those of 1880 or 1886. The Prime Minister was infirm and backed by a far from enthusiastic or unanimous Cabinet. And the bill itself was by no means a perfect piece of draft legislation. In addition there was Gladstone's strong suspicion that it would not make the statute book. It therefore had a good deal of gesture politics in it. All this makes the more heroic his last parliamentary *tour de force*. Essentially it was he who took the bill through the House of Commons in the most strenuous parliamentary session on record. The Chancellor of the Exchequer gave some rather grudging help on the financial clauses, and the Irish Secretary was constantly at the GOM's side. But Morley was not long on parliamentary experience, and was in any event a scratchy violin compared with the resonant organ notes which the Prime Minister was still able to produce. It was an organ which did not just produce great volumes of solemn sound. There was widespread agreement that he was supple, subtle, erudite, good-humoured and sometimes very amusing. His committee-stage speeches were almost entirely spontaneous. They almost had to be, for as he wrote to a correspondent on 4 March he could not see to read any notes which he might have made. On 11 May when Chamberlain had delivered one of his most vicious attacks at the end of a 'clause stand part' (that is, fairly general) debate, Gladstone after hesitating until the last moment about whether to speak, rose at the dinner-hungry time of just after 8.00 p.m. but nonetheless delighted the House, according to Morley, with 'one of the most remarkable performances that ever was known'. 'I have never seen Mr. Gladstone so dramatic, so prolific of all the resources of the actor's art,' wrote another observer. 'The courage the audacity and the melodrama of it were irresistible.'[5] Gladstone himself wrote of the occasion: 'I seemed to be held up by a strength not my own. Much fatigued.'[6]

That incident also illustrates what was the one criticism of his parliamentary handling of the bill. The reply to Chamberlain was not strictly necessary. The division might have taken place immediately after Chamberlain; instead the debate was stimulated to such an extent that the vote was postponed until two hours into the following day's sitting. Gladstone exposed a lot of surface, which meant that with an opposition trying to spin things out he was a helpful minister to have on the other side. Morley referring back sixty years from 1893 thought that an Althorp might have expedited matters more. Looking forward almost the same length of time it is probable that an Attlee might have done so too.

On the other hand Gladstone's resilience and expansive good humour could sometimes unravel parliamentary knots. Morley describes another afternoon of obstruction when no progress at all had been made until the dinner adjournment. Gladstone had gone off 'haggard and depressed' briefly to fulfil a dining engagement. When Morley returned to the chamber around 10.00 p.m. he found Gladstone on his feet making 'a most lively and amusing speech on procedure' which ungummed the works. He sat down a different man, and turned compliments from his colleagues by saying: 'To make a speech of that sort, a man does best to dine out; 'tis no use to lie on a sofa and think about it.'[7]

Yet overall it was his courage and his endurance, the latter triumphing over frequent complaints of exhaustion, even more than his debating skill, which made his conduct of the marathon so memorable. In different parts of the House, even among his bitterest opponents, there was a sense of witnessing a magnificent last performance by a unique creature, the like of whom would never be seen again. One evening during the bill's passage Lord Randolph Churchill, admittedly then on the edge of his decline into incoherence, accosted Albert (later fourth Earl) Grey, a prominent Liberal Unionist: 'And that is the man you deserted,' he said of Gladstone. 'How could you do it?'[8] There were at least two ironies to this exchange. The first was that Churchill's last successful speech in the House, delivered on 23 February on Welsh Church disestablishment, had been a most violent attack on Gladstone. The second was that the accused deserter Grey was the son not only of Queen Victoria's former private secretary who had travelled to Hawarden twenty-five years before to give to Gladstone his first opportunity to form a government, but also of the former Miss Caroline Farquhar, who had so sharply rejected his amorous overtures at Polesden Lacey another thirty-five years before that.

A marathon the progress of the bill most certainly was. Gladstone moved the second reading on 6 April and carried it, after nine nights of debate, on the 21st, by a majority of forty-three. He wound up from 11.05 p.m. to 1.00 a.m. before an overflowing House. Of a total membership of 670, 651 voted, 4 were tellers, 14 were paired and one was the Speaker. The committee stage started on 8 May and continued until 27 July, consuming, together with guillotine and procedural motions, parts of fifty-three parliamentary days. During this stage of the proceedings Gladstone made over eighty speeches, sometimes as many as four in a single day. Between 7 and 25 August another ten days were devoted to the report stage. Third reading was secured after three parliamentary days, late at night on Friday, 1 September.

By then the greater part of eighty-two sittings had been devoted to the bill. Even this rate of progress had been achieved only by the use at both committee and report stages of the still relatively unfamiliar 'guillotine' (although there was a good precedent in the Conservative use of it for the Irish Crimes Bill of 1887). When the blade fell on the night of Thursday, 27 July, there were nine divisions in a row, a form of parliamentary torture, particularly on a foetid July night, of which more cruel regimes might have been proud.

But there was also, in Gladstone's words, 'the sad scene never to be forgotten'.[9] Chamberlain, always one on whichever side he was for provoking bitterness, launched a fierce attack on Gladstone whom he accused of behaving like an imperious and cruel god (reminiscent of those of Lucretius whom Gladstone himself had so memorably summoned to the attention of the House in a Bradlaugh debate ten years before). As ten o'clock, the terminal time, approached, Chamberlain moved towards his derisory conclusion: 'The Prime Minister calls "black" and they say it is good: the Prime Minister calls "white" and they say it is better. Never since the time of Herod has there been such slavish adulation.'[10] The biblical allusion was typically provocative, but not wise. T. P. O'Connor, who had the distinction of being the only Nationalist MP elected from outside Ireland (by the Scotland division of Liverpool) started a widely taken up shout of 'Judas.' Within seconds this led to an almost unprecedented outbreak of fighting on the floor in which the ringleaders appear to have been J. W. Logan, Liberal MP for Harborough, and Hayes Fisher, Conservative MP for Fulham. Between them they got about forty members in a battling mass around the end of the clerks' table. Speaker Peel, who, the House being in committee, was not in the chair, was sent for and quickly restored order, but the incident horrified Gladstone, who referred to it on the next day as 'last night's catastrophe' and on the day after that, when some sort of apologies were exchanged, wrote of getting 'the wretched incident to a close'.[11] Its only benefit was that it somewhat restored his relations with Arthur Balfour, who as leader of the opposition dealt with the matter elegantly.

The majority for the third reading was thirty-four, which showed a slight but uncomfortable decline from the forty-three of the second reading. Three Liberals voted against and two abstained, at least one of them because of the removal of the restriction on the voting rights of Irish MPs. Gladstone greeted the result with 'This is a great step. Thanks be to God.'[12] But his mood was not one of rejoicing or of optimism. Nor should it have been. He had shot his last bolt. On the next day (a Saturday) he wrote: 'Saw . . . Lord Stanmore: an uneasy conversation. I was rather upset by that or some other cause: and spent the day mainly on my back.'[13] Stanmore, who had been made a peer only that year, was the Arthur Gordon who had been his ADC in the Ionian Isles in 1858, had since held several colonial governorships, and in 1893 had just completed a (good) life of his Prime Minister father, the fourth Lord Aberdeen. He was, however, showing ingratitude for his Gladstone-bestowed peerage to the extent of making trouble about voting in the Lords for the Home Rule Bill. (He eventually did so, however.) The near unanimity with which Gladstone's old connections and associates were reluctant to support him can hardly have been a solace.

On the Monday he moved a business motion which provided for Parliament after a six-week break from 21 September to be recalled on 2 November and to sit indefinitely until the government's business was completed. During this autumn session (on 4 September Parliament was still nominally in its normal summer session) the government would take the whole of the time of the House and pursue its two other major measures, the Local Government (or Parish Councils) Bill and the Employers' Liability (or Industrial Accidents) Bill. Gladstone then departed by the night train to Perthshire, once again the guest of the ever welcoming Armitstead, but this time at his impressively named Black Craig Castle in the Forest of Clunie. There he stayed for three weeks of deserved rest, leaving Harcourt in charge in the House of Commons. But his holiday enthusiasm was less than usual. On the first day: 'Drive and walk: 2 miles entirely knocked me up. . . . Early bed, worked on Odes of Horace: pleasant but how difficult.' And on the second: 'Worked on Odes: so slow. Backgammon with Mr. A. I have fallen back another step or stride in the power of reading.'[14]

While the Commons was dealing with minor business and the Prime Minister was driving about the Perthshire Highlands and tinkering with his Horatian translations, the House of Lords was indulging in one of the seismic actions of its history. Yet it was an earthquake almost without noise or excitement, if that is a possible concept. On 8 September, after four short days of debate, it rejected the bill which was the centre of the government's programme and on which the Commons had spent eighty-two days by a vote of 419 to 41. It was a division without precedent, both for the size of the majority and for the strength of the vote. There were only 560 entitled to vote, and 82 per cent of them did so, even though there was no incentive of uncertainty to bring remote peers to London.

The breakdown of the vote, as well as its overall shape, was at once remarkable and profoundly unsatisfactory to Gladstone. Not a single bishop voted for the Bill, whereas both archbishops, the senior trio of London, Durham and Winchester, together with no less than seventeen other diocesans, voted against it. Many of these, including both Canterbury (Benson) and York (Maclagan), had of course been appointed by him. Nor did any duke vote for the Bill, although twenty-two (an almost incredible turn-up) voted against it. So did Gladstone's nephew Lyttelton, as well as, amongst those with whose persons or titles Gladstone had been closely associated, Ampthill, Rothschild and Wolverton (newly succeeded, not Gladstone's old Whip). On the other hand the heirs to Granville, Russell and Northbourne (James) remained loyal. So did Acton.

It was an enormity, but it was one which had become so widely discounted in advance, with the subject so exhausted by discussion, that the result was received with calm, almost with boredom. Magnus wrote that 'not a dog barked from John O'Groat's to Land's End'. What was even more surprising was that Gladstone hardly growled. He did not mention the result in his diary, either for that day or for the next. He received a visit from Sir Henry Ponsonby, who came over from Balmoral. But Ponsonby was more concerned to discuss the burning question of whether the Duke of Edinburgh, Queen Victoria's second son who had succeeded as Duke (and princeling) of Coburg could continue to keep the whole or part of his British civil-list allowance, which subject did indeed occupy not only Gladstone but Harcourt and Rosebery as well for a considerable part of the autumn. Ponsonby also,

Gladstone noted, 'brought a message half inviting me to a limited visit [to Balmoral], which I think is well meant'[15] – but was not taken up. Neither Prime Minister nor private secretary sought a constitutional discussion. Gladstone's other occupation that day and the next was to read the official life of W. H. Smith, the stationer–politician, which should have been reasonably calming.

It is sometimes alleged that Gladstone proposed an immediate dissolution but was frustrated by his colleagues. There is no evidence for this, although what is certainly the case is that had he proposed it he would have been so resisted. But he did not. And the facts that he neither went to London nor summoned a Cabinet until the first days of November are a firm indication to the contrary. His tactics were subtler and different from that. He knew that he could not mount a successful electoral indictment of the Lords on the Irish issue alone. During the general election of 1892 he had been seized with the obvious truth that English and Scottish votes could not be adequately sustained on a purely Irish diet. (It was an extraordinary Unionist conceit that Gladstone's Irish policy was based on an opportunistic craving for votes, which was almost the reverse of the truth.) He now fully saw the need for 'British' measures, which had perhaps not been the case in 1886.

This was the reason why he was determined to bring an exhausted Parliament back in early November and drive it up to Christmas and beyond with work on the Employers' Liability and Local Government Bills. If the Lords again proved recalcitrant, which they did (they mutilated the Employers' Liability Bill beyond repair and seriously weakened the Parish Councils measure), then an anti-Lords dissolution would attract him. This was a course which he urged from Biarritz, to which in 1894 he had once again made a January–February retreat, even though Parliament was still grinding on with what was still nominally the interminable 1893 session. But by then his final and essentially suicidal dispute with his colleagues over the naval estimates had assumed such proportions that his views on a dissolution had become a staking out of a personal position rather than a practical leadership of a Cabinet. Apart from anything else, it is difficult to believe that in the winter of his eighty-fifth year, he could have sustained the physical demands of a highly charged election campaign. He nevertheless remained convinced for his remaining four years, which is of course fully compatible with the 'staking out' theory, that a signal opportunity of regaining the Liberal initiative and beleaguering the Lords was then lost.

The labours to which he subjected the House of Commons (including mostly himself) were indeed extraordinary. It sat until Friday, 22 December, and was brought back on Wednesday the 27th, in which interval he had snatched only five days at Brighton. The House was therefore sitting, which it had not done in any of the previous sixty-two years which his membership had spanned, on his 29 December birthday. Balfour and others were suitably gracious about the anniversary, although they cannot have been pleased at having their Christmases so truncated. On New Year's Day the House ploughed on with its work on parish and district councils, as it did, tempered with other bits of business, for most of the winter. Gladstone's escape to Biarritz lasted from 13 January to 10 February 1894, but the session was still going on his return, and indeed continued until 1 March, when his last words in the House were a reluctant acquiescence to the Lords' amendments to the Local Government Bill. Then, after an interval of no more than a weekend, the 1894 session began, but without Gladstone.

The issue of increased naval expenditure began to obtrude in the summer of 1893, although Gladstone did not much engage with it until December, being preoccupied with the Irish Bill until September and then away from London until November. In 1889 the Salisbury government had launched a sustained programme of increased warship-building. This had provoked a response by other European powers, particularly France and Russia, who were then moving into the alliance in support of which Britain was to fight the First World War, although this orientation was not obvious at the time. Then in June 1893 two British men-of-war, *Camperdown* and *Victoria*, collided with vast loss of life. The combination of circumstances produced a naval panic, which was carefully fanned by *The Times* and some other newspapers. It cannot be said that it was wholly logical. It was not obvious, for instance, that the answer to British ships running into each other was to have more of them. But the clamour was enthusiastically and not surprisingly taken up by the admirals. Given the persistent British affiliation to a 'blue water' theory of defence they swept along without too much difficulty the Queen, the Tories and the more imperially minded members of the Liberal Cabinet. And even such a Little Englander as Harcourt, although at first sceptical as a Chancellor of the Exchequer should have been, saw increased naval expenditure (the sum involved was £3 million plus) as preferable to the possible alternative of entangling alliances.

Even more key than Harcourt was Spencer, the First Lord of the Admiralty. It is always tempting to think of Spencer, perhaps because of his venerable beard, as older than he was. He was in fact twenty-six years' Gladstone's junior, succeeded to his fine possessions at the age of twenty-two, was given the Garter by Palmerston when he was only twenty-nine, first became Viceroy of Ireland at thirty-three, and in 1893 was still well under sixty. He was in no way a jingo, as he was to show at the time of the South African War by inclining more to the Campbell-Bannerman pro-Boer than to the Rosebery Liberal Imperialist position. He was not a clever man, but he was a great gentleman, and he had the fortitude to stand almost alone of the high Whigs as a steady Home Rule ally of Gladstone's. He also had a deep regard for and loyalty to the Grand Old Man. He was not exactly an intimate – no Latin tags were exchanged – but he was never reported as making a disparaging remark about Gladstone, at a time when there were only too many flying around behind the cupped hands of his colleagues.

Spencer could probably take on only one unconventional policy at a time. At any rate he swallowed the demands of the admirals whole, and once he had done so he was a more formidable adversary for Gladstone than any other member of the Cabinet would have been. They never quarrelled, although Gladstone made some most violent remarks about Spencer's policy, but never his person. Indeed, even after Gladstone had been overwhelmingly defeated in his own Cabinet by Spencer, the First Lord was still the man whom, if he had been asked by the Queen, which he was not, he would have named as his chosen successor. But Spencer, totally untinged by malice, unmovable once he was convinced where his duty lay, and impossible to defeat by dialectic because that was not the currency in which he dealt, was a fatal foe. Yet Spencer, by a supreme irony because of the quality of his central loyalty, was the spike on which Gladstone chose to immolate his final premiership.

Nonetheless Gladstone won the first round. For 19 December Lord George Hamilton, who had been First Lord in the previous government, put down a 'greater navy' motion. The Cabinet was persuaded to treat it as one of no confidence and Gladstone refuted it in what turned out to be his last major (or, to be more accurate, semi-major) speech in the House of Commons. It gave him a 'troubled night physically, in brain only' (whatever that meant) beforehand. 'This is certainly the weakness of old age unfitting me for Parliamentary effort,'[16] he added. It also gave him a majority of thirty-six. But it was not a majority against a larger navy. It was a party majority against this being decided by Hamilton rather than by Spencer. This was recognized by Gladstone, who wrote pessimistically after the debate: 'The situation almost hopeless when a large minority allows itself to panic and joining hands with the professional elements works on the susceptibilities of a portion of the people to alarm.'[17]

Over his short Christmas holiday Gladstone's opposition to the Admiralty proposals strengthened and deepened. He sometimes expressed it in extreme terms. When they were first expounded in Cabinet he asked in a resonant aside whether there were any plans for the enlargement of Bedlam. And in February, when he had had plenty of time to calm down, he informed Edward Hamilton that 'I can only characterize those who put [these proposals] forward as mad or drunk.'[18] Yet he was far from being without a rational case, and it was probably best expressed again to Hamilton and also in mid-February:

> He again and again said it was not a question of amount: he would swallow any amount of expenditures, however reckless it might appear to be, for such purposes as converting all our ironclads into wooden ships on the assumption that naval policy has gone through a transformation, or (say) doubling the Education grant. No. It was a question of policy. Russia and France had gone ahead with their ship-building, solely owing to our Naval programme of 1889 for which we had to thank the late Government; and now we were to 'go one better', thus directly challenging Europe in the race of armaments. It was his conviction that this competitive action of ours would accelerate some great European catastrophe: these vast armaments must lead to some flare-up – probably the absorption of small states and the break-up of Italy. He could not be party to this.[19]

And a few weeks later he added to Hamilton: 'If I stood alone in the world on this question, I could not be moved: so strongly am I convinced that this large increase to the Navy will lead to disaster in Europe – *Europe* is my watchword.'[20] It sounded a little hysterical, yet who is to say that his sombre view of the likely consequences of competitive armaments was not given strong reinforcement twenty years later?

The first critical phase of the dispute was reached in early January 1894. Then Gladstone realized how isolated he was. Even Harcourt, who was against the increased naval expenditure on merits, nonetheless disagreed violently with Gladstone on tactics, believing that there was, regrettably, no sensible alternative to accepting Spencer's demand: by thinking otherwise Gladstone was displaying irresponsibility. Harcourt gave vent to his spleen at a lunch with the ubiquitous Hamilton on 5 January.

> Mr. G. has already twice brought the Liberal party to grief – first in 1874 and afterwards in 1886; and now he proposes taking a step which would mean its complete smash up, after it has been partially set on its legs again with infinite trouble. He does not care a rush for the party. So long as the party suits his purpose, he uses it. The moment the question of his own personal convenience turns up, or he finds himself out of touch with the party, he is ready to discard it regardless of all consequences. I consider it mean and shabby of him.[21]

Harcourt, beyond the habitual extremity of his language, was in a very jumpy state at this time because he had his own strong personal reasons for wanting Gladstone to survive in office and believed that the latter's behaviour was making this impossible. Harcourt much wanted to be Prime Minister, and as the senior and dominant figure after Gladstone on the government front bench he obviously had a high claim. But it was becoming gradually borne in on him that, because of his overbearingness in Cabinet, none of his colleagues wanted to serve under him. Even John Morley preferred Rosebery. And a Rosebery premiership was anathema to Harcourt. At this stage he did not believe that he could serve under him (Rosebery, who knew he was on safe ground here, said that he could serve *under* Harcourt; what he could not bear was the thought of serving *over* such an intolerable colleague), and that his political career would be brought to an abrupt end. Harcourt was therefore in favour of the *status quo* but on grounds of convenience and not of respect for Gladstone's current faculties and performance.

Nor was even Morley, the other most committed Little Englander, and one on much closer personal terms with Gladstone than was Harcourt, a dependable ally. The best that Gladstone could record him as being was 'sympathetic'. Gladstone needed more than sympathy. He needed fighting support, and that was not forthcoming. Wednesday, 3 January, was a terrible day:

> I have felt myself hard hit from a combination of circumstances: I seem to stand alone. . . . my sleep is a good deal disturbed. . . . The perpetual more or less dark fog odd to say contributes: I have always been open in a degree to this influence. Today I saw Spencer 1–2 and explained everything. In tone and temper, there was nothing to be desired. Of substantial progress hardly any. We agreed that in any case I ought to wind up the present Session [that is, continue well into February, as opposed to resigning immediately].[22]

The fog, which that week shrouded London with the full intensity of a Sherlock Holmes-style pea-souper, became a recurrent theme of

Gladstone's. When on the following Monday he came back from a weekend in Brighton he told Morley that he was rapidly travelling along a 'road that leads to total blindness'. 'You are all complaining of fog,' he added. 'I live in fog that never lifts.'[23] Morley found Gladstone on this (and some adjacent occasions) lacking in nobility, and he retaliated by himself writing about it in his diary with singular meanness, very different from the uplifting picture of Gladstone as a hero at bay that he gave in his great Gladstone biography, although he admittedly passed over the final period with considerable speed. Morley wrote:

> This was perhaps the most painful thing about it – no piety, no noble resignation, but the resistance of a child or an animal to an uncomprehensible & (incredible) torment. I never was more distressed. The scene was pure pain, neither redeemed nor elevated by any sense of majestic meekness before decrees that must be to him divine. Not the right end for a life of such power, & long and sweeping triumph.[24]

On the following day Gladstone confronted the Cabinet. It was in one sense a true confrontation, for there was no one on his side, with the possible exception of Shaw-Lefevre, the First Commissioner of Works, who although an admirable man much concerned with the preservation of open spaces, was hardly a heavyweight minister. In another sense 'confrontation' was too gladiatorial a word, for Gladstone knew that he was beaten before he started. 'On Tuesday I have to go to the stake (so to speak) and perhaps the sooner the better,' he had written to Morley from Brighton on the Sunday, and had struck a note in that letter which was much more engaging than Morley's diary entry. 'I once made a speech of 3 hours in Cabinet,'* he almost jauntily wrote. 'This will not be so long.'[25] However, he did speak for fifty minutes, and from one of the most elaborate and schematically prepared speaking notes (largely illegible to him) which he had ever used. Nonetheless he had occupied the Sunday at Brighton not only by working on this and writing to Morley and others but by producing a substantial monograph on the changes (and improvement) in church music during his lifetime. He was an amazing man. Almost anyone else would have been preoccupied with his Tuesday battle and an obsessive sense of grievance stemming from his knowledge that it was already lost. And so, most assuredly, it was. His fifty-minute oration did not shift the position of a single member of the Cabinet.

Four days later he retreated to Biarritz accompanied by Armitstead,

* Explaining the budget of 1853 (his first). See p. 150, above.

Mrs Gladstone, his daughter Mary with her child Dorothy Drew, and Lord Acton. He left everyone in considerable doubt about what he would do next. Was he going to return to resign, or, as many thought likely, to come back rejuvenated and announce that he was swallowing the naval estimates and staying on? And, if he resigned, was he to go quietly on grounds of increasing infirmity, or was he to make an issue of the naval quarrel, stay in Parliament and fulminate against his colleagues? It was a striking fact that the long-running Cabinet naval row never got into the newspapers. It justified Hamilton's comment: 'Mr G's Cabinets have been able to keep their own counsel ever since Chamberlain and Dilke ceased to be colleagues.'[26] It also set an example which modern Cabinets would find hard to follow.

There was the additional lurking fear that Gladstone might indulge in one last exercise in the prerogatives of a Prime Minister and try to force a dissolution of Parliament. This would have been in the tradition (not a happy one) of 1874, when his dissolution was just as much against Cardwell's army estimates as it was against the Tories. Fortunately, perhaps, that precedent was not much noticed, although one or two of his Cabinet colleagues – Harcourt in particular – had a naive faith that they were going to catch him out, and even force a change in his position, on the basis that in 1860 when Chancellor under Palmerston he had accepted, and even defended, a bigger increase in naval spending than anything which Spencer was currently putting forward.

Towards the end of his month at Biarritz Gladstone increased the tension, probably deliberately, by sending to Welby (the permanent secretary of the Treasury) a request to know immediately the minimum number of days between (i) dissolution and the assembly of the new Parliament, and (ii) that assembly and the taking of votes on the various estimates, including the naval ones. It was a good gamesmanship ploy. He also sent back, via his own chief of staff, Algernon West, who had come out for a few days, a definite proposition for an immediate dissolution on the accumulated sins of the Lords. It was turned down unanimously, and Gladstone made no attempt to act unilaterally. Harcourt nevertheless described Gladstone's proposal as 'the act of a selfish lunatic'.[27]

There was ambiguity about Gladstone's mood during that last visit to Biarritz. The weather was mostly wet, although 'wild but soft' in his rather good oxymoron for one aspect of the Basque climate. He made numerous expeditions, which did not point to low spirits, to St Jean de Luz, to San Sebastián, to Bayonne, to Cambo-les-Bains, to St Jean Piedde-Port, and when one of these drives was not on the agenda he got pleasure out of going with his wife to the Rocher or the Phare (two Biarritz promontories) to look at the fierce seas.

On the other hand when Algernon West came out (instigated by Harcourt) to try to persuade Gladstone to give way, or at least to compromise, he got short shrift. Hamilton, who saw West after he got back wrote: '[He] was in the depths of despair. Nobody knew, he said, what he had been through at Biarritz; he never got a civil word out of Mr. G., who either fulminated against everybody as if they were all criminals or treated everything with the greatest levity.'[28] Gladstone provided some confirmation by writing (20 January): 'I had with W[est] my tenth [?] long conversation on the coming events.... He is most kind and loyal: but weary talk casts no light whatever on the matter.' And even with his son Herbert (by now Asquith's under-secretary at the Home Office), who also came out, there was some trouble. 'Polemical talk with Herbert. He argued as well as any. I hope I have now nearly done.'[29]

Also at Biarritz he engaged spiritedly but not generously in a final honours joust with the Queen. The Marquess of Lansdowne was about to return after five years as Viceroy of India. Before that he had been Governor-General of Canada, so that his public service (although he was still under fifty) was great. On the other hand he had led the flight of the Whigs from Liberalism by his 1880 resignation from a junior position in Gladstone's second government. He obviously had to receive some high honour. The Queen was in favour of a dukedom or a Garter, or maybe both. But there was no Garter vacancy. He would therefore have had to be given an 'extra' one for which there was no precedent since the Duke of Wellington. Gladstone thought there was no question of his deserving this. He saw his record as Viceroy as 'very chequered'. Nor did he want to make him a duke (about which Lansdowne himself was also reticent). On both issues Gladstone entered into an elaborate defence in depth. A step from a marquessate to a dukedom, he argued with more pedantry than persuasiveness, was qualitatively different from any other elevation in the peerage. He thought a Grand Cross of the Bath would do perfectly well. The Indian Secretary, Kimberley, was doubtfully on his side. It was in a way the encapsulation of Gladstone's relations with the Queen. He was probably by a narrow margin right on the merits, although he would have been very hard put to it to explain why his own Westminster dukedom was more appropriate than a Lansdowne one would have been. But Disraeli, had he been alive, in office and aware of what the Queen wanted, would have happily given Lansdowne the dukedom, the 'extra' Garter, and the GCB as well. In this little final skirmish Gladstone, while convincing himself that he was discharging his duty to maintain the value of honours, exhibited many of the traits which, in combination with her prejudices, ruined his relations with Victoria.

When he got back to London on 10 February ('Luxurious journey: but bad [Channel] passage'),[30] Gladstone continued to keep his colleagues on tenterhooks. Except for Asquith as a minister, Morley as a companion and Spencer as a *grand seigneur* he did not have much of a view of them, and was at least half happy that they should swing in the wind. He held a brief Cabinet on the 12th, to which he gave no hint of his intentions. There was a sense of anti-climax when he adjourned it after merely an hour's discussion on the Lords' amendments to the Parish Councils Bill. On Saturday the 17th he held a Cabinet dinner. Every member came. They were eager more for the news than for the food. But again nothing happened, even when Rosebery, with perhaps less than his vaunted subtlety, suggested that they ought to make sure that the doors were closed and that there were no waiters or others behind the screens. Gladstone wrote: 'I believe it was expected that I should say something. But from my point of view there is nothing to be said.'[31]

Algernon West thought that he was waiting to see what the Lords did with the Parish Councils Bill: 'and they may alter things, for in the case of a dissolution I should go to the country with them' – 'them' referring not back to 'they' but to his Liberal colleagues. As, however, the one thing his Liberal colleagues were determined not to do was to 'go to the country' this was not a meaningful promise or threat. And it has to be set against the view of Hamilton, who for all his occasional Roseberyite disloyalty both knew and understood Gladstone better than did West. Hamilton recorded on 17 February that he was 'convinced that Mr. G. has never really vacillated since the Admiralty decision was taken by Cabinet before he went to Biarritz'.[32] He was going, but he nonetheless felt at least enough resentment against his colleagues to enjoy playing a game with them on the way.

There was no further Cabinet until Friday, 23 February. On this occasion, after the attitude of the government to the Lords' amendments to the Local Government Bill (hostile acquiescence) had been fixed and the Prorogation speech (end of the session) agreed, Gladstone announced that its delivery would be the moment of his resignation, but did so only as the Cabinet was breaking up, so that no one else had a chance to say anything. However, there was another Cabinet on the Monday, and nobody seems to have said much on that occasion either, although Gladstone had seen both Harcourt and Rosebery (together; it cannot have been an easy triangle) to tell them of an interview which he had had with Ponsonby, the Queen's secretary. The purport of this interview was for Gladstone to authorize Ponsonby to tell the Queen he was about to resign, provided that the Queen would agree to pass the information on to no one else. The Queen refused to give the assurance. It was a preposterous refusal to a farcical request. The idea that the Sovereign would not agree to accept a confidence from her Prime Minister was disgraceful. Equally it was not very fruitful to make an issue of secrecy about an event which was the gossip of London. Like the issue of Lansdowne's honours it showed that they never could fail to rub each other the wrong way.

On Wednesday, 28 February, he eventually saw her, most exceptionally and conveniently at Buckingham Palace (where she had not come, needless to say, to effect an easy changeover but to hold a drawing room). By the time of the formal replacement of Gladstone by Rosebery she had retreated to Windsor. Of this first resignation interview, however, Gladstone provided a very good throw-away account on the borderline of irony, which was not normally his strongest weapon:

> I had an audience of the Queen, for 30 or 35 minutes today: doubtless my last in an official capacity. She had much difficulty in finding topics for an adequate prolongation: but fog and rain and [her] coming journey to Italy all did their duty and helped. I thought I never saw her looking better. She was at the highest point of her cheerfulness. Her manner was personally kind throughout.[33]

The next event was the so-called 'blubbering Cabinet' of the following day, Tuesday, 1 March. The sobriquet was the dismissive title which Gladstone himself subsequently gave it, although at the time he wrote of it as 'a really moving scene'. However, I prefer the account of the occasion given by Asquith, a man of cool judgement who had been given a great opportunity by Gladstone, who admired his historical resonance, but was at that time a friend and ally of Rosebery's, and with his brilliant career ahead of him naturally looked more to the future than to the past. Thirty years later Asquith wrote:

> Before the Cabinet separated, Lord Kimberley (the senior member), who was genuinely moved, had uttered a few broken sentences of affection and

> reverence, when Harcourt produced from his box and proceeded to read a well-thumbed MS of highly elaborated eulogy. Of those who were present there are now few survivors; but which of them can forget the expression of Mr. Gladstone's face, as he looked on with hooded eyes and tightened lips at the maladroit performance?[34]

That afternoon Gladstone also made his last appearance in the House of Commons. He was there for one and three-quarter hours. He answered questions and then spoke on the Lords' amendments to the Local Government Bill. He withdrew the government's opposition to them 'under protest', and warned that if, as seemed likely, the Lords had abandoned their traditional 'reserve and circumspection' then the conflict between them and the elected House 'when once raised, must [in due course] go forward to an issue. . . . Having said this, and thanking the House for the attention they have given me,' he concluded, 'I have only to signify that it is the intention of the Government to acquiesce in the amendments which have been made by the House of Lords.'[35] These were the last words that he spoke in the chamber, where in its different guise before the great fire of 1834, he had first spoken sixty-one years earlier. Indeed he never again entered the Palace of Westminster, although he retained his nominal membership until the general election fifteen months later. It appeared to suit his Edinburgh constituents better that way.*

Twenty-four hours later he went to Windsor to 'dine and sleep'. His conversation with the Queen, as part of the general company, was, he wrote 'long and courteous, but of little meaning'. The next morning he was waylaid by Ponsonby on his way to the St George's Chapel service. Ponsonby trailed the disadvantages of having a peer as Prime Minister. Gladstone refused to be drawn, either then or at a resumed conversation an hour later. If the Queen asked his views direct or if Ponsonby did it at her express command, he would of course give them; 'but . . . otherwise my lips must be sealed'.[36] Ponsonby could not say he had been

* Whether it suited the government Whips, who were operating on a fairly small and unstable majority, may have been another matter. They managed, however, to get him permanently paired with the even older Charles Villiers (b. 1802), who after several decades of never visiting his Wolverhampton constituency had since 1886, when following a Radical middle age he became a Liberal Unionist, decided rarely to visit Westminster either. Unlike Gladstone, however, he continued after the 1895 election, and was still an MP when he died aged ninety-six. He also established a record of drawing a ministerial pension for thirty-two years. Appropriately he had been chairman of the Poor Law Board in the long Palmerston–Russell government and was making sure that he did not swell the numbers of those for whom he had been responsible.

so commanded and so nothing more was said. Nor was there the slightest mention of the succession when Gladstone later saw the Queen and formally handed over his letter of resignation. She thanked him profusely – but only for what he had done in the matter of the Duke of Edinburgh (become Coburg) retaining his British annuity. She also opined that German oculists were better than English ones. And so, after fifty-three years as a Privy Councillor, twenty-seven of them in the service of the Crown, and twelve of them in the highest office, it was all over. Ponsonby informed him that the Queen had sent for Rosebery, to whom he could not object on the ground that he was a peer, for as we know he would, if asked, have advised Spencer. Nor was the news of the beginning of Rosebery's unfortunate premiership in any way a surprise to Gladstone, although he obviously felt deeply the complete absence of any consultation or even direct prior information on the point.

He then went back to London on what he described as 'the Council train' (there had been a Privy Council at Windsor that morning), finished off his translation of the Odes of Horace ('But *what* is it worth?') and dined with Lord Kimberley.[37] He still had to receive the Queen's jejune reply to his letter of resignation,* which perhaps hurt the most of the lot, and then to begin a very leisurely move out of 10 Downing Street. Rosebery at least had the advantage of not being in a hurry for that perquisite of office; he did not occupy it for nearly a year.

* *Windsor Castle, 3rd March 1894*

Though the Queen has already accepted Mr Gladstone's resignation and has taken leave of him, she does not like to leave his letter tendering his resignation unanswered. She therefore writes these few lines to say that she thinks, after so many years of arduous labour and responsibility, he is right in wishing to be relieved at his age of these arduous duties, and she trusts [he will] be able to enjoy peace and quiet, with his excellent and devoted wife, in health and happiness, and that his eyesight may improve.

The Queen would gladly have offered a peerage to Mr Gladstone, but she knows that he would not accept it. (*Letters of Queen Victoria*, 3rd series, II, pp. 372–3).

—— 36 ——

The Closing of the Doors of the Senses

THERE WERE JUST OVER fifty months between Gladstone leaving office and his death. During this twilight zone he was half-blind and half-deaf. The first infirmity greatly restricted his reading but not to any comparable degree his writing. Equally the second made him an inhibited listener (and transactor of any form of business) but left his ability to talk, in favourable circumstances, mainly anecdotally and reminiscently but sometimes analytically, largely unimpaired. He was untormented by the loss of office and, with the exception of one issue, viewed the political scene with detachment, feeling little enthusiasm for the Rosebery–Harcourt government, which staggered on for fifteen months, and only limited virulence against its successor, the third Salisbury administration, which included Liberal Unionists. Only one issue, and that at one remove a nostalgic one, the Armenian massacres, constituted enough of a jerk upon his memory to cause him, once in 1895 and again in 1896, to make his final political speeches. This state of semi-infirm equilibrium persisted until the autumn of 1897 when, at the age of almost eighty-eight, he became afflicted with a painful disease, which after a few months was diagnosed as terminal, and which made him long for the end, an event for which over many years previously he had regarded it as necessary, and even easy, to be well prepared.

Nevertheless, three and a half years before the beginning of the 1897 plunge, he had experienced a significant and downward change of gear in his life. On 24 May 1894 he had a cataract operation. It was carried out at Dollis Hill by a young but leading St Thomas's eye surgeon. Mary Gladstone (Drew) wrote a typically graphic account: 'Mr. Nettleship came at 9 with Dr H[abershon] and without any delay drew out the cataract. Father had cocaine drops in his eye and was totally unagitated; it only lasted a moment and was perfectly done. Mama and I in the next room with the door open. . . .'[1] This led to eight weeks of rough convalescence, much of it lying in darkness, which phase came to an end only on 19 July, when Nettleship conducted an examination and pronounced that the results of the operation were not wholly satisfactory. A supplementary operation on 20 September at Hawarden was envisaged, but although Nettleship duly attended in North Wales at that time, he decided against a further attempt. Hope of a significant improvement was therefore abandoned, although Gladstone was substantially more physically mobile and intellectually active after late July than he had been during the eight weeks following the operation. He was able to go to Hawarden at the beginning of August, and his regime there included a daily drive, an occasional short walk and making the maximum use of the hours of daylight (when he could see better) to sit at his desk and do written work. Against the habits of his lifetime he could no longer go each day to early church because bowel trouble somewhat obscurely prevented his getting up before ten o'clock.

More important as a station on the way to the tomb than the partial failure of the operation, however, was the fact that it caused him (or maybe provided an excuse) to give up writing his journal. His last daily entry, after sixty-nine years and ten and a half months, was for 23 May 1894. He next made an entry for 19 July (there had been illness breaks before, but always much shorter), and then, after only two intermediate entries, he defined on 1 September his diary policy for the future: 'After breaking up the practice of seventy years, I now mean to proceed by leaps and bounds, making an occasional note.'[2] In fact he added only a dozen subsequent entries over the next two and a half years, his final one being on 29 December 1896, his eighty-seventh birthday.

For the outside observer this drew across his life a new screen of opaqueness which was almost as obfuscating as the perpetual fog in which he had complained to Morley of having to live. It became no longer possible to trace his day-to-day movements and activity from a single source. Obviously a great deal can be put together from letters, from the records of others and from his own sporadic writings. But there was no longer a wholly reliable budget of time against which the recollections of others and indeed of himself could be measured. This had the objective effect of putting the short remainder of his life more in the shadows.

It may also have had a considerable subjective effect. Once the discipline of the diary had gone, so a significant part of the framework and of the purpose of Gladstone's life had gone with it. The diary was not just a record. It was his account book with God for his expenditure of 'the most precious gift of time'. As such its filling, particularly with items of duty, whether they were letters written or journeys completed or meetings conducted or books read or articles composed, gave him a sense of fulfilment, and indeed an incentive to keep his nose to the grindstone in order to be able to make the entries. Once that was gone his life was much more a matter of drifting towards the end. Minutes became more for passing than for saving.

His vitality and the width of his interests were such that he could endure this loosening of incentive and framework without sinking into the torpor which most would regard as natural for the second half of their eighties (and some for their sixties or earlier). He abandoned his old pattern of travel. He no longer made expeditions, either at home or abroad, for sightseeing or political reasons, but only for those of health, which broadly meant avoiding the not very fierce North Wales winter. His Italian days were over. So with one exception were his Scottish ones. He stayed with Armitstead in Perthshire in the early autumn of 1897, but he never went for a last look at Fasque, or even to say goodbye to the Edinburgh constituents when he ceased to be their member in the summer of 1895. Just as he could accuse the Queen of treating him as he had treated his Sicilian mule of 1838,* so others could have accused him of doing the same with his several constituencies.

He abandoned also those tours of English cathedral cities, interspersed with halts at conveniently situated great houses, which had been an earlier feature of his life.† The only exception was in the spring of 1895,

* 'There was the fact staring me in the face, I could not get up the smallest shred of feeling for the brute, I could neither love nor like it.' (Memorandum written on 20 March 1894 and published in *Diaries*, XIII, p. 403.)

† It could be said that by that stage he had no need for such tours, except that the pleasure of movement and sightseeing is not in general marred by having been there before. Gladstone knew Britain (excluding Ireland) exceptionally well. There was no English county that he had not visited, although his two Cornish visits came late in life, and were both, the one in 1880 and the other in 1889, in the form of landings from a cruise ship. His ubiquity was almost equally true of the Scottish counties. He may have missed Kirkcudbrightshire and Wigtownshire in the hidden south-west corner, but nowhere else. Nor is it easy to think of an old cathedral which might have eluded him. Ripon is a possible gap, and Llandaff a probable one, the latter not entirely by accident, for of all the economically important areas of Britain the South Wales coalfield was the only one which he never visited. In 1825 he went into the eastern edge of Monmouthshire. In 1852 he went to Pembrokeshire by boat from Bristol and then, fringing the valleys, to Brecon and rural mid-Wales. And in 1887 he made a major political visit to Swansea and delivered 'whistle-stop' speeches in Cardiff and Newport on the way back. But he never went to the Rhondda or Merthyr Tydfil or Aberdare. Those close-packed Glamorgan valleys already contained about half the population of Wales, but it was not untypically North Walian that they were almost the only enclave of Britain to which he never penetrated.

when he went for four days to the Lincoln deanery, to which epitome of close splendour he had appointed his Wickham son-in-law in one of his last and entirely appropriate acts of patronage. He went only rarely to London, and then mostly as a staging post to somewhere beyond. An exception was in July 1896, when he perhaps unwisely attended a royal wedding (that of the Wales's daughter to the future King of Norway) and thought that the Queen (in contrast to the Prince) took inadequate notice of 'a lady [Mrs Gladstone] of 84 who had come near 200 miles to attend the service'.[3] On this occasion, as on a few others, the Gladstones stayed, not out at Dollis Hill, but with their son Henry and his Rendel wife in Whitehall Court, part of the pinnacled palace, built by Waterhouse mainly for the National Liberal Club, of which Gladstone had laid the foundation stone in 1884. It was on the site of the house, among others, in which Peel had died forty-six years earlier.

Among old resorts, Gladstone went for a three-week visit to Penmaenmawr at the end of October 1896. It was the first return for nearly ten years. There was no sea-bathing or even climbing of the Gwynedd hills, but he found the house – Plas Mawr – more comfortable than hitherto, and the visit left a sufficient glow of pleasure that Catherine Gladstone went back in 1899 during her two brief years of widowhood. On the other hand Biarritz was never revisited during the interval between office and the grave. It was superseded by Cannes, where the comforts of Lord Rendel's villa and the relative beneficence of the winter climate convinced Gladstone that it would massage his constitution. But it was all for health and not for interest. At Biarritz, a few years before, he could at least look at the wild seas and make inland drives into the Pyrenees. At Cannes, apart from Lord Acton's intermittent presence, it was healthful repose rather than stimulus which was on the menu. It was an old man's rest home, and it was appropriate that when he left it for the last time in February 1898 he should have gone immediately to Bournemouth, its nearest English equivalent, for a final and unhappy month away from home.

Cannes was central to his years of decline. He was there from early January to late March 1895 (with a side excursion to Cap Martin), from the end of December 1895 to early March 1896, and from January 1897 for another couple of months, and then for a final painful visit from late November of that year to the retreat to Bournemouth in February 1898. It was extraordinary the virtues which the English of that epoch attributed to the unreliable winter weather of the Côte d'Azur. Its exaggerated reputation brought Queen Victoria to Cimiez for a season during Gladstone's penultimate visit, and they met briefly in a Cannes hotel for the last time. The Queen came over to Cannes to visit what Gladstone described as 'a copious supply of Hanoverian royalties'. Princess Louise, later Duchess of Argyll, got the Gladstones to come to tea with her, and then slipped them into her mother's presence. It would be difficult to present the occasion as one of reconciliation. The Queen wrote: 'Mr. and Mrs. Gladstone came in for a moment, both looking much aged'[4] (which appeared to give her satisfaction). Gladstone set the visit at ten minutes rather than 'a moment', but made it clear that the Queen had brought it to an end and propelled them into a mêlée of Hanoverians. 'To speak frankly,' he wrote, 'it seemed to me that the Queen's peculiar faculty and habit of conversation had disappeared.'[5]

The Queen in the South of France was composing herself for the rigours of her Diamond Jubilee, which took place on and around 22 June 1897. Although he was the senior Privy Councillor (he believed himself to be the second senior, but a search even with the aid of the Privy Council Office fails to reveal a rival) as well as the most famous British statesman, the Gladstones do not seem to have been invited to perform any special participatory role. In view of the highly imperialist tone of the proceedings this was perhaps as well, but it was an added slight. The Colonial premiers, however, made a pilgrimage to Hawarden after the London festivities, and the Prince and Princess of Wales were also briefly there in that summer.

Apart from these three long sessions in the Alpes Maritimes, Gladstone's only other expedition beyond the shores of Britain was another northern-waters cruise for a fortnight in June 1895. Sir Donald Currie was again the provider, and the places visited were Hamburg, Kiel for the Kaiser's opening of the new canal, and Copenhagen. Gladstone recorded it in a then rare diary entry and in a mixed but above all flat way, contrasting with his previous exuberance of holiday enjoyment: 'Cruise to the Baltic in the Tantallon Castle. We did not see the places we mainly wished, but the weather was very good, the hotel incomparable [Where? How one misses the daily entry!] and the sanatory effect admirable!'[6]

His intellectual vigour at least for the two years or so between his recovery from the cataract operation and the end of 1896 was greater than might be inferred from this somewhat flaccid account of his sea trip. Indeed immediately after his return he exceptionally spent five days in London, mostly working in the British Museum on material relating to the eighteenth-century divine Joseph Butler, Bishop first of Bristol and later of Durham, to whom Gladstone devoted the main part of his post-Prime Ministerial energies. He prepared and annotated a new edition of Butler's works, which was published in February 1896, and was followed a few months later by a 150,000-word theological volume of his own, entitled *Studies Subsidiary to the Works of Bishop Butler*. Although it bore the Clarendon imprint, which is the Oxford University Press's seal of academic quality, it was bereft of an index, a deficiency much more common then than a century later. But it was a spirited work of not very subtle theology, including some philippics against 'Mr Bagehot, Mr Leslie Stephen and Mr Matthew Arnold' (two of them dead), whom he saw as detractors of Butler.

Butler was the central work of Gladstone's twilight years, but by no means the only one. When he went out of office he had four tasks on hand, and three of them he completed. In spite of his diary claim that he had 'finished' his version of the Odes of Horace on the day that he came back from his resignation audience at Windsor, he in fact did a good deal of subsequent tidying-up work on them. They were a form of high-grade crossword puzzle for him, which suited his fading eyesight well. His translations were eventually published by John Murray in late 1894.

The third task which he had on hand in March 1894 was a long article on the Atonement which he wrote for the *Nineteenth Century* and which was published in its September number. With his unique capacity always to seek (and find) a rebound, he had begun work on this not altogether recreational subject, which he curiously mingled with a review of Annie Besant's *Autobiography* (a chapter of which also engaged with the Atonement), on 18 February 1894. That was a day when the whole of the London political world was obsessed with the question of whether or not he really was going to resign, and when he himself (according to Algernon West at least) was still waiting to see what the House of Lords would do to the Parish Councils Bill before finally making up his mind.

The fourth task was the autobiography which he had started, at an even more strange moment than the article on the Atonement, at Dalmeny during the 1892 election campaign. By then he knew that he was going to be Prime Minister again (at eighty-two), although with a small majority which, as he put it, was 'the heaviest weight I can bear'. Yet, because he could not read, he chose that extraordinary moment to start on an autobiography. This, however, he never completed, despite vast if slightly vague financial incentives. There was a firm offer from

Cassell of £5000 (£250,000 today) in 1891, which could have been supplemented by at least an equivalent amount from Putnam's of New York. Hamilton however recorded that in 1887 he had been offered, probably through his friendly acquaintance Andrew Carnegie, the then fantastic sum of £100,000 (£5 million today) for full rights in a full-scale autobiography. It would have been tempting, first because Gladstone liked to have money, not to spend on himself, but to give away alike to his descendants and to his eleemosynary causes; and second, because Disraeli, at the height of his fame and for all his writer's professionalism, had earned no more than £10,000 for his semi-autobiographical *Endymion* (1880). But the temptation, if it was seriously there, was resisted, and the contract was not made.

This was as well, for Gladstone never got near to completing the autobiography. In the five years to 1897, he wrote interesting fragments about both his early life and his old age (weaker on the middle), rather but not excessively self-justificatory, but anything approaching a continuous whole was elusive. Had he achieved completion he would have anticipated the mid- and late-twentieth-century pattern, which affectively began with Lloyd George, of it being almost obligatory for Prime Ministers (and others) to sell their lives dearly. As it was he nominally stuck to and, together with Rosebery and Salisbury, rounded off the nineteenth-century tradition of leaving others to write biographies rather than oneself taking the first cut of the cake. Nevertheless Gladstone's outpouring of written words, some but not most solipsistic, was on a scale which no other Prime Minister except Churchill has ever rivalled. It is matched, again with this solitary exception, only by the enormous bibliography from others which has accumulated around his name.

Although he resisted, or found insubstantial, the extreme literary blandishments of Mammon, he nonetheless distributed very considerable sums during these final years, and gave the impression of doing so from a satisfactorily elastic bran-tub. In November 1895 he made his main bequest (apart from the site and 20,000 books) to the St Deiniol's residential library which he had founded at Hawarden. When the transactions were complete he wrote: 'I am now 40m. poorer than this day week. All right: & may God prosper the work.'[7] By 40m he meant of course £40,000 or 40 mille, which was mostly his way of expressing large sums of money, and not £40 million. But allowing for the change in the value of money it meant that he had endowed the St Deiniol's trust with approximately a modern £2 million. Such underpinning has been one reason why a remotely situated and strongly theological library has more than maintained its vitality over the changes of a century which have not been naturally helpful to such an institution.

In the autumn (1896) after the St Deiniol's transaction he 'completed the arrangement for a third and probably last partition of property among my children'. He calculated that until then each of his three surviving sons had received £27,000 from him, and each of his three surviving daughters £15,000. (The discrimination, while there, was not gross by the standards of the time.) He further calculated that his remaining capital amounted to about £58,000 ('besides copyrights if they are worth anything'), and decided to distribute almost all of it by giving another £10,000 to each of his sons, which meant that they had each done nearly as well as St Deiniol's, and another £5000 to each of his daughters, which brought them up to a modern million apiece. In addition he had written in December 1893 of arranging 'my little money presents for the 13 grandchildren'. This left him with disposable assets of at most £15,000. Nonetheless his will was eventually proved at £57,000, much of which was made up of collections and personal possessions which were not easily disposable.[8]

This sloughing off (but not dissipation) of capital seemed to give him a positive satisfaction: 'It is a comfort and relief to me thus to narrow and reduce my temporal cares. God be thanked.'[9] Any shortage of income from the £15,000 was balanced, substantially but not extravagantly, by his having an annuity of £3400 a year as a charge upon the Hawarden estate, which he had made over after the death of Sir Stephen Glynne in 1874 first to his eldest son Willy Gladstone and then, when he died in 1891, to Willy's son, William Glynne Charles Gladstone, who had been born in 1885. By the 1890s the estate had been restored (mainly by the efforts of Gladstone himself) from its mid-century vicissitudes to a fine upper-medium-sized property of 7000 acres and 2500 inhabitants, producing an income of £10,000 to £12,000 a year and carrying relatively light debts. Indeed it was sufficiently attractive that Gladstone, to whom it briefly reverted between son and grandson, had to fight off a determined attempt by Lord Penrhyn, the slate-quarry magnate and inhabitant of the vast Victorian castle further along the North Wales coast, to contest the succession and get it back for his wife, the daughter of the Revd Henry Glynne.

His grandson and heir naturally became an important symbol of the future for Gladstone. When Millais painted his third and last Gladstone picture in 1889 the boy was portrayed standing by the chair of the

GOM. Eight years after that Gladstone wrote him a long testamentary letter, to be read when the recipient was older and the writer probably dead, in which he expressed some remarkably conservative sentiments about the ownership of land, local leadership and the structure of county society. The Hawarden estate should be a leading influence in Flintshire. 'Should it be possible, through favouring influences, to reunite to it the lands which it has lost, or other lands, I contemplate such a contingency with satisfaction. Society cannot afford to dispense with its dominant influences.'[10] The outlying Glynne lands were not regained, but otherwise the boy in the brief time available to him more than fulfilled his grandfather's hopes. When he was killed in France in April 1915, at the age of twenty-nine, he had been President of the Oxford Union and was currently Lord Lieutenant of Flintshire and Liberal member of Parliament for Kilmarnock Burghs. The estate then passed to the descendants of Stephen Gladstone, the second and clergyman son, and in a later generation was reunited, not with the lost local lands, but in a more dramatic swoop with old Sir John Gladstone's Fasque estate in Kincardineshire. The late-twentieth-century Sir William Gladstone became the seventh holder of the baronetcy to which Peel nominated John Gladstone as in effect a recognition of the early Cabinet services of W. E. Gladstone. This he inherited by the normal automatic rules of succession. Fasque he inherited separately by the decision of his bachelor uncle Albert, Stephen Gladstone's son, who had previously received it in the same way from another bachelor uncle of his own, Thomas Gladstone's son. In 1985, Sir William Gladstone also became Lord Lieutenant of Clwyd (which includes Flintshire), a tribute not only to him but also to the solidity with which the GOM secured the future of his family as 'a leading influence' in the county.

Gladstone's final intervention in politics was a reprise, inevitably in a very minor key, of his explosive re-entry in the summer of 1876, twenty years before. The Armenians were a thousand miles from the Bulgarians and on the other side of the Black Sea, but they were nonetheless roughly in the same part of the world in British eyes, their oppressors were the same Constantinople regime, easily portrayed as a cruel and lustful oriental despotism, and Gladstone swept down in both cases like an avenging prophet from the hills, providing some justification for Harcourt's diatribe to Hamilton about his destructive effect upon the Liberal party.* Of course in 1896 his force and capacity for follow-

* See pp. 610–11, above.

through was immensely less than in 1876. On the other hand he was on the second occasion dealing with a more thin-skinned and selfish, even if, in the context of the time, equally right-of-centre Liberal leader. Hartington in the second half of the 1870s was not particularly selfish and at least had the advantage of being phlegmatic. Rosebery in the second half of the 1890s was looking even more urgently than usual for an excuse to flounce.

When therefore Gladstone went on 24 September 1896 to Hengler's Circus in Liverpool, which although a vast arena was, he claimed, one of the most agreeable in which to speak, and there delivered an hour and twenty minutes of denunciation of the Turks and demanded that the British government should take somewhat unspecified action against them, it had more effect on the internecine warfare within the Liberal party than on that in the area between the Black and Caspian Seas. Rosebery resigned from the leadership twelve days later, citing this as the 'last straw on his back' and complaining that it would enable 'discontented Liberals to pelt [him] with [Gladstone's] authority'.[11] But Harcourt was Rosebery's real trouble, even though he too did not approve of Gladstone's speech. To him, although – or maybe because – he was leader in the Commons, Rosebery absolutely refused to speak. The Liberal party was in fact stultified until it got rid of both of them and, although the last Gladstone eruption was from a party point of view self-indulgent, its objective results were not bad. Two years after Rosebery, Harcourt flounced in turn, and the party moved on to Campbell-Bannerman and Asquith and the possibility of revival.

The Liverpool speech was Gladstone's last direct impact upon politics, and a typical one. (His indirect impact of course lingered for decades, through his legend, his friends, his enemies, his disciples, his youngest son, his photographs in innumerable – mostly Nonconformist – cottage homes.) But it was not absolutely his last speech. That came only on 2 August 1897, when he addressed the Hawarden Horticultural Society. It is easy to imagine the semi-feudal, late-Victorian scene, with fine blooms exhibited at the beginning of the holiday season, and the sonorous if somewhat exhausted voice, no doubt with a felicity of elevating, slightly portentous allusion which had always been his forte, advising his listeners to continue to cultivate their gardens in a seemly and traditional way.

Early that autumn Gladstone entered his final decline. At his great age, which never failed to surprise him and which was of course much more exceptional then than today, a quiet subsidence might have been expected and deserved. Alas, it was not to be. He developed a cancer of the cheek, which first showed itself through an unpleasant catarrh and advanced to an extreme neuralgic pain. It was not diagnosed until the following March, but it caused him much misery in the meantime. He stayed with Armitstead in Perthshire in October, and Morley, who joined them there, thought that, although he was already complaining, it was the last time that he heard Gladstone talk with 'all the freedom, full self-possession, and kind geniality of old days'. With peculiar vividness he retailed an exchange between Armitstead and Gladstone which revealed both the obsequiousness of the host and the dismissive fatalism which was then settling on Gladstone. 'Oh, sir, you'll live ten years to come,' Armitstead had said. 'I do trust that God in his mercy will spare me that' was Gladstone's sombre reply.[12]

A month later Hamilton saw Gladstone in London on his way to Cannes. Hamilton sounds more breezy than sympathetic:

> When I began talking to Mr. G. and asking him about himself he was very glum, put on his well known black-look and complained that the neuralgia which had taken hold of one side of his face was most distressing and completely incapacitated him from serious writing or reading. He has always made the most of his ailments, partly due to the extraordinary immunity from troubles which he has enjoyed during his long life; so one must make allowance for some exaggeration; and I tried to persuade him that all his neuralgia would fly at the sight of Cannes.'[13]

It did not. That Cannes visit, which lasted nearly three months, was miserable for Gladstone, and must have been so too for his wife (who was herself better than a year before, although perhaps moving into a world of her own), his host (Rendel) and others of the party. He returned to England on 22 February 1898, and went straight to Bournemouth. Why? He had never been there before in his life, and it is a most unGladstonian place. If it was in search of a mild winter climate, why did he not stay at Cannes, or even go to the place which frequently records the warmest winter temperatures in Britain – Hawarden, rivalled only by Colwyn Bay a few miles further along the coast? Or was it in search of a particular doctor? It was certainly the case that at Bournemouth he was for the first time diagnosed properly and hopelessly. When he left there on 22 March it was consciously to return home to die. He wanted the end, and if he was not exactly stoical about the pain, he was so about the outcome. The prognosis also brought out his theatrical side. When the party left Bournemouth he turned to the assembled crowd at the railway station and said: 'God bless you all, and this place, and the land you love.'

He and his party arrived at Hawarden on a beautiful early-spring evening, but his perception of this or anything else was becoming confused. After the fatal diagnosis he was heavily sustained by pain-killing drugs. Music also helped, although the recordings to which he listened must have been almost as scratchy as those of his own voice which survive from the epoch. There were nine weeks between his return and the end. There were a few upward spirals. He last walked out of the castle on 9 April, and he last came down to dinner on the 18th, when he talked with animation of the Oxford and Cambridge boat race, his mind going back to the first one, which he had seen rowed at Henley sixty-nine years before. His family were in constant attendance. Rosebery and Morley paid farewell visits. Messages of goodwill were abundant, the most welcome being a felicitously drafted one from the Hebdomadal Council at Oxford. Gladstone roused himself to dictate to his daughter Helen a reply in at least equally memorable terms to 'the God-fearing and God-sustaining University of Oxford. I served her, perhaps mistakenly, but to the best of my ability. My most earnest prayers are hers to the uttermost and to the last.' He died in the early morning of Ascension Day, which that year fell on 19 May.

The obsequies were magnificent. He who had been so sparing of honours for himself in life was allowed by his family and without any sign of attempted prior prohibition by himself to be treated in death far more grandly than Peel or Disraeli before him, or Asquith or Lloyd George after him. The only comparable non-royal funerals of the past 150 years have been those of the Duke of Wellington and of Churchill. The House of Commons adjourned immediately on receipt of the news, and on the following day tributes were paid by Balfour and Harcourt in the Commons and by Salisbury and Rosebery in the Lords. All four were notable. Resolutions for a Westminster Abbey burial were carried unanimously. The body was brought by special train to the adjacent Underground station before lying in state in Westminster Hall, with a great file-past of the famous and the obscure alike. The Abbey funeral was on Saturday, 28 May. The pall-bearers were the Prince of Wales and his son the Duke of York (later King George V); Lord Salisbury and Lord Rosebery; Lord Kimberley and Sir William Harcourt; Arthur Balfour and the Duke of Rutland (who as Lord John Manners had been Gladstone's fellow member for Newark during the Peel government;

and Lord Rendel and Mr Armitstead. It was a nicely balanced ten, although among Liberals both Spencer and Morley (the latter presumably excluded as a non-believer) would have been more appropriate than Harcourt, and Rutland was a substitute for Argyll, who was unable to be present, and defensively explained to *The Times* that it was not because of recent political differences. The Queen, unfailing to the last, telegraphed to the Prince of Wales to ask what was the precedent he had followed and whose advice he had taken in acting in such a capacity. He rather splendidly replied that he knew of no precedent and had taken no advice.

Even in her relatively warm telegram to Catherine Gladstone the Queen could not bring herself to refer to Gladstone as more than 'one of the most distinguished statesmen of my reign'.[14] What she could not recognize was that he was the quintessential statesman of her reign, its epitome and, almost as much as herself, its symbol. His death announced the conclusion of the Victorian age only a little less clearly than did her own two and a half years later.

References

1. A Liverpool Gentleman?

1 Bagehot, *Biographical Studies*, p. 86.
2 Checkland, *The Gladstones*, pp. 414–15.
3 *Ibid.*, p. 129.
4 Brooke and Sorenson (eds), *The Prime Ministers' Papers: W. E. Gladstone*, I. p. 21.
5 *Ibid.*, pp. 18–19.
6 *Diaries*, I, p. 74.
7 *Diaries*, I, p. 74.
8 Brooke and Sorenson (eds), *The Prime Ministers' Papers: W. E. Gladstone*, I, p. 28.
9 *Ibid.*, pp. 24–5.
10 *Diaries*, I, p. 360.
11 Brooke and Sorenson (eds), *The Prime Ministers' Papers: W. E. Gladstone*, I, p. 30.
12 *Diaries*, I, p. 259.
13 Magnus, *Gladstone*, p. 9.
14 *Diaries*, II, p. 63.
15 Tennyson, *In Memoriam.*
16 Martin, *Tennyson: The Unquiet Heart*, p. 74.
17 *Diaries*, I, pp. 290–1.
18 *Ibid.*, p. 386.
19 *Ibid.*, p. 347.
20 Morley, *Life of Gladstone*, I, p. 74.
21 Commons Hansard for 22 April 1866.
22 Brooke and Sorenson (eds), *The Prime Ministers' Papers: W. E. Gladstone*, I, p. 40.

2. *A Grand Tour Ending at Newark*

1 *Diaries*, I, p. 551.
2 *Ibid.*, pp. 562–3.
3 Magnus, *Gladstone*, p. 4.
4 Matthew, *Gladstone 1809–1874*, p. 6.
5 *Diaries*, I, p. 97.
6 *Ibid.*, I, p. 272.
7 *Gleamings of Past Years*, VII, p. 219.
8 *Diaries*, I, p. 413.
9 *Ibid.*, p. 453.
10 *Ibid.*
11 *Ibid.*, p. 460.
12 *Ibid.*, p. 462.
13 *Ibid.*, p. 428.
14 *Ibid.*, p. 463.
15 *Ibid.*, p. 495.
16 Brooke and Sorenson (eds), *The Prime Ministers' Papers: W. E. Gladstone*, I, pp. 142–3.
17 Magnus, *Gladstone*, p. 16.
18 Shannon, *Gladstone*, p. 40.
19 *Diaries*, I, p. 592.
20 Morley, *Life of Gladstone*, I, p. 93.
21 *Diaries*, II, p. 33.

3. *A Clumsy Suitor*

1 Gordon, *The Earl of Aberdeen*, p. 111.
2 *Ibid.*, p. 116.
3 *Ibid.*, p. 176.
4 Shannon, *Gladstone*, p. 224–50.
5 *Diaries*, I, p. 338.
6 *Ibid.*, p. 139.
7 Maxwell, *Clarendon*, II, p. 224.
8 Goldwin Smith, *My Memory of Gladstone*, p. 18.
9 Commons Hansard for 30 July 1838.
10 *Diaries*, II, p. 502.
11 Harris, *Attlee*, p. 525.

4. Peel's Apprentice

1 *Diaries*, II, p. 580.
2 Battiscombe, *Mrs Gladstone*, p. 31.
3 *Ibid.*, p. 82.
4 *Diaries*, II, pp. 639–40.
5 *Ibid.*, p. 608n.
6 *Ibid.*, p. 614.
7 *Ibid.*, III, p. 5.
8 *Ibid.*, p. 21.
9 *Ibid.*, p. 29.
10 Bagehot, *Biographical Studies*, p. 6.
11 Gash, *Sir Robert Peel*, II, pp. 185–6.
12 *Ibid.*, p. 186.
13 Morley, *Life of Gladstone*, I, p. ??
14 Commons Hansard for 3 July 1850.
15 *Diaries*, IV, p. 224.
16 Morley, *Life of Gladstone*, I, p. 372.
17 *Ibid.*, p. 373.
18 *Ibid.*
19 *Ibid.*
20 *Ibid.*, p. 374.
21 *Ibid.*, p. 613.
22 Shannon, *Gladstone*, . 62.
23 *Diaries*, III, p. 4[illegible]
24 *Ibid.*, IV, p. 200
25 *Ibid.*, p. 20–2.
26 *Ibid.*, III, p. 130.
27 Fletcher, *Mr Gladstone at Oxford*, p. 83.
28 Brooke and Sorenson (eds), *The Prime Ministers' Papers: W. E. Gladstone*, I, pp 247.

5. Orator, Zealot and Debtor

1 Morley, *Life of Gladstone*, I, pp. 191–2.
2 *Ibid.*, p. 280.
3 Lathbury, *Letters on Church and Religion of William Ewart Gladstone*, I, p 339.
4 *Diaries*, III, p. 483.

5 Morley, *Life of Gladstone*, I, p. 311.
6 Faber, *The Oxford Apostles*, pp. 170–1.
7 Ker, *John Henry Newman*, p. 90.
8 Faber, *The Oxford Apostles*, p. 170.
9 Matthew, *Gladstone 1809–1874*, p. 70.
10 *Ibid.*
11 *Diaries*, III, pp. 416–70.

6. Mid-Century Frenzy

1 Dugdale, *Arthur James Balfour*, II, p. 55.
2 Tilney Bassett (ed.), *Gladstone to His Wife*, p. 68.
3 *Diaries*, III, pp. 506–7.
4 *Ibid.*, p. 530.
5 Morley, *Life of Gladstone*, III, p. 485.
6 *Ibid.*, I, p. 350.
7 Shannon, *Gladstone*, I, p. 201.
8 *Diaries*, III, p. 653.
9 *Ibid.*, p. 655.
10 *Ibid.*, p. 658.
11 Commons Hansard for 16 December 1847.
12 *Diaries*, IV, pp. 47–8.
13 *Ibid.*, p. 146.
14 *Ibid.*, p. 142.
15 *Ibid.*, p. 142
16 *Ibid.*, p. 144.
17 *Ibid.*, pp. 174–5.
18 Brooke and Sorenson (eds), *The Prime Ministers' Papers: W. E. Gladstone*, I.
19 *Diaries*, IV, p. 353.

7. *Ladies of the Night*

1 *Diaries*, III, p. 491.
2 *Ibid.*, pp. 492–3.
3 *Ibid.*, IV, p. 36n.
4 *Ibid.*, p. 37.
5 *Ibid.*, p. 55.
6 *Ibid.*, p. 117.

7 Ivor (Bulmer-)Thomas, *Gladstone of Hawarden* pp. 241–2.
8 Magnus, *Gladstone*, p. 107.
9 *Diaries*, IV, p. 319.
10 *Ibid.*, p. 586.
11 *Ibid.*, p. 124.
12 *Ibid.*, p. 133.
13 *Ibid.*, p. 207.
14 *Ibid.*
15 *Ibid.*, p. 210.
16 *Ibid.*, pp. 214–15.
17 *Ibid.*, p. 229.
18 *Ibid.*, p. 230.
19 *Ibid.*, p. 233.
20 *Ibid.*
21 *Ibid.*, p. 235.
22 *Ibid.*, pp. 295–6.
23 *Ibid.*, p. 319.
24 *Ibid.*
25 *Ibid.*, p. 325.
26 *Ibid.*, p. 336.
27 *Ibid.*, p. 342.
28 *Ibid.*, p. 344.
29 *Ibid.*, p. 346.
30 *Ibid.*
31 *Ibid.*, V, p. 422.
32 *Ibid.*, IV, p. 586.
33 Mathew, *Gladstone 1809–1874*, p 93.

8. The Tremendous Projectile

1 Morley, *Life of Gladstone*, I, p. 261.
2 Shannon, *Gladstone*, I, p. 223.
3 Tilney Bassett (ed.), *Gladstone's Speeches*, pp. 109–54.
4 *Diaries*, p. 304–6.
5 *Ibid.*, IV, p. 305.
6 *Ibid.*, pp. 306–7.
7 *Ibid.*, pp. 307–8.
8 *Ibid.*, p. 322.
9 Morley, *Life of Gladstone*, I, p. 400.

10 *Ibid.*, p. 411.
11 *Diaries*, IV, pp. 317–18.
12 Chadwick, *The Victorian Church*, I, p. 296.
13 *Letters of Queen Victoria*, 1st Series, II, pp. 325–6.
14 Walpole, *Life of Lord John Russell*, II, pp. 120–1.
15 Chadwick, *The Victorian Church*, I, p. 303.
16 Commons Hansard for 25 March 1851.
17 Letter from Gladstone to Richard Gressell, his Oxford University constituency chairman.

9. The Chancellor Who Made the Job

1 Blake, *Disraeli*, p. 305.
2 *Ibid.*
3 *Diaries*, IV, p. 475.
4 Blake, *Disraeli*, p. 345.
5 Tilney Bassett (ed.), *Gladstone to His Wife*, p. 94.
6 *Ibid.*
7 *Ibid.*
8 Commons Hansard for 16 December 1852.
9 *Diaries*, IV, p. 477.
10 Full correspondence published in Monypenny and Buckle, *Life of Disraeli*, III, pp. 476–80.
11 Morley, *Life of Gladstone*, I, p. 451.
12 *Ibid.*, p. 466.
13 *Diaries*, IV, p. 515.
14 *Ibid.*
15 Commons Hansard for 18 April 1853.
16 *Letters of Queen Victoria*, 1st Series, p. 542.
17 Morley, *Life of Gladstone*, I, p. 469.
18 Shannon, *Gladstone*, p. 272.
19 Greville, *Diaries*, 3rd Series, I, p. 59.
20 Brooke and Sorenson (eds), *The Prime Ministers' Papers: W. E. Gladstone*, I, p. 65.
21 *Diaries*, IV, p. 579.
22 Morley, *Life of Gladstone*, I, pp. 511–12.

10. The Decline and Fall of the Aberdeen Coalition

1 Letter from Aberdeen to Gladstone, 5 December 1856.
2 Protheroe, *Life of A. P. Stanley*, I, p. 434.
3 See the essay by V. H. H. Green, former Rector of Lincoln College in the (1993) *Illustrated History of the University of Oxford*.
4 *Letters of Queen Victoria*, 3rd Series, III, p. 11.
5 Morley, *Life of Gladstone*, I, p. 511.
6 *Ibid.*, I, p. 510.
7 *Diaries*, IV, p. 621.
8 Morley, *Life of Gladstone*, I, p. 540.
9 Brooke and Sorenson (eds), *The Prime Ministers' Papers: W. E. Gladstone*, I, p. 82.
10 *Diaries.*, V, p. 21.
11 *Ibid.*

11. Health and Wealth

1 *Diaries*, IV, p. 522.
2 *Ibid.*, p. 525.
3 *Ibid.*, V, p. 42.
4 *Ibid.*, IV, p. 562.
5 *Ibid.*
6 Morley, *Life of Gladstone*, I, p. 483.
7 *Diaries*, IV, p. 621.
8 *Ibid.*, p. 568.
9 *Ibid.*, p. 579.
10 *Ibid.*, V, p. 423.
11 *Ibid.*, p. 62.
12 *Ibid.*, p. 68.
13 Morley, *Life of Gladstone*, I, p. 563.

12. A Short Odyssey for a British Ulysses

1 *Diaries*, V, p. 279.
2 Morley, *Life of Gladstone*, I, pp. 587–8.
3 G. W. E. Russell, *Gladstone*, p. 140.

4 Morley, *Life of Gladstone*, I, p. 589.
5 *Diaries*, V, p. 315.
6 Speech at Blackpool, 24 January 1884 (James, *Lord Randolph* Churchill, pp. 136–7.
7 *Diaries*, V, p. 339.
8 *Ibid.*, p. 340.
9 *Ibid.*, p. 343.
10 *Ibid.*, p. 349.
11 *Ibid.*, p. 367.
12 *Ibid.*, pp. 351–8
13 *Ibid.*, p. 373.

13. The Hostile Partnership with Palmerston

1 Magnus, *Gladstone*, p. 144.
2 Blake, *Disraeli*, p. 396.
3 Southgate, *The Most English Minister*, p. 453.
4 *Ibid.*, p. 452.
5 Parker, *Life and Letters of Sir James Graham*, II, p. 388.
6 *Diaries*, V, p. 399.
7 Maxwell, *Life of Clarendon*, II, p. 186.
8 Bailey (ed.), *The Diary of Lady Frederick Cavendish*, I, pp. 92–3.
9 *Diaries*, V, p. 402.
10 Guedalla, *Palmerston*, p. 453.
11 *Diaries*, V, p. 410.
12 *Ibid.*, p. 410n.
13 Republished in 1879 in *Gleanings of Past Years*, pp. 131–79.
14 *Diaries*, V, p. 418.
15 *Ibid.*, pp. 434–5.
16 *Ibid.*, VI, p. 47.
17 Guedalla, *Palmerston*, p. 453.
18 Guedalla (ed.), *Gladstone and Palmerston*, p. 126.

14. God's Vicar in the Treasury

1 *Diaries*, V, p. 410.
2 *Ibid.*, p. 415.
3 *Ibid.*, p. 421.

4 Hinde, *Richard Cobden*, p. 285.
5 *Diaries*, V, p. 424.
6 Hinde, *Richard Cobden*, pp. 285–95.
7 Guedalla (ed.), *Gladstone and Palmerston*, pp. 115–18.
8 *Ibid.*, p. 123.
9 *Ibid.*, p. 124.
10 *Diaries*, V, p. 463.
11 *Ibid.*, p. 462.
12 Guedalla (ed.), *Gladstone and Palmerston*, p. 123.
13 *Diaries*, V, p. 464.
14 Tilney Bassett (ed.), *Gladstone's Speeches*, pp. 288–90.
15 *Ibid.*, p. 273.
16 *Diaries*, V, p. 485.
17 *Ibid.*, p. 495.
18 *Ibid.*, p. 506.
19 *Ibid.*, p. 541.

15. *The People's William*

1 *Diaries*, VI, p. 51.
2 *Ibid.*, p. 163.
3 *Ibid.*, p. 179.
4 *Ibid.*, p. 24.
5 Guedalla (ed.), *Gladstone and Palmerston*, pp. 169–70.
6 *Ibid.*, p. 176.
7 *Diaries*, VI, p. 48.
8 Guedalla (ed.), *Gladstone and Palmerston*, pp. 176–9.
9 Shannon, *Gladstone*, I, p. 423.
10 Morley, *Life of Gladstone*, II, p. 79.
11 *The Times*, 9 October 1862.
12 Morley, *Life of Gladstone*, II, p. 80.
13 Brooke and Sorenson (eds), *The Prime Ministers' Papers: W. E. Gladstone*, I, pp. 133–4 and 250
14 Magnus, *Gladstone*, p. 152.
15 *Diaries*, VI, pp. 152–3.
16 *Ibid.*, p. 153.
17 Gladstone's 'Secret Account Book', finally tabulated in 1897, the last year of his life.
18 *Diaries*, VI, p. 199.

19 Tilney Bassett (ed.), *Gladstone to His Wife*, pp. 160–3.
20 *Diaries*, VI, p. 170.
21 *Ibid.*, p. 246.
22 *Ibid.*, p. 127.
23 *Ibid.*, p. 167.
24 *Ibid.*, p. 18.
25 Commons Hansard for 11 May 1864.
26 Guedalla (ed.), *Gladstone and Palmerston*, pp. 279–87.
27 *Ibid.*, p. 318.
28 *Ibid.*, pp. 297–8.
29 *Ibid.*, p. 300.
30 *Diaries*, VI, pp. 326–32.
31 Guedalla (ed.), *Gladstone and Palmerston*, p. 335.
32 *Diaries*, VI, p. 370.
33 Guedalla (ed.), *Gladstone and Palmerston*, p. 348.

16. Disraeli's Foil

1 *The Diary of Charles Adams*, p. 368.
2 *Diaries*, VI, p. 102.
3 Tilney Bassett (ed.), *Gladstone's Speeches*, p. 359.
4 Brooke and Sorenson (eds), *The Prime Ministers' Papers: W. E. Gladstone*, I, p. 92.
5 *Diaries*, VI, pp. 449–50.
6 Magnus, *Gladstone*, p. 184.
7 Morley, *Life of Gladstone*, II, pp. 217–18.
8 *Diaries*, VI, p. 472.
9 Morley, *Life of Gladstone*, II, p. 216.
10 Blake, *Disraeli*, p. 542
11 *Ibid.*, p. 477.
12 *Ibid.*, p. 458.
13 Brooke and Sorenson (eds), *The Prime Ministers' Papers: W. E. Gladstone*, I, p. 94.
14 Morley, *Life of Gladstone*, II, pp. 222–3.
15 *Diaries*, VI, p. 588.
16 *Ibid.*, p. 511.
17 *Ibid.*, p. 513.
18 Blake, *Disraeli*, p. 421.
19 Holland, *Life of Wilberforce*, III, p. 227.

20 *Diaries*, VI, p. 521.
21 Brooke and Sorenson (eds), *The Prime Ministers' Papers: W. E. Gladstone*, I, p. 95.
22 Blake, *Disraeli*, p. 421.
23 *Diaries*, VI, p. 536.
24 Morley, *Life of Gladstone*, II, pp. 172–3.
25 *Diaries*, VI, p. 566.
26 *Ibid.*, pp. 565–79.
27 *Ibid.*, p. 586.

17. 'My Mission is to Pacify Ireland'

1 Hammond, *Gladstone and the Irish Nation*, pp. 68–9.
2 Tilney Bassett (ed.), *Gladstone to His Wife*, p. 124.
3 Hammond, *Gladstone and the Irish Nation*, p. 79.
4 *Ibid.*, p. 80.
5 *Diaries*, VI, p. 588.
6 Blake, *Disraeli*, p. 502.
7 *Diaries*, VI, p. 628.
8 Morley, *Life of Gladstone*, II, p. 250.
9 *Diaries*, VI, p. 638.
10 Article by Ashley in the *National Review* for June 1898.
11 Memorandum by General Charles Grey included in *Letters of Queen Victoria*, 2nd Series, I, p. 560.
12 *Diaries*, VI, p. 641.
13 *Ibid.*, p. 645.
14 *Ibid.*

18. A Commanding Prime Minister

1 *Diaries*, VI, p. 654.
2 *Ibid.*, pp. 655–6.
3 *Ibid.*, VII, p. 4.
4 *Ibid.*, p. 14.
5 *Ibid.*, p. 15–16.
6 *Ibid.*, p. 22.
7 *Ibid.*, p. 20.
8 *Ibid.*, pp. 14 and 18–19.

9 *Ibid.*, p. 175.
10 *Ibid.*, p. 101.
11 Morley, *Life of Gladstone*, II, p. 279.
12 Letter from Temple to Sir T. Acland, 12 March 1869.
13 Morley, *Life of Gladstone*, II, p. 264.
14 *Diaries*, VII, p. 43.
15 *Ibid.*, p. 78.
16 Morley, *Life of Gladstone*, II, p. 271.
17 *Diaries*, VII, p. 104.
18 *Ibid.*, p. 106.
19 *Ibid.*, p. 114.
20 *Ibid.*, p. 120.
21 *Ibid.*, p. 118.
22 Davidson, *Life of Archbishop Tait*, II, p. 45.
23 *Diaries*, VII, pp. 126–7.
24 *Ibid.*, p. 114.
25 *Ibid.*, p. 141.
26 *Ibid.*, p. 155.
27 *Ibid.*, p. 175.
28 *Ibid.*, p. 141.
29 *Ibid.*, p. 152.
30 *Ibid.*, p. 167.
31 *Ibid.*, p. 171.
32 *Ibid.*, p. 158.
33 *Ibid.*, p. 197.
34 Matthew, *Gladstone 1809–1874*.
35 *Diaries*, VII, p. 206.
36 *Ibid.*, p. 208.

19. Irish Land and European War

1 Hammond, *Gladstone and the Irish Nation*, p. 93.
2 *Ibid.*, p. 107.
3 *Ibid.*, p. 98.
4 *Diaries*, VII, p. 228.
5 Guedalla (ed.), *The Queen and Mr Gladstone*, p. 24.
6 *Ibid.*, p. 408.
7 Morley, *Life of Gladstone*, II, p. 292.
8 *Ibid.*

9 *Diaries*, VII, p. 301.
10 *Ibid.*, p. 309.
11 Matthew, *Gladstone 1809–1874*, p. 203.
12 Morley, *Life of Gladstone*, II, p. 313.
13 *Ibid.*
14 Guedalla (ed.), *The Queen and Mr Gladstone*, pp. 283–94.
15 Jenkins, *Sir Charles Dilke*, p. 60.
16 Morley, *Life of Gladstone*, II, p. 328.
17 *Diaries*, VII, p. 372.
18 *Gleanings of Past Years*, IV, pp. 197–259.

20. Sovereign and Prime Minister

1 Guedalla (ed.), *The Queen and Mr Gladstone*, p. 8.
2 *Ibid.*, pp. 14–15.
3 *Ibid.*, pp. 207–8.
4 *Ibid.*, p. 210.
5 *Ibid.*, p. 215.
6 *Ibid.*, p. 255–6.
7 *Ibid.*, p. 260.
8 *Ibid.*
9 *Ibid.*, p. 261.
10 *Ibid.*, p. 315.
11 *Ibid.*, p. 296.
12 *Ibid.*, p. 271.
13 *Ibid.*, p. 267.
14 *Ibid.*, p. 315.
15 *Ibid.*, pp. 317–18.
16 Elizabeth Longford, *Victoria R.I.*, p. 584.
17 Guedalla (ed.), *The Queen and Mr Gladstone*, pp. 328–30.
18 *Ibid.*, p. 333.
19 *Ibid.*, pp. 333–4.
20 *Diaries*, VIII, p. 40.
21 *Ibid.*, p. 42.
22 Tilney Bassett (ed.), *Gladstone to His Wife*, p. 192.
23 Guedalla (ed.), *The Queen and Mr Gladstone*, p. 66.
24 *Ibid.*, p. 353.
25 *Ibid.*, p. 360.
26 Magnus, *King Edward the Seventh*, p. 117.

27 Guedalla (ed.), *The Queen and Mr Gladstone*, p. 347.
28 *Ibid.*, p. 381.
29 *Ibid.*, p. 382.
30 *Ibid.*, p. 383.
31 *Ibid.*, p. 391.
32 *Ibid.*, p. 397.
33 *Ibid.*, p. 399.
34 *Ibid.*, p. 400.

21. *'Ever and Anon the Dark Rumbling of the Sea'*

1 *Diaries*, VII, p. 517.
2 Guedalla (ed.), *The Queen and Mr Gladstone*, p. 373.
3 *Ibid.*, p. 372.
4 Balfour, *Chapters of Autobiography*, p. 70.
5 *Diaries*, VIII, p. 219.
6 Tilney Bassett (ed.), *Gladstone to His Wife*, pp. 195–6.
7 *Diaries*, VIII, pp. 219–20.
8 *Letters of Lord Aberdare*, I, p. 351.
9 *Diaries*, VIII, p. 255.
10 Commons Hansard for 13 February 1873.
11 Guedalla (ed.), *The Queen and Mr Gladstone*, pp. 408–9.
12 Morley, *Life of Gladstone*, II, p. 445.
13 *Ibid.*, p. 444.
14 *Diaries*, VIII. p. 302.
15 *Ibid.*, p. 300.
16 Brooke and Sorenson (eds), *The Prime Ministers' Papers: W. E. Gladstone*, I, p. 112.
17 Guedalla (ed.), *The Queen and Mr Gladstone*, pp. 417–18.

22. *Defeat and Retirement*

1 *Diaries*, VIII, p. 368.
2 Guedalla (ed.), *The Queen and Mr Gladstone*, p. 427.
3 *Diaries*, VIII, p. 368.
4 *Ibid.*, p. 442.
5 Article in *Fortnightly Review*, October 1874.
6 Matthew, *Gladstone 1809–1874*, p. 223n.

7 *Diaries*, VIII, p. 451.
8 *Ibid.*, pp. 449–53.
9 *Ibid.*, p. 456.
10 *Ibid.*, p. 461.
11 Guedalla (ed.), *The Queen and Mr Gladstone*, pp. 444–5.
12 *Diaries*, VIII, p. 464.
13 *Ibid.*, p. 456.
14 *Ibid.*, p. 470.
15 *Ibid.*, p. 472.
16 Blake, *Disraeli*, p. 550.
17 Chadwick, *The Victorian Church*, II, p. 36.
18 *Diaries*, VIII, p. 518.
19 *Gleanings of Past Years*, VI, pp. 127–8.
20 *Diaries*, VIII, p. 526.

23. *The Temporary Withdrawal*

1 *Diaries*, IX, p. 29.
2 *Ibid.*, p. 141.
3 *Ibid.*, p. 29.
4 *Ibid.*, p. 115.
5 Tilney Bassett (ed.), *Gladstone to His Wife*, p. 212.
6 Disraeli's letter to the Queen, 15 March 1875.
7 *Diaries*, IX, p. 265.
8 *Ibid.*, p. 64.
9 *Ibid.*, p. 147n.
10 *Ibid.*, p. 77.
11 *Ibid.*, p. 71.
12 *Ibid.*, p. 261.
13 *Ibid.*, p. 138.

24. *'Of All the Bulgarian Horrors Perhaps the Greatest'*

1 *Diaries*, IX, p. 150.
2 *Ibid.*, p. 151.
3 *Ibid.*, p. 152.
4 Monypenny and Buckle, *Life of Disraeli*, VI, p. 60.
5 Blake, *Disraeli*, p. 603.

6 Morley, *Life of Gladstone*, II, p. 554.
7 Magnus, *Gladstone*, p. 243.
8 Commons Hansard for 10 July 1876.
9 Magnus, *Gladstone*, p. 245.
10 Monypenny and Buckle, *Life of Disraeli*, VI, pp. 356–7.
11 *Gleanings*, I, p. 204.
12 Commons Hansard for 12 August 1876.
13 *Diaries*, IX, p. 200.
14 *Ibid.*, p. 297.
15 *Ibid.*, p. 410.
16 *Ibid.*, p. 415.
17 *Ibid.*, p. 199.
18 Morley, *Life of Gladstone*, II, p. 562.
19 *Diaries*, IX, p. 212.
20 *Ibid.*, p. 214.
21 *Ibid.*, p. 216.
22 Commons Hansard for 20 May 1898.
23 *Diaries*, IX, pp. 223–4.
24 *Ibid.*, p. 240.

25. *Midlothian Beckons*

1 *Diaries*, IX, p. 333.
2 *Ibid.*, p. 334.
3 *Ibid.*, p. 440.
4 *Ibid.*, p. 421.
5 *Ibid.*, p. 307.
6 *Ibid.*, p. 421.
7 *Ibid.*, p. 319.
8 Blake, *Disraeli*, pp. 705–6.
9 Matthew, *Gladstone 1875–1898*, p. 47.
10 *Diaries*, IX, p. 386.
11 Tilney Bassett (ed.), *Gladstone's Speeches*, p. 555.
12 *Diaries*, IX, p. 371.
13 *Ibid.*, p. 373.
14 *Ibid.*, p. 374.
15 *Ibid.*, p. 435.
16 *Ibid.*, p. 439.
17 *Ibid.*, p. 446.

18 Morley, *Life of Gladstone*, II, p. 587.
19 Magnus, *Gladstone*, p. 261.
20 *Diaries*, IX, p. 461.
21 Morley, *Life of Gladstone*, II, p. 595.
22 *Diaries*, IX, p. 463.
23 *Ibid.*, p. 283.
24 Morley, *Life of Gladstone*, II, p. 582.
25 Foster, *Lord Randolph Churchill*, p. 127.
26 *Diaries*, IX, p. 464.
27 Morley, *Life of Gladstone*, II, p. 591.
28 *Diaries*, IX, p. 464.
29 *Ibid.*, p. 466.
30 Bailey (ed.), *The Diaries of Lady Frederick Cavendish*, II, p. 241.
31 Jackson, *The Last of the Whigs*, p. 262.
32 *Ibid.*, p. 99.
33 *Diaries*, IX, p. 471.
34 Morley, *Life of Gladstone*, II, pp. 610–11.
35 *Ibid.*, p. 498.
36 *Ibid.*, pp. 499–501.
37 *Ibid.*, p. 502.
38 *Ibid.*, p. 501.

26. Victory, Where Are Thy Fruits?

1 Ponsonby, *Henry Ponsonby*, p. 184.
2 Jackson, *The Last of the Whigs*, p. 112.
3 *Letters of Queen Victoria*, 2nd Series, III, p. 80.
4 Memorandum written by Gladstone, 22 April 1880, printed in *Diaries*, IX, pp. 504–5.
5 *Letters of Queen Victoria*, 2nd Series, III, p. 84.
6 *Diaries*, IX, p. 506.
7 *Ibid.*, p. 507.
8 *Letters of Queen Victoria*, 2nd Series, III, p. 85.
9 Dilke Papers, 43934, 149.
10 Garvin and Amery, *Life of Joseph Chamberlain*, I, p. 301.
11 Hammond, *Gladstone and the Irish Nation*, p. 328.
12 Jenkins, *Sir Charles Dilke*, p. 168.
13 *Diaries*, IX, p. 526.
14 *Ibid.*, p. 557.

15 *Letters of Queen Victoria*, 2nd Series, III, p. 116.
16 Morley, *Life of Gladstone*, III, pp. 19–20.
17 *Diaries*, IX, p. 559.
18 *Ibid.*, p. 562.
19 *Ibid.*, p. 564.
20 *Ibid.*

27. *Gladstone Becomes the Grand Old Man*

1 1879 letter from Dilke to Mrs Mark Pattison (his future wife).
2 *Diaries*, IX, p. 655.
3 *Ibid.*, X, p. 2.
4 *Ibid.*, p. 52.
5 Thorold, *The Life of Henry Labouchère*, p. 144.
6 Bahlmann (ed.), *The Diary of Sir Edward Walter Hamilton 1880–1885*, I, pp. 190–1.
7 Matthew, *Gladstone 1875–1898*, p. 278.
8 *Diaries*, XI, pp. 656–7.
9 *Ibid.*, pp. 659–60.
10 Matthew, *Gladstone 1875–1898*, p. 279.
11 *Diaries*, X, p. 24.
12 *Ibid.*, p. 94.
13 *Ibid.*, p. 396.
14 *Ibid.*, p. 168.
15 *Ibid.*, p. 386.
16 Magnus, *Gladstone*, p. 308.
17 *Letters of Queen Victoria*, 2nd Series, III, p. 241.
18 *Ibid.*, p. 395.
19 Bahlmann (ed.), *The Diary of Sir Edward Walter Hamilton 1880–1885*, II, pp. 486–7.
20 Commons Hansard for 16 May 1882.
21 *Diaries*, X, p. 264.
22 Bahlmann (ed.), *The Diary of Sir Edward Walter Hamilton 1880–1885*, I, p. 310.
23 Dilke Papers, 43926 30.
24 Jenkins, *Sir Charles Dilke*, p. 169.

28. *The Cloud in the West Darkens*

1 Garvin and Amery, *Life of Joseph Chamberlain*, I, p. 332.
2 Speech at the Cloth Hall banquet, Leeds, 8 October 1881.
3 Bahlmann (ed.), *The Diary of Sir Edward Walter Hamilton 1880–1885*, II, pp. 454, 558 and 701.
4 Interview with R. Barry O'Brien for O'Brien's 1898 biography of Parnell. The circumstances of the interview and Gladstone's words are in pp. 353–67 of the second volume of the work.
5 *Ibid.*, pp. 357–8.
6 Recorded in Asquith's diary for 16 October 1891, published in his *Fifty Years of Parliament* (1926).
7 1891 conversation with Henry Harrison, recorded in Harrison's *Parnell Vindicated*.
8 Jenkins, *Sir Charles Dilke*, pp. 204–5.

29. *The Third Reform Bill*

1 Martin, *Tennyson*, pp. 540–1.
2 Gwynn and Tuckwell, *Life of Sir Charles Dilke*, II, p. 63.
3 Bahlmann (ed.), *The Diary of Sir Edward Walter Hamilton 1880–1885*, II, p. 500.
4 *Ibid.*, p. 567.
5 *Ibid.*, pp. 516–17.
6 *Diaries*, XI, p. 144.
7 Bahlmann (ed.), *The Diary of Sir Edward Walter Hamilton 1880–1885*, II, p. 644.
8 Guedalla (ed.), *The Queen and Mr Gladstone*, p. 617
9 *Letters of Queen Victoria*, 2nd Series, III, p. 539.
10 Guedalla (ed.), *The Queen and Mr Gladstone*, p. 623.
11 *Diaries*, XI, p. 193.
12 Jenkins, *Sir Charles Dilke*, p. 19.
13 Bahlmann (ed.), *The Diary of Sir Edward Walter Hamilton 1880–1885*, II, p. 750.

30. Murderer of Gordon?

1 Bahlmann (ed.), *The Diary of Sir Edward Walter Hamilton 1880–1885*, I, p. 65.
2 Commons Hansard for 14 June 1882.
3 *Diaries*, X, pp. 290–1.
4 *Ibid.*, p. 292.
5 Bahlmann (ed.), *The Diary of Sir Edward Walter Hamilton 1880–1885*, I, p. 340.
6 *Diaries*, X, p. 335.
7 *Ibid.*, XI, p. 218.
8 Matthew, *Gladstone 1875–1898*, pp. 135–6.
9 Pollock, *Gordon: The Man Behind the Legend*, pp. 139–40.
10 Jenkins, *Sir Charles Dilke*, p. 179.
11 Ramm (ed.), *Political Correspondence of Mr Gladstone and Lord Granville*, II, p. 150.
12 Bahlmann (ed.), *The Diary of Sir Edward Walter Hamilton 1880–1885*, II, p. 545.
13 Ramm (ed.), *Political Correspondence of Mr Gladstone and Lord Granville*, II, p. 151.
14 Dilke Papers, British Museum, 43938 76.
15 *Ibid.*, 43926 30.
16 *Diaries*, XI, p. 182.
17 Pollock, *Gordon: The Man Behind the Legend*, p. 301.
18 Bahlmann (ed.), *The Diary of Sir Edward Walter Hamilton 1880–1885*, II, p. 788.
19 Guedalla (ed.), *The Queen and Mr Gladstone*, II, p. 326.
20 Bahlmann (ed.), *The Diary of Sir Edward Walter Hamilton 1880–1885*, II, p. 789.
21 Guedalla (ed.), *The Queen and Mr Gladstone*, II, p. 326.
22 *Diaries*, XI, p. 289.
23 Bahlmann (ed.), *The Diary of Sir Edward Walter Hamilton 1880–1885*, II, p. 797.
24 *Diaries*, XI, p. 354.
25 *Ibid.*, p. 362.

31. Slow Road to Damascus

1 *Diaries*, XI, p. 359.
2 Matthew, *Gladstone 1875–1898*, p. 286.
3 Bahlmann (ed.), *The Diary of Sir Edward Walter Hamilton 1885–1906*, p. 17.
4 *Diaries*, XI, p. 378.
5 *Ibid.*, p. 456.
6 Ramm (ed.), *Political Correspondence of Mr Gladstone and Lord Granville*, II, p. 414.
7 *Ibid.*
8 *Diaries*, XI, p. 443.
9 *Ibid.*, pp. 447–8.
10 *Ibid.*, p. 455.
11 *Letters of Queen Victoria*, 2nd Series, III, p. 711.
12 Quoted in Hammond, *Gladstone and the Irish Nation*, pp. 449–50.
13 *Ibid.*, p. 445.
14 *Diaries*, XI, p. 448.
15 *Ibid.*, p. 450n.
16 Hammond, *Gladstone and the Irish Nation*, p. 440.
17 Bahlmann (ed.), *The Diary of Sir Edward Walter Hamilton 1885–1906*, p. 14.
18 The whole letter is reproduced in Appendix I of *Diaries*, XI, pp. 663–7.
19 This paper is published in full in *ibid.*, pp. 429–30.
20 Parnell's paper is given in Hammond, *Gladstone and the Irish Nation*, pp. 422–3.
21 *Diaries*, XI, p. 425.
22 *Ibid.*, p. 411.

32. Schism and Failure

1 Brooke and Sorenson (eds), *The Prime Ministers' Papers: W. E. Gladstone*, I, p. 110.
2 *Diaries*, XI, p. 484.
3 *Letters of Queen Victoria*, 3rd Series, I, p. 34.
4 *Ibid.*, p. 35.
5 *Diaries*, XI, p. 485.
6 *Letters of Queen Victoria*, 3rd Series, I, p. 36.
7 Garvin and Amery, *Life of Joseph Chamberlain*, II, p. 172.

8 Dilke Papers, British Museum, 43927 25.
9 Ramm (ed.), *Political Correspondence of Mr Gladstone and Lord Granville*, II, p. 445.
10 Marsh, *Joseph Chamberlain*, p. 222.
11 Hammond, *Gladstone and the Irish Nation*, p. 493.
12 Bahlmann (ed.), *The Diary of Sir Edward Walter Hamilton 1885–1906*, pp. 33–4.
13 *Diaries*, XI, p. 526.
14 Tilney Bassett (ed.), *Gladstone's Speeches*, p. 644.
15 Bahlmann (ed.), *The Diary of Sir Edward Walter Hamilton 1885–1906*, p. 34.
16 *Diaries*, XI, p. 549.
17 Bahlmann (ed.), *The Diary of Sir Edward Walter Hamilton 1885–1906*, p. 36.
18 *Diaries*, XI, p. 567.
19 *Ibid.*, p. 581.
20 *Ibid.*, p. 585.
21 *Ibid.*, p. 583.
22 *Ibid.*, pp. 579–80.
23 *Ibid.*, p. 592.
24 Memorandum by Gladstone quoted in Morley, *Life of Gladstone*, III, pp. 347–8.
25 *Letters of Queen Victoria*, 3rd Series, I, pp. 168–9.
26 *Diaries*, XI, p. 583.
27 *Ibid.*, p. 594.

33. 'The Union – and Disunion – of Hearts'

1 *Letters of Queen Victoria*, 3rd Series, I, p. 658.
2 *Diaries*, XII, pp. 209–10.
3 Matthew, *Gladstone 1875–1898*, p. 301.
4 *Diaries*, XII, p. 193.
5 *Ibid.*, p. 254.
6 Kee, *The Laurel and the Ivy*, p. 548.
7 *Ibid.*
8 Morley, *Life of Gladstone*, III, p. 435.
9 *Ibid.*, p. 431.
10 Kee, *The Laurel and the Ivy*, p. 557.
11 *Methodist Times*, 20 November 1890.

12 Birrell, *Gladstone*, p. 125.
13 Hammond, *Gladstone and the Irish Nation*, p. 666.
14 *Diaries*, XII, p. 340.
15 Lyons, *Charles Stewart Parnell*, p. 468.

34. The Leaden Victory

1 *Diaries*, XII, pp. 258–9.
2 *Ibid.*, p. 350.
3 Morley, *Life of Gladstone*, III, pp. 452–3.
4 Shakespeare's *Henry VIII*, Act III, scene ii.
5 *Diaries*, XII, p. 354.
6 Tilney Bassett (ed.), *Gladstone to His Wife*, p. 254.
7 *Diaries*, XII, p. 270.
8 *Ibid.*, p. 407.
9 *Ibid.*, p. 393n.
10 *Ibid.*, p. 370.
11 *Ibid.*, p. 410.
12 *Ibid.*, XIII, p. 36.
13 Report in *The Times*, 27 June 1892.
14 *Diaries*, XIII, p. 36.
15 *Ibid.*, p. 37.
16 Bahlmann (ed.), *The Diary of Sir Edward Walter Hamilton 1885–1906*, p. 158.
17 *Diaries*, XIII, pp. 38–9.
18 *Ibid.*, p. 42.
19 *Ibid.*, p. 43.
20 L. V. Harcourt's unpublished diary (Harcourt papers).
21 Magnus, *Gladstone*, p. 293.
22 Bahlmann (ed.), *The Diary of Sir Edward Walter Hamilton 1885–1906*, p. 159.
23 *Diaries*, XIII, pp. 46–7.
24 *Ibid.*, p. 51.
25 *Ibid.*, p. 58.
26 Bahlmann (ed.), *The Diary of Sir Edward Walter Hamilton 1885–1906*, p. 159.
27 *Letters of Queen Victoria*, 3rd Series, II, p. 132.
28 Bahlmann (ed.), *The Diary of Sir Edward Walter Hamilton 1885–1906*, p. 172.

29 *Ibid.*, p. 176.
30 *Diaries*, XIII, p. 67.
31 Magnus, *Gladstone*, p. 403.
32 *Diaries*, XIII, p. 113.
33 *The Times*, 25 October 1892.
34 The memorandum is published in full in *Diaries*, XIII, pp. 122–6.
35 *Letters of Queen Victoria*, 3rd Series, II, p. 176.
36 *Diaries*, XIII, p. 138.
37 *Ibid.*, p. 149.
38 *Ibid.*, pp. 161–3.
39 Bahlmann (ed.), *The Diary of Sir Edward Walter Hamilton 1885–1906*, p. 165.
40 *Ibid.*, p. 176.

35. Last Exit to Hawarden

1 *Diaries*, XIII, p. 178.
2 *Ibid.*, p. 193.
3 *Ibid.*, p. 194.
4 *Ibid.*, p. 201.
5 Morley, *Life of Gladstone*, III, p. 499.
6 *Diaries*, XIII, p. 236.
7 Morley, *Life of Gladstone*, III, p. 501.
8 Magnus, *Gladstone*, p. 417.
9 *Diaries*, XIII, p. 271.
10 Commons Hansard for 27 July 1893.
11 *Diaries*, XIII, p. 272.
12 *Ibid.*, p. 285.
13 *Ibid.*, p. 286.
14 *Ibid.*, p. 288.
15 *Ibid.*, p. 290.
16 *Ibid.*, p. 341.
17 *Ibid.*, p. 342.
18 Bahlmann (ed.), *The Diary of Sir Edward Walter Hamilton 1885–1906*, p. 237.
19 *Ibid.*, p. 236.
20 *Ibid.*, p. 247.
21 *Ibid.*, p. 217.
22 *Diaries*, XIII, p. 349.

23 From Morley's diary for 8 January 1894, cited in Matthew, *Gladstone 1875–1898*, p. 350.
24 *Ibid.*
25 *Diaries*, XIII, p. 353.
26 Bahlmann (ed.), *The Diary of Sir Edward Walter Hamilton 1885–1906*, p. 225.
27 *Ibid.*, p. 233.
28 *Ibid.*, p. 234.
29 *Diaries*, XIII, pp. 363–4.
30 *Ibid.*, p. 375.
31 *Ibid.*, p. 378.
32 Bahlmann (ed.), *The Diary of Sir Edward Walter Hamilton 1885–1906*, p. 238.
33 *Diaries*, XIII, pp. 385–6.
34 Asquith, *Fifty Years of Parliament*, I, pp. 216–17.
35 Commons Hansard for 1 March 1894.
36 *Diaries*, XIII, p. 390.
37 *Ibid.*, pp. 389–90.

36. The Closing of the Doors of the Senses

1 Mary Drew, *Diaries and Letters*, p. 425.
2 *Diaries*, XIII, p. 419.
3 *Ibid.*, p. 426.
4 *Letters of Queen Victoria*, 3rd Series, III, p. 146.
5 Brooke and Sorenson (eds), *The Prime Ministers' Papers. W. E. Gladstone*, I, pp. 173–4.
6 *Diaries*, XIII, p. 423.
7 *Ibid.*
8 Matthew, *Gladstone 1875–1898*, pp. 375–6.
9 *Diaries*, XIII, p. 427.
10 Magnus, *Gladstone*, p. 433.
11 James, *Rosebery*, p. 392.
12 Morley, *Life of Gladstone*, III, p. 525.
13 Bahlmann (ed.), *The Diary of Sir Edward Walter Hamilton 1885–1906*, pp. 344–5.
14 *Letters of Queen Victoria*, 3rd Series, III, pp. 249–50.

Select Bibliography

Books by Gladstone

The Gladstone Diaries, 14 vols, ed. M. R. D. Foot (vols 1 and 2), ed. M. R. D. Foot and H. C. G. Matthew (vols 3 and 4), ed. H. C. G. Matthew (vols 5–14)

The State in its Relations with the Church, 2 vols (1838)

Church Principles Considered in their Results (1840)

Translation of Farini's *Lo Stato Romano*, 4 vols (1852)

On the Place of Homer in Classical Education and in Historical Inquiry, an Oxford Essay, (1857)

A Chapter of Autobiography (1868)

Juventus Mundi: The Gods and Men of the Heroic Age of Homer (1876)

The Church of England and Ritualism (1875)

Homeric Synchronism: An Enquiry into the Time and Place of Homer (1869)

Gleanings of Past Years 1844–78, 8 vols (1879)

Landmarks of Homeric Study (1890)

The Impregnable Rock of Holy Scripture (1890)

The Odes of Horace (1896)

The Works of Joseph Butler (ed.) (1896)

Studies Subsidiary to the Works of Bishop Butler (1896)

Later Gleanings (1897)

Together with innumerable long magazine articles in, *inter alia*, the *Edinburgh Review*, the *Quarterly Review*, the *Nineteenth Century*, the *North American Review*, on literary, religious, political and historical subjects, a few of which were published in *Gleanings*.

Books Directly About Gladstone

Major works

John Morley: *Life of Gladstone*, 3 vols (1903)
Philip Magnus: *Gladstone* (1954)
Richard Shannon: *Gladstone* I: *1809–1865* (1982)
H. C. G. Matthew: *Gladstone 1809–1874* (1986)
H. C. G. Matthew: *Gladstone 1875–1898* (1995)
J. L. Hammond: *Gladstone and the Irish Nation* (1938)
S. G. Checkland: *The Gladstones 1764–1851* (1971) [a history of the family with much about W.E.G.'s father, Sir John Gladstone]

Collections of letters or speeches

Philip Guedalla (ed.): *Gladstone and Palmerston* (1928) [mainly letters]
Philip Guedalla (ed.): *The Queen and Mr Gladstone*, 2 vols (1933) [mainly letters]
A. Tilney Bassett (ed.): *Gladstone's Speeches* (1916)
A. Tilney Bassett (ed.): *Gladstone to His Wife* (1936) [letters]
Agatha Ramm (ed.): *Political Correspondence of Mr Gladstone and Lord Granville*, 4 vols (1952–62)
D. C. Lathbury: *Letters on Church and Religion of William Ewart Gladstone*, 2 vols (1910)

Biographical essays or studies of Gladstone from particular angles

G. W. E. Russell: *William Ewart Gladstone* The Queen's Prime Ministers Series (1891)
G. W. E. Russell: *Mr Gladstone's Religious Development* (1899)
C. R. L. Fletcher: *Mr Gladstone at Oxford, 1890* (1908)
F. W. Hirst: *Gladstone as Financier and Economist* (1931)
Mary Drew (née Gladstone): *Acton, Gladstone and Others* (1924)
Mary Drew: *Diaries and Letters* (1930)
Viscount (Herbert) Gladstone: *After Thirty Years* (1928) [his father seen in retrospect]
G. T. Garrett: *The Two Mr Gladstones* (1936)
Francis Birrell: *Gladstone*, Great Lives Series (1933)
E. J. Feuchtwanger: *Gladstone* (1975)

Penelope Gladstone: *The Gladstones: Portrait of a Family 1839–1889* (1989)
Peter J. Jagger: *Gladstone: The Making of a Christian Politician* (1991)
Goldwin Smith: *My Memory of Gladstone*

General

Henry Adams: Charles Francis Adams
Evelyn Ashley: *Henry John Temple: Life of Viscount Palmerston*, 2 vols (1879)
H. H. Asquith: *Fifty Years of Parliament*, 2 vols (1925)
Walter Bagehot: *Biographical Studies*
W. R. Bahlmann (ed.): *The Diary of Sir Edward Walter Hamilton 1880–1885*, 2 vols (1972)
W. R. Bahlmann (ed.): *The Diary of Sir Edward Walter Hamilton 1885–1906* (1993)
John Bailey (ed.), *The Diary of Lady Frederick Cavendish*, 2 vols (1927)
A. J. Balfour: *Chapters of Autobiography* (1930)
Georgina Battiscombe: *Mrs Gladstone* (1956)
Robert Blake: *Disraeli* (1960)
John Brooke and Mary Sorenson (eds): *The Prime Ministers' Papers: W. E. Gladstone*, vols I and II (1971 and 1972)
Frank Callanan: *The Parnell Split 1890–91* (1992)
Lady Gwendoline Cecil: *Life of Robert Marquess of Salisbury*, 4 vols (1921–32)
Owen Chadwick: *The Victorian Church*, 2 vols (1966 and 1971)
Owen Chadwick: *Acton and Gladstone* (1976)
Owen Chadwick: *Newman* (1983)
Winston Spencer Churchill: *Lord Randolph Churchill*, 2 vols (1906)
Marquess of Crewe: *Lord Rosebery*, 2 vols (1931)
Randall Davidson: *Life of Archbishop Tait*, 2 vols (1891)
Blanche Dugdale: *Arthur James Balfour*, 2 vols (1936)
Max Egremont: *Balfour* (1980)
Geoffrey Faber: *The Oxford Apostles* (1933)
Lord Edmond Fitzmaurice: *Life of Earl Granville*, 2 vols (1905)
R. F. Foster: *Lord Randolph Churchill: A Political Life* (1981)
R. F. Foster: *Charles Stewart Parnell: The Man and His Family* (1976)
R. F. Foster (ed.): *Modern Ireland 1600–1972* (1988)
R. F. Foster: *Paddy and Mr Punch* (1993)
A. G. Gardiner: *The Life of Sir William Harcourt*, 2 vols (1923)
J. L. Garvin and Julian Amery: *Life of Joseph Chamberlain*, 3 vols by Garvin (1932–4), 2 vols by Amery (1969)

Norman Gash: *Sir Robert Peel after 1830* (1972)
Arthur Gordon: *The Earl of Aberdeen*, The Queen's Prime Ministers Series (1893)
Lord Stanmore (Arthur Gordon): *Sidney Herbert: A Memoir*, 2 vols (1906)
Charles Greville: *Diaries*, 3rd series, 2 vols (1887)
Philip Guedalla: *Palmerston* (1926)
Stephen Gwynn and Gertrude Tuckwell: *Life of Sir Charles Dilke*, 2 vols (1917)
Kenneth Harris: *Attlee* (1982)
Henry Harrison: *Parnell Vindicated: The Lifting of the Veil* (1931)
T. M. Healy: *Letters and Leaders of My Day*, 2 vols (1928)
Wendy Hinde: *George Canning* (1973)
Wendy Hinde: *Richard Cobden* (1987)
Bernard Holland: *Life of the [8th] Duke of Devonshire*, 2 vols (1911)
Patrick Jackson: *The Last of the Whigs: A Political Biography of Lord Hartington* (1994)
Robert Rhodes James: *Rosebery* (1963)
Robert Rhodes James: *Lord Randolph Churchill* (1959)
Roy Jenkins: *Asquith* (1964)
Roy Jenkins: *Sir Charles Dilke: A Victorian Tragedy* (1958)
T. A. Jenkins: *Gladstone, Whiggery and the Liberal Party 1874–86* (1988)
Robert Kee: *The Laurel and the Ivy* (1993)
A. L. Kennedy: *Salisbury* (1953)
Ian Ker: *John Henry Newman* (1988)
Sidney Lee: *King Edward VII: A Biography*, 2 vols (1925 and 1927)
Elizabeth Longford: *Victoria R.I.* (1964)
Elizabeth Longford: *Wellington: Pillar of State* (1972)
Elizabeth Longford: *A Pilgrimage of Passion: Life of Wilfrid Scawen Blunt* (1979)
F. S. L. Lyons: *Charles Stewart Parnell* (1977)
Philip Magnus: *King Edward the Seventh* (1964)
P. T. Marsh: *Joseph Chamberlain* (1994)
Robert Bernard Martin: *Tennyson: The Unquiet Heart* (1980)
Herbert Maxwell: *Life of Clarendon*, 2 vols (1913)
W. F. Monypenny and G. E. Buckle: *Life of Disraeli* (Earl of Beaconsfield), 6 vols (1910–20)
John Morley: *Recollections*, 2 vols (1917)
David Newsome: *The Convert Cardinals: Newman and Manning* (1993)
Conor Cruise O'Brien: *Parnell and His Party 1880–90* (1957)
R. Barry O'Brien: *Charles Stewart Parnell*, 2 vols (1898)
S. L. Ollard: *A Short History of the Oxford Movement* (1915)
C. S. Parker: *Sir Robert Peel from His Private Papers*, 3 vols (1891–9)

C. S. Parker: *Life and Letters of Sir James Graham* (1906)
Jonathan Parry: *The Rise and Fall of Liberal Government in Victorian Britain* (1993)
John Pollock: *Gordon: The Man Behind the Legend* (1993)
Arthur Ponsonby: *Henry Ponsonby: His Life from His Letters* (1942)
John Prest: *Lord John Russell* (1972)
R. E. Protheroe: *Life of A. P. Stanley* (1893)
E. S. Purcell: *Life of Cardinal Manning*, 2 vols (1896)
T. Wemyss Reid: *Life of W. E. Forster* (1888)
T. Wemyss Reid: *Life of Richard Monckton Milnes, 1st Lord Houghton* (1891)
Jane Ridley: *The Young Disraeli* (1994)

Index

ABOUT THE AUTHOR

Roy Jenkins was born in South Wales in 1920. He was educated at Balliol College, Oxford, where he was awarded a first-class degree in Philosophy, Politics and Economics. During the second world war, he served with the Royal Artillery and then worked as a cryptographer for British intelligence. First elected a member of parliament in 1948, Roy Jenkins represented the Stechford constituency of Birmingham for over twenty-five years. In Labour governments of the 1960s and 1970s, he served as Minister for Aviation; Home Secretary, a post he held twice; and Chancellor of the Exchequer. From 1970 to 1972 he was deputy leader of the Labour Party. In 1977 Roy Jenkins became president of the European Commission, returning to British politics in 1981 when he helped found the Social Democratic Party, leading the party for a time in the early 1980s. He won the Glasgow Hillhead seat for the SDP, representing it in the House of Commons from 1982 to 1987. In 1986 Roy Jenkins was elected Chancellor of Oxford University and the following year accepted a peerage and took his seat in the House of Lords as Lord Jenkins of Hillhead. A prolific writer and journalist, he is the author of biographies of Asquith, Truman and Baldwin, and of other historical and political works. Lord Jenkins and his wife, Jennifer, have three children, Charles, Cynthia, and Edward. They live in Oxfordshire and London.

ABOUT THE TYPE

The text of this book was set in Janson, a misnamed typeface designed in about 1690 by Nicholas Kis, a Hungarian in Amsterdam. In 1919 the matrices became the property of the Stempel Foundry in Frankfurt. It is an old-style book face of excellent clarity and sharpness. Janson serifs are concave and splayed; the contrast between thick and thin strokes is marked.